STUDIES IN CHRISTIAN HISTORY AND THOUGHT

Holy Spirit and Religious Experience in Christian Literature ca. AD 90–200

STUDIES IN CHRISTIAN HISTORY AND THOUGHT

A full listing of all titles in this series
appears at the close of this book

STUDIES IN CHRISTIAN HISTORY AND THOUGHT

Holy Spirit and Religious Experience in Christian Literature ca. AD 90–200

John Eifion Morgan-Wynne

Foreword by James D.G. Dunn

Wipf and Stock Publishers
199 W 8th Ave, Suite 3
Eugene, OR 97401

Holy Spirit and Religious Experience in Christian Literature ca. AD 90-200
By Morgan-Wynne, John Eifion
Copyright©2006 Paternoster
ISBN: 1-59752-724-6
Publication date 6/1/2006
Previously published by Paternoster, 2006

This Edition reprinted by Wipf and Stock Publishers
by arrangement with Paternoster

Paternoster
9 Holdom Avenue
Bletchley
Milton Keyes, MK1 1QR
Great Britain

STUDIES IN CHRISTIAN HISTORY AND THOUGHT

Series Preface

This series complements the specialist series of *Studies in Evangelical History and Thought* and *Studies in Baptist History and Thought* for which Paternoster is becoming increasingly well known by offering works that cover the wider field of Christian history and thought. It encompasses accounts of Christian witness at various periods, studies of individual Christians and movements, and works which concern the relations of church and society through history, and the history of Christian thought.

The series includes monographs, revised dissertations and theses, and collections of papers by individuals and groups. As well as 'free standing' volumes, works on particular running themes are being commissioned; authors will be engaged for these from around the world and from a variety of Christian traditions.

A high academic standard combined with lively writing will commend the volumes in this series both to scholars and to a wider readership.

Series Editors

Alan P.F. Sell, Visiting Professor at Acadia University Divinity College, Nova Scotia, Canada

David Bebbington, Professor of History, University of Stirling, Stirling, Scotland, UK

Clyde Binfield, Professor Associate in History, University of Sheffield, UK

Gerald Bray, Anglican Professor of Divinity, Beeson Divinity School, Samford University, Birmingham, Alabama, USA

Grayson Carter, Associate Professor of Church History, Fuller Theological Seminary SW, Phoenix, Arizona, USA

In memory of
Gwynne Henton Davies (1906–98)
Baptist Minister
University Professor
College Principal
Prophet
Man of God

Contents

Foreword by James D.G. Dunn xv

Preface xvii

Abbreviations xix

Chapter 1
Introduction 1
1. The Present State of Research 1
   I 1
   II 2
   III 3
      EXCURSUS 3
2. A Brief Survey of the Experience of the Spirit in the First
Two Generations 9
   Summary 14
3. Problems and Aims 15

Chapter 2
Syria 20
1. Gospel of John 22
   A. Divine Presence 24
      SUMMARY 30
   B. Divine Illumination 30
      SUMMARY 34
   C. Divine Power 34
   Summary 34
2. The Johannine Epistles 35
   A. Divine Presence 36
   B. Divine Illumination 39
   C. Divine Power 42
   Summary 43
3. The Didache 44
   A. Divine Presence 45
   B. Divine Illumination 47
   C. Divine Power 47
   Summary 48
4. Matthew's Gospel 49
   C. Divine Power 53

Summary..53
5. Ignatius of Antioch..53
   A and B. Divine Presence and Illumination................................53
   C. Divine Power..56
   Summary..58
6. The Odes of Solomon..58
   A. Divine Presence..59
   B. Divine Illumination..73
   C. Divine Power..74
   D. Other Features...76
   Summary..78
      EXCURSUS...78
7. Tatian...80
   A. Divine Presence..81
   B. Divine Illumination..82
   C. Divine Power..82
   Summary..83
8. Conclusion..83

Chapter 3
Asia Minor...**87**
1. John of Patmos...89
   A and B. Divine Presence and Illumination................................90
      SUMMARY...92
   C. Divine Power..92
   D. Other Features and Summary..95
2. The Pastoral Epistles..96
   A. Divine Presence..96
   B. Divine Illumination..99
   C. Divine Power..102
   Summary..103
3. Jude..104
4. 2 Peter..105
   Summary..108
5. The Letter of Barnabas..109
   A. Divine Presence..110
      SUMMARY...115
   B. Divine Illumination..116
   C. Divine Power..116
   Summary..117
6. Polycarp's Letter to the Philippians...118
   Summary..119
7. The Martyrdom of Polycarp..119

Summary 120
8. Asia Minor Montanism 120
   A. *Divine Presence* 121
   B and C. *Divine Illumination and Power* 123
   Summary 124
      EXCURSUS 125
9. Conclusion 126

Chapter 4
Greece **128**
1. Corinth and 1 Clement 129
2. 2 Clement 130
   Summary 133
3. Conclusion 134

Chapter 5
Rome **135**
1. 1 Peter 139
   A. *Divine Presence* 140
      SUMMARY 143
   C. *Divine Power* 143
      SUMMARY 145
2. 1 Clement 146
   A. *Divine Presence* 147
      SUMMARY 150
3. The Shepherd of Hermas 150
   A and B. *Divine Presence and Illumination* 152
   C. *Divine Power* 154
      SUMMARY 162
4. Justin Martyr 164
   A. *Divine Presence* 165
      SUMMARY 169
5. Valentinian Gnosticism 170
   5.1. The Author of the Gospel of Truth 171
   A and B. *Divine Presence and Illumination* 172
   C. *Divine Power* 176
   Summary 176
   5.2 Heracleon 177
      SUMMARY 180
   5.3 Ptolemaeus 180
      SUMMARY 182
      EXCURSUS 182
6. Conclusion 185

Chapter 6
Southern Gaul **189**
1. The Letter of the Church at Lyons and Vienne 190
   A. Divine Presence 190
   B. Divine Illumination 192
   C. Divine Power 192
   Summary 195
2. Irenaeus 195
   A. Divine Presence 199
      SUMMARY 210
   B. Divine Illumination 211
      SUMMARY 211
   C. Divine Power 212
      SUMMARY 217
   Summary 218
3. The Valentinian Marcus 218
   Summary 219
4. Conclusion 219

Chapter 7
Northern Africa **222**
1. The Passion of Perpetua and Felicitas 223
   A. Divine Presence 224
   C. Divine Power 224
   Summary 225
2. Tertullian 226
   A. Divine Presence 229
      SUMMARY 236
   B. Divine Illumination 236
      SUMMARY 239
   C. Divine Power 239
   Summary 249
3. Conclusion 249

Chapter 8
Egypt **252**
1. Clement of Alexandria 253
   A. Divine Presence 255
   B. Divine Illumination 256
   C. Divine Power 258
   Summary 261
2. Theodotus 262
   A. Divine Presence 262

C. Divine Power	267
Conclusion	268
3. Conclusion	269

Chapter 9
Conclusion 271
I	271
II	274
III	277
IV	281
V	282
VI	285
VII	287
VIII	290

Appendix 1
Who were the Spiritual? A Second-Century Debate 292
1. Justin Martyr	292
2. Irenaeus and the Valentinian Gnostics	293
3. Tertullian and the Catholics	297
4. Conclusion	300

Appendix 2
The Meaning ἀκοίμητον πνεῦμα in Ignatius' Letter to Polycarp 1.3 302
Summary	306

Appendix 3
The Experience of the Spirit in the Odes of Solomon 307
I	307
II	308
III	309
IV	310
V	311

Appendix 4
The 'Delicacy' of the Spirit in the Shepherd of Hermas and in Tertullian 313
1. The Shepherd of Hermas	313
2. Tertullian	314
3. Concluding Remarks	316

Appendix 5
The Cessation of the Holy Spirit from Judaism in Justin Martyr, Irenaeus and Tertullian ... 317
1. Justin Martyr ... 317
2. Irenaeus ... 319
3. Tertullian ... 319
4. Other Evidence ... 321
5. Older Roots ... 322
6. Conclusions ... 322

Select Bibliography ... 325

Author Index ... 351

Scripture Index ... 357

Foreword

When John Morgan-Wynne initially suggested his thesis topic for his Durham PhD I was very excited—for three reasons.

One was that I was unaware of any study focused on the subject of the Holy Spirit in the early patristic church beyond the classic but rather pedestrian study of H.B. Swete, *The Holy Spirit in the Ancient Church* (London: Macmillan, 1910), now almost a century old. Here indeed was opportunity for and need of a fresh study, not least in the light of all that had been happening in twentieth-century Christianity since the emergence of Pentecostalism, and latterly of the variously described 'charismatic movement'. John, with his fine knowledge of ancient Greek and his well-honed skills in exegeting the nuances of New Testament Greek, was ideally placed to fill this gap.

Another was that my own research into the Holy Spirit in the New Testament had brought home to me the crucial importance of what we can describe here simply as 'the experience of the Holy Spirit' in the beginnings of Christianity. My impression then was the common one, as John indicates, that this vitality of spiritual experience largely waned in the post-apostolic age, with the upsurgence of Montanism as a kind of throwback to the primitive enthusiasm depicted in the Acts of the Apostles. But I recognized that this perception needed to be thoroughly tested. And once again, John was the obvious man for the task.

The other was the frustration I often experienced over the lack of porousness in the boundary between New Testament studies and Early Church studies. The former rarely 'transgressed'(!) beyond the first century, while the latter often treated the New Testament in a perfunctory way or as simply a sort of precursor to the real study of emerging doctrine and ecclesiology. The consequence was a kind of disjunction or roadblock between the first and second centuries, or even a sense that the post-apostolic age constituted a kind of 'fall' from the Garden of Eden sublimity of the primitive Church. What was needed were more inquiries which deliberately straddled the two centuries and could properly examine questions of continuity and discontinuity. And this was precisely what John proposed and has produced.

The outcome was very much what I had hoped for. Here readers will see full documentation of the degree to which 'the experience of the Holy Spirit' continued to be vital in the late first century and through the second century, and recognition of its continuing importance. At the same time we see aspects and issues which were often more hidden in the first century writings (the New Testament): tensions between Christians claiming the same Spirit; the Spirit as a bone of contention as well as a crucial touchstone; the diversity of experiences attributed to the Spirit; and, regrettably, in too many cases claims to the Spirit functioning as part of a supersessionist depreciation of Judaism.

Particularly important, as John shows, was the recognition of the need for *discernment*: how to recognize spiritual experiences as experiences of the Spirit, how to discern false prophecy from true (1 John, Didache and Hermas offer some interesting 'tests'); how to recognize the voice of the Spirit in groups or movements which bubble up outside the mainstream of emerging 'orthodoxy' (Montanism as an important case study); and generally how to retain the freshness and spontaneity of experience of the Spirit when good order and ecclesiastical hierarchy and structure are becoming more and more important (and constricting). The fact that these are still questions for Christianity today, at global as well as local level, makes John's study all the more relevant and with lessons of considerable potential value for pastors and church leaders today.

John's study poses several other issues and questions of continuing relevance. Especially important is the question concerning the relation and role of the Spirit in the still active issue of the relation between scripture and tradition: has the Spirit, in effect, been imprisoned in or subordinated to one ('I believe in God the Father, God the Son, and the Holy Scripture') or other ('I believe in God the Father, God the Son, and the Holy Church')?! But equally important is the issue of whether, to what extent and how does contemporary Christianity genuinely look to the Spirit for inspiration and guidance in ethical issues; is there really room for the 'prophet' in today's Christianity, alongside the 'teacher' and the 'priest'?

These are some of the questions which John's work has raised for me. In a day when we still need to recover the vitality of the Spirit—or rather to be revitalized by the Spirit—in local and ecumenical Christianity, John's volume provides some invaluable case-studies from the early days of Christianity, when the moulds and structures were still at an early stage of formation. The degree to which we experience what John talks about as strange and rather foreign is the degree to which we need to be reawakened to the sensitivities and potential which the early church(es) knew so well.

James D. G. Dunn
Emeritus Lightfoot Professor of Divinity,
University of Durham
February, 2006

Preface

This work began life as a doctoral thesis, which was prepared under the supervision of Professor J.D.G. Dunn and presented to and accepted by the University of Durham in 1987. I wish to place on record my deep indebtedness for Professor Dunn's stimulating, incisive advice and his insistence that I should always be keeping in mind the broader picture, during the time I worked under his guidance.

At the time of completion, I had just moved from being New Testament Tutor at Regent's Park College, Oxford (1965-87) to become Principal at Bristol Baptist College (the oldest surviving Free Church theological college). A heavy teaching and administrative load, coupled with preaching engagements, left little time for trying to prepare the thesis for submission for a publisher's consideration. I served at Bristol till 1993 when I had a heart attack and agreed to step down, and I returned to the pastorate, at Ilkley Baptist Church, West Yorkshire, whom I served 1994-2002. Now in retirement, I have returned to the thesis, encouraged by the Revd. Dr. Anthony R. Cross of Paternoster, for whose initial kindly prodding and subsequent guidance and practical help in preparing the work in the required format I am very grateful.

I have decided to retain the format of the thesis—of looking at three areas of Christian experience: a sense of the presence of the Divine; of guidance or illumination; of ethical empowerment—and the basic approach of examining and exegeting the passages of each author. We are what we have become, and I was trained first in the Honours School of Modern History and then in the Honours School of Theology at Oxford. In both I learned the importance of going back to the text and seeking patiently to get it to yield up its meaning. I hope that in getting immersed in the trees, I have not lost sight of the wood, and certainly Professor Dunn was assiduous in reminding me to keep in mind the total 'landscape'.

In the seventeen years since 1987, inevitably a fair amount of secondary literature germane to my theme in both the New Testament and early Patristic fields has been published. Currently, I am a fair way from a library able to offer full coverage of this literature. I would like to thank the officials of the Brotherton Library, Leeds University, for allowing me to use the theology section on an ad hoc basis, while I have made use of the Inter-Library Loan system. If I have missed some vital article or monograph, I can only apologise in advance. Even so, the bibliography is rather long, due to the large field of Christian literature which we have attempted to cover.

I have sought throughout to use inclusive language, believing this to be entirely right and proper, but sometimes it has proved difficult and I hope that where I have not been successful, readers will make allowances. I have of course retained masculine language where that was clearly the intention of the writer (e.g. where the writer would assume the holder of a church office had to be a man).

The person in whose memory this book is dedicated is someone to whom I owe more than I can ever calculate and who, as the years passed by, became increasing a 'father in God' to me. I was one of his first students at Regent's Park College in

1958, when he became its Principal after nearly a decade as the first Professor of Old Testament at Durham, and then served under him as his New Testament Tutor from 1965 until his retirement in 1972. I learned from him, first hand as it were (and also from the written works of the late Joachim Jeremias of Göttingen) that one could be both scholar and preacher, that detailed study of the Scriptures and a passionate commitment to the Gospel could go hand in hand. I have sought throughout my ministry, in pastorate and college work, to hold these two together. I hope that this book may in some small way contribute to the work of today's church as it seeks to serve the Kingdom of God and the Gospel of Jesus Christ.

I also gladly acknowledge the support in all my ministry of my dear wife, Enid, partner and friend now for over forty years.

John E. Morgan-Wynne
Ilkley, 2005

Abbreviations

AB	Anchor Bible
AB	Analecta Biblica
ACW	Ancient Christian Writers
AG	Analecta Gregoriana
AGSU	Arbeiten zur Geschichte des Spätjudentums und Urchristentums
AH	Adversus Haereses (Irenaeus)
AKG	Arbeiten zur Kirchengeschichte
ANCL	Ante-Nicene Christian Library
ATANT	Abhandlungen zur Theologie des Alten und Neuen Testaments
BJRL	*Bulletin of the John Rylands Library*
BTS	Biblische-theologische Studien
BU	Biblische Untersuchungen
BZ	*Biblische Zeitschrift*
CBQ	*Catholic Biblical Quarterly*
CBQMS	Catholic Biblical Quarterly Monograph Series
CB	Coniectanea Biblica
CQR	*Church Quarterly Review*
DCB	Dictionary of Christian Biography
EB	Études Bibliques
EKKNT	Evangelisch-Katholischer Kommentar zum Neuen Testament
EPM	Études de philosophie médiévale
EQ	*Evangelical Quarterly*
EvTh	*Evangelische Theologie*
ETSE	Esthonian Theological Society in Exile
FTS	Frankfürter Theologischen Studien
FRLANT	Forschungen zur Religion und Literatur des Alten und Neuen Testamentes
HE	Historia Ecclesiastica (Eusebius)
HJ	*Heythrop Journal*
HzNT	Handbuch zum Neuen Testament
HTKNT	Herders theologischer Kommentar zum Neuen Testament
HTR	*Harvard Theological Review*
HUT	Hermeneutische Untersuchungen zur Theologie
ICC	International Critical Commentary
JBL	*Journal of Biblical Literature*
JEH	*Journal of Ecclesiastical History*
JJS	*Journal of Jewish Studies*
JPT	*Journal of Pentecostal Theology*
JSNTSS	Journal for the Study of the New Testament Supplement Series
JTS	*Journal of Theological Studies*
KAV	Kommentar zu den apostolischen Vätern

MBPS	Mellen Biblical Press Series
MBT	Münsterische Beiträge zur Theologie
MTS	Münchener theologischen Studien
NCB	New Century Bible
NHS	Nag Hammadi Studies
NICNT	New International Commentary on the New Testament
NT	*Novum Testamentum*
NTAbh.	Neutestamentliche Abhandlungen
NTD	Das Neue Testament Deutsch
NTS	*New Testament Studies*
NTTS	New Testament Tools and Studies
OBS	Österreichische biblische Studien
OBO	Orbis Biblicus et Orientalis
OCA	Orientalia Christina Analecta
RB	*Revue Biblique*
RHE	*Revue d'histoire ecclésiastique*
RHPR	*Revue d'histoire et philosophie religieuses*
SAC	Studies in Antiquity and Christianity
SANT	Studien zum Alten und Neuen Testament
SBEC	Studies in the Bible and Early Christianity
SBLDS	Society for Biblical Literature Dissertation Series
SBLMS	Society for Biblical Literature Monograph Series
SBS	Stuttgarter Bibelstudien
SBT	Studies in Biblical Theology
SC	*Second Century*
SC	Sources Chrétiennes
SHAW	*Sitzungsberichte heidelbergen Akademie der Wissenschaften*
SJT	*Scottish Journal of Theology*
SM	*Studia Moralia*
SNT	Supplements to Novum Testamentum
SNTSMS	Society for New Testament Studies Monograph Series
SNTW	Studies in the New Testament and its World
SPAW	*Sitzungsberichte preussischen Akademie der Wissenschaften*
SSAW	Schriften des Sektion für Altertumswissenschaft
ST	*Studia Theologica*
STL	Studia Theologica Lundensia
TDNT	Theological Dictionary of the New Testament
ThZ	*Theologische Zeitschrift*
TLZ	*Theologische Literaturzeitung*
TNTC	Tyndale New Testament Commentary
TU	Texte und Untersuchungen
VC	*Vigiliae Christianae*
WBC	Word Biblical Series
WMANT	Wissenschaftliche Monographien zum Alten und Neuen Testament

WUNT	Wissenschaftliche Untersuchungen zum Neuen Testament
ZThK	*Zeitschrift für Theologie und Kirche*
ZKg	*Zeitschrift für Kirchengeschichte*
ZKT	*Zeitschrift für katholische Theologie*
ZNW	*Zeitschrift für neutestamentliche Wissenschaft*

CHAPTER 1

Introduction

1. The Present State of Research

A considerable amount of literature has appeared since the Second World War on the theme of the Holy Spirit, and another work on such a topic needs justification. Three reasons may be offered.

I.

The first reason concerns the nature of the secondary literature, which often leaves the reader with a sense of dissatisfaction. When examined, we observe firstly a tendency to departmentalize research into NT and Patristic studies. This is due partly to the traditional reverence which Christian scholars feel towards the NT as the primary documents of the Christian faith,[1] and partly to modest reluctance on the part of specialists in one field to venture into the other field.[2] In the famous 'Kittel' article on Spirit by E. Schweizer, the NT section comprised pp. 396-451 of the English translation, while section F on the post-apostolic Fathers consisted of half a page!

Then, secondly, this literature is often very limited in theme or is now to be judged inadequate.

The survey in the excursus to this chapter will illustrate these two points. While we are not in any way denigrating the careful and illuminating work that has gone on, the tendency to departmentalize and separate off NT and Apostolic Fathers and later writers is artificial and arbitrary. Concerning our theme of the Spirit there tends to be a cut-off point around AD 100. Scholars look at the early Palestinian church or Paul or the Fourth Evangelist. But what was the experience of other, later

---

[1] E.g. E. Schweizer, *Neotestamentica* (Zurich: Zwingli Verlag, 1963), p. 233: 'The New Testament is part of the tradition, therefore necessarily expressed in human language, limited by contemporaneous possibilities of understanding, imperfect, and yet standing in an unique position as the beginning of the tradition, historically close to the incarnate Word of God and sign for its "once-for-allness".'

[2] E.g. E. Schweizer, *Church Order in the New Testament* (London: SCM, 1963), p. 139, who wrote in a footnote (in the section 'The Conception of the Church in the Apostolic Fathers'): 'A summary treatment is all that is possible without specialist knowledge of patristics'. There are some noteworthy exceptions and names like H. Lietzmann, R. Knopf and H. von Campenhausen in Germany and G.W.H. Lampe and J.N.D. Kelly in Britain spring to mind.

Christians? If it be true that an intense awareness of the Spirit's presence and power was the hallmark of the earliest generation (as suggested by Acts and Paul), did that continue for much longer or did Christianity settle down to become something more 'domesticated' and 'bourgeois'? Did Christianity begin in a revivalist outburst and then simmer down into something more 'respectable'? To pursue the study over into the second century is vital to secure an answer. To stay on the NT side within the first century or to start in the second century will leave the question unanswered. In a similar way, to set up the Apostolic Fathers as an entity and omit the Odes of Solomon (if an early second century date for them is preferred) would be unjustifiable. All extant Christian literature ought to be investigated in order to obtain as complete a view as possible.

Thus, since Weinel[3] (see below), there has not really been an overall survey of the period ca.AD 90 to ca.200, which might be termed the third to fifth generations.

So, our criticism concerns (a) the departmentalisation of study, leaving unanswered a major question concerning whether experience of the Spirit continued as a vital part of Christianity; (b) treatments limited to a particular author; (c) inadequate treatments, confining themselves to the listing of references and very little else; (d) and the lack of scrutinising what religious experience lay behind statements concerning the Spirit.

II.

The second major reason for the present study lies in the extent of the era to be covered. It could be described as the transition period from 'earliest Christianity' to the 'Great Church'. We might expect that this period could offer an interesting era for an examination of the experiences attributed to the Spirit. We will be looking at the period that lies between the break with the synagogue (roughly the 90s, without implying any theory of when the pronouncement against 'heretics' known as the Birkath-ha-Minim may have been introduced into the worship of the synagogue) and the era around the end of the second century, by which time those features associated with the so-called 'Great Church' had emerged (ministry, creed/rule of faith, catechumenate, sacramental system, sense of universal destiny). The founding period of the first two generations was over; the church was settling down and entering an era of consolidation.

There is a tendency to assert that as far as the experience of the Spirit is concerned, it is a period of decline. Thus, R. Knopf many years ago asserted that in the era AD 70-150 the work of the Spirit was often demanded more dogmatically than actually experienced in a living way; there was a receding of spiritual gifts in the post-apostolic period, though all were believed to have the Spirit; and the Spirit's activity could be observed especially in 'the pneumatic aristocracy' of

---

[3] H. Weinel, *Die Wirkungen des Geistes und der Geister in nachapostolischen Zeitalter bis auf Irenäus* (Tübingen: Druck von H. Lampp, 1899).

apostle, prophet and teacher.[4] In more recent times, U. Luz has said that by about the end of the first century experiences of the Spirit had generally receded.[5] Is this type of verdict in fact correct?

III.

The third reason is the contemporary situation. There has been in recent decades a considerable renewal of interest in the Holy Spirit due to the so-called Charismatic Movement, which has cut across denominational boundaries and often resulted either in the establishment of separate house/community churches or the changing of the character and style of worship in some 'older' churches. Arguably, a study of how Christian writers in the third to fifth generations—the period after the first wave of enthusiasm in the early generations—felt about the Spirit will be of interest to the church today. This is not to bow to the 'cult of the relevant', but to acknowledge that to some degree our research quests are determined by our own contemporary interests.

These, then, are the reasons why we feel that the present study can justify itself.

EXCURSUS

Survey of Some of the Secondary Literature on the Spirit in NT and Patristic Literature up to ca.AD 200.

1. In NT studies, focus has been particularly centred on three areas:

(a) *The primitive church's experience of the Spirit.* Detailed examination of Acts has been carried out. Areas of particular interest have been the nature of the Pentecost experience (glossolalia/foreign languages), the relation of the Holy Spirit and baptism, the link between the Spirit and mission, whether the Spirit is an essential part of the Christian life or a *donum superadditum* granted to various individuals to enable them to carry out divinely appointed tasks, and the place of Spirit-inspired prophets. Apart from the standard commentaries, we may list the following important contributions: G.W.H. Lampe, 'The Holy Spirit in the Writings of St. Luke', in D.E. Nineham (ed.), *Studies in the Gospels* (Oxford: Blackwell, 1955), pp. 159-200; G.R. Beasley-Murray, *Baptism in the New Testament* (London: Macmillan, 1962), pp. 104-22; J.H.E. Hull, *The Holy Spirit in the Acts of the Apostles* (London: Lutterworth, 1967); J.D.G. Dunn, *Baptism in the Holy Spirit* (London: SCM, 1970), pp. 38-102, and *Jesus and the Spirit* (London: SCM, 1975), pp. 93-196; J. Kremer, *Pfingstbericht und Pfingstgeschehen* (Stuttgart: KBW Verlag, 1973); G. Haya-Prats, *L'Esprit force de l'église: sa nature et son activité d'après les Actes des Apôtres* (Paris: Les Éditions du Cerf, 1975); M-A. Chevalier, *Souffle de Dieu* (Paris: Beauchesne, 1978), pp. 160-215; R. Stronstad, *The*

---

[4] R. Knopf, *Das nachapostolische Zeitalter* (Tübingen: Mohr, 1905), pp. 344, 406 and 403 respectively.

[5] U. Luz, 'The Disciples in the Gospel according to Matthew', in G. Stanton (ed.), *The Interpretation of Matthew* (London: SPCK), p. 107 (originally published in *ZNW* 62 [1971], pp. 141-71).

Charismatic Theology of St. Luke (Peabody, MA: Hendrickson, 1984); J.B. Shelton, *Mighty in Word and Deed: The Role of the Holy Spirit in Luke-Acts* (Peabody, MA: Hendrickson, 1991); R.P. Menzies, *Empowered for Witness: The Spirit in Luke-Acts* (Sheffield: Sheffield Academic Press, 1994) (= revised edition of *The Development of Early Christian Pneumatology with special reference to Luke-Acts* (Sheffield: JSOT Press, 1991);[6] W.H. Shepherd, *The Narrative Function of the Holy Spirit as a Character in Luke-Acts* (Atlanta, GA: Scholars, 1994); M. Turner, *Power from on High* (Sheffield: Sheffield Academic Press, 1996); M. Wenk, *Community-Forming Power: The Socio-Ethical Role of the Spirit in Luke-Acts* (Sheffield: Sheffield Academic Press, 2000).

(b) *Paul's view of the Spirit.* Apart from the issue of the relation of the Spirit and the risen Christ (with 2 Cor. 3.17 proving contentious), the Pauline antithesis of flesh and Spirit and its ethical implications has been explored. The idea of spiritual gifts (especially in relation to 1 Cor. 12–14) and the question of Spirit versus office have been much ventilated. The eschatological dimension of Paul's understanding of the Spirit has received due recognition. Among some significant contributions we may mention N.Q. Hamilton, *The Holy Spirit and Eschatology in Paul* (Edinburgh: Oliver & Boyd, 1957); I. Hermann, *Kyrios und Pneuma* (SANT 2; München: Kösel, 1961); K. Stalder, *Das Werk des Geistes in der Heiligung bei Paulus* (Zurich: EVZ-Verlag, 1962); W. Pfister, *Das Leben im Geist nach Paulus* (Freiburg: Universitätsverlag, 1963); J.D.G. Dunn, '2 Corinthians 3.17—The Lord is the Spirit', *JTS* 21 (1970), pp. 309-20, *Jesus and the Spirit*, pp. 197-342, and *The Theology of Paul the Apostle* (Edinburgh: T. & T. Clark, 1998), pp. 413-41; C.F.D. Moule, '2 Corinthians 3.18b, καθάπερ ἀπὸ κυρίου πνεύματος', in H. Baltensweiler and B. Reicke (eds.), *Neues Testament und Geschichte* (Tübingen: Mohr, 1972), pp. 232-37; D.J. Lull, *The Spirit in Galatia* (Chico, CA: Scholars Press, 1980); J.A. Davis, *Wisdom and Spirit: An Investigation of 1 Cor. 1.18–3.20 against the Background of Jewish Sapiential Traditions in the Greco-Roman Period* (Lanham, MD: University Press of America, 1984); F.W. Horn, *Das Angeld des Geistes: Studien zur paulischen Pneumatologie* (Göttingen: Vandenhoeck & Ruprecht, 1992); G.D. Fee, *God's Empowering Presence: The Holy Spirit in the Letters of Paul* (Peabody, MA: Hendrickson, 1994); M. Turner, *The Holy Spirit and Spiritual Gifts Then and Now* (Carlisle: Paternoster, 1996), pp. 103-35; S.J. Hafemann, *Suffering and Ministry in the Spirit* (Carlisle: Paternoster, 2000), and its sequel, *Paul, Moses, and the History of Israel* (Milton Keynes: Paternoster, 2005).

(c) *The Fourth Evangelist's teaching about the Spirit.* A good deal of discussion has centred on the background of παράκλητος, which has been illuminated by the emphasis on the legal background of the Fourth Gospel, and on the Spirit as

---

[6] Stronstad, Shelton and Menzies may be mentioned as the most substantial works from Pentecostal scholars stimulated by James Dunn's *Baptism in the Holy Spirit* (whose sub-title was *A Re-examination of the New Testament Teaching on the Gift of the Holy Spirit in relation to Pentecostalism Today*). Dunn responded, by invitation, to these scholars' and others' works, in his article 'Baptism in the Spirit: A Response to Pentecostal Scholarship on Luke–Acts', *JPT* 3 (1993), pp. 3-27.

Christ's alter ego. It has been widely assumed that the more developed teaching in John is due to the delay of the Parousia and the death of the apostolic generation, but K. Haacker's suggestion (*Die Stiftung des Heils. Untersuchungen zur Struktur der Johanneischen Theologie* [Stuttgart: Calwer Verlag, 1971]) that John is concerned with the problem of how Christianity copes with following Jesus when it no longer has his physical presence with it seems more true to the thrust of the Farewell Discourses.[7] Apart from commentaries on John, we may mention the following significant studies: G. Bornkamm, 'Der Paraklet im Johannesevangelium', in *Festschrift für R. Bultmann* (Stuttgart: Kohlhammer, 1949), pp. 12-35; D.E. Holwerda, *The Holy Spirit and Eschatology in the Gospel of John* (Kampen: Kok, 1959); F. Mussner, 'Die Parakletspruch und die apostolischen Tradition', *BZ* 5 (1961), pp. 56-70; O. Betz, *Der Paraklet* (AGSU 2; Leiden: Brill, 1963); R.E. Brown, 'The Paraclete in the Fourth Gospel', *NTS* 13 (1966–67), pp. 113-32 (reprinted in his *The Gospel according to John XIII-XXI* [London: Chapman, 1971]), pp. 1135-44; H. Windisch, *The Spirit-Paraclete in the Fourth Gospel* (Philadelphia: Fortress, 1968 [ET of *Die fünf johanneischen Parakletsprüche* (1927), and *Jesus und der Geist im Johannesevangelium* (1933)]; G. Johnston, *The Spirit-Paraclete in the Gospel of John* (Cambridge: Cambridge University Press, 1970); E. Bammel, 'Jesus und der Paraklet in Johannes 16', in B. Lindars and S.S. Smalley (eds.), *Christ and Spirit in the New Testament* (Cambridge: Cambridge University Press, 1973), pp. 199-216; U.B. Müller, 'Die Parakletvorstellung im Johannesevangelium', *ZThK* 71 (1974), pp. 331-77; F. Porsch, *Pneuma und Wort. Ein exegetischer Beitrag zur Pneumatologie des Johannesevangelium* (FTS 16; Frankfurt: Knecht, 1974); E. Franck, *Revelation Taught: The Paraclete in the Gospel of John* (CB NT series 14; Lund: Gleerup, 1985); G.M. Burge, *The Anointed Community: The Holy Spirit in the Johannine Tradition* (Grand Rapids, MI: Eerdmans, 1987); C. Dietzfelbinger, 'Paraklet und theologischer Anspruch im Johannesevangelium', *ZThK* 82 (1985), pp. 389-408; U. Schnelle, 'Johannes als Geisttheologe', *NT* 40 (1988), pp. 17-31; C.S. Keener, *The Spirit in the Gospels and Acts: Divine Purity and Power* (Peabody, MA: Hendrickson, 1997), pp. 135-189; J. Becker, 'Das Geist- und Gemeindeverständnis des vierten Evangelisten', *ZNW* 89 (1998), pp. 217-34; J. Rahner, 'Vergegenwärtigende Erinnerung: die Abschiedsreden, der Geist-Paraklet und die Retrospektive des Johannes-evangeliums', *ZNW* 91 (2000), pp. 72-90; C. Bennema, *The Power of Saving Wisdom: An Investigation of Spirit and Wisdom in Relation to the Soteriology of the Fourth Gospel* (WUNT 148; Tubingen: Mohr Siebeck, 2002).

The weight of research has fallen on these three areas in the NT, though discussions of the role of the Spirit in other NT writings have occasionally appeared, especially on the Synoptic Tradition, of which we may mention: H. Windisch 'Jesus und Geist nach synoptischen Uberlieferung', in S.J. Case (ed.), *Studies in Early*

---

[7] Recently, C. Dietzfelbinger, *Paraklet*, p. 396, and J. Rahner, *Vergegenwärtigende Erinnerung*, p. 74 (see above), have also stressed the departure of Jesus and how the revelation of Jesus is to continue, as the issue being dealt with in Jn 13.31–14.31.

Christianity (New York: Century, 1928), pp. 209-36; C.K. Barrett, *The Holy Spirit in the Gospel Tradition* (London: SPCK, 1947); Dunn, *Jesus and the Spirit*, pp. 41-92; Chevalier, *Souffle*, pp. 81-225; Keener, *The Spirit*, pp. 1-134. There have also been some studies on the implications of what the NT says about the Spirit for Christian doctrine: A.W. Wainwright, *The Trinity in the New Testament* (London: SPCK, 1957), pp. 199-234; J.V. Taylor, *The Go-Between God* (London: SCM, 1972); G.W.H. Lampe, *God as Spirit* (Oxford: Clarendon, 1977); C.F.D. Moule, *The Holy Spirit* (London and Oxford: Mowbray, 1978).

2. On the Patristic side, we have a few monographs or articles on the Spirit in the Apostolic Fathers and later second-century writers. T. Rüsch examined the teaching on the Spirit in Ignatius, Theophilus and Irenaeus (*Die Entstehung der Lehre vom heiligen Geist bei Ignatius von Antiocha, Theophilus von Antiocheia und Irenäus von Lyon* [Zurich: Theologischer Verlag, 1952]). The treatment is fairly brief—a chapter per author and within each chapter little exploration of the experience of the Spirit emerges. H. Opitz investigated the pneumatology of Clement and Hermas, in his *Ursprünge frühkatholischen Pneumatologie* (Berlin: Evangelische Verlagsanstalt, 1960). He was particularly interested in the comparative religious background of the Roman church's concept of the Spirit as revealed by these two authors—even here the late Jewish background and similarities with Qumran material need to be considered far more than he did—and not with religious experience per se. He felt that Clement is strongly influenced by Stoic philosophy (Seneca, Epictetus); Hermas, on the other hand, is indebted to the Roman genius concept, as it had been spiritualized and internalized in Stoicism. The Roman experience of the Spirit combined Christian tradition and Stoic philosophy, and thus enabled it to both remain Christian and pursue its victorious way in the world. J. Reiling included a chapter on prophecy and the Spirit in his important monograph, *Hermas and Christian Prophecy* (SNT 37; Leiden: Brill, 1973), but his attention was confined to Mandate XI and he did not, therefore, range any further.

Of the Apologists, Justin's view of the Spirit's relation to the Logos has usually attracted more attention than anything else. A short article on what Justin lets us discern of contemporary experience of the Holy Spirit's working has appeared from the present writer ('The Holy Spirit and Christian Experience in Justin Martyr', *V.C.* 38 [1984], pp. 172-77).

An extremely important monograph came from W-D. Hauschild, *Gottes Geist und der Mensch, Studien zur frühchristlichen Pneumatologie* (München: Chr. Kaiser Verlag, 1972). Hauschild investigated the concept of the Spirit in Clement of Alexander, Origen and Valentinian Gnosticism. He then briefly examined Tatian and Irenaeus. His major interest was in examining the idea of the formation of the true man through the Spirit, and he believed that the late second-century theologians were more influenced by late Jewish than by early Christian ideas. In other words, the focus of his attention was basically anthropological: pneumatology is a way in which the elect or elite express their sense of being something special within humanity. This became ontologised in Valentinian Gnosticism. Thus, Hauschild's interest was a limited one. Whether he does justice to someone like Irenaeus is doubtful.

To H.J. Jaschke we owe a work on Irenaeus' pneumatology: *Der heilige Geist in Bekenntnis der Kirche. Eine Studie zur Pneumatologie des Irenäus von Lyons im Ausgang vom altchristlichen Glaubensbekenntnis* (Münster: Aschendorff, 1976). A first section surveyed credal formulae to the fourth century and argued for the primitiveness of a trinitarian baptismal faith, which was the basis of the later three-article confession of faith. Thus, Irenaeus' pneumatology is set against a traditional background. Then Jaschke discusses Irenaeus' views—the Spirit in the unity of the Trinitarian God; the Spirit's role in the application of God's work of salvation (in the Christ event; OT prophecy; creation); and the Spirit's activity in the church (the church as the place of the Spirit; truth and understanding through the Spirit; the renewal of humans by the Spirit). A good deal of Jaschke's attention is directed to inter-Trinitarian relationships and to the church as the place where the Spirit is active in guiding into the truth. His section on the renewal of humans by the Spirit is fairly brief and is not a major centre of interest. There is room for further work here.

Until recently we were dependent for a study of Montanism on older works, such as N. Bonwetsch, *Die Geschichte des Montanismus* (Erlangen: Andreas Deichert, 1881); P. de Labriolle, *La Crise Montaniste* (Paris: Ernest Leroux, 1913); and W. Schepelern, *Der Montanismus und die phrygischen Kulte: Eine religionsgeschichtliche Untersuchung* (Tübingen: Mohr, 1929), together with some recent articles (to mention a few) by H. Kraft, 'Die altchristliche Prophetie und die Entstehung des Montanismus', *ThZ* 11 (1955), pp. 249-71 (dealing with prophecy before and in Montanism); K. Aland, 'Der Montanismus und die kleinasiatische Theologie', *ZNW* 46 (1955), pp. 109-16, and 'Bermerkungen zur frühchristlichen Eschatologie', in *Kirchengeschichtliche Entwurfe* (Gütersloh: Gerd Mohn, 1960), pp. 105-48, (emphasizing the movement's orthodoxy in the early days and its Asia Minor theology); A.F. Walls, 'The Montanist "Catholic Epistle" and its NT Prototype', in F.L. Cross (ed.), *Studia Evangelica* III (TU 88; Berlin: Akadamie-Verlag, 1964), pp. 436-46; H. Paulsen, 'Die Bedeutung des Montanismus fur die Herausbildung des Kanons', *VC* 32 (1978), pp. 1-32; R.E. Heine, 'The Role of the Gospel of John in the Montanist Controversy', *SC* 6 (1987), pp. 1-19; 'The Gospel of John and the Montanist Debate at Rome', in *Studia Patristica* XXI (Leuven: Peeters, 1989), pp. 95-100. Now, however, we not only have an edition of Montanist oracles through R.E. Heine, *The Montanist Oracles and Testimonia* (Macon, GA: Mercer University Press, 1989), but we also have a full-length study of the movement, which not only draws together recent research but makes its own contribution, by C. Trevett, *Montanism: Gender, Authority and the New Prophecy* (Cambridge: Cambridge University Press, 1996). Trevett looks at the beginnings and spread of Montanism, its teaching on various subjects, the role of women within it (a special interest of the author) and, finally, its fate.

Discussion of Montanism is inevitably controlled by the fact that the sources are limited and are generally transmitted through hostile channels. The issue of ecstasy as a sign of the Spirit's inspiration is clearly a major topic because the controversy between the catholics and the Montanists centred on this. T.D. Barnes' *Tertullian* (Oxford: Clarendon, 1971; reissued with a postscript, 1985) has a chapter on Montanism, while H. Bender looked at Tertullian's pneumatology in *Die Lehre über den heiligen Geist bei Tertullian* (München: Max Hueber Verlag, 1961), though he did little more than group the references thematically, and he asked few questions of the material. G.L. Bray, *Holiness and the Will of God, Perspectives on the Theology of Tertullian* (London: Marshall, Morgan & Scott, 1979), considered that Tertullian's major preoccupation was sanctification, made possible through the coming of the Spirit (before the imminent end), though he did not in fact devote much attention to the role of the Spirit. R. Kearsley, *Tertullian's Theology of Divine Power* (Edinburgh: Rutherford House and Carlisle: Paternoster, 1998), looks at Tertullian's theology through the concept of divine power, and within the chapter on the new creation there are a few pages on the Spirit's role (pp. 83-88), though we shall have to examine whether Tertullian's belief that Christians enjoy the Spirit's power is not in the end overshadowed by his stress on what they ought to do.

There have been a couple of more popular surveys of the work and gifts of the Spirit in the post-NT period. They tend to list the references to the Spirit without lengthy discussions: S.M. Burgess, *The Spirit and the Church: Antiquity* (Peabody, MA: Hendrickson, 1984), and R.A.N. Kydd, *Charismatic Gifts in the Early Church* (Peabody, MA: Hendrickson, 1984).

3. There are some exceptions to the general rule about departmentalized study. H. Weinel, *Die Wirkungen des Geistes und der Geister in nachapostolischen Zeitalter bis auf Irenäus* (Tübingen: Druck von H. Lampp, 1899), straddled the NT and early Patristic period. He covered the post-Pauline period up to Irenaeus and saw his study as a continuation of the work of his teacher, H. Gunkel, *The Influence of the Holy Spirit: The Popular View of the Apostolic Age and the Teaching of the Apostle Paul* (Philadelphia: Fortress, 1979, ET of *Die Wirkungen des heiligen Geistes nach der populären Anschauung der apostolischen Zeit und der Lehre des Apostels Paulus* [Göttingen: Vandenhoeck & Ruprecht, 1888]). Weinel examined the areas of speech, writing, healings, miracles, symbolic actions, martyrdom, ethical victory over sinful behaviour, visions, auditory experiences, baptism, laying-on of hands, prayer, asceticism, and certain sensory experiences (taste, smell, touch), etc. The treatment is a history of phenomena associated with the Spirit, and the reader does not receive a clear idea of what particular authors thought overall nor of their geographical distribution, though Weinel succeeded in making out his case that the experience of the Spirit and spirits continued to live on after the first generation, in many, vivid ways. At several points Weinel utilised the then comparatively new approaches of psychology in an endeavour to understand the various texts. Over a hundred years have elapsed since Weinel wrote, and it may be reasonably maintained that a new study is not out of place.

H. Swete's two separate volumes, *The Holy Spirit in the New Testament* and *The Holy Spirit in the Ancient Church* (London: Macmillan, 1910 and 1912 respectively), were presumably conceived as complementing one another to afford a survey of the teaching in the church from earliest days to Chalcedon. He hardly did more than list references to the Spirit in each writer, and made little attempt to ask questions of the text. As such, his work has a limited usefulness and certainly needs to be superseded in the English-speaking world.

More recently, G.W.H. Lampe, *The Seal of the Spirit: A Study of the Doctrine of Baptism and Confirmation in the New Testament and the Fathers* (London: Longmans, Green, 1951, 2nd edn, 1967), is also an exception to the general rule. Lampe investigated the relation of the Spirit and baptism with special reference to the concept of the seal of the Spirit. Thus, his theme was a very narrow one, pursued out of interest in the Anglican church's debate whether the giving of the Spirit took place in baptism or confirmation.

In conclusion, then, we feel confident that there is room for a look at the whole issue of how far Christian religious experience was interpreted in terms of the Holy Spirit in the period suggested.

2. A Brief Survey of the Experience of the Spirit in the First Two Generations

In this section we shall seek to assess very briefly Christian experience of the Holy Spirit from the church's inception to ca.AD 90 to provide the background to our study. From those sources which exist in this period, we want to ascertain how far believers' Christianity was determined by an ongoing experience of the Spirit. What did Christians mean by claiming that they had 'received' God's Spirit? What did their sense that the presence and power of the Spirit was impinging on their lives involve? Were they conscious of a power transcending human nature, helping them in worship and prayer, as they spoke the Christian message, and as they struggled against the temptations and vices of the world around them? Or, put another way, what experiences did they have which they 'naturally' attributed to the Spirit?

a) *Paul* is our only direct witness to the first generation. From occasional statements which he makes about himself, we learn that he was aware of the Spirit's presence and power in his life and ministry. He claimed (i) to speak with tongues, though preferring rational utterance in church. Glossolalia is one of the gifts of the Spirit, though not to be overrated (1 Cor. 14.18); (ii) to have had ecstatic experiences (2 Cor. 5.13a;[8] 12.1-4); (iii) to perform miracles through the Spirit's power (Rom. 15.19; cf. 2 Cor. 12.12). Presumably he had some sense of power flowing through him; (iv) to speak through the Spirit's inspiration (in 1 Cor. 2.4 the conscious antithesis to cultivated rhetorical techniques suggests spontaneous utterance). He had a sense of the words flowing out of him and the hearers being gripped by what he said;[9] (v) to give rulings through the Spirit: 1 Corinthians 7.40

---

[8] C.K. Barrett, *The Second Epistle to the Corinthians* (London: A & C Black, 1973), p. 166, and Dunn, *Jesus and the Spirit*, pp. 215-16, both accept a reference to an ecstatic state in Paul's words.

[9] Cf. Dunn, *Jesus and the Spirit*, p. 247.

could mean either the 'blinding flash'[10] or the product of careful and perhaps prolonged thought and consideration.

When we broaden our consideration from Paul personally to what he said to and about the congregations, then we find that he can describe a Christian in terms of the Holy Spirit: 'Anyone who does not have the Spirit of Christ does not belong to him' (Rom. 8.9). The very phraseology suggests that 'having' the Spirit is a *conscious*—almost (one might say) quantifiable—experience.

On the other hand, nowhere does Paul suggest that a Christian has not received the Spirit[11] *(*e.g. 1 Thess. 4.8; 1 Cor. 12.3, 13; 2 Cor. 3.17-18; Gal. 3.2-5, assume his readers' possession of the Spirit). The assumption of 1 Corinthians 12 is that the Spirit has given a gift or gifts to everyone for the common good, to benefit the church as a whole, to build it up. A whole list of gifts is enumerated, all dispensed by one and the same Spirit (vv. 8-11, 28-30; cf. Rom. 12.6-8).

How far does Paul assume *conscious* experience of the Spirit? He says that believers:

(i) receive the Spirit. His question to the Galatians points to a definite awareness of the fact (Gal. 3.2,[12] 14; cf. Rom. 8.15; 1 Cor. 2.12; 2 Cor. 11.4).

(ii) walk or live by the Spirit (Gal. 5.16, 25; Rom. 8.4) or are led by the Spirit (Gal. 5.17-18; Rom. 8.14). The language suggests an awareness of strength imparted to resist temptation and follow what is good or a sudden illumination which gives certainty concerning God's will or the right conduct.[13] Thus, in the tussle between the indwelling Spirit and the individual as still living in this age, the Spirit proves the stronger force (Gal. 5.18).[14] Here we might mention that the Spirit helps our weakness, especially our inadequacy of expression in prayer.

(iii) cry out, in prayer or confession, through the Spirit's prompting (Gal. 4.6; Rom. 8.15).[15]

(iv) believers' bodies individually are temples of God's Spirit (1 Cor. 6.19; possibly 2 Cor. 6.16, where the individual believer and unbeliever are envisaged).

---

[10] Dunn, *Jesus and the Spirit*, p. 224, opts for this.

[11] C.L. Mitton, *Ephesians* (London: Oliphants, 1976), p. 59, is typical in stating 'Paul felt that he could assume that anyone who was a believing Christian had received the Holy Spirit. It was a privilege granted to all believers, not to only a few.'

[12] See Dunn, *Baptism*, p. 113; H.D. Betz, *Galatians* (Hermeneia; Philadelphia: Fortress, 1979), p. 132.

[13] Betz, *Galatians*, p. 281; Dunn, *Jesus and the Spirit*, p. 225, pertinently remarks that in Paul the Spirit cannot be reduced to some rationally construed claim of God, while the attempt to reduce Paul's concept of guidance to the level of Bible study misunderstands him at a fundamental level.

[14] Betz, *Galatians*, p. 280, sees Gal. 5.17 as pre-Pauline and 5.18 as Paul's own doctrine, a view accepted by F.F. Bruce, *The Epistle to the Galatians* (Exeter: Paternoster, 1982), p. 245.

[15] Dunn, *Jesus and the Spirit*, p. 240, takes κρᾶζον as 'a cry of some intensity, probably a loud cry, and perhaps (but less likely) an ecstatic cry', while Betz, *Galatians*, pp. 132, 210, thinks that the term does have the ring of ecstasy.

(v) are not to quench the Spirit (1 Thess.5.19), which is probably a reference to the exercise of spiritual gifts, through which the Spirit manifests himself.

(vi) are to use spiritual gifts to contribute to worship, the impression created being that of spontaneous rather than prepared contributions, and these are seen as gifts of the Spirit (1 Cor. 14.26-28). The dramatic effect of prophecy on an 'outsider' is deemed to be the Spirit's work (vv. 24-25).

On the other hand, there are passages which suggest that Paul would not exclude thoughtful consideration leading to action as the Spirit's work. The Spirit's activity could inspire both spontaneous action and hard thinking. For example, Christian giving as expounded in 2 Corinthians 8–9 may be both a spontaneous gesture of generosity (8.2,5) and the careful working out of Christian principles and responsibilities. Then, again, discerning God's will could be both a spontaneous, intuitive awareness (possibly Gal. 2.2; 1 Cor. 15.51; 2 Cor. 12.9; Rom. 11.25) or the result of exercising intelligent, rational thinking on a topic or problem (hence Paul's appeal to judge a matter (1 Cor. 10.15; 11.13) and to be mature in thinking (1 Cor. 14.20); and his stress on the need for the mind to be renewed (Rom. 12.1-3) and engaged (1 Cor. 14.14, 19) and his exhortation to take into consideration what is honourable in the sight of men and women (2 Cor. 8.21; Phil. 4.8). Furthermore, the qualities of love listed in 1 Corinthians 13 seem as likely to be the result of gradual transformation as of instant change[16] (e.g. patience, lack of envy), while at 2 Corinthians 3.18 Paul speaks of our being transformed, which suggests an ongoing process. Love must be pursued continually (1 Cor. 14.1).

Thus, we may say that there has emerged a combination of (to put the matter colloquially) 'something hit me' and the calm, rational, sober working out of a Christian response.

This albeit sketchy survey shows that for Paul personally and his congregations Christianity was directed by the Spirit of God, and this was a matter of something often felt in a dramatic way. From the moment of commitment to Christ, all aspects of the Christian life (worship, prayer, ethics, service, miracles, decisions, etc.) were connected with the Spirit.

(b) *Pre-Lucan Material in Acts* corroborates the impression left by the Pauline evidence. However much Lucan shaping of the material may have occurred, most scholars would accept that the experience of the Spirit was embedded in the traditions which came to Luke. Primitive Christianity was a movement which originated through the impact made by Jesus of Nazareth and by the belief that God had raised him after he had been crucified, coupled with the sense that the Holy Spirit of God had been poured out on the followers of Jesus.

---

[16] So also Betz, *Galatians*, p. 287, on the fruit of the Spirit; and against Dunn, *Jesus and the Spirit*, pp. 224-25, who sees love as the inner compulsion of God's Spirit coming to concrete expression in loving word and deed.

That the phrase 'in the last days' in the Joel quotation in Acts 2 is hardly likely to have been added by Luke himself[17] suggests a pre-Lucan use of Joel 2 to explain the early Christians' sense of God's Spirit in their midst, inaugurating the last days (Paul's eschatological view of the Spirit in Rom. 8.23; 2 Cor. 1.22 and 5.5, agrees with this). The earliest congregations had a sense of invasion by divine power, which they explained as due to the outpouring of God's Spirit in fulfillment of Joel 2.

This experience resulted in:

(i) prophecy (11.28a;[18] 21.10-11[19]—the tension between 21.4 and 10-11 may be historical and illustrate the impossibility of objectivity in assessing claims to guidance by the Spirit); cf. Acts 13.1; 15.32; 21.9 for mention of specific prophets by name.

(ii) inspired speech. The phrase 'filled with the Holy Spirit' at 4.8; 13.9 may be Lucan, but the idea tallies with Paul's view of utterance through the Spirit (1 Cor. 12.8-10; 14.24-33; Rom. 15.18-19).

(iii) the ability to heal (cf. Rom. 15.19; Heb. 2.4).

(iv) glossolalia—perhaps taken to be speaking in a foreign language (Acts 2.4,8; 10.46; 19.6).[20]

(v) visions (frequent in Acts).

(vi) pronouncements of judgment like that on Ananias and Sapphira, which presupposed the sense of the Spirit's indwelling the congregation and its leaders (Acts 5.1-11; cf. 1 Cor. 5.3-5; 14.24-25).

(vii) guidance and direction from the Spirit. There seems a scholarly consensus that in practice either a prophet claimed to utter a message directly from the Spirit or a prophetic word was recognized there and then as a word from the Spirit: 13.2; 15.28; 16.7, have all been understood in these ways. Clearly there is a difference between 'what happened' and how the event was written up. We can partially penetrate the latter (whether Lucan or pre-Lucan) to discern the primitive church's sense of the Spirit's directing the church's mission and internal life.

We have sought in this brief survey only to mention passages where there is widespread agreement on their pre-Lucan character. The picture that emerges coheres at several points with the picture which Paul offers,[21] as indicated.

---

[17] So rightly Dunn, *Jesus and the Spirit*, p. 160, against E. Haenchen, *The Acts of the Apostles* (Oxford: Blackwell, 1971), p.179, who opts for the B reading, but this is most likely to have been an assimilation to the original Joel quotation.

[18] Even Haenchen, *Acts*, p. 378, accepts that Luke received a tradition about Agabus' prophecy.

[19] Haenchen, *Acts*, p. 605, seems again to accept the broad historicity of the story. If Luke had invented the episode, he would hardly have mentioned that the Jews would tie Paul up (cf. H. Patsch, 'Die Prophetie des Agabus', *TZ* 28 [1972], pp. 230-31).

[20] See the study by C. Forbes, *Prophecy and Inspired Speech in Early Christianity and its Hellenistic Environment* (Peabody, MA: Hendrickson, 1997), for a thorough investigation of this theme.

[21] Cf. Dunn's comments, *Jesus and the Spirit*, pp. 169, 195.

Luke's gaze is on the mission of the church, not so much the internal life. So, what he offers is inevitably partial and incomplete. Yet, within his own terms of reference, he offers, as far as the experience of the Spirit is concerned, a reasonably reliable picture of a movement which believed that it had been baptized in the Holy Spirit (cf. Acts 1.5; 11.16).

c) *Lucan Redaction*. In order to avoid unnecessary reduplication we shall only briefly comment here on Luke himself as a witness to second generation Christianity. Luke clearly saw the Spirit as the best of all the Heavenly Father's good gifts (Lk. 11.13 over against Mt. 7.11). He sees the Spirit as the motive power behind the church's mission (Lk. 24.49). We need only instance a few examples where his editorial hand is widely accepted. At Acts 1.8, the programmatic sentence links Spirit, power and mission, and sets the scene for the rest of Acts. Luke seems to have set the Jewish and Gentile 'Pentecost' in chapters 2 and 10 in parallel. The 'encounter' between Christianity and paganism in the person of Simon Magus shows that the Holy Spirit is more powerful than pagan magic (8.14-24). In Paul's farewell speech to the Ephesian elders, it is asserted that the Holy Spirit appoints leaders to care for the congregations (20.28, though there is no interest in ministerial succession).

The overall impression is of the church surging forward on its God-intended task of mission, empowered by the Spirit. There is resistance and opposition, but these do not really thwart the onward march of the Spirit-inspired mission. Luke leaves the reader with the gospel being proclaimed 'quite openly and without hindrance' (μετὰ πάσης παρρησίας ἀκωλύτως) at Rome, the centre of the Roman empire (28.31).

There is widespread agreement that Luke has heightened an existing emphasis and that he takes great pleasure in recording words and deeds deemed to be inspired by the Spirit (for all the so-called 'early catholic' features allegedly present in Acts). Thus did someone in the post-apostolic period look back on the beginnings of the church and no doubt also reflected current experience in his description.

We assume that *Ephesians* is by a Paulinist and is a product of the second generation of the church.[22] The author exhorts his readers not to get drunk with

---

[22] Cf. C.L. Mitton, *The Epistle to the Ephesians: Its Authorship, Origin and Purpose* (Oxford: Clarendon, 1951), and *Ephesians* (NCB; London: Oliphants, 1976); J. Gnilka, *Der Epheserbrief* (HTKNT Band X.2; Freiburg-Basel-Wien: Herder, 1971); D.G. Meade, *Pseudonymity and Canon: An Investigation into the Relationship of Authorship and Authority in Jewish and Earliest Christian Tradition* (Grand Rapids, MI: Eerdmans, 1987), pp. 139-57; R. Schnackenburg, *The Epistle to the Ephesians* (Edinburgh: T. & T. Clark, 1991); J.D.G. Dunn, *The Theology of Paul the Apostle* (Edinburgh: T. & T. Clark, 1998), p. 13 (n. 39). Defenders of Pauline authorship include E. Percy, *Die Probleme der Kolosser- und Epheserbriefe* (Lund: Gleerup, 1946), esp. pp. 179-356; A. van Roon, *The Authenticity of Ephesians* (Leiden: Brill, 1974); H. Schlier, *Der Brief an die Epheser: Ein Kommentar* (Düsseldorf: Patmos, 1957); J.A.T. Robinson, *Redating the New Testament* (London: SCM, 1976), pp. 62-64; F.F. Bruce, *The Epistles to the Colossians, to Philemon and to the Ephesians* (NICNT; Grand Rapids, MI: Eerdmans, 1984); A.T. Lincoln, *Ephesians* (WBC 42; Waco, TX: Word, 1990); D. Guthrie, *New Testament*

alcohol but to be filled with the Spirit (5.18). If the author is contrasting alcoholic inebriation with spiritual experience, we may ask whether he was thinking of something 'felt', something exhilarating which heightened one's emotions and led to praise and thanksgiving (5.19).[23]

All have been sealed by the promised Spirit at their conversion (1.13; 4.30). Nothing is said as to the nature of this experience,[24] whether it is an exuberant or non-ecstatic type of sensation. The Spirit seems to be a sign of God's ownership and a protection to ensure safe arrival at the Last Day (see 4.29, 31).[25]

Twice the author prays for the gift of the Spirit for his readers: for wisdom and understanding of spiritual things (1.17)[26] and for inner strengthening (3.16), presumably in the fight against evil and temptation (6.10-20).

The Spirit indwells the church (2.22), helps to create unity (4.3-4) and is the means of access in Christ for Jew and Gentile to God (2.18).

Summary

Both Paul and the traditional material in Acts show that first generation Christianity was conscious of having received the Spirit of God and this experience consisted both of dramatic aspects (stimulus to speak, power to perform certain deeds like healing and miracles, sudden flashes of insight into God's purposes, etc.) as well as what we might call sublimation of the normal in a non-ecstatic manner—ethical

---

Introduction, (Leicester: Apollos and Downer's Grove, Illinois: InterVarsity Press, 4th edn (rev.), 1990), pp 496-528; L.M. McDonald and S.E. Porter, *Early Christianity and its Sacred Literature* (Peabody, MA: Hendrickson, 2000), pp. 482-85 ('Authentic Pauline authorship is as reasonable a choice as the alternatives'). A mediating position is taken by J. Muddiman, *A Commentary on the Epistle to the Ephesians* (London-New York: Continuum, 2001), pp. 2-36 (an expansion of a genuine letter by Paul, the letter to the Laodiceans, and to be dated ca.90). R.P. Martin, *New Testament Foundations: A Guide for Christian Students, Vol. 2: Acts-Revelation* (Exeter: Paternoster, 1978), pp. 227-33, 238, argues for Lucan authorship after Paul's death, and sees Ephesians 'as a last ditch stand by a well-known representative of Paul in his final attempt to regain Asia for the Pauline gospel' (p. 233).

[23] So H. Schlier, *Epheserbrief*, pp. 245-50; M. Barth, *Ephesians* (AB; New York: Doubleday, 1974), p. 582; Mitton, *Ephesians*, pp. 189-90; Schnackenburg, *Ephesians*, pp. 237-38.

[24] Barth, *Ephesians*, pp. 140-41, equates it with the fact that they glorify God and confess Jesus as Lord, and he thinks of the continual flow of strength from God to men and women; for Barth, the phrase is equivalent to 'supplying the Spirit'. On p. 143, he speaks of it in terms of the designation, appointment and equipment of the saints for public ministry.

[25] See Lampe, *Seal*, pp. 1-18.

[26] That God's Spirit is thought of here and not the human spirit is also the view of Schlier, *Epheserbrief*, pp. 75-81; J. Gnilka, *Epheserbrief*, p. 90; and Schnackenburg, *Ephesians*, p. 74; though there may be a thin line of distinction in practice between the Spirit who bestows wisdom and the spirit which has received wisdom from the Spirit.

growth, maturity of character, the use of gifts and abilities like administration, practical service, etc.

If Luke and the author of Ephesians are in any way typical of second generation Christianity, this sense of the Spirit's presence continued in vivid and unabated fashion. There are signs of developing institutions, but at this stage office and Spirit are not seen as antithetical; rather, office is created by the Spirit (Acts 20.28) or the ascended Lord (Eph. 4.11). Luke sees the Spirit as mighty power (Acts 1.8) carrying the church onward and forward on its mission (e.g. 16.6, 8, 10) and superior to all pagan forms of wonder-working magic (8.4-24; 19.11-20). In Ephesians, Christians ought to be filled and strengthened by the Spirit by whom they have been sealed.

3. Problems and Aims

If the earliest generation certainly and the next generation probably understood its Christian life as characterized by the experience of the Holy Spirit in the ways already described, we now face the question: did that experience continue to be central and dominant in the era AD 90-200? Did Christians of this period see their Christianity in such terms?

A word of caution needs to be sounded here. If a rose would smell as sweet by any other name, we ought to remember that other phrases might convey the same experience as Spirit-phraseology (e.g. 1 Cor. 12.4-6 is surely a triple way of describing the same basic experience). Thus, the lack of mention of the Spirit need not of itself indicate that what characterized the earlier Christianity of the first and second generations was absent. That first generation found it natural to speak in a certain way. It is possible that the same experience could be included within different phraseology. Other expressions would have to be taken into consideration.[27]

Another factor which also has to be taken into consideration is the genre of a work and its aim. Is the subject matter treated of such a nature that we would naturally expect references to the Holy Spirit? How is silence about the Spirit to be evaluated—when is it significant and when accidental or covered by other phrases? If the topic is Christian behaviour, then we might expect to hear mention of the Spirit, but criticism of false teaching, allegorical interpretation of the OT, rules concerning the administration of baptism, fasts and the agape/eucharist, need not contain references to the Spirit, and so absence of them needs occasion no surprise.

The organisation of the material presents some problems. Arguably, the most neutral approach would be to examine each author individually, but the question may justly be posed whether this does not result in a skeleton, a portrait without any flesh and blood. An alternative or variant of this approach would be an arrangement according to date, though basically the same objection might be raised here also.

In the end, we have decided on a geographical arrangement. A few years ago, J.P. Meir and R.E. Brown (in their book on *Antioch and Rome* [New York-Ramsey:

---

[27] Luz, *Disciples*, p. 113, has said with regard to Mt. 28.20, that the formulation 'I am with you' probably means in effect the same as what is said with the catch-word 'Spirit'.

Paulist, 1983], pp ix, 213) admitted that some areas of their work were speculative, but claimed that research is only advanced by such probes (even if it is by stimulating others to produce better suggestions). I have arranged the material in this book in the same spirit. I am aware that the geographical arrangement has its drawbacks, since there is no certainty about the provenance of, for example, Jude and 2 Clement, while dispute continues over that of John's Gospel and Epistles, the Didache and Barnabas. Nevertheless, none of the positions here adopted are outlandish, and all can call on considerable scholarly support.

Actually, the geographical approach is not novel. It was used effectively fifty years ago by L. Goppelt in his *Christentum und Judentum im ersten und zweiten Jahrhundert* (Gütersloh: Mohn, 1954) and more recently by H. Koester in his *Introduction to the New Testament, Vol. 2: History and Literature of Early Christianity* (Philadelphia: Fortress, 1982) and by J.M.G. Barclay, *Jews in the Mediterranean Diaspora* (Berkeley-Los Angeles-London: University of California Press, 1996).

The advantage of the geographical arrangement is that it puts a little more 'flesh and blood on the bones' and enables us to appreciate some of the diversity and variety of church life and Christian experience in the period chosen. Within the geographical arrangement, we also use the author by author and the chronological one, so that in a sense the two different approaches are being married. Of course, a given writer may not necessarily be typical of the church in the region where the author wrote. Tertullian is a possible instance that springs to mind, but precisely his polemical references to other Christians whom he deemed unspiritual are helpful in gauging the spiritual temperature in North Africa at the end of the second century.

While geographical location may not arouse passionate feelings, the issue of dating can be a much more sensitive one. There will be readers who affirm the traditional authorship of NT writings and their dating, and will, therefore, disagree with some of the positions adopted in this work. Clearly, our 'road map' of Christian experience in relation to the Holy Spirit will differ, if, for example, 1 Peter, the Pastoral Epistles, John's Gospel and the Johannine Epistles are pulled back before AD 70. Readers who disagree with my position on dating will have to make the necessary adjustments. Those who do date the NT writings to the period before AD 70 have to cope with a 'tunnel period' before the writings of the Apostolic Fathers appear from 1 Clement and the *Didache* in the 90s onwards.[28] I hope that those who disagree with my positions on dating will realize that I have reached them only after much careful thought. For myself there is no conflict between the acceptance of pseudepigraphy within the NT (and OT) and the acceptance of the authority of the Scriptures in all matters of faith and conduct for the Christian church as a whole and for individual Christians.

---

[28] Robinson, *Redating*, pp. 312-335, sought to overcome this by dating the *Didache* to 40-60; 1 Clement, early 70s; the *Epistle of Barnabas*, ca.75; and *the Shepherd of Hermas* to ca.85.

Not all aspects of the work of the Holy Spirit will be investigated. That would be impossible to achieve at any depth within reasonable limits of space and would be possible only at the cost of becoming a mere catalogue of references. So, we have selected three areas of experience of the Spirit to examine in the authors of our period.

When Christians from NT times to the present day have spoken about experiencing the Holy Spirit, they have meant a variety of things, but certainly the following are included:

(i) What we may call *a sense of God's wholly-other presence, a sense of the numinous, some sort of ecstatic experience, a sense of being surrounded or pervaded or overwhelmed by or caught up into the divine.* The human personality seems to be invaded by an outside power and this occasions feelings of intense joy or fear. Or it may be described as a sense of something welling up within a person's inner being, bringing heightened emotional sensations. Such an experience may well be described in terms of the Holy Spirit.

This rapturous experience may not remain wholly 'internalised', as it were, but may lead to some sort of utterance—the proclamation of a word deemed to come from God which has been heard or perceived internally, a word which may be one of judgment/threat, or of deliverance/promise/reassurance/comfort. The speaker feels moved or impelled to utter 'on the spot' or on the nearest occasion possible the message received. (Equally, of course, it may be that the Spirit's inspiration is claimed for a word or written work which is the result of careful prior preparation.)

Deeds may also flow from this experience. Thus, recipients may feel impelled to heal or perform some miracle or action because they have become the channel of the Spirit's power.

What we have thus described is a felt or conscious experience of God's Spirit, rather than an evaluation after the event. It is not a case of looking back with hindsight and claiming that one was led by the Spirit, but rather a conscious awareness of a power outside of oneself at work in and through one.

Why did the early Christians ascribe such experiences to the Spirit of God? The answer must lie within their heritage. In the OT and Hebraic-Judaic tradition the Spirit was associated with power. The Spirit is pictured as invading and impelling to action (often unusual and bizarre). There was a link between the Spirit and the miracle-working prophets like Elijah and Elisha, while Micah and Ezekiel claimed to speak through the inspiration of the Spirit. The Joel quotation together with Numbers 11.29 ('Would that all the Lord's people were prophets') and Isaiah 11.1-10 (taken as referring to the messiah) would afford specific OT support. There was, then, a cultural and theological framework at hand for early Christians to use.

(ii) What we may call *illumination or guidance*, which leads to a deeper understanding of God's purposes in general and the individual congregation or believer's situation in particular, so that a course of action becomes imperative because willed and revealed by God's Spirit. The link of truth and the Spirit is involved in this aspect: believers know that they are in possession of divine truth because the Spirit has revealed it to them. This may be contrasted with the ignorance of the world or the benighted condition of 'heretics'. There may be a polemical thrust in the claim to be led by the Spirit: we are led by the Spirit, but you are not.

Once again, the impartation of this wisdom and understanding could be over a period and be linked with study, meditation, preparation, all of which could be seen as means which the Spirit uses to guide and direct into what is God's will and way. We could call this 'mediated' guidance, whereas the sudden realisation of being confronted and possessed by the truth might be termed 'immediate' inspiration and guidance by the Spirit.

(iii) What we may term *ethical empowering*. By this we mean when the Christian becomes conscious of being helped by divine power and assisted in a course of action or the development of character, or when grappling with temptation and base desires, and indeed in the ultimate test of loyalty to Christ, namely martyrdom. Believers feel borne along by resources other than their own. They may feel utterly helpless in the face of circumstances, but precisely at this point they become aware of the help of God's Spirit. Thus, temptation may be resisted, greater patience exercised, sterner endurance maintained, more love expended, fuller commitment to God's service shown and so on. Through all these ways the Christian character is matured and deepened and Christ is formed in us.

These three areas, then, will provide the focus of our study as we explore the era ca. AD 90-200, to discover how far later Christians maintained the initial experience of the activity of God's Spirit, which, as we have briefly seen, was a hallmark of the Christianity of the first and second generations. In the chapters which follow, these three areas will be designated 'Divine Presence'; 'Divine Illumination'; and 'Divine Power', respectively (these are merely convenient labels meant to encapsulate what has just been described). Sometimes we have felt that the first two of these cannot be too rigidly separated, and so they have occasionally been treated together. Sometimes a fourth section has been included, to discuss other factors germane to evaluating the author's stance vis-à-vis the Spirit.

It must be emphasized, in order to avoid any possible misunderstanding, that these three aspects are not being seen as chronologically sequential. Thus, our 'Divine Presence' section may include an initial experience but is not confined to that. The material under 'Divine Illumination' is not to be thought of as immediately sequential to 'Divine Presence', but may occur at moments along the Christian life. Our 'Divine Power' section is clearly an ongoing sense, not something experienced at one particular point. In these three areas, then, were the members of the Christian church in the transition period between the primitive period and the 'Great Church' conscious of the Holy Spirit?

Finally, we mention briefly a point to which we shall return later: how is a claim to have received the Spirit or been inspired by him to say or do something, to be established? Like Israel in connection with prophecy, Christianity from the beginning faced the problem of evaluating claims by people within its ranks to spiritual experience and directives. Paul had to tackle this at Corinth, and if Acts 20.22 and 21.4 embody historical tradition, then members of the Tyre congregation and Paul's entourage faced the problem of deciding between conflicting interpretations or whether the Spirit had cancelled an earlier command. How could they be sure that a claim to the Spirit's inspiration was true and not merely a reflection of personal wishes? We shall see that this recurs specifically as a problem in our period and in general confronts the historian at every point: can objective tests be applied to weigh the claims made? Or is it a hopeless task to differentiate between subjective and objective aspects of experience?

Chapter 2

Syria

The Christian gospel must soon have been taken over the border of northern Israel, since there were Christians at Damascus before Paul's conversion (Acts 9.1-2), which is generally reckoned to have taken place between AD 32-34. We learn very little about the church at Damascus from Acts, other than that they received Paul through the agency of a devout person called Ananias (Acts 9.17-19a). Paul was baptized and spent some time there preaching in the synagogues that Jesus was the messianic Son of God (Acts 9.19b-22). It was, however, the members of the group around Stephen, the so-called 'Hellenists' (Greek-speaking Jewish Christians in Jerusalem), who eventually brought the Christian message to the capital of Syria, Antioch (Acts 11.19-26). There they preached the gospel to non-Jews and converted them. So the church at Antioch was a mixed congregation from its inception.

Barnabas, Paul and others appear to have been the first leaders of the church (Acts 13.1). The church sent out Barnabas and Paul to preach the gospel and they went to Cyprus and southern Galatia (the so-called first missionary journey, see Acts 13–14).

According to Paul (Gal. 2.1-10), an important meeting took place between the representatives of the Jerusalem and Antioch churches. Paul says that he and Barnabas went up, taking Titus (an uncircumcised Gentile believer) with them, in order to ensure that he was not and had not been preaching 'in vain'. The three Jerusalem leaders (Peter, James and John) accepted that his preaching was a valid expression of the gospel and 'added nothing' to it (Gal. 2.6-8). Only they asked Paul to remember the poor Christians in Jerusalem (2.9-10). Whether Luke in Acts gives us any account of this meeting is a matter of considerable debate. Either the meeting took place during the visit of Paul and Barnabas with relief for the economically hard pressed Jerusalem church (Acts 11.28-30), in which case Luke is silent about it (and what he gives in Acts 15.1-29 is a subsequent 'conference' called to sort out the problem of how Jewish and Gentile Christians could enjoy table fellowship together), or Luke's account is given in Acts 15.1-29, according to which the cause of the meeting was the visit to Antioch of certain conservatively inclined Jewish Christians from Jerusalem who insisted that Gentile converts needed to be circumcised and keep the law of Moses. The ultimate outcome of the gathering in Jerusalem mentioned in Acts 15 was that Gentiles Christians were not required to be circumcised but were asked to observe certain requirements which would take note of Jewish sensibilities, and thus enable table fellowship to take place between Jewish and Gentile Christians.

The differences between these two accounts have engendered a vast volume of scholarly discussion. We cannot enter into the discussion of these knotty issues here.[1] Even allowing for the fact that Paul as a participant had his own 'agenda' and that he had his eyes on the situation in Galatia which was a very difficult one for him, Paul's account should, as a matter of methodological principle, be given priority, especially as he said that he was 'on oath' in giving his account (Gal. 1.20).

Subsequent to the Jerusalem meeting, Peter paid a visit to Antioch, and had enjoyed table fellowship with Gentile believers. But, under pressure from James, Peter withdrew from this table fellowship, as did Barnabas and other Jewish Christians. Paul saw this as a move destructive of the fellowship of the mixed congregation at Antioch and he had what seems to have been a serious disagreement with Peter, whom he rebuked to his face (Gal. 2.11-14). That Paul is silent on the outcome probably indicates that he failed to change the decision taken by Peter and Barnabas. It looks as if after this Paul moved into a position more independent of Antioch in his work as an apostle of Christ charged with taking the gospel to the Gentiles.

Traditionally, Matthew's Gospel has been associated with Antioch. Assuming this to be correct, Matthew's Gospel shows us a church conscious of its heritage from the Old Covenant (e.g. 5.17-20) and yet open to the non-Jewish world (28.18-20). If Matthew's Gospel was written for a city church, many scholars place the *Didache* in rural Syria. It is quite possible that the two documents were composed around the same period, at the end of the first or beginning of the second century.

Recently, a significant group of scholars has placed the origin of the Gospel and Epistles of John in Greek-speaking Syria, even if later some Johannine Christians may have moved to Ephesus.

In the early years of the second century we know that Ignatius was the bishop of the church at Antioch, and he was a firm advocate of an organisation of bishop-elders-deacons for the churches. But we know nothing of the fortunes of the Antioch church for the greater part of the second century.

Tatian settled there for a while, probably after the martyrdom of his teacher, Justin, at Rome in the 160s. He moved in a strongly ascetic direction and appears to have become the leader of those called the Encratites. In the last quarter of the century one of the so-called Apologists, Theophilus, was bishop of the church at Antioch.

As to the more Syriac speaking area east of Antioch, later in the second century, a Christian community was established in Edessa, even though Edessa did not become

---

[1] Suffice to say that if the visit mentioned by Paul in Galatians 2 took place at the time of the visit mentioned in Acts 11, then Galatians is the earliest extant letter of Paul, and the dispute at Antioch mentioned in Galatians 2.11-14 was the cause of the so-called Jerusalem conference of Acts 15 and the so-called 'decree' was intended to sort out the issue of table fellowship. If the visit of Galatians 2 is that recorded in Acts 15, we are left with a problem that Luke has mentioned a visit to Jerusalem by Paul at Acts 11 which Paul has not apparently mentioned in Galatians 1-2.

part of the Roman empire until AD 216. Although Syriac was the language of Edessa, many educated people did speak Greek as well as Syriac. We have the Odes of Solomon from a Syriac speaking Christian, while Tatian composed a harmony of the four gospels in Syriac and this was used for a long time in the Syriac church. The most famous Edessan Christian was Bardesanes (AD 154-220). He was born of pagan parents. According to Eusebius, he moved from Valentinian Gnosticism and became an able defender of Christianity, including writing against the ideas of Marcion, although Eusebius regarded him as not quite orthodox (*HE*, 4.30).

1. Gospel of John

I shall assume that a group of Johannine Christians were responsible for the actual publication of the Gospel in the form in which we now have it—they were the 'we' of 21.24-25. The roots of the Gospel go back to the witness of one who is described as 'the disciple whom Jesus loved' (whether we identify him with the apostle John or a Jerusalem follower of Jesus). That witness was developed over a period, in the distinctive way which characterizes the Fourth Gospel over against the Synoptics, in the preaching and teaching within the 'Johannine' churches, and finally committed to writing by a gifted individual.[2]

Although traditionally the Fourth Gospel has been associated with Ephesus, more recently a few notable scholars have advocated Syria as the Gospel's place of origin.[3] The reasons are as follows:

---

[2] Substantially, this is the view of scholars like (to name but a few) R. Schnackenburg, *The Gospel according to St. John*, Vol. I (London: Burns & Oates, 1968), pp. 72-74, 100-4; R.E. Brown, *The Gospel according to John I-XII* (AB 29A. New York: Doubleday, 1966), pp. xxxiv-xxxix, lxxxvii-cii; modified in *An Introduction to the Gospel of John* (ed. by F.J. Moloney. New York: Doubleday, 2003), pp. 62-69, 78-86, 189-99; G.R. Beasley-Murray, *John* (WBC 36. Waco, Texas: Word Books, 1987), pp. xliv-liii, lxvi-lxxv; F.J. Moloney, *The Gospel of John* (Sacra Pagina 4. Collegeville, Minnesota: Liturgical Press (Michael Glazier), 1998), pp. 1-9; R.P. Martin, *Foundations, Vol.I*, pp. 281-82 and S.S. Smalley, *John: Evangelist and Interpreter* (Exeter: Paternoster, 1978), pp. 80-2, 119-21. For those who maintain authorship by the apostle John, see L. Morris, *Studies in the Fourth Gospel* (Exeter: Paternoster, 1969), pp. 139-292, and *The Gospel according to John* (NICNT. Grand Rapids, Michigan: Eerdmans, rev. ed.,1994), pp. 4-25; J.A.T. Robinson, *The Priority of John* (London: SCM, 1985); D. Guthrie, *Introduction*, pp. 252-83; D.A. Carson, *The Gospel according to John* (Grand Rapids, MI: Eerdmans, 1991), pp. 68-81.

[3] For example, see J.H. Charlesworth, 'Qumran, John and the Odes of Solomon', in J.H. Charlesworth (ed.), *Qumran and John* (London: Geoffrey Chapman, 1972), p. 136, who looks to 'N. Palestine and Syria for the provenance of the Odes and of at least one recension of John'. W.G. Kümmel, *Introduction to the New Testament* (London: SCM, rev. ed., 1975), p. 247; D.M. Smith, 'Johannine Christianity: Some Reflections on its Character and Delineation', *NTS* 21 (1975), pp. 237-38; O. Cullmann, *The Johannine Circle* (London: SCM, 1976), p. 98, lists Syria and Transjordania as the two main possibilities. K. Wengst, *Bedrängte Gemeinde und verherrlichter Christus: Der*

(i) Since the discovery of the Dead Sea Scrolls, it has been felt that the dualistic approach and language of John's Gospel fits into the type of Judaism reflected in the Scrolls.

(ii) The attitude of the Gospel to John the Baptist and his followers is held to reflect a situation in which there was tension, if not hostility, between the two movements, and this is more likely in the Syria-Transjordan area.

(iii) Ignatius of Antioch reflects a knowledge of Johannine thought, ca.AD 112-117.

(iv) The Gospel's lack of acceptance until the time of Irenaeus fits better with an origin in (say) eastern Syria rather than a busy and important centre like Ephesus, i.e. a more 'backwater' situation.

(v) The *Odes of Solomon* which show affinities to the thought of the Fourth Gospel originated in Syria.

(vi) Gnosis flourished early in Syria, and John seems to be open to the questions behind gnosis, especially a gnosis influenced by Judaism.

(vii) This takes account of the links and the dissimilarities with the book of Revelation.[4] If some Jewish Christians, acquainted with an early stage of Johannine thought, migrated to Asia Minor before AD 70,[5] one of them or a pupil or descendant of one of them could have written Revelation ca.AD 90. It is highly unlikely that the Gospel and Revelation were written by the same author, for the eschatology is too different. But echoes of Johannine thought are part of the thought of John of Patmos who wrote Revelation.

(viii) Polycarp could have met John in Palestine or Syria, and Irenaeus made a genuine mistake that Polycarp knew John in Ephesus. It must be noted, however, that neither Polycarp himself in his *Letter to the Philippians* nor the *Martyrdom of Polycarp* claim any link with the apostle John.

---

historischer Ort des Johannesevangeliums als Schüssel zu seiner Interpretation (Neukirchen-Vluyn: Neukirchener Verlag, 1981), p. 80, posits the region of Batanea and Gaulanitis (to which J. Ashton, *Understanding the Fourth Gospel* [Oxford: Clarendon, 1991], pp. 196-98, is not unsympathetic). Charlesworth had been anticipated to a certain extent by a number of scholars who postulated the Johannine tradition moving from Jerusalem to Antioch and then to Ephesus, such as T.W. Manson, *Studies in the Gospels and the Epistles* (Manchester: Manchester University Press, 1962), pp. 120-21 (reprint of a 1947 Rylands Library lecture); R.H. Lightfoot, *St. John's Gospel* (Oxford: Oxford University Press, 1956), pp. 5-6; R. Schnackenburg, *John* I.152. B. Lindars, *The Gospel of John* (London: Oliphants, 1972), p. 44, is more cautious: 'the choice lies between Ephesus and Syria, but no certainty on this issue is possible.'

[4] See the discussion in Elisabeth Schüssler Fiorenza, 'The Quest for the Johannine School: The Apocalypse and the Fourth Gospel', *NTS* 23 (1977), pp. 402-27, who believes that the author of Revelation was familiar with the Johannine (and also the Pauline) tradition without belonging to it: he was rather at home within, and indeed was the leader of, an early Christian prophetic-apocalyptic school.

[5] As Eusebius, *HE* 3.31.3, 39.9 and 5.24.2 implies. See U.B. Müller, *Zur frühchristlichen Theologiegeschichte* (Gütersloh: Gerd Mohn, 1976), p. 48.

(ix) Papias of Hierapolis in Asia Minor does not seem to have been acquainted with the fourth gospel or its traditions.[6]

(x) The Syrian origin means that we do not have to postulate Pauline and Johannine schools existing separately and in virtual isolation from one another in Ephesus.

(xi) If the Fourth Gospel contains a protest of some sort against increasing trends of sacramental and ministerial hierarchy,[7] what Ignatius reveals in his letters could provide the foil (just as much, and even better, than the Pastorals for Ephesus).

It cannot be said that these points amount to certainty, but they cumulatively make out a better case for Syria than for Ephesus. We shall, therefore, proceed on the assumption that the fourth gospel and Johannine epistles originated in Syria, even if the Johannine tradition may have moved to Ephesus later.

A. *Divine Presence*

A natural starting point in our quest for the Johannine understanding of the believer's experience of the Spirit is the discussion of the new birth, birth ἄνωθεν in 3.3-13. It very soon becomes clear that ἄνωθεν does not primarily mean 'a second time', as Nicodemus takes it (3.4), but 'from above', by the Spirit, as 3.6 puts it, or from God, as 1.13 had expressed it.

Birth 'from above' is vital for someone to see or enter the Kingdom of God. Because this birth is from above, it cannot be effected from within the 'realm' of flesh: neither the world nor human beings can achieve it. We have already been informed of this in the prologue, when birth from God was contrasted with birth from blood, the will of the flesh or the will of a man (1.13). These very terms—flesh and blood, a man's will—evoke the whole area of human effort and striving. Only 'Spirit' can bring about the birth from above or birth 'of water and the Spirit', as 3.6 shows: 'What is born of flesh is flesh, and what is born of the Spirit is spirit'.

Verse 8 propounds the mysterious nature of birth from above. The wind (also πνεῦμα) blows where it wishes. People hear its sound, but do not know whence it comes or whither it goes. Just as there is a mystery about the wind, 'so is the case with every one born of the Spirit'.

Whether or not baptism is in mind at verse 5,[8] the Spirit is the *vital* element in the birth from above. Water is not mentioned outside verse 5; only the Spirit is. The

---

[6] See U.H.J. Körtner, *Papias von Hierapolis* (Göttingen: Vandenhoeck & Ruprecht, 1983), especially pp. 173-76, 197-98.

[7] See J.D.G. Dunn, *Baptism in the Holy Spirit* (London: SCM, 1970), pp. 188-90, 193-94; *Jesus and the Spirit* (London: SCM, 1975), p. 359; *Unity and Diversity in the New Testament* (London: SCM, 1977), pp. 118-19, 168-71.

[8] Among those in favour of a reference to baptism are O. Cullmann, *Early Christian Worship* (London: SCM, 1953), pp. 75-78; G.R. Beasley-Murray, *Baptism in the New Testament* (London: Macmillan, 1962), pp. 228-29; Schnackenburg, *John* I, pp. 369-70; F. Porsch, *Pneuma und Wort: ein exegetischer Beitrag zur Pneumatologie des*

role of the Spirit is paramount in the experience of birth from above.[9] Without the activity of the Spirit, such a birth does not take place. No Spirit—no birth from above. The Spirit is the sine qua non of all genuine Christian experience. He stands at the entry into it as the creative force who brings it about. This subjective experience of birth by the Spirit has its objective basis in Jesus' being lifted up on the cross and to glory, as 3.14-16, following on 3.3-8, shows.

If we seek now to press behind the language to the experience described, we may say in the first place that while people may not understand the origin, movement and destination of the wind, they do hear it, i.e. they know its effects. The οὕτως draws the parallel with the birth from above. We may surmise that this birth is mysterious in *how* it takes place, but the fact *that it takes place and that one is aware of it is assumed*.[10]

In the second place, the image of birth from above, which is also new birth, is the language that we would expect from those who have been 'twice born',[11] i.e. whose spiritual experience has been dramatic and startling, something which is sharply delineated in the memory. This is the terminology of the instant conversion experience. In later Christianity, those who have had such an experience have turned to this type of Johannine language—'born again Christians'. This is the language of those who are most conscious of a sharp distinction between themselves and their milieu ('the world'). As Burge puts it, 'Divine birth through the Spirit marked the Johannine Christian...this begetting...primarily denoted the dramatic reception of the

---

Johannesevangeliums (FTS 16; Frankfurt: Knecht, 1974), pp. 125-30; U. Schnelle, 'Johannes als Geisttheologe', *NT* 40 (1988), pp. 25, 28. Dunn, *Baptism*, pp. 182-94, dissents from this (the majority) view. I side with Dunn in my 'References to Baptism in the Fourth Gospel', in S.E. Porter and A.R. Cross (eds.), *Baptism, the New Testament and the Church* (Sheffield: Sheffield Academic Press, 1999), pp. 121-26. G.M. Burge, *The Anointed Community* (Grand Rapids, MI: Eerdmans, 1987), pp. 165-66, believes that the evangelist probably intended 'his readers to draw the connection with their own experience of rebirth, Christian baptism and the Spirit'.

[9] So, e.g., Beasley-Murray, *Baptism*, p. 230; Schnackenburg, *John 1*, p. 369; Dunn, *Baptism*, pp. 183-94, and *Unity and Diversity*, p. 170; Schnelle *Geisttheologe*, p. 27. Burge, *Anointed Community*, p. 167, comments that 'the role of water in rebirth is wholly and exclusively defined in terms of the Spirit', and goes on to say that 'the water (or Christian baptism) is only theologically meaningful if it is accompanied by the experiential presence of the Spirit' (p. 169).

[10] Thus I want to put it more strongly than Schnackenburg, *John I*, pp. 373-4, who writes, 'The wind is also a mystery as to its origin and goal, but it still remains a reality, perceptible by means of its sound ("voice"), recognisable through the effects... And hence the Spirit is also recognisable through the effects which he produces in man'. Porsh, *Pneuma und Wort*, p. 124, says that being born of the Spirit 'takes place *through the opening of the human heart* to the witness of the Revealer who speaks God's word' (my italics).

[11] Cf. Weinel, *Wirkungen*, p. 42. J. Becker, 'Das Geist- und Gemeindeverstandnis des vierten Evangelisten', *ZNW* 89 (1998), p. 223, refers to birth by the Spirit in Jn. 3.5-8 as 'a highly individual event'.

Holy Spirit' and he goes on later to speak of 'the exuberant spiritual (or pneumatic) vitality known within the community'.[12]

Alongside the image of new birth from above, we have that of living waters which the thirsty drink. We turn to 7.37-39, within which verse 39 constitutes an interpretative comment by the final writer. This comment agrees with the standpoint of the farewell discourses that the Paraclete-Spirit only comes when Jesus goes from this world to the Father. Here the 'commentator' says that the Spirit was not yet ('given' is a correct, though secondary, addition), because Jesus had not yet been glorified, a reference to his crucifixion-exaltation.

Verses 37-38, however they are to be punctuated, offer a promise on the lips of the Johannine Jesus of living water (comparable to the offer of living bread in chapter 6). The promise is offered to the thirsty one who is invited to come to Jesus and believe on him and drink. The scriptural quotation may support either why the thirsty one should come to *Jesus*—namely, because living water flows out of him to satisfy the thirst of others, or the idea that the living water will gush forth from *the believer*.

Both ideas are actually Johannine. The first fits the general Christological emphasis in the Gospel, while the second possibility agrees with the promise to the Samaritan woman (4.14). Since, however, in the fourth gospel Jesus bestows the Spirit from the Father and is, therefore, the mediating source of the Spirit for believers, it is more likely that the believer is pictured as coming to Jesus to drink from *him*.[13] Otherwise, the believer comes to Jesus and drinks; then he or she, in turn, becomes the source for others. Nothing, however, is actually said in the text about the direction in which the rivers will flow (nor in 4.14).

So, verse 39 offers a pneumatological reinterpretation of an originally Christological statement. (One could say that in reinterpreting vv. 37-38 in terms of the Spirit, the evangelist is like Luke interpreting the 'good things' of the Q saying, now recorded in Matthew 7.11, as the Holy Spirit in Luke 11.13). Why should the evangelist feel impelled to take this step? The answer can only lie in the direction that *for him experience of the risen, exalted Jesus and his life-giving power was the experience of the Holy Spirit*. The streams of living water were available because the Holy Spirit was given to those who believed in Jesus.

The 'original' promise, though set in the earthly ministry of Jesus, the incarnate word, was really a promise from the Jesus-lifted-up-on-the-cross-and-into-glory. Behind the incarnate Word in the pages of the gospel stands the exalted Word returned to the Father. The Son of Man had to be lifted up in order to confer life (3.14-15). Through 7.39, the evangelist, from the standpoint of his own understanding and experience, sees the living waters as none other than the gift of the Spirit. Whereas

---

[12] Burge, *Anointed Community*, pp. 171, 177.

[13] So e.g. Schnackenburg, *John II*, p. 154; Brown, *John I*, pp. 319-21; Dunn, *Baptism*, p. 179; Burge, *Anointed Community*, p. 93; Schnelle, *Geisttheologe*, p. 24; C.S. Keener, *The Spirit in the Gospels and Acts: Divine Purity and Power* (Peabody, MA: Hendrickson, 1997), p. 160. For the contrary view, see C.K. Barrett, *The Gospel according to St. John* (London: SPCK, 2nd ed., 1978), pp. 326-27.

in chapter 6 the proffered gift of the bread of heaven is firmly equated with Jesus, the promise of 7.37-38 allowed scope to carry through the reinterpretation and, in a sense, prepare the way for the position enunciated in the farewell discourses through the Paraclete sayings (assuming a growth of the farewell discourses to their present shape in chaps. 13-17[14]).

7.39, then, offers us an important clue into the Gospel writer's approach. The gift of Jesus, which in some sense is Jesus himself, is the Holy Spirit. What, then, of the imagery used in these verses? Does the picture used of drinking living water to quench one's spiritual thirst evoke an experience which is specific, definite and vivid? Are the component phrases such as to evoke something precise and noteworthy in the believer's experience and memory? We think so. In the moment of believing in Jesus, the Johannine type of believer was aware of a different dimension of experience, such as can very or even most effectively be described in terms of slaking thirst (especially in a middle eastern setting). The thirsty drink, and their parched throat is moistened, thirst quenched and vitality renewed. The language can be claimed to point to a dramatic religious experience of memorable dimensions.

We turn now to a consideration of certain promises made by Jesus in the farewell discourses, in the context of the announcement of his impending departure (13.33, 36; 14.2) and his attempt to calm the disciples' troubled hearts (14.1, 27-28). A vital part in this process of encouragement is the promise of the Paraclete-Spirit. At Jesus' request, the Father will give them the Spirit that he might be with them forever (14.16; note that the same phrase μεθ' ὑμῶν, plus ἤμην is used of Jesus' presence with his disciples during his ministry at 16.4b). If the intention is to administer comfort to the disciples who feel that they will soon be like orphans, the evangelist presumably thinks in terms of a conscious experience of the Spirit.[15] In contrast to the world, the disciples already know him because he abides alongside of them but will be in them (14.17). At the moment, the Spirit is *alongside* them, because he abides in Jesus (1.32-33; 3.34), but (after Jesus' glorification) he will be *in* the disciples.[16]

---

[14] See H. Windisch, *The Spirit-Paraclete in the Fourth Gospel* (Philadelphia, PA: Fortress, 1968 [= a translation of two articles, entitled *'Die fünf johanneischen Parakletspruche'* (1927) and *'Jesus und der Geist im Johannesevangelium'* (1933)]), pp. 1-26, who assumed that the Paraclete sayings constituted a final layer in the farewell discourses; cf. to some extent J. Becker, 'Die Abschiedsreden Jesu im Johannesevangelium', *ZNW* 61 (1970), pp. 224, 227, 237-38. We have to reckon with a number of farewell discourses—so Becker, pp. 229-36, 246; R.E. Brown, *The Gospel according to John XIII-XXI* (hereafter *John II*) (AB 29A; New York: Doubleday, 1971), pp. 581-604; U.B. Müller, 'Die Parakletenvorstellung im Johannesevangelium', *ZThK* 71 (1974), pp. 31-77; Schnackenburg, *John III*, pp. 89-93, 123-25; J. Painter, 'The Farewell Discourses and the History of the Johannine Christianity', *NTS* 27 (1981), pp. 525-43. See U. Schnelle, 'Die Abschiedsreden im Johannesevangelium', *ZNW* 80 (1989), pp. 64-79, for a challenge to this approach and for a defence of the evangelist's working over Johannine school traditions.

[15] Cf. Lindars, *John*, p. 477; Schnackenburg, *John III*, pp. 75-76.

[16] For a defence of ἔσται, see my 'A Note on John 14.17b', *BZ* 23 (1979), pp. 93-98.

The new relationship will be a deeper one than during the earthly ministry. Though they knew of the Spirit's activity, his relationship to them was an external one (παρ' ὑμῖν μένει), but the new relationship will be an inner one (ἐν ὑμῖν ἔσται). The relationship of indwelling, designated by the ἐν formula, denoted intimacy and closeness. It is inconceivable that the evangelist could use this formula to denote the intimacy and closeness of the relationship both of Jesus and the Father and of Jesus and the disciples, and then use it at 14.17 of the Paraclete and the disciples but mean something different by it.

This interpretation is reinforced by a consideration of the terms employed to designate what the Spirit does vis-à-vis the disciples: 'he will teach you all things, that is, he will recall to your remembrance' (14.26); 'he will guide you...he will announce to you' (16.13-15). The pupil-teacher type of relationship here envisaged confirms the point just made. The Spirit is conceived in personal terms as one who instructs and informs the disciples (just as Jesus had done in his ministry).[17]

Further confirmation is afforded by two other facts. The first of these is the proximity of the first Paraclete saying, with its promise that the Father will give the Paraclete to be with the disciples forever (14.16-17), to 14.18-19, the promise that Jesus himself will come to his disciples: 'I will not leave you as orphans, I will come to you. Yet a little while, and the world will see me no more, but you will see me; because I live, you shall live also'. The picture of the orphan well suits the situation of the disciples soon to be bereft of their Master. But the assurance theme continues: they will not be left as orphans. 'I will come to you'. The language shifts from the gift of the Paraclete (vv. 16-17) to Jesus (vv. 18-19). It would seem that either 14.18 refers to the resurrection[18] or the coming of the Paraclete-Spirit is the coming of Jesus.[19] But an either-or approach is probably not the best one here.

We may claim that verses 18-19 do not speak of a temporary experience of Christ.[20] That being so, we may go on to claim that the parallelism of thought in the two passages is deliberately employed by the evangelist to interpret an original promise of Jesus' return at Easter to indicate his permanent presence with his disciples.[21]

That this interpretation is correct is confirmed by the frequently made observation that the Paraclete-Spirit will do everything that Jesus did (being with the disciples,

---

[17] Cf. Porsch, *Pneuma und Wort*, pp. 216, 239, 389.

[18] So E.C. Hoskins (and F.N. Davey), *The Fourth Gospel* (London: Faber & Faber, 2nd ed., 1947), p. 459; Lindars, *John*, p. 481.

[19] So Porsch, *Pneuma und Wort*, p. 241; Burge, *Anointed Community*, pp. 138-39, 147.

[20] Brown, *John II*, pp. 645-46.

[21] R. Bultmann, *The Gospel of John* (Oxford: Blackwell, 1971), pp. 617-18; D.E. Holwerda, *The Holy Spirit and Eschatology in the Gospel of John* (Kampen: Kok, 1959), pp. 65, 76; Brown, *John II*, pp. 644-45; Burge, *Anointed Community*, pp. 138-39.

teaching, bearing witness, convincing, revealing the truth, not speaking on one's own authority, glorifying one's sender and not oneself).[22]

The conclusion is inescapable: the fourth evangelist saw the experience of the risen Jesus as the experience of the Paraclete-Spirit. Or, to put the matter the other way round, the Spirit is the presence of Jesus with the disciples.[23] However he might have expressed this dogmatically.[24] he did assert that the Christian life is a life lived in conscious fellowship with the Spirit. Believers would know the presence of the Spirit indwelling them. This was a coming of Jesus to believers and a 'seeing' of Jesus by believers.

The second factor is the proximity (this time in the reverse order) of the promise that Jesus and the Father will come and dwell with believers (14.23) and the promise in the second Paraclete saying that the Father will send the Paraclete-Spirit to the disciples (14.26). The promise of 14.23 is set in the context of a question used to set up a reply: Judas (not Iscariot) asked 'Lord, what has happened that you will manifest yourself to us and not to the world?' (14.22). At one level, the question is surprising, since a distinction between believers and the world is a commonplace of Johannine thought; at another level, it enables the evangelist to deal again with the question of Jesus' relationship to his followers in the future. The answer to Judas is 'If someone loves me, they will keep my word and my Father will love them and we will come to them and make our abode with them' (14.23). Because of that oneness which exists between the Father and the Son, for Jesus to come to the believer means in fact that the Father comes too: they both take up residence in believers. They dwell in them.[25] The vivid language of taking up residence points to a conscious awareness of the experience.

Yet in 14.26 comes the second Paraclete saying, promising that the Father will send the Paraclete in Jesus' name. We are forced to say, therefore, that from the point of view of *experience*, the evangelist can talk of believers receiving the Spirit or Jesus and the Father dwelling with them, and mean the same thing.

---

[22] See Brown, *John II*, pp. 1140-41 (originally, 'The Paraclete in the Fourth Gospel', *NTS* 13 [1966-67], pp. 126-28).

[23] Burge, *Anointed Community*, p. 147: 'the Paraclete serves as the presence of Jesus while Jesus is away'. Schnelle, *Geisttheologe*, p. 19, denies this sort of statement. He seems to assume that this implies an identification of the Paraclete and Jesus. Scholars who make this sort of statement do not imply any such thing, however—see the next footnote. It is a statement about experience, not dogmatics. C. Dietzfelbinger, 'Paraklet und theologischer Anspruch im Johannesevangelium', *ZThK* 82 (1985), p. 398, helpfully put it that by means of the Paraclete, Jesus is present in the way appropriate to him so that the community on its side can be the community in the way appropriate to it. Subsequent to both Burge and Schnelle, Becker, *Geist- und Gemeindeverstandnis*, p. 227, also stated that the Paraclete-Spirit is the presence of the exalted and glorified One.

[24] Barrett, *John*, p. 464: 'We ought not to suppose that John simple [sic] confounds Jesus with the Holy Spirit'; cf. Schnackenburg, *John III*, p. 77.

[25] Cf. Lindars, *John*, p. 482, on 14.23: 'an interior apprehension of Jesus and the Father in the hearts of those who love Jesus'.

We return to 14.17 in the light of our intervening discussion. If the words of 14.17 are to comfort, they must surely suggest conscious awareness of a presence, real though invisible, of one who 'takes the place' of Jesus.

SUMMARY

While it is not the intention of the evangelist to describe in detail the subjective experience of believers, an examination of two images associated with the Holy Spirit—new birth from above and living waters—both suggest heightened, dramatic experience, while the employment of his famous immanence language in 14.17 also points to a sense of awareness on the part of believers that the Spirit dwells in them.

B. Divine Illumination

Our second area of interest is that of illumination: how wisdom and understanding, the ability to discern spiritual or divine truth, are imparted.

This is most emphatically a role of the Spirit in John. The second Paraclete saying announces: 'He will teach you all things—that is,[26] he will recall to your remembrance all that I have said to you' (14.26). Just as Jesus taught, so will the Paraclete. The Spirit's task is to recall all that Jesus said, but this is not mere remembering, but a remembering with deeper understanding, as 2.22 and 12.16 make abundantly clear (13.7 ought to be taken in the same way). The Spirit's task is to teach by reminding the disciples of the meaning of Jesus' words.[27] Here there is both binding to the past and freedom for the future. The link with Jesus' revelation is decisive,[28] but there is the possibility left open for reinterpretation of that past revelation to new situations and ongoing needs.[29]

The Spirit is the teacher of believers, but what he teaches is linked closely with what Jesus taught. As Jesus is the 'exegete' of the Father (1.18), so the Paraclete-Spirit is the 'exegete' of the Son. We catch a glimpse of the fact that the evangelist

---

[26] I assume the καὶ to be epexegetic (or explanatory): it explains the previous διδάξει πάντα (an alternative translation might, therefore, be 'He will teach you all things by recalling to your remembrance all that I have said to you'): Bultmann, *John*, p. 626 (footnote 6); Schnackenburg, *John III*, p. 83; Brown, *John I*, pp. 450-51 (who says that the last two lines of v. 26 are in synonymous parallelism); Porsch, *Pneuma und Wort*, p. 265; E. Franck, *Revelation Taught* (Lund: Gleerup, 1985), p. 42.

[27] Porsch, *Pneuma und Wort*, pp. 261-65, esp. 265; Burge, *Anointed Community*, pp. 212-13; Franck, *Revelation Taught*, pp. 50-51; Schnelle, *Geisttheologe*, p. 21; Rahner, *Vergegenwärtigende Erinnerung*, pp. 76-79.

[28] As Barrett, *John*, p. 467, maintains, there is for John no independent revelation through the Paraclete, but only an application of the revelation in Jesus; Porsch, *Pneuma und Wort*, p. 258; Burge, *Anointed Community*, p. 213.

[29] Dunn, *Jesus and the Spirit*, p. 352, seems to go further than this, when he maintains that the thought of 14.26 'must include some idea of new information, new revelation', but then seems to qualify this by saying 'even if that new revelation is in effect drawn out of the old by way of reinterpretation'; cf. similarly, *Unity and Diversity*, p. 198: 'the new truth of revelation' is 'set in correlation with the original truth of Jesus'.

is grappling with the relation of the contemporary experience of the Spirit and the past revelation of the incarnate Word in Jesus' historic ministry.[30]

The final Paraclete saying (16.12-15) confronts us with the same issues as the second saying. Its opening verse apparently asserts the incompleteness of Jesus' revelation, due not to inadequacy on his part, but weakness on the part of the disciples. Verse 13a continues with the assertion 'But when he, the Spirit of truth, comes, he will guide you into all the truth', as if suggesting that he will complete what Jesus has been unable to pass on. There seems thus far the idea of new revelation, filling up what is lacking.[31] We shall see in a moment whether this is the correct interpretation, or whether this impression needs modifying.

The activity of the Spirit in leading into the whole truth is grounded in the 'for' clause of v. 13b: the Spirit does not speak on his own initiative or authority. Rather, he will say what he will hear—it is not said whether from the Father or Jesus or both. The future tense λαλήσει could support either that new truth is in mind or that the Spirit is interpreting the past via what he 'hears'.

The passage continues (v. 13c) 'and he will declare things to come to you' or 'interpret'[32] events to come for you' (τὰ ἐρχόμενα). To what is the evangelist referring with the phrase 'things/events to come'? Various interpretations have been suggested. Some think that eschatological events, or, at any rate, future events are in mind, so that the whole clause is seen as a veiled reference to Christian prophets[33] (with sometimes the book of Revelation being specifically mentioned). Yet this interpretation does not accord with the evangelist's realized eschatological viewpoint and is not really convincing. Another suggestion has been the forthcoming passion,[34] on the basis that the evangelist refers to the passion in the arrest scene at 18.4 in the phrase that Jesus knew πάντα τὰ ἐρχόμενα ἐπ' αὐτον. The context in the arrest scene makes it abundantly clear what the phrase refers to, whereas there is no such specific context in 16.13, though of course in general the context is that of

---

[30] Dunn, *Jesus and the Spirit*, pp. 351-52; *Unity and Diversity*, p. 198.

[31] This is the interpretation of Müller, *Parakletenvorstellung*, pp. 74-75 (Müller notes the greater independence of the Paraclete in ch. 16 than in ch. 14: see pp. 69, 73); E. Bammel, 'Jesus und der Paraklet in Johannes 16', in B. Lindars and S.S. Smalley (eds.), *Christ and Spirit in the New Testament* (Cambridge: Cambridge University Press, 1973), p. 207.

[32] See note 36 below for explanation of this possible translation.

[33] So G. Johnston, *The Spirit-Paraclete in the Gospel of John* (Cambridge: Cambridge University Press, 1970), pp. 39, 137-41; Lindars, *John*, p. 505; Müller, *Parakletenvorstellung*, p. 72; M.E. Boring, *The Continuing Voice of Jesus: Christian Prophecy and the Gospel Tradition* (Louisville, KY: Westminster/John Knox, 1991), pp. 146, 178.

[34] Barrett, *John*, p. 490, who combines this idea with that of events in the future, namely the Spirit makes the Final Judgment operative by convincing the world. R.H. Lightfoot, *St. John's Gospel* (Oxford: Oxford University Press, 1956), p. 287, comes close to this view when he remarked 'this will include explanation and interpretation of the *events now imminent* (cf. 2.22; 12.16)' (italics mine). Burge, *Anointed Community*, p. 215, is sympathetic.

Jesus' departure to the Father. The phrase in the arrest scene is probably too weak support for a view that is per se not unattractive.

A third possibility is the meaning of what happens to the church, in the light of what Jesus accomplishes for the salvation of the world in his cross-exaltation.[35] That is to say, the Paraclete-Spirit will not announce anything new, but will constantly interpret what Jesus has said and done with reference to the ongoing situation of the church.[36] On this view, the καὶ which introduces the clause under consideration could be epexegetic (explanatory) and the 'for' clause of v. 13b could be parenthetical. If this is allowed, our clause helps to explain the idea of leading into all the truth:[37] this involves applying the past revelation in Jesus to fresh situations. That this is the most satisfactory solution will be confirmed by considering vv. 14-15.

The aim of the Paraclete-Spirit is to glorify Jesus and he does so because he takes what belongs to Jesus and declares it to the disciples. This seems to say exactly what was said at 14.26:[38] he will recall to their remembrance what Jesus said. Just as the activity of 'causing to remember' involved interpretation and explanation, so also the activity of taking what belongs to Jesus (given him by the Father, cf. 3.35) and declaring it likewise involves explanation and interpretation, a re-presentation. Verses 14-15 clearly, then, affirm the completeness of what Jesus had said and done.

We discern, then, two possibilities of taking vv. 12-15:

(a) The view which sees some tension between vv. 12-13 and vv. 14-15. Put more exactly, it is suggested that vv. 12-13 point boldly in one direction (new truth), with vv. 14-15 'applying the brakes' (there must be a link with the revelation given by the historical Jesus). On this approach, the evangelist is walking a tightrope: he wants to affirm new truth, yet is concerned to anchor that new truth firmly in the past revelatory work of Christ.[39]

(b) Alternatively, verse 12 is taken to mean no more than that Jesus cannot do the explaining, with this being left to the Paraclete-Spirit (vv. 13-15). This eliminates the idea of new truth and stays within the idea of drawing out the significance and

---

[35] Hoskyns (and Davey), *John*, p. 486 ('the new order which results from the departure of Jesus').

[36] Schnackenburg, *John III*, p. 135; Brown, *John II*, p. 716 (Brown draws on the researches of I. de la Potterie on the verb ἀναγγέλλω in Jewish apocalyptic literature; on p. 708, he writes, 'There the verb is used to describe the interpretation of mysteries already communicated in dreams or visions. The declarative interpretation deals with the future by seeking a deeper meaning in what has already happened'); Porsch, *Pneuma und Wort*, p. 298. W. Thüsing, *Die Erhöhung und Verherrlichung Jesu im Johannesevangelium* (Münster: Aschendorff, 1960), pp. 150-51, 153, sees the phrase as having a comprehensive meaning, embracing all that should happen in the time of the Paraclete, inaugurated by the 'hour'; it is a very broad concept which embraces the entire execution of the work of salvation by the Spirit/disciples.

[37] So Porsch, *Pneuma und Wort*, pp. 298, 300.

[38] Schnackenburg, *John III*, pp. 143-44, who speaks of 'relecture' [a second reading] of 14.26; Porsch, *Pneuma und Wort*, p. 290.

[39] See Dunn, *Jesus and the Spirit*, p. 352; *Unity and Diversity*, p. 198; Boring, *Continuing Voice*, p. 79.

implication of what Jesus had already revealed. This might receive support from 16.25: 'I have said these things to you in figures of speech; the hour is coming when I will no longer speak to you in figures of speech, but I will tell you about the Father plainly'. How will Jesus speak about the Father openly? He will do so through the Paraclete-Spirit. The speaking 'in figures of speech' relates to the incarnate ministry; the speaking 'plainly' comes through the Paraclete-Spirit.[40]

In the end, the difference between these two views is probably one of degree, rather than kind, a difference of emphasis rather than an unbridgeable gulf. Our preference is for the latter interpretation, because it can do justice to the element of reinterpretation without involving the idea of tension, while also being in line with the general standpoint of the Gospel, that he who is the incarnate and now glorified Word has spoken all that is needful for us to know the Father and have eternal life.[41]

The contrast between veiled and open speech mentioned in 16.25 points us to the work of the evangelist. He and the tradition within which he stood has so interpreted the works and words of Jesus that what was implicit has become explicit, what was below the surface is now drawn out fully.[42] It is difficult to escape the conclusion that the evangelist believed that the Paraclete-Spirit was at work in his own writing. Indeed, the Paraclete sayings constitute a legitimating or authorization of the Johannine interpretation of the tradition.[43]

There is probably another indirect reference to the work of the Paraclete-Spirit at the end of the 'High Priestly Prayer', although the Spirit is nowhere specifically mentioned.[44] Jesus says that he has already made known the Father's Name to the disciples and he will make it known (17.26). How can Jesus *continue* to reveal the

---

[40] Porsch, *Pneuma und Wort*, pp. 291, 297, 303; Burge, *Anointed Community*, p. 214.

[41] Burge, *Anointed Community*, pp. 216-17, has an excellent discussion on what he calls the Johannine hermeneutic, which combines freedom and control, inspiration and tradition: the power of the Spirit 'means declaring the word of Jesus afresh and not departing from the historic anchor'. Rahner, *Vergegenwärtigende Erinnerung*, pp. 82-88, in a discussion of whether John has melded the 'two horizons' (Gadamer), argues very strongly that the horizon of the past story of Jesus retains its abiding significance, but that the evangelist is seeking to bring to new power and validity that historical horizon (the Christ event)'s claim to truth.

[42] See e.g. Schackenburg, *John I*, p. 182; Dunn, *Jesus and the Spirit*, pp. 351-52; Porsch, *Pneuma und Wort*, pp. 295, 300-2, 305; Burge, *Anointed Community*, p. 216.

[43] This is the view of many scholars: e.g. Brown, *John II*, p. 1142 (who goes so far as to say that the Beloved Disciple is an 'incarnation of the Paraclete'); Schnackenburg, *John III*, p. 149; Dunn, *Jesus and the Spirit*, p. 352 ('John would undoubtedly regard his own gospel as the product of this inspiring Spirit'); *Unity and Diversity*, pp. 75-78; Porsch, *Pneuma und Wort*, pp. 264-65; Müller, *Parakletenvorstellung*, pp. 49, 51, 77; U. Wilckens 'Der Paraklet und die Kirche', in D. Lührmann and G. Strecker (eds.), *Kirche*, (Tübingen: Mohr, 1980), p. 198; Burge, *Anointed Community*, p. 217; Dietzfelbinger, *Paraklet*, p. 405; Schnelle, *Geisttheologe*, p. 22.

[44] As Schnackenburg points out, *John III*, p. 197.

Father to his disciples except through the Spirit, who takes the revelation given in Jesus and applies it in interpretative fashion to disciples in the future?[45]

How does, in fact, the Spirit-Paraclete teach and guide into all the truth? The third Paraclete saying (15.26-27) can perhaps offer a helpful clue here. This saying concerns the role of the Paraclete vis-à-vis the world, as does the fourth saying (16.7-11). The lawsuit which was in progress during the ministry of Jesus continues. The Paraclete is a witness against the world and will seek to convince it of the rightness of Jesus' case and how completely in the wrong is the world's case. The Paraclete will bear witness to Jesus (15.26), and then immediately we read that the disciples who have been with Jesus from the beginning will also bear witness (v. 27). It seems that the two statements, conjoined by καὶ, are to be taken together: that is, the Paraclete bears witness *through* that of the disciples, who represent all subsequent believers, the church.

In the light of this, it seems a fair assumption that the Paraclete was believed in Johannine circles to work through teachers and preachers of the word in order to guide the believing community of Jesus into the truth. Without diminishing the conviction that all believers are born of the Spirit and live in his life giving power, there are in the Johannine churches those who are specially gifted to be teachers and preachers. There would be a mutual interplay between the Spirit-guided teachers and the Spirit-indwelt congregation, and the result would be that the whole community would be led into, and built up in, the truth that is in Jesus.

SUMMARY

John strongly emphasizes the didactic role of the Spirit of Truth. He explains and interprets the truth incarnate in Jesus. The promise of his guidance into all the truth is made to every believer. This activity is a major facet of what the Paraclete-Spirit achieves.

C. Divine Power

Ethical empowerment is not a facet of the Spirit's work on which John dwells. Ethical issues as such do not occupy his attention, so it occasions no surprise that the Spirit as power in the believer's life to overcome evil and follow good is not a topic of discussion as it is in Paul's letters (e.g. Galatians and Romans).

Summary

Our examination of John's Gospel has revealed a spirituality deeply marked by a consciousness of God's Spirit. Christian experience begins in birth from God by the Spirit into a new life (3.3-8).

---

[45] Barrett, *John*, p. 515; Brown, *John II*, p. 781; Schnackenburg, *John III*, p. 197; Beasley-Murray, *John*, p. 305.

Language can vary: the Father and Jesus come to the believer and make their home with him or her (14.23); believers 'abide' in Christ and he in them like a vine and its branches (15.1-17); the Spirit flows from the Father through the Son to the believer like water gushing forth from a spring (7.37-39). But whoever was finally responsible for the shape of the gospel saw the Christian life in terms of life in the Spirit, as John 7.39 and the Paraclete sayings amply testify.

What may have originally been references to the Easter experience of reunion with the Master now alive again, are reinterpreted by means of the idea of Jesus' place being taken by the Paraclete-Spirit, gift of the Father through the Son (14.16-17 with 18-19; 14.23 with 26). All that Jesus had done in his earthly ministry is continued in the post-Easter era by the Spirit. Scholars have used various modes of expression to convey this: the Spirit is the presence of Jesus now returned to the Father; the Spirit is Christ's alter ego; one experiences Jesus in and through the Spirit; the indwelling Paraclete-Spirit is the indwelling Jesus, and so on.

Johannine Christians were deeply conscious of the Spirit's presence in their midst as the one who guided into all the truth. That truth had been brought by Jesus, and the Spirit's ongoing task was to interpret what Jesus had said and done in such a way as to deepen faith and love and obedience towards Jesus, and thus help the followers of Jesus continue his ministry in the world. The Paraclete-Spirit's ongoing ministry was to glorify Jesus in this way.

As there is an outward movement from the Father in the Son and in the Spirit, so also there is a return movement, as it were, as the Paraclete-Spirit enables believers to know Christ, to believe in him as the messiah, Son of God and Saviour of the world, and to see in him the Father. The Spirit glorifies Christ, who in turn glorifies the Father.

We endorse the verdict of Burge, when he commented that the Johannine Christian's sense of identity consisted in being 'born of God' and 'abiding in the Spirit' and this 'persevered as the central distinctive of Johannine discipleship.'[46]

2. The Johannine Epistles

I shall assume that the author of 1 and 2 John was someone different from the author of the Fourth Gospel (though many scholars would accept common authorship[47]),

---

[46] Burge, *Anointed Community*, p. 177. Cf. the verdict of Schnelle, *Geistheologe*, p. 26: 'As in Paul, the bestowal of the Spirit is also in the Johannine school the primary datum of the Christian existence.'

[47] E.g. B.F. Westcott, *The Epistles of St. John* (Cambridge and London: MacMillan, 2nd ed., 1886), pp. xxx-xxxii (the apostle John); R. Law, *The Tests of Life: A Study of the First Epistle of St. John* (Edinburgh: T. & T. Clark, 1909), pp. 50-51, 339-63 (the apostle John); A.E. Brooke, *The Johannine Epistles* (ICC; Edinburgh: T. & T. Clark, 1912), pp. i-xxvii, lxxvii-lxxix (the Elder John); W.F. Howard, 'The Common Authorship of the Johannine Gospel and Epistles', *JTS* 48 (1947), pp. 12-25; W.G. Wilson, 'An Examination of the Linguistic Evidence Adduced against the Unity of Authorship of the First Epistle of John and the Fourth Gospel', *JTS* 49 (1948), pp. 147-

but from within the 'Johannine circle'. Though some scholars have argued for the priority of the Epistles,[48] most scholars believe that 1 and 2 John were written a few years after the Gospel, during which a secession of some members of the Johannine communities took place.[49] The tremendous stress on the unity of Christ's followers in the Gospel (10.16; 11.51-52; 17.20-23) was no doubt intended to meet the incipient signs of, and to stave off, the breakaway, but it did not succeed. It is in this situation that the Elder, by means of 1 and 2 John, sought to encourage those Christians who had not broken away (3 John deals with a different situation altogether).

A. Divine Presence

One of the tests given by the writer to his readers to enable them to reassure themselves that they are Christians is mentioned at 3.24, and this test quite clearly identifies their experience of God's presence with the Holy Spirit: 'We know that He [God] abides in us by the fact that He has given us of His Spirit.' God's indwelling in Christians is equated with the Spirit whom God has given them.

A somewhat similar test is given at 4.13: 'We know that we abide in Him and He in us by the fact that He has given us of His Spirit.' The abiding concept is made mutual here: we abide in God as well as He abides in us. The sign and guarantee of this is that God has given us His Spirit.[50]

If this test is to be meaningful, it can only involve *conscious awareness of the Spirit*.[51] Believers can proceed from this conscious awareness to the conclusion that

---

56; J. Schneider, *Die Kirchenbriefe* (NTD 10; Göttingen: Vandenhoeck & Ruprecht, 1961), p. 139 (the Elder John mentioned by Papias, p. 189); Kümmel, *Introduction*, pp. 310-12 (author of the Gospel and Epistles is unknown to us); Robinson, *Redating*, p. 307, and *Priority*, pp. 113-14 (the apostle John); I.H. Marshall, *The Epistles of John* (NICNT; Grand Rapids, MI: Eerdmans, 1978, p. 46 (the Gospel and Epistles were written either by John the apostle who was known as the Elder or by a follower of the apostle who was known as the Elder); Guthrie, *Introduction*, pp. 858-66 (the apostle John).

[48] See the list in R.E. Brown, *The Epistles of John* (AB 30; New York: Doubleday, 1983), p. 33, to which should now be added G. Strecker, 'Die Anfänge der johanneischen Schule', *NTS* 32 (1986), pp. 31-47, esp. 47 (note 50); *The Johannine Letters* (Minneapolis, MN: Fortress, 1996), p. xlii; and his pupil, U. Schnelle, *Antidocetic Christology in the Gospel of John* (Minneapolis, MN: Fortress, 1992), p. 235.

[49] 1 John 2.19; 4.1c, 5a; 2 John 7. See Brown, *Epistles*, pp. 32-35, 69-71, 97-101, for a discussion; also his *The Community of the Beloved Disciple: The Life, Loves, and Hates of an Individual Church in New Testament Times* (New York: Paulist Press, 1979), pp. 93-144.

[50] The phrase ἐκ τοῦ πνεύματος αὐτοῦ is a partitive genitive, as maintained by Marshall, *Epistles*, p. 219; Brown, *Epistles*, p. 466.

[51] Cf. C.H. Dodd, *The Johannine Epistles* (London: Hodder & Stoughton, 1946), p. 115, 'immediate spontaneous unanalysable awareness of a divine presence in our life'; R. Schnackenburg, *Die Johannesbriefe* (Freiburg-Basel-Wien: Herder, 2nd ed., 1963), p. 209 (where Schnackenburg wrote 'Er muss also erfahrbar sein' ['He must also be

they enjoy the presence of God. There is a 'theological' conclusion to be drawn from experience.

Brown has challenged this on the grounds that the Elder's opponents could also claim inner experience of the Spirit,[52] so that the Elder would be 'playing into the hands' of his opponents by suggesting such a test. However, Schnackenburg's description of 3.24 and 4.13 as stereotyped expressions which stem from church instruction,[53] probably helps us understand the progression of the Elder's thought. It makes sense of the progression of his thought if we have (i) a piece of church tradition (3.24), but, in view of the fact that this can no longer unmask the opponents, then (ii) a warning in 4.1, 'Test the spirits, to see whether they are from God'.

The Elder is forced by the situation in which he finds himself to introduce certain qualifications to the church tradition. He 'hedges' the tradition around by tests. (He is thus rather like Paul who ordered the Thessalonians *both* not to quench the Spirit and not despise prophecy *and* to test everything—see 1 Thess. 5.19-21. Acceptance and critical evaluation go hand in hand).

The mere claim to inspiration and possession of the Spirit does not *ipso facto* mean that the claim is justified. There is a 'spirit of error' around as well as the Spirit of Truth (4.6); there are false prophets as well as genuine ones (4.1). Antichrist has his servants as well as the true God and His messiah and Son.

So, what are the tests which the writer suggests? There are two tests by which the Elder 'hedges' around the tradition. The first test devised is a doctrinal one (4.2-3). The incarnation (Jesus as the Messiah *come in the flesh*[54]) becomes the touchstone for the claim to inspiration by God's Spirit. Those who deny this belong to the world: what they say has its origin in worldly ideas, standards and motives, and as a result gains a hearing from the world (4.5). The writer includes himself and his readers in the resounding claim: 'We are of God' (4.6).

---

experiencable'], which appears rather less emphatically in the English translation of the 7th edition of 1984 as 'it is an experience open to all', *The Johannine Epistles* (Tunbridge Wells: Burns & Oates, 1992, p. 191) and p. 242 (ET, p. 219)—the author 'is absolutely sure that everyone begotten by God can be aware of their possession of the Spirit and experience it in its inner effects'; Marshall, *Epistles*, p. 219 ('various experiences might be in mind'); J.M. Lieu, *The Theology of the Johannine Epistles* (Cambridge: Cambridge University Press, 1991), p. 45 (the Spirit 'is also seen as something outward and recognisable which can confirm the validity of claims to inner experience').

[52] Brown, *Epistles*, p. 466.

[53] Schnackenburg, *Epistles*, pp. 191, 219.

[54] This is certainly not the only possible translation of Χριστὸν εν σαρκὶ εληλυθότα and it is rejected by many scholars. It seems to me that what we have here is one particular Johannine confession of faith—Jesus is the Christ/Messiah (as at 2.22; 5.1)—now expanded by the crucial 'come in the flesh', to meet the crisis of false belief in the Johannine congregations (cf. V.N. Neufeld, *The Earliest Christian Confessions* [Leiden: Brill, 1963], pp. 103-104, 106). See Brown, *Epistles*, pp. 492-94, and S.S. Smalley, *1, 2, 3 John* (WBC 51; Dallas, TX: Word, 1984), pp. 221-23, for full discussions of the various possibilities of translating 4.2.

This section on testing the spirits shows that while all Christians have God's Spirit (3.24; 4.13), some are inspired by the Spirit for proclamation of the Christian message. The generality of Christians will recognize those specially gifted and the validity of their message (4.6b).[55]

The second test of whether the readers are of God and have His Spirit indwelling them comes in 4.7-12, namely whether love is present in their lives, for love is the supreme characteristic of God and has been demonstrated in the incarnation (God sent His Son, 4.9) and the crucifixion (Jesus as the atoning sacrifice or expiation for our sins, 4.10). Therefore, 'Beloved, if God so loved us, we ought also to love one another' (4.11). When Christians do love one another, 'God abides in us and His love is perfected in us' (4.12). Then comes 4.13 already mentioned and we cannot but be struck by the parallel expressions in 4.12 and 4.13:

v.12 God abides in you	Love as the sign of this.
v.13 we abide in Him and He in us.	The Spirit as the sign of this.

The test that God's presence in us is guaranteed by His Spirit within us turns out to be very close to the test that love is a sign that God indwells us. Bultmann believed that 'the receiving of the Spirit is therefore likewise historicized'.[56] I doubt whether this is a correct interpretation. The Elder has not surrendered the direct sense of the Spirit's presence: he has been forced, however, to bring into play two tests (doctrinal and ethical) to ensure the truly divine origin of the experience of the Spirit, in order to counteract his opponents. True belief and conduct attest that our experience is genuinely one of *God's* Spirit.

We ought here to add a reference to the phrase 'the one who is born of God', which is used eight times of Christians and once of Jesus himself (5.18b). As one born of God, the Christian does not and cannot sin (3.9 twice; 5.18a); overcomes the world (5.4) and loves others born of God (5.1). As signs of birth from God, the Elder lists doing what is right (2.29), loving (4.7) and believing (5.1). Once God is Himself described as He who has begotten His children (5.1).

What was said above on the Fourth Gospel need not be repeated here. Those who use such language are usually those conscious of a dramatic conversion experience, and it is quite probable that the Elder has John 1.13 and 3.1-10 in mind, i.e. that the Spirit of God is the agent of this. Phrases like 'born of God' or 'born of the Spirit' would be part of the 'in-language' of the Johannine community.[57] At the same time,

---

[55] Marshall, *Epistles*, p. 209: 'It is by their response to the preaching of the true church that it is possible to discern those who are directed by the spirit of truth, i.e. the Holy Spirit, and the spirit of falsehood or error.'

[56] R. Bultmann, *The Johannine Epistles* (Philadelphia, PA: Fortress, 1973), p. 60.

[57] Schnackenburg, *Epistles*, pp. 154-55, speaks of being born of God as a fixed Johannine concept, while Brown, *Epistles*, p. 386, believes 'that divine begetting was part of the language of admission to the Johannine community'. See H. Leroy, *Rätsel und Missverständnis: Ein Beitrag zur Formgeschichte des Johannesevangelium* (Bonn: Peter

the fact that the author lists the characteristics of the one begotten by God is an indication that the morale and confidence of the congregation(s) have been shaken by the secession and that the Elder has to offer pastoral encouragement.

B. Divine Illumination

We turn to the second area of the Spirit's activity with which we are concerned, that of illumination and guidance into knowledge of the truth.[58]

The first passage to which we must turn is that of 2.18-27, in which we have a triple use of χρῖσμα (anointing). Many in the past and still today believe that this is a reference to the Holy Spirit.[59] The main reason is that the activities of the anointing are the same as those predicated of the Paraclete-Spirit in the Fourth Gospel.[60] In addition, the use of 'anoint' at Luke 4.18, Acts 10.38 and 2 Corinthians 1.21 in connection with the Spirit is referred to as additional support, though 1 John does not actually use the verb itself. However, usage outside of the Johannine writings cannot really lend much additional support. It is the argument about activities on which this case stands or falls.

An alternative viewpoint was put forward by C.H. Dodd: he argued that the 'anointing' stands for the Christian gospel, the truth of the Christian faith.[61] Dodd cited in support a passage from Ignatius' letter to the Ephesians (17.1-2), where Ignatius warned not to be anointed with the ill-odour of the prince of this world's doctrines. This is not so compelling as might seem at first sight, since Ignatius accompanies his verb with a prepositional phrase which indicates that teaching is in mind, whereas in 1 John that is not so. Then, Dodd also argued that in 1 John the word of God/truth is said to remain in Christians (e.g. 2.14; 2 Jn. 2), but Schnackenburg has a case here when he points out that the expressions used of anointing favour a personal interpretation of the metaphor.[62] Finally, Dodd maintained that his interpretation avoids the dangers of subjectivism, but this is an argument designed to appeal to the modern reader and does not of itself contribute to an exegesis of the text.

Hanstein, 1968), for a treatment of this theme of 'in-language' in respect to the Fourth Gospel.

[58] This is the chief function of the Spirit in 1 John according to Schnackenburg, *Johannesbriefe*, pp. 215 [The English translation, *The Johannine Epistles*, p. 195, seems to me to weaken the original].

[59] F. Hauck, *Die Kirchenbriefe* (NTD 10; Göttingen: Vandenhoeck & Ruprecht, 1949), p. 130; Schneider, *Kirchenbriefe*, p. 157; Schnackenburg, *Epistles*, p. 141; Brown *Epistles*, p. 348; W. Grundman, article on χρίω in *TDNT*, Vol. IX (Grand Rapids, MI: Eerdmans, 1974), p. 572; Boring, *Continuing Voice*, p. 104.

[60] Schnackenburg, *Epistles*, p. 141; Brown, *Epistles*, p. 346.

[61] Dodd, *Epistles*, pp. 58-64; supported by Lieu, *Theology*, pp. 29-30.

[62] Schnackenburg, *Epistles*, p. 192, and also p. 141, note 39.

More recently, several scholars have combined the two views outlined and suggested that the anointing refers to both the Spirit and the word of God.[63] This view rests very much on the link between the Spirit and word/proclamation in the Fourth Gospel, though there tends to be a difference of emphasis among its proponents, with some stressing the word of God but the word administered and confirmed by the work of the Spirit, while others stress the Spirit using the word.[64]

The discussion has been useful in order to highlight the link between Spirit and word. Probably, this was a 'given' in Johannine circles and a nuance which could be taken for granted (part of its 'in-language').[65] It is somewhat tautologous to say that the anointing 'teaches about everything' if χρῖσμα meant Spirit and word in equal fashion, but meaningful if it meant Spirit who uses the word of preachers and teachers. Burge has well summed up the matter in his comment: 'the anointing stands apart from the word as independent but finds its primary function in confirming the word and applying it in the present schism'.[66]

Proceeding on this assumption that the primary reference is to the Spirit, the following things are said: the Spirit is a gift from God (v. 20); all believers possess the Spirit who abides in them (v. 20) and so everyone has knowledge (v. 20—note the emphatic position of 'all', πάντες[67]), because the Spirit is the teacher and instructor of believers (v. 27) and he imparts truth, not falsehood (v. 27). These statements are made against the background of the necessity to confess Jesus as the Christ as a means of having fellowship with the Father, who is the donor of the Spirit (vv. 22-23).

The didactic role of the Spirit is quite clearly stressed in this passage. He gives the truth and so all believers have knowledge and do not require human teachers—assertions which offer some support to the view widely held today that the Johannine communities were charismatic congregations without much structure or hierarchy, but which ought not to be pressed too literally, in view of the heavy stress on the tradition 'from the beginning'[68] and the need to continue faithfully in that tradition as 'a part of the authenticity of where they now stand',[69] all of which

---

[63] I. de la Potterie, *La vie selon l'Esprit. Condition du Chrétien* (Paris: Les Éditions du Cerf, 1965), pp. 141-42 (= *The Christian Lives by the Spirit* [Staten Island: Alba, 1971], pp. 114-15); Dunn, *Baptism*, pp. 195-200; Porsch, *Pneuma und Wort*, pp. 116-17, 260; Marshall, *Epistles*, p. 155.

[64] Of scholars mentioned in footnote 57, de la Potterie, Porsch and Marshall are in the former category and Dunn in the latter.

[65] I disagree with Lieu's argument (*Theology*, p. 29) that it would be strange for the Elder to use a different term from Spirit for the same reality. If χρῖσμα was part of a vocabulary common to him and his readers, there would be no problem—varying his terms would not create any difficulty.

[66] Burge, *Anointed Community*, p. 175.

[67] The reading πάντες is to be preferred to πάντα (all things). There seems to be unanimity amongst commentators on this.

[68] See 1.1-4; 2.7, 24; 3.11; 2 Jn. 5-6.

[69] Lieu, *Theology*, p. 30.

argues for the presence of teachers within the congregations. The formulation is probably over-exaggerated as a polemical thrust against those who have broken away.[70]

The Spirit's role in illumination is further touched on in the passage 5.6-8. The Spirit is experienced here as one who bears witness because he is (or brings) the Truth. To whom does the Spirit bear witness? Clearly in the epistle believers are being addressed and they have just been reminded that it is their faith which overcomes the world (5.4b), a faith which is explained as believing that Jesus is the Son of God (v. 5), who came (from heaven) δι' ὕδατος καὶ αἵματος (v. 6a). The writer stresses that he came not just with[71] water but with water and blood (v. 6b), by which he wishes to stress the full humanity of Jesus the Son of God.[72] In other words, it is not just a question of belief, but of correct belief.

Then comes the statement about the Spirit's bearing witness (v. 6cd). The present participle utilized indicates a continuing activity, grounded on the close association of the Spirit and truth. The fact that here only the Spirit is mentioned suggests that a primary significance is being accorded to the Spirit as witness-bearer. The author then draws in other factors which bear witness: 'There are three who bear witness, the Spirit and the water and the blood, and the three are one' (vv. 7-8). Although many scholars have argued for a switch in meaning of water and blood in verses 6 and 8, from historical events in the life of Jesus in verse 6 to the Christian sacraments in verse 8,[73] perfectly good sense results by assuming the same meaning in both verses:[74] verse 6 asserts the full human experience of Jesus Christ, while verse 8 asserts that to the believing congregations the events, experience and impact of that human life continue to bear witness, because the Spirit bears witness through them. To use the language of the fourth gospel, the Spirit takes what belongs to Jesus and declares and interprets its meaning to believers. The Spirit is the interpreter

---

[70] Boring, *Continuing Voice*, p. 116, comments that the relation to tradition can be used as a criterion of true and false prophecy.

[71] I assume the διά to be one of attendant circumstances, i.e. indicating the set of circumstances accompanying someone or something.

[72] Considerations of space forbid a detailed examination of this much discussed sentence. Suffice to say that it is unlikely to refer to Jesus' baptism and crucifixion, despite the popularity over the years of this view, which is linked with the belief that the author was combating a docetic view which said that the divine Spirit descended on Jesus at his baptism. If this were so, the writer would be playing into the hands of the proponents of this putative false teaching; but for the writer of 1 John, Jesus is the Word incarnate from birth, not from baptism (cf. the Johannine tradition in Jn. 1.14). Perhaps I can refer to some observations made on 1 Jn. 5.6-8 in my 'References to Baptism in the Fourth Gospel', pp. 131-34.

[73] E.g. Westcott, *Epistles*, p. 182; Hauck, *Kirchenbriefe*, pp. 149-50; Dodd, *Epistles*, pp. 130-31; Schnackenburg, *Epistles*, pp. 235-38; Bultmann, *Epistles*, p. 80; J.L. Houlden, *The Johannine Epistles* (London: A. & C. Black, 1973), p. 128.

[74] E.g. Schneider, *Kirchenbriefe*, p. 183; Marshall, *Epistles*, pp. 237-39 (both say that a sacramental meaning is possible at a secondary level); Dunn, Baptism, pp. 200-204.

of Jesus, his life, his deeds and words (cf. Jn. 14.26; 16.12-15, with concrete examples of this at 2.22; 12.16). It is this inner coherence of meaning which tells against Margaret Barker's interpretation of the three witnesses as the Spirit at creation, the water issuing from the throne and the blood of the Day of Atonement.[75]

The community of Johannine believers experienced the Spirit as the one who guides into the truth, enabling it to understand aright the meaning and significance of the events of Jesus who revealed the Father and brought eternal life to the world.

C. Divine Power

The thought of the Spirit as ethical empowerment figures in the letters if the expression God's 'seed' (σπέρμα) which abides in the believer (3.9) is taken to be a metaphor for the Holy Spirit.[76] The association of God's seed and being begotten by God creates a strong probability that this is so. The abiding of God's 'seed' in believers enables them to avoid sinning—they do not sin (3.6; 5.18). Indeed, the writer goes further at 3.9: they cannot sin because they have been born of God.

These statements, rather akin to Paul's 'indicative' assertions, seem to draw on the late Jewish hope of sinlessness in the Age to Come due to the presence of God in the midst of His people,[77] plus the Johannine conviction that Christians were born of God by His Spirit who now indwelt them. The author is well aware that Christians sin (e.g. 2.1; 5.16[78]) and he sharply rebuts claims to sinlessness (made by

---

[75] M. Barker, *On Earth as It is in Heaven: Temple Symbolism in the New Testament* (Edinburgh: T. & T. Clark, 1995), p. 57. In Johannine thought, the *Word* is the mediator of creation (Jn. 1.1-3, 10). Furthermore, the Fourth Evangelist relativized the importance of the temple in John 4. And if there is any typology in the Johannine passion story, it is the Passover, not the Day of Atonement.

[76] So, e.g., Hauck, *Kirchenbriefe*, p. 135; F. Büchsel, article on γεννάω, *TDNT*, Vol. I (Grand Rapids, MI: Eerdmans, 1964), pp. 671-72; Schnackenburg, *Epistles*, p. 175; Schneider, *Kirchenbriefe*, p. 163; Brown, *Epistles*, p. 411; Burge, *Anointed Community*, p. 176. Some scholars speak more generally of the new life principle implanted by the divine begetting: Law, *Tests*, p. 389; Brooke, *Epistles*, p. 89; and Dodd, *Epistles*, p. 75. As might be expected in the light of how they take the 'anointing', de la Potterie, *La vie*, pp. 213-24; Dunn, *Baptism*, p. 198; Porsch, *Pneuma und Wort*, p. 115; Marshall, *Epistles*, pp. 186-87, combine Word and Spirit, as does S. Schulz, article on σπέρμα in *TDNT*, Vol. VII (Grand Rapids, MI: Eerdmans, 1971), p. 545. Bultmann, *Epistles*, p. 52 (note 37) sits on the fence.

[77] Cf. I. de la Potterie, 'L'impeccabilité du chrétien d'après 1 Jean 3.6-9', in *L'Évangile de Jean: Études et Problemes* (Recherches Bibliques 3; Bruges: Desclée de Brouwer, 1958, pp. 161-77 [reprinted in *La vie selon l'Esprit*, pp. 197-216 (= *The Christian lives by the Spirit*, pp. 175-196)]; J. Bogart, *Orthodox and Heretical Perfectionism in the Johannine Community as Evident in the First Epistle of John* (Missoula, MT: Scholars, 1977), pp. 105-106; Lieu, *Theology*, p. 59.

[78] 1 John 5.16-17 seems to be evidence of a certain moral casuistry, not incompatible with a strong sense of the Spirit's presence. Bogart, *Perfectionism*, p. 48, calls it a casuistic compromise.

those who seceded?) in 1.8, 10. Nonetheless, 3.9 plus 3.6 and 5.18 witness to a conviction that the indwelling seed/Spirit of God, as the agent of the divine birth, is also the agent who maintains Christians in ways of holy and Christlike living. The Spirit is the source of the so-called Johannine 'perfectionism', which fits into the Johannine dualism of those who are of God and those who are of the world/devil.[79]

As mentioned above, a test of whether Christians have the Spirit is whether they love their fellow Christians (2.10; 3.10-11.14, 23; 4.7-12, 20-21; 5.1-2). To love is a sign of being born of God (4.7), which is itself the work of the Spirit. At this point, the Johannine and Pauline approaches concur on the importance of love as a sign of the Spirit.

Summary

Lieu, in a comment about the tests of behaviour, wrote: 'We do not see ruthless attack against some external opposition but a genuine wrestling with the implications of religious experience'.[80] She is certainly right in what she affirms, even if we may not necessarily concur in what she denies (rather than an either-or choice, it might be better to embrace a both-and approach). In the Johannine congregations the experience of the Spirit continued to be prominent. Nevertheless, because of the schism, the author is compelled to reassure his readers of their Christian standing, and one of his tests aimed at producing this assurance is their experience of the Spirit, though this has now to be wedded to correct belief in order to undermine the claims of those who had left.

In setting up tests, 1 John was not introducing something new into Christianity, since in the first generation Paul had been compelled to do the same. Paul indicated three tests: the confession of Jesus as Lord (1 Cor.12.1-3); whether a spiritual gift builds up the congregation (1 Cor.12.7; 14.12); and love as the greatest sign and fruit of the Spirit (1 Cor.12.31b–14.1a). His confessional test, while appropriate in the Corinthian situation, would be singularly vague in other contexts, where more precision would be needed. This is exactly what we find in 1 John: the older confessions 'Jesus is the Christ' and 'Jesus is the Son of God' needed to be expanded by 'come in the flesh'. The test is related to the current controversy. The older confession marked Johannine Christians off from the synagogue (e.g. Jn. 9.22); now, that confession is expanded to provide a pointer to the true Christian as opposed to the false.

Many years ago, Schweizer pointed to the dangers, inherent in setting up doctrinal tests, of sliding into rigidity in mere orthodoxy and losing the 'spiritual glow'.[81] The point was well made and needs to be pondered on, but we do not feel that that stage had by any means been reached in the Johannine Epistles. Burge was surely

---

[79] See Dunn, *Jesus and the Spirit*, pp. 355-56, for a brilliantly concise assessment of Johannine perfectionism; also Bogart, *Perfectionism*, for an attempted reconstruction of the differences between the Elder and his opponents on the issue of perfection.

[80] Lieu, *Theology*, p. 51.

[81] E. Schweizer, *Church Order in the New Testament* (London: SCM, 1961), p. 129.

right in his judgment: 'Any community which holds John 3:1-15 as its charter of discipleship is bound to exhibit a profound spiritual vitality...the immediacy of the divine presence retained its validity in the community. Christian identity is first found in birth through the Spirit.'[82]

The sense of guidance of the Spirit is also emphasized by the author, though clearly the confidence of his readers had been shaken by the schismatics' claim to possess the truth. At the same time, there is a strong emphasis on keeping to that which they had heard from the beginning: the Spirit had opened their spiritual eyes to the truth within the Johannine gospel and they must keep to it. This too has its dangers, but then we must remember that the churches were in the middle of a crisis. In such a situation, it is not unnatural to emphasize holding fast to the traditions already received.

Ethical empowering too is part of the experience if, as we assume, behind the expression 'seed of God' there lies the thought of the Holy Spirit: the Spirit produces holiness of life (sinlessness) in believers. Balancing this, however, is a realistic awareness that Christians do sin, (though in Jesus Christ we have a permanent advocate with the Father [2.1-2]) and the motivation that, as our hope is in Jesus and his appearing (3.2), Christians will seek purity in the knowledge that their master is righteous, pure and holy (3.3) and that at the End we shall be like him (3.2bc).

3. The Didache

The Didache may also be located in Syria, probably composed about AD 90-100.[83]

---

[82] Burge, *Anointed Community*, p. 171.

[83] So A. Adam, 'Erwagungen zur Herkunft der Didache', *ZKg* 68 (1957), pp. 1-47, esp. 47, where he says that an E. Syrian destination is highly probable, a date ca.90-100 a well-grounded hypothesis and Pella as the specific place of composition a hypothetical supposition; L. Goppelt, *Christentum und Judentum* (Gütersloh: Gerd Mohn, 1954), p. 186; D.E. Aune, *Prophecy in Early Christianity* (Grand Rapids, MI: Eerdmans, 1983, p. 310, who sets the Didache in 'the congregations of Syria-Palestine at the turn of the first century'; Boring, *Continuing Voice*, p. 83 (Syria and the last third of the first century): K. Niederwimmer, *The Didache* (Minneapolis, MN: Fortress, 1998), pp. 52-54, cautiously postulates Syria-Palestine and ca.110-20. J. Danielou, *The Theology of Jewish Christianity* (London: Darton, Longman & Todd, 1964), pp. 28-30, locates the development of the document in Syria after 70, with an origin in the earliest Jerusalem community and with our document having undergone some touching-up later than the second century. J-P. Audet, *La Didachè* (Paris: Gabalda, 1958), pp. 187-210, esp. 199 and 210, locates it in Syrian Antioch but dates it between 50-70. Robinson, *Redating*, p. 327, places it between 40 and 60, but does not discuss location. M. Goguel, *L'Eucharistie dès origenes à Justin Martyr* (Paris: Fischbacker, 1910), p. 230, dates it to ca.100 but locates it in Palestine. On the other hand, A. von Harnack, *Die Lehre der Zwölf Apostel* (TU 2; Leipzig: Akademie-Verlag, 1884), pp. 159, 168-69, placed it in Egypt and in the period 140-65, and F.E. Vokes, *The Riddle of the Didache* (London: SPCK, 1937), pp. 216, 218, also placed it in Egypt, but dated it to the end of the second century or

A. Divine Presence

Interestingly, the Didache orders the congregation to remember the person who speaks the word of God (where Barn. 19.9-10 has the command to remember the Day of Judgment night and day and to love the one who speaks of the Lord as 'the apple of one's eye'), for such a person is clearly regarded as mediating the presence of God;[84] 'Where the lordship [= presumably the proclamation of the lordship and authority of God or Christ] is, there is the Lord'. From chapters 9–15, it is clear that those who proclaim the word are regarded as Spirit-inspired (e.g. 11.7-12). Where such people proclaim the word of God and of Christ, there the congregation experience the sense of their divine presence, for we may assume that this proclamation takes place in worship.[85]

In the sections dealing with the Agape prayers[86] (9.1–10.7) (although the point is not affected if these prayers are for the Lord's Supper[87]), God the Father is thanked for having made His holy Name to dwell in their hearts (10.2) and for having bestowed spiritual food and drink and eternal life on them through His Son (10.3). Since the Name stands for the person, the phrase in the prayer implies God's presence in their hearts and this could be an indirect reference to the Spirit. Likewise, what is meant by the 'spiritual food and drink' clearly has some association with the Holy Spirit: they are food and drink produced and supplied by the Spirit to the deepest levels of human personalities.

Thus, in the prayers of the congregations, grateful acknowledgment is made for the experience of God's presence and sustaining power and for the inward blessings given through the Spirit.

The concept of the Spirit's presence inspiring someone to utter a word from God is clearly attested in chapters 11–15, as already stated. The congregation or

---

beginning of the third as an anti-Montanist document. A. Vööbus, *Liturgical Traditions in the Didache* (Stockholm: ETSE, 1968), pp. 12-14, contents himself with speaking of the document as 'hoary with antiquity', because of the uncertainties in being more precise, but locates it in Egypt.

[84] J. Lawson, *A Theological and Historical Introduction to the Apostolic Fathers* (New York: Macmillan, 1961), p. 76, takes this reference as an allusion to Spirit-filled prophets, and, though there is no specific reference to the Holy Spirit, he is probably right.

[85] So D.E. Aune, *The Cultic Setting of Realised Eschatology in Early Christianity* (Leiden: Brill, 1972), p. 182.

[86] So M. Dibelius, 'Die Mahl-Gebete der Didache', *ZNW* 37 (1938), pp. 32-41; Vokes, *Riddle*, pp. 177-207; R. Bultmann, *The Theology of the New Testament* (London: SCM, Vol. I, 1955), p. 145; J. Jeremias, *The Eucharistic Words of Jesus* (London: SCM, 2nd ed., 1966), p. 118; Niederwimmer, *Didache*, pp. 142-43. Audet, *Didache*, pp. 372-424, esp. 407, accepts 10.6 as a transition to the Eucharist, but sees 9.1–10.5 as a 'vigil' celebrating the coming of the Kingdom of God.

[87] J.R. Harris, *The Teaching of the Twelve Apostles* (London: Clay and Baltimore: John Hopkins University Press, 1887), p. 89; Lawson, *Introduction*, pp. 90-91; Vööbus, *Liturgical Traditions*, p. 63. Goguel, *Eucharistie*, pp. 243-44, believed that chs 9-10 dealt with prayers for a private Eucharist and ch. 14 was about a public one.

congregations for which the Didachist wrote had in the past highly respected itinerant apostles and prophets who from time to time visited them. They are inspired by the Spirit, but the congregations have had some unfortunate experiences from charlatans.

There are a number of indications of the respect for such inspired prophets. A prophet is allowed to lead prayers of thanksgiving at the Agape as he feels led (10.7) and is not bound by the fixed prayers appended in 9.1-10.6. At 15.1-2, the author stresses that the resident bishops and deacons perform the same service and deserve *the same respect and honour* as the itinerant prophets and teachers.

In addition, the instruction is given 'You must not test or pass judgment on any prophet who speaks by the Spirit (ἐν Πνεύματι), for every sin will be forgiven, but this sin will not be forgiven' (11.7[88]). Clearly, the traditional logion about blasphemy against the Holy Spirit, now found in the Synoptic Gospels, has been reapplied to apostolic/prophetic figures in the church life of the day. What originally referred to Jesus' ministry (in view of Mk. 3.28-29) is here applied to the risen Lord's messenger: as the Lord himself was endowed with the Spirit, so are his servants, the prophets.[89]

Yet immediately this instruction is qualified, suggesting that 11.7 is the older material and 11.8-9 is a development,[90] due to the problem of discerning a true prophet from a false one, a true Spirit-directed utterance from a counterfeit one. So, what are the qualifications? The first test is one of conduct. 'But not every one who speaks by the Spirit (ἐν Πνεύματι) is a prophet, but only if he has the ways of the Lord. Therefore, the false prophet and the (true) prophet will be known by their ways' (11.8; cf. 11.10). Then, secondly, certain utterances allegedly made in the Spirit are branded as inauthentic. Two examples are given. 'If a prophet who orders a meal by the Spirit (ὁρίζων τράπεζαν ἐν Πνεύματι), he must not eat of it himself' (11.9). The meaning of this phrase is much disputed, but it may refer to an Agape

---

[88] Cf. too 11.11, where it is said that they must not judge a true prophet 'who acts for the earthly mystery of the church' (ποιῶν εἰς μυστήριον κοσμικὸν ἐκκλησίας). Paraphrasing, we could render as 'who performs an action to set forth the earthly mystery of the church'. We cannot be certain of what is meant by this phrase, but it may be a case of a symbolic action, a 'spiritual marriage' by a prophet, to set forth the mystery of Christ and his church (so von Harnack, *Lehre*, p. 44.; R. Knopf, 'Die Lehre der zwölf Apostel', in *Die apostolischen Vater* (HzNT Erganzungs-Band; Tübingen: Mohr, 1923), pp. 32-33; H. von Campenhausen, *Ecclesiastical Authority and Spiritual Power in the Church of the First Three Centuries* (London: A. & C. Black, 1969), p. 73 (note 119); G. Bornkamm, article on μυστήριον, *TDNT*, Vol. IV (Grand Rapids, MI: Eerdmans, 1967), p. 825; Boring, *Continuing Voice*, p. 137; Niederwimmer, *Didache*, pp. 180-81. Audet, *Didache*, p. 452, speaks of an apocalyptic mime drama, but what did he mean by speaking of 'the disorders' which such a mime drama could easily involve?

[89] Boring, *Continuing Voice*, p. 219, sees the Didachist's interpretation of the saying in connection with prophecy, as representing an actual memory of the original setting of the logion about the blasphemy against the Spirit. He does not accept that this was an original saying of Jesus—wrongly in my opinion.

[90] Boring, *Continuing Voice*, p. 83: 'Such inconsistencies denote a developing *tradition* rather than composition by a single author.'

meal, perhaps as anticipating the messianic banquet.[91] Reading between the lines, it looks as if some charlatans had claimed the Spirit's inspiration as a means of obtaining a good meal. The second example comes at 11.12: 'If someone says by the Spirit, Give me money or something else [that is, for himself], you must not listen to him. But if he asks for others in need, let no one condemn him'. Again, it is obvious that some had claimed to be Spirit-inspired for their own financial advantage.

Some so-called prophets have discredited their vocation by greed and gluttony. This has necessitated drawing up some tests, but not the outright rejection of the idea of inspiration by the Spirit.

B. Divine Illumination

The Didache does not dwell on the Spirit's role as illuminator, as guide into truth and knowledge, though knowledge is one of God's gifts mediated through Jesus, for which thanks are offered (9.3; 10.3).

C. Divine Power

There is one reference to the Holy Spirit in the Two Ways section (chapters 1–6) and as this is also found in Barnabas, we may assume that it belonged to the original source used by both authors. At 4.10 it is said that God comes to those whom the Spirit 'has prepared'. Here the meaning is that the Spirit is active[92] in all[93] believers' lives so that when the eschatological coming of God takes place, they are ready to enjoy fellowship with God. The idea is not elaborated, but presumably refers to making believers pure and holy, and so fit for God's presence.

Taking chapters 1–6 as a whole, there is no other word about divine help and succour in the fulfilling of the demands made. Indeed, in the last section of this part of the work, we read 'If you (sing.) are able to bear the whole yoke of the Lord, you will be perfect; but if not, do what you can' (6.2). If pressed, this seems to open up the way to thinking of two classes of Christians, the perfect and the non-perfect triers. Can such a division claim any support from any NT writers? Occasionally Paul speaks of those who are perfect or mature ($\tau\acute{\epsilon}\lambda\epsilon\iota o\iota$). For Paul men and women

---

[91] So Harris, *Teaching*, p. 103; Vokes, *Riddle*, pp. 169, 178; Lawson, *Introduction*, p. 94. However, Knopf, *Apostolischen Vater*, p. 31, thinks of a meal for the poor, not an Agape, and he is followed by Niederwimmer, *Didache*, p. 179, while Audet, *Didache*, pp. 450-52, refers to the vigil celebrating the coming of God's Kingdom of 9.1–10.6.

[92] I assume this translation. The Greek could be rendered as 'those for whom God has prepared the Spirit', in which case the Spirit is an eschatological gift. But, as the Spirit is already active in the congregations, this interpretation should be rejected.

[93] That is, irrespective of such social distinctions as masters and slaves. Actually, Audet, *Didache*, pp. 338-40, refers this text to the human spirit and he compares it with Mt. 5.3, 8. He sees a contrast between external éclat and righteousness of heart and spirit, but this is hardly convincing.

were 'children' before Christ/faith came (Gal. 4.1, 3). The pre-Christian period is one of infancy; since Christ and the era of faith, we have 'come of age'. However, not all Christians realize this maturity. Thus, Paul criticized the Corinthians for acting like children in Christ (1 Cor. 3.1). They were not fully controlled by the Spirit but by their own egos, and he urged them not to be children but 'mature' in understanding (1 Cor. 14.20). He claimed to speak wisdom among the 'mature' (1 Cor. 2.6),[94] but, basically, all his ethical demands are addressed to the entire congregation.

It is interesting to see how Paul can ask for respect for those who admonish the Thessalonians on the one hand, while on the other hand he exhorts the whole congregation to admonish the idle (1 Thess. 5.12, 14). In Galatians, he can ask the 'spiritual' among them to restore an offender with gentleness, which is one of the virtues which the Spirit produces in all believers, and so, in theory, all could engage in the task of restoration (Gal. 5.23; 6.1). Is the Didachist in line with this? He seems to be resigned to a double standard, whereas Paul sees the childhood/maturity schema of Galatians 4.1, 3 as normative. The Corinthians have failed to capitalize on this, and are sternly rebuked for it.[95]

Much the same could be said as the result of a comparison with Hebrews (5.11–6.12; 10.14). Possibly the Didachist knew of Matthew 19.21, but I doubt it. Here the question of dates of composition of the two works is crucial, for the use of 'perfect' at Matthew 19.21 is redactional.

We may say, then, that the distinction drawn by the Didachist seems to represent a standpoint different from that within Paul and Hebrews. He has not introduced the concept of the Holy Spirit as divine aid in ethical living into the Two Ways section.

Summary

The contribution of the Didache to our subject is disappointingly meagre. We might have expected more about the Spirit's help in living out the commands imposed in the Two Ways, while it is clear that unworthy prophets are in circulation and the 'old ideas' are having to be re-scrutinized and rules drawn up to protect congregations.

If we ask after the reason why the Didache says so little about the Spirit, we might speculate whether the unworthy prophets were themselves the very reason

---

[94] In Phil. 3.15, Paul believes that those who are τέλειοι will think the way he does. Some commentators like F.W. Beare *The Epistle to the Philippians* (London: A. & C. Black, 1959), pp. 130-31, and J. Gnilka, *Der Philipperbrief* (Freiburg-Basel-Wien: Herder, 1968), p. 201, believe that Paul may be taking up a slogan of his opponents ironically, but B. Witherington, *Friendship and Finances in Philippi* (Valley Forge, PA: Trinity Press International, 1994), p. 96, strongly rejects this and maintains that excessive mirror-reading and speculation about opponents is 'not in order here', for the problem is a potential, not an actual, one.

[95] C.K. Barrett, *The First Epistle to the Corinthians* (London: A. & C. Black, 1976), p. 69, wrote, 'All Christians are potentially *perfect* or *mature* in Christ (Col. 1.28), though only some are actually what all ought to be.'

why the Spirit does not figure prominently. Could it be that their claims to be inspired by the Spirit, accompanied by unworthy conduct, produced a backlash against stressing the Spirit? Alternatively, if 'spiritual experiences' were tending to be more limited, this might in turn produce a restrictive coalescing of Spirit and prophecy, with people coming to expect only prophets to possess the Spirit. If the latter is accepted, then this means that a vital element of early Christianity had been surrendered, whereas the first suggestion explains the silence in terms of a clash of viewpoints within the congregations.

On either viewpoint, we might have a situation, not the same as, but not entirely dissimilar to, that behind 3 John, where a local congregational leader, Diotrephes, has banned the travelling preachers who have set forth with the Elder's blessing. Clearly Diotrephes has taken an extreme step of actually refusing admission to these travelling preachers; the Didache insists on applying tests. Diotrephes has risen to leadership, whether he bore a specific title or not; the Didache wants bishops and deacons appointed. We are, in the Didache, at a point of transition; we are further on in that transition in the 3 John situation. The Elder represents the more charismatic type of leadership within a series of congregations which he and others visit in the course of their missionary preaching. In one particular congregation, Diotrephes has acquired position and leadership, and resents the—to him—interference of visiting evangelists. We have a clash between (incipient) 'Office' and 'Spirit' in the Johannine stream of Christianity. The seeds of this kind of conflict are there in the Didache.

4. Matthew's Gospel

Prime facie, Matthew's Gospel, probably written in the last decade of the first century or the first decade of the second century[96] in Syria,[97] might not seem to have

---

[96] Those who so date the Gospel include G.D. Kilpatrick, *The Origins of the Gospel according to St. Matthew* (Oxford: Clarendon, 1946), p. 130; G. Strecker, *Der Weg der Gerechtigkeit* (Göttingen: Vandenhoeck & Ruprecht, 2nd ed., 1966), p. 36; J.P. Meier, *Law and History in Matthew's Gospel* (Rome: Biblical Institute Press, 1976), p. 7; F.W. Beare, *The Gospel according to St. Matthew* (Oxford: Blackwell, 1981), pp. 7-8; J.A. Overman, *Matthew's Gospel and Formative Judaism* (Minneapolis, MN: Fortress, 1990), pp. 153-54. Those favouring the 80s include D.R.A. Hare, *The Theme of Jewish Persecution of Christians in the Gospel according to St. Matthew* (SNTSMS 6; Cambridge: Cambridge University Press, 1967), p. 166; D. Hill, *The Gospel of Matthew* (NCB; London: Oliphants, 1972), pp. 49-50; and G. Stanton, *A Gospel for a New People* (Edinburgh: T. & T. Clark, 1992), p. 378, with Kümmel. *Introduction*, p. 84, opting for 80-100. A number of scholars who accept the apostle Matthew as author place the composition of the Gospel to the sixties: E.J. Goodspeed, *Matthew, Apostle and Evangelist* (Philadelphia, PA: Winston, 1959), pp. 5-19, 57-98; N.B. Stonehouse, *Origins of the Synoptic Gospels* (Grand Rapids, MI: Eerdmans, 1963), pp. 46-47; Robinson, *Redating*, pp. 103-107; R.H. Gundry, *Matthew: A Commentary on his Literary and Theological Art* (Grand Rapids, MI: Eerdmans, 1982), pp. 601-22; R.T. France, *Matthew: Evangelist and Teacher* (Exeter: Paternoster, 1989), pp. 77-80; L.

much to contribute to our theme. There is only one reference to the Spirit's help given to the disciples in this Gospel, namely the strictly limited promise of 10.20: when hauled before hostile tribunals, the disciples will be inspired what to say by the Holy Spirit. While disciples after Easter are to be baptized in the name of the Father, Son and Holy Spirit, it is not actually said that the disciples will be given the gift of the Spirit (unlike the Gospels of Luke and John). Why?

Suspicion of the charismatic type of figure[98] seems, on the one hand, to be even more strongly expressed in this Gospel than in the Didache. Thus, the Sermon on the Mount contains a warning against Christian false prophets whose conduct will reveal that they are not what they claim (7.16-20),[99] and a warning that many who have prophesied, exorcised and healed in the name of Jesus will nonetheless be excluded from the eschatological kingdom (7.21-23). A distinction is drawn between using religious jargon ('Lord, Lord') and doing the heavenly Father's will (7.21).

Yet, on the other hand, this should not be taken to mean that Matthew is opposed 'root and branch' to 'charismatic activity', as the editorially shaped 17.17-20 and

---

Morris, *The Gospel according to Matthew* (Leicester: IVP, 1992), pp. 11-15; Guthrie, *Introduction*, pp. 43-53 (non-committal about the date). D.A. Schlatter, *Der Evangelist Matthäus: Seine Sprache, sein Ziel, seine Selbtstandigkeit* (Stuttgart: Calwer, 1948), pp. viii-xi, believed that the author was Matthew, a disciple of Jesus, a Palestinian Christian, but offered no view on the actual date of composition, though on p. 706 he reveals that he thought Matthew wrote well after the scare that Caligula intended to put a statute of himself in the temple.

[97] See B.H. Streeter, *The Four Gospels* (London: Macmillan, rev. ed., 1930), pp. 500-507, for the 'classic' statement of the Gospel's place of composition at Antioch. The vast majority of scholars, if not following Streeter's precise position, at least opt for Syria, with some exceptions being Kilpatrick, *Origins*, pp. 130-34, who suggests one of the Phoenician cities to the south of Antioch, and Overman, *Matthew's Gospel*, p. 159, who advocates Sepphoris or Tiberias.

[98] Among scholars who believe that Matthew was attacking miracle-working charismatics are G. Barth, 'Matthew and the Law', in G. Bornkamm, G. Barth and H.J. Held, *Tradition and Interpretation in Matthew* (London: SCM, 1963), pp. 162-64; P. Bonnard, *L'Évangile selon saint Matthieu* (Neuchâtel: Delachaux & Niestlé, 1963), pp. 103-105; R. Hümmel, *Die Auseinandersetzung zwischen Kirche und Judentum* (München: Chr. Kaiser Verlag), 1963, p. 27; W.D. Davies, *The Setting of the Sermon on the Mount* (Cambridge: Cambridge University Press, 1964), pp. 199-206; Hill, *Matthew*, pp. 151-53; É. Cothenet, 'Les Prophètes chrétiens dans l'Évangile selon Matthieu', in M. Didier (ed.), *L'Évangile selon Mathieu* (Gembloux: Duculot, 1972), p. 300; E. Schweizer, *Matthäus und seine Gemeinde* (Stuttgart: KBW Verlag, 1974), pp. 140-41; J.A. Kingsbury, 'The verb AKOLOUTHEIN ("To Follow") as an Index of Matthew's view of his Community', *JBL* 97 (1978), pp. 70, 72; Beare, *Matthew*, pp. 195-97; Aune, *Prophecy*, p. 219, 222-24; Overman, *Matthew's Gospel*, pp. 118-19; Boring, *Continuing Voice*, pp. 69, 104, 177, 255. This suggestion is denied by Strecker, *Weg*, pp. 137-38, while Stanton, *Gospel*, p. 49, urges caution in trying to be precise.

[99] Against D. Hill, 'False Prophets and Charismatics: Structure and Interpretation in Matthew 7.15-23', *Biblica* 57 (1976), pp. 327-48, who takes vv. 15-20 of the Pharisees and only vv. 21-23 of Christian charismatics.

23.34 (par. Lk. 11.49); and the instructions in chapter 10 for missionaries,[100] who represented Jesus and who are described as prophets (10.40-41), show. Indeed, Schweizer has gone so far as to describe the Matthean church thus: 'Matthew presupposes healings and similar miracles still going on in the church. In its preaching the church is a church of the prophets'.[101] This seems to me to be going far too far, and, as his view, if correct, would have considerable implications for our study, we need to examine it in detail. There are several reasons why it ought to be rejected.

Schweizer's view assumes that because so many so-called 'sentences of Holy Law' occur in Matthew, this reflects the Matthean church situation at the stage when the Gospel was composed,[102] but this need not be the case at all. Furthermore, the challenge of K. Berger[103] to E. Käsemann has shown that linking such sayings to prophets is not justified, though Berger's own stress on a sapiential-paraenetic Sitz im Leben may be equally too one-sided.[104]

Following on from this, Schweizer's view ignores that sometimes Matthew includes material which is not entirely congruous with his own stance (e.g. 10.23; 23.2-3; possibly 10.5-6, though see 15.24). Also, there are signs in the Gospel of an attempt to make the absolute teaching of Jesus 'workable': e.g. 19.9 (cf. 5.32), which permits divorce for adultery; 5.37, which allows a mild oath (Yes yes, No no);[105] 5.21-26, with its grading of outbursts of anger against a brother. This hardly suggests the itinerant charismatic who has renounced all to follow and serve Jesus. Furthermore, the passage 23.8-12 suggests a conflict within the leadership of the Matthean church, but the terms used point more to teachers, and presumably resident ones, while 23.34 mentions 'wise men and scribes' alongside of prophets, where the Lucan parallel has 'prophets and apostles' (11.49). We may suspect Matthean redaction here.

Schweizer exaggerates when he asks whether for Matthew Jesus' journeys in chapters 2–4 are the model for all wandering prophets.[106] Much more likely is

---

[100] Cf. Boring, *Continuing Voice*, p. 71, whose description of Mt. 10 as 'a manual of conduct for Christian prophets and teachers on their missionary journeys' would be widely accepted.

[101] E. Schweizer, 'The Law and Charismatic Activity in Matthew's Gospel', *NTS* 16 (1969-70), p. 226.

[102] Kingsbury, '*AKOLOUTHEIN*', p. 63. (The phrase 'Sentences of Holy Law'—Sätze heiligen Rechtes—appears to have been coined by E. Käsemann in an article 'Sätze heiligen Rechtes im Neuen Testament', *NTS* 1 [1954-55], pp. 248-60, translated in *New Testament Questions of Today* [London: SCM, 1969], pp. 66-81.)

[103] K. Berger, 'Zu den Sogennanten Sätzen heiligen Rechts', *NTS* 17 (1970-71), pp. 10-40.

[104] See the balanced discussion in Aune, *Prophecy*, pp. 237-40.

[105] See Strecker, *Weg*, pp. 133-34.

[106] Schweizer, *Law and Charismatic Activity*, p. 221, and *Matthäus und seine Gemeinde*, p. 147.

Stendahl's suggestion[107] that there is a focus on places in these chapters, and support for this comes from John's Gospel which shows that Jesus' links with Galilee were offensive (7.27, 41-42, 52; cf. 6.42). We reject also Schweizer's tentative suggestion that the OT quotations inserted in 8.17, 12.18-21 and 13.35 are aimed to set forth Jesus as the charismatic healer and prophetic revealer of God's mysteries.[108] More convincing is the view that they afford backing for aspects of Jesus' ministry in the controversy with Pharisaic Judaism (his miracles of healing; his withdrawal in the face of opposition and his gentleness exemplified in his secrecy; his speaking in parables).

Finally, there are various hints that Matthew's Gospel originated in a wealthy congregation.[109] This fits in better with the picture of a settled congregation with an ordered structure rather than the kind of charismatic activity envisaged by Schweizer.

For these reasons, therefore, we reject the view propounded by Schweizer. What 7.15-23 does show us is that even charismatic activities may be unchristian if not accompanied by what was in Matthew's opinion true obedience to God. Interestingly, there is no mention of miraculous activity in the Great Commission[110] (though miracles were part of early Christian activity, as shown by 2 Cor. 12.12; Rom. 15.19; Heb. 2.4; Acts; the longer ending of Mk. 16.17-18) and the promised help in mission is described not in terms of the Holy Spirit (as in Acts 1.8; Jn. 20.21-22), but in terms of the risen, exalted Lord's permanent presence (Mt. 28.20; cf. 18.20). There may be stylistic reasons for this: Matthew may wish to balance the God-with-us of the opening of the Gospel (1.23) with the Lord Jesus-with-us. Or it may reflect a desire on the part of the evangelist not to overemphasize the idea of inspiration by the Spirit, for fear of playing into the hands of the charismatic prophet-miracle workers of whom he disapproved. These two suggestions are not necessarily mutually exclusive, and the stylistic reason could have operated alongside of the other. In the light of the evidence surveyed, we believe that it is conceivable that the charismatic experiences were viewed with some caution by Matthew and that he preferred to speak of Jesus' living presence in the assembled congregation (18.20) and in the mission of the church (28.20), though we cannot overlook the promise of the Spirit's aid to missionaries interrogated before hostile tribunals (10.19-20).

---

[107] K. Stendahl, 'Quis et Unde? An Analysis of Mt. 1-2', in W. Eltester (ed.), *Judentum Urchristentum Kirche* (Berlin: Topelmann, 1960), pp. 94-105.

[108] Schweizer, *Matthäus und seine Gemeinde*, p. 146.

[109] Kilpatrick, *Origins*, p. 125; Kingsbury, '*AKOLOUTHEIN*', pp. 67-68, 71.

[110] This is stressed by G. Bornkamm, 'The Risen Lord and Earthly Jesus: Matthew 28.16-20', in J.M. Robinson (ed.), *The Future of our Religious Past* (London: SCM, 1971), pp. 213-216, esp. 216. Cf. the hint of this point also in an earlier article, which appeared first in *EvTh* 10 (1950-51), pp. 16-26, and now translated into English, by O. Michel, 'The Conclusion of Matthew's Gospel', in G. Stanton (ed.), *The Interpretation of Matthew* (London: SPCK, 1983), pp. 30-41.

C. Divine Power

This picture is confirmed when we consider the ethical stress in Matthew's Gospel. Matthew does not insinuate any references to the Spirit's power to help the follower of Jesus. He emphasizes the need to produce right living in God's sight and the fact of the judgment at the End. He retains a structure of gracious deed and imperious demand in chapters 4.23-25 and 5–7, and records a saying about making the tree sound and then the fruit will be good (12.33), which appears to be his own redaction of a Q saying (Lk. 6.43/Mt. 7.17-18). It could be that Matthew believed that the sonship relationship to the Heavenly Father generated (as it were) the motivation and the power to do God's will.

Summary

If we put Matthew and the Didache side by side, their pictures seem to complement each other, perhaps from the side of a more wealthy, settled city congregation (Matthew) and the side of the more rural area congregation (Didache). From both the past and the present, there comes evidence of itinerant missionary preachers/prophets who performed miracles, and yet in the present there is some suspicion (Didache) and even hostility (Matthew) towards them because of abuses. While neither wishes to deny the activity of the Spirit, both agree that claims to the Spirit's inspiration need to be evaluated carefully, lest the faithful be deceived by those who are unworthy.

5. Ignatius of Antioch

Ignatius was bishop of the church at Antioch. In his letter to the church at Rome, he says that the Syrian church now 'has God as its shepherd in place of me; Jesus Christ only—and your love—will be its bishop' (Rom. 9.1). Through his letters we catch a vivid glimpse of him while being transported from Antioch to Rome in chains (Eph. 21.2; Rom. 5.1). He passed through Asia Minor guarded by ten soldiers (Rom. 10.5) and from Smyrna he wrote to the Ephesians, Magnesians, Trallians and Romans, while he penned letters to the Philadelphians, Smyrneans and Polycarp from Troas. The charge against him is not specified, while the date of his martyrdom cannot be set with any certainty, and estimates vary from ca.AD 107 to 117.

We meet a startling paradox in Ignatius: a charismatic institutionalist. Ignatius was a firm advocate of order in church life, centred on one bishop, a group of elders and deacons (though not every one by a long way was well disposed to this development). Yet in his extant letters, written on the way to martyrdom at Rome, he reveals his own charismatic nature and experience.

A and B. Divine Presence and Illumination

In his letter to the Philadelphians, Ignatius refers to an incident which had happened while he was among them. Although unacquainted with the division and tension in the church, of which certain people wished to keep him in the dark, he was inspired by the Spirit of God to speak a word very relevant to that situation. Ignatius describes the Spirit as one who, because God's Spirit, 'is not deceived ....for he knows whence he comes and where he goes, and brings to light things that are hidden' (Phld. 7.1). Whether Ignatius knew John's Gospel or not, he here applies to the Spirit language which in John's Gospel is used both of the wind in the analogy figuring in the dialogue with Nicodemus (Jn. 3.8) and also of Jesus himself (Jn. 8.14).[111] Knowledge of one's origin and destiny gives a spiritual awareness denied to others, and this enables the Spirit to be aware of the situation.

A further indication that Ignatius believed that he was under the Spirit's control is the fact that he 'shouted out' and 'spoke *with a loud voice*, with God's voice' (Phld. 7.1).[112]

The first word which he uttered was a brief command: 'Pay attention to the bishop and the eldership and the deacons' (Phld. 7.1). This is, of course, a message that Ignatius was constantly emphasizing. Although some suspected him of having prior knowledge of the division caused by some, Ignatius maintains before God that that was not so. What he 'learned' (intuitively) was not due to human information; rather,

'The Spirit was proclaiming, speaking in this way:
Do nothing apart from the bishop;
Keep your flesh like God's temple;
Love unity; flee divisions;
Be imitators of Jesus Christ as he was of His Father.' (7.2)

As Aune has said, 'Ignatius views these inspired utterances as a divine confirmation of the very values which he himself seeks to inculcate in the congregations he visited and addressed by letter'.[113]

Trevett points out that Ignatius' utterance was 'tested', although no member of that word group for testing (διάκρισις; διακρίνω) is actually used.[114] Clearly, Ignatius was challenged and his word discussed.

---

[111] C. Maurer, *Ignatius und das Johannesevangelium* (Zurich: Zwingli-Verlag, 1949), pp. 25-30, believes that here Ignatius' thought flits from one NT text to another—John 8.14; 3.8; 1 Corinthians 14.24-25, while W.R. Schoedel, *Ignatius of Antioch* (Hermeneia; Philadelphia, PA: Fortress, 1985), p. 206, leaves open the question of whether Ignatius was dependent on John or knew a formula apart from the Fourth Gospel.

[112] Schoedel, *Ignatius*, p. 205: 'He shared with many others in the Graeco-Roman world the belief that a sudden loud utterance marked the inrush of the divine'; cf. Aune, *Prophecy*, pp. 292, 435-36; C. Trevett, *A Study of Ignatius of Antioch in Syria and Asia* (Lewiston: Edwin Mellen, 1992), p. 135.

[113] Aune, *Prophecy*, p. 293.

[114] Trevett, *Ignatius*, p. 136. She refers to the testing of prophecy in the early churches as revealed by 1 Cor. 12.8-9; 14.29 and 37; 1 Thess. 5.19-20; 1 John 4.1; Didache 11.7-8; 12.1; Hermas, Mandate 11.7,11 and 16.

Thus, we have a pattern of a (claimed) inspiration by the Spirit leading to the utterance of a word related to a situation of which he was ignorant. Ignatius was not cognizant of what was going on in the church, but became the mouthpiece of the Spirit to utter a message pertinent to it. Thus, 'inspiration' and 'illumination' are conjoined in this passage from Philadelphians.

The idea of the inspiration of the Spirit leading to speech probably occurs also in Ephesians 5.1. Here Ignatius refers to the short conversation which he had with the bishop of Ephesus. This conversation was not purely human but inspired by the Spirit (πνευματικήν). He points out how fortunate the Ephesians are to have such a leader permanently among them. We may well suspect a polemical thrust behind this laudatory section. Elsewhere Ignatius enjoins submission to and respect for bishop Onesimus (Eph. 2.2; 4.1, 3; 6.1; 20.2), and perhaps it was the itinerant preachers (Eph. 7.1; 9.1) who had created some discontent towards the resident bishop. Perhaps, in the light of what Ignatius says at Ephesians 6.1 – 'The more that someone sees the bishop silent, let that person respect him all the more' – we may conjecture that Onesimus was not very vocal.[115] So, Ignatius' comment about a 'spiritual conversation', by helping to emphasize the quality as opposed to the quantity of the words (or their rhetorical shaping), proffers support for the criticized bishop.

Later on in the letter (Eph. 8.2), Ignatius contrasts those who are 'fleshly' and those who are 'spiritual'. To this contrast he adds another, that between faith and unbelief and what kind of behaviour each type of person exhibits (we shall return to this in our section C shortly). Ignatius concludes by praising the Ephesians because even what they do on the level of the flesh, their physical actions, is 'spiritual',[116] for they 'do all things in Jesus Christ'. Ignatius then proceeds to commend the Ephesians for another of their actions: namely, the refusal to give credence to some who passed through Ephesus with an 'evil teaching' (Eph. 9.1). We may conclude that one feature of those who are 'spiritual' is the ability to know the truth from error and so refuse to listen to the purveyors of false doctrine: such indeed the Ephesians have showed themselves to be by their refusal to listen to these false teachers.

When Ignatius claims in Trallians 5.2 to be able to understand heavenly things and the arrays of angels and the gatherings of the spiritual powers, this may point to the receipt of divine revelations.[117] While the Spirit is not specifically mentioned, the context implies that Ignatius is Spirit-inspired in contrast to his readers who are 'babes',[118] though Ignatius does stress that this knowledge does not make him already a disciple, i.e. a perfect one who already has perfect knowledge of God.

---

[115] So Schoedel, *Ignatius*, p. 56.

[116] This must be seen against the background of Ignatius' fight against the docetists and his stress on the importance of the flesh, both for Jesus Christ and us.

[117] So Aune, *Prophecy*, p. 294.

[118] H. Schlier, *Religionsgeschichtliche Untersuchungen zu den Ignatiusbriefen* (Giessen: Topelmann, 1929), p. 140, correctly believes that in Trallians 5.1 Ignatius is pneumatic, while the church members are the babes (νήπιοι).

C. Divine Power

After referring to those whom he considers false teachers, whose behaviour he finds wanting and whom the Ephesians should at all costs shun (Eph. 7.1), Ignatius reflects on Jesus Christ, who is both 'fleshly and spiritual, begotten and unbegotten, God in man...from Mary and from God, first capable of suffering and then impassible' (Eph. 7.2). Ignatius will pick up the first pair in this series of antitheses in chapter 8 as he considers the Ephesians who have not allowed themselves to be deceived and who wholly belong to God (Eph. 8.1).

> 'Those who are fleshly cannot do spiritual things,
> nor the spiritual do fleshly things,
> just as faith (cannot do) the things of unbelief,
> nor unbelief (do) the things of faith.
> What you do even on the level of the flesh is spiritual;
> For you do everything in Jesus Christ'. (8.2)

The first two lines in our arrangement could be a piece of tradition and is certainly reminiscent of Pauline teaching (and in their antithetical character akin to Jn. 3.6).[119] The third and fourth lines expand the first two with another antithetical pair: faith and unbelief. Trevett sees this pair as emphasizing 'a different division of humankind from that of the sarkikoi-pneumatikoi':[120] presumably she means by this a different way of looking at the division of humanity, since, as Schoedel noted, against Schlier's attempt to see here a Gnostic doctrine of the two races of humanity, that the antithesis is in fact Pauline, as seen in Romans 14.27.[121] We assume that Ignatius has given us a different way of looking at humanity from a fleshly-spiritual antithesis, namely, a faith-unbelief antithesis.

The last two lines in our arrangement are clearly Ignatius' comment. While he may not here be consistent terminologically, the sense is clear. Because one belongs to God, because one is in Jesus Christ, because one is of the Spirit, the Christian can live obediently and righteously and in conformity with God's will in the world, in the realm of the flesh, amidst the physical and material pressures and needs of everyday life. In his involvement in this world of flesh, Jesus Christ is the model for Christians (cf. Eph. 7.2). The Ephesians have followed his example and live in a godly way in a union of flesh and spirit (cf. Magn. 13.1), above the reach of destructive lusts (Eph. 8.1).

In chapter 9, Ignatius continues his reference to itinerant teachers and the response to them on the part of the Ephesians. Their refusal to listen to these teachers is explained as due to the fact that they are stones of a temple prepared beforehand by

---

[119] Schoedel, *Ignatius*, p. 23, refers to these lines as 'an older view' and as 'the tradition', and later in the commentary (p. 64) refers to Rom. 8.5; 1 Cor. 2.14-15; Gal. 5.16-26.

[120] Trevett, *Ignatius*, p. 161.

[121] Schoedel, *Ignatius*, p. 64.

God the Father for His dwelling place (Eph. 9.1). The imagery is somewhat complicated and may be set out as follows:

The engine for lifting the stones into place = the cross
The rope = the Holy Spirit
The crane = faith
The way which leads to God = love.

That Ignatius had daily conduct in mind is shown both by the reference to faith and love and by the fact that he immediately goes on to envisage Christians' being like a religious procession in which a shrine and sacred objects are carried around: Christians carry God and Christ around, 'adorned in every way with the commands of Jesus Christ'. The thought is that, just as pagans during their religious processions put on special clothes, in honour of the deities they worship, so the obedience of Christians to the commands of their Lord and Master is their spiritual garments which reveal their allegiance and loyalty to God and Christ.

In this picture of a shrine, the 'objective' basis of the building process is the cross, while the 'subjective' side comprises the help of the Spirit and the exercise of faith and love by Christians.[122] It is not straining the sequence of thought to believe that Ignatius here envisaged the help of the Spirit in the exercise of faith and love and obedience to the commands of Jesus Christ.[123] But it must be admitted that he has not developed the idea with crystal clarity.

Finally, we turn to Romans 7, where yet another spiritual experience of Ignatius is described, and here the link with martyrdom is made. Ignatius says that he is writing to the Romans in the midst of life, yet longing for death. His physical desire has been crucified. Within him there is only living water, which speaks within him: 'Come to the Father'. There can be little doubt that the 'living water' is a symbolic way of describing the Spirit.[124] The Spirit within has extinguished love for the world

---

[122] Cf. W.C. Weinrich, *Spirit and Martyrdom: A Study of the Work of the Holy Spirit in Contexts of Persecution and Martyrdom in the New Testament and Early Christian Literature* (Washington DC: University of America Press, 1981), pp. 122-23: 'the life of the Christian community' is 'a life in the passion of Christ by the power of the Spirit... The activity of the Spirit is intimately connected with the cross.'

[123] In disagreement with Schoedel, *Ignatius*, p. 68, who does not think that ethical injunctions are in mind, and C.C. Richardson, *The Christianity of Ignatius of Antioch* (New York: Columbia University, 1935), p. 99, who denied that in Ignatius the Spirit transforms the moral nature and takes 9.1 as intellectual. Given the stress of 8.2b, there is surely no need to exclude ethical injunctions from Ignatius' intentions. Certainly P. Meinhold, *Studien zu Ignatius von Antiochen* (Wiesbaden: Steiner, 1979), pp. 67-72, discusses this passage in his chapter on the ethics of Ignatius.

[124] So also W. Bauer, 'Die Ignatienbriefe', in *Die apostolischen Väter* (Tübingen: Mohr, 1920), p. 252; Schlier, *Untersuchungen*, p. 146; Bultmann, *John*, p. 185 (footnote 1); H. Paulsen, *Studien zu Ignatius* (Göttingen: Vandenhoeck & Ruprecht, 1978), p. 126; Weinrich, *Spirit and Martyrdom*, p. 133; Schoedel, *Ignatius*, p. 185. Some scholars see here a reference to baptism: H-W. Bartsch, *Gnostisches Gut und*

and all love of material things (7.2-3). The Spirit is urging him on to martyrdom that he may attain to fellowship with God the Father.

Summary

The idea of the Spirit cannot be said to be dominant in Ignatius. Certainly, Ignatius himself had had experiences which he attributed to the Spirit of God. He became the spokesman and vehicle of that Spirit who revealed to him things which of himself he could not have known. He also experienced the inner urge and compulsion to martyrdom as the Spirit's invitation to come to the Father. Yet he seems to find it more natural to express himself in terms of 'Christ mysticism'.

Ignatius envisaged the Spirit as working in all church members and it is the Spirit who aids to a truly spiritual life of obedience in the world.[125]

So Ignatius is an interesting blend, but he leaves us with the impression in the end that he has swung the weight of his influence onto the development of ministry.[126] So much has he stressed the role of the bishop and the need not to do anything without him that in practice the likely outcome would be a curbing of the expectation of the Spirit's free and sovereign work in the congregation as a whole. Around roughly the same time in Asia Minor (as we shall see), the Pastoral Epistles reveal a similar tendency to link the Spirit with the ministerial Office: the bishop/elders guard the tradition through the help of the Spirit.

6. The Odes of Solomon

Whether composed originally in Syriac or Greek, these Christian hymns have been variously dated to ca.AD 100; sometime in the middle to latter half of the second century; and even in the second half of the third century. We shall assume a cautious approach here and adopt a date early in the second half of the second century, thus

---

Gemeindetradition bei Ignatius von Antiochen (Gütersloh: Bertelsmann, 1940), pp. 110-11. and Lawson, *Introduction*, p. 131; while Aune, *Prophecy*, p. 294, combines the two interpretations: 'metaphorical use of an oracular form to indicate the implications for him of his baptism and subsequent possession of the Spirit of Christ'. This seems to be a wholly unnecessary importation of baptism into a context which makes perfectly good sense when taken as an experience of the Spirit, which the writer describes in language drawn from Jn. 4.14; 7.37-39. Interestingly, A. Benoit, *Le Baptême chrétien au second siècle* (Paris: Presses Universitaires de France, 1953), p. 79, sees baptismal language from Paul being used in the phrase that Ignatius' desire has been crucified, but he makes no reference to the living water phrase.

[125] Trevett, *Ignatius*, p. 137, observed: 'To judge from the number of references to it, the Holy Spirit did not have a very significant place in Ignatius' writings but he certainly knew of its importance for the life of the Christian communities.'

[126] Cf. Meinhold, *Studien*, p. 9, who commented that the pneumatic in Ignatius wills the self-sacrifice of the pneumatic and subordinates himself to the episcopal office and church institutions; there is a similar view in Trevett, *Ignatius*, p. 137.

allowing some response in the Odes to Marcionite theology, while also doing justice to the strong Jewish Christian flavour of the Odes.[127]

No other extant Christian work of the second century is so vibrant with the intensity of Christian experience, of present experience of the Spirit and of fellowship with the risen Lord Jesus than these Odes. This may be due to an 'accident of survival' and had other works come down to us, the Odes might not stand so isolated in this respect. The language is exuberant and the imagery is intense, bordering on the erotic, or, perhaps we should say, the amatory. As H. Chadwick has said, 'The inward experience of the believer is described in enthusiastic and impassioned terms of palpable feeling' and he also remarked on the Odist's 'uninhibited freedom of expression'.[128]

A. Divine Presence

We turn first to explore the Odes for a sense of being inspired or seized by the Spirit. There are a number of Odes which in all probability deal with what we may term the conversion experience. Ode 11.1a says that the Odist's heart was pruned and its flower appeared. The horticultural metaphor used implies some experience which enabled the writer to undergo (we might say) the full flowering of his personality and life. 'Then grace sprang up in it' and his heart 'produced fruits for the Lord' (v. 1bc).[129] The 'for' of verse 2 grounds this idea of divine grace appearing in his life, and we then appear to have a repetition of the basic idea expressed in the pruning picture:

> 'For the Most High circumcised me by His Holy Spirit.
> Then he uncovered my inward being towards Him,
> And filled me with His love.
> And His circumcising became my salvation...
> And I was established upon the rock of truth,
> Where He had set me'. (vv. 2-3a, 5)

This experience is brought about by God through His Holy Spirit. As physical circumcision marked the Israelite child as a member of the covenant people, so this spiritual circumcision has marked the Odist as belonging to God. The circumcision metaphor confirms that we are dealing with the initial Christian experience.

In verse 6, the imagery switches to imbibing living waters and becoming inebriated. This intoxication did not cause ignorance, but, on the contrary, in this

---

[127] See the excursus at the end of this section for some indication of scholarly opinion on dating the Odes.

[128] H. Chadwick, 'Some Reflections on the Character and Theology of the Odes of Solomon', in P. Granfield and J.A. Jungmann (eds.), *Kyriakon, Festschrift für J. Quasten* (Münster: Aschendorff, Vol. I, 1970), pp. 269 and 270 respectively.

[129] Unless otherwise stated, all translations are taken from J.H. Charlesworth (ed.), *The Odes of Solomon* (Chico, CA: Scholars, 1977).

turning to the Most High, the Odist abandoned vanity and folly. That someone should use imagery of drunkenness strongly suggests an overpowering and intense experience.

This present experience of God is compared to the present entry into Paradise, a motif which appears frequently in the Odes, as Aune has stressed:[130]

> 'And from above He gave me immortal rest,
> And I became like the land that blossoms and rejoices in its fruits....
> And He took me to His Paradise,
> Wherein is the wealth of the Lord's pleasure. (vv. 12,16)
> I beheld blooming and fruit-bearing trees.... 16a
> From an immortal land (were) their roots. 16d
> And a river of gladness was irrigating them, 16e
> And round about them in the land of eternal life.' 16-17 [131]

This is indeed realized eschatology.[132] That this is not a one-off mystical experience (akin to 2 Cor. 12.1-9) seems to be proved by words which occur within the praise called forth from the Odist to the Lord for this experience and which speak of growth:

> 'Blessed, O Lord, are they
> Who are planted in Thy land....
> And who grow in the growth of Thy trees
> And have passed from darkness into light.' (vv.18-19)

And the Odist speaks of the remnant, planted in Paradise and bearing fruit (cf. 20.7 for another reference to the present experience of Paradise).

Ode 11, then, shows that the Holy Spirit is the agent of this conversion experience which leads into God's Paradise. As a result of conversion, the Odist experiences such fellowship with the Lord that only the language of lovers apparently suffices to express his feelings.

We turn to Ode 3 for an illustration of this.[133] The Lord's prior love has taught the Odist to love (v.3):

---

[130] Aune, *Cultic Setting*, p. 185; 'The Odes of Solomon and Early Christian Prophecy', *NTS* 28 (1982), pp. 441-43; *Prophecy*, pp. 297-98.

[131] Verse 16adef only occurs in the Greek text of the Bodmer Papyrus XI (G); and is accepted as authentic by Charlesworth, *Odes*, pp. 12, 56-57.

[132] A motif in the Odes which Aune has stressed: see *Cultic Setting*, pp. 185-87; *Prophecy*, p. 298.

[133] J.R. Harris, *The Odes and Psalms of Solomon* (Cambridge: Cambridge University Press, 2nd ed., 1911), p. 90: 'The author is a mystic, with a doctrine, or rather an experience, of union with the Son.'

> 'I love the Beloved and I myself love Him' (v.5a);
> 'I have been united (to Him), because the lover has found the Beloved.' (v.7a)

There then follows a series of three statements which assert that union with the Lord makes the believer what the Lord is:[134]

> 'Because I love Him that is the Son, I shall become a son.
> Indeed he who is joined to Him who is immortal,
> Truly shall be immortal.
> And he who delights in the Life
> Will become living.' (vv. 7b-9)

Then there immediately follows a statement about the Spirit.

> 'This is the Spirit of the Lord which is not false,[135]
> Which teaches the sons of men to know His ways.' (v. 10)

What is the link between the preceding sentences verses 7-9 and this verse? Why does the Odist say 'This is the Spirit of the Lord'? Aune has taken this formulation as equivalent to a claim to inspiration which backs up a prophetic statement.[136] I am not convinced that this is the right explanation, for two reasons. In the first place, what has preceded this statement of 3.10 is not a prophetic statement. Rather, it is a celebration of the spiritual relationship between the believer and the Lord; it is spiritual love poetry, not a word from God to humans. Secondly, Ode 3 is nothing like Revelation 2-3 or 1 Corinthians 14.37-38, which Aune cites as comparable.

We suggest a different interpretation: the Odist has in mind the union of the Son and the believer, which creates sonship, immortality and life for the believer.[137] Language used about this may be fluid and variable. As in the NT writers may speak of being united with Christ or that the Spirit dwells within them, so here the Spirit of the Lord is envisaged as creating and sustaining the union. The knowledge of the Lord and his ways which the Spirit imparts leads to the loving relationship which this Ode expresses.

Ode 25 may also be considered at this point.

---

[134] Akin to, but even more strongly expressed than, 2 Cor. 3.18 and 1 Jn. 3.1-2.

[135] H.J.W. Drijvers, 'Die Oden Salomos und die Polemik mit den Markioniten im Syrischen Christentum', Symposium Syriacum 1976, *OCA* 205 (1978), pp. 49-50, detects here a thrust directed against the Marcionites, who taught that the Creator-God deceived human beings.

[136] Aune, *Odes and Prophecy*, pp. 438-39; *Prophecy*, pp. 296-97.

[137] For this reason we query the assertion of R. Abramowski, 'Der Christus der Salomo-Oden', *ZNW* 35 (1936), p. 57: 'In the end there is no distinction between the real and adopted sons.'

'I was rescued from my chains
And I fled unto Thee, O my God.'[138] (v. 1)

He has been saved by grace (v. 4b). The Odist also uses the imagery of light: God has given him a lamp as a result of which no darkness dwells in him (v. 7). Then he continues:

'And I was covered with the covering of Thy Spirit
And I removed from me my garments of skin.' (v. 8)

The imagery of a change of clothing is utilized here. The phrase 'the garments of skin' stands for the pre-conversion state of the believer[139] (a person as 'flesh' as at 20.3). The believer at conversion is given new clothes, and so a new nature: God's Spirit dwells with the believer.

Verse 9 includes another picture: God's right hand exalted the writer and caused sickness to pass from him.

'And I became mighty in Thy truth,
And holy in Thy righteousness.' (vv. 9-10)

Probably sickness is here a metaphor for the pre-conversion state.[140]

Thus far, we have seen that Odes 11, 3 and 25 describe religious experience in terms of union with Christ brought about by the Spirit.

The Odist uses the concept of 'seal' and we need to examine his usage to see whether he was thinking of the Spirit. We turn to Ode 4.

'For who shall put on grace and be rejected?
Because Thy seal is known;
And Thy creatures are known to it.' (vv. 6-7)

Bernard thought that baptism was in mind,[141] but the phrase could equally refer to the reception of the Spirit as part of the conversion experience (repentance, faith,

---

[138] Here he experiences the release which in 10.1-3 he helps others to achieve. Harris, *Odes*, p. 126, says, 'In this Psalm we are back again in the region of personal experience.'

[139] There may be an allusion to Gen. 3.21 here. So Harris, *Odes*, p. 68, who took 'the garments of skin' to represent the body and assumed the spiritual conversion and regeneration of the soul was in mind.

[140] Against J.H. Bernard, *The Odes of Solomon* (Texts and Studies VIII; Cambridge: Cambridge University Press, 1912), p. 108, and Aune, *Cultic Setting*, p. 187, both of whom espouse the literal interpretation.

[141] Bernard, *Odes*, pp. 448-54 (in accordance with his general approach to the Odes, which is adopted by G.W.H. Lampe, *The Seal of the Spirit* [London: Longmans, Green, 1951], pp. 111-14 [not entirely with conviction, it should be added!]. A.C. Headlam,

baptism, entry into the church). The Lord places his seal (the Spirit) on believers: they know the Spirit and the Spirit knows those who are the Lord's creatures. This interpretation would certainly fit verse 9 also:

> 'Thou hast given to us Thy fellowship,
> Not that Thou wast in need of us,
> But that we are always in need of Thee'

(cf. earlier in verse 3 'Thou hast given Thy heart, O Lord, to Thy believers') and also it would fit verse 10:

> 'Sprinkle upon us Thy sprinklings,
> And open Thy bountiful springs which abundantly supply us with milk and honey'.

The images of gentle showers descending, springs gushing forth, entry into the promised land of milk and honey, would all be congruous with the experience of the Spirit—an interpretation which is strengthened by the fact that the image of God's pouring out streams of water = the Holy Spirit upon Jacob-Israel, His servant, in an overall New Exodus setting, occurs in Isaiah 44.1-3.[142]

But will the interpretation seal = Holy Spirit fit what is said about the seal here?

> 'And Thy hosts possess it
> And the elect archangels are clothed with it.'

While at first sight strange, the thought that the angels experience God's Spirit is not impossible and is better than Bernard's view that 'it is as a seal which the heavenly host recognize... the splendour of baptismal grace is like the splendours of the heavenly host.'[143] Bernard's view labours under several difficulties. Firstly, he is too much influenced by later Christian writers like Cyril of Jerusalem and Basil. How later Christian writers regarded baptism is no certain guide for a writer in the second century. Then, it is difficult to see the meaning of the assertion that the heavenly host possess the baptismal sign. Thirdly, there is nothing in the text which says that the heavenly host recognize the seal—Bernard reads that into the text at v.

'The Odes of Solomon', *CQR* 71 (1911), p. 292, wrote of the Odes: 'The writer...is thinking primarily of the new life he is experiencing and not of baptism. Baptism may have provided language to express his own spiritual experiences, but it is not of baptism that he is thinking.'

[142] J.R. Harris and A. Mingana, *The Odes and Psalms of Solomon* (Manchester: Manchester University Press, Vol. 2, 1920), pp. 228-229, and Charlesworth, *Odes*, pp. 24-25, deny any reference to baptism in Ode 4, against Bernard, *Odes*, p. 53, and J.A.F. Gregg, ' The Odes of Solomon', *ICQ* 6 (1913), p. 23.

[143] Bernard, *Odes,* p. 51.

7. Finally, the text does not say that the splendour of the seal is like the splendours of the heavenly host.

If the seal = the Spirit who brings the fellowship of the Lord, then the Odist is saying that believers on earth experience what the angels in heaven experience.[144]

The idea of a seal also occurs in Ode 8. Speaking of his own and to them, Christ says:

> 'And before they had existed,
> I recognized them;
> And imprinted a seal on their faces.' (v. 13)

Here the meaning can only be a mark of ownership which is based on Christ's foreknowledge and which distinguished those who came to faith in Christ. The seal as a mark of ownership could quite naturally be taken as the Spirit.

So, then, our investigation suggests that the two occurrences of 'seal' in the Odes can be treated alike. In Ode 4 the reference may be to the Holy Spirit, and this could also fit Ode 8 where the sealing process finds its ultimate basis in the foreordaining knowledge of Christ.

If the Spirit is involved in the conversion experience, he is also involved in the ongoing Christian life.

The opening verses of Ode 28 use the imagery of the parent doves' extending their wings over their young as an analogy of the Spirit's activity towards the Odist:

> 'So also are the wings of the Spirit over my heart.
> My heart continually refreshes itself and leaps for joy,
> Like the babe who leaps for joy in his mother's womb.' (vv. 1c-2)

The Spirit provides continual protection and nourishment for the Odist. The Spirit is the 'spiritual mother' of the Odist.

Then the thought moves on to that of the Odist's being at rest through trust in Christ, for Christ is completely trustworthy. Christ has greatly blessed him. 'My head is with him' (v. 4); the picture of his head resting in Christ is that of a lover in the beloved's lap, in view of verse 7:

> 'And immortal life embraced me,
> And kissed me.'

Then comes a reference to the Spirit who is within him and who cannot die because the Spirit is life. No wonder the Odist can contemplate the destruction of this mortal frame with equanimity and knows that neither 'dagger' nor 'sword' can separate him from Christ (v. 5; cf. Rom. 8.35-39).

---

[144] Another motif within the Odes which is stressed by Aune, *Cultic Setting*, p. 187; *Odes and Prophecy*, p. 452.

We again have the language of realized eschatology in connection with the Spirit in Ode 36:

'I rested on the Spirit of the Lord,
And she lifted me up to heaven
And caused me to stand on my feet in the Lord's high place.' (vv. 1-2a)

If here the Odist uses the language of the Spirit, he can also speak elsewhere of the Lord who dwells in his blessed ones (e.g. 32.1).

We now turn to Ode 38, where the writer pictures himself like a root planted and watered by the Lord (vv. 18-21). Because of such care, this plant's roots penetrate deeply, and the plant springs up and spreads out,

'And the Lord alone was glorified
In His planting and in His cultivation.' (v. 20)

It would certainly be consonant with his thought if behind this imagery was the idea of the Spirit who enables him to grow up as a lovely plant.

Ode 19 calls for attention also. In imagery strange to Western ears, the Odist speaks of the believer being given a cup of milk through the sweetness of the Lord's kindness. The Son is the cup; the Father is milked; the Spirit does the milking (v. 2): the Father is the source of what is given, the Son is the channel and the Spirit ensures the transmission. Then in verse 4 the Odist says:

'The Holy Spirit opened her bosom[145]
And mixed the milk of the two breasts of the Father.'

The picture seems to be that the Spirit milks the breasts of the Father[146] and then imparts that milk through her own breasts.

Verse 5 opens 'Then she gave the mixture to the generation[147] without their knowing', though some received it. This points to the incarnation, as verses 6-7 show:

'The womb of the virgin took (it)
And she received conception and gave birth.
So the Virgin became a mother with great mercies.'

---

[145] H.J.W. Drivers, 'The 19th Ode of Solomon', *JTS* 31 (1980), p. 341, translates 'opened her womb'. He argues that the Holy Spirit functions as the womb of the Father from where His grace and truth (the milk of His two breasts) = His only begotten Son are born. M. Lattke, *Die Oden Salomos* (OBO 25.1; Göttingen: Vandenhoeck & Ruprecht, 1979), p. 129, rendered by 'bosom' (seinen Busen).

[146] Harris, *Odes*, p. 117, took the breasts of the Father as meaning the old and new covenants.

[147] Drijvers, '19th Ode', p. 340, and Lattke, *Oden*, p. 129, translate 'to the world'.

The cup imagery is dropped after its initial mention in verse 1.

We can describe the contents of this Ode as primarily the Incarnation.[148] But, what the Spirit produced from the Father in the virgin can be offered to believers.[149] This milk, this spiritual nourishment, is from the Father in the Son *through the Spirit*. Clearly, the Spirit's work in mediating the Son *continues*, since the Odist celebrates what has been given to *him*. It is through 'the breasts' of the Spirit that we receive the Father's gift in the Son.

Summarizing, we may say that Odes 19, 26 and 36, and possibly 38, afford evidence that the Spirit is the mainspring of the life of the Christian, though equally we have seen places where the language is that of the Lord's indwelling his believers.

A final facet of our inquiry into a sense of inspiration by the Spirit is that of inspiration for composing the Odes. This is a prominent theme in the Odes.

> 'As the wind glides through the harp
> And the strings speak,
> So the Spirit of the Lord speaks through my members,
> And I speak through His love.' (6.1-2)

With these words, the Odist shows clearly how conscious he is of being the mouthpiece of the Spirit. The image itself might almost suggest passivity, but we ought not to press the language too far.[150] The Spirit destroys what is alien and so everything that the Odist speaks comes from the Lord (v. 3). The Lord is described as keen that what had been given to believers through His grace should be known.

> 'His praise He gave us on account of His name;
> Our spirits praise His Holy Spirit'. (v. 7)

Believers like the Odist praise the Lord's Holy Spirit because the Spirit is the one who mediates all the blessings of salvation. This praise is meant in the Lord's plan to reverberate outwards, so that others may learn of His grace.

There then follows the picture of a stream which not only reaches to the Temple[151] but spreads over the surface of the whole earth.[152] This symbolizes the spread of the Christian message.[153]

---

[148] Cf. Drijvers, '19th Ode', p. 349.

[149] Drijvers, '19th Ode', speaks of a doctrine of recapitulation: how to regain the lost paradise.

[150] Bernard, *Odes*, p. 56, says that this type of language is often found in orthodox Syrian writers.

[151] This may be due to the influence of Ezek. 47; cf. Harris, *Odes*, p. 97; Barnard, *Odes*, pp. 56-57; A.E. Abbott, *Light on the Gospel from an Ancient Poet* (Cambridge: Cambridge University Press, 1912), p. 128. Perhaps it is also an indication that the author is a Jewish Christian.

> 'And all the thirsty upon the earth drank,
> And thirst was relieved and quenched
> For from the Most High the drink was given.' (v. 11)

A blessing on those who are the ministers of that drink follows, 'who have been entrusted with the water' (v. 12). The 'water' is the gospel, the Christian message[154] (we must not equate water and the Spirit as in the Johannine manner[155]), but the inspiration is clearly, in the light of verses 1-2, the Holy Spirit.

As Spirit-inspired messengers, speakers, ministers of the word, they dispense the water of life in that word:

> 'They have refreshed the parched lips
> And have roused the paralyzed will.
> Even living persons who were about to expire,
> They have held back from death,
> And limbs which had collapsed,
> They have restored and set up.
> They gave strength for their coming,
> And light for their eyes,
> Because everyone recognized them as the Lord's
> And lived by the living water of eternity.' (vv. 14-18)

This is a moving description of what the preacher achieves.

If the harp figures in the simile of 6.1, it figures again in Ode 14, as a metaphor this time. The Odist prays:

> 'Teach me the odes of Thy truth
> That I may produce fruits in Thee.
> And open to me the harp of Thy Holy Spirit,
> So that with every note I may praise Thee, O Lord.' (vv. 7-8)

The picture seems to be that of the Odist overhearing within himself the music of the Spirit, and then reproducing this in praise to the Lord. His whole aim is to glorify and praise the Lord. He covets the blessings of inspiration in order that he may 'produce fruits in Thee' (v. 7), i.e. that he may be useful in the service of

---

[152] Harris, *Odes*, p. 97, says, 'The writer is exultant in his universalism... The writer is as universal as St. Paul.'

[153] Charlesworth, *Odes*, p. 32.

[154] Against Bernard, *Odes*, p. 58, who takes the passage as a reference to baptism on the grounds that the baptismal waters were conceived of by the early commentators as a draught for the thirsty.

[155] As Abbott, *Light*, p. 118, does. He entitles the Ode 'The River of the Spirit of God'.

Christ.[156] He wants to be a means of blessing to others and so bring glory to the Lord.

Ode 16 begins with the Odist's work in composing hymns. As the ploughman steers his ploughshare and the helmsman steers his ship, so the Odist's occupation is to praise the Lord by composing hymns:

> 'My art and my service are in his hymns,
> Because His love has nourished my heart,
> And His fruits He poured unto my lips.
> For my love is the Lord;
> Hence I will sing unto Him.' (vv. 1-3)

The Lord's love has evoked the Odist's love and art. Conscious of the prior love of the Lord which nourishes his heart, the Odist sings forth praise by composing hymns. He cries out:

> 'I will open my mouth,
> And His Spirit will speak through me
> The glory of the Lord and His beauty,
> The work of His hands,
> And the labours of His fingers,
> For the multitude of His mercies
> And the strength of His Word.' (vv. 5-7)

Creation and nature are the themes of the Odist inspired by the Spirit of the Lord, and creation occupies the centre of the hymn in this Ode (vv. 9-20). Even nature is among 'the multitude of His mercies'.

Though there is no express mention of the Spirit in Ode 26, this Ode deals with the art of the Odist and the harp theme links it with Odes 6 and 14 previously considered.

> 'I poured out praise to the Lord,
> Because I am His own.
> And I will recite His holy ode,
> Because my heart is with Him.
> For His harp is in my hand,
> And the odes of His rest shall not be silent.' (vv. 1-3)

---

[156] Aune, *Odes and Prophecy*, p. 447, notes how often in the Odes the symbol of fruit is connected with speech, particularly inspired or prophetic speech (cf. 8.2; 10.2; 12.2; 14.7; 16.2).

The union of 'heart with heart' calls forth composition out of sheer gratitude. The Odist belongs to the Lord and this evokes his praise, a praise which he sees as universal, spreading to all points of the compass (vv. 5-7).

A series of rhetorical questions pose the question of inspiration, for the theme far outstrips our human capabilities.[157]

> 'Who can write the odes of the Lord,
> Or who can read them? .....
> Or who can press upon the Most High
> So that He would recite from his mouth?' (vv. 8, 10)

Death may remove the Odists, but the subject of their interpretation will remain. The Odists stand serene, at rest: they are like a river whose spring gushes forth increasingly and whose waters flow to the relief of those who seek rest.

We now return to Ode 36, whose opening verse we mentioned earlier: the Spirit lifts the Odist heavenwards to stand before the Lord in all His glory and perfection, 'where I continued glorifying (Him) by the composition of His odes'. The heavenly experience is the source of inspiration. From his fellowship with the Lord, brought about by the Spirit, the Odist composes the Lord's hymns.

Finally, we turn to the last Ode. The Lord promises

> 'And I will be with those
> Who love me....
> Then I arose [= resurrection[158]] and am with them,
> And will speak by their mouths.' (42.4,6)

The risen Christ asserts his fellowship with those who love him and promises that he will speak through them. In the light of the Odes as a whole, this must mean either the composition of Odes and Hymns or the preaching of the gospel (not the promulgation of sayings of prophets into the tradition of the earthly Jesus[159]).

Thus we may say that Odes 6, 14, 16 and 36 establish the link between the Odist's work and the inspiration of the Spirit, with Ode 42 speaking of the risen Christ's inspiration. This establishes a base which permits us to draw in other references in the Odes which deal with the composition of hymns and their

---

[157] Cf. Harris, *Odes,* p. 127, 'The creature cannot express God's praise fully; if he could, he would no longer be a creature: he would be the Word, and not the interpreter of the Word.'

[158] So Charlesworth, *Odes*, p. 147; Lattke, *Oden*, p. 183 ('ich bin auferstanden'); Aune, *Odes and Prophecy*, p. 44; *Prophecy*, p. 297.

[159] See D. Hill, 'On the Evidence for the Creative Role of Christian Prophets', *NTS* 20 (1974), pp. 265-68, for a criticism of how Gunkel, von Soden and Bultmann have used this passage.,

composers, even though the Spirit is not specifically mentioned: 10.1-3; 12.1-4, 10-12; 21.8, together with 7.17-29.[160]

The evidence surveyed leaves no doubt whatsoever: the Odist believed himself the vehicle of the Spirit in the composition of the Odes. The language employed—the journey to heaven, the harp, streams of water flowing forth to refresh others—evince the sense of ecstatic experience, of divine inspiration, resulting in the writing of the Odes.

Before we move from Section A to section B, there is an issue which we ought to discuss. We have seen the uninhibited way in which the Odist expresses his sense of fellowship and union with Christ. This is the subjective side. But is there anything objective which 'controls' the personal experience and prevents it from dissolving into mere subjectivity? In other words, are there any 'tests' which the Odist offered, in the same way as in the first generation Paul, and in the third generation, the Didachist and the author of 1 John, provided for their congregations?

H. Chadwick has maintained that the consistently Christian character of the Odes is unambiguous,[161] and that they are orthodox and are not written to be the vehicle of any overt or hidden deviation from the apostolic tradition of the faith.[162] Charlesworth also denied that the Odes are gnostic,[163] and other scholars have also strongly supported the orthodoxy of the Odes.[164]

Certainly God is the creator (4.15; 7.7-12; 16.8-16) and Christ the pre-existent Son, who descended (16.18; 21.1; 28.19; 41.14) to become incarnate (7.4, 6, 20-21; 17.6; 31.1-11; 41.4, 12). Certain of the events of his earthly life are mentioned together with his cross and passion (7.10; 28.9-18; 31.8-10; 42.2) and his resurrection (17.7; 41.12; 42.6) after descending to hell and freeing the captives there (17.9-16; 22.7; 24.5; 42.10).

If various commentators have discerned docetic overtones here and there (17.6; 28.17; 41.8; 42.10; cf. 7.4), we might call it a naïve docetism. Charlesworth rightly

---

[160] Aune, *Odes and Prophecy*, pp. 448-49, refers this Ode about the coming of the Lord to the Parousia, though concedes that there may be some proleptic anticipation of this. It is possible, however, to take the theme to be the Incarnation and to explain the use of eye witness type language as due to the intensity of spiritual communion with Christ, so that such language falls naturally from the lips. The inspiration of the Spirit is such that everyone is as equidistant from Christ as any generation, even the first, in one sense, while in another sense, subsequent generations depend on that first generation.

[161] Chadwick, *Reflections*, p. 267.

[162] Chadwick, *Reflections*, p. 270.

[163] J.H. Charlesworth, 'The Odes of Solomon—not Gnostic', *CBQ* 31 (1969), pp. 357-69.

[164] E.g. F.M. Braun, *Jean le Théologien et son Évangile dans l'Église ancienne:* (Paris: Gabalda, 1959), p. 232: 'The doctrine of the Odes is in substantial accord with the orthodoxy of the "Great Church"'; J. Carmignac, 'Un Qumranien converti au Christianisme: l'auteur des Odes de Salomon', in H. Bardtke (ed.), *Qumran-Probleme* (Berlin: Deutsche Akademie der Wissenschaften zu Berlin, 1963), pp. 77, 84-90, 91-92.

suggests that the Odes were composed in a milieu which, 'though it may have contained docetic tendencies, apparently neither knew of nor professed gnosticism'.[165]

The experience of salvation is entirely due to God's grace. Terms like redeemed (9.5; 35.7; 38.17) and justified (9.10-12; 17.2-3; 25.12; 29.5) are used, and imagery like release from captivity and chains (10.3; 17.4, 12; 25.1), the passage from death to life (3.8-11; 6.15; 15.8-10; 22.8-10; 31.7) or from darkness to light (6.17; 10.1; 11.11, 14; 12.3; 14.2; 15.2; 21.3, 6; 25.7; 31.1-2; 32.1; 41.4, 14) and entry into paradise (6.16-24; 11.14-21; 20.7).

The fellowship of believers is assumed, but not conceptualized much (17.16 members and the head; 42.8-9 the bridegroom and bride). Present eschatology is uppermost, but occasionally the note of future hope is struck (8.22; 9.4, 7; 18.7; 33.12; possibly, 7.12-24; though even here one cannot be absolutely certain).

All these affirm that the Odist stands within the main currents of the Christian faith. His experience takes place within a framework of doctrine that was in line with mainstream orthodoxy.

Alongside this framework of doctrine, we are struck by the frequency of the idea of 'truth' in the Odes. Of course, 'truth' may not of itself help us to answer our question about an objective basis for the Odist's experience, not least because there is a subjective side to our apprehension of truth and, furthermore, because in the author's milieu there might be considerable divergence of opinion about what is truth, and the claim to have the truth might be polemical/apologetic and involve the denial that others possess the truth.

We, therefore, turn to a brief consideration of the idea of truth in these Odes. It might be doubted whether the Odist would have understood the distinction which we make between objective and subjective. There is in many Odes an interpenetration of these two aspects. Truth is not something abstract or theoretical or even purely intellectual. At times we may suspect that possession of the truth and fellowship with Christ are interchangeable. There are various reasons for this.

Firstly, Christ is himself identified with Truth. 'He was and is the Truth' (38.5). At his Incarnation, error perished; it was submerged by the truth of the Lord (31.2).

Then, secondly, we find several examples where, within the same Ode, the author passes from a statement about truth to one similar or identical about Christ. In the first Ode, the Lord is likened to a crown set on the Odist's head (v. 1). Then the Odist says that the crown of truth has been plaited for him (v. 2), to follow this up by asserting that the Lord lives on his head (v. 4). The Odist speaks of the Most High uncovering his inner being to Him (11.2), and then says that he has been established upon the rock of truth (v. 5). On another occasion, the Odist can speak of hearing the Lord's truth and acquiring knowledge (15.4-5), and immediately go on to say that he repudiated the way of error and went towards the Lord (v. 6). The phrases to walk in the Lord and to go after truth are juxtaposed in Ode 17 (vv. 4b-5). Or again, the Odist can say that the truth led him and the Lord went with him (38.1,

---

[165] Charlesworth, *Odes not Gnostic*, p. 37.

4a). We might also note that a blessing is pronounced on those who have known the Lord in His truth (12.13).

Thirdly, there is what we may call an inescapable existential challenge thrown out by truth to men and women. People are confronted by truth and error, and a decision has to be made. This emerges with particular force in Odes 33 and 38, where we meet the figure of the Corruptor, the Evil One, who leads people into error. Over against this figure, there stands that of Truth in Ode 38, while in Ode 33 we meet the figure of the virgin, probably a symbol for the church, the fellowship of those who have come to know the truth and, therefore, 'the place' where truth may be found. It is, of course, these Odes where Drijvers has claimed to detect polemic against Mani and his followers. Even if we cannot follow him in placing the Odes in the late third century, he is surely right in detecting polemical overtones in the descriptions (writers use this kind of language when they are most conscious of something in their environment which stands in complete opposition to what they believe and stand for). For our purposes here, we may leave it unresolved whether a specific personality and his followers are in mind (and Marcion and the Marcionite church could be candidates in the second half of the second century) or whether, more generally, the hostile world is in the author's mind.

Another aspect of the truth which deserves mention here is its missionary dimension: receiving the truth carries with it a responsibility for spreading the truth abroad. Knowing the truth leads to proclamation.[166] Ode 12.1 illustrates this perfectly:

> 'He has filled me with words of truth,
> That I may proclaim Him'.

The Odist can pray to be taught the Odes of the Lord's truth that he may write such compositions as will praise the Lord, with the implication that others may be incited to praise Him also (14.7-8; akin to this is the plea in 18.4 for the Lord not to dismiss His word from the Odist 'for the sake of those who are in need').

What, then, are the results of this for our theme? Certainly, we cannot neatly separate truth into objective and subjective compartments, for they are intertwined in the Odes. Given the overall orthodoxy of the theology of the Odes, however, we must conclude that there is a framework within which the ecstatic and enthusiastic experience of the Spirit takes place. If it be objected that in general there are no safeguards built into an approach such as is exemplified by the Odes, it can only be rejoined that neither in the end can a structured hierarchical framework prevent people from 'going it their way' if they are so minded.

---

[166] This missionary concern, which is a feature of the Odes in general, is stressed by Charlesworth, *Odes not Gnostic*, p. 361. In his edition of the *Odes,* p. 39, he commented on 7.26 ['Confess His power And declare His grace'] 'Note the missionary zeal of this verse', an interpretation challenged by P. Southwell in his review in *JTS* 25 (1974), p. 508. Even if this verse could just as well be taken as an exhortation to the redeemed, in general Charlesworth's stress is a correct interpretation of the outlook of the Odes.

We return to our original question about tests. Here we need to bear in mind the literary genre of the Odes and ask whether we might expect to find such tests in this type of composition. Of course, poems and hymns may be as polemical as other literary forms and may, by what they assert, proffer a standard by which truth may be measured. However, where a polemical note is struck in Odes 33 and 38, the Odist has not in fact gone into precise details. Thus, in the end, the literary genre probably exercised a determinative influence on the fact that precise tests are lacking in the Odes rather than that the idea of them was per se unacceptable to such a writer.

To some extent, the Odes are unique in the intensity of their experience of the Spirit and the risen Lord. Their exuberance and extravagance of language almost put them in a category of their own. They give the impression that they could fit in with Johannine spirituality. They express *directly* what can be *inferred* from the fourth gospel. They treat of religious experience, while we have to deduce that from what the fourth evangelist says. When we have made allowances for the different literary genres, it is not forcing the evidence to conjecture that the Odes *could* stem from one of the Johannine congregations.[167] Perhaps, if Johannine Christianity came into mainstream Catholic Christianity, as R.E. Brown suggested,[168] compositions like the Odes were an ultimate casualty. Perhaps their experience was too individualistic and unsacramental to fit entirely comfortably with the 'Great Church' and its hierarchical structure. On the other hand, they were preserved, and the later spirituality of the Syrian Church did stress the Spirit, so that presumably some section of the Syrian church found them congenial.

B. Divine Illumination

We have just mentioned the frequency with which 'truth' appears in the Odes and suggested that while truth had its subjective side, there was an objective side, and this was exemplified in the overall orthodox position of the Odes.

There are occasions when the Spirit is seen as the source of that illumination which has led to the Odist's understanding of the truth. Indeed, in Ode 3 it is said that it is

'the Spirit of the Lord which is not false
Which teaches the sons of men to know His ways.' (v. 10)

---

[167] This puts the matter more cautiously than Charlesworth, 'Qumran, John and the Odes of Solomon', in J.H. Charlesworth, (ed.) *John and Qumran* (London: Geoffrey Chapman, 1972), p. 135: 'The Odes and John shared the same milieu and it is not improbable that they lived in the same community', which view also depends on an early date for the Odes, of course. See the cautious estimate of R.J. Murray, *Symbols of Church and Kingdom: A Study in Early Syriac Tradition* (Cambridge: Cambridge University Press, 1975), p. 25: 'The milieu certainly seems Judaeo-Christian, not sectarian-Gnostic, and perhaps not far in date and milieu from the Fourth Gospel and Ignatius.'

[168] Brown, *The Community of the Beloved Disciple*, p. 159.

To describe the Spirit negatively as 'not false' is by implication to characterize him as the Spirit of Truth. The Spirit is the teacher of believers: he enables them to know the ways of the Lord.

One facet of the conversion experience, brought about through being circumcised by the Holy Spirit, is that the Odist 'ran...in the way of truth' (11.3). He says 'I received His knowledge / And I was established upon the rock of truth / Where He had set me' (11.4b-5).

Ode 25, which mentions the removal of the Odist's garments of skin and how he has been clothed with the Spirit's covering (v. 8), also uses the lamp picture: the Lord has given him a lamp on both his right and left (= totality), so that there might be nothing of darkness in him (v. 7). The Odist claims 'And I became mighty in Thy truth' (v. 10a). All that the Odist is or has is due to the Lord and His Spirit. The Lord is his helper (vv. 2b, 6b); He is with him (v. 4a). From Him comes the Odist's strength (v. 6a). The Odist has been clothed with the Lord's Spirit (v. 8a).

The link between the imparting of truth and the Spirit can probably also be seen in Ode 14.7a, 8a:

'Teach me the Odes of Thy truth...
And open to me the harp of Thy Holy Spirit'.

What the Holy Spirit will produce through him are poems full of truth.

There are places where the Odist refers to his possession of the truth without mention of the Holy Spirit (17.5 and the whole of 38, where truth is personified as a guide; 33.8, where the church, symbolised as a virgin, possesses the truth; and the battle imagery where truth is locked in deadly combat with falsehood and will be victorious, in 18.6-7a; 25.10-11; 31.1-2, 7-11).

Odes 12 and 14 give us the indicative and petitionary sides of this whole question. The Odist claims that the Lord filled him with words of truth to proclaim Him, and so, like the flowing of waters, truth flows from his mouth (12.1-2). Yet he prays to be taught the Odes of the Lord's truth in 14.7-8.

C. Divine Power

We ask now whether the thought of the Spirit's empowerment in the ethical sphere is present in the Odes.

Ode 11, already considered above as celebrating the conversion of the Odist through the Holy Spirit, mentions the present experience of Paradise. Christians are those who are planted in the Lord's land (11.18). They are described as those 'who turn from wickedness to Thy pleasantness' (v. 20); they 'work good works' (v. 20). The Odist pictures Christians as trees filled with fruit (v. 23), which could refer to good works (? the fruit of the Spirit) or may be poetic imagery and not to be pressed allegorically.

Though the Holy Spirit is not specifically mentioned in these verses, it is clear that the good works stem from the experience of Paradise: God's grace leads to ethical endeavour. It is not improbable that the Holy Spirit is envisaged as the author of these good works.

Ode 25, already considered in relation to the experience of conversion, spoke of the removal of garments of skin (the pre-conversion nature) and the being covered by the Holy Spirit's covering (v. 8). Then the Odist says

> 'And I became mighty in Thy truth
> And holy in Thy righteousness'. (v. 10)

The experience of God's Spirit thus led to holy and righteous living.

We shall briefly mention three other Odes where the ethical life is underlined without express mention of the Spirit. Ode 8 commences

> 'Open, open your hearts to the exultation of the Lord,
> And let your love abound from the heart to the lips
> In order to bring forth fruits to the Lord, a holy life'. (vv. 1-2a).

We note a combination of ideas—the opened hearts, and love expressing itself in praise and holy living. Later, in verse 6, the Lord is said to be the helper of His followers.

In Ode 13, believers are exhorted to sing praises to the Spirit of the Lord (v. 2b). Then comes the command:

> 'And wipe the paint from your face
> And love holiness and put it on'. (v. 3)

The clearly pejorative connotation of the paint on the face[169] stands for worldly/immoral living; the opposite is holiness. The Christian, who is turned to the Lord as a mirror and who sings praise to the Spirit, will as a consequence turn from wrong living to the holy lifestyle which reflects the Lord's own character.

The Odist claims to be a priest of the Lord (20.1). This is then unfolded in verses 4-5:

> 'The offering of the Lord is righteousness
> And purity of heart and lips.
> Offer thy inward being faultlessly;
> And let not thy compassion oppress compassion[170]
> And let not thyself oppress anyone'.

---

[169] Charlesworth, *Odes*, p. 65, points to Ezek. 23.40; 2 Kgs. 9.30; Jer. 4.30.

[170] So Charlesworth's translation. Harris. *Odes*, p. 117, renders 'And let not thy heart do violence to heart, nor thy soul to soul', while Lattke, *Oden*, p. 131, offers 'And let not your flesh oppress (another) flesh'. On any of these translations, it looks as if we are dealing with synonymous parallelism.

Verse 6 consists of very practical directions reminiscent of OT moral regulations. We feel justified in believing that the Odist had the help of the Spirit in mind for the empowering of this 'spiritual worship' that reaches into the very practicalities of life and exhibits a concern that amidst the glow of spiritual experiences the outworking of faith in daily life should not be neglected but prosecuted with the utmost vigour and comprehensiveness.[171]

D. *Other Features*

Before we draw our examination of the Odes to a close, there is one further phenomenon that needs discussion, because of its bearing on our themes, namely that parts of an Ode or sometimes a whole Ode is in fact *Christ* speaking. On this general point, there is widespread agreement amongst editors of the Odes, even if they differ on specific details.[172]

Harris-Mingana wrote in their expository notes on Ode 8: 'This is the first of the Odes that is clearly marked with a dual personality, *the Odist becoming at a certain point in the song the Lord Himself*'[173] (italics mine), while Charlesworth observed that 'the Odist and the risen Christ coalesce making it virtually impossible to separate them'.[174]

It may be best to start our enquiry from the last Ode.

'Then I arose and am with them,
And will speak by their mouths'. (42.6)

This of itself does not demand the phenomenon to which we have referred. What it does mean is the belief that the living Christ speaks in and through his followers. He gives his message through them. But what we need to ask, even more in the light of 42.6, is why, then, the Odist wrote as he did? Why did he not explicitly introduce what was Christ's part as a 'word of the Lord'? Is this due purely to the 'rules' of style? Charlesworth clearly thought not, for he wrote: '*No linguistic device announces the shift in speakers, only the thoughts of the passage reflect it*' (my italics).

From the standpoint of analogies, we could think of the following:

---

[171] In view of the evidence of section C, plus the general point about the literary genre of the Odes, H. Chadwick is perhaps less than fair to the Odist when he says (*Reflections*, p. 269) that the author was not particularly interested in virtue, moral conflict or the training of character.

[172] Thus, Harris and Mingana and Charlesworth agree in observing this feature in Odes 8, 10, 17, 22, 28, 31, 41 and 42; Harris and Mingana also have Christ or Wisdom speaking in Ode 33, whereas here Bernard and Charlesworth think that it is the church as the perfect virgin who stands up and preaches from v. 5 onwards. On the other hand, Lattke does not mark off the sections where Christ speaks.

[173] Harris and Mingana, *Odes*, pp. 256-57.

[174] Charlesworth, *Odes*, p. 126.

(a) how in the OT prophets, the speaker may begin with 'Thus says the Lord' and an oracle follows, but at times the prophet 'becomes' Yahweh, as it were, and speaks in the first person as if he were God (e.g. Isa. 22.15-25: verses 17-18 speak of what Yahweh will do in the third person, whereas verses 19-23 continues in the first person 'I will...').[175]

(b) the pseudonymous works of the intertestamental period, but here the whole work is clothed in the form of the utterance of a figure of the past. D.S. Russell (elaborating ideas of H. Wheeler Robinson) has suggested that the apocalypticists regarded themselves not as original writers at all, but as representatives of a tradition. 'As spokesman of the tradition, they were in fact, spokesmen of the seer himself and could justifiably assume his name', and a little later he goes on to ask whether the writer may not have thought of himself 'as in some way an 'extension' of his [ancient seer] personality.... By assuming his name, he would thereby be sharing in his very character and life'.[176] This viewpoint has come under criticism since, and one of its critics, D.G. Meade[177] has looked at examples of pseudonymous literature both from the Hebrew prophetic, wisdom and apocalyptic traditions and from the NT, and has maintained the thesis that 'authorship is not primarily a statement of literary origins, but of authoritative tradition'.

We need not go into the discussion of whether Russell is correct for Jewish apocalyptic, but we could pose the question 'How might someone who felt indwelt by God's Spirit/the risen Christ and who felt himself to be the mouthpiece of the risen Christ, express messages which he believed came from the Spirit/risen Christ?' I suspect that Russell's way of putting things may come closer to the truth about the Odist, whether he is correct or not about Jewish apocalyptic.

(c) Presumably, something not dissimilar may lie behind the Johannine Jesus' discourses if they represent meditations spoken aloud to the believing congregations before they were committed to writing.[178]

These three analogies form a useful background against which we may set the phenomenon under observation. We have already explored the Odist's sense of inspiration: he is the lyre plucked by the Spirit. Given this sense of inspiration and his rootage in Jewish tradition, we may see how he comes to speak *ex ore Christi*.

---

[175] See the treatment of this phenomenon in A.R. Johnson, *The One and the Many in the Israelite Conception of God* (Cardiff: University of Wales Press, 2nd ed., 1961), pp. 32-37. On p. 33, Johnson wrote 'The true prophet, then, ...for the time being...was an active "Extension" of Yahweh's Personality and, as such, *was* Yahweh—"in Person."' This phenomenon is apparently still encountered today in prophetic utterances in the charismatic movement.

[176] D.S. Russell, *The Method and Message of Jewish Apocalyptic* (London: SCM, 1964), pp. 134 and 138.

[177] D.G. Meade, *Pseudonymity and Canon* (Grand Rapids, MI: Eerdmans, 1987). The sentence quoted as Meade's thesis appears several times: see pp. 43, 53, 55, 69, 72, 91, 101-2, 139, 157, 161, 179, 186, 190, 193, 207.

[178] So, e.g., Lindars, *John*, pp. 51-54; and *Behind the Fourth Gospel* (London: SPCK, 1971), pp. 59-60.

In that conviction of union with Christ, inspired by the Spirit, he feels himself to be a channel for his beloved Master and Lover to speak through him.

This phenomenon is, then, further support for the centrality of the Spirit in the religious experience of the Odist.

Summary

Our investigations into the place and role of the Spirit in the three chosen areas, plus the phenomenon in which Christ himself speaks in certain Odes, show without any doubt that in the Christian experience of the author and presumably his community, the Spirit was of considerable and decisive importance. In this part of the Christian church, the members were conscious of a very direct and intimate experience of the Spirit at work in their lives, from their conversion onwards. An ecstatic element is all too obvious in these hymns. They are vibrant with first-hand experience and they proclaim it in no uncertain terms. The language and imagery used are signs of the immediacy of communion with their Lord in the power of the Spirit.[179]

Though aware of the power of error to lead astray, they exhibit few doubts about the Spirit's inspiration, and in this way they could be said to differ from 1 John and the Didache. Here again, the differing literary genres need to be remembered, and this may well urge some caution against overstating the differences. In a 'charismatic song-book', we would not expect to find analyses of those deemed inspired by an evil/false spirit. Nonetheless, the unhappy experiences of the Elder's and the Didachist's congregations have left their mark in their writings in a way that is not discernible in the Odes.

In all this, these writings deserve a place alongside of John's Gospel in the primacy afforded to the Spirit in their religious life.

EXCURSUS

The Date of the Odes of Solomon (see footnote 127)

Supporting a date ca.100 or early second century we may list A. von Harnack and J. Flemming, *Ein judisch-christliches Psalmbuch aus dem ersten Jahrhundert* (TU 35; Leipzig: J.C. Hinrichs, 1910); J.R. Harris, *The Odes and Psalms of Solomon*

---

[179] Some remarks of A.C. Headlam, *Odes*, are worth quoting. The work 'embodies the devotions of a pious, somewhat mystical, mind...who walks with God, who is carried away by the contemplation of the wonderful redemption which he has experienced and records' (pp. 275-76); 'the author is a devout man with spiritual insight and a deeply religious mind who is describing a wonderful experience which has happened to him, a new life, a new joy, a new hope, a new salvation' (p. 294); 'Here we have in this long-forgotten voice from the dead a wonderful pourtrayal [sic] of the loftiest motives that won souls to Christ when the Gospel was a new message, when it flashed into the world as a revelation of truth and love and joy, when it came as a spiritual refuge for all who sought the Lord, when it corresponded to all that was loftiest in human aspiration, when it gave an assurance and hope of the glorious life in eternity with the Most High through the blessedness of the spiritual union with Him on earth' (p. 297).

(Cambridge: Cambridge University Press, 2nd ed., 1911), pp. 58, 66, 89; J.R. Harris and A. Mingana, *The Odes and Psalms of Solomon* (Manchester: Manchester University Press, 1920), pp. 61-69; J. Labourt and P. Batiffol, *Les Odes de Salomon: Une oeuvre chrétienne des environs de l'an 100-120* (Paris: Gabalda, 1911); J.H. Charlesworth, 'Qumran, John and the Odes of Solomon', in J.H. Charlesworth (ed.), *John and Qumran* (London: Geoffrey Chapman, 1972), p. 109, and *The Odes of Solomon* (Chico, CA: Scholars, 2nd ed., 1977); D.E. Aune. *Prophecy in Early Christianity* (Grand Rapids, MI: Eerdmans, 1983), p. 286; B. Layton, *The Gnostic Scriptures* (London: SCM, 1987), p. 364.

In favour of a date in the second half of the second century are J.H. Bernard, *The Odes of Solomon* (Texts and Studies VIII; Cambridge: Cambridge University Press, 1912), p. 4 (AD 150-190); J. de Zwaan, 'The Essene Origin of the Odes of Solomon', in R.P. Casey, S. Lake and A.K. Lake (eds.), *Quantulacunque* (London: Christophers, 1937), pp. 298, 302 (ca.AD 200); G.W.H. Lampe, *The Seal of the Spirit* (London: Longmans, 1951), p. 111; F.M. Braun, *Jean le Théologien et son Évangile dans l'Église ancienne* (Paris: Gabalda, 1959), pp. 238-41 (late second century); J. Danielou, *The Theology of Jewish Christianity* (London: Darton, Longman & Todd, 1964), p. 31 (note 106). In a letter to me dated 7 August 1984, Dr S. Brock of Oxford University intimated that he favoured a late second century date. In a personal conversation, the late Dr R.J. Murray informed me that Dr B. McNeil in an unpublished Cambridge PhD thesis had espoused a mid-second-century date.

More recently, in a series of publications, H.J.W. Drijvers has argued for a date ca.275: see 'Die Oden Salomos und die Polemik mit den Markioniten im syrischen Christentum', Symposium Syriacum 1976, *Orientalia Christiana Analecta* 205 (1978), pp. 39-55; 'Kerygma und Logos in den Oden Salomos dargestellt am Beispiel der 23 Ode', in A.M. Ritter (ed.), *Beiträge zu den geistesgeschichtlichen Beziehungen zwischen Antike und Christentum (Festschrift für Carl Andreson)* (Göttingen: Vandenhoeck & Ruprecht, 1979), pp. 153-172; 'The 19th Ode of Solomon: Its Interpretation and Place in Syrian Christianity', *JTS* 31 (1980), pp. 337-55; 'Odes of Solomon and Psalms of Mari', in R. van Broek and M.J. Vermaseren (eds.), *Studies in Gnosticism and Hellenistic Religions* (Leiden: Brill, 1981), pp. 117-30; 'Facts and Problems in early Syriac-speaking Christianity', *The Second Century* 2 (1982), pp. 157-75.

In response to such a late dating, we might pose the following general points:

(i) Do traces of a response to Marcionite teaching (e.g. the emphasis in the Odes that the Lord is not jealous 3.6; 7.3; 11.6; 15.6; 17.12; 20.7; 23.4[180]) necessarily demand a date as late as the third century?

---

[180] Drijvers, *Polemik*, pp. 41-52, criticises the translation of these verses offered by Harris, Bauer and Charlesworth, because they obscure the fact that there is a reference to the fact that 'the Lord knows no jealousy'. Drijvers regularly translates the Syriac by the German word *Missgunst* (cf. the translation of Lattke, Oden, on these verses, where he regularly employs the German *Neid*).

(ii) Are the suggested parallels in Odes 33 and 38 to Manicheean literature (see *Odes and Mani*, pp.118-30, for Drijvers' list) sufficiently striking or could they belong to that 'common stock' of religious expressions on which both writers may have drawn? And while the corruptor and those whom he has corrupted, a false bridegroom and bride, could stand for Mani and his followers, the imagery could apply in a more general fashion to the evil one and the world.

(iii) Is the Odist's understanding of the Spirit really dependent on Tatian, *Oratio ad Graecos* 13? Do the Odes reflect a body-soul-Spirit view as *Oratio* 13 does? Is Tatian's statement that 'If the soul gains union with the divine Spirit, it is not unaided but mounts to the realms above, where the Spirit leads it' (13.2), really the inspiration for Ode 36.2, or could the Odist be applying to the believer the kind of assertion made in the Fourth Gospel about Jesus (e.g. Jn. 3.13; 8.23; 13.1) and the promise that believers should be where he is (12.26; 13.36; 14.3; 17.24)? See Aune, *Cultic Setting*, p. 185; *Odes and Prophecy*, pp. 440-42; *Prophecy*, pp. 297-98, for the Heavenly Journey motif.

7. Tatian[181]

Born east of the Euphrates, of non-Christian parents, Tatian was eventually, after a long preoccupation with contemporary philosophy, converted at Rome, possibly through the influence of Justin to whom Tatian refers appreciatively. He later broke away from the church (probably ca.172) and returned to the east. For a while he was in Antioch, and then he founded his own school in Mesopotamia and produced his *Harmony of the Four Gospels* (the *Diatessaron*), which was used in the Syrian church until the fifth century.

Tatian was the author of an apologetic work, *Oratio ad Graecos*, which forms the basis for our reconstruction of his thought. For Tatian, human beings were originally created body-soul-Holy Spirit. 'The bond of the flesh is soul, but it is the flesh which contains the soul' (15.2), while the Spirit of God was originally the soul's companion (13.2).

The soul was not immortal, but mortal, and it was the receptacle of the Spirit. 'We have knowledge of two different kinds of spirits, one of which is called soul, but the other is greater than the soul; it is the image and likeness of God. The first human beings were endowed with both, so that they might be part of the material world and at the same time above it' (12.1). Or, to put the matter another way, 'the Spirit's home is above, but the soul's birth is below' (13.2).[182]

---

[181] Quotations from M. Whittaker (ed.), *Oratio ad Graecos* (Oxford: Oxford University Press, 1982). For biographical details, see *Oratio ad Graecos* 42; 35.1; 18.2, and also Eusebius, *HE* 4.29.1; *Chronicle*, 12.

[182] It is worth pointing out that Tatian has equated the image and likeness of God in Genesis 1.26-27 with the Holy Spirit and appears to stand within a line of interpretation of Genesis 2.7, which took what God breathed into humans as Spirit, not πνοή. See W-D. Hauschild, *Gottes Geist und der Mensch* (München: Chr. Kaiser Verlag, 1972), p. 199.

When humans sinned, the Spirit left them. 'The Spirit became originally the soul's companion but gave it up when the soul was unwilling to follow it' (13.2). Tatian asserts that free will has destroyed us: God is not the author of our lamentable state, but we ourselves, though born free, have become slaves of sin through our own fault (11.2). The result of the Fall, then, is that human beings became mortal. 'The creature made in the image of God, when the more powerful Spirit departed from him, became mortal' (7.3).

Tatian describes the soul's wings as 'the perfect Spirit but the soul cast it away because of sin, fluttered like a nestling and fell to the ground, and, once removed from heavenly company, yearned for association with inferiors' (20.1).

Bereft of the Spirit, humans become enmeshed in the material. When the soul lives on its own, 'it inclines down towards matter and dies with the flesh' (13.2). However, Tatian believed that the soul kept a spark of the Spirit's power within it (τὸ ἔναυσμα, 13.2), and so this does enable humans to make a response to the truth.

A. Divine Presence

Tatian used three images which could be taken to indicate a conscious experience of the Spirit. Firstly, he speaks of the soul's ascent to heaven through the Spirit. Tatian encourages his readers to search for what they once possessed but lost. They should link the soul to the Holy Spirit and occupy themselves with the union ordained and willed by God (15.1). If the soul enters into union with the Divine Spirit, it is not unaided in its struggle against the downward pull of matter, 'but mounts to the realms above where the Spirit leads it, for the Spirit's home is above...' (13.2).

Language, which in John's Gospel is applied to Christ (he comes from above and returns there) is in the *Oration* applied to the one who responds to the truth,[183] to the Word of God, to the Spirit. With the Spirit as companion, the soul is drawn upwards.

Secondly, there is the idea of the temple indwelt by God through His Spirit. The human constitution is like a temple and God is willing to dwell in it through the Spirit, His representative (διὰ τοῦ πρεσβεύοντος, 15.2) (If humans were not so constituted, we would only be superior to the animals in having articulate speech and would not be a likeness of God 15.3). The idea of the believer as a temple indwelt by the Spirit picks up material from NT writings (1 Cor. 3.16-17; 6.19-20; Eph. 2.19-22; 1 Pet. 2.5).

Thirdly, Tatian used the picture of the rediscovery of lost property or coin. Conversion is a rediscovery of one's own lost property or treasure. Tatian exploited the idea of hidden treasure from the Matthean parable to illustrate his point. The Word of God is seen as holding power over our property through a certain hidden treasure. When we dug it up, we were covered with dust, but through this we are given the opportunity of re-establishing our property. 'For everyone who recovers

---

[183] Hauschild, *Gottes Geist*, p. 202.

his property obtains power over very precious wealth' (30.1). The Word of God's power over us may be referred to the spark of the Spirit in us.[184] This is like hidden treasure. If we through that spark respond and obey the Word of God, if we channel our efforts in this direction and do not dissipate our energies, then the hidden treasure is recovered, though it has to be cleaned up because of its long involvement in the material.

Given the brevity and the genre of the *Oration*, we cannot claim too much, but these pictures are congruous with a definite awareness of the Spirit's activity in the believer's experience.

B. Divine Illumination

Because it was separated from the Spirit, the soul could no longer see things that are perfect, and so, in its search for God, went astray into idolatry (13.2-3). The ignorant soul is in darkness. If it is ignorant of the truth, it dies and is dissolved with the body (13.1).

When Tatian says that 'you will easily comprehend the Godhead, when the (power) which makes souls immortal has come upon you', the inference is clearly that without the Spirit we do not comprehend God.

He can also speak of God's Spirit dwelling among those who lived righteously, or of those souls who were obedient to wisdom attracting to themselves the kindred Spirit (τὸ πνεῦμα συγγενές, 13.3). In intimate union with the soul of such persons, the Spirit announced by predictions to other souls what had been hidden to them (13.3). In line with this, Tatian can say that we have learned through the prophets what we did not know. The prophets used to foretell what other souls did not know. They were convinced that the Spirit, in union with the soul, would obtain immortality (τὸ οὐράνιον ἐπένδυμα τῆς θνητότητος τὴν ἀθανασίαν: lit. 'the heavenly garment of mortality, immortality' = the heavenly garment of immortality to put on over our mortality). Without the Spirit, the soul is doomed to mortality; with the Spirit, the soul receives heavenly clothing and will enjoy immortality (20.3).

There are, then, hints of the Spirit's role in illuminating believers with the truth.

C. Divine Power

Tatian also speaks of those who are guarded by God's Spirit and who are thus able to perceive the bodies of demons (15.3). Armed with the breastplate of the heavenly Spirit, a person will be able to protect (σῶσαι) all that is encompassed by matter (16.3): while Tatian is here thinking of diseases and disorders that demons inflict on us through the material, the idea is capable of extension into the ethical field, for Tatian saw demons behind the immorality of the theatre and the shows (22.1), and he

---

[184] M. Elze, *Tatian und seine Theologie* (Göttingen: Vandenhoeck & Ruprecht, 1960), p. 99.

stressed the chasteness of Christian women and girls in contrast to standards among their pagan counterparts (33.2).

The picture of the recovery of the buried treasure states that it has to be cleaned up because of its long involvement in the material. This has implications for behaviour and conduct obviously.

Again, there are hints of a connection between the Spirit and ethics, but the genre of the work hardly called for elaboration of this.

Summary

The role of the Spirit is, therefore, crucial for Tatian. Conversion, however intellectually conceived,[185] takes place when the union of soul and Spirit is effected.

The spark of the Spirit retained by humans does enable a response to be made: like responds to like. This was true of people in pre-Christian times, like the prophets, who continue to teach us by what they said. Not that Tatian accords in the *Oration* any decisive significance to the incarnate ministry of Christ or his cross and resurrection as either redemptive or revelatory. There is no salvation-history thinking or promise-fulfillment approach. The name of Jesus Christ is never mentioned and oblique references seem limited to 13.3 and 21.1. For Tatian, the Logos seems only to have a cosmological function,[186] and the person of Jesus is not mentioned as a revealer of truth. It is the divine Spirit who lifts humans above and so has a soteriological function.[187]

So union (or reunion) with the Spirit is a restoration to what a person was before they sinned. Indeed, the true person is one who 'has advanced far beyond his humanity towards God Himself' (15.2). Tatian here is thinking of the union of Spirit and soul. This union is open to all. As Tatian says, 'It is possible for everyone who is naked to get this adornment [the immortality which the Spirit gives] and race back to his ancient kinship' (20.3).

8. Conclusion

The evidence surveyed affords ample proof of how a great deal of religious experience in Syrian Christianity continued to be ascribed to the activity of God's Spirit.

We may detect a division between western Syria (dominated by Antioch) and eastern Syria, or, rather, the division may be between a rich, prosperous city-congregation (Matthew), which moved towards a structured form of ministry (Ignatius) and was suspicious of the older type of itinerant, charismatic miracle-worker, and more rural situated congregations. The *Didache* confirms this suggestion. Its rules reveal both a respect for and suspicion towards itinerant

---

[185] See Elze, *Tatian*, pp. 34-40, for his discussion of Tatian's understanding of truth; and cf. Hauschild, *Gottes Geist*, p. 204.

[186] Elze, *Tatian*, pp. 81-83.

[187] Hauschild, *Gottes Geist*, pp. 203, 205-206.

prophets: the former reflects the older tradition of eastern Syria; the latter, more recent experiences. Nonetheless, the respect lingers on.

In the eastern area of Syria, we find that the Spirit holds a vital place in the Johannine congregations. The Spirit takes the place of Jesus who has gone to the Father. He will be with Christians forever and will be in them. The pattern of religious experience prized in this stream of Christianity is that of rebirth by the Spirit, the dramatic conversion which comes upon a person as mysteriously as the wind and which seems to well up within like fountains of flowing water.

The Johannine Epistles speak of God's giving us His Spirit, and this was a conscious experience, since believers know thereby that God abides in them. Believers are born of God, and this is clearly the work of the Spirit and betokens a dramatic experience.

The 'hymn book' called the *Odes of Solomon* reverberates with an exuberant sense of the Spirit's presence and inspiration. He lifts believers into paradise and enables them to commune with Christ like lovers. The amatory imagery points to the intensity of the experience. Believers are in the hands of the Spirit like a lyre plucked by the musician.

Tatian too knows of the union between the Spirit and believers: the συζυγία ordained by God enables the soul to mount to realms above, the Spirit's home. An alternative image is that the Spirit dwells in believers like a temple. The Spirit comes upon believers and the spark within is rekindled.

This intensity of experience associated with the Spirit in many documents from Syrian Christianity is akin to that reflected in the Jerusalem and Pauline congregations of the first generation.

By contrast Matthew does not appear to stress the Spirit as the origin of Christian experience. He speaks of the risen Lord's presence, both in church meetings (18.20) and mission (28.20), and he knows of much charismatic activity which is not accompanied by the doing of God's will, which for him probably means carrying out the love of neighbour part of the Double Love Command. If this is correct, we would have an interesting case of virtually parallel phenomenon in the Matthean and Johannine congregations: both have experience of those who claim to be inspired, and yet are not characterized by love of neighbour or brother. Both Matthew and the author of 1John reject such people as non-Christian (Mt. 7.23; 1 Jn. 2.19). The difference is that in Matthew there is not any doctrinal aberration such as is discernible in 1 and 2 John.

From western to eastern Syria, then, we catch a glimpse of how some members of the Christian congregations prized spiritual experiences and phenomena to such an extent that they became negligent of the practical outworking of Christianity in love. Since Paul faced the same problem at Corinth, it looks as if this feature was endemic in the earliest generations and may be a constant danger of this type of Christianity.

The Spirit is certainly seen as the teacher and guide of the church in the Johannine congregations, according to the Gospel (14.26; 16.12-15) and Epistles (1 Jn. 2.20, 27; 5.6-8), but we see how concerned the fourth evangelist was to show that while the Spirit imparts new truth, he does so by drawing that out of what Jesus had already taught and said. Likewise, the author of 1 John appealed to his hearers to adhere to 'what they had heard from the beginning'. Interestingly, Matthew also insists on the primacy of what Jesus had already commanded (28.20): the earthly Jesus' teaching is normative. There is, perhaps, more room in the Fourth Gospel's approach for new facets of truth (though in practice Matthew 'actualises' the tradition about Jesus for the needs of his congregation), but both Matthew and John appear to be aware of the dangers inherent in claiming the Spirit's guidance and direction for new teaching: there are to be new developments of the old rather than completely new developments.

The Odist also associates the Spirit and truth, and he believes that the Lord's Spirit teaches us to know His ways (3.10). Sometimes he personifies Truth as a guide who leads or accompanies him (17.5). While we surmised earlier that the Odist might not have been averse to doctrinal tests, it remains true that his own work exhibits traces of what has been called a naïve docetism. Clearly, then, in his milieu, there might be the danger of others going further in a docetic direction, as in the case of the Johannine congregations.

This in turn raises the question of whether the ideal proposed by the fourth evangelist can, in practice, be effective without some sort of church structures (just as the same question must be raised of Paul's vision of a charismatic community). R.E. Brown felt that it was not: 'The very fact that a Paraclete-centred ecclesiology had offered no real protection against schismatics ultimately caused [the author of the Epistles]'s followers to accept the authoritative presbyter-bishop teaching structure which in the second century became dominant in the Great Church but which was quite foreign to the Johannine tradition'.[188] (Of course, the episcopal structure was itself incapable of preventing heretical or schismatic movements as the later story of the church shows!). It looks as if Diotrephes was, in fact, if not in name, virtually bishop of his congregation, and incipient structures were already emerging within the NT period in this branch of Christianity.

We observed how Ignatius believed that he was prompted by the Spirit to command the Philadelphians to obey the bishop and avoid divisions. Spirit and Office are here linked in indissoluble unity. Ignatius was annoyed that there were some who had the bishop's name on their lips, but in everything acted apart from him (Magn. 4.1).

Less prominent is the association of the Spirit and the ethical side of Christianity. The Johannine Epistles speak of God's seed abiding in the believer, and this should lead to sinless perfection (1 Jn. 3.6, 9; 5.18). In the *Didache*, on the other hand, the author never inserts the idea of the Spirit's help into his redaction of the Two Ways. Ignatius, however, sees the Spirit as enabling believers to live obedient lives pleasing to God in the flesh. The Spirit is the rope which helps to lift

---

[188] Brown, *Community of the Beloved Disciple*, p. 147. Brown felt that historically the two groups within the Johannine community were swallowed up by the Great Church and by the Gnostic movement respectively (pp. 145-162).

stones (= believers) into place in the temple of God, which is in the process of being erected, but probably in the end Christ-mysticism dominates his thinking. The Odist believed that the Spirit lifted him to Paradise, and, as a result, he turned from wickedness to holy, righteous living (25.10) and to do good works (11.18, 20). The implication of Tatian's teaching—that conversion is the recovery of hidden treasure which has to be cleaned up—is ethical purification from embroilment in pagan idolatry and wicked ways.

Is there any reason why the association of the Spirit and ethics is not so prominent in the writings surveyed? To some extent, the occasion for the documents and their literary genre may account for this, but not (one feels) entirely. Thus, in the farewell discourses of the Fourth Gospel, there would be room for some treatment of the ethical side of Christianity. And why did the *Didache* feel happy enough with taking over the Jewish Two Ways and not editing it more thoroughly?

We have to ask whether the Spirit's link with the ethical side of Christianity was not so prominent generally in Syrian Christianity as was the case with Paul. Did the Spirit tend to be associated with our categories A and B rather than C, i.e. uplifting experiences, phenomena like prophecy, exorcisms, healings, a sense of guidance and illumination, etc? This might be the conclusion which we should draw when we put together both the paucity of evidence in section C and the evidence that some Christians stressed charismatic experiences without bothering about love (see section A).

The total impression is that, in writers where mention of the Spirit attains to anything like prominence, the stress is on experience. The Gospel and Epistles of John, the Odist and Tatian, all in their various ways describe the Spirit as a living reality who produced certain effects in their lives: images like new birth, spring water bubbling up, entry into paradise, ascending on high, all emphasize the experiential side. Then again, the Gospel of John has worked out a view of the Spirit's work as teacher of Christians and, to a lesser extent, the Odist also speaks of the Spirit's leading him into the truth.

In a comparison with the picture of first and second generation Christianity, Syria 'stands up' well. There is no concern about the delay of the Parousia. The sense of the Spirit's presence in the believer's life presumably alleviated this problem.

Chapter 3

Asia Minor

Next to Syria, Asia Minor was an obvious and natural target for the Christian mission. Paul worked in both the south-eastern end (Cilicia, Gal. 1.21) and the western end (i.e. the Roman province of Asia). He said that a good opportunity for preaching the gospel existed in Ephesus, though equally there was much opposition (1 Cor. 16.8). Later, a similar opportunity existed at Troas, but personal factors prevented his using it (2 Cor. 2.12-13). In Romans 16.5 he mentions one Epaenetus as the first convert to Christ in 'Asia'. There is broad confirmation of this from Acts, where Luke records missionary preaching by Paul and Barnabas in Pamphylia, Pisidia, Lycaonia and Cilicia (Acts 13–14) and says that Paul had a ministry of over two years at Ephesus, though he records few stories about it (Acts 19).

Churches existed in Laodicea, Colosse and Hierapolis when Colossians (whether by Paul or not) was written. Epaphras, one of Paul's coworkers, was the first to preach the gospel at Colosse (Col. 1.7) and he may have founded the church at Laodicea and Hierapolis too (Col. 4.13). On the assumption that the Pastorals represents a third-generation Paulinist's attempt to apply the Pauline inheritance to the situation in his day, we can see that rules to guide the choice of church officers were already in operation in the churches of Ephesus and on the island of Crete, and, a decade or two later, Ignatius' letters show that a ministry of bishop, elders and deacons was established in the western area churches, even if not to the liking of everyone.

The book of Revelation was written to churches in the western area, as were the majority of the letters of Ignatius a decade or more later, while the bishop of Antioch was on his way to Rome and eventual martyrdom.

1 Peter shows that at the time of writing congregations existed in northern Asia Minor, and this receives confirmation from an extra-biblical source, the letters of the younger Pliny, who was governor of Bithynia and Pontus under Trajan. His correspondence with the emperor reveals that 'a great many individuals of every age and class, both men and women, are being brought to trial, and this is likely to continue. It is not only the towns, but villages and rural districts too which are infected through contact with this wretched cult'. The temples 'had been almost entirely deserted for a long time'; worship in these temples 'had been allowed to lapse'; and 'scarcely anyone could be found to buy the meat of those animals reared to be sacrificial victims'. Some claimed to have ceased being Christians twenty years previously, others some two or more years before. Two women, of slave status,

were called 'deaconesses', whom Pliny tortured to try and secure more information and evidence (see *Letters of the Younger Pliny*, Book 10.96).

During the course of the second century, two of the outstanding leaders were Polycarp, who in his late eighties was martyred (?155-56), and Polybius, who was bishop of Ephesus ca.190. Both of them were in touch with Christians at Rome over the date and manner of observance of Easter. Polycarp's standing was such that he journeyed to Rome to explain Asia Minor custom on this issue to leaders of the church there. He and Anicetus, the then bishop, agreed to differ and parted amicably. By the last decade of the century, Rome's attitude hardened, and, despite Polybius' letter, Victor, bishop of Rome, excommunicated all those who did not agree with Rome's position.

The account of the *Martyrdom of Polycarp* sheds light on a number of facets of Christianity in the middle of the second century. There is a sense of 'brotherhood' which linked the church at Smyrna, who drew up and sent the account, not only with the church at Philomelium, the immediate recipients of it, but also 'the holy and universal church sojourning in every place' (*Inscr.*). The church at Smyrna requested that the account should be sent to 'the brothers farther off' (20) (Compare the reference to the fact that Polycarp spent two hours in prayer before being led off under arrest, this prayer being for those whom he had met and for 'all the universal church throughout the world', 8.2).

Polycarp was clearly well known. When one Germanicus had been killed in the arena, the crowds yelled out 'Away with these atheists; let search be made for Polycarp' (3). Later on, in the stadium, the crowds shouted out 'This is the teacher of Asia, the father of the Christians, the destroyer of our gods, who teaches many not to sacrifice (to them) or worship (them)' (12.2).

The Jews are depicted as joining in with the Gentiles in calling for Polycarp to be put to the lion (12.2) and then, when it had been decided that Polycarp should be burned to death, assisting in constructing the pile of wood on which Polycarp was to be burned (13.1). They also took a leading role in trying to prevent Christians from collecting Polycarp's body (17.2; 18.1).

We might mention the fact that when the Roman proconsul tried to persuade Polycarp to say that Caesar was lord, Polycarp asserted that he had served Jesus Christ as lord for eighty-six years and that Christ had done him no wrong—how could he blaspheme his King who had saved him? (10.2). Assuming that Polycarp was expressing himself loosely here, rather than thinking precisely of his baptism as a believer, Polycarp must have been born in the early 70s of the first century and grown up in the immediate sub-apostolic period.

Finally, we may mention the idea of a 'veneration' of the martyr. The Christians at Smyrna gathered Polycarp's bones, which they describe as being 'more valuable than precious stones and finer than refined gold' and put them in a suitable place (18), and there they promise to gather with gladness and joy to commemorate and celebrate 'the birthday' of Polycarp's martyrdom, conscious that by such a ceremony they will help train and prepare those who may be called upon to be martyrs in the future.

In the second half of the century, the movement known as Montanism originated in Phrygia in Asia Minor. Its leaders, Montanus and two women, Priscilla and Maximilla, claimed to be prophets, the instruments of the Paraclete, and delivered oracles which they claimed were of divine inspiration. The movement probably got under way in the late 150s. By the 170s, the churches began to take serious note of it and sought to combat it. Eusebius tells us that there were public disputations (e.g. Ancyra in Galatia, *HE* 5.16.4; cf. 5.16.16-17). Clearly, the movement caused dissension between Christians. The main points at issue were the inspiration of the Spirit and prophecy. From Asia Minor, it won support in North Africa and even at Rome.

The letter which Polybius of Ephesus wrote to Victor of Rome, already referred to, reveals something of the sense of history which he and presumably many other Christians of Asia Minor had. 'In Asia great luminaries sleep and will rise on the day of the Lord's coming' (*HE* 5.24.2). He mentions that Philip and two of his daughters are buried in the province (5.24.2). John the apostle is buried at Ephesus (5.24.3), while among martyrs there have been Polycarp and Thraseas, bishop of Eumenaea, buried at Smyrna; Sagaris, bishop of Laodicea, and buried there; Papirius of Smyrna, Polycarp's succesor; and Melito, bishop of Sardis and buried there (5.24.4-5). The last named, who had remained celibate, is accorded the high praise that he 'had lived his life entirely in the Holy Spirit' (τὸν ἐν ἁγίῳ Πνεύματι πάντα πολιτευσάμενον). Polybius mentions with some pride that seven members of his own family had been bishops and that he was the eighth (24.6).

We turn now to an examination of those documents which we assume originated from Asia Minor.

1. John of Patmos

We shall assume here that the book of Revelation was composed about the early nineties in western Asia Minor, when the Emperor Domitian was intent on being acknowledged as divine. Older material may well have been incorporated, but the actual composition was in the last few years of Domitian's reign.[1]

---

[1] So e.g. E. Stauffer, *Christ and the Caesars* (London: SCM, 1955), pp. 147-91; E. Lohse, *Die Offenbarung des Johannes* (Göttingen: Vandenhoeck & Ruprecht, 1960); A. Feuillet, *The Apocalypse* (New York: Alba, 1965), p. 91; A. Satake, *Die Gemeindeordnung in der Johannesapokalypse* (Neukirchen-Vluyn: Neukirchener Verlag, 1966), p. 193; G.B. Caird, *The Revelation of St. John the Divine* (London: A. & C. Black, 1966), p. 6; G.R. Beasley-Murray, *The Book of Revelation* (London: Oliphants, 1974), p. 38; J.M. Court, *Myth and History in the Book of Revelation* (London: SPCK, 1979); McDonald and Porter, *Sacred Literature*, p. 557. On the other hand, the case for an early date for the book, in the late 60s, is argued by Robinson, *Redating*, pp. 221-53, esp. 248-53; Margaret Barker, *The Revelation of Jesus Christ* (London: T. & T. Clark, 2000), pp. xi-xiii, with Josephine M. Ford, *Revelation* (AB 38; New York: Doubleday, 1975), arguing that chs 4–22 were composed between 60 and 70, and D.E. Aune, *Revelation 1-5* (WBC 52a-c; Waco, TX: Word Books, 1997), p. lviii, postulating a two-

A and B. Divine Presence and Illumination

It is evident that the author believed that he was the recipient of certain experiences which he attributed to the Holy Spirit[2] and that he felt inspired by the Holy Spirit to deliver a message to the churches as a result of those experiences. John tells us at the beginning that he was 'in the Spirit' on the Lord's Day (1.10) and that he received a message to deliver to the seven churches (1.11). In this state he both heard and saw the risen Christ (1.12-20). The state of being 'in the Spirit' designates an extraordinary experience during which the seer is overwhelmed by the presence of the numinous.[3] The normal boundaries of sense are transcended, and John saw and heard the risen Jesus who had been exalted to heaven.

A similar phrase is used as the prelude to a vision of God's throne and of the heavenly throng (4.2). He heard a voice summoning him 'Come up hither and I will show you what must take place after these things' (4.1). Then he said 'Immediately I was in the Spirit'. Whereas in chapter 1 John was given a Christophany on earth, in chapter 4 he claimed to have been transported to heaven.

Two other instances of 'transportation' occur, both attributed to the agency of the Spirit (ἀπήνεγκέν με…ἐν πνεύματι). The first occasion is when an angel carried John into the desert to behold the great whore and the divine judgment on her (17.3-18). Secondly, when an angel led him to a very high mountain to give him a vision of the heavenly city, the new Jerusalem (21.10). To experience the heavenly world and to be a recipient of a divine revelation is not within the control or prerogative of humans—people need to be taken out of themselves by the Spirit to have such experiences.

While all these are specific references, they undergird the whole work and help to present it as a product of the Spirit's influence.[4] Of course, during the visions and auditions in the rest of the work, John receives explanations from an angel-interpreter.[5] In this, the work is following apocalyptic tradition, and the presence of the angel-interpreter must not be allowed to weaken the fact that the Spirit is the source of John's inspiration.

---

stage composition, with a first edition in the 60s and a final editing during late in Domitian's reign or, more likely, during the early part of Trajan's reign.

[2] I assume that, however skilful a literary artist John of Patmos may be, he is describing some real experiences; cf. Aune, *Prophecy*, p. 275.

[3] Cf. Ford, *Revelation*, p. 382; R.J. Bauckham, 'The Role of the Spirit in the Apocalypse', *EQ* 52 (1980), pp. 67, 71 (reprinted in *The Climax of Prophecy* [Edinburgh: T. & T. Clark, 1993], pp. 152, 159); Boring, *Continuing Voice*, p. 126; against R.L. Jeske, 'Spirit and Community in the Johannine Apocalypse', *NTS* 31 (1985), p. 464, who believes that 'in the Spirit' is 'a relational symbol', linking John with the community from which he is separated, 'rather than a privately experiential one'.

[4] Cf. the feature at the end of the Seven Letters: 'Let the one who has ears to hear what the *Spirit* says to the churches' (in parallel with the opening word from the exalted Christ).

[5] Boring, *Continuing Voice*, pp. 180-81, draws attention to the close association of the Spirit and angels in Revelation.

We may now draw into our study the phenomenon where an utterance ascribed to the Spirit may have been a prophetic word:

(a) 14.13, where the Spirit responds to God's blessing pronounced on dead Christians with 'Yes; let them rest from their labours, for their works follow after them'. What the prophet said[6] is traced back to its origin and the human vehicle is allowed to fade out of the picture.[7]

(b) 22.16-17. The Spirit and the Bride probably represent the prophetic leader(s) and the believing community respectively[8] (rather than the believing community indwelt by the Spirit[9]). The congregation follows the lead of the prophet inspired by the Spirit and invites the Lord Jesus to come.

(c) 19.10. The much discussed phrase 'the witness of Jesus', which is 'the Spirit of prophecy', is probably an objective[10] rather than subjective[11] genitive (as at 1.9; 12.17; and even 1.2[12]), i.e. the testimony *about* Jesus (his ministry, death and resurrection) is what the Spirit takes and places on the lips of the prophet. The Spirit who prompts the prophet to speak a word leads him to bear witness to Jesus who is the crucified and triumphant Warrior-Lamb.

---

[6] Aune, *Prophecy*, p. 283; A. Farrer, *The Revelation of St. John the Divine* (Oxford: Clarendon, 1964), p. 226; Bauckham, *Role of the Spirit*, p. 73 (*Climax*, p. 160).

[7] Cf. E. Schweizer, article on πνεῦμα, in *TDNT*, Vol. VII (Grand Rapids, MI: Eerdmans, 1968), p. 449

[8] So Caird, *Revelation*, p. 287; Beasley-Murray, *Revelation*, pp. 344-45; J. Sweet, *Revelation* (London: SCM (Pelican), 1979), p. 318; F.F. Bruce, 'The Spirit in the Apocalypse', in B. Lindars and S.S. Smalley (eds.), *Christ and Spirit in the New Testament* (Cambridge: Cambridge University Press, 1973), p. 343; Bauckham, *Climax*, p. 160 (though on pp. 166-67, Bauckham interprets the prayer as a moment when 'the eschatological church is becoming present reality already'); Boring, *Continuing Voice*, p. 101.

[9] So Schweizer, πνεῦμα, p. 450; E. Lohmeyer, *Die Offenbarung des Johannes* (Tübingen: Mohr, 1926), p. 178, though he also sees the Spirit as working through a prophet; Farrer, *Revelation*, p. 226.

[10] So, e.g., I.T. Beckwith, *The Apocalypse* (New York-London: Macmillan, 1919), p. 729; H. Strathmann, article on μάρτυς, *TDNT*, Vol. IV (Grand Rapids, MI: Eerdmans, 1967), p. 501; Bruce, 'Spirit', p. 338; Ford, *Revelation*, p. 312; G.W.H. Lampe, 'The Testimony of Jesus is the Spirit of Prophecy', in W.C. Weinrich (ed.), *The New Testament Age* (Macon, GA: Mercer University Press, 1984), pp. 245-58.

[11] So Farrer, *Revelation*, pp. 194-95; Caird, *Revelation*, p. 238; Beasley-Murray, *Revelation*, p. 276; A.A. Trites, *The New Testament Concept of Witness* (SNTSMS 31; Cambridge: Cambridge University Press, 1977), pp. 156-58; D. Hill, *New Testament Prophecy* (London: Marshall, Morgan & Scott, 1979), pp. 89-90; Weinel, *Spirit and Martyrdom*, pp. 74-76; Bauckham, *Climax*, p. 161. Boring, *Continuing Voice*, pp. 150-51, claims that both senses are present.

[12] In agreement with Lampe, *Testimony*, p. 254. At Rev. 12.11, the witness is borne by Christ's faithful followers to and about him, so that subjective and objective senses are both present.

SUMMARY

The author represented his work as a message from the risen Lord through the Spirit to himself for onward transmission to the churches. Prophets are active in the worshipping community. Prompted by the Spirit, they bear witness in their proclamation to Jesus the crucified and exalted one, while they may have led the congregation to respond in ejaculatory prayer.

C. Divine Power

To some it is surprising that nowhere in the whole book does the author, whose pastoral aim to encourage the congregations facing imminent persecution is clear, ever mention the help of the Spirit in either strengthening Christians to bear witness (as in Mk. 13.9, 11) or helping them to endure the physical pain of persecution.[13] But this omission may be more apparent than real. Bauckham has challenged this assumption, and he has referred in the first place to the reference to the Spirit in the crucial vision of the Lamb who bore the marks of slaughter before the throne of God, in chapter 5.[14] The lamb is described as having seven horns and seven eyes, which are interpreted as 'the seven spirits of God sent forth into the world' (τὰ ἑπτὰ Πνεύματι τοῦ Θεοῦ ἀπεσταλμένοι εἰς πᾶσαν τὴν γῆν, 5.6. [the 'seven spirits' is a way of referring to the one Holy Spirit in all the fullness of his power]). Many scholars had observed the allusion to Zechariah 4.1-14, where the seven lamps on the golden lampstand are said to represent 'the eyes of the Lord which range through the whole earth'. Bauckham claims that the eyes of the Lord 'indicate not only his ability to see what happens throughout the world but also his ability to act powerfully wherever he chooses'.[15] The Zechariah 4 passage contains the famous warning 'This is the word of the Lord to Zerubbabel, Not by might, nor by power, but by my Spirit, says the LORD of Hosts' (v. 6), and, of course, John had already mentioned 'the seven spirits who are before His throne' in 1.4 and 4.5. What is new in chapter 5 is in the first place the change from ranging to being *sent* (God sends His Spirit) and the close association made between the Lamb and the Spirit (expressed by means of saying that the Lamb's seven eyes are the seven spirits of God).

Bauckham further comments that 'the seven spirits are sent out into all the world to make his [the Lamb's] victory effective throughout the world'.[16] The Spirit is sent after the death and exaltation of Christ the Lamb who has conquered through his death, to help actualize the triumph of the cross-exaltation.

Thus, to the discerning reader, John's reinterpretation of the language from Zechariah would convey the idea that the Spirit had been sent into the world to help

---

[13] An omission noted by Ford, *Revelation*, p. 19.
[14] See Bauckham, *Climax*, pp. 162-65; *The Theology of the Book of Revelation* (Cambridge: Cambridge University Press, 1993), pp. 110-15.
[15] Bauckham, *Climax*, p. 164; *Theology*, p. 112.
[16] Bauckham, *Climax*, p. 165; cf. *Theology*, p. 114.

Christians in their task of making known the claims of the slaughtered and triumphant Lamb, the Lord Jesus Christ. To the one who had ears to hear, John's description of the Spirit would be saying something similar to the dominical promise recorded in Mark 13.11, though with a larger horizon than just hostile tribunals or courts.

The other passage on which Bauckham places a great deal of emphasis is that of the Two Witnesses in chapter 11.[17] While the Spirit is not expressly mentioned, the fact that the role of the witnesses is prophetic witness ('and they shall prophesy', v.3), and for John the Spirit inspires prophecy, makes it not unreasonable to assume that for John the Spirit is the power enabling the witness to be borne.

In a book which deals so profusely in symbols, we naturally ask whom or what do the two prophetic witnesses stand for? They are described as the two olive trees and the two lampstands which stand before the Lord, another allusion to Zechariah 4 and to the priestly and kingly figures mentioned there. However, rather than having individuals in mind, John is thinking of the believing church in its corporate role as prophetic witness to God, Christ and the Gospel.[18] Material from Zechariah is 'recycled' and given a new application. In the Book of Revelation, it is the church as a whole which has been redeemed to act as kings and priests to God (1.6; 5.10; 20.6; cf. 3.12, 21). The figure 'two' probably also fulfils the requirement of Deuteronomy 19.15, a prescription which exerted considerable influence on the early church. In addition, John in 1.20 identified the seven lampstands with the seven churches to which the following letters were addressed.

Features of two great OT prophetic figures, Moses and Elijah, are transferred to these two witnesses, in vv. 5-6: the use of fire and the power to inflict drought recall the career of Elijah, while that of turning water to blood and inflicting plagues reminds of Moses (the motif of fire proceeding from their mouths may be a blending of the idea of God's word as a consuming fire in Jeremiah 5.14 and the image of the sword of Christ's mouth [1.16; 2.12,16; 19.15], itself probably dependant on the picture of a descendant of Jesse slaying the wicked with the breath of his lips in Isaiah 11.4, in which case we would again have a link with the prophetic tradition). These are not meant to be taken literally as if supernatural powers will be bestowed on the church in its witness. These traits serve to underline the continuity of prophetic witness under the old and new covenants and to remind the church of John's day that prophets like Moses and Elijah had stood up to the political tyrants of their day and borne witness to God.

In the task of the two witnesses there is to be a pattern repeated from the ministry of the Lamb: witness, opposition, defeat, death and vindication (v. 7). The Beast is only allowed to attack and overcome them when their task has been accomplished.

Where they bear witness and are martyred is called 'the great city'. For those with Spirit-inspired perception 'it is called Sodom and Egypt, where their Lord was also

---

[17] Bauckham, *Climax*, pp. 273-83; *Theology*, pp. 113-14.

[18] Caird, *Revelation*, p. 134; Beasley-Murray, *Revelation*, pp. 178-79, 181; Sweet, *Revelation*, p. 185; Bauckham, *Climax*, p. 274, and *Theology*, p. 84; Aune, *Revelation*, p. 631.

crucified' (v. 8). In a sense, it is anywhere where men and women hear the gospel of Christ and reject it and persecute the messengers. For John's readers, it would be pre-eminently the city of Rome, the heart of the Roman empire (and, derivatively, in those cities of Asia Minor which had adopted emperor worship and sold their souls to such satanically-inspired, idolatrous falsehood).

Their vindication is described in terms of resurrection (v. 11) and exaltation to heaven (v. 12), suggestive of a parallel to and sharing in the experience of Jesus. This sequence produces fear (vv. 11,13) and then those who have survived the great earthquake (v. 13a), which is a symbol of divine intervention in judgment on human wickedness (God is at work in and through the prophetic witness of His people), 'gave glory to the God of heaven', which is an indication of repentance and turning back to God.[19]

Once again, it must be said that to the discerning hearer there would be a message that the Spirit would help in the role of prophetic witness to which the churches were summoned in a hostile and alien world, to bring people to repentance and faith.

If John of Patmos believed that the Spirit enabled God's faithful people to bear witness in a hostile world, we are probably justified in assuming that he believed that same Spirit would protect believers against the seductive blandishments of the 'great whore', Babylon-Rome. In this connection, we might briefly mention that the view which sees John of Patmos as a rigorous ascetic on the basis of a literal interpretation of 14.4 ought to be rejected.[20] 'The 144,000 who have not defiled themselves with women' is an instance of the spiritualization of holy war regulations (Deut. 23.9-10) and means those who have not been seduced by the spiritual whore, Babylon-Rome.[21]

John may have been a rigorist, but that should not be based on 14.4, or, for that matter, on his rejection of the Nicolaitan compromise with the world (2.14-16, 20-23), which would be comparable to Paul's insistence that Christians should not participate in idolatrous worship (1 Cor. 10.14-22). Whether Montanus was influenced by a literal interpretation of Rev. 14.4 we cannot say. This text could have been a contributory factor in the rise of asceticism/celibacy in Christianity, but that was not its original meaning.

---

[19] So Caird, *Revelation*, pp. 141-42; Beasley-Murray, *Revelation*, p. 187; Sweet, *Revelation*, p. 189; Aune, *Revelation*, p. 628; Bauckham, *Climax*, pp. 273-83, and *Theology*, pp. 84-87.

[20] Against M. Kiddle, *The Revelation of St. John* (London: Hodder & Stoughton, 1940), pp. 267-71; M. Black, 'The Dead Sea Scrolls and Christian Origins', in M. Black (ed.), *The Scrolls and Christianity* (London: SPCK, 1969), pp. 100-101; Boring, *Continuing Voice*, p. 136.

[21] So rightly Caird, *Revelation*, p. 179; Beasley-Murray, *Revelation*, p. 223; Sweet, *Revelation*, p. 222; Bauckham, *Climax*, pp. 230-32; Elisabeth Schüssler Fiorenza, *The Book of Revelation: Justice and Judgment* (Philadelphia, PA: Fortress, 1985), pp. 190-91; Aune, *Revelation*, p. 848.

D. Other Features and Summary

Thus far the concordance takes us. What we have gleaned so far is valuable, but we need to press our inquiry beyond the mere occurrence of the word 'spirit'. We need also to ask questions about the author and his standing in, and attitude towards, the churches of Asia Minor. We have to account both for the author's being soaked in OT language and imagery and his thinking Semitically while writing Greek, and for echoes of the Johannine tradition accompanied by considerable differences between Revelation and the Fourth Gospel, too deep to allow common authorship.

These factors could point to the fact that the author was a Jewish Christian who had migrated from Palestine just before the Jewish War or was a descendant of that group.[22] We would, then, have a prophetic figure who claimed to be inspired by the Spirit, who moved from being in contact with the Johannine stream of Christianity into the Pauline communities around Ephesus in Asia Minor.[23]

He does not refer to any structured leadership in the seven letters to the churches. Such an omission is surprising since we know (in view of Acts 20, Eph. 4 and the Pastorals) that the Pauline congregations moved to a more structured organization in the post-Pauline period.[24] The silence is probably deliberate—and revealing. Throughout the book, the congregations are addressed as 'saints', and 'prophets' are coupled with them at 16.6; 18.24 (at 18.20 we have 'saints and apostles and prophets'), i.e. the leaders = the prophets and the members = the saints. This fits the suggested picture of the author as a Spirit-inspired prophet. His silence concerning the emerging forms of ministry reflects his dislike or suspicion or indifference to them. He sat loose to structures.[25] For him, the Spirit speaks directly to the congregation. In the (to him) imminent crisis of the end of the world, of which Domitian's megalomaniac claims were a symptom and of which the emerging conflict between church and state was a part, the Spirit was urging him to deliver a message to the churches, to steel the nerve and put iron into the soul of God's people to stand firm.

If the trend in Asia Minor around the end of the first and the beginning of the second century was towards increased institutionalism and developing structures, then

---

[22] So G. Bornkamm, article on πρέσβυς, in *TDNT*, Vol.VI (Grand Rapids, MI: Eerdmans, 1969), pp. 669-70; Satake, *Gemeindeordnung*, pp. 192-93; Müller, *Theologiegeschichte*, pp. 46-50.

[23] Bornkamm, πρέσβυς, p. 667, thinks that John has nothing to do with the Pauline congregations. But how many Christian congregations were there in a place like Ephesus?

[24] Cf. e.g. Bornkamm, πρέσβυς, p. 667; Dunn, *Unity and Diversity*, p. 115; Aune, *Prophecy*, p. 205.

[25] Cf. Aune, *Prophecy*, pp. 205-206; Bauckham, *Role of the Spirit*, p. 72. We view with scepticism Schweizer's theory that 'the whole church was understood in principle, at least in this passage, as a church of prophets' (*Church Order*, p. 135), accepted by Hill, *New Testament Prophecy*, pp. 89-90. In 19.10 the brothers are fellow church members who have received the witness about Jesus from the prophets. More nuanced is Dunn, *Unity and Diversity*, p. 121: 'a church that lives through and out of prophecy'.

in many respects John of Patmos was untypical. He stood for a certain type of Christianity in which the Spirit is deemed to be active and the prophet is his agent. But he was not by any means the 'norm' of Asia Minor Christianity at the turn of the century.

2. The Pastoral Epistles

With the majority of scholars we believe that the Pastorals represent the attempt by a sincere Paulinist to apply the Pauline tradition to the problems facing the Pauline congregations at the turn of the century.[26] They are of special interest, therefore, insofar as they should reveal to us whether Paul's own emphasis on the Spirit's role in the church's life continued to play a dominant part or not, some forty years or so after the apostle's death.

A. Divine Presence

The idea of ecstatic experience in which believers are overwhelmed by a sense of the Divine invading their life strikes one as foreign to the general ethos of the Pastorals. These letters present us with a picture of the church settling down in the world.[27] A number of scholars would maintain that the ideal is that of good citizenship with the author wishing 'to become part of the world'[28] and emphasizing sobriety, moderation

---

[26] Advocates of a non-Pauline authorship include P.N. Harrison, *The Problem of the Pastoral Epistles* (Oxford: Oxford University Press, 1929); M. Dibelius and H. Conzelmann, *The Pastoral Epistles* (Philadelphia, PA: Fortress, 1972); C.K. Barrett, *The Pastoral Epistles* (Oxford: Clarendon, 1963); N. Brox, *Die Briefe an Timotheus und Titus* (Regensburg: Pustet, 1969); Kümmel, *Introduction*, pp. 258-72; Dunn, *Jesus and the Spirit*, pp. 347-50; *Unity and Diversity*, pp. 114-16; A.T. Hanson, *The Pastoral Epistles* (London: A. & C. Black, 1982); and L. Oberlinner, *Die Pastoralbriefe* (Freiburg-Basel-Wien: Herder, 3 Vols., 1994–96). H. von Campenhausen, 'Polykarp von Smyrna und die Pastoralbriefe', *SHA* 51 (1951), pp. 5-51, attributed the Pastorals to Polycarp. Defenders of Pauline authorship include J. Jeremias, *Die Briefe an Timotheus und Titus* (NTD 9; Göttingen: Vandenhoeck & Ruprecht, 1947); C. Spicq, *Les Épitres Pastorales* (EB; Paris: Gabalda, 1947); D. Guthrie, *The Pastoral Epistles* (TNTC; London: Tyndale, 1957), and *Introduction*, pp. 607-49; E.E. Ellis, *Paul and His Interpreters* (Grand Rapids, MI: Eerdmans, 1961), pp. 49-57; J.N.D. Kelly, *The Pastoral Epistles* (London: A. & C. Black, 1963); G. Fee, *The Letters to Timothy and Titus* (Grand Rapids, MI: Eerdmans, 1988); McDonald and Porter, *Sacred Literature*, pp. 489-97. Some argue for genuine Pauline notes worked into letters by a Paulinist: P.N. Harrison, *The Problem of the Pastoral Epistles*, and *Paulines and Pastorals* (London: Villiers, 1964); J.D. Miller, *The Pastoral Letters as Composite Documents* (Cambridge: Cambridge University Press, 1997); and I.H. Marshall (with P.H. Towner), *The Pastoral Letters* (ICC; Edinburgh: T.& T. Clark, 1999), pp. 83-92 (but disclaiming our ability to trace precisely authentic Pauline material).

[27] Schweizer, *Church Order*, p. 77.

[28] Dibelius-Conzelmann, *Pastorals*, pp. 39-41.

and contentment. At the same time, it is easy to exaggerate this side: we ought not to forget that the author shows himself well aware of the dangers of the pursuit of wealth and the love of money (1 Tim. 6.9-10, 17-19) and warns against becoming a prey to worldly lusts (Tit. 2.12). It is a matter for regret that Demas has 'loved this present world' and has left Paul (2 Tim. 4.10). A Christian should be like a soldier who does not get entangled in the affairs of everyday civilian life in order that he might give satisfaction to his commanding officer (2 Tim. 2.4). Persecution is the lot that believers can expect in this world (2 Tim. 3.12), and their hope ultimately lies outside this world order and rests on the glorious coming of Christ (Tit. 2.13). In the contrast scheme, effectively used at Titus 3.3-7, the readers are reminded of the past life which they have left behind, because Christ has redeemed them from all wickedness (Tit. 2.14). So, while it is important that the church should have a good reputation among outsiders (e.g. 1 Tim. 3.7; 6.1; cf. Tit. 2.5, 9-10), the cutting edge between church and world has not been lost sight of by any means. We ought not to exaggerate the so-called 'bourgeois ethics' of the Pastorals, which has been so roundly dismissed by some as symptomatic of the decline of the post-Pauline congregations from the heights of their founder's Christianity.[29] We need to maintain a correct balance on this issue.

If the author's ideal is that Christians should be able to lead a quiet and peaceable life, in all godliness and holiness (1 Tim. 2.2), we might well not expect to find any stress on the sovereign freedom of the Spirit. And, of course, in letters which advise office-holders on 'how men ought to behave themselves in God's household' (1 Tim. 3.15) and which offer criteria for the conduct of the office-holders themselves, we do not expect to find extensive discussions on the role of the Spirit in the religious experience of believers in general. There is, however, one passage in Titus which may be characterized as part of the Pauline tradition, both because of the Pauline idea of justification by grace enshrined in it and because it is rounded-off by the formula 'Faithful is the saying': 3.4-8a. The passage affirms that God has not saved us on the grounds of our own good works, but due entirely to His mercy:

'According to His mercy, He saved us through the washing of rebirth and renewal (διὰ λουτροῦ παλιγγενεσίας καὶ ἀνακαινώσεως) by the Holy Spirit whom He poured out on us richly through Jesus Christ'.

Assuming that παλιγγενεσία and ἀνακαίνωσις are virtually synonymous,[30] representing the same event viewed from slightly different terminological angles, the Holy Spirit is the agent who effects rebirth.

The passage asserts that God's act of saving us by His mercy and not our deeds is experienced as rebirth or renewal brought about by the Holy Spirit, as being justified and as becoming an heir of God with the hope of eternal life. All this is bestowed on

---

[29] E.g. E. Käsemann, *Jesus Means Freedom* (London: SCM, 1969), p. 95.
[30] So Lampe, *Seal*, p. 60; Dibelius and Conzelmann, *Pastorals*, p. 149; Beasley-Murray, *Baptism*, pp. 210-11; Dunn, *Baptism*, p. 166; Barrett, *Pastorals*, p. 142; Kelly, *Pastorals*, p. 252; Brox, *Pastoralbriefe*, pp. 307-308; Fee, *1 and 2 Timothy, Titus*, p. 204; P. H. Towner, *The Goal of our Instruction* (Sheffield: Sheffield Academic Press, 1989), pp. 115-117; Oberlinner, *Titusbriefe*, p. 175; Marshall, *Pastorals*, p. 321.

us by God's gracious kindness through Jesus Christ. The verb 'saved' is, in effect, parallel to the verb 'poured out'[31] (which probably evokes Joel 2.28, which is alluded to also in Rom. 5.5 and quoted, of course, in Acts 2.17): God's saving act towards us is experienced in the outpouring of His Spirit upon us.

Most commentators assume that baptism is in mind.[32] Certainly the author's views on ordination suggest that probably, whatever may have been the original reference of the faithful saying, the author linked the experience described in it with baptism administered to those who had heard the gospel message and responded in faith to Christ. In other words, there is a holding together of the Gospel message, the response in faith and baptism, and the encounter with God in Christ through the experience of God's Spirit.

Thus, this passage affirms that at the beginning of the Christian life lies an experience of God's grace and mercy, part of which consists of the outpouring of God's Spirit on the believer and the awareness of a new life. The idea of a new mode of existence, contained in 'rebirth' and 'renewal', is underlined by the contrast between v. 3, which deals with the past life, and vv. 4-7, which are centred on the revolutionary change through God's generous outpouring of the Spirit ("once...but now...").

But is this tradition, in which an experience defined in terms of the Spirit is apparently regarded as the norm, also one which is normative for the author of the Pastorals? We need to remember that he is well aware of the dangers of formalism and emptiness in the religious life: at 2 Timothy 3.1-5, he refers to those who have the form of godliness but deny its power (v. 5). Ideally, then, the true religious life is marked by power, which is surely a reference to the Spirit.[33] This would suggest that his reference to the tradition at Titus 3.4-7 is no formal one.

These two passages (Tit. 3.4-7 and 2 Tim. 3.5)[34] warn against too easily dismissing the religious experience of the Pastorals as a decline from Paul. At the same time, many of the exhortations within the letter do not make use of the Spirit. Are, then, these two passages enough to counterbalance the overall impression? We shall return to this point at the end of our discussion.

---

[31] Dunn, *Baptism,* p. 166; Towner, *Goal,* pp. 56-57, 116.

[32] In addition, R. Schnackenburg, *Baptism in the Thought of St. Paul* (Oxford: Blackwell, 1964), p. 11; Beasley-Murray, *Baptism,* pp. 210-16. Note Dunn's shift from thinking of the conversion experience (*Baptism,* p. 168) to believing that the Pastor possibly read the faithful saying in a more strongly sacramental sense than it originally bore (*Unity and Diversity,* p. 159). Towner, *Goal,* pp. 115-17, maintains that the passage is an exposition of the role of the Spirit in the conversion process and that water baptism is not primarily in mind—at most, there may be an incidental or secondary allusion to it.

[33] So rightly, Marshall, *Pastorals,* p. 775.

[34] To which possibly 2 Timothy 1.14 should be added, if the phrase 'the Holy Spirit who dwells ἐν ἡμῖν' is a reference to all Christians, which is how Guthrie, *Pastorals,* p. 134, and Barrett, *Pastorals,* p. 98, take it, while Oberlinner, *Zweiter Timotheusbrief,* p. 52, sees at least an implicit reference to all Christians.

If Titus 3.4-7 and 2 Timothy 3.5 refer to all church members, the Christian minister is also considered to be the recipient of God's Spirit. In 2 Timothy 1.6-7, Timothy is urged to stir up the gift of God which was in him through the laying-on of hands by Paul.[35] This gift of God may be neglected (1 Tim. 4.14) and may need to be stirred up into activity as one might fan into flames the dying embers of a fire (2 Tim. 1.6). Fear and timidity may be factors in the quenching of this gift. But Timothy should remember that God did not give him the Spirit who inspires cowardice but the Spirit who imparts power and love and self-discipline (Πνεῦμα δειλίας ἀλλὰ δυνάμεως καὶ ἀγάπης καὶ σωφρονισμοῦ). The Holy Spirit is in mind here, not the human spirit. God gave the Holy Spirit who himself mediates power, love and self-control. There is, then, a 'grace' of ordination,[36] which the Christian minister needs to keep active or else he will fail in his task of maintaining a bold and fearless witness. It seems almost a static idea of the Spirit rather than the Spirit as event or encounter; the Spirit is latent within the office-holder and can be 'turned up' by human will. But this way of putting the matter must not be pressed too sharply because the Spirit does impel to action.[37] Timothy and the contemporary office-holder must allow the Spirit freedom to enable their work.

Further, if this gift is mediated by the laying-on of hands as the 'gateway' to the work of ministry, we have arrived at the idea of office.[38] Laying-on of hands inevitably sets up a boundary between those who can and those who cannot exercise ministerial functions. The Spirit is envisaged as working through the official channels of the church to equip the minister for his work.[39]

B. Divine Illumination

The Pastorals seem to envisage truth as something which is given, a body of doctrine which was transmitted originally by Paul and then by his successors (Timothy, faithful men) and which must be handed on in tact to the next generations. The imagery of a deposit (παραθήκη, 1 Tim. 6.20; 2 Tim. 1.12, 14) emphasizes this idea: something has been deposited and entrusted for safekeeping.

---

[35] The difference over against 1 Tim, 4.14 (the gift is given by means of the laying-on of hands by the elders) can be explained by the testatory character of 2 Timothy. Thus, 1 Tim. 4.14 probably reflects the actual conditions of the author's day; 2 Tim. 1.6-7, on the other hand, reflects the pseudepigraphical nature of the letters and helps to give office an apostolic origin. Cf. Hanson, *Pastorals*, pp. 94, 121; Oberlinner, *Erster Timotheusbrief*, p. 210.

[36] Dunn, *Unity and Diversity*, p. 352: 'a clear theology of ordination has emerged'; see the detailed treatment of H. von Lips, *Glaube-Gemeinde-Amt (zur Verständnis der Ordination in den Pastoralbriefen)* (Göttingen: Vandenhoeck & Ruprecht, 1979), esp. pp. 206-22, 240-65.

[37] Marshall, *Pastorals*, p. 696, emphasises that the Spirit is here understood as something dynamic.

[38] E.g. von Campenhausen, *Ecclesiastical Authority*, pp. 106-19.

[39] Cf. Dunn, *Jesus and the Spirit*, p. 348: 'Charisma has become the power of office'.

This is the 'sound doctrine' (1 Tim. 1.10; 6.3; 2 Tim. 1.13; 4.3; Tit. 1.9; 2.1) which stands over against heretical perversions of it. The idea of new interpretations is ruled out. Speculation is discouraged (1 Tim. 1.3-4; 4.7; 2 Tim. 2.14, 23; Tit. 3.9). *The* faith must be adhered to (1 Tim. 5.8; 2 Tim. 3.14; 4.7; Tit. 1.13). Truth is already known and does not need any additions or alteration. The church's task is to be the bulwark of that truth (1 Tim. 3.15) and to resist heretical distortions of it.

In accordance with this idea, Timothy is told to guard 'the good deposit' (2 Tim. 1.14), and then the writer gives the means by which the tradition may be preserved faithfully: 'through the 'Holy Spirit who dwells in us' The Holy Spirit who indwells Timothy will assist him in his role as guardian of the tradition. How he will do so is not specified. The deposit, Paul's teaching, must be handed-on undiminished to future generations. In the midst of dangerous speculations, the Christian minister's duty is to eschew all debate and discussion, and authoritatively proclaim the truth. Any idea that the Spirit may reinterpret and reapply the Christian tradition to the differing needs and problems of successive generations seems to be absent.[40]

The difference in tone and ethos between 1 Corinthians 12–14 and the Pastorals is unmistakable. Where in the former it is the Spirit's sovereign, free working in equipping people for service which is uppermost, in the Pastorals it is *office and tradition* which stand to the fore and the Spirit is *an aid to the office-holder in maintaining the status-quo of the tradition.*[41]

We ought to say a word about references to prophecy in 1 Timothy 1.18; 4.14, which have been taken by some scholars to show that prophecy was still alive in the Pauline churches after the apostle's death. Whereas 1.18 could point to a Spirit-inspired utterance without specifying the occasion, 4.14 contains a tension between the concept of laying-on of hands by the elders (suggesting testing and recognition before admission to office) and that of prophecy (which implies spontaneous choice by a Spirit-inspired figure). A possible solution could be that 1.18 is part of the pseudonymous framework recalling the ethos of 1 Corinthians 12–14 (the prophet discerns those fitted for service), while at 4.14 the author reflects the practice of his own day. But this suggestion still leaves us with the question what was envisaged in the phrase διὰ προφητείας μετὰ ἐπιθέσεως τῶν χειρῶν at 4.14? The first question to be sorted out is whether, in the absence of the definite article with προφητείας, διὰ is here used with the accusative plural or the genitive singular? In the former case, more than one prophetic utterance would have preceded ordination: the laying on of hands would take place *because* a person had been pointed out by prophets (that is, prophetic discernment of a person's abilities stood at the beginning of a process which culminated in ordination and the imparting of divine charisma). In the latter case, a preeminent role would be given to the prophetic utterance *in* the act

---

[40] Schweizer, *Church Order*, p. 80: 'The problem of reinterpretation...is not seen at all'.

[41] Dunn, *Jesus and the Spirit*, p. 349 'Spirit and charisma have become in effect subordinate to office, to ritual, to tradition'; cf. *Unity and Diversity*, p. 361.

of ordination, and it would be accompanied by the role of the elders in laying on of hands.

Our answer to this question will probably depend on whether we think that there is room or not within the picture painted by the Pastorals for the spontaneous activity of prophets alongside of the bishop(s)/elders and deacons structure described for us in the Pastorals. While it may be true that the letters do not give us a total picture of the life of the churches for which the author wrote,[42] they are all we have to go on, and they do seem to depict a situation in which authority is concentrated in the hands of the elders, perhaps presided over by the senior elder who as president might well command increasing respect and authority. It is not easy to see how the elders could rule and yet there be room for the unpredictable activity of the prophet to utter the dictates of God.[43] The structures, with rules laid down for the bishop/elders and deacons, but no corresponding ones for prophets, do not seem to leave much scope for non-official functions in the congregations.

If this is so, why then did the author use the word 'prophecy'? Oberlinner reduces the significance of 'prophecy' to 'prayer',[44] but it is difficult to see how προφητεία can mean prayer, even if there is an association between prayer and prophecy,[45] while surely the author could have written the word commonly used for prayer, προσευχή, if an ordination prayer was what he had in mind. Is, however, 'prophecy' used with a somewhat reduced sense of 'ministry of the word'? This is how both Hill and von Lips have interpreted the phrase,[46] and they may be right. It could be that the author intended to endow the word spoken on such occasions with extra authority and chose to use the word 'prophecy' with all its resonances of God's speaking through His spokesmen. We could then imagine one of the bishops/elders either uttering a word about someone and this word was held to be from God, or, at the service of setting aside someone, preaching in such a way as to express their conviction about the suitability of the person concerned and to assure them of the divine equipment for their work. This seems to fit in with the overall picture of the Pastorals and could fit the use of the word προφητεία.

What, then, is the result of this consideration of the passage? Negatively, we would have to rule out a major role for prophets in the church life of the author of the Pastorals. Positively, it suggests a momentous significance for 'ordination', and fits in with the command in 1 Timothy 5.22 not to lay hands on anyone too hastily, which suggests a careful testing process before someone was admitted to the ministerial office. God is the ultimate donor (ἐδόθη is the 'divine passive') of the

---

[42] So A. Sand, 'Anfänge einer Koordinieriung verschiedener Gemeindeordungen nach den Pastoralbriefen', in J. Hainz (ed.), *Kirche im Werden,* (München-Paderborn-Wien: Schöningh, 1976), p. 219.

[43] Cf. von Lips, *Glaube-Gemeinde-Amt,* pp. 245-46.

[44] Oberlinner, *Erster Timotheusbriefe,* p. 211.

[45] G. Friedrich, article on προφήτης, *TDNT,* Vol. VI (Grand Rapids, MI: Eerdmans, 1968), pp. 852-53.

[46] Hill, *Prophecy,* p. 140: 'perhaps in the sense of the liturgy of the Word'; von Lips, *Glaube-Gemeinde-Amt,* p. 246, esp. n. 326.

gift (χάρισμα) for ministry, but it would be mediated through the prophetic type word accompanied by the laying on of hands by the elders. And that ministry is for the service of the congregation (e.g. 1 Tim. 4.11-13).[47]

C. Divine Power

One scans the Pastorals in vain for any direct reference to the Spirit's help in fulfilling the ethical ideal held up by the writer. There are moments when reliance on the Spirit for attaining the virtues demanded could have been mentioned and this motif exploited to good effect. Thus, in 1 Timothy 2.9-10, a contrast between outward cosmetics and inner adornment by the Spirit leading to good works could have been introduced; or at 1 Timothy 4.9 the Spirit's help in the training for godliness would not be unexpected nor at 1 Timothy 6.17-19 in the exhortations to the rich to be generous. In the imagery of the different utensils in a house at 2 Timothy 2.20-21, a reference to the Spirit would be appropriate and thoroughly 'Pauline' (likewise in Tit. 2.1-12).

When we add to this the absence of any reference to the Spirit in the church rules on the desirable qualifications for the office of bishop/elder, deacon/deaconess (1 Tim. 3.1-13; 5.17-20; Tit. 1.5-9), we are once more faced with the question whether the faithful saying of Titus 3.5-7 represents an inheritance from the past rather than a powerful force for the present. The dominant impression is that more is said about ethical performance and good works than divine help in the realization of them. Here we sense a shift in emphasis in the Pastorals over against the genuine Paul. As in Paul, Christians are engaged in fighting the good fight, but Paul's sense of the Spirit's help to overcome 'ungodliness and worldly desires' is absent.

This said, it must be pointed out on the other hand that the Pastorals do provide a theological under-girding for the ethical demand, as several scholars have recently convincingly shown.[48] One of them, L.R. Donelson, however, significantly comments in his conclusion that 'the Pastorals proffer, in contrast to this spirit-ethic [namely, of Paul], clear ethical norms and reliable authorities...Given the theological fact that Jesus is not accessible and that the spirit keeps relatively quiet, these letters suggest that the ordained and educated clergy can provide a version of Christianity that is reasonable and moral'.[49]

All this is not to deny that there is a vital Christianity in the Pastorals,[50] a passionate concern for the truth and the correct formulation of doctrine and a deep

---

[47] Marshall, *Pastorals*, p. 566, dissents from this line of approach, and believes that we should interpret the passage in the light of 1.18 and Acts 13.1-2.

[48] L.R. Donelson, *Pseudepigraphy and Ethical Argument in the Pastoral Epistles* (Tübingen: Mohr, 1986), pp. 67-113, 129-54, 199-202; Towner, *Goal*, pp. 47-244; F. Young, *The Theology of the Pastoral Letters* (Cambridge: Cambridge University Press, 1994), pp. 24-46.

[49] Donelson, *Pseudepigraphy*, p. 201.

[50] Cf. Dibelius and Conzelmann, *Pastorals*, pp. 40-41: 'A genuine expression of an existence in the world based on faith'.

conviction that good deeds must characterize the lives of Christians. Yet we must record the conviction borne in upon the reader that in terms of religious experience the Holy Spirit does not seem a dominant factor.

Summary

The difference between Paul and a third generation Paulinist in their approach to the Spirit is considerable. In Paul, the Spirit bestows gifts on all members of the church for the common good; without the Spirit there is no church life. Over against this stress, we have reached the stage in the Pastorals where office and ordination have emerged. It is true that Paul rated ministries of the Word higher than other services (1 Cor. 12.28 puts apostles, prophets and teachers above the rest), but he accords a significant role to the *whole* membership of the congregation which does not appear to be the case with the Pastor, who concentrates on the office-holders, and puts the responsibility of guiding the spiritual life of the congregation on them. In the milieu of the Pastorals the voice of the prophet does not seem likely to be heard, for the development has gone in the direction of order and institution.

The silence of the Pastorals on the equipping of office-holders by the Spirit is striking: their moral qualities are laid out, but there is not much stress on the Spirit (only 2 Tim. 1.6-7, 14).

The idea of a fixed, unalterable body of belief which the Christian minister must guard has emerged. The Spirit helps in guarding this tradition (2 Tim. 1.14), not in imparting new insights into God's plan and purpose. Faced with aberrant teaching, 'the faith', already defined, has to be adhered to not only for the wellbeing but also the preservation of Pauline Christianity.

Ethical exhortation is part of the work of the ministry, but mention of the Spirit as divine aid is on the whole lacking. 2 Timothy 3.5 reminds us that the author knew the distinction between the outer forms and the inner power of Christianity, but the idea of 'walking in the Spirit' does not appear to be the way in which he would naturally describe the Christian life.

It is true that the traditional saying Titus 3.5-7 is included, but the overall impression created by the Pastorals is that any intensity of experience of the Spirit is not a feature of the Pauline congregations by the turn of the century. In forty years, we seem to have moved a long way from the distinctive heart of the Pauline view of Christianity. The Pastorals let us glimpse how Pauline congregations had settled down to face the ongoing haul of history and the appearance of 'heresy'. The Pauline enthusiasms seem muted on the whole. An enthusiastic movement has had to develop structures and institutions to ensure that the initial impulse did not 'run into the sand'.

3. Jude

We shall proceed on the assumption, held by most scholars,[51] that the letter of Jude is a pseudonymous writing (although defenders of Jude as its author are not wanting[52]). A corollary of this is that it is virtually impossible to determine the place of origin or the destination of the letter with any certainty. Kümmel, Vögtle and Neyrey,[53] for example, denied that we can know anything about the place of Jude's composition. Nevertheless, we have opted to include the letter in our Asia Minor section because it was used by 2 Peter and there is a case for locating 2 Peter in Asia Minor (see the next section),[54] while on the other hand Jude was not accepted as authoritative in the Syriac-speaking church.[55]

---

[51] So declares A. Vögtle, *Das Judasbrief. Der zweite Petrusbriefe* (EKKNT 23; Solothum/Düsseldorf: Benziger and Neukirchenen-Vluyn: Neukirchener Verlag, 1994), p. 5.

[52] Those who accept that the writing is actually by Jude, a brother of Jesus, include C.E.B. Cranfield, *I & II Peter and Jude* (London: SCM, 1960), p. 148 (the date is put between 80-100, p. 146); Robinson, *Redating*, pp. 170-73, 198 (between 60-62); R. Bauckham, *Jude, 2 Peter* (WBC 50; Waco, TX: Word Books, 1983), pp. 14-16 (with a date in the 50s possible, p. 13), and *Jude and the Relatives of Jesus in the Early Church* (Edinburgh: T. & T. Clark, 1990), esp. pp. 134-78; Guthrie, *Introduction*, pp. 902-905 (written somewhere between AD 65 and 80); McDonald and Porter, *Sacred Literature*, p. 542 (between AD 50 and 80). J.N.D. Kelly, *The Epistles of Peter and Jude* (London: A. & C. Black, 1969), pp. 231-4, accepts pseudonymity and dates to 80-90 or even nearer the end of the century. J. Schneider, *Die Kirchenbriefe* (NTD 10; 9th ed. Göttingen: Vandenhoeck & Ruprecht, 1961), pp. 123-24, neither rules Jude's authorship out nor rules it in. J. Knight, *2 Peter and Jude* (New Testament Guides; Sheffield: Sheffield Academic Press, 1995), p. 26, considers that it is possible that Jude wrote the letter, but that we cannot be sure. If Jude were written by a brother of Jesus, then the letter might have been written in Palestine before AD 70. The convincingly well-marshalled arguments of Bauckham (following E.E. Ellis, 'Prophecy and Hermeneutic in Jude', *Prophecy and Hermeneutic in Early Christianity: New Testament Essays* [WUNT 18; Tubingen: Mohr, 1978, pp. 221-36]) that the letter is a highly skilled midrashic composition, may, ironically, have actually weakened his case on the authorship level. The skills needed for the midrashic type of composition demand some form of training such as potential rabbis underwent, yet the criticism of the Nazareth villagers recorded at Mk. 6.3 indicates that they did not regard Jesus' siblings as anything out of the ordinary. Bauckham himself (*Jude, 2 Peter*, p. 15), admits that the language of the letter is the real difficulty in the way of accepting Jude as author, but his argument that Jude could have picked up rhetorical skills in the course of missionary travels, while a possibility, does not, it would seem, answer the point which we have raised.

[53] Kümmel, *Introduction*, p. 302; J.H. Neyrey, *2 Peter, Jude* (AB 37C; New York Doubleday, 1993), p. 31; and Vögtle, *Judasbrief*, p. 12.

[54] This argument is, admittedly, not very strong, as the letter could have been written well away from Asia Minor but brought there and used by the author of 2 Peter.

[55] E.M. Sidebottom, *James Jude 2 Peter* (London: Thomas Nelson, 1967), p. 101; Bauckham, *Jude, 2 Peter*, p. 16; Vögtle, *Judasbrief*, p.13.

It is difficult to reach firm conclusions on the basis of such a small sample as Jude's 25 verses. We shall not be able to carry through our tripartite division because of the small size of the letter.

The possession of the Spirit appears to have been claimed by the false Christians attacked,[56] but this is denied to them by Jude. In vv. 19-21 we have a sharp antithesis ('they..., but you...'). The false Christians are described as unspiritual and they do not have the Spirit (Πνεῦμα μὴ ἔχοντες). In this criticism, the author may be turning back on the 'heretics' a claim which they had made, to be 'spiritual', and perhaps, therefore, above all questions of morality. Certainly severe criticism is made of their alleged licentious behaviour in vv. 4, 8, 11-12, but this may be standard anti-heretical polemic and 'smear tactics'.

The Holy Spirit is associated with prayer as one feature of the Christian life. Christian prayer is uttered by the help of the Spirit. Is this understood in some ecstatic sense? Probably not. The thought is presumably that God calls men and women to pray, and He assists them to do so by the Spirit, in shaping thoughts and their consequent expression within the parameters of 'the faith'.

In the closing doxology, praise is ascribed to God who is able to keep us from falling and ultimately to set us before His glorious presence without blemish, vv. 24-25. In this description of God, it is His continuous help which is highlighted. It is not always easy to be sure whether a doxology like this is traditional[57] and just taken over, or whether it is composed *ad hoc* to fit the particular situation.

Such as the evidence is, it suggests that the Spirit was not a neglected element in Jude's religious experience and outlook. He judged the heretics as lacking in the Spirit and he believed that Spirit-led prayer was a vital facet of the Christian life and that God bestows His help to maintain Christians in an ethically acceptable lifestyle.

4. 2 Peter

There can be no absolute certainty about where and to whom 2 Peter[58] was written, but there is some reason for accepting Asia Minor.[59] The author described his

---

[56] Kelly, *Epistles*, pp. 284-85; Neyrey, *2 Peter, Jude*, p. 91.

[57] So Kelly, *Epistles*, p. 290.

[58] The vast majority of scholars opt for pseudonymity (see, e.g., Kümmel, *Introduction*, pp. 302-5, Neyrey, *2 Peter, Jude*, p. 128; and Vögtle, *Zweite Petrusbrief*, pp. 122-25), including conservatively inclined ones (like Cranfield, *I & II Peter and Jude*, p. 148; Schneider, *Kirchenbriefe*, p. 100; Kelly, *Epistles*, pp. 235-37; Martin, *Introduction*, 2.383-88; Bauckham, *Jude, 2 Peter*, pp. 158-62; McDonald and Porter, *Sacred Literature*, pp. 539-42). Exceptions are M. Green, *The Second Epistle General of Peter and the General Epistle of Jude* (TNTC; Leicester: IVP, 1968); Robinson, *Redating*, pp. 173-99; Guthrie, *Introduction*, pp. 811-42 (cautiously).

[59] So Kelly, *Epistles*, p. 237; T. Fornberg, *An Early Church in a Pluralistic Society: A Study of 2 Peter* (CB NT Series 9; Lund: CWK Gleerup, 1977), pp. 122, 125, 147. Similarly, Robinson, *Redating*, pp. 197-98. Bauckham, *Jude, 2 Peter*, p. 159, believes that 2 Peter was written at Rome and sent to the same churches as 1 Peter in Asia Minor

writing as his second letter addressed to them and this points to the same addressees as 1 Peter. Fornberg believed that the slight Jewish and the strong Hellenistic influences in the letter were congruous with the cultural environment of the interior of Asia Minor.[60]

As with Jude, the sample is small. There is one specific reference to the Holy Spirit (1.21). Although this refers to the OT writers,[61] the passage is worth examining closely because of its implications. We shall assume the following translation for 1.19-20: 'We possess the prophetic word as something very reliable,[62] to which you do well to pay attention, until the Day dawns and the Daystar rises in your hearts, knowing of first importance that all prophetic scripture is not a matter of private interpretation'.[63]

The issue here is of wrong interpretation of the OT put forward by false teachers[64] (cf. 3.16). This gives to προσέχοντες the nuance of 'Pay attention to *the correct interpretation*'. Christians must study the OT, but not in an individualistic manner. Why is there an attack on 'private' interpretation of Scripture? What is the alternative to it? The opposite of a private individual's interpretation is that of the church or the churches in which the writer worships and works (rather than that of the author personally himself, since this would run the risk of transgressing the rule being enunciated[65]).

(see p. 161, for a measured assessment of the idea of a Petrine circle at Rome, which he is prepared to accept only in a very loose sense. Vögtle, *Zweite Petrusbrief*, p. 125, is sceptical).

[60] Fornberg, *Early Church*, pp. 121-48

[61] See Neyrey, *2 Peter, Jude*, p. 179, for the view that the 'prophetic word' is a reference to the event of the Transfiguration understood as a prophecy of Christ's return in glory, but this seems a rather complicated and far from natural explanation.

[62] Taking βεβαιότερον as elative, thereby avoiding the idea that the prophetic word is more reliable than God's voice. Cf. Bauckham, *Jude, 2 Peter*, p. 223; Vögtle, *Zweite Petrusbrief*, p. 170.

[63] Against M. Green, *2 Peter and Jude*, pp. 90-92, and Bauckham, *Jude, 2 Peter*, pp. 229-33, both of whom favour 'No prophecy arises from the prophet's own interpretation'. See Kelly, *Epistles*, pp. 323-24, for decisive criticism of this line of interpretation. Neyrey, *2 Peter, Jude*, p. 181, comments: 'Implied in the argument in 1: 19-21 is the value put in the ancient Mediterranean culture on being a group-orientated person rather than an individualist'. Knight, *2 Peter*, p. 62, also accepts that 'private interpretation' is being opposed.

[64] Cf. R. Knopf, *Die Briefe Petri und Juda* (KEKNT; Göttingen: Vandenhoeck & Ruprecht, 1912), p. 281.

[65] Against Vögtle, *Zweite Petrusbrief*, pp. 172-78, who argues that the author is looking ahead to the OT passages which he will adduce later (3.4-9) and claiming that these will not be subjected to a 'wilful interpretation' (eigenwilligen Auslegung). Arguably, Vögtle draws too sharp a distinction between what is to be interpreted and who is to do the interpretation, especially in the light of the author's criticism of those who distort not only Paul's writings but also 'the other scriptures also' (3.16). We cannot exclude the false teachers from consideration in vv. 19-21.

The phraseology here reveals a conflict between how the church at large was taking the OT and how some individuals within it were teaching it. Kelly's comment is judicious and worth quoting: 'The notion of the official church as the appointed custodian of scripture is evidently taking shape'.[66]

The reason why a private, individualistic interpretation of the OT is ruled out is given in the 'for' clause of v. 21. Verse 21 points us to how prophecy originated and draws a distinction between human will and divine inspiration. 'No prophecy was ever produced by human will, but, as people were moved by the Holy Spirit, they spoke from God'. Here prophecy is traced to the activity of the Holy Spirit and God's will. The Holy Spirit moved individuals and they prophesied.[67] The implication is that the Spirit gave the prophecy and *he will interpret it too*.

Can we say what was the aim of our passage? After all, it seems fairly commonplace to stress that prophecy is of divine origin under the inspiration of the Holy Spirit. Two possibilities present themselves:

(a) The argument proceeds on the following lines. The Holy Spirit prompted prophecy, not the individual prophet's own will. Therefore, the interpretation of that prophecy must rest not with any individual person, but with *those officially recognized teachers and expositors who, because of their being set part by the church, are those endowed with the Spirit*. The italicized part of this statement is inference but legitimate inference. To balance the opposition to private interpretation, we must have the official teaching; to balance the Spirit's inspiration of prophecy, we must have the Spirit's guidance of those entrusted with the teaching ministry. There is no place here really for the spontaneous charismatic utterance of prophet or teacher.

(b) There were actually those who asserted that the prophets did speak by their own will. E. Molland[68] has argued that such a viewpoint is in fact found in *The Preaching of Peter* section of the *Pseudo-Clementines*.[69] OT prophecy was of human origin and the so-called prophets were not divinely inspired and died without having known the truth. Molland dates *The Preaching of Peter* around the same period as 2 Peter. Even if a later date be preferred,[70] the actual tradition embodied in it could date from much earlier.

---

[66] Kelly, *Epistles*, p. 324; cf. K. Schelkle, *Die Petrusbriefe. Der Judasbrief* (HTKNT 13.2; Freiburg-Basel-Wien: Herder, 1961), p. 202; E. Käsemann, *Essays on NT Themes*, (London: SCM, 1964), p. 190; Dunn, *Unity and Diversity*, p. 358.

[67] For a similar viewpoint in Hellenistic Judaism, see G. Friedrich, article on προφήτης, in *TDNT*, Vol. VI (Grand Rapids, MI: Eerdmans, 1968), pp. 821-23, and amongst the rabbis, P. Schäfer, *Die Vorstellung von heiligen Geist in der rabbinischen Literatur* (München: Kösel Verlag, 1972), pp. 21-69.

[68] E. Molland, 'La These: "La prophétie n'est jamais venue de la volonté de l'homme" (2 Pierre 1.21) et les Pseudo-Clementines', *Studia Theologica* 9 (1955), pp. 67-85.

[69] Both Methodius (d.311) and Epiphanius (ca.315-403) said that the Ebionites asserted that what the prophets spoke was the product of their own imagination.

[70] G, Strecker, *Das Judentumchristentum in den Pseudoklementinen* (TU 70; Berlin: Akademie-Verlag, 2nd ed., 1981), p. 219, dates to ca.AD 200.

The evidence adduced by Molland is impressive, and he seems to have made out his case[71] that precisely the standpoint denied in 2 Peter 1.21 was asserted by the group behind *The Preaching of Peter* (the second and third generations of Ebionites do not seem to have been as anti-the OT prophets as they). On the other hand, the charges of licentious behaviour brought by the author does not seem to fit them. It seems better to be somewhat cautious and accept that the evidence adduced by Molland shows that such views were current, without wishing to identify the opponents attacked in 2 Peter specifically as Ebionites.[72]

In actual fact, the two possibilities (a) and (b) are not mutually exclusive. The way 2 Peter combats the false position held by either the Ebionites behind *The Preaching of Peter* or others still demands the belief that God's Spirit was behind the original inspiration of OT prophecy and its exposition in the church's life.

We may summarize as follows: the problem in 2 Peter is not Christian versus Jew, but what the author deems to be 'true' Christianity versus what he deems 'false' Christianity. One of the contentious issues is the OT. Against a group which disparaged it, the church of 2 Peter stoutly defended it. It was of divine origin and inspired by the Holy Spirit. As such, it was authoritative, though its exposition should be entrusted to official teachers and not left to the whim of any individual. So important is the OT that the church will not surrender it or brand parts of it as inferior. The Holy Spirit is behind it and this means that the church must pay attention to it.

If this is a correct discernment of the implication of the author's thought, then we have here a further 'footprint' of the onward trend in the direction of institutionalism. The handling of scripture is confined to the recognized teaching office of the church. We have moved a considerable way from the conviction that the Spirit endows every member with some gift and that he may choose anyone through whom to reveal God's will and teach the truth.[73]

Summary

There is evidence that 2 Peter wished to confine the exposition of the OT (and such Christian writings as the letters of Paul—3.15-16) to the officially appointed teachers of the church. By implication, theirs is the activity of the Spirit.

This kind of approach, designed to eliminate expositions unacceptable to the author, is inimical to notions of the spontaneous inspiration of the Spirit who may impart insight and understanding to anyone. Such freedom has become dangerous,

---

[71] Kelly, *Epistles*, p. 325, assents to it.

[72] Bauckham, *Jude 2 Peter*, p. 234, is also reluctant to endorse Molland's thesis, though it should be observed that he dates 2 Peter to 80-90 (p. 158) and locates the discussion in 2 Peter within the debate about true and false prophecy stretching back into OT times.

[73] Schelke, *Petrusbriefe*, p. 202, said that when 2 Peter linked Spirit and office, Pauline teaching that every Christian is Spirit-gifted has no longer been retained.

for, under the claimed inspiration of the Spirit, teaching has been circulated which the author deems 'destructive heresies' (2.1).

It is not surprising, therefore, that the Spirit is not a prominent theme. There is no attempt to 'rescue' the Spirit from the false teachers. Silence on this topic is deemed the best policy, and denunciation of the bad ethical consequences of the false teaching is offered. Rather akin to the approach of the Pastorals, 2 Peter has tied Spirit and the teaching office together.

The author stresses the need for strenuous moral effort in that section which is to be very much 'Peter's legacy' (1.3-11) which the readers can remember for the future (1.12-15). But he does maintain the link between God's saving action and our response, between grace and ethics. He says that all that makes for a godly life has been given to us through the knowledge of Him who called us by His own glorious power, through which precious and very great promises have been given to us (1.3-4). It is for this very reason that believers should make every effort to produce a whole series of virtues (1.5). The list begins with faith and ends with love (1.5-7). They should not be like some who have forgotten that we have received cleansing from past sins (1.9). Therefore, they should make every effort to make their calling and election sure (1.10). The final entry into the kingdom of Christ is a gift generously supplied by God (1.11). This link acknowledged, there is no explicit mention of the Spirit as our aid to maintain this strenuous moral effort, which the author urges the recipients to show in the light of the hope of Christ's coming and the final judgment (e.g. 3.11-13, 14, 17), no doubt to accentuate the difference between the lifestyle advocated by him and the unacceptable lifestyle of his opponents. In moral seriousness, the author is on a par with John of Patmos or the Montanist leaders, but where they emphasize the Spirit, it seems that 2 Peter represents the opposite pole: the Spirit does not bulk large in his thought. One could say that Montanism in emphasizing prophecy and the Spirit was harking back to the original phase of Christianity, whereas in 2 Peter we see that the sense of an original, normative *Urzeit*, to which the church looks back (1.12-15, 16-18; 3.1-2) and from which apostolic tradition it must live, produced a different emphasis from that found in Montanism. 2 Peter stressed tradition; Montanism, experience of the Spirit.

5. The Letter of Barnabas

The exact location where Barnabas was written cannot be determined. Some of the arguments used in the discussion about this do not carry conviction because of their very general nature (thus, allegorical exegesis was not confined to Alexandria;[74] knowledge of Jewish traditions was not limited to Palestine or Syria;[75] the first area

---

[74] So rightly P. Prigent and R.A. Kraft, *L'Épître de Barnabé* (SC; Paris: Les Éditions de Cerf, 1971), p. 22; K. Wengst, *Tradition und Theologie des Barnabasbriefes* (Berlin-New York: Walter de Gruyter, 1971), p. 114; and against J. Quasten, *Patrology I* (Utrecht-Antwerp: Spectrum Publishers, 1950), p. 79.

[75] Against Prigent and Kraft, *Barnabé*, p. 23.

to show awareness of the work is not necessarily a guide to its origin). H. Windisch said that the author possibly lived in Egypt, but either Asia Minor or Greek-speaking Syria were conceivable.[76] In 1971, K. Wengst argued for Western Asia Minor, believing that the school, within which Barnabas stood, shared with the group attacked by Ignatius in Philadelphians 8.2 a view of the timeless validity of Scripture.[77] While his view falls short of proof, we have decided to follow his lead and place Barnabas in our Asia Minor section (despite recent support for Egypt from W. Horbury and J.N.B. Carleton-Paget[78]).

As to date, a number of scholars accept that there is an allusion to Hadrian's building of a new city, Aelia Capitolina, with a temple dedicated to Jupiter, on the site of the old Jerusalem in 132, and so date the letter to the early 130s.[79] Recently, there has been some support for a date in the reign of Nerva (96-98), on the grounds that Nerva's friendliness towards the Jews might have encouraged hopes that the temple would be rebuilt.[80] We need not enter into a discussion of this particular issue.

A. Divine Presence

A good deal of this letter consists of allegorical and midrashic interpretations of the OT, seeking to wrest it from the Jews[81] and treating it wholly as a Christian book, the very details of which pointed to Christ. Can we discern anything that would help us understand whether this writer saw the Spirit as central to religious experience?

---

[76] H. Windisch, 'Der Barnabasbrief', in *Die apostolischen Väter III* (HzNT Ergänzsband. Tübingen: Mohr, 1920), p. 413.

[77] Wengst, *Tradition*, pp. 113-18. R. Hvalvik, *The Struggle for Scripture and Covenant: The Purpose of the Epistle of Barnabas and Jewish-Christian Competition in the Second Century* (WUNT 82; Tübingen: Mohr, 1996), p. 41, thinks that the provenance of the work is still an open question and contents himself with 'Greek-speaking eastern part of the Mediterranean'.

[78] W. Horbury, 'Jewish-Christian Relations in Barnabas and Justin Martyr', in J.D.G. Dunn, *Jews and Christians: The Parting of the Ways, AD70–135* (Grand Rapids, MI: Eerdmans, 1999), pp. 329, 336; his student, J.N.B. Carleton-Paget, 'The Outlook and Background of the Epistle of Barnabas' (Cambridge PhD thesis, 1991), p. 24, thinks that Wengst makes too much of a single verse in Ignatius, *Philadelphians* 8.2, and adheres to Alexandria as the place of composition (see pp. 25-26, 148-50).

[79] Windisch, *Barnabasbrief*, p. 412; Wengst, *Tradition*, p. 113; F.M. Braun, 'La lettre de Barnabé et l'Évangile de St. Jean', *NTS* 4 (1957-58), p. 119; Hvalvik, *Struggle*, p. 23.

[80] See Horbury, *Relations*, pp. 320-21, and Carleton-Paget, *Outlook*, pp. 5-19, 161. The argument that Barnabas would have exploited the defeat of Bar Kochbar's revolt (Carleton-Paget, *Outlook*, p. 17) can be countered by the fact that the Temple had been destroyed in AD 70 and that was the reference in 16.3-4.

[81] See Hvalvik, *Struggle*, for an exposition of the work from this standpoint. Cf. also Horbury, *Relations*, pp. 323-27, and Carleton-Paget, *Outlook*, e.g. pp. 114-118, though not in the same detail. All three see Barnabas' anti-Judaism as motivated by fear of Jewish proselytising.

Joel 2.28-32, a passage which we might have expected the author to have exploited, is not quoted directly, but it does seem to be alluded-to early on in the letter. At 1.2 the writer says that he rejoices because God's commandments are so great and rich towards them and because the grace of the spiritual gift which they have received is so innate (ἔμφυτον). To what is Barnabas referring by this 'spiritual gift'? In the light of the reference to God's commandments, and because later at 9.9 he refers to 'the innate (ἔμφυτον) gift of His teaching',[82] it looks as if author is thinking of teaching.[83]

However, Barnabas continues in 1.3 to give an additional reason for his joy at the readers: 'I truly see amongst you the Spirit poured out upon you from the rich fountain of the Lord'. Since Barnabas knows the readers, his use of the phrase 'I truly see' suggests that he has witnessed at first hand tangible evidence for the Spirit's presence. We are not told whether the evidence is in the form of miracles or ethical qualities, but the balance points in favour of the latter, as he goes on to say 'Because great faith and love dwell among you in hope of His life' (1.4).

The expression which Barnabas uses at 1.3—ἐκκεχυμένον.... Πνεῦμα ἐφ' ὑμᾶς from the rich fountain of the Lord'—is interesting. The verb ἐκχύνω is used of the outpouring of the Holy Spirit at Acts 10.45 and its older form ἐκχέω at Acts 2.17 (Joel 2.28) and Titus 3.5. If Joel 2.28-32 was an early Christian testimonium,[84] then the use of such a word in Barnabas can hardly be accidental. He might be wishing to parallel the experience of his readers with that of the first generation, and the phrase 'the rich fountain of the Lord' is conducive to such a thought.

For Barnabas, faith is an initial stage, and he hopes by what he writes to perfect the readers' knowledge (1.5). There are three instructions from the Lord: 'the hope of life constitutes the beginning and end of faith; right conduct is the beginning and end of God's judgment; love is the witness of and rejoicing based on works done by right conduct' (1.6). Whether Prigent is correct or not in thinking that 1.6 is a gloss by the author to define knowledge,[85] the function of 1.6 is certainly to explain the knowledge, and it does so in an ethical direction.[86] We would, then, have a cluster of ideas—faith, Spirit, knowledge, ethics. Knowledge and ethics develop from a basis of faith and the outpouring of the Spirit.

---

[82] Manuscripts G and L have διδαχῆς, while S and H have διαθήκης. Windisch, *Barnabasbrief*, p. 356, accepts διδαχῆς.

[83] Against Windisch, *Barnabasbrief*, p. 303, who refers the phrase to the readers' 'full possession of the Spirit'.

[84] So C. H. Dodd, *According to the Scriptures* (London: Nisbet, 1952), pp. 46-48; B. Lindars, *New Testament Apologetic* (London: SCM, 1961), pp. 36-38, 253. It may have been this which caused Paul to use ἐκχύνω at Rom. 5.5.

[85] Prigent and Kraft, *Barnabé*, pp. 76-77. See Hvalvik, *Struggle*, pp. 49-50, 61-62, for the importance of γνῶσις for Barnabas; knowledge of God's will and requirements is also connected with a right understanding of Scripture (p. 83). Carleton-Paget, *Outlook*, p. 30, aptly says that ethics and exegesis are partners in Barnabas.

[86] Cf. Wengst, *Tradition*, p. 12.

To begin like this creates the impression that the Spirit is of central significance for Barnabas. Yet 2.2 runs: 'The aids and allies of faith are fear and patience, long-suffering and self-control. If these continue in a pure manner in matters which concern the Lord, then wisdom, understanding, skill, knowledge rejoice with them'. Are these to be understood as the outgrowth of the Spirit so richly poured out on them according to 1.3?

Believers should seek out those things which can save them and flee from all wickedness (4.1). Their faith will not avail them if in these wicked days they succumb to evil ways (4.9-10). So the appeal rings out: 'Let us become spiritual; let us become a perfect temple for God' (4.11: γενώμεθα πνευματικοί, γενώμεθα ναὸς τέλειος τῷ Θεῷ). So far as they can, let them strive to keep God's commandments for they will receive from Him according to their deeds (4.11-12). Taken on their own, we have a moral demand without a theological under girding. If, however, 4.11 is taken with 1.2-3, we would have a 'Become what you are' idea.

We turn now to consider the use which Barnabas makes of the new creation and new temple themes. In chapter 6, we seem to have a midrash on the paradise and promised land traditions (v. 8, citing Ex. 33.1-3), applying them first to Jesus (v. 9) and then to Christians (vv. 11-16).[87] In vv. 11-16, to enter the promised land is the new creation based on forgiveness (cf. v. 14, where Ezek. 11.19 and 36.26 are also quoted: 'Behold, the Lord says, I will take out of those [that is, whom the Spirit of the Lord foresaw] the stony hearts and place [in them] hearts of flesh', which is interpreted as referring to Christ who was to come in the flesh and dwell in us. The concept of the Lord's dwelling in us leads over into the thought of our being a holy temple for the Lord (v. 15), the temple imagery not being elaborated, however.

Christians are the ones whom the Lord has brought into the good land (v.16). The milk and honey of the Exodus 33 quotation are then likened to our nourishment by faith in God's promise and by the word. This nourishment means that we shall live in the future as lords over the earth (vv. 18-19). The new creation, then, transports Christians into paradise.

Most interpreters see a reference to baptism in the theme of new creation (probably due to the concept of becoming like children in v. 17;[88] the clear link later in 11.11 between baptism and forgiveness/cleansing; and the assumed link elsewhere in Christian literature between baptism and new creation/life). This may be correct, but it is not explicit. The stress is on what the Lord does to us: 'He renewed us....

---

[87] N.A. Dahl, 'La terre où coulent le lait et le miel selon Barnabé 6,8-19', in *Aux Sources de la Tradition Chrétienne, Mélanges offerts à M. Goguel* (Neuchâtel-Paris: Delachaux & Niestlé, 1950), pp. 62-69; P. Prigent, *L'Épitre de Barnabé I-XVI et Ses Sources* (Paris: Gabalda, 1961), pp. 84-90; Prigent and Kraft, *Barnabé*, pp. 120-21; Wengst, *Tradition*, pp. 27-29; Carleton-Paget, *Outlook*, p. 87; Hvalvik, *Struggle*, p. 181.

[88] Verse 17 'The child is first kept alive by honey, then by milk. So in similar fashion, therefore, we also are kept alive...'. Windisch, *Barnabasbrief*, p. 338, quotes references which indicate a widespread view in antiquity that a child was first fed on honey and milk.

He made us another type...as if He were recreating us, v. 11.... He made a second creation, v. 13...we have been created anew [i.e. by God],' v. 14...(we) whom He brought into the good land', v. 16.

The thought of predestination as the activity of the Spirit emerges in the gloss ('that is, from those whom the Spirit of the Lord foresaw') at v. 14, introduced into the Ezekiel 36.26 quotation to explain whose stony hearts will be replaced. Presumably, the Spirit is also envisaged as the agent of the new heart, while the Lord's dwelling in our hearts for His abode is suggestive of the Spirit's activity.

In this passage, the new creation theme is clearly emphasized. It suggests a conscious experience of a break between the old and new life. The imagery of entry into the promised land reinforces this, with its idea of passing from the barren wilderness to the fertile land. Then also, the idea of our hearts becoming a 'temple' for God strengthens the impression that the Spirit is important in the initial and ongoing Christian experience.

We turn next to the passage 11.9. Barnabas possessed a series of OT passages on water (baptism) and the cross.[89] He provided an introduction to them in 11.1a, and chapter 11 gives us references to both water/baptism and cross, with chapter 12 offering references solely to the cross. Though the aim is to show that Israel would not receive the baptism which brings the forgiveness of sins (11.1b), some of the material used and explained is significant for our theme. Barnabas explains Psalm 1.3-6 (which he describes as God's word through a prophet) as meaning 'Blessed are they who set their hope on the cross and went down into the water', a clear reference to baptism (11.6, 8). He follows this up with the words of 'another prophet' (though exactly which prophet is uncertain) 'The land of Jacob was praised above the whole earth',[90] and by asserting that this means that He will glorify 'the vessel of His Spirit' (11.9). To whom does the 'vessel' refer? In the context, the writer is thinking of what God has done for Christians. Barnabas has interpreted 'the land of Jacob' allegorically of the believer who has received God's Spirit and so the believer could be said to be a vessel 'containing' God's Spirit. Instead of using the word 'praised', he has opted to use the word 'glorify'. In giving believers His Spirit, God has glorified them.[91]

Next follows Ezekiel 47.1, 7, 12, verses which are applied to Christians (11.10). 'We go down into the water full of sins and filth and we come up bearing fruit in (our) hearts because we have the fruit of the fear and hope in Jesus through the Spirit' (11.11). Again, the reference to baptism is unmistakable. It marks a point of transition from one mode of life, tainted by the pollution of sin, to another whose characteristics are reverent fear towards and hope in Jesus and the possession of the

---

[89] While Prigent, *Barnabé I-XVI*, pp. 97-98 and Prigent and Kraft, *Barnabé*, p. 165, think of a fresh recourse to the tradition which inspired 6.8-18 (just considered), Wengst, *Tradition*, p. 40, believes that vv. 9-11 are traditional material.

[90] Possibly an inexact reference to Zeph. 3.19 or Ezek. 20.6.

[91] R. Knopf, *Das nachapostolische Zeitalter* (Tübingen: Mohr, 1905), p. 282; Prigent, *Barnabé I-XVI*, p. 97; Prigent and Kraft, *Barnabé*, p. 165, take the phrase as a reference to the believer.

Spirit. The Spirit-filled believer fulfils the OT prediction that beautiful trees laden with life-giving fruit will grow along the banks of the river of paradise.[92] Then Barnabas repeats the words 'Whoever eats of them will live forever' and says that this means: 'Whoever (He says) hears these things which are being spoken and believes will live forever'.

Thus, we may say that the sequence of thought is:

(i) the conversion experience which includes the human response to Jesus and the experience of the Spirit and which is associated with baptism (v. 11a);

(ii) the experience of the Spirit restores believers to paradise: they become like a tree with life-giving fruit (v. 10; cf. Ezek. 47);

(iii) recapitulation: faith in the message proclaimed is the means of receiving life (v. 11b—where we might have expected that believers become the source of life to others[93]). This way of putting the matter should warn us against too hastily assuming that baptism automatically per se effects all this.[94] Repentance and faith are clearly of crucial significance. Although the exact nature of the fruit is not specified, it probably is to be taken in this context as the spiritual blessings imparted to the believer.[95] Christians already bear this fruit in their hearts when they rise from the water (this would not preclude in another context the deduction that this spiritual experience had ethical consequences, but that is not the theme here).

Finally, in this section, we turn to 16.6-10. Although Wengst accepts these verses as traditional material utilized by Barnabas,[96] Prigent believed that Barnabas was himself responsible for vv. 7-10[97] and felt that it was parallel to 6.14-15. Here Prigent seems to be on stronger ground, in view of not only the parallel passage 6.14-15 but the hortatory nature of the material and the use of the first person plural.[98]

Barnabas begins by asking whether there is a temple of God and affirms that there is (v. 6). Before the readers believed in God, their hearts were corrupt and weak, a temple built with hands and full of idolatry and demons, because they did what was contrary to God. The change and transformation from this state is described thus: 'Because we have received the forgiveness of sins and have hoped in (His) Name, we have become new, as if created again from the beginning' (16.8).

---

[92] Prigent, *Barnabé I-XVI*, p. 98: 'The baptized is integrated into paradise where he can eat the fruit refused to Adam' (cf. Prigent and Kraft, *Barnabé*, p. 165).

[93] Prigent-Kraft, *Barnabé*, p. 166: 'Note that our author is no longer sensitive to the primitive paradisal emphasis'.

[94] As Benoit, *Baptême*, pp. 34-49, seems to assume.

[95] Cf. Benoit, *Baptême*, p. 47, who equates the fruit with the grace of the Spirit given in baptism.

[96] Wengst, *Tradition*, pp. 51-53.

[97] Prigent and Kraft, *Barnabé I-XVI*, pp. 71-83, esp. 80-83; cf. Carleton-Paget, *Outlook*, p. 111: Barnabas has taken over anti-temple material and given it a radical twist.

[98] Verse 6a 'Let us enquire'; v. 7a 'I find, therefore'; vv. 7, 8b 'Understand'; vv. 8b-9a 'How?' v. 8 'See to it that'.

So, the conversion experience is described in terms of:

(i) our hoping in the name of Jesus;
(ii) our receiving forgiveness;
(iii) our being made new, a restoration of the first creation.

The language is striking and draws a sharp antithesis between before and after conversion. Now God dwells in us. Clearly this refers to the Spirit's presence in believers.

The presence of God by His Spirit in believers leads to our speaking for God: 'He prophesies in us, dwells in us, opens for us who are enslaved to death the door of His temple, that is the mouth, gives us repentance, leads us into the immortal temple' (v. 9).

In this piling up of phrases to describe Christians, two refer to God's speaking through us—the first and third (He prophesies in us and He opens our mouth). All this prepares the way for v. 10: 'For the one who longs to be saved [= the pagan] looks not at the human person, but on Him who indwells such a one and speaks through him. They are astonished at this because they have never heard the One who is speaking (such words) from the human mouth nor have they ever longed to hear (such words). This is the spiritual temple built for the Lord'.

God's Spirit in the believer, then, speaks to convince and convict non-Christians and bring about their conversion. There is no reference here to glossolalia.[99] Rational speech expounding the Christian message is in mind (cf. the beginning of v. 9 'The word of faith, the calling of His promise, the wisdom of the ordinances, the commands of the teaching').

It seems as if we become part of the corporate temple of God (16.9) and thus individual temples with whom God dwells (16.8), a blend of corporate and individual which is also found in Paul at 1 Corinthians 3.16 and 6.19-20. There is a mixing of metaphor insofar as we are both led into the temple and our mouths are the door of the temple (for others to enter) v.9.

SUMMARY

Barnabas, whose OT exegesis reached extreme positions because of his anti-Jewish stance, stood in the mainstream of Christian thought in his stress on the dramatic effect of the conversion experience (within which baptism finds its place). The work of the Spirit in this renewal process is crucial. The language used is that of those who are 'twice born'. The move from paganism to Christianity has been decisive and memorable, and is attributed to God's gracious outpouring of His Spirit. Christians are cleansed and made new.

The writer seems to use five images, not always elaborated or clearly distinguished, associated with the work of the Spirit and its effects. These are:

---

[99] Cf. Prigent and Kraft, *Barnabé*, p. 195: 'For Barnabas the Spirit manifests himself in a gnostic reading of scripture rather than by glosslalia as in the Pauline churches'.

Entry into paradise (11.9-11: Barnabas applying traditional material);
New or second creation (6.13, 14a, 18-19, with v. 14 being a gloss by Barnabas);
Promised land flowing with milk and honey (6.13b, 16b, 17: Barnabas using traditional material);
Temple for God (4.11-12; 6.15: Barnabas' comments);
Outpouring of the Spirit as from a fountain (1.3: Barnabas' formulation). Furthermore, Christians become the channel for God to speak through and to prophesy to others.

B. Divine Illumination

While Barnabas stresses the need for deeper knowledge and understanding of God's way of salvation (2.10; 1.4-5)[100] and the erroneous nature of the present time (4.1), he hopes that he has not omitted anything of what concerns salvation (17.1). It is probably about himself that he is thinking when he writes: 'Therefore, we ought to give all the more thanks to the Lord because He has made known to us things past and has made us wise about present matters and we have understanding about the future' (5.3; cf. 6.10).

Despite his disclaimers that he is not a teacher (1.8; 4.6, 9), he in fact expounds the OT scripture in a 'pneumatic' way, offers instructions and passes on *Schulgut*[101] (material current in a 'school') as well as his own individual interpretations (e.g. 9.9). He speaks as one who rightly perceived God's commands as the Lord willed. 'Because of this, He circumcised our hearing and hearts that we might understand these things' (10.12). The plural here probably embraces Christian teachers over against Jewish lack of understanding (a theme which runs right through the letter[102]).

At no point does Barnabas actually claim inspiration by the Spirit for this illumination and understanding. It is probably implied, however, in the circumcision of the ears and hearts passage just quoted (cf. Deut. 30.6; Rom. 2.29) and is 'below the surface' in other passages where his knowledge is said to be a gift (5.3; 6.10).

C. Divine Power

We need not repeat what was said earlier about the reference to the Spirit in the Two Ways section shared by Didache 4.10 and Barnabas 19.7. Like the Didachist, Barnabas did not further obtrude the idea of the Spirit's help into that section. In the concluding chapter, he prays that God who rules the whole world may grant them wisdom, understanding, knowledge of His commands and patience (21.5) and he asks

---

[100] See Hvalvik, *Struggle*, pp. 61-62, for a stress on Barnabas' use of words connected with knowledge, learning and understanding.

[101] W. Bousset, *Judischer-Christlicher Schultrieb in Alexandria und Rom* (Göttingen: Vandenhoeck & Ruprecht, 1915), pp. 312-13, followed by many subsequent scholars, e.g. Wengst, *Tradition*, pp. 8, 12, 55; Hvalvik, *Struggle*, p. 330.

[102] Rightly stressed by Hvalvik, *Struggle*, e.g. pp. 132, 136, 169, 187-88, 204, 323-4

them to be 'taught by God, seeking what the Lord requires from you and doing (it) that you may be found (acceptable) in the Day of Judgment' (21.6). Here reliance on God's aid and directing is clearly expressed.

Lampe believes that there is a connection with the Spirit when Barnabas says that love is the witness full of the joy and gladness of the works done in righteousness (1.6).[103] But this really depends on reading the Pauline concept of love as the chief fruit of the Spirit into the passage.

Within the main body of the letter (chs. 2–16), the new/holy temple for the Lord has ethical implications (6.15; 16.7-10), but Barnabas does not exploit them, nor does he develop in an ethical direction (at 11.10) the idea of Christians, filled with the Spirit, being like the fruit-bearing trees mentioned in the vision of Ezekiel 47.1-12.

Summary

The further investigations in sections B and C have not added any further substantial material. Had Barnabas expanded 5.3 and 10.12, he would probably have referred to the Spirit. Ethical implications are involved in his teaching on baptism and the idea of the Spirit in our hearts at 11.11. We may say that although there are not many references to the Spirit and although the subject matter treated is not all that conducive to expatiating on the Spirit, nonetheless enough evidence has emerged to suggest that the Spirit is important for Barnabas in the Christian religious experience (see section A). If we discount Barnabas' disclaimers as an expression of modesty, perhaps aiming not to create a gulf between him and the recipients of his work, we may think of him as an itinerant teacher who visits congregations from time to time (cf. Did. 11-12; Hermas Sim. 9.25)[104] or sends communications to instruct the faithful in his absence (Interestingly, he does not address bishops/elders and deacons). That he allowed his modesty to prevail to this extent is significant. Does it also reflect an age when Spirit-endowed itinerant teachers were open to some suspicion? We have seen the evidence of this in Syria in the Didache and Matthew, and how a local church leader, Diotrephes, resented the itinerant missioners of the Elder (3 John). We have also seen how in the Pastorals, Jude and 2 Peter some teachers/prophets were denied the Spirit's inspiration for what was deemed their heretical teaching and loose life-style. The itinerant teacher was less controllable than

---

[103] Lampe, *Seal*, p. 65: 'In Barn. 1.6 "joy" is the fruit of the ἀγάπη which is the Spirit's supreme gift'.

[104] Papias of Hierapolis is quoted by Eusebius, *HE* 3.39.4, as saying that he gathered information from 'those who followed the elders about what the elders reported that the apostles had said and what Aristion and the Elder John were saying'. Papias preferred oral testimony to the written word. If we accept a date of ca.110 for the composition of Papias' (now lost) *Five Books of Exposition* (with Körtner, *Papias*, p. 94) and can assume that Papias lived and worked on after that, we are near the time of Barnabas' activity.

a church-based one. If 2 Timothy 3.6 and 4.3 show the difficulties in controlling local teachers, how much more would itinerant ones be 'loose canons'!

It may be that Barnabas represents a successor of the itinerant Spirit-filled teacher/prophet. He has a definite church base, from which he draws traditional material (Schulgut) and to which he adds his own pneumatic exegesis. With the passage of time, some of the intensity of experience has faded and Barnabas does not parade the Spirit as the source of his teaching. He does, however, think of the Spirit as active in the conversion process and that seems the main facet of the Spirit's work which emerges in a work primarily devoted to showing how the OT is a Christian book, completely misunderstood by the Jews but properly understood by Christians.

6. Polycarp's Letter to the Philippians[105]

Polycarp was bishop of the church at Smyrna (*Ign.Pol.Inscr.*; *Mart.Pol.* 16.2). He had been asked by the church at Philippi to forward their letter to the church at Antioch (13.1) and to send them copies of Ignatius' letters to the Asia Minor churches (13.2).

This letter contains only one specific reference to the Holy Spirit, and that in a quotation from Paul (Gal. 5.17) without elaboration, at 5.3. There is within the letter a combination of statements which recognize our dependence on God's grace and those which demand human effort. Thus, if we are saved by grace, not works (1.3), our future resurrection to a blessed state depends on our doing God's commands and abstaining from all forms of wickedness (2.2; cf. 5.2).[106] Polycarp recognizes that faith is the mother of us all and is accompanied by hope and love (3.2-3). We need to put on the armour of righteousness (4.1), forsaking the wrong lifestyles of false teachers and entreating God not to bring us to testing (7.2). We need to imitate Jesus' endurance (8.2). No one who cannot govern himself should be in a position of church leadership, for how can he enjoin others to refrain from covetousness and to be pure and truthful (11.2)? Yet the letter also contains a prayer request that God may build up the readers in all Christian virtues (12.2).

---

[105] P.N. Harrison *Polycarp's Two Epistles to the Philippians* (Cambridge: Cambridge University Press, 1936), has proved that our present letter probably originally consisted of (a) ch. 13 (? + 14), a covering note to the collection of Ignatius' letters, sent soon after the martyr's death, and (b) chs 1–12, a letter sent to the church at Philippi ca.135.

[106] Cf. the comment of A. Chester, 'The Parting of the Ways: Eschatological and Messianic Hope', in J.D.G. Dunn (ed.), *Jews and Christians: The Parting of the Ways, AD 70–135* (Grand Rapids, MI: Eerdmans, 1999), p. 300: 'The main emphasis of Polycarp's Epistle to the Philippians is moral...the main concern...[is] Polycarp's insistence that those whom he addresses live as good citizen [sic] (πολιτεύομαι) in the present, in order to have any future reward at all'.

Summary

In view of the esteem in which Polycarp was held as a notable teacher, faithful leader, a man of prayer and a distinguished martyr, it is interesting that he makes no reference to the Holy Spirit. We may speculate whether there were any local factors which might lead to hesitation to mention the Spirit: did the false teachers claim such an inspiration? On the other hand, the atmosphere is like that of the Pastoral Epistles, without our needing to agree with von Campenhausen's theory that Polycarp actually wrote them.

7. The Martyrdom of Polycarp

This document, probably composed shortly after Polycarp's death, is a letter from the church at Smyrna to the church at Philomelium, but it was also intended for a wider audience of the church in general.[107]

It has only two references to the Spirit, both within the prayer of Polycarp when he was tied to the stake (recorded in ch. 14). The first described the blessed state, to which Polycarp hoped to be admitted shortly, as immortal and due to the Holy Spirit (14.2). This reference to the incorruptible state effected by the Spirit seems to find a proleptic realization in the fact recorded in chapter 15 that the fire made a wall round the body of the martyr and a fragrant smell ensued (15.2,3). In the end, his body was, of course, burned (18.1). The other is a Trinitarian doxology at the close of the prayer. Neither reference helps us.

What is more pertinent is the sense of God's grace surrounding both the holy Polycarp and the other martyrs. Polycarp was so full of God's grace that, when arrested, he poured forth prayer for two hours (7.2), while at the hour of the torture of his colleagues, the Lord stood by them and conversed with them. They gave heed to Christ's grace and so were able to despise this world's tortures. Such was the nobility, endurance, love of the Master and bravery of the martyrs, that they did not even cry out or groan (2.2-3). Thanks are given to God because the devil did not prevail against them (3.1).

Polycarp told the guards not to bother to nail him to the stake, for God who had enabled him to endure the fire would enable him to remain unmoved at the pile (13.3), a reference to God's sustaining help.[108]

---

[107] See Weinrich, *Spirit and Martyrdom*, pp. 165-66, for a criticism of von Campenhausen's theory of a double redaction of *The Martyrdom*. Weinrich also refers (p. 177, note 4) to L.W. Barnard, 'In Defence of Pseudo-Pionius' Account of Polycarp's Martyrdom', *Kyriakon: Festschrift für Johannes Quasten* (Münster: Aschendorff, Vol. 1, 1970), pp. 192-204, for a similar criticism.

[108] Weinrich, *Spirit and Martyrdom*, p. 170, believes that behind the heavenly voice's command to Polycarp to be strong and play the man, there is an implied allusion to the promise of God's presence and help in certain OT passages like Deut. 31.6, 8, 23; Josh. 1.9; 1 Chron. 28.20; 2 Chron. 32.7; cf. Dan. 10.19. Yet why omit such a marvellous promise for such an ordeal?

The doxology of 20.2 is addressed to 'Him who is able to bring us all by His grace and liberality to His heavenly kingdom, through His servant, the only-begotten Jesus Christ'. Perhaps a traditional doxology in use in worship, it represents the conviction that only through God's help can we enter His kingdom.

Summary

This work offers us a negative conclusion, namely that its author did not have recourse to the Spirit to describe the divine help which assisted Polycarp to endure his martyrdom, nor did he use the idea of the Spirit's help in bearing verbal testimony (as in Mk. 13.11; Lk. 12.11-12). In both cases, the silence seems to be significant. Neither the trance in which Polycarp saw his pillow burning with fire (5.2) nor the heavenly voice which exhorted him to be strong and play the man (9.1) were attributed to the Spirit's agency.

Polycarp is venerated as a glorious martyr, an apostolic and prophetic teacher and a bishop (16.2), a man of blameless life (17.1), but any enduing by the Spirit is not mentioned. Von Campenhausen sees in this document the first unmistakable tendencies to a cultic veneration of the martyr[109] (e.g. 18.1-2, where Polycarp's bones are said to be more valuable than precious stones and gold and that there should be a yearly commemoration of his martyrdom).

It would be a curious coincidence, if 156/7 is accepted for the commencement of Montanism, that the *Martyrdom* is silent about that Spirit which Montanism claimed had just come on its prophetic leaders.

8. Asia Minor Montanism

The original home of Montanism was Asia Minor, though it spread widely beyond this area. We need not go into the dispute over the date of its commencement here: 156/7 (so Epiphanius, *Panarion* 48.1-2) or 171-77 (Eusebius, *Chronicle* 287-88; *HE* 4.27; 5.3.4; cf. 5 *Preface*; 5.3.4).[110] It is sufficent for our purpose that it is a phenomenon of the second half of the second century.

In our quest for the religious experience of Montanus and his earliest followers, we must bear in mind that our two major sources, Eusebius and Epiphanius, are hostile to Montanism and we must reckon with this.

---

[109] H. von Campenhausen, *Die Idee des Martyriums in der alten Kirche* (Göttingen: Vandenhoeck & Ruprecht, 2nd ed., 1964), p. 80. He also notes that the author places no real emphasis on the idea of witness before the world (p. 87) and that he is concerned to shape the story of Polycarp's martyrdom on the model of Christ's passion and so hold up Polycarp for imitation because he had repeated the ideal martyrdom, that of Christ (pp. 83-84).

[110] See the Excursus at the end of this chapter.

A. Divine Presence

The ecstatic experience of the Spirit must have been a feature of Montanism, for both the surviving oracles and the fact that it was the basic issue between Montanists and their catholic opponents are evidence of this.

We shall first look at the evidence of the oracles themselves. One oracle suggests that the Montanist leaders believed that the prophet was a totally passive instrument of the Holy Spirit. This oracle used the analogy of a lyre plucked by a musician. The prophet is totally possessed and used by the Spirit: a totally 'other' activity impinges upon him/her and he/she receives this. The oracle runs: 'For immediately Montanus said: "Look—a person is like a lyre and I am fallen upon like a plectron; the person sleeps, but I am awake. Behold, it is the Lord who gives ecstasy to men's hearts and gives (different) hearts to men" ' (*Panarion* 48.4). The oracle thus draws a distinction between the person (ἄνθρωπος) and the ἐγώ, the latter being drawn out into an ecstatic state by the Lord. The human agent is passive ('sleeps'), but the Lord 'awakes' him/her.

This theory of the ecstatic state or trance underlies those oracles where Montanus and the two prophetesses, Priscilla and Maximilla, expressed their conviction that they were the agents and mouthpiece of the triune God. From Montanus we have: 'I am the Lord God omnipotent who dwells in a person'; 'I am neither an angel nor an ambassador, but I the Lord God the Father have come'[111] (both quoted in *Panarion* 48.11) and 'I am the Father and the Son and the Paraclete' (quoted by Didymus of Alexandria, *de Trinitate* 3.41.1). Maximilla (as cited in *Panarion* 48.12) announced 'Children of Christ, listen to what he says: do not listen to me but listen to Christ'. Clearly, such statements could be twisted by opponents to accuse them of claiming to be God (cf. Eusebius, *HE* 5.14.1).

That in this ecstatic state, brought about by the inspiration of the Spirit, the prophet(-ess) was overwhelmed and overpowered emerges in an oracle of Maximilla: 'The Lord has sent me as a supporter, revealer and interpreter of this enterprise, promise and covenant, and I have been compelled, whether I want to or not, to learn the knowledge of God' (*Pan.* 48.13.1).[112] Maximilla has been forced willy-nilly to learn about God and join in the task of spreading the knowledge acquired to others.[113]

Maximilla protested against the persecution directed against her. She was driven like a wolf from the sheep. 'I am not a wolf: I am word and Spirit and power' (Eusebius *HE* 5.16.17, quoting from the Anonymous[114] who was himself quoting from a collection made by Asterius Orbanus).

---

[111] C. Trevett, *Montanism: Gender, Authority and the New Prophecy* (Cambridge: Cambridge University Press, 1996) p. 81, sees this as 'charismatic exegesis of LXX Isaiah 63.9, with the promise of God's loving intervention'.

[112] Or 'The Lord of this enterprise, promise and covenant, has sent me as (its) supporter, revealer and interpreter, etc.'.

[113] Trevett, *Montanism*, pp. 164-66, comments that her understanding of the γνῶσις of God was at odds with another γνῶσις which distorted the God-Christian relationship.

[114] So called because Eusebius, though using him as a source in *HE* 5.16-17, does not name him.

Secondly, from the catholic side there comes evidence that Montanus and others were 'inspired' and about the ecstatic nature of their experience. The burning question was not whether Montanus was 'inspired', but whether his inspiration was of God or the devil. The catholic bishops' attempt to exorcise the leaders of Montanism[115] reveals an acceptance of possession/inspiration, but a belief in its demonic origin. Also, catholic martyrs would not associate with Montanist martyrs 'because they refused to agree with the spirit in Montanus and the women',[116] i.e. for them it was an evil spirit. Apollonius, an anti-Montanist writer, accused Priscilla and Maximilla of deserting their husbands from the moment that they were filled with the evil spirit (*HE* 5.18.3).

Catholic sources speak of an ecstatic state in connection with Montanus, Priscilla and Maximilla. The Anonymous writer said that Montanus 'became obsessed and suddenly fell into frenzy and convulsions. He began to be ecstatic and to speak and to talk strangely, prophesying contrary to the custom which belongs to the tradition and succession of the church from the beginning'.[117]

Another catholic writer, Miltiades, wrote a treatise arguing that a prophet did not have to speak in ecstasy and that neither the OT nor NT nor the post-NT prophets (Amnia in Philadelphia and Quadratus are specified) were ecstatically inspired (*HE* 5.17.1-2). 'But the false prophet speaks in ecstasy, after which follow ease and freedom from fear; he begins with involuntary ignorance, but turns to involuntary madness of soul, as has been said before' (*HE* 5.17.2-3).

Are these descriptions of glossolalia? Possibly,[118] but on the other hand the oracles are intelligible and those recording them never suggest that the words were first unintelligible and then were interpreted. Probably it is a case of some form of trance in which intelligible words were uttered. When catholic writers branded what was said as 'bastard utterances', it was because the *content* of what was said was repugnant.

Was this experience confined to Montanus, Priscilla and Maximilla, or were there other figures in the movement who claimed to be Spirit-filled? While Maximilla did not expect a prophet after her before the End, there are a number of references in Eusebius' account which imply that many of the earliest leaders were considered to be inspired by the Spirit. 'Just then for the first time the disciples of Montanus and Alcibiades and Theodotus in the region of Phrygia were winning a wide reputation for prophecy' (*HE* 5.3.4). These followers claimed to be prophets in fulfillment of Matthew 23.34 (*HE* 5.16.20).

Montanists claimed to have produced many martyrs and regarded this as proof of 'the power of what is called among them the prophetical spirit' (*HE* 5.16.20). Then also, the composition of a catholic epistles by Themiso (*HE* 5.18.5), in imitation of

---

[115] Eusebius, *HE* 5.16.8, 16-17; 5.18.12-13; 5.19.3.

[116] Eusebius, *HE* 5.16.22.

[117] *HE* 5.16.7. See P. Labriolle, 'La polémique antimontaniste contre le prophétie extatique', *RHLR* 11 (1925), pp. 97-145.

[118] Trevett, *Montanism*, pp. 89-91, accepts that glossolalia figured among the earliest prophets.

the NT letters, could be taken as implying a claim to be inspired by the Spirit with a message.

Apollonius in his exposure of the Montanist Alexander asks 'Let the prophetess tell us about Alexander who calls himself a martyr, with whom she banquets' (*HE* 5.18.6). Now, since Apollonius was writing after the Anonymous who himself claimed to be writing thirteen years after the death of Maximilla (*HE* 5.16.19), self-evidently the prophetess must be someone other than Maximilla! The present tense points to figures current at the time of writing.[119] Whether this prophetess is the same as a certain Quintilla is impossible to say, but Quintilla was a later figure in the movement and the 'Quintillians' were named after her.[120]

All this evidence points to others who claimed to be Spirit-inspired and to prophesy rather than just the three leaders. The ecstatic experience impelling someone to prophesy and credited to the Spirit's leading was a comparatively wide one.

B and C. Divine Illumination and Power

If the ecstatic trance was one feature of Montanism's view of the Spirit, this was wedded to the conviction that the Spirit had a message for the churches. The Spirit gave a word to the prophet to deliver to the churches. The doctrinal orthodoxy of the Montanist movement in its early decades is widely recognized.[121] Its message was not primarily doctrinal, but concerned with spiritual discipline and personal holiness.

Epiphanius quotes an oracle distinguishing between the righteous person and the little ones [or the least]. 'What to say about the superman who will be saved? For the righteous (he says) will shine a hundred times more than the sun; and the least among you to be saved will shine a hundred times more than the moon' (*Pan.* 48.10). The future tenses point to the eschatological consummation. Labriolle is probably right in suggesting that 'the little ones' are those who have not attained so

---

[119] So P. de Labriolle, *La Crise Montaniste* (Paris: Ernest Leroux, 1913), p. 584; H.J. Lawlor and J.E. Oulton, *Eusebius' Ecclesiastical History II* (New York–Toronto: Macmillan and London: SPCK, 1928), p. 177. D. Powell, 'Tertullianists and Cataphrygians', *VC* 29, (1975), p. 43, thinks that Apollonius was describing a revival on a lower plane of prophecy after a period of silence.

[120] See Trevett, *Montanism*, pp. 167-70, for a discussion of Quintilla.

[121] Labriolle, *Crise*, pp. 106, 123-24; W. Schepelern, *Der Montanismus und die phrygischen Kulte* (Tübingen: Mohr, 1929), p. 25; K. Aland, 'Der Montanismus und die kleinasiatische Theologie', *ZNW* 46 (1955), p. 113, and 'Bemerkungen zum Montanismus und zur frühchristlichen Eschatologie', *Kirchengeschichtliche Entwurfe*, Gütersloh: Gerd Mohn, 1960), pp. 117, 137; Trevett, *Montanism*, pp. 84, 144, 155. Indeed, J.G. Davies, 'Tertullian *de Resurr. Carnis* LXIII: A Note on the Origins of Montanism', *JTS* 6 (1955), pp. 90-94, sees it as a protest against false teaching (Gnosticism).

high a degree of ethical merit as 'the righteous person' who fulfils the extra demands made by Montanus.[122]

Apollonius said of Montanus: 'It is he who taught the annulment of marriage, who enacts fasts' (*HE* 5.18.2), and this indicates a Montanist stress on abstinence from marriage and on fasting. This is further revealed in Apollonius' challenge against their habit of calling Priscilla a virgin (*HE* 5.18.3).[123] This ethical rigorism may have had its roots in the imminent expectation of the end, an expectation revealed by Maximilla's announcement that there would be no prophet after her, but only the Consummation (*Pan.* 48.11; cf. *HE* 5.16.18-19).[124]

A stern discipline is imposed, yet, in none of the surviving sources in Eusebius or Epiphanius, is there really any hint that the Spirit is an aid or power to assist in achieving this high standard of morality and piety. The two major themes of B and C seem to fuse together. The Paraclete inspires the prophetic announcement of stern measures to promote holiness. Spiritual or holy law is given. What is imposed must be fulfilled. But *how* it is fulfilled is not indicated. Our sources for Asia Minor give the impression of a charismatic legalism, but they may be fragmentary at this point.

Summary

Our survey of the sources for Asia Minor Montanism reveal that there was a strong ecstatic element in the experience of the Spirit for the leaders and their followers. In what appears to have been a trance-like state, they uttered messages believed by them to be from God's Spirit. They put great emphasis on personal holiness and sought to impose a rigorist ethical approach to life, without our sources giving any indication that they proclaimed the Spirit's help in the realization of this ethical ideal.

Within our survey, Montanism has most affinity with John of Patmos. They share a stress on ecstatic experiences in the Spirit and the conviction that the Spirit impels a person to prophesy within the context of an imminent expectation of the End. They share an ethical rigorism and tolerate no compromise with the world (in the case of John of Patmos, the Nicolaitans; in that of the Montanists, the less spiritually-minded catholic Christians). A difference would be that whereas John of

---

[122] Labriolle, *Crise*, pp. 44-45. Trevett, *Montanism*, pp. 84-86, sees it as less an oracle than a reminiscence of a debate between Montanus and a second party concerning salvation. It is for her an example of the creative use of Mt. 13.40-43 and Rev. 21. But she declines to identify 'the righteous person' and 'the little ones'.

[123] The oracle about not forgiving sinners lest others be encouraged to sin, attributed by Tertullian to the Paraclete (and not specifically to Montanus, Priscilla or Maximilla) in *de Pudicitia* 21, further illustrates the concern for ethical rigorism as a feature of the movement.

[124] So H. Kraft, 'Die altkirchliche Prophetie und die Entstehung des Montanismus', *TZ* 11 (1955), pp. 249-271; Aland, *Bermerkungen*, pp. 126-27. Trevett, *Montanism*, p. 99, is more cautious about apocalyptic fervour and points (p. 104) to the fact that Montanus and his associates organised the movement. Yet organisation and apocalyptic fervour are not incompatible, as the apostle Paul illustrates.

Patmos appears to have sat loose to ecclesiastical structures, Montanus organized his movement with a hierarchical structure, a point which undermines the view that Montanism was a protest against hierarchical organization.

It is tempting to assume that a linear connection between John of Patmos and Montanism existed, but the historian cannot make this assertion, given the meagreness of the sources. The connecting links in the chain do not exist in the present state of the evidence. Yet Montanists did claim a prophetic succession and pointed to Agabus, Judas Barsabbas and Silas, Philip's daughters, Amnia and Quadratus, and on to Maximilla and Priscilla (*HE* 5.17.4).[125] We know that Papias was influenced by the Book of Revelation and maintained chiliastic teaching, as did Irenaeus, a native of Asia Minor. Both were bishops, however. Whether prophetic groups persisted without leaving any literary trace (a not impossible eventuality) we just cannot say: the earlier date of 156/7 for the start of Montanism would make such a continuance more credible.

EXCURSUS (SEE FOOTNOTE 110)

In favour of 156/7 as the start of Montanism, we may mention G.S.P. Freeman-Grenville, 'The Date of the Outbreak of Montanism', *JEH* 5 (1954), pp. 7-15; H. Kraft, 'Die altkirchliche Prophetie und die Entstehung des Montanismus', *TZ* 11 (1955), pp. 269-70; A.F. Walls 'The Montanist "Catholic Epistle" and its New Testament Prototype', in F.L. Cross (ed.), *Studia Evangelica III* (TU 88; Berlin: Akademie-Verlag, 1964), p. 437; R.M. Grant, *Augustus to Constantine* (London: Collins, 1971), pp. 158-59; L.W. Barnard, *Athenagoras* (Paris: Beauchesne, 1972), p. 75; H. Paulsen, 'Die Bedeutung des Montanismus fur die Herausbildung des Kanons', *VC* 32 (1978), pp. 40-41, who reiterates the telling point (made by G. Salmon in *DCB* 3, p. 937) that the difference between Epiphanius and Eusebius may be due to the difference between the actual commencement and the time when the Church began to condemn it. R.L. Fox, *Pagans and Christians* (Harmondsworth: Viking, 1986), p. 405, wrote that 'the mid-150s or later 160s are both possibilities', and Trevett, *Montanism*, p.32, placed it in the 160s. J.M. Ford, 'A Note on Proto-Montanism in the Pastoral Epistles', *NTS* 17 (1970-71), p. 338, placed it between 126 and 172.

Scholars in favour of 171 include P. de Labriolle, *La crise Montaniste* (Paris: Ernest Leroux, 1913), p. 12; H. Chadwick, *The Early Church* (Harmondsworth: Penguin, 1967), p. 52; T. Barnes, 'The Chronology of Montanism', *JTS* 21 (1970), pp. 403-408; W.H.C Frend, *The Rise of Christianity* (London: Darton, Longman & Todd, 1984), pp. 253, 265.

For a full discussion, see now Trevett, *Montanism*, pp. 26-45, who believes that Montanism was energetic in the 160s, and that catholic rejection began in the 170s and was complete by the 190s, with attitudes hardening on both sides then (i.e. not dissimilar to Salmon's position).

---

[125] See the discussion in Trevett, *Montanism*, pp. 33-35.

9. Conclusion

Roughly at the beginning of our period we meet two strikingly different standpoints, those of John of Patmos and the author of the Pastoral Epistles. The former believed that he was inspired by God's Spirit to deliver a prophetic word to the churches, and seems to have been a charismatic leader who stood somewhat aloof from the institutionalism developing in Asia Minor. This very development is exemplified by the Pastoral Epistles, which, while incorporating a traditional saying like Titus 3.5-7 which stresses the Spirit's renewing power, does not on the whole express the Christian life in general or the ministerial character in particular in terms of the Holy Spirit. Spirit has become subordinated to office. The Pastorals seem more typical of what was to follow.

If 2 Peter and Barnabas date from around the same era, we have again an interesting contrast. The former ties explanation of the OT to the churches' authorized teachers and denies the right of ordinary individuals to interpret it. Though he speaks of God's power and grace, he does not quite seem to combine these and the ethical demand into an integrated and harmonious whole. Barnabas, on the other hand, mentioned the Spirit as cleansing and renewing Christians on whom he has been richly poured. Believers are a new creation brought about by God's power/Spirit and constitute the new temple in which the Spirit dwells. Indeed, the Spirit restores believers to paradise in the present. Believers become a vehicle for God to speak through and convince others. The evidence suggests that the Spirit was a meaningful part of religious experience for Barnabas and that he attributed various facets of it to the Spirit's work.

It is interesting, in view of the undoubtedly wide respect for Polycarp and his spiritual qualities, that in his own letter and the account of his martyrdom the Spirit does not figure at all or only marginally.

In the second half of the century we meet Montanism, a movement whose leaders saw themselves as mouthpieces of the Spirit and who saw their ecstatic experiences as the sign and confirmation of the Spirit's presence and inspiration. The catholic bishops resisted Montanus and his followers. Did they warrant the severe strictures levelled against them by the Montanists? In public disputation, the bishops do not appear to have been very successful, but this might only mean that they were less glib of tongue and swift of thought and repartee than the Montanists. It need not necessarily be a guide to spirituality. If Polycarp and Polycrates were in any way typical of the Asia Minor episcopate in this era, the spiritual qualities of the church's leadership were not by any means negligible, even if dramatic ecstatic experiences were foreign to them. But, of course, they may have been exceptional amongst the bishops.

The overall impression is that the Asia Minor churches moved more quickly to a hierarchical structure than did the majority of the Syrian churches and that as the century wore on, except for Montanism, dramatic and ecstatic type experiences were more a thing of the past compared with Syrian Christianity.

If we glance back to the first and second generations, we are struck by the change. One letter of the genuine Pauline corpus was written from Ephesus, namely 1

Corinthians. The difference in terms of the place accorded to the Spirit in 1 Corinthians by Paul and that in most of our sources in Asia Minor in our period is striking. Virtually all religious experience, individual and corporate, is traced back to the Spirit in 1 Corinthians. Ephesians, a second generation Paulinist's work, assumed that all Christians have been sealed by the Spirit. It was natural for him to exhort his readers to go on being filled with the Spirit and to pray that they might be strengthened and guided into wisdom by the Spirit.

But the Pauline stress on the Spirit as undergirding all Christian experience is nowhere prominent in Asia Minor of the second century. Even in Montanism there has not survived any indication that the Spirit's power to help believers to fulfil its stern ethical demands was stressed.

CHAPTER 4

Greece

Paul brought Christianity to Greece as 1 and 2 Corinthians demonstrate. While he may not have been too successful at Athens (Acts 17.16-34 mentions some converts, two of whose names Luke records at v. 34), he founded what turned out to be a lively church at Corinth. As we have seen, 1 and 2 Corinthians contain much material about the Spirit. Any attempt to work out the final state of relationships between Paul and the church is complicated by scholarly division over the analysis of 2 Corinthians. If 2 Corinthians 10–13 do not precede 2 Corinthians 1–9,[1] then it looks as if the loyalty of the Corinthians was still suspect; if 2 Corinthians 10–13 do precede chs 1–9, then some sort of reconciliation had been effected.

Extant literature from or about the churches in Greece in our period is unfortunately meagre or uncertain. Thus, 1 Clement supplies us with some information about the state of the church at Corinth, but the provenance and date of 2 Clement are uncertain. That it was associated with 1 Clement in the Alexandrine uncial MS of the NT (fifth century) is evidence of some supposed connection, but 2 Clement was not ascribed to Clement of Rome by those fourth century Fathers who quote it. Most scholars date it to the second quarter of the second century,[2] but are divided on whether the work originates from Corinth or Rome, though its association with 1 Clement referred-to above suggests the former.[3]

The apologist Athenagoras was associated with Athens, but his two works offer us no material germane to our theme.

---

[1] As C.K. Barrett has persuasively demonstrated in 'Titus', in E.E. Ellis and M. Wilcox (eds.), *Neotestamentica et Semitica* (Edinburgh: T. & T. Clark, 1969), pp 1-14, and *A Commentary on the Second Epistle to the Corinthians* (London: A. & C. Black, 1973), pp. 18-21.

[2] E.g. J.B. Lightfoot, *The Apostolic Fathers*, Part I, Vol. 2 (London: MacMillan, 1890), pp. 201-204, dated it between 120-40: J. Quasten, *Patrology*, Vol. I (Westminister, MD: Neuman, 1950), to about 150, though recently K.P. Donfried, *The Setting of Second Clement in Early Christianity* (SNT 38; Leiden: Brill, 1974), argued for ca.98-100 and saw it as a sermon published at Corinth by a church elder, shortly after the impact made by 1 Clement and the successful reinstatement of the elders.

[3] So Lightfoot, *Apostolic Fathers*, pp. 197-201; Quasten, *Patrology*, p. 53.

1. Corinth and 1 Clement

Here we will only be concerned with what information Clement provides about the Corinthian church, although of course he is not an unbiased reporter. He was intervening from Rome on behalf of the ejected elders and sought their restoration to their former office and the voluntary exile of the ringleaders of the revolt. He is thus an opponent of those who had spearheaded the successful opposition to the former incumbents. He is not an umpire adjudicating in the dispute.

From what Clement says about these ringleaders, is there anything which contributes to our theme? He accuses them of arrogance, unruliness and jealousy (14.1) and also of boastful and arrogant words (21.5; 57.2). He emphasizes the need for modest, humble and true speech (21.7; 30.1, 3; 35.5; 38.2; 48.5).

It cannot be affirmed with certainty, but it is possible that the ringleaders were charismatics[4] who prided themselves on what they claimed were Spirit-inspired utterances. Alternatively, some scholars have suggested that they may have been itinerant missionaries with similar claims.[5] Some of the teaching on speech in 1 Clement is fairly standard, but the plea to display wisdom in works, not words (38.2), may be significant.

If this conjecture is correct, the division at Corinth looks like a split between the established officeholders and a charismatic group who did not think that the elders were spiritual enough and prided themselves on their powers of utterance. In other words, it could have been a renewal of elements similar to those of the situation in Paul's day as reflected in his correspondence. That they had persuaded the congregation to follow their lead suggests that they had managed to impress the members with their spiritual gifts.

---

[4] So W. Wrede, *Untersuchungen zum ersten Clemensbrief* (Göttingen: Vandenhoeck & Ruprecht, 1891), pp. 34-35; F. Gerke, *Die Stellung des ersten Clemensbrief innerhalb der Entwicklung der altchristlichen Gemeindeverfassung und des Kirchenrechts* (TU 47; Leipzig: Akademie-Verlag Berlin, 1931), pp. 65-68; P. Meinhold, 'Geschehen und Deutung im ersten Clemensbrief', *ZKG* 58 (1939), pp. 99-117, 127-8; H. Opitz, *Ursprünge frühkatholischer Pneumatologie* (Berlin: Evangelische Verlagsanstalt, 1960), pp. 111-17; G. Bornkamm 'The History of the Origin of the so-called Second Letter to the Corinthians', in K. Aland (ed.), *The Authorship and Integrity of the New Testament* (London: SPCK, 1965), p. 81; Donfried, *Setting*, pp. 8-9. On the other hand, A. von Harnack, *Das Schreiben der romischen Kirche an die korinthische aus der Zeit Domitians (1 Clemensbrief): Einfuhrung in die alte Kirchengeschichte* (Leipzig: Hinrichs, 1929), pp. 91-92, saw the dispute just as a struggle for power between two cliques in the congregation.

[5] R. Knopf, 'Der erste Clemensbrief', in *Die apostolischen Väter* (Tübingen: Mohr, 1923), p. 131; B.E. Bowe, *A Church in Crisis: Ecclesiology and Paraenesis in Clement of Rome* (Minneapolis, MN: Fortress, 1988), p. 152.

2. 2 Clement

In this sermon (17.3; 19.1), the Spirit is certainly not a dominant motif, and some scholars maintain that we have moved into an atmosphere of moralism.[6] It must be stated, however, in fairness to the author, that he begins his sermon with an emphatic statement of the gospel of salvation by grace. Christians are saved by Christ's mercy and compassion (1.7; 2.7; 3.1), which has been expressed in what he has done for us when we were enveloped in darkness and blinded in understanding, erroneously worshipping idols and perishing (1.6-7; 2.6-7).

The author encourages the hearers to 'think big' about their salvation (1.1-2). The Christian life is to be seen as a response of gratitude for so great a salvation. 'What recompense, therefore, shall we give to him? Or what fruit worthy of what he has given to us? And how many mercies do we owe him?... What praise, therefore, shall we give to him? Or what payment (shall we give to him) in recompense for those things that we have received?' (1.3, 5).

The immediate ethical appeal is based on the conviction that Christ came to call sinners (2.4-5) and that he has called us when we were perishing (2.7). 'Seeing, therefore, that he bestowed so great a mercy on us, it follows first of all that we...' (3.1). Twice, later on, the link between the salvation brought by Christ is made the basis for the ethical appeal. At 9.2, he says 'In what (state) were you saved? In what (state) did you recover your sight?... Therefore, we, as the temple of God, ought...', and at 9.5 he speaks of Christ the Lord who saved us. Further on in the address, at 15.5, the ethical summons is grounded on the prior reception of God's or Christ's graciousness: 'Since, therefore, we have received so great kindness, let us...'.

All this said, we note, on the other hand, how the author constantly emphasizes the need for pure, holy and righteous living in order to secure the rest and life of God's kingdom (4.3; 5.1, 5-6; 6.7-9; 7.1-5; 11.6-7). It is this constant emphasis which has attracted the adverse criticism and which, it is held, overlays the note of salvation as gracious gift. Christians must keep their baptism, referred to as a 'seal' in 7.6; 8.4, 6, pure and undefiled (6.9) or else they will be tormented in hell (7.6).[7] The author summons his readers to keep 'the flesh' pure, in order to receive eternal life (8.4, 6). In chapter 14, to be dealt with below, the 'flesh' which must be kept pure and undefiled is the church. If we guard her (the church) in the flesh, we shall receive her again 'in the Holy Spirit' (14.3). It is clear that in chapter 14 the gift of the Spirit is a future, eschatological one: 'So excellent is the life and immortality

---

[6] T.F. Torrance, *The Doctrine of Grace in the Apostolic Fathers* (Edinburgh: Oliver & Boyd, 1948), pp. 126, 132, bluntly says that 2 Clement is much inferior to 1 Clement and is 'characterised by a more blatant moralism...the least evangelic of all the writings of the so-called Apostolic Fathers'. See Lawson, *Introduction*, pp. 9-16, 179-81, for a general discussion and a balanced assessment of the issue of whether there was a decline in spirituality in the post-apostolic church.

[7] Lampe, *Seal*, pp. 103-104, commented, 'Baptism imprints upon mortal flesh a seal, which must be preserved intact by righteous living.... We are in the unpauline atmosphere of works.'

which this flesh can receive if the Holy Spirit is joined to it' (κολληθέντος αὐτῇ τοῦ πνεύματος τοῦ ἁγίου, 14.5).

This is similar in sense to 11.6-7 where we read, 'If, therefore, we have done righteousness in God's sight, we shall enter His kingdom and receive His promises'.[8]

One might say that the author believes that we are 'in' the state of salvation by grace, but that we 'stay in' by doing God's will and will receive the (future) salvation if we obey God's commands. To borrow a current phrase from Pauline studies, the thought of 2 Clement is akin to or is a form of 'covenantal nomism'.

There is a point in the sermon where the homilist refers to a teaching with which he strongly disagrees and which may afford a lead into our theme. At 9.1, he says: 'Let not any of you say that this flesh is not judged nor rises'.[9] What attitude lies behind this viewpoint?

A number of possibilities suggest themselves. It could be that such people emphasized the immortality of the soul and considered that the body (flesh) was vastly inferior. Yet, even on this view, would not 'the soul' be liable to judgment as the agent of our willing and doing? Thus, a dominical saying like Matthew 10.28 (par. Lk. 12.4-5) *could* be taken in such a dichotomist way by someone not familiar with the Semitic thought world in the background of the saying.

Was it, then, a form of docetism which regarded what was done in the flesh (body) as unimportant?[10] This could explain the over-emphasis, as some would see it, on moral teaching in the homily. We know from other sources that in the second century, if not before, the church faced this form of aberrant teaching.

A third possibility has recently been suggested—that there were 'pneumatics' who claimed to have been saved and were seeking to move the congregation in a libertine and gnosticizing direction.[11]

Before trying to reach a conclusion on this issue, let us first examine the actual emphases of the homilist's teaching in the hope that these may shed further light on the opponents. The author first argues that Christians were saved and received their spiritual sight here and now, in the flesh, in this world (9.2). He draws a parallel between this being saved and the future glorious salvation: both take place in the flesh (9.4). In other words, he teaches a future resurrection of the flesh. He draws a

---

[8] Lampe, *Seal*, p. 100, cites 11.7 as an example of the view that God's Kingdom can be gained by merit.

[9] The people who are propounding this sort of teaching seem to be referred to at 10.5, when the homilist says, 'If they were doing these things [wickedness and ungodliness] on their own, it would be bearable; but now they are persisting in passing on evil teaching to innocent souls, without realising that they will receive a double judgment, they and those who listen to them'.

[10] Lawson, *Introduction*, p. 187: 'the doctrine condemned here may be some form of Gnosticism'.

[11] Donfried, *Setting*, pp. 145, 149, 179. He compares their teaching with 1 Corinthians 15.12 and 2 Timothy 2.18. Donfried's suggestion ties in with his early dating of the homily and his view of a 'gnostic' threat at Corinth in Paul's day.

further parallel between Christ and believers: Christ who preexisted as 'spirit' became flesh and called us, and so we shall receive our (eschatological) reward in the flesh (9.5).

He had in the previous section of his address pointed out that after we have 'departed out of the world', there is no further opportunity to repent. It is how we behave in this life which will determine our destiny hereafter (8.1-6). Conduct here and now is, therefore, all-important.

In general, throughout the letter, he emphasizes the twofold contrast:

to enjoy worldly pleasures now	eternal punishment hereafter;
repentance, obedience to God, and pursuit of virtue now,[12]	eternal bliss hereafter.

The opponents whose teaching he abhors 'do not know how great the torment which present enjoyment brings, and what delights the future promise involves' (10.4). At 17.4, the homilist refers to the coming of the Lord Jesus, and then continues: 'And unbelievers will be amazed when they see the kingdom of the world given to Jesus, saying Woe to us, for You were and we did not know and did not believe' and then refers to 'the judgment when people shall see those among us who lived ungodly lives and dealt falsely with the commandments of Jesus Christ. But the righteous, having done good and endured torments and hated the (evil) pleasures of the soul, when they see how those who have gone astray and denied Jesus by their words or by their deeds are punished with terrible torments in unquenchable fire, will give glory to their God, saying There will be hope for those who have served God with their whole heart' (17.5-7).

Towards the end of his address, he exhorts his hearers, 'Let us, therefore, practise righteousness so that we may be saved in the end. Blessed are those who obey these commands. Though they may endure affliction for a little while in the world, they will gather the immortal fruit of the resurrection. Therefore, do not let the godly be upset if they endure distress in the present time: a blessed time awaits them. They shall live again in heaven with their ancestors, and shall rejoice through an eternity free from sorrows' (19.3-4).[13]

Furthermore, without deeds to back up Christian teaching, the faith will be insulted by Gentiles (13.3-4).

The author may have adopted the tactic of briefly alluding to the viewpoint of those with whom he disagreed (9.1; 10.5), but not engaging in a theological discussion with them, either because he felt himself not gifted enough, or because he felt sure such discussion profitless and only unsettling to the congregation. His emphasis upon moral effort now to be followed by eternal bliss with Christ in the Kingdom cannot be said to help us further to gain a profile of those whom he

---

[12] Repentance: 8.1-3; 9.8; 13.1; 16.1,4; 17.1; 19.1; obedience to God: 3.4; 5.1; 8.4; 9.11; 10.1; 11.1; 17.3; 18.1; pursuit of virtue and goodness: 4.3; 10.1, 2; 15.3; 16.4; 17.7; 19.3.

[13] See also for a similar contrast 5.1-7; 6.1-7; 9.4; 11.1; 15.5; 20.1-4.

opposes, as such a stress could fit either docetists or charismatics who did not stress ethical advance in the Christian life.

The bipolarity of his view of salvation—saved by Christ's incarnate ministry and death in the past and to be saved in the future Kingdom of God at Christ's second coming—comes out in the discussion about Christ and the Church in chapter 14. He says that the church preexisted (it was spiritual, created before the sun and moon) (14.1-2). It was revealed in the flesh of Christ who was in his preexistence himself spirit, but became flesh in the incarnation (14.3). The present church on earth is the body of Christ (14.2) and is the female in the Genesis 1.27 passage about God's having created male and female in His image and likeness, as Christ is the male: i.e. the church is the bride of Christ. On earth, the present church (σάρξ) is a copy of the original (ἀντίτυπος τοῦ πνεύματος, 14.3). If we do God's will, we shall belong to the first (i.e. spiritual) church. Otherwise, no one who defiles the copy will receive the original. To deal insultingly with the flesh = church disqualifies us from receiving the Spirit to enjoy eternal life (14.4). At the second coming of Christ, the church (now flesh) will become spirit. Thus, there is a movement Spirit-flesh-Spirit.

The ethical consequences of this are both negative and positive: negatively, if one defiles the 'flesh' (= the church), then one will not receive the Kingdom of God; positively, if one guards the flesh (= the church), then one will receive the Spirit in union with Christ the Bridegroom. Clearly, the reception of the Spirit through union with Christ is an eschatological one.

It fits in with this when the homilist exhorts the hearers to keep the seal which they have received (= baptism) pure and undefiled (6.9; 7.6; 8.4, 6), or else they will be tormented in hell.

In all this emphasis on the need for a high ethical standard in the Christian life, we miss the note of the Spirit's help and strength. There is no mention of divine aid along life's way and amid its struggles and difficulties in the present. Human effort is stressed. Reward awaits us: complete possession by the Spirit to fit us to enjoy eternal life.

Summary

Judged by this one sermon, the author does not see the Holy Spirit as central in the believer's present experience and life.

We have suggested that the term 'covenantal nomism' might with some justice be applied to 2 Clement. We have been saved, but to continue on to the perfect salvation, we need to live an upright, morally pure life, to eschew all the pleasures and vices of this world, to be ready for any sacrifice and to bear any persecution or distress. So great is that emphasis that some feel that the author has veered over into sheer moralism and a works-righteousness. This would not be entirely fair, but the dangers are there.

If we were to generalize, he is akin, in his moral stress, to the Epistle of James within the canon.

3. Conclusion

It seems best not to attempt a summary and comparison in view of the uncertainty of the provenance of the evidence reviewed and of the sparseness of what is offered by it in any case. We do not really have enough firm evidence to proffer any generalization about the religious experience of Christians in Greece in the second century. It would be unwise to assume that 2 Clement was typical, even if we were sure that it originated in Greece.

CHAPTER 5

Rome

The exact origins of Christianity in Rome are not known to us.[1] Paul refers to no outstanding figure as the founder (had Peter, for example, been its founder, Paul would have had to have mentioned him in Romans). It seems likely, therefore, that those who took the Christian message to Rome were not necessarily evangelists specifically sent out for that purpose. They are not to be associated with either Peter or Paul.

The statement of Acts 18.2 that Claudius expelled the Jews from Rome dovetails into the report in the Roman writer Suetonius (ca.AD 75–ca.140)[2] that Claudius expelled the Jews from Rome because of disputes over 'Chrestus', which is presumably a garbled form of Christos. If this is a correct surmise, it shows that the Christian preaching had stirred up serious disagreement and friction. This could have been the occasion when Christians separated from the synagogues in Rome.

When Paul wrote to the church there, it was a well-established and prestigious community with a wide reputation (Rom. 1.8) and one which, if favourable to him, could form a launching pad to a mission in the west Mediterranean area (Rom. 15.29). Romans 9–11 reveals that Christians at Rome were racially mixed and consisted of Jewish and Gentile believers, with the latter in the majority.

From Romans 16 (assuming that chapter 16 was an integral part of the letter to Rome), there appear to be a number of house churches in existence: this is certainly the case at vv. 5, 14 and 15, while Lampe believes that there must have been at least

---

[1] The latest study, using the most recent archaeological discoveries plus a detailed examination, in the literary and inscriptional sources, of every single person thought to be a Christian, is P. Lampe, *Die stadtrömischen Christen in den ersten beiden Jahrhunderten* (Tübingen: Mohr, 1987), a revised and partially updated edition of which has now been translated: *From Paul to Valentinus: Christians at Rome in the First Two Centuries* (Minneapolis, MN: Fortress, 2003). Other works which may be profitably consulted are A. von Harnack, *The Expansion of Christianity in the First Three Centuries* (London: Williams & Norgate/New York: Putnam's, 1904), Vol. 2, pp. 379-95; G. la Piana, 'The Roman Church at the End of the Second Century', *HTR* 18 (1925), pp. 201-77; 'Foreign Groups in Rome during the First Centuries of the Empire', *HTR* 20 (1927), pp. 183-403; K.P. Donfried (ed.), *The Romans Debate* (Minneapolis, MN: Fortress, 1977), esp. pp. 100-19; G. Lüdemann, 'Zur Geschichte des altesten Christentums in Rom', *ZNW* 70 (1979), pp. 86-114; R.E. Brown and J.P. Meier, *Antioch and Rome* (New York: Paulist, 1983), pp. 92-104.

[2] *Life of Claudius* 25.4. Cf. Dio Cassius, (ca.AD 160-post 229) *History of Rome* 60.66.6.

a further five, a conclusion which he arrives at by assuming that 'those of the household of Aristobulus' (v. 10) and 'those of the household of Narcissus' (v. 11) were slaves or freedmen of these two individuals who themselves were not Christians and who are not personally greeted (unlike in vv. 5, 14 and 15); by assuming that the remaining 14 persons greeted by name would belong to at least two other house churches; and by assuming that there would be a house church in Paul's hired quarters mentioned in Acts 28.30-31.[3]

Much earlier, P.S. Minear, on the basis of his study of Romans 14–15, postulated five different theological groupings and referred to 'so many scattered house-churches in greater Rome, many of whom were isolated either by distance, by ethnic background or by hostility'.[4]

The Acts' narrative mentions Christians at Puteoli with whom Paul stayed a week (Acts 28.14), and confirms that Christians already existed in Rome when Paul was finally brought there under arrest, for they met him outside the city (Acts 28.15). Lampe sees in a Christian presence at Puteoli a pointer to the fact that Christians had come to Rome from the east along the trading route which still in Nero's time entered Rome via the harbour at Puteoli (Ostia first rose to prominence under the Flavian emperors).[5]

After the great fire in Rome which destroyed so much of the city, Nero diverted suspicions away from himself and on to Christians for having started the blaze (so Tacitus, *Annals*, 15.44.2-8; Suetonius, *Life of Nero*, 16.2). Many Christians were put to death (Tacitus uses the phrase 'a huge multitude of Christians', while Clement in 1 Clem. 6.1 refers to 'a great multitude of the elect'). Both Peter and Paul were martyred according to tradition in Rome in this persecution. Theologically, the Roman church was independent of these two figures. How much actual influence they exerted during their period in the city cannot be measured. Clement utilized their martyrdom within his 'jealousy' section, though not actually emphasizing that it was at Rome that they perished (1 Clem. 5).

On the basis of the ancient *tituli* (titles or designations) of parishes, at least twenty of which probably have a pre-Constantine origin, Lampe believes that the earliest Christians were to be found in the Trastevere district and the Appian Valley from the Porta Capena to the River Almone. Anyone coming to Rome from the east would tend to be sucked first into these two regions, both inhabited by the poorer people, and possibly the Aventine and smaller Aventine districts and the Mars Field on either side of the via Lata/Flamina. If in these last named areas, this would suggest that some had risen up the social ladder.[6]

Clement's letter from the church at Rome to that at Corinth shows that, however many different house churches there may have been in the city, they obviously kept in touch and had commissioned both Clement to write the letter and three people

---

[3] Lampe, *Christen*, pp. 301-302 (*Christians at Rome*, pp. 359-60).
[4] P.S. Minear, *The Obedience of Faith* (London: SCM, 1971), p. 27, and pp. 8-17 for discussion.
[5] Lampe, *Christen*, pp. 3-4 (*Christians at Rome*, pp. 9-10).
[6] Lampe, *Christen*, pp. 10-52 (*Christians at Rome*, pp. 19-60).

(Claudius Ephebus, Valerius Bito and Fortunatus, mentioned at 65.1) to take the letter to Corinth as representatives of the church at Rome. At the very least the sending of the letter shows, furthermore, Rome's contacts with a sister church in the east. The letter is one of exhortation rather than an attempt to impose a solution to a problem within the Corinthian congregation.

Hermas, author of *The Shepherd of Hermas*, confirms that there was someone in charge of what we can call 'foreign correspondence', indeed someone called Clement (who may or may not be identical with the author of 1 Clement). Hermas also reveals that there was a woman called Grapte who had been appointed to instruct the widows and orphans and who should receive a copy of Hermas' book.[7]

Lampe believes that as the second century wore on, especially in the second half, the person in charge of the foreign correspondence increased in prestige until by the end of the century, though not before, we have the monarchical episcopate in Rome.[8]

It is in Ignatius' letter that we see what reputation the Roman church had acquired: 'worthy of God, worthy of honour, worthy of felicitation, worthy of praise, worthy of success, worthy in purity and having the presidency in love, walking in the law of Christ and bearing the Father's name, filled with the grace of God without wavering and filtered clear from every foreign stain' (Ignatius, *Rom.Insc.*). The fact that Ignatius begs the church not to try and intervene to save him from martyrdom raises the question of whether the church had some members who could exert influence in 'high places' in the Imperial court.

Though Clement includes a warning to the rich (38.2), he also reveals that many Roman Christians had actually sold themselves into slavery in order both to help others get their freedom and to help feed others (55.2). Quite apart from the sacrificial spirit displayed, this report also reveals that there must have been many in desperate need in the various house churches to evoke such conduct.

Hermas knows of many rich Christians, business people of both sexes. He himself had once been wealthy, but for whatever reason had 'come down in the world' and was economically much poorer than he had once been. Hermas rebukes the rich Christians for fearing lest they would be expected to help their poorer brothers and sisters, and he tries his hardest to inculcate a more generous approach in them and to encourage them to cut down their business interests lest their Christian faith should be swamped.[9]

The economic standing of its adherents did improve as the decades of the century wore on. This seems to be suggested by Tertullian's comment that the Roman church returned Marcion's gift of two hundred thousand sesterces, when it expelled him from its membership ca.144 (*de praes.haer.* 30). Justin reveals that each house church had a fund for the needy, controlled and administered by the 'president'

---

[7] *The Shepherd of Hermas*, Vision 2.4.3.

[8] Lampe, *Christen*, p. 340 (*Christians at Rome*, pp. 403-404).

[9] See Carolyn Osiek, *Rich and Poor in the Shepherd of Hermas: An Exegetical-Social Investigation* (Washington DC: Catholic Biblical Association, 1983); Lampe, *Christen*, pp. 71-78, 182-200 (*Christians at Rome*, pp. 88-99, 218-36).

(*Apol.I.* 67.6; 13.1; 14.2). A little later, Dionysius, bishop of Corinth (fl.180) speaks of how the Roman church sent help to other churches outside of Italy, including Christians in the mines. He also reveals in one of his letters how Soter (166-74) had enlarged this enterprise (Eusebius *HE* 4.23.10).

All this noted, it remains true that even by the end of the second century most Christians were members of the poorer classes according to the character Octavius in the writer Minucius Felix's imaginary dialogue, *Octavius*, between a Christian and a pagan friend.[10]

This might seem to suggest that the rich were giving generously if the Roman church was able to send aid to other Christians as well as help its own. Christianity was penetrating the upper stratum of society and by the end of the century, when Commodus was emperor (180-92), it had adherents among men and especially women of senatorial rank and members of the imperial household (as Irenaeus, *AH* 4.30.1 maintains and Lampe has shown[11]).

Rome acted as a magnet to so many, and certain 'heretical' teachers like Marcion and Valentinus as well as 'orthodox' ones like Justin Martyr were present and active in Rome around the middle years of the second century.

The presence in Rome of many believers who originated from Asia Minor and who had different customs, especially in respect to the observation of the date of Easter (called the Quartodecimans), led to contacts between Rome and Asia Minor leaders like Polycarp. Polycarp visited Rome and he and Anicetus (155-66) exchanged views, agreed to disagree and parted amicably (Eusebius, *HE* 5.24.16-17). The issue of the date of Easter flared up again as a cause of dispute in the time of Victor (bishop of Rome 189-99), who excommunicated those who followed the eastern dating.

This leads us on to mention another feature of Roman Christianity in our period. The geographical separateness of the different house churches, even if their elders or presbyters kept in touch with one another and held consultations, had at least two, if not three, consequences. It meant in practice theological pluralism. There was variety of beliefs and theological emphases among Christians. There was, furthermore, it would seem, a fair degree of tolerance of differing viewpoints. If the various house churches were not rubbing up against one another, theological friction was less likely to arise.[12]

Thus, for example, it looks as if Valentinus was never condemned during his period in Rome, while the Valentinian Florinus was a presbyter at Rome until Irenaeus spurred Victor on to depose him. The 'monarchian' Theodotus, and two of his pupils, Asclepiodotus and another Theodotus, were active in Rome until Victor withdrew fellowship from them. According to Tertullian, one bishop of the Roman church was favourably disposed to Montanism and was nearly on the point of recognizing it, but was in the end dissuaded from doing so, much to Tertullian's

---

[10] Minucius Felix, *Octavius*, 36.3,5-7; also 37.7; 16.5.

[11] *Christen*, pp. 270-87 (*Christians at Rome*, pp. 321-34).

[12] See Lampe, *Christen*, pp. 320-44 (*Christians at Rome*, pp. 381-408), for a full discussion.

disgust. It is not certain exactly who this bishop was, but it may have been Eleutherus (174-89), Victor (189-99) or Zephyrinus (199-217).

Finally, this diversity probably retarded the emergence of what we have come to know as the 'monarchical episcopate'. It was not till the end of the century that such emerged, in the person of Victor (189-99).

The language of those writings which emanated from Rome in our period was Greek, and this may confirm what is deducible from other data like the names which Christians bore, that Roman Christianity was not predominantly indigenous but 'fed' by people coming to Rome from the east, whether as free or as slaves (in this, the Christian community only reflected the population of Rome in general). In the final decade of the second century Victor, possibly a North African by origin, was elected and, according to Jerome, he wrote in Latin. Eventually, Latin emerged by the middle of the third century as the language of the Roman church.

Within our period a number of documents come from members of the Christian community in Rome, and to these we now turn.

1. 1 Peter

With probably the majority of modern scholars we shall here assume that 1 Peter is a pseudonymous work,[13] composed at Rome, during Domitian's reign, later rather than earlier.[14] The letter is written to encourage and support Christians who, the author believes, are about to face the outbreak of persecution (4.12-17). Suffering of various kinds, ranging from ostracism to social abuse to harassment, is assumed to

---

[13] We may mention as examples F.W. Beare, *The First Epistle of Peter* (Oxford: Blackwell, 1958); Kümmel, *Introduction*, pp. 296-98; E. Best, *1 Peter* (London: Oliphants, 1971); L. Goppelt, *A Commentary on 1 Peter* (Grand Rapids, MI: Eerdmans, 1993); J.H. Elliott, *1 Peter* (AB 37B; New York: Doubleday, 2000), pp. 120-30 (who gives a full list on p. 125). McDonald and Porter, *Sacred Literature*, p. 536, conclude their discussion by stating that the majority view today is that 1 Peter is pseudonymous. Among defenders of Petrine authorship we may mention E.G. Selwyn, *The First Epistle of St. Peter* (London: Macmillan, 1946), pp. 7-38; C.E.B. Cranfield, *I and II Peter and Jude* (London: SCM, 1950), pp. 13-16; J. Schneider, *Die Kirchenbriefe* (NTD 10; Göttingen: Vandenhoeck & Ruprecht, 1961); C. Spicq, *Les Épitres de saint Pierre* (Paris: Gabalda, 1966); J.N.D. Kelly, *The Epistles of Peter and of Jude* (London: A. & C. Black, 1969) (with considerable hesitation), pp. 30-33; Robinson, *Redating*, pp. 140-69; Martin, *New Testament Foundations*, Vol. 2, pp. 330-35; J.R. Michaels, *1 Peter* (WBC 49; Waco, TX: Word, 1988), pp. lxii-lxvii (a possibility); Guthrie, *Introduction*, pp. 762-81. For a fuller list, see Elliott, *1 Peter*, p. 118. Defence of Petrine authorship is usually accompanied by the attribution of an important role in the writing of the letter to Silvanus on the basis of 5.12 (but see Elliott, *1 Peter*, pp. 871-74, for a critique of taking διὰ Σιλουανοῦ in this way and not of the bearer of the letter).

[14] There is fairly widespread unanimity on the view that Babylon in 1 Pet. 5.13 is a cryptogram for Rome; see e.g. Selwyn, *First Epistle*, p. 243; Beare, *First Epistle*, p. 183; Schneider, *Kirchenbriefe*, p. 98; Spicq, *Épitres*, p. 181; Kelly, *Epistles*, pp. 218-20; Best, *1 Peter*, p. 178; Robinson, *Redating*, p. 151; Elliott, *1 Peter*, pp. 882-87.

be the destiny of Christians loyal to their faith (1.6-7; 2.12; 3.13-17; 4.4), but 4.12 mentions the imminent likelihood of something more severe, a contingency which supports the dating of the letter ca.AD 90, when Domitian was becoming more and more suspicious of any danger to his own position.

In the salutation of 1Peter, the readers are greeted as resident aliens, elect of God, part of His scattered people in certain areas of Asia Minor. Their elect status, which contrasts sharply with their social status,[15] is grounded in three factors (1.2): God the Father's foreknowledge; their being set apart for God's service by the Holy Spirit (ἐν ἁγιασμῷ Πνεύματος); and Jesus' sacrificial death which affords liberating power to live obediently for God. God the Father's foreknowledge is actualized through the atoning death of His son and the power of the Holy Spirit, to draw us away from entanglement with the world and its desires and into the sphere of service.

What experience lies behind this phraseology? The conversion experience is certainly important in 1 Peter. A sharp line of demarcation is drawn between the past, pagan, immoral life and the present Christian life (1.14, 18, 21; 2.9-10; 4.2-4). This 'before' and 'after' contrast shows that conversion was experienced as a dramatic and vivid turning point, part of which was the sense of the Spirit at work to remove believers from an alien, evil sphere into the sanctifying sphere of God's holy love. The Spirit drew them from evil to God and, within that relationship thus created, they are exposed to God's sanctifying power. The phrases used in 1.1-2 would certainly help to compensate for the readers' separation from the world and their becoming the focal point of feelings of resentment on the part of former pagan friends (4.1-6). The language would help to cement and intensify group consciousness.[16]

The description of 1.1-2 creates the presupposition that the Spirit will be central for this writer,[17] a presupposition strengthened by the fact that at the close of the blessing (1.3-12), the author refers to the activity of the Holy Spirit twice: first, in inspiring the OT prophets (1.11) and, secondly, in empowering those who preached the gospel to the readers in the Christian mission (1.12). Whether this is borne out by the rest of the letter must now be seen.

A. Divine Presence

At 2.4-5 the Lord Jesus is described as a living stone rejected by men but elect and precious to God. The readers must come to him as living stones. There is an obvious parallelism between living stone and living stones. If we ask why can Christians be described as 'living', the prior description of them at 1.23 springs to mind: they 'have been born again not of mortal but immortal seed through God's living and abiding word' (cf. 2.2 'newborn babes'). The rebirth image is used in

---

[15] J.H. Elliott, *A Home for the Homeless* (Philadelphia, PA: Fortress, 1981), esp. pp. 59, 120.

[16] Elliot, *Home for the Homeless*, pp. 116, 127, 133-34, 226-27.

[17] Dunn, *Baptism*, p. 222, came to the conclusion that 1 Peter is close to Paul in its pneumatology.

connection with God's word (supported by Isaiah 40.6-8 with its sharp distinction between mortals' and God's word). In terms of Christian experience, there is not much difference between the word of God mentioned in 1.23 and the Spirit of God of (say) 1.2: both in the end signify the power of God at work.[18]

The author of 1 Peter goes on to offer certain descriptions of the Christian church, including the assertion that the members are an οἶκος πνευματικός. Should we here translate a spiritual (as opposed to a material) temple or a household filled with the Spirit? Most commentators and translations assume the former, but this has been vigorously challenged by Elliott, who favours the lattter.[19] What are the arguments on which a decision must be based? There are four points to take into consideration.

(i) If 2.4 and 5 prepare the way for and interpret the blocks of material in vv. 6-8 (a 'Stone' complex) and 9-10 (a 'People' complex) respectively,[20] then the πνευματικός of v. 5 interprets βασίλειον of v. 9, which is a noun, not an adjective, namely a 'palace' or 'royal residence'. This means that the 'royal house' is the household in which the Holy Spirit resides. Both οἶκος and βασίλειον express the elect and covenantal nature of the community which belongs to God. The focus of thought is not, therefore, on the cultic role of the Christian community, but on its election and its holiness.[21]

(ii) If temple were in mind, ναός would be used. Though Best argued that the LXX uses ναός and the verb 'to build' (οἰκοδομέω) for the temple, in the NT it is ναός which is used of Christians at 1 Corinthians 3.16; 2 Corinthians 6.16; Ephesians 2.21-22 as temples (while οἶκος τοῦ Θεοῦ is used for God's household at Hebrews 10.21; cf. 3.2-6).

(iii) πνευματικός does not mean metaphorical or immaterial or spiritual, but created or filled by the Spirit. Words of the –ικός group describe the essence and

---

[18] Dunn, *Baptism*, p. 222: 'In the light of 1.12 we should probably think of the regenerative power of the Word in 1.23 as being due to the Spirit'.

[19] *The Elect and the Holy* (Leiden: Brill, 1966), pp. 148-59: e.g. 'The royal house of the Eschaton, the elected βασίλειον of the Messianic Age, is the house created and sustained by the Divine Spirit. The house of the Divine King is in reality the house of the Divine Spirit' (p. 159). Elliott cites P. Vielhauer, *OIKODOME: Das Bild vom Bau in der christlichen Literatur vom NT bis Clemens Alexandrinus* (Karlsruhe: Tron, 1940), pp. 146-47, and J. Blinzer, 'IERATEUMA. Zur Exegese von 1 Petr. 2.5 u. 9', in *Episcopus: Festschrift für Kardinal Michael von Faulhaber* (Regensburg: Gregorius, 1949), pp. 49-65, as also sharing this view. It was rejected by C.F.D. Moule in a review of Elliott's book in *JTS* 18 (1967), pp. 472-73. Elliott has reiterated his view in less detail in *1 Peter*, p. 418.

[20] So Elliott, *Elect and Holy*, pp.148-59; *1 Peter*, p. 408; partially accepted by E. Best, '1 Peter ii.4-10—A Reconsideration', *NT* 11 (1969), p. 271: 'The OT texts offer proof texts of statements made in vv4f.'

[21] Elliott, *Elect and Holy*, pp. 141, points to 'elect' in v. 4 of Christ and 'elect race' of Christians in v. 9, together with the terms associated with Israel as God's covenant people in the passage; *1 Peter*, pp. 419, 444-47.

nature of that to which they belong.[22] In any case, there does not appear to be a specific polemic against the Jewish or pagan temples in this part of the letter, though there is a contrast between before and after conversion together with exhortations to a different lifestyle based on the assertions of the change which has come over the readers (1.13-2.3).

(iv) If household is the meaning, there would then be no sharp transition from being the temple to being priests who offer sacrifices, as on the traditional understanding and translation; rather, two thoughts are developed: members of a royal household are filled by the Spirit, to make them priests to offer sacrifices.

We believe that Elliott has made out a strong case for the translation 'a household filled by the Spirit'. Such a phrase would be compensation language, meeting the needs of those who had left their previous 'collectives' and securities for Christ's sake,[23] rather than being temple language serving as polemic against those who said that Christian worship was unacceptable to God as it lacked animal sacrifice and temple.[24] The verse, then, becomes significant for our purpose, because an important description of the church has utilized the idea of its being filled by the Spirit. We are entitled to say that for this author, when the congregation gathered together, the Spirit's presence was experienced.

We must also consider 4.10-11, because of the occurrence of the word 'gift' (χάρισμα). A fairly literal translation of verse 10 (the structure of which is obliterated in modern English translations) is: 'Inasmuch as [καθώς] each has received a gift, use[25] it among yourselves as good stewards of the manifold grace of God'. This clearly assumes that each member of the Christian church has received a spiritual gift ('each' is placed emphatically outside the καθώς clause to which it belongs) and that each must use it for the common good. The variety of gifts assumed in the καθώς clause is confirmed by the manner in which the readers are exhorted to utilise their gift: 'as good stewards of the grace of God which manifests itself in various ways.' Christians are but stewards of what God has given them. What they have received they must exercise for the wellbeing of the congregation. God's grace is manifold and multifaceted. The word 'grace' (χάρις) here clearly picks up gift (χάριμα). God's grace manifests itself in gifts; gifts are God's grace in action, they are a specific illustration or realisation of God's grace.[26]

---

[22] Bauer, *Lexicon*, p. 685: 'In the great majority of cases it refers to the divine πνεῦμα...caused by or filled with the (divine) Spirit, pertaining to or corresponding to the (divine) Spirit'.

[23] Elliott, *Home for the Homeless*, p. 132.

[24] As C.F.D Moule argued, 'Sanctuary and Sacrifice in the Church of the New Testament', *JTS* 1 (1950), pp. 29-41.

[25] Here in the Greek a participle (διακονοῦντες) is used with the sense of an imperative (this usage appears elsewhere in 1 Peter and also elsewhere in the NT. See D. Daube, 'Appended Note: Participle and Imperative in 1 Peter', in E.G. Selwyn, *The First Epistle of St. Peter* [London: Macmillan, 1946], pp. 467-88).

[26] So similarly for Paul: see Dunn, *Jesus and the Spirit*, pp. 206-207, 253-54.

Two types of gifts are singled out for specific mention: speaking (which, while including a wide range of forms of speaking, seems to have in mind primarily some form of communication of God's message) and practical service. If people are involved in preaching, they should use this gift as if they were ministering 'the oracles of God'; if some are engaged in serving, they must do so through the strength which God supplies. God's help in using His own gifts in His service is highlighted. God strengthens Christians for His work. There is an implicit reference to the Spirit here: though not mentioned explicitly, the Spirit is in the author's mind.

Is this a deliberate selection of two characteristic types of 'gifts', or had they become limited with the passage of time to preaching and a range of practical service? This second suggestion seems an unnecessarily restrictive view of Christian life in the nineties. We think that the former view has much to commend it, the more so if preaching and teaching activities were being discharged by the eldership whose existence the author clearly assumes (5.1-5). 4.10-11 would reflect a 'high view' of preaching, without minimising other forms of Christian service since these also came from God. In a household or family, there were many duties even if there was one paterfamilias. In any case, it would be odd for the writer to speak of God's grace which manifests itself in various ways and then be able only to find two examples of it.

If we hold together 4.10-11 and 5.1-5 (the message to the elders), we are at a stage of transition in the life of the congregations represented by the author: the older view (if we may so describe it) of every member being gifted by the Spirit still prevailed, but an eldership form of government had also been established for some time. That being so, there would be the danger that over a period of time gifts and tasks would be concentrated in the hands of the elders, but that stage had certainly not been reached in 1Peter.

SUMMARY

The texts surveyed so far reveal a conviction that the Christian life begins in an experience of the Holy Spirit's activity, and that within the Christian community his presence continues to be experienced, while he endows individuals with gifts to serve the congregation and helps them to use these gifts beneficially.

C. Divine Power

Before we turn to seek for any specific evidence for the Spirit's help in the moral life and other related aspects of the Christian way, we mention the firm anchoring of the Christian life in God's redemptive activity in Christ and the way in which ethical demands are grounded in what God has done for us (e.g. 1.3, 13-25; 2.9-10). If Christ is held out as an example (2.21-25; possibly 3.18-20) and indeed God Himself (1.14-16), it is not that either is a distant figure to be emulated, but the Spirit is active in mediating God's strength and help to achieve that ideal.

The first piece of evidence is 2.5, where the readers are reminded that they are a holy priesthood to offer 'spiritual sacrifices' acceptable to God through Jesus Christ. What are these 'spiritual sacrifices'? Pursuing Elliott's contention that v. 5 prepares the way for vv. 9-10, we must include the proclamation of God's gracious salvation, ranging from spreading the gospel (2.9[27]) to conversational witness (3.15) to the witness based on character and conduct, even without verbal communication (3.1). Doing good should probably also be included, as this is a key concept in the letter (2.12, 15; 3.13, 16; cf. 2.20; 3.17) and contributes to the spread of Christianity.[28] If this is correct, then 1 Peter would be akin to Romans 12.1-2 and Hebrews 13.16 in seeing our whole lives as a sacrifice to God. Another corollary would be confirmation that 'spiritual sacrifices' (πνευματικὰς θυσίας) means sacrifices 'produced or inspired by the Spirit,'[29] not just spiritual as opposed to physical or material, since doing good is expressed in concrete, practical situations. In the context, there is no specific polemic against animal sacrifice, whether in Judaism or paganism, although there may be an implied criticism, just as at 1.18 their previous life and traditional customs were branded as futile.

Under ethical empowering we may also include 4.14. The readers are not to consider the fiery trial which will come upon them with testing force as something strange. On the contrary, they are to rejoice and think of themselves as sharing in the sufferings of Christ. If they are insulted for the name of Christ, they must count themselves as blessed. A reason is given for counting oneself as blessed in a 'because' clause, the Greek of which is very difficult: τὸ τῆς δόξης καὶ τὸ Θεοῦ Πνεῦμα ἐφ᾽ ὑμᾶς ἀναπαύεται. The Spirit seems to govern the two genitives, 'glory' and 'God', though the repetition of the article (here τὸ) is rare.[30] Assuming this (though one might have expected the reverse order, namely 'the Spirit of God, that is the Spirit of glory'), what function does the first genitive 'of glory' play? Is

---

[27] Against D.L. Balch, *Let Wives be Submissive* (Missoula, MT: Scholars, 1981), pp. 132-36, who denies a missionary thrust here and stresses that in 2.4-7 unbelievers are rejected and that sacrifices are offered to God, not human beings. In response, it may be argued that the concept of spiritual sacrifices offered to God does not exclude the possibility of their being expressed in terms of service to one's fellow men and women, while 3.1, 15 should be noted as evidence that conversions from paganism to Christianity were still hoped for, despite 2.4-7.

[28] Cf. W.C. van Unnik, 'The Teaching of Good Works in 1 Peter', *NTS* 1 (1954-55), pp. 108-109; 'Christianity according to 1 Peter', *ExpT* 68 (1956-57), p. 83.

[29] Elliott, *Elect and Holy*, pp. 175-76, 183, 197; Kelly, *Epistles*, pp. 91-92; Best, *1 Peter*, p. 103.

[30] F. Blass and A. Debrunner, *A Greek Grammar of the New Testament* (trans. R.W. Funk; Cambridge: Cambridge University Press/Chicago: University of Chicago, 1961), para. 269(6), p. 141. This led Selwyn, *First Epistle*, pp. 222-24, to opt for 'the presence of glory, that is the Spirit of God' (followed by Weinrich, *Spirit and Martyrdom*, pp. 64-66, and Best, *1 Peter*, p. 164), but why did not the writer use παρουσία as the noun governing 'glory'?

the meaning God's glorious Spirit[31] or God's Spirit who will glorify you? In the former case, the genitive acts adjectivally as a description of the Spirit; in the latter case, it describes the action of the Spirit or what the Spirit imparts and may be described as a genitive of direction and purpose.[32] The context tilts the balance of probability in favour of the latter sense.[33] The phrase 'of glory' picks up the reference to the revelation of Christ's glory when Christians will rejoice (4.13). The Spirit who will transform Christians into a state of glory at the End is already resting on them in times of persecution.

Why has the author used the language of the Spirit's resting upon rather than indwelling Christians? There may well be some influence here from Isaiah 11.2 (possibly even Num. 11.25-26): what was predicted of the Messiah will also be true of his followers. As Christ's followers, Christians participate in the Spirit who equipped him for his messianic task, and the Spirit's resting on them will also enable them to glorify God in persecution. What, we may ask, is the specific experience which lies behind the verb 'rest'? We are left to conjecture, but we may postulate a sense of the nearness of God's presence over against the fearful prospect of human foes and a heightened sense of joy and peace, even when faced with persecution.

1 Peter, then, encourages Christians, faced with persecution and slander at the hands of their Gentile neighbours, with the thought that God's Spirit will rest upon them in such trials. They do not face hardships on their own, because God's Spirit will be with them. More than that, he will prepare them for that day when Christ's glorious revelation takes place.

The promise here is, then, a limited, though significant, one: help in times of difficulty occasioned by fidelity to one's calling as a Christian. It recalls the traditional promise of the Spirit's help in time of persecution and interrogation (Mk. 13.11; Lk. 12.11-12). Actually, since persecution in one form or another seems likely to be the norm, it is perhaps incorrect to call this promise 'limited'. If persecution is an all-pervasive probability, the promise correspondingly becomes increasingly valid.[34]

SUMMARY

1 Peter is a small document dominated in the main by the theme of persecution and what ought to be Christian conduct and witness in such a situation. Notwithstanding this, the letter reveals an approach which sees the Christian life commmencing in

---

[31] Blass-Debrunner, *Greek Grammar*, para. 442(16), p. 228, treat the two genitives as a hendiadys, as does Elliott, *1 Peter*, p. 782.

[32] See Blass-Debrunner, *Greek Grammar*, para. 166, p. 92, though they do not themselves place 1 Peter 4.14 in this category.

[33] Beare, *First Epistle*, p. 224; Spicq, *Épîtres*, p. 156; Kelly, *Epistles*, p. 187, all describe the Spirit as the source and imparter of glory.

[34] It would be unwise, on the basis of this verse, to assume that for the author the Spirit did not constantly dwell in the hearts of Christians, as Beare, *First Epistle*, p. 166, alleges.

the activity of the Spirit (1.2), being sustained and developed by the Spirit (2.5, 9), supported in persecution by the Spirit (4.14) and endued with various gifts by the Spirit for God's service.[35]

Brief as the references to the Spirit are, their implications are far-reaching: the beginning and continuance of such a life, service during its course, and help at crises points like persecution, all are linked to the Holy Spirit. There is no extensive meditation on the work of the Spirit, but enough references to suggest the importance of the Spirit for the author.

What we have summarised above appear as major themes in connection with the Spirit in Paul. As Christians are set apart for God's service in their conversion for 1 Peter, so for Paul a Christian confesses Jesus as Lord by the Spirit's help and has been made to 'drink' of the Spirit. The church as the household indwelt by the Spirit is akin to Paul's idea of the church as the temple of the Spirit, and the thought of each member equipped with their gift (with that gift being seen as an expression of God's grace in action) is obviously close to Paul's exposition of this theme in 1 Corinthians and Romans. With the idea of Christians' offering spiritual sacrifices, we can compare Romans 12.1, where the offering our bodies is seen as living and holy sacrifice well pleasing to God which constitutes a form of worship (cf. Phil. 4.18). Though Paul never speaks about the special help from the Spirit in persecution, he did say of the Thessalonians that they had received the word amidst much affliction with joy inspired by the Holy Spirit (1 Thess. 1.6), so that belief, persecution, joy and Spirit could all be associated.

Thus, 1 Peter emerges favourably from a comparison with Paul (there are some basic similarities without our needing, however, to assume direct literary dependence of 1 Peter on Paul for this material). The comparison suggests that this author had maintained the stress of the first generation on the Holy Spirit as a distinctive quality of the Christian life.

We must now see if that is so of other authors writing from Rome in our period.

2. 1 Clement

1 Clement is a lengthy letter, written by a leader of the Roman church on its behalf, appealing for peace and concord in the church at Corinth, soon after the persecution of Domitian about AD 96. Either a group within the church[36] or some itinerant

---

[35] Dunn, *Baptism*, p. 223, said that for 1 Peter the essence of Christianity lies in the experience of receiving the Spirit. Kelly, *Epistles*, p. 43, wrote that the Spirit's sanctifying action 'became real for the Asian Christians in their moment of faith which led them to Christ and supremely in their baptism...; these events are probably in mind here (1.2). But the Spirit is continually present in the daily life of believers, developing their faith and deepening their sanctification (cf. 1.15; 3.15)'.

[36] So, e.g., W. Wrede, *Untersuchungen*, pp. 25-26, 34-35: A. von Harnack, *Einführung in die alte Kirchengeschichte: Das Schreiben der römischen Kirche an die korinthische aus der zeit Domitians (1 Clemensbrief)* (Leipzig: J.C. Hinrichs, 1929), pp.

visiting missionaries[37] had persuaded the members to eject the elders from office. Clement pleads for the reinstatement of the dismissed elders, as he believes that they had done nothing wrong but had carried out their duties in exemplary fashion (see especially chapters 44, 46-47, 54, 57). He suggests self-imposed exile on part of the ringleaders of the revolt, though the church might suggest to where they might withdraw (54.2).

Most of Clement's references to the Holy Spirit are related to the inspiration of the prophets and other OT writings (e.g. 8.1; 13.1; 16.2; 45.2). Once he refers to 1 Corinthians as written by Paul under the inspiration of the Spirit (47.3). Two passages refer to the apostles: after the resurrection they went forth to preach with assurance born of the resurrection and the Holy Spirit (42.3), and from amongst the converts of their mission they appointed men as bishops and deacons after having tested them by the Spirit (42.4).

A. Divine Presence

In seeking to determine whether the Holy Spirit was of any significance for Clement's religious experience, 2.2 is of vital importance. In chapters 1-2 Clement praised the previous faith and piety of the Corinthians. They were humble and free from arrogance, heeding God's words (2.1). As a result (οὕτως), a profound and rich peace and an insatiable desire to do good was given to all and 'a full outpouring of the Holy Spirit came upon all'. Three things, therefore, seem to be governed by the 'as a result': peace, the desire to do good and the gift of the Holy Spirit. This has led scholars to speak of the Holy Spirit as a reward for the good Christian conduct previously described (1.1-2.1),[38] and certainly the sequence of thought tends in that direction. It should be noted that the whole community experienced the abundant outpouring. If the tense of the verb is pressed, then the imperfect indicative active ἐγίνετο suggests a continuous outpouring unless the imperfect be deemed ingressive, but even this would point to the start of something that presumably continued.

Is this outpouring the initial gift of the Spirit or a subsequent outpouring? One would be inclined to assume the latter. It will be helpful at this point to draw 46.6 into the discussion. There Clement asks why there were factions and strife amongst the Corinthians (46.5)? He then calls to mind certain factors which ought to have obviated such conditions: 'Do not we have one God and one Christ and one Spirit of grace who was poured out (ἐκχυθὲν) upon us? And (do we not have) one calling in Christ?' In other words, they worship and serve the one God who has been revealed to them in the person of His son; they have been redeemed by the one Saviour,

---

91-92; Meinhold, *Geschehen*, pp. 82-129; A.W. Ziegler, *Neue Studien zum ersten Klemensbrief* (München:Manz, 1958), esp. p. 58.

[37] So Knopf, *Der erste Clemensbrief*, pp. 130-31; Bowe, *Crisis*, p. 152.

[38] E.g., Knopf, *Der erste Clemensbrief*, p. 46, though A. Jaubert, *Clément de Rome. Épître aux Corinthians* (SC 167; Paris: Les Editions du Cerf, 1971), p. 74 (note 2), thinks that it is difficult to decide from this verse.

Christ; they have experienced the one Spirit of grace poured out on them. Their common experience of God, Christ and the Spirit should have kept them a united fellowship.

What Clement says reveals his conviction that the Corinthians have the Spirit in the present (the initial 'Do not we have' governs the whole sentence), but this Spirit was poured out on them in the past (ἐκχυθὲν).

Thus, 46.6 can help us decide the question to what 2.2 refers. There was an initial outpouring of the Holy Spirit, and then a subsequent outpouring of the Spirit because of the humble and obedient attitude of the Corinthians.[39]

We note that both passages assume that all the Corinthians have received the gift of the Spirit; both use the same word root—at 2.2 the noun 'outpouring' and at 46.6 the verb 'to pour out', this word root possibly being used as a reminiscence of the Joel quotation employed to interpret early Christian experience of the Spirit; and while 2.2 may have the connotation of reward lurking in the context, 46.6 uses the expression 'Spirit of grace'.

To explain the differences of emphases, we must realise the tendentious character of chapters 1–3 and be wary of seeing in them an exact, historically accurate account of the spiritual history of the Corinthian church,[40] a position surely confirmed by 1 and 2 Corinthians, since these letters do not support the idea of a golden era at the beginning of that church's history. In his chapter 2, Clement builds up a picture of the past to show that jealousy and envy struck even at a spiritually exalted period when God had poured out His Spirit, which leads into the theme of jealousy and its baneful effects in chapters 4–6. Clement has his eyes on the situation at Corinth from the very beginning of his letter, even though overtly he does not seem to come to it till chapter 40. He shapes his description of the past in order to have a message for the contemporary situation.

We may say, however, that 2.2 supports 46.6 in the assumption that all Christians are thought of as receiving the Spirit. Whether this is a traditional concept without being a living experience must be discussed shortly.

Once Clement claims that he has written the letter through the Holy Spirit, and hopes, therefore, to find obedience to its suggestions (63.2; cf. 59.1 where Clement warns against disobeying what God [possibly the Lord Jesus Christ] has spoken through him). The polemical thrust of this remark is obvious: over against both the ringleaders of the trouble at Corinth who may have been charismatics[41] and the

---

[39] Thus we agree with the conclusion of Bowe, *Crisis*, p. 149, note 104, but disagree with the way in which she appears to reach this conclusion. She links the initial gratuitous outpouring with 2.2 and their present enjoyment with 46.5, whereas we have seen the initial outpouring referred to in the τὸ ἐκχυθὲν of 46.6.

[40] So correctly K. Beyschlag, *Clemens Romanus und der Frühkatholizismus* (Tübingen: Mohr, 1966), pp. 193, 329-337. D.G. Horrell, *The Social Ethos of the Corinthian Correspondence: Interests and Ideology from 1 Corinthians to 1 Clement* (Edinburgh: T. & T. Clark, 1996), p. 268, calls it 'an ideological use of history', 'a highly perspectival use of history'.

[41] Wrede, *Untersuchungen*, pp. 34-35; Meinhold, *Geschechen*, pp. 99-117.

whole congregation, Clement claims divine inspiration for the position advocated in the letter.

We now need to broaden our inquiry to take into consideration the general tenor of 1 Clement and move beyond the mere occurrence of the word 'Spirit'.

Clement quotes the OT extensively and he does so to meet the problems of the Corinthian church,[42] though within that overarching aim, it is true that he uses the OT chiefly for its moral message.[43] He does not use the OT in a promise-fulfilment pattern, but to reinforce his ethical appeal directed to the situation in Corinth. A classic example is his citation of the whole of Isaiah to back up his assertion that Jesus came not with arrogant pomp but in lowliness, and thus furnished us with an example which we who 'have come under the yoke of his grace' should copy (chap. 16). No use is made at any point in the letter of the atoning aspects of the Servant's work in Isaiah 53.

The lengthy expositions of jealousy and envy, humility, and order, are all intended to bring about peace and concord, of which the restoration to office of the unfairly deposed elders is a vitally important part.[44] Since Paul declared love, peace, patience, gentleness, self-control to be the fruit of the Spirit, we might have expected a writer following him to have exploited this at some point, if the Spirit had been central in his religious experience. Yet Clement does not do so.

Can it be that Clement avoids mentioning the Spirit for 'tactical' reasons? If the ringleaders of the trouble at Corinth were themselves charismatics, who claimed to be inspired and led by the Spirit, then to have stressed the Spirit would have played into their hands. The apostle Paul, of course, did not avoid the subject, and, for example, in 1 Corinthians 12–14, while affirming the centrality of the Spirit in Christian experience, sought to show the Corinthians a sounder evaluation of spiritual gifts. Paul had pointed the way. It is hard not to think that Clement was astute enough to see the advantages of using Paul if that had been the way he wished to go. That he did not is significant. 'Silence' at this point may speak volumes.

Clement has been seen by many as a representative of that 'Early Catholicism',[45] which, it is alleged, was setting-in in many parts of the church at the end of the first and in the early second centuries.[46] Without entering into the debate about 'Early

---

[42] Ziegler, *Neue Studien*, p. 45; D.A. Hagner, *The Use of the Old and New Testaments in Clement of Rome* (Leiden: Brill, 1973), pp. 131-32; Bowe, *Crisis*, p. 26.

[43] So the well known dictum of Wrede, *Untersuchungen*, p. 76, that scripture in 1 Clement is the great book of ethical examples, accepted by O. Knoch, *Eigenart und Bedeutung der Eschatolgie im theologischen Aufriss des ersten Clemensbriefes* (Bonn: Peter Hanstein Verlag, 1964), p. 412.

[44] Cf. the careful analysis of the structure of 1 Clement by G. Brunner, *Die theologische Mitte des 1 Klemensbriefes* (Frankfurt: Verlag Josef Knecht, 1972).

[45] Beyschlag, *Clemens Romanus*, esp. pp. 350-51; also, though without specifically mentioning the issue, the analysis of Clement's thought by Knoch, *Eigenart*, would certainly endorse this assessment.

[46] See, e.g., E. Käsemann, *NT Questions*, pp. 236-51; W. Marxsen, *Der Frühkatholizismus im Neuen Testament* (Neukirchen: Neukirchener Verlag, 1958); J.H.

Catholicism', we can say that Clement stresses office in the church; invokes the apostolic institution of the pattern of bishops and deacons (chs 42–44); and emphasises order in the cosmos and in the church as a reflection of the divine nature (chs 20, 37–38). He is theocentric rather than Christocentric.[47] His stress is on the ethical and moral side of Christianity. He does not seem to exhibit much sense of the history of God's saving activity,[48] and the OT heroes seem Christians before Christ, with Christ universalising a message of repentance which had been proclaimed before his coming.[49]

In other words, the fewness of references to the Spirit in such a long work and the general ethos of the letter cohere together to produce the conviction that the Spirit was not the centre of the Christian life for Clement.[50]

SUMMARY

We have surveyed the extremely few references to the Spirit in 1 Clement and we have examined the general ethos of the letter. These combine to produce the conviction that the Spirit was not central to the Christian life for Clement. His tremendous stress on order and pattern in the church and his strong ethical emphasis together suggest that the concept of the free, sovereign, unexpected, explosive activity of the Spirit would be uncomfortable, perhaps even threatening, to Clement. While he may have claimed to be in line with Paul, we can only say that on the issue of the relation of the Spirit to the Christian life and experience, Clement was un-Pauline. Where Paul held together order and Spirit, in 1 Clement the balance has tipped wholly to the side of order, and the Spirit has been subordinated to order.

3. The Shepherd of Hermas

The next piece of Christian literature emanating from Rome is *The Shepherd of Hermas*. I shall assume the view that the work is the product of a period extending perhaps from ca.AD 100 to 140.[51] The earliest portions may have overlapped with

---

Elliott, 'A Catholic Gospel: Reflections on "Early Catholicism" in the New Testament', *CBQ* 31 (1969), pp. 213-33. See Dunn, *Unity and Diversity*, pp. 341-66, for a useful survey.

[47] Beyschlag, *Clemens Romanus*, p. 350; Knoch, *Eigenart*, pp. 100, 150, 160-61, 309, 420-48. Harnack, *1 Clemensbrief*, p. 61, described Clement's theology as 'a living theism'.

[48] Wrede, *Untersuchungen*, pp. 97-99; Harnack, *1 Clemensbrief*, pp. 66-71; Knoch, *Eigenart*, pp. 411-18.

[49] See 7.4-7; Harnack, *1 Clemensbrief*, pp. 78-79; Knoch, *Eigenart*, pp. 266-68, 418.

[50] Wrede, *Untersuchungen*, pp. 106-107: 'πνεῦμα is not a characteristic concept in the letter'; Harnack, *1 Clemensbriefe*, p. 75, noted the renewed outpouring of the Spirit in 2.2 and 46.6, but said that there was no pneumatic enthusiasm in the letter or the church.

[51] This is the view of R. Joly, *Hermas le Pasteur* (SC 53; Paris: Les Editions du Cerf, 1958); 'Hermas et le Pasteur', *VC* 21 (1967), pp. 201-18; L.W. Barnard, *Studies in the Apostolic Fathers and their Background* (Oxford: Blackwell, 1966), pp. 154, 156 (modified somewhat to emphasise the distinctiveness of Visions 1–4 and Vision 5 to the

Clement if the Clement of Vision 5.4.3 is the same as the author of 1 Clement, as many scholars believe. On the other hand, the *Muratorian Canon* stated that Hermas was the brother of Pius I and wrote during Pius' episcopate (ca.140-155). The theory of composition over a period could accommodate these two points, plus the fact that within the work there are examples of the development and extension of imagery, (e.g. the tower in Vision 3 is much elaborated in Similitude 9), suggesting that Hermas took up and reworked earlier material of his.

There is far more on the Spirit in *The Shepherd* than in 1 Clement. In one sense, this is what we might expect, since Hermas receives visions under the inspiration of the Spirit (e.g. Vision 1.1.3) and instructions from a heavenly being (the Shepherd), while Clement is rational, sober and non-mystical.

Before we look at Hermas' references to the Spirit, it will be as well to formulate an impression of his position or standing in the church at Rome. While the messages he receives are to be handed on to the leaders of the church (Vision 2.2.6; 2.4.2-3), it seems as if Hermas feels himself to be inferior to the elders, judging by the scene when the Lady has to bid him sharply to sit down, whereas Hermas was avoiding the seats as fitting for the elders but not for himself (Vision 3.1.8-9). Indeed, L.W. Barnard has gone so far as to formulate the position as follows: 'It seems very probably that this is a reflection of his own feelings when first allowed to deliver one of his visions to the Roman church... Behind this scene we sense a certain reluctance in recognizing Hermas' prophetic gift... The Roman church...must have sensed the strangeness of his visions'.[52] On the other hand, it has been correctly pointed out that in Mandate 11, Hermas does not have to argue for prophecy — it is

---

end, in 'The Shepherd of Hermas in Recent Study', *HJ* 9 [1968], p. 32); J. Reiling, *Hermas and Christian Prophecy* (Leiden: Brill, 1973), pp. 23-24; N. Brox, *Der Hirt des Hermas* (Göttigen: Vandenhoeck & Ruprecht, 1991), p. 25 (adding that the problem of dating has not really been solved); Carolyn Osiek, *Shepherd of Hermas: A Commentary* (Hermeneia; Minneapolis, MN: Fortress, 1999), p. 19. Lampe, *Christen*, p. 172, note 157 (*Christians at Rome*, p. 206, note 1), also dates it towards the middle of the second century.

Recently, J.C. Wilson has argued for a date 'towards the end of the first century, perhaps even as early as 80 AD' (*Toward a Reassessment of the Shepherd of Hermas: Its Date and Pneumatology* [Lewiston: Mellen, 1993], p. 7. For him (pp. 9-61), the *terminus a quo* is the Neronian persecution of AD 64-65 and the *terminus ad quem* is the rise of Clement to the Roman episcopate 92-100, if the episcopate had developed by then. He points out that Origen took the Hermas of Romans 16.14 as the author of *The Shepherd*. But the references to persecution can hardly be pinned down with such precision; the evidence for a monarchical episcopate at Rome before well on in the second century, if not towards the very close, is very insecure; and Origen's opinion about the Hermas of Romans 16.14 can hardly carry much weight. Fox, *Pagans and*, p. 381, places it in the 90s and rejects the idea of a staged composition, while H.O. Maier, *The Social Setting of the Ministry as Reflected in the Writings of Hermas, Clement and Ignatius* (Waterloo, ON: Wilfred Laurier University Press, 1991), p. 58, also dates the work 'some time near the end of the first century'.

[52] Barnard, *Studies*, pp. 153-54.

accepted;⁵³ but what he aims to do is to offer tests to distinguish the true and the false prophet and offer criticism of those Christians who turn to the latter. Furthermore, Hermas is strongly convinced of the reality of his call to proclaim a second repentance, and he certainly does not mince his words at times in criticizing the existing church leaders; indeed, in the same Vision 3, he is commanded to summon them to repent and cleanse their hearts, for they are carrying poison in their hearts, they are hard-hearted and they need to stop their quarrelling with one another (3.9.7-10), while in Similitude 8.7.4 they are accused of quarrelling over 'the chief places' and in Similitude 9.26.2 some deacons are accused of embezzling the funds which should have been used for the benefit of widows and orphans, though 9.27.1-3 knows of bishops, probably the same as elders/presbyters, who have properly cared for widows and the needy and have been hospitable to visitors. Barnard may have somewhat exaggerated the position, therefore, and while there may be some respect for the office of elders, it does not necessarily mean that Hermas had a sense of inferiority over against the individual holders of the office.

If this is a correct reading of the situation, then we have to say that Hermas is not necessarily typical of the leadership of the Roman church at the time.⁵⁴ We shall have to remember this, as we consider how representative in the Roman church his views about the Spirit might have been.

A and B. Divine Presence and Illumination

In Vision 1.1.3, Hermas recounts how, when on a journey to Cumae, he fell asleep and the Spirit took hold of him (καὶ πνεῦμα με ἔλαβεν) and brought him through a place with no roads to a level country where he began to pray and was granted a vision of Rhoda, his former owner, whom he had desired. She bids him repent.

Vision 2.1.1 is similarly introduced by a reference to the Spirit's taking hold of him (this time αἴρει is used) and leading him away to the same place, a year later. This time an aged woman appears. The remaining visions do not contain a reference to the Spirit. The third one follows frequent fasting and entreaty to the Lord to give him the promised further revelation. Twenty days later he has a fourth vision in which he meets the great beast while walking along the Campanian way. Finally, the glorious figure of the Shepherd appears to him to pass on commands and parables (Vision 5).

Although the two occurrences of 'Spirit' lack the article, we have here assumed that the Spirit of God is meant,⁵⁵ on the grounds that these references are reminiscent

---

⁵³ Osiek, *Shepherd*, pp. 23, 240-41.

⁵⁴ Brox, *Hirt*, p. 23, says that Hermas is only typical for one or possibly one part of many congregations of Rome.

⁵⁵ Against Dibelius, *Hirt*, pp. 430, 432, and Osiek, *Shepherd*, pp. 41, 43, both of whom assume 'a spirit' and acknowledge the possibility of a play on spirit/wind in πνεῦμα, and against Brox, *Hirt*, pp. 81, 543, who maintains that the spirit who catches Hermas away is an angel, but the echoes of Ezekiel and Revelation seem too striking to allow this.

of both the experiences described by John of Patmos in the book of Revelation (17.3; 21.10), with which they would be roughly contemporary if Visions 1–4 were dated ca.AD 100, and of Ezekiel's experiences (Ezek. 8.3; 11.1, 24; cf. 40.2).

It is worth pointing out that Hermas receives these visions when he is on his own and not within the worshipping and praying community (the importance of the believing congregation is something stressed in Mandate 11), though, after the initial vision, the visions are to be passed on to the church, for they contain messages for the church (2.4.2-3; 3.8.11; 4.4.5-6; and 5.7 leads on into the Mandates for the church). Though received in solitude, the messages are for God's people in the church.

When Hermas speaks about true and false prophecy in Mandate11, the link between the Holy Spirit and inspiration to speak comes out clearly.[56] Whereas the false prophet gives answers to inquiries from people, the true Spirit of God speaks when God himself determines, not human beings (11.2, 8). From what Hermas says, the false prophet is really a fortune-teller or diviner, giving people information that would be beneficial to them in their various concerns and business enterprises. The false prophet receives money for his advice, whereas 'can the divine Spirit receive money and prophesy? It is not possible for a prophet to do this...' (11.12). Again, the implication is that God's Spirit cannot be controlled or induced by humans. So Hermas can conclude that the false prophet is not filled with the power of the divine Spirit, whereas the true prophet is filled by the Holy Spirit (11.2, 8).

The true prophet responds to the 'atmosphere' of a gathering of godly people: 'When the person who has the divine Spirit comes into an assembly of righteous persons who have faith in the divine Spirit and intercession is made to God by the gathering of those persons, then the angel of the prophetic Spirit who is attached to the person fills that person, and he, filled with the Holy Spirit, speaks to the multitude as the Lord wills. In this way, then, the Spirit of the Deity shall be manifest. This, then, is the greatness of the power as touching the Spirit of the Deity of the Lord' (11.9-10). It is as if the believing congregation indwelt by the Spirit provides the right setting for the Spirit to inspire the true prophet to speak.

The reverse is said about the false prophet: 'when he comes into the assembly full of righteous persons who have the Spirit of Deity and intercession is made from them, that man is emptied and the earthly spirit flees from him in fear and that man is struck dumb and is totally shattered, being unable to utter a word' (11.14). The false prophet is thus exposed. His 'emptiness' is shown up. The conclusion is: 'Trust the Spirit who comes from God and has power' (11.17).

---

[56] We note that in this description the true prophet appears to have the Holy Spirit (the author uses ὁ ἔχων τὸ πνεῦμα τὸ θεῖον at 7, 8, 9 and 14, or πνευματοφόρος εἶναι at 16) and yet is also filled with the Holy Spirit (πληθεὶς τῷ πνεύματι τῷ ἁγίῳ at 9) for a particular occasion to deliver a message from God. This is comparable to the way in Acts both Peter and Paul are men of the Spirit and equally are said to be filled with the Spirit on particular occasions (Acts 4.8; 13.9. The same seems true of Stephen too in Acts 6.10; 7.55). Cf. Wilson, *Reassessment*, pp. 100-101.

Hermas illustrates the difference between the Divine Spirit and earthly spirits: a squirt of water ejected upwards falls to the ground, whereas a hailstone falling from above is painful when it lands on someone's head (11.18-20). 'Small things falling from above on earth have great power. So likewise the divine Spirit coming from above is powerful' (11.21). Clearly, in this line of argument, God's Spirit is powerful, so powerful as to cause lesser spirits to flee, whereas the earthly spirit has 'no power for it comes from the devil' (11.17).

Both in the Visions and Mandate 11 the Spirit is seen as the power behind the prophet's inspiration, in visions and prophecy. He impels the prophet to speak God's word to the congregation.

C. Divine Power

Of greatest interest really is the ethical side of Hermas' teaching on the Spirit. For Hermas, a person's flesh is a vessel, in whom the Holy Spirit may dwell. God makes the Spirit dwell in it (Mand. 3.1; 5.2.7; 10.2.5-6; Sim. 5.7.1). This is analogous to certain Christological statements which Hermas makes: God made the Holy Spirit dwell in the Son's flesh (Sim. 5.6.5); and this flesh served and co-operated with the Spirit; and, as a result, was chosen to be the Spirit's companion (Sim. 5.6.6). On the analogy of the reward to the Son who had served the Spirit blamelessly, 'all flesh in which the Holy Spirit has dwelt shall receive a reward if it be found undefiled and spotless' (5.6.7).[57] To defile the flesh is to defile the Spirit who is its partner (5.7.1-2).

There is no flesh-Spirit antithesis such as we find in the NT, in Paul and John especially. Of course, for Paul the body is the temple of the Spirit and the Christian is called on to glorify God in the body, but 'flesh' and 'Spirit' are a person under sin and a person in Christ respectively. Hermas is using 'flesh' of a person's physical being —hence the idea of the vessel in which the Spirit dwells. Thus, at this point, Hermas illustrates how in the post-apostolic era the Pauline distinction between σῶμα and σάρξ[58] tended to fall into disuse.

When we press the inquiry into Hermas' understanding further, we are confronted by a (in one sense) bewildering blend of the Spirit seen on the one hand in terms of power, strength, help and assistance for the Christian, and on the other hand the Spirit as delicate and powerless in the face of opposition from evil. We shall first set out this combination.

There is a very long and involved allegory in Similitude 9. Without going into all the details, we may mention that it is concerned (as in Vision 3) with a Tower (which represents the church) and a variety of stones (which represent people fit or

---

[57] Wilson, *Reassessment*, p. 135, remarks that here Hermas is drawing the implications for human beings of his parable about the Son, namely that Christians must live undefiled lives to gain salvation, a position which, Wilson points out, is very different from Paul's.

[58] Paul was not always consistent in his terminology: e.g., he could refer to the need to put to death the deeds of the body (Rom. 8.12).

not fit to be part of the tower). The tower is built on a rock (in vision 3 it was built on waters, which is an allusion to baptism) and has a door (the Son of God is in fact both of these). Twelve virgins are seen by Hermas standing near the tower and then they carry the stones through the gate (contrast Vis. 3.8.2 where Hermas saw seven women standing around the Tower and where the seven are explained as faith, self-control, simplicity, knowledge, innocence, reverence and love, and it is said that whoever serves them and can master their works will be part of the tower, 3.8.8). These twelve virgins are said to be faith, temperance, power, patience, simplicity, guilelessness, purity, cheerfulness, truth, understanding, concord and love. There is an increase here from seven in the earlier writing (Vis. 3) to twelve: in Vision 3, the number seven may have been chosen because it is the perfect number[59] or because seven represents the same type of thinking as in Revelation, where the seven spirits stand for the Holy Spirit, while the number twelve in Similitude 9 may evoke the number of the twelve tribes of Israel and, possibly, since entry into God's Kingdom depends on receiving these virgins, there may be the symbolism of God's true people, the new Israel, in the background.

One aspect of the allegory is that these virgins bring stones for incorporation into the building of the tower, at which point the colour of the stones becomes white. This indicates the spiritual transformation brought about by the Holy Spirit (represented by the virgins) to enable believers to be received into the kingdom of God. If the stones are not carried by the virgins, they cannot change their colour and so cannot become part of the tower (Sim. 9.2-4).

These virgins are virtues personified, and yet they also stand for 'the powers of the Son of God' (9.13.2) who is the Spirit of God (9.1.1; cf. 5.5.2). Later, the virgins are described as holy spirits. In other words, the one Holy Spirit's activities are personified as virgins (9.13.2).[60]

Another level of the allegory comes in Similitude 9.13. The imagery shifts to putting on appropriate garments. Believers need to clothe themselves with the garment of these virgins in order to enter the kingdom of God (9.13.2-3). A distinction is drawn between just bearing the name and bearing the power. The first is not enough; the second is vital (Hermas knows the same point which 2 Tim. 3.5 makes). Those deemed fit to belong to the tower are those who have believed in the Lord through His Son and have clothed themselves with these spirits (9.13.5, 7). The close link between the Holy Spirit and an ethical lifestyle pleasing to God is thus set forth.

Thus, several themes meet us in this allegory: believing and bearing the name, which are to be linked with baptism, the need to progress and go on beyond baptism, and in the strength of the Holy Spirit to live a life in step with God's will and way.

---

[59] Dibelius, *Hirt*, pp. 472-73.

[60] Later, in 9.24.2, in yet another allegory—that of the seventh mountain—believers are described as those 'clothed in the Holy Spirit of these virgins'. They are people who show mercy and help people. 9.24.4 concludes with an exhortation to believers to remain as they are, 'for you have received of his Spirit'.

Verbal confession is not enough; faith must work itself out in moral virtues and deeds.

In the allegory, the opposite of the twelve good virgins are the twelve women clad in black (9.13), who represent vices (9.15). Some believers are guilty of desiring them and wanting to put on their power and put off the garment and power of the virgins (9.13.8), as a result of which they were rejected from the house of God (9.13.9). Clearly, we have here a picture of believers succumbing to evil influences and temptations, which lure them away from full loyalty to Christ, from following the guidance of the Spirit and from fellowship with their fellow-believers (such as the temptation for the rich to get more and more entangled in business affairs to the detriment and possible destruction of their faith, which is touched on for example in Sim. 8.8.1; 9.20.1-2).

By contrast those believers who 'put on these spirits (of the virgins) will become one spirit and one body... They all received the name of the Son of God and the power of these virgins. By receiving these spirits they were strengthened...' (9.13.5, 7). Two points may be made. Firstly, there is the idea of becoming one spirit and one body, which may have been influenced by the kind of assertion now visible at Ephesians 4.4[61] or possibly by Paul's assertion that the believer who is an organ or member of Christ and joined to the Lord is one spirit with him (1 Cor. 6.17). For Paul, the believer is bodily part of Christ and one spiritually with him, and this is followed in 1 Corinthians 6.19 by Paul's assertion that our bodies are the temple of the Holy Spirit. For Paul, in experience, our union with Christ and the indwelling of the Spirit are the same. In Hermas, the expression is intended to assert the unity of believers, which stems from a common experience of 'the powers of the virgins', i.e., the Holy Spirit.

The other point is that the association of these virgins and power is clearly set forth. Believers are strengthened when they receive the power of these virgins/Holy Spirit.[62]

We need not repeat the evidence of the Spirit's power in Mandate 11 when Hermas was writing about true and false prophecy, but we may now note the ethical dimension involved in the true and false prophets. Their characters differ: the latter are arrogant and constantly push themselves to the fore, whereas the true prophet is gentle, tranquil, humble and morally upright. The implication is clearly that there are some qualities of character incompatible with inspiration by the Spirit, while

---

[61] So Osiek, *Shepherd*, pp. 235-36.

[62] There is a mixture of the virgins standing for personification of virtues and for the Holy Spirit and also of one Holy Spirit and holy spirits, which can be all rather confusing! John of Patmos had, of course, spoken of seven spirits standing for the one Spirit of God (so there is no need to accuse Hermas of a contradiction here, as Wilson, *Reassessment*, p. 154, rightly pointed out). Paul's list of the fruit of the Spirit in Gal. 5.22 could easily lead another author into the kind of allegory we find in Similitude 9 in Hermas, while the figure of a woman standing for God's people in the OT could be 'midwife' to the use of virgins = the Spirit of God. See below, pp. 160-61, for further discussion of possible influences on Hermas' modes of expression.

there is a character which the Spirit shapes and which he can use. Similarly, desire for money is not harmonious with the Spirit (Mand. 11.12). Power and morality go hand in hand. It is not a question of the true prophet 'browbeating' others, as it were, but power is exercised in a way commensurate with the highest ideals of Christian character produced by the Spirit of God.

In two passages, then, Similitude 9 and Mandate 11, Hermas' view of the Spirit as power and, therefore, as an aid to believers emerges quite clearly and distinctly.[63]

Alongside of this strand, we meet another, in which the Spirit appears as delicate and lacking in power. The relevant passages are:

(a) the Spirit as a deposit (Mand. 3.2). The Spirit[64] whom God made to dwell in the flesh is a deposit which we have received from the Lord.

This Spirit is true and free from lies. If, therefore, believers speak lies, they in effect become thieves. They have cheated the Lord. 'If they return a lying spirit, they have defiled the commandment of the Lord and have become robbers' (3.2). When Hermas is alarmed at this, because in his business affairs he has not told the truth, the Shepherd says 'You ought as a servant of God to walk in the truth, and a bad conscience ought not to dwell with the Spirit of truth nor bring grief to the Spirit who is holy and true' (3.4).

The Shepherd says that when believers love and speak the truth, the Spirit will be found true among all people and the Lord will be glorified (3.1).

We miss here any idea of the Spirit's renewing power helping believers to speak the truth and eschew falsehood. All the emphasis is on our capacity to maintain truthfulness. The concept of the Spirit is a static one. God has given a deposit, but believers may lessen the value of this and may not return the deposit intact. They can 'change' the Spirit from a truthful into a lying one.[65]

---

[63] We ought also to mention Mandate 12, which begins with the Shepherd encouraging Hermas to remove himself from all evil desires and to clothe himself in the good and holy desire (12.1.1). The longing for luxury items is mentioned among these evil desires (12.2). When Hermas says that the commandments of the Lord are hard and perhaps impossible to keep (12.3.4), he is rebuked angrily by the Shepherd. When the Shepherd sees that Hermas is frightened by his anger, he says that God created the world for the sake of the human race and subjected it to it: 'If humans are the Lord (κύριος) of all creatures made by God and master (κατακυριεύει) all of them, cannot they master (κατακυριεῦσαι) the commandments? Those who *have the Lord* (τὸν Κύριον) *in their hearts* can master (κατακυριεῦσαι) all these commandments' (12.4.3). This is an alternative way of expressing the help and power of the Spirit to the believer. (Note the allusion to Psa. 8.6 and the play on words: κύριος and κατακυριεύω.)

[64] Against Brox, *Hirt*, p. 198, who assumes that the human spirit is in mind here. But note that in 3.1 the Shepherd refers to the Lord 'who dwells in you' and that in 3.4 the Shepherd says that an evil conscience should not dwell μετὰ τοῦ πνεύματος τῆς ἀληθείας and that no servant of God should bring sadness upon τῷ πνεύματι τῷ σεμνῷ καὶ ἀληθεῖ. In terms of *experience* all three of these phrases point to the Spirit of God being in mind.

[65] Dibelius, *Hirt*, p. 502, bluntly says 'This is not the early Christian concept of the Holy Spirit of God'.

A different interpretation of this passage has been proposed by Carolyn Osiek in her recent commentary. She takes τὸ πνεῦμα to be the human spirit 'that supports the presence of God, but that is to be in perfect communion with the indwelling holy spirit which inspires to do good',[66] and in a later comment on Mandate 5.2 she says 'the whole attempt to distinguish one good spirit from another and from the "spirit of God" begs the question and would have been beside the point for Christian writers at this period, when many Jewish and Jewish-Christian writers found spirit-possession, either good or bad, as a viable way to explain the otherwise inexplicable changes and contrasts in human behaviour'.[67] In one sense, this would remove the difficulty. However, in the next example to be considered, Osiek accepts that the Holy Spirit is in mind,[68] so that it is not clear as to why she has come to a different conclusion in the two passages.

(b) the Spirit as a new garment given to a launderer in Similitude 9.32.3. Hermas imagines that a person sends a new garment to the laundry. If it comes back torn, its owner is justifiably angry with the launderer and complains bitterly. So also, the Lord will be angry with us unless we restore the Spirit[69] to Him as whole as we received it. Again the emphasis is on what believers do with the Spirit rather than on what the Spirit does to believers.

(c) the Spirit as delicate in Mandates 5 and 10.

The Holy Spirit is delicate[70] and needs plenty of space in which to live or otherwise feels restricted, choked, contaminated and unable to serve the Lord (5.1.3). The Holy Spirit feels hindered if an evil spirit enters a Christian, and he finds the place where he is living impure and inconvenient. The evil spirit may be a bad temper (5.1.3), double-mindedness (9.1.1-12) and sadness (10.1.1-3), and the devil is associated with these vices (e.g. bad temper 5.1.3). For both spirits to dwell in someone is inconvenient and evil for that person in whom they dwell (5.1.4). Hermas uses the illustration of wormwood added to honey, which is then rendered bitter and ruined (5.5).

Hermas speaks of overcrowding. 'When all these spirits dwell in one vessel, where the Holy Spirit also dwells, that vessel cannot contain them but is overcrowded' (5.2.5-6). The Holy Spirit is delicate and unaccustomed to dwell with an evil spirit or harshness and so departs from such a person and seeks to dwell with gentleness and tranquillity (5.2.5-6). The result of that abandonment is that the person is filled with evil spirits (5.2.7).

In Mandate 10, the Shepherd says that grief wears out the Holy Spirit (10.1.1) and grieves Him (10.2.2). The first of these statements needs examining, for in full

---

[66] Osiek, *Shepherd*, p. 107.
[67] Osiek, *Shepherd*, p. 119.
[68] Osiek, *Shepherd*, p. 257.
[69] Brox, *Hirt*, p. 463, also appears to accept that the Holy Spirit is in mind.
[70] Dibelius, *Hirt*, p. 514, sees this delicacy as 'a strange characteristic' in the Christian Holy Spirit. Brox, *Hirt*, p. 243, sees the 'spirit' here as the good 'I' of an individual person.

it runs: 'it wears out the Holy Spirit and yet again it saves (καὶ πάλιν σώζει).[71] This statement is then really elucidated in 10.2.2-6. Angry temper embitters people and allows grief to enter their heart. However, this grief *leads people to repent* because of their wickedness *and so* they are able to receive salvation (10.2.4: αὕτη οὖν ἡ λύπη δοκεῖ σωτηρίαν ἔχειν ὅτι τὸ πονηρὸν πράξας μετενόησεν).

The phrase 'seems to have salvation' of v. 4 clearly alludes to the earlier phrase 'and yet again it saves' of v. 1. Strangely, in view of its importance, the thought of salvation does not occur in the remainder of 10.2.4-6. The Shepherd goes on to say that both double mindedness and angry temper grieve the Holy Spirit (10.2.4), and pleads that grief be put away so that the Holy Spirit may not be oppressed (10.2.5).[72]

Two further points may be made. Firstly, a sad person's prayer lacks power and efficacy. The delicate Spirit's power is lessened by the presence of sadness. Hermas uses the illustration of vinegar mixed with wine producing a less pleasant quality. In the same way, sadness mixed with the Holy Spirit does not have the same power of prayer or praise (10.3.2-3).[73]

Secondly, the Spirit prays to God to be allowed to depart from a sad person. It is to avert this possibility that the Shepherd encourages people to put away sadness and not to oppress the Spirit who indwells them 'lest he petitions God[74] and turns away from you' (10.2.5). We could say, then, that in Hermas there is a triumvirate of vices—sadness, bad-temper and double-mindedness—which expels the Holy Spirit from the believer. On this teaching, the Holy Spirit may be polluted by evil spirits and retreats before them. There is no thought of battle and conflict or of the believer's being helped to victory by the Spirit. Evil seems able to nullify the effect of the good Holy Spirit completely.

The material just surveyed thus agrees in general and presents an antithesis to the idea of the Spirit as power and assistance for the believer.

---

[71] Dibelius, *Hirt*, pp. 534, 517-19, sees this as an attempt at Christianising extra-Christian material.

[72] Brox, *Hirt*, pp. 241-48, believes that the distinction between two types of grief is Hermas' own work, inserted into a previous piece of tradition, which saw sadness as wholly undesirable and in need of eradication from the believer's life. He, therefore, attributes the phrase 'and again saves' in 10.1.2 and the references to grief inducing repentance leading to salvation in 10.2.3-4 to Hermas. If these are removed, a consistent and uniform denunciation of grief, doubt and double-mindedness and a demand for their removal from the Christian's life result.

[73] Dibelius, *Hirt*, p.518, again sees this as an attempt at Christianising material drawn from pagan sources.

[74] We have left the translation of ἐντεύξηται in general terms, as does Osiek, *Shepherd*, p. 135, on the assumption that κατὰ σοῦ is secondary. Both Lightfoot, *The Apostolic Fathers*, p. 433, and Dibelius, *Hirt*, p. 534, however, assume that κατὰ σοῦ is original, and this inevitably forces the verb to carry an element of accusation against the unsatisfactory Christian.

Of these two strands in Hermas, the weakness strand is the unusual one which calls for explanation.[75] Are there any precedents for this type of thought? We may rule out some previously offered explanations which suggest that Hermas was influenced by pagan thought: Opitz's view that Hermas was indebted to a Stoicized form of the Roman concept of a person's genius[76] or Dibelius' suggestion that Hermas' thought was akin to the form of demonology found in the Pseudo-Clementine Homilies (9.11) and Porphyrius' *de abstinentia*.[77] Neither of these really explains the delicacy of the Spirit.

Was a possible influence exercised here by the thought of Romans 7–8 if, as many scholars believe, they refer to Christian experience? Did Hermas think in a similar way —that the strand which envisages the weakness and delicacy of the Spirit draws on Romans 7, while the idea of the power of the Spirit rests on Romans 8? While presumably Romans continued to be known and read at Rome, the Pauline influence on *The Shepherd of Hermas* as a whole is not great, and, furthermore, it is not a question of the weakness of the Spirit himself in Romans 7. We may set aside the idea that Romans 7–8 influenced Hermas.

In the OT, one writer said that God's Spirit abandoned Saul and an evil spirit tormented him (1 Sam. 16.14). Outside the OT, 4 Ezra (post AD 70 in its present form) speaks of the disastrous consequences of Adam's sin: the law was in the heart of the people but also wickedness, and the result was that what was good departed and what was evil remained (3.22). There is no specific mention of the Spirit/spirits here, but there is the idea of the retreat of good before evil.

More significant is the Hebraic-Judaic concept of sin as affecting the holiness of (for example) the Temple[78] and indeed causing the Divine glory to depart from it (Ezek. 10.18; 11.22-23). God will remain only while His dwelling place is pure. If the individual is now considered the temple or vessel of the Spirit, the same idea could apply: God's Spirit will withdraw from the individual who is not pure and holy. In the post-exilic period, there is a lament that the people's sins have created a barrier between them and God, and have made Him hide His face from them so that He no longer hears their prayers (Isa. 59.1-2), but this is followed by a description of Yahweh's intervention (59.15b-19).

The situation has to a large extent been altered by the discovery of the Dead Sea Scrolls, and, in particular, the *Manual of Discipline* (3.13–4.26), which envisages two spirits contending fiercely in the universe and in people's hearts until the End, when the spirit of evil will be destroyed. W.D. Davies, commenting on the two spirits (truth and error) in the *Manual of Discipline*, wrote, 'The emphasis in the

---

[75] Cf. J-P. Audet, 'Affinites litteraires et doctrinales du Manuel de Discipline', *RB* 60 (1953), pp. 64-65, commented on Mandate 5.2.4-7: 'The most remarkable feature of this passage is undoubtedly that of the sullying of the Holy Spirit. To my knowledge, the idea is only found twice outside the Shepherd and that is in the Damascus Document'.

[76] Opitz, *Frühchristliche Pneumatologie*, pp. 136-49, esp. 142-49.

[77] Dibelius, *Hirt*, pp. 517-19.

[78] See M. Newton, *The Concept of Purity at Qumran and in the Letters of Paul* (Cambridge: Cambridge University Press, 1985), pp. 6-7, 37, 41, 51.

Scrolls is not on the invasive transcendent character of the two spirits, but on their enduring presence and persistence until the End: they suggest not an inrush of specially given energy but, if we may so express it, two constant currents of good and evil forces in conflict',[79] while A.R.C. Leaney remarked that truth 'has been contaminated with the ways of evil, during the dominion of perversity until the set time'.[80]

Two passages from the *Zadokite Fragment* (or *Damascus Document*), to which J-P. Audet drew attention,[81] deserve to be quoted, for they contain references to the sullying or polluting of the Spirit. They are, firstly, 'Such men have desecrated the Holy Spirit within them and with mocking tongue have opened their mouths against the statutes of God's covenant' (7.12 = 5.11); and, secondly, 'Let no man sully the Holy Spirit within him' (8.20 = 7.4).

We ought also to mention the fact that Philo of Alexandria asserted that it was impossible for the divine Spirit to remain in a mind contaminated by the appetites of the flesh (see *de Gigantibus* 19, 20, 28–31, 53–54).[82]

These passages from the OT and intertestamental writings form a cogent background against which to set that part of the strand within Hermas' teaching on the Spirit which particularly concerns us. However, in the actual use of 'delicate' (τρυφερός), Hermas almost seems unique. LSJ record no examples in classical Greek of this word's being used of the gods or spirits. The occurrences in the LXX are not helpful.[83] It seems as if Hermas' application of the word 'delicate' to God's Spirit is unparalleled.

Overall, however, it must be concluded that Hermas' Jewish background exerted a considerable influence on him. Hermas found it natural to express himself in the way that we have seen.

At the same time we ought to take into consideration what we may call the pastoral situation. Many have been critical of Hermas as a theologian and dismissed him as theologically confused and shallow, but if we approach the problem from a pastoral rather than a dogmatic theological one,[84] there may be a way forward.

Hermas as a person with a pastoral concern knew that the level of Christian commitment and discipleship varied within the church, and he sought to grapple

---

[79] W.D. Davies, *Christian Origins and Judaism* (London: SPCK, 1962), pp. 164-65.

[80] A.R.C. Leaney, *The Rule of Qumran and its Meaning* (London: SCM, 1966), p. 154.

[81] Audet, 'Affinites litteraires', pp. 64-65.

[82] M.E. Isaacs, *The Spirit of God: A Study of Pneuma in Hellenistic Judaism and its Bearing on the New Testament* (Heythrop Monographs 1; London: Heythrop College, 1976), p. 19, has commented: 'Philo asserts that it is precisely because of the incorporeal and moral nature of the spirit, that it cannot remain a permanent possession of man, who is corporeal and sinful'.

[83] Neither Isaiah 58.13 where the returned Jews are promised Yahweh's blessing if they will keep the Sabbath holy and call it τρυφερός (delightful), nor Baruch 4.26, which calls God's faithful ones His 'delicate ones', are relevant for our purposes.

[84] Cf. what R. Joly wrote in his commentary *Hermas Le Pasteur*, p. 33, 'Hermas is and wanted to be a moralist, he does not make himself out to be a theologian'.

with why some Christians displayed so little Christ-like qualities. This, together with his Jewish heritage[85] (the departure of God's presence or the good; the two spirits within a person; the bad actions driving away the good inclination; the contamination of truth by evil; the Two Ways moral teaching) could provide an intelligible background and explanation of why he expressed himself as he did. However, to explain is not to excuse. In allowing what we have called the 'weakness' strand to find expression within his work, Hermas was weakening an emphasis which predominated in the earliest Christian generations and which is there as one strand in his own writings, namely the Spirit as power to uplift and assist Christians in their struggle against evil and their quest to do God's holy will.

SUMMARY

Hermas mentions the Spirit twice in connection with his visions as if this was the 'expected' thing. The more literary these visions are seen to be, the more these two references become a sign of what was associated with prophetic visions, i.e., the Spirit is the source of inspiration for a prophet. This is confirmed by the discussion of true and false prophecy in Mandate 11: the Holy Spirit inspires the true prophet and the believing congregation within which prophecy takes place, in a mutual interplay of appropriate milieu and inspired person.

There is a fair amount of material which links the Spirit with how the Christian should behave. One strand assumes that the Spirit empowers the Christian. The one Holy Spirit is variously described as holy spirits and as virgins who are the personifications of virtues. Furthermore, the believing congregation indwelt by the Spirit is too powerful a resistant to the false prophet whose false spirit flees from him, leaving him 'dumb'.

On the other side, the Spirit is viewed as either something which can be harmed, impaired or diminished (for which believers are responsible and which they ought to preserve and return intact to God) or as delicate, too weak to withstand the power of evil and forced to leave the believer (whose own behaviour, especially sadness, bad temper and double-mindedness, may choke and restrict the Spirit and cause him to flee).

The striking fact is that Hermas has more material in section C than any other writer examined thus far, not only in Rome but also Syria and Asia Minor. Why is

---

[85] Wilson, *Reassessment*, p. 71, considered that Hermas' pneumatology stemmed from the same intellectual environment as Qumran and the *Testaments of the Twelve Patriarchs*. Brox, *Hirt*, p. 543, spoke about the the two spirits teaching being in Hermas' *Umwelt*, and believes (p. 218) that the idea of antagonistic spirits who dwell in people interprets with massive spatial categories the moral alternatives set before human beings. Osiek, *Shepherd*, pp. 31-34, locates it in the Two Ways tradition of moral teaching, with personification of the Two Ways as two spirits competing for the human heart, and she draws in *The Manual of Discipline* for comparison. Dibelius, *Hirt*, pp. 517-19, writing before the discovery of the Dead Sea Scrolls, was on the right lines when he asserted that Hermas' pneumatology was closely related to the spirit concept to be found in the *Testaments of the Twelve Patriarchs*.

this so? Hermas' major interest lies in this area: he feels called by God to offer sinful Christians one more chance of repentance before the End. The ethical concern is thus uppermost. But, in the end, Hermas seems to have little to offer: Christians can put on 'the powers of the virgins', yet on the other hand, he portrays a weak, sensitive, delicate Spirit who will withdraw if evil holds too much sway in the human life and heart.

Although there are hints in 1 John and the *Odes of Solomon* of the Spirit's ability to produce Christ-like love and holiness in the believer, ethics were tending to become autonomous and not seen as both response to God's grace and enabled by God's grace in the Spirit's power, as evidenced by the Didache [Syria]; Jude, 2 Peter, Polycarp, Montanism [Asia Minor]; 2 Clement [Greece]; and Clement of Rome. In some instances, ethical performance seems to lead to salvation rather than being a product of it. The moralistic note, discernible in some of Hermas' ethical teaching,[86] fits into this apparently developing pattern. We are constrained to say that we have come a long way from the position of Paul in NT times.

In the position we have adopted, we have taken an approach which differs from that of Carolyn Osiek in her commentary on *The Shepherd of Hermas*. She maintains that 'The Holy Spirit is not always a distinctive figure, but one of the many good spirits of God. Translation may skew the meaning by capitalization when a more generic reference is intended.... In some contexts, the term "holy spirit" is probably a general term for one of the many spirits that come from God and do God's work. There are other contexts, however, in which something more must be meant. Examples include *Sim.* 5.6.5 or *Sim.* 9.1.1, where the Shepherd reveals that it was the Holy Spirit who spoke to Hermas in the form of the church. In these passages, a particular theological designation must be intended: that Spirit which is closest to God and is the most authoritative representative of God.'[87] She is critical of Dibelius' view that the teaching on spirits is lightly christianized and of N. Brox who does not think that the teaching is Christian in origin or quality, and she protests that in such discussions what constitutes 'Christian' is rarely specified and usually means consonant with the canonical Gospels or Paul.[88] She considers that the teaching on spirits in Hermas may be considered very Christian.

We would subscribe to the position that the important thing is not the origin of material but the use made of it. In an allegory, there cannot, in principle, be any objection to the portrayal of the Spirit of God as a group of women, particularly with the long history of personifying the people of God in the OT and NT as a woman. Furthermore, John of Patmos could picture the Spirit as seven spirits before the throne of God. Also, the existence of evil spirits is widely accepted in the NT, and, for example, 1 John can exhort his readers 'Do not believe every spirit but test the spirits to see whether they are of God' (4.1) and contrasts God's Spirit with an

---

[86] Stressed by T.F. Torrance, *The Concept of Grace in the Apostolic Fathers* (Edinburgh: Oliver & Boyd, 1953), pp. 116-119, if somewhat one-sidedly.
[87] Osiek, *Shepherd*, p. 33.
[88] Osiek, *Shepherd*, p. 31, note 240.

evil spirit which produces the antichrist who is revealed in the false prophets who have now left the church (4.2-3).

We have already referred to passages in the NT which speak of Christians by their conduct nullifying the influence and activity of the Spirit (1 Thess. 5.19; Eph. 4.30), and the behaviour of Ananias and Sapphira and of Simon Magus (Acts 5.1-11; 8.18-24) could be quoted as illustrations of this.

It is not a question of trying to deny that Hermas is 'Christian', but we do think, however, that what we have called the 'weakness' strand in Hermas' teaching on the Spirit is open to criticism by comparison with what we have seen to be the experience of the first two generations of the Christian community.[89] Furthermore, granted that the New Testament writings constitute the primary documents of the Christian faith, what other criteria can be employed by which to judge other writings produced within the Christian tradition? Tradition must be tested by Scripture.

4. Justin Martyr

Justin Martyr was a Gentile, born at Flavia Neapolis (Shechem/Nablus) in Samaria ca.AD 100. In his spiritual pilgrimage, Justin moved eventually from Platonism to Christianity. He taught at Ephesus where, according to Eusebius,[90] he engaged in his disputation with Trypho. He eventually moved to Rome ca.AD 150, where he established a 'school'. He wrote two *Apologies*, the first ca.AD 155 and the second ca.AD 161, and subsequently *Dialogue with Trypho* before he was martyred at Rome ca.AD 165.[91] Thus, Justin was a well-travelled person and was no doubt acquainted with Christianity in many areas, but, since we know that he taught and was martyred in Rome, it seemed appropriate to include Justin in our section on Rome. Roman Christians and non-Christians could hear Justin's teaching in the middle decades of the second century.

---

[89] To this extent ,therefore, we also disagree with Reiling, *Hermas*, p. 143, who states 'As far as this experience [the presence of the Spirit] is concerned, Hermas is in the main stream of first and second century Christianity'. Although Reiling does mention that the Holy Spirit is delicate (pp. 72, 102) or gentle (pp. 34,40), he does not discuss this aspect in pp. 127-43 which is headed 'The Presence of the Spirit' as part of his chapter on 'Prophecy and the Church'.

[90] Eusebius, *HE* 4.18.6.

[91] For details of Justin's life, see *Dial.* 1; *Apol.II*.12; and the discussions in L.W. Barnard, *Justin Martyr* (Cambridge: Cambridge University Press, 1967), pp. 1-13; C.I.K. Story, *The Nature of Truth in "The Gospel of Truth" and in the Writings of Justin Martyr* (Leiden: Brill, 1970), pp. xiii-xv; E.F. Osborn, *Justin Martyr* (Tübingen: Mohr, 1973), pp. 6-10; F. L. Cross and E.A. Livingstone (eds.), *The Oxford Dictionary of the Christian Church* (Oxford: Oxford University Press, 2nd ed., 1974), p. 770.

A. Divine Presence

In *Apology I.*61, Justin describes conversion as both a divine act and human response. The divine side is indicated by such phrases as made new, reborn, washed, illumined; the human side, by repentance, belief, choice, dedication. Justin uses the language of being born again in contrast with our first, natural birth.[92] Christian conversion is a momentous occasion: it involves a passage from darkness to light, i.e., an illumination and a washing clean from moral defilement. That conversion was a 'felt' experience is confirmed by *Dialogue* 8.1: when the old man, instrumental in his conversion, finished speaking, Justin says 'a fire was kindled in my soul'. How far is this associated in Justin's thought with the activity of the Holy Spirit? A number of passages suggest that he did link the two.

In the first place, he applied the reference to the Spirit brooding over the waters in Genesis 1.1-2, to the waters of baptism, since he speaks of demons erecting the image of the pagan goddess, Kore, at springs, in imitation of Christian custom (*Apol.I.*64.2). Given that baptism is a focal point within the conversion experience, this passage implies that the Spirit is active in it.

Secondly, Justin can speak of Christians as those who have been baptized by the Holy Spirit. 'What need, then, of circumcision have I who have been witnessed to by God? What need of that (other) baptism have I who have been baptized with the Holy Spirit?' (*Dial.* 29.1). Circumcision and proselyte baptism ('that (other) baptism') are set in parallelism and belong together as constituent parts of initiation into Judaism. On the other side, being 'witnessed-to by God' and being 'baptized with the Holy Spirit' belong together as parts of becoming a Christian. By baptizing the believer with the Holy Spirit, God witnessed to His acceptance and ownership of the believer. The lack of circumcision—the state in which God created the Gentiles—is no matter for reproach, therefore. Justin here speaks for Christians in general as is shown by the fact that both before and after this passage he used the first person plural (e.g., 'our sacrifices'; the Scriptures are 'not yours, but ours'). There is no specific reference to water baptism here. Justin only employs the language of being baptized by the Holy Spirit. This surely shows that this was vitally important for him. Being baptized by the Spirit is an essential feature of conversion. Furthermore, the use of the perfect participle passive βεβαπτισμένῳ suggests a past event with continuing consequences: baptism is not an experience limited to the past but has lasting and permanent effects. The gift of the Spirit is an abiding one.

---

[92] Barnard, *Justin Martyr*, p. 10, denies that Justin was a 'twice born' Christian. 'He experienced nothing like a dramatic conversion of a St. Paul or a St. Augustine. Christianity was for him the true philosophy and throughout his days he retained the impress of his passage from an imperfect to a perfect philosophy'. But, while Justin may have progressed through various stages of philosophical conviction, he was still prepared to use dramatic language for his and other Christians' embracing of Christianity. Barnard has ignored the language from *Apol. I.*61; 65-66 and *Dial.* 8.1.

Thirdly, Justin also speaks of Christians' having received a spiritual circumcision through baptism (*Dial.* 43.2-3). He contrasts Enoch and those like him who observed or followed this spiritual circumcision and Christians who received it through baptism. Since Christians were sinners, they received it because of God's mercy and all can obtain it in a similar way.

Under 'spiritual circumcision' Justin can only mean that the gift of the Holy Spirit has been imparted by God by His mercy to forgiven sinners, as is confirmed by what he says at *Dialogue* 114.4: by this 'second circumcision God circumcises us from idolatry and simply all forms of evil; our hearts have been circumcised from wickedness'. Justin then gives the positive side of this act of circumcision. Christians 'rejoice to die because of the name of the beautiful rock who both causes the living water to burst forth into the hearts of those who through him (Christ) have loved the Father of all and gives those who wish to drink the water of life'. The imagery of living water or water of life can be confidently thought of as nothing less than the gift of the Holy Spirit in the life of believers.[93]

The two sides of spiritual circumcision are the putting away of wickedness and the receiving of the living waters = the Holy Spirit. Baptism may be the occasion, but the important thing is receiving the Spirit, here described as spiritual circumcision because it involves both the putting off of evil and receiving the living water. The imagery of living water bursting forth from Christ the rock into the hearts of Christians again points to a specific, vivid and memorable experience.

In the fourth place, in a section of the *Dialogue* where Justin contrasts Jews and Christians, he reveals what distinguishes the church from the Jewish people: it is, on the human side, faith and, on the divine side, the Spirit. 'It is necessary for us here to observe that there are two seeds of Judah and two races, as there are two houses of Jacob: the one begotten by blood and flesh, the other by faith and the Spirit' (135.9-10). The Jews are a race produced by the normal process of human reproduction; Christians are given birth 'through faith and the Spirit' (ἐκ πίστεως καὶ Πνεύματος).

Earlier in the chapter, Justin, arguing that Christians are the true Israelites and seed of Jacob, applied Isaiah 42.1-4 to Christ, not to the patriarch Jacob (135.3). 'As therefore he calls the Christ Israel and Jacob, so also we, who have been quarried out of the belly of Christ, are the true Israelite race' (135.4-5). Since Isaiah 42.1-4 contains the reference to God's giving His Spirit to His servant, it is reasonable to believe that here Justin was thinking that Christians have also received the Spirit.

Fifthly, possibly *Dialogue* 54.1 should be mentioned. Justin is exegeting Genesis 49.11: 'He shall wash his robe in wine and his garment in the blood of the grape'. This meant that Christ would wash believers in his blood. 'For the Holy Spirit called those, who received forgiveness of sins through him, his robe, among whom he is continually present in power and will be visibly present at his second coming'. Believers enjoy the continual presence of Christ. We may well have here that

---

[93] Cf. the imagery of Jn. 4.14 and 7.37-39, though in actual fact Justin quotes Jer. 2.13 in support.

phenomenon observable in the NT where, in terms of Christian experience, the risen Christ and the Spirit are identical and interchangeable.

The concept of the Spirit's gifts of speech and deed is also present in Justin's writings, as we can see from the following four passages. Firstly, Trypho referred to Justin's statement (based on Isa.11.1-10) that Christ was filled with the powers of the Spirit, and claimed that this implied that he lacked them prior to this (*Dial.* 87.2). Justin countered[94] by arguing that, whereas famous OT figures had had only one power, all these powers found their accomplishment in Christ. Justin then said that when Christ came, the Spirit 'rested', immediately adding the comment 'that is, after he [Christ] had come, he [the Spirit] ceased [to impart his gifts]' (87.5).

Justin's theory is that in the OT era the Spirit was active, although only imparting one or two gifts to men. He then endowed Jesus with all the powers mentioned by Isaiah. He 'rested' in the sense that he did not inspire anyone else from the Jewish nation then or subsequently (cf. 'For after him no prophet has arisen among you...it was necessary that such gifts should cease from you'). After Christ's ascension the Spirit resumed his activity —in those who believe in Christ (87.5) and whom Christ deems worthy. As Justin puts it, 'from the grace of his Spirit's power (Christ) imparts (gifts) to those who believe in him, according as he deems each one worthy'.

To justify this argument, Justin quotes both Psalm 68.18 and Joel 2.28-29:[95]

'He ascended on high,
He led captivity captive,
He gave gifts to men and women [literally, the sons of men]
And, again, in another prophecy it is said:
And it shall come to pass after this, I will pour out my Spirit on all mankind, and on my male servants and my female servants, and they shall prophesy' (87.6).

Justin immediately goes on to say: 'Now, it is possible to see amongst us both women and men who possess gifts from the Spirit of God' (88.1). It is clear that Justin has in mind specific and special gifts which the Spirit imparts. Otherwise he would not have phrased his statement as he does, with particular individuals in mind.[96]

---

[94] Justin has here carried through a certain play on words: he has interpreted the compound verb ἀνεπαύσατο (rest) as equivalent to ἐπαύσατο (bring to an end, stop, leave off). For further discussion of this theory of Justin, see Appendix 5.

[95] See note 100 below for a discussion on how these OT quotations may have come to Justin.

[96] Benoit, *Baptême*, pp. 171-73, believes that two concepts of the Spirit are juxtaposed without Justin's clearly distinguishing them: (a) the Spirit bestows his gifts on certain members of the church (χαρίσματα, 82.1; 88.1); (b) the Spirit is given to all who believe (δόματα, 39.2; 87.5). If we examine 87.3-88.1, we see, however, that

We note in passing that women as well as men are said to possess these gifts, though Justin does not dwell on this feature.[97] While such a statement functions to indicate the fulfilment of the Joel quotation, Justin is clearly referring to actual facts which he can recall. It is interesting too that he makes this statement, immediately after his somewhat abbreviated quotation of Joel which nonetheless concluded 'and they shall prophesy', *before* the rise of Montanism.

Secondly, earlier in *The Dialogue* Justin claimed that 'the prophetical gifts remain with us, even to the present day' (82.1). Again, this statement is interesting in view of the widespread assumption that prophecy ceased before Montanism revived it. Justin goes on to say that these prophetic gifts should be a sign to Trypho and his friends that the ancient Jewish gifts have been transferred to Christians.

In the third place, elsewhere (*Dial.* 39.2) Justin applied the passage 1 Kings 18 about the 7,000 who had not worshipped Baal to Jewish Christians who were becoming disciples of Christ and abandoning the way of error. Each of them, as they are worthy, receives gifts: 'for one receives the Spirit of understanding, another (the Spirit) of counsel, another (the Spirit) of might, another (the Spirit) of healing, another (the Spirit) of foreknowledge, another (the Spirit) of teaching, another (the Spirit) of the fear of God'. Here πνεῦμα must be God's Spirit, not the human spirit, as the link with healing and teaching shows. God's Spirit imparts these δόματα which range from gifts of spiritual understanding (understanding, counsel, foreknowledge, fear of God)[98] to miracles (might, healing). While there may be some influence of the Isaiah 11.1-10 passage on Justin's language here, it is equally clear that he has not derived all his terminology from there. Again, as in chapter 87, Psalm 68 with its reference to gifts is quoted to substantiate Justin's remarks.

Finally, in addition to the miracles mentioned in 39.2, we find evidence for exorcisms in Justin's day both elsewhere in *The Dialogue* and in *Apology II*. Christian believers find that all demons and evil spirits are subjected to them when they command them (*Dial.* 76.6). So powerful is Christ's name that Christians do not need to use fumigations and incantations, as Jewish and Gentile exorcists do (30.3; 85.3). In *Apology II* Justin refers to past and present exorcisms of innumerable demoniacs throughout the world and at Rome, although other exorcists who used incantations and drugs were impotent to effect their cure (6.6).

Justin, then, believed that some Christians had received special gifts of the Spirit in fulfilment of Psalm 68 and Joel 2. *Dialogue* 88.1 quoted above has in mind some, not all Christians. In *Dialogue* 87.5, Justin says that after the ascension Christ imparts gifts to believers 'as he deems each worthy', while in *Apology II*.6 he refers to a specific group of Christian exorcists (πολλοὶ τῶν ἡμετέρων ἀνθρώπων). It is

---

Justin uses δυνάμεις in 87.3-4, δόματα in 87.5-6 and χαρίματα in 88.1, and it is difficult to see any real distinction in the sense behind the different terminology.

[97] Justin appears to be more liberal than the author of the Pastorals (1 Tim. 2.9-15) (and the person responsible for 1 Cor. 14.34-35 if these verses are an interpolation).

[98] Cf. *Dial.* 10.4, where Trypho is credited with the statement, with which Justin no doubt concurred: 'Will the human mind see God at any time, if it is uninstructed by the Holy Spirit?'

clear that, given the style of *The Dialogue*, Justin cannot have been making up these references to gifts. They were part of his argument, which would collapse unless they did occur and were visible.

SUMMARY

Justin held that all Christian believers have received the Holy Spirit (through faith and baptism) and this marked them off from the Jews, the old people of God and the first circumcision. This experience is the heart of conversion. Justin's use of the language of rebirth and being made new argues for a dramatic experience attending conversion.

Some Christians have received special gifts of the Spirit in fulfilment of Psalm 68 and Joel 2. Prophecy is still current as is the power to perform miracles, healings and exorcisms, while special spiritual wisdom and understanding are granted to some. In terms of scriptural support, Justin may be drawing on a tradition current in Christian circles. Both Ephesians and Justin use Psalm 68 and take the 'gifts' bestowed on people to mean the risen Lord's gifts through his Spirit. There could be at least an allusion to the original form of Psalm 68.19 in Acts 2.33 with its use of λαβών ('having received'),[99] which would agree with the MT and LXX, together with Joel 2.28. The value of Psalm 68.19 for the early Christians was the combination of the ideas of ascending and gifts. An exegetical tradition which drew together Psalm 68 and Joel 2 to support Christian experience of the Spirit may have developed: Acts 2 and Ephesians 4 would be the start of the process and Justin could be an heir to it.[100]

Whereas in Ephesians the gifts are people capable of holding certain offices in the church, in Justin the gifts are activities (cf. *Dial.* 39.2), i.e. Justin is closer in fact to 1 Corinthians 12 than to Ephesians 4, though both he and Ephesians use Psalm 68.

Justin Martyr, then, becomes evidence that in 'popular' Christianity[101] of the mid-second century the experience of the Holy Spirit was part of the life and

---

[99] This is accepted by B. Lindars, *New Testament Apologetic* (London: SCM, 1961), pp. 44, 50, 51 (Lindars does not mention Justin's use of Psa. 68).

[100] P. Prigent, *Justin et l'Ancien Testament* (Paris: Gabalda, 1964), pp. 12, 113-15, 321, 326, suggested that Justin was utilising in *Dial.* 87 a section from his own *Syntagma*, a treatise against heresies, in which the divinity of the exalted, glorified Christ, who is reigning now and will come in glory, was celebrated and proved by Psalms 19, 24, 47, 72, 99 and 110, Daniel 7 and Isaiah 66, and the claim that the Exalted One gave the Spirit to men was backed up by Isaiah 11, Psalm 68 and Joel 2. O. Skarsaune, *The Proof from Prophecy: A Study in Justin Martyr's Proof Text Tradition* (Leiden: Brill, 1987), pp. 196-98, however, comes to a different conclusion: that in *Dial.* 87–88 Justin was working with two sources, one of which understood Jesus' baptism as a messianic anointing with the Spirit, in fulfillment of Isaiah 11.2-3, which Justin felt was too risky and open to an adoptionist Christology and so suppressed it, while the other stressed Christ as the second Adam fully endowed with his power before his baptism (*Dial.* 88.2).

[101] H. Chadwick, 'Justin Martyr's Defence of Christianity', *BJRL* 47 (1964-65), p. 293, has said that Justin's theology deserves 'the epithet "popular" in the sense that he wants to stress the points prominent in the mind of ordinary Christian folk with a

discipleship of Christians. Far from playing a negligible role, the Spirit was an important ingredient in the life of the church.[102]

5. Valentinian Gnosticism

Born in northern Egypt and educated at Alexandria, Valentinus moved to Rome where he lived and worked ca.AD 136-155, possibly as late as AD 165.[103] According to Tertullian, he was apparently in and out of membership of the church there[104] and had at one time (ca.AD 143) hopes of becoming the bishop,[105] but whether Tertullian had access to really accurate information must remain an open question.[106]

Markschies argues that we must reconstruct Valentinus' thought from the fragments of his teaching quoted by Clement of Alexandria and Hippolytus, and not rely on what is said by Irenaeus, as Irenaeus was better informed about Valentinus' successors than Valentinus himself. He maintains that Valentinus' pupils developed their master's teaching.[107] Certainly, Tertullian said that teaching on aeons was a major point of difference between Valentinus' pupils and their master.[108]

Lampe points out that fellowship with the Valentinians went on in the second century for far longer than with Marcion and his followers.[109] Justin did not attack

---

practical concern for moral responsibility and a devotion quickened to life by the dramatic story of the divine acts of redemption through Christ and the work of the Holy Spirit'. Thus, Justin may be a good guide to what ordinary Christian folk thought and felt on the topic of the Holy Spirit.

[102] This dissents from the view of Story, *Nature of Truth*, p. 147, who asserts that the relationship of the Holy Spirit to the actual life of the Christian receives little attention in Justin's writings and says that 'neither from D.29.1 nor D.87.6–88.1 can one conclude that the Holy Spirit has significant role to play in the daily life of Christians'.

[103] So Irenaeus, *AH* 3.4.3, and repeated by Eusebius, *HE* 4.10.

[104] Tertullian, *Praescr. Haer*.30.

[105] Tertullian, *Adv. Val.* 4.

[106] C. Markschies, *Valentinus Gnosticus? Untersuchungen zur valentinianischen Gnosis mit ein Kommentar zu den Fragmenten Valentins* (WUNT 65; Tübingen: Mohr, 1992), pp. 309, 311, doubts the accuracy of Tertullian, and believes that he was better informed about the Valentinians but knew only gossip about Valentinus. The charge of desiring highest honours and moving into heresy as a result of failure is a not uncommon charge in anti-heretical propaganda.

[107] Markschies, *Valentinus Gnosticus?*, pp. 291-318, 335-36, 376-407.

[108] Tertullian, *Adv. Val.* 4.2. In 4.3, Tertullian made the significant comment, 'Ita nusque iam Valentinus, et tamen Valentiniani qui per Valentinum' ('So Valentinus [is] nowhere now, and yet Valentinians [exist], who [arose] through Valentinus').

[109] Lampe, *Christen*, p. 329 (*Christians at Rome*, p. 391). On pp. 257-63 (*Christians at Rome*, pp. 298-311), he mentions both a marble inscription from the second century and a marble gravestone, dating from the end of the second or beginning of the third century, with two inscriptions arranged in hexameter, both of which point to a Valentinian congregation which gathered in the home of a socially privileged Valentinian in the suburbs on the Via Latina.

Valentinus in his two *Apologies*, and even in the later *Dialogue against Trypho* he is more critical of Valentinians than of Valentinus. In the 190s, Victor accepted the Valentinian Florinus as a presbyter and only moved to depose him at the instigation of Irenaeus who wrote to Victor.[110]

Who, then, were the major followers of Valentinus? It is from Hippolytus' *Refutation of Heresies* 6.30 that we learn the names of some of them: in the 'eastern school', Theodotus, Marcus, Axionicus of Antioch and Bardesanes of Edessa, and in the so-called 'Italian school', Ptolemaeus, Heracleon and Secundus. While there are variations and developments of thought, some common features run through the thinking of these 'Valentinians'. As these common features have been adequately described by scholars in the past,[111] we need not spend time in describing the whole Valentinian system. Suffice to say that all thirty aeons between the supreme deity and the demiurge (the inferior creator who is ignorant of the supreme deity) are spiritual and one of them is the Holy Spirit (not the 'orthodox' Holy Spirit), and that there are three classes of people—pneumatics (in whom a spiritual seed has been sown by Sophia), psychics and hylics. The first-named have to be awakened to their true nature through the revelation of the saviour, to be reunited with an angelic partner.

In order not to prolong our inquiry beyond reasonable limits, we propose to confine ourselves to a discussion of *The Gospel of Truth* and two of the Italian school, Ptolemaeus and Heracleon.

5.1. The Author of the Gospel of Truth[112]

Scholarship is divided as to whether Valentinus or an early pupil/colleague of his is the author of the GT.[113] For our purposes, all that matters is that the GT is probably the earliest example of a Valentinian Gnostic writing that we possess.

---

[110] Irenaeus, *Syrian Fragment* 28; cf. Eusebius, *HE* 5.20.4 for a letter of Irenaeus to Florinus himself.

[111] F.M.M. Sagnard, *La Gnose valentinienne et le Témoignage de saint Irénée* (Paris: Gabalda, 1947); H. Jonas, *The Gnostic Religion* (Boston: Beacon, 2nd ed., 1963); K. Rudolph, *Gnosis* (Edinburgh: T. & T. Clark, 1983); R. Berthouzoz, *Liberté et Grâce suivant la Théologie d'Irénée de Lyons* (Fribourg-Paris: Éditions Universitaires Fribourg & Les Éditions du Cerf, 1980).

[112] All quotations are from the translation by K. Grobel, *The Gospel of Truth* (London: A. & C. Black, 1960).

[113] Among those who accept Valentinus as the author of the Gospel of Truth (hereafter *GT*) are W.C. van Unnik, '"The Gospel of Truth" and the New Testament', in F.L. Cross (ed.), *The Jung Codex* (London: A.R. Mowbray, 1955), p. 81; Grobel, *Gospel of Truth*, pp. 19, 26-27; R.M. Grant, *Gnosticism and Early Christianity* (New York: Harper & Row, 2nd ed., 1966), p. 128; B. Standaert, 'L'Évangile de Vérité: Critique et lecture', *NTS* 22 (1976), pp. 243-75; B. Layton, *The Gnostic Scriptures* (London: SCM, 1987), p. 251; Jacqueline A. Williams, *Biblical Interpretation in the Gnostic Gospel of Truth from Nag Hammadi* (Atlanta, GA: Scholars, 1988), pp. 4-5; Judith H. Wray, *Rest as a Theological Metaphor in the Epistle to the Hebrews and The Gospel of Truth* (Atlanta, GA: Scholars,

A and B. Divine Presence and Illumination

The vivid distinction which the *GT* draws between the pre- and post-conversion states[114] leaves no doubt that a genuine and dramatic experience is being described. There are three pictures which are employed for the pre-conversion state:

(a) anguish or terror which envelopes the person like a fog, thus giving Plane (Error) her opportunity to deceive (17.10-11);

(b) drunkenness in which a person is not their true self (22.16-19);

(c) the experience of nightmares during which people try and do things but are unable to do so (28.28–30.12).

While these images are favourite gnostic themes, as Jonas has shown,[115] the *GT* is one of the earliest gnostic writings we actually possess and there is no reason why literary skill and personal experience may not have been fused to make the powerful impact of (for example) the nightmare section. To what experiences do these images point? We may say that they point to a sense of alienation vis-a-vis the world, of not being one's true self and needing to discover who one really is. The individual does not 'see' where they are going; like a drunken person they have no control over their direction and are in a stupefied state, not their true self. They seek but never achieve their true goal in life, like a person in a nightmare strives but never accomplishes what they aim to do. These are powerful images for a particular human predicament and need, and suggest that the author of *GT* starts from the experience of alienation over against the world and of inner dividedness. He is aware of being a 'foreigner' in the world and of a lack of inner peace and harmony. While these images do not convey the sense of man's sinful state vis-s-vis a holy God, it would not be fair to say that there is an indifference to sin.[116] But the starting point could

---

1998), p. 99. However, since the extremely learned and thorough monograph of Markschies, *Valentinus Gnosticus?*, the attribution of *GT* to Valentinus himself must now be regarded as extremely doubtful (Earlier, Rudolph, *GNOSIS*, p.319, had denied that Valentinus was the author). However, the precise issue of authorship is not of particular concern to us: what matters is that the *GT* is probably the earliest known sample of Valentinian theology. Grobel remarks that if the author is a pupil of Valentinus, he would seem to be an 'earlier' one than Ptolemy or Heracleon because he is less involved in the mythological-heterodox trend than they (*Gospel of Truth*, p. 26).

[114] In using the language of conversion, it can be seen that I am in agreement with A. McGuire, 'Conversion and Gnosis in the Gospel of Truth', *NT* 28 (1986), pp. 338-55, who criticised A.D. Nock, *Conversion: The Old and the New in Religion from Alexander the Great to Augustine of Hippo* (Oxford: Oxford University Press, 1933), pp.10-16, for denying that 'conversion' was the appropriate term to use of Gnostic experience and for preferring 'adhesion'. In fact, McGuire describes the *GT* as the 'Gospel of conversion' (p. 354).

[115] Jonas, *Gnostic Religion*, pp. 49-74.

[116] See M.R. Desjardins, *Sin in Valentinianism* (Atlanta, GA: Scholars, 1990), esp. pp. 3, 118, 129-31. Desjardins contends that the Valentinians were not indifferent to sin or ethics. See pp. 80-83 for a discussion of the two occurrences of sin in the *GT* (32.37 and 35.25-26). People commit sin because they live in a state of ignorance and error, but

be formulated as residing not so much in a theological but anthropological understanding of life, though this latter does have a theological aspect (namely, that God/the divine is alien to the world).[117]

What reverses this state so graphically described? The concept of a 'call' plays a part in the GT (as in gnosticism generally).[118] The Father calls the gnostic (21.25-27); He pronounces their name (21.28–22.15).

Of course, it is the basic revelation of the Son in his incarnation which enables the separation between the unknown Father[119] and the gnostic to be abolished: (34.28-29, 32; 38.21-24; 40.27-28). What was achieved then becomes actualised in the call of the gnostic.

Once the call is received, the pre-conversion state is reversed. The gnostic wakes up as from sleep (30.13-19) or sobers up after drunkenness (22.16-20) and becomes their true self: they know 'whence they came and whither they go' (22.13-15); that they are from above (22.3-4) and came from out of God (27.11-14). The state of forgetting is abolished (18.5-12, 16-18; 37.37-39). They receive light to replace darkness (24.32–25.3, 12-18; 35.27-29; 32.23, 32-34). They receive rest (42.21-22; 35.23, 25-27) instead of torment (31.21-22, 26-27). They have a sense of completeness (19.3-7; 25.35–26.15; 34.28-32; 36.1-13; 42.31-33; 43.19-23). Warmth replaces coldness (34.28-29, 32). There is a reorientation or conversion.[120]

What part, if any, is the Spirit thought to play in the experience of this conversion or call? 'For everyone who loves the Truth...attaches themselves to the Father's mouth by means of His tongue as they receive the Spirit, this [the Spirit] being the revelation of the Father and the manifestation of Himself to the aeons' (26.32–27.8). The expressions 'Father's mouth' and 'tongue' stand for God's revelation and the means of revelation. In this passage the means of revelation is the Holy Spirit, from whom the gnostic receives the revelation (what comes from the Father's mouth).

We have here a parallel between the heavenly and the earthly. The Father has revealed Himself to His aeons, but also to the gnostic. What happens to the aeons also happens at an earthly level to the gnostic, the lover of truth.[121] We also observe

---

the Father like a doctor treating a sick patient seeks of His grace to offer forgiveness and rest.

[117] What we have described accounts for why Gnosticism has proved such a source of interest to modern existentialists: see, e.g., Jonas, *Gnostic Religion*, pp. 320-40.

[118] See e.g. Jonas, *Gnostic Religion*, pp. 74-91; W. Foerster, *GNOSIS I* (Oxford: Oxford University Press, 1972), pp. 2, 20.

[119] This description appears at 17.8, 22; 18.32; 20.2; 30.34.

[120] McGuire, *Conversion*, p. 344; she states that the individual response is part of the mythic process by which the Entirety [Grobel uses Totality] returns to the Father. Individual conversions participate in the collective conversion or restoration of the Entirety (pp. 348-49).

[121] Both Sagnard, *Gnose valentinienne*, p. 244, and B. Aland, 'Gnosis and Christentum', in B. Layton (ed.), *The Rediscovery of Gnosticism* (Leiden: Brill, 1979),

a 'filiation' of names.[122] Elsewhere the Son or Word is described as the one who reveals the Father; here Spirit is used.

That the Spirit is involved in the process of revelation can be seen in the passage which begins with a beatitude on 'the one who has returned to themselves and awakened' and 'on Him who has opened the eyes of the blind' (30.12-16). Whereas Grobel[123] assumes that the latter refers to the Father or Jesus, Story[124] believes that the Holy Spirit is the one who is in mind and this certainly fits in with the continuation of the passage in vv. 16-31: 'and the swift Spirit followed him up after he had caused him to wake up. Having given hand to him, who was stretched out on the ground, he set him on his feet, though he had not yet (ever) risen up. And he gave them means of understanding the gnosis of the Father and the revealing of his Son, for when they had seen him and heard him, he permitted them to taste him and smell him and lay hold of the beloved Son'.

The Spirit wakes up the sleepers and helps them to their feet. The Spirit brings the call and enables those called to return to themselves. He helped them understand the Father's gnosis and what the Son has revealed. The Spirit deepens the believer's understanding of the Son[125] and permitted the believer to 'taste and smell and lay hold of the beloved Son'. The language may owe something to 1 John 1.1-3, but certainly goes beyond it (taste, smell) and, in that very fact, probably reveals the experience underlying the passage under consideration.

The writer continues: 'Having been revealed, he teaches them concerning the Father, the Incomprehensible One, having breathed into them that which is in the Thought, (thereby) doing His will. Many receive the light, they turn to Him' (30.32-35).

The mention of 'breathing' evokes John 20.22, but the Johannine passage is the Johannine Pentecost and the fulfilment of the promise of the Spirit made earlier in the course of the gospel, whereas the *GT*'s use is detached from any prior anchorage and used to convey the author's particular slant. The phrase may be intended to suggest the gift of the Holy Spirit as the agent who mediates gnosis ('That which is in the Thought', i.e., teaching concerning the Incomprehensible Father).

We come across the idea of 'breath' in another passage 34.9-14, and here Grobel believes that there is a double sense of 'breath' and Spirit:[126] 'It is not the ears that

---

p. 335, maintain that each individual event of redemption is only the subsequent accomplishment of the first inner-divine event.

[122] Cf. Sagnard, *Gnose valentinienne*, p. 240.

[123] Grobel, *Gospel of Truth*, p. 119.

[124] Story, *Nature of Truth*, p. 19.

[125] Story, *Nature of Truth*, p. 20, believes that here the *GT* is akin to the Fourth Gospel's teaching on the Holy Spirit in Jn. 16.12-15, especially v. 14, that the Spirit expounds the teaching and revelation of the Son.

[126] Grobel, *Gospel of Truth*, p. 151. Story, *Nature of Truth*, p. 26, also sees a reference to the Spirit in the passage: 'The Father's aroma can only be sensed by the gift of the Spirit (34.9-12)'.

smell the aroma but it is the breath which has the sense of smell and is wont to bring it to him for him and to submerge (him?) in the aroma of the Father'.

The Spirit (the breath of God) utilizes human breath to convey the divine aroma to those who breathe it in. If 'the sons of the Father are His aroma' (so 33.39–34.1), which He loves, then the idea of conveying that aroma to someone means that they become sons of the Father. They are awakened to the fact that they are 'from the Father' (33.32). The redeemed realize their origin, and this aroma 'takes them up to the Place out of which they came forth' (34.15-16).

Another passage mentions breathing. After saying that the return of the redeemed is called repentance (35.23), the writer goes on: 'This is why Imperishability breathed out, and followed after the one who had sinned: in order that He might give them rest. For forgiveness is to remain behind in the Light within the Lack' (35.24-28). If we follow Grobel in taking Imperishability as abstract for concrete,[127] i.e. the Imperishable One (= the Father), then what is His breathing out but the gift of the Spirit? As at 30.16 the Spirit followed the awakened person, so here the Spirit follows the sinner to impart forgiveness, light, rest (to replace the darkness and restless anguish already noted).

There is a passage on anointing (36.17–37.3) where we may well also detect a reference to the Spirit. Our writer says that finding the unchangeable light of the truth is 'why it was said about the Christ in their midst "Seek and they shall receive" a return—they who were perplexed—and He will anoint them with the anointing'. Grobel takes the anointing as probably Spirit baptism.[128] This anointing is from the merciful Father. Those anointed are complete (36.17-20). The experience of the Spirit completes the one whose origin is from above. There then follows the complicated illustration of the jars, smeared around the stopper to seal them, which distinguishes between full and partially full jars.

The Spirit is also experienced as power. After a reference to the incarnation (31.4-7) and the teaching ministry which gave life (31.9-15), *GT* continues: (the Son) 'gave them thought and wisdom and mercy and salvation and the Spirit of power from the infinitude of the Father and from the kindness. He caused the torments and scourging to cease...and with power he abolished them and defeated them by gnosis' (31.15-22, 26-27; cf. 26.18-27). Clearly, then, the Spirit is one of the Son's gifts, with the Father remaining the ultimate source ('the infinite and kind Father'). The link of Spirit and power receives emphasis from the fact that gnosis is powerful to end the torments and anguish of illusory existence (cf. 28.19-28). The Spirit will enable those illumined to defeat Plane and her confusion themselves (cf. 31.32-33: 'By his victory he becomes stability to those who were staggering').

Towards the end of the *GT*, the author contemplates the rest of the redeemed, whether it is here and now[129] or the ultimate, eschatological rest.[130] They rest in Him who rests (42.21-22). The Father is in them and they are in the Father (42.26-

---

[127] Grobel, *Gospel of Truth*, p. 163.
[128] Grobel, *Gospel of Truth*, p. 169.
[129] So Wray, *Rest*, pp. 136-37.
[130] Grobel, *Gospel of Truth*, pp. 191, 193 (note 602) lists the two possibilities.

30). They are complete, indivisible in the Good One, 'lacking nothing at all but giving rest,[131] being fresh in the Spirit' (42.31-33). The Spirit confers all blessings on the redeemed in the Place from where they originally came and whither they have returned (41.25-28). They do not descend to Hades (42.18), but all are at rest in Him who is perfect rest. Contemplating this eventuality, the author says: 'And His children are complete and worthy of His name, for it is children of this sort that the Father Himself desires' (43.19-23). There seems to be a realised eschatological standpoint here, which makes the reference to God's Spirit all the more significant.[132]

C. Divine Power

The aspect of the Spirit's help in ethical transformation is not dwelt upon in the *GT*. However, we intend here to mention a passage in Clement of Alexandria's *Stromateis* II.114.3-6, where he is discussing Valentinus,[133] because this does reveal the idea of the ethical transformation of the gnostic by God in Valentinus' thought. Before conversion, the heart is like an inn often filled with filth by men who live there licentiously and who have no regard for the place because it belongs to another. The heart is unclean and the abode of many demons. 'Through God alone is it possible for the heart to become pure when every evil spirit is banished from the heart... When the Father who alone is good visits it, it is sanctified and becomes bright with light; and the one who has such a heart will be proclaimed blessed, for they will see God' (Mt.5.8).[134]

Summary

It cannot be said that the Holy Spirit is a dominant or central theme in the *GT*.[135] He is seen as the gift of the Father. His task is to reveal the Father and the Son, and he

---

[131] Following Grobel, *Gospel of Truth*, p. 199, note 626 (and not his translation on p. 198); Layton, *The Gnostic Scriptures*, p. 264; and Wray, *Rest*, p. 136.

[132] I have left out of this survey 24.10-11; 26.34–27.1, which are regarded by Grobel, *Gospel of Truth*, pp. 93 and 109 respectively, as interpolations, though Story, *Nature of Truth*, pp. 147-48, does not treat them as such.

[133] This is a fragment accepted as genuinely from Valentinus by Markchies, *Valentinus Gnosticus?*, pp. 54-82. For a full translation, see Pearson, *Gnostic Scriptures*, pp. 244-45.

[134] Desjardins, *Sin*, p. 132, believes that this fragment has 'a decidedly Pauline flavour' and that in his argument 'Valentinus' emphasis on the human need for external amd unmerited help is far more Pauline than Clement's plea to Christians to follow the law and struggle to overcome their fleshly passions on their own'.

[135] Cf. Grobel, *Gospel of Truth*, p. 22: 'The (Holy) Spirit is not prominent in the meditation'. By contrast, Story, *Nature of Truth*, p. 176, believes that the *GT* tries to fulfil the lack of emphasis which, he claims, exists in Justin on the work of the Holy Spirit. We have already queried Story's assessment of Justin and we are not inclined to follow him in his verdict about *GT* and the Spirit.

is experienced as power. He transports the redeemed into the aroma of the Father, gives rest and refreshment and completion. But the references are few and sparse, and the impressive quality of the meditation is not dependent on them

Is the link between the Spirit and experience which we have nonetheless discerned any different from what can be discerned in writings from within the 'orthodox' wing of Christendom? I do not think so. The difference comes in the interpretation given to the experience. This, of courses, raises the question whether an experience understood differently eventually in the course of time becomes a different experience. This whole issue will be discussed at greater length in our final conclusion to the entire study.

5.2. Heracleon[136]

Clement of Alexandria called Heracleon 'the most celebrated of Valentinus' school' (*Stromateis* 4.9). We owe the survival of any of Heracleon's teaching to the fact that Origen incorporated some of it in his own commentary on John's gospel. It thus appears that Heracleon himself was the first known commentator on the fourth gospel.

Heracleon has an ontological explanation of the pneumatics: they are 'of the same substance' (ὁμοούσιοι) with the Father and may be described as spirit because He is spirit. However, the pneumatic seed is lost in or intertwined with matter.

In the extant fragments, Heracleon took the cleansing of the temple (Jn. 2) and the Samaritan episode (Jn. 4) as illustrative of the pneumatic. He interpreted the forty-six years of John 2.20 as follows: six refers to matter and forty to the inbreathing and to the seed (contained) in the inbreathing. (This assumes the idea of Sophia using the Demiurge to breathe the pneumatic seed into the elect). The cord and the wood which formed the whip constructed by Jesus to cleanse the temple are taken to symbolize the Spirit and the cross respectively. By these means the Saviour purifies and cleanses the pneumatics, separating them from the rest who are evil, and so the church consists no longer of a den of robbers and merchants but is a house of his Father.

We have to ask whether this process of separation indicates a definite 'felt' experience of the power and energy of the Spirit. We cannot be dogmatic at this point, but we could say that at least the language is consistent with it. The pneumatics are conscious of a moment when they became pneumatic and thus were separated from others. The basis for this feeling was the experience of the Spirit, and the Cross' upright beam becomes a symbol of the line of separation, while the cross beam symbolizes Christ's reaching out to form or fashion both Sophia in the heavenly realm and the pneumatics on earth.

As for the Samaritan woman, her sexual involvement with six husbands is a symbol of the involvement in matter which causes ignorance, i.e., ignorance of God,

---

[136] All quotations which follow are from Foerster, *GNOSIS I*. The number of the fragment will be given and then the page reference in Foerster.

of the worship agreeable to Him and of those things essential for true life. At the same time, her request to Jesus for the water of life reveals a dissatisfaction with worldly life.

Heracleon taught that a response was called-for from the pneumatic, and this can be illustrated by the way in which he interpreted this episode of the Samaritan woman. Faith was needed to secure release from this involvement in the material and to cast away the passions resulting from false relations and to come to the saviour both to receive gnosis and so that the pneumatic might receive her heavenly bridegroom (the heavenly counterpart). Heracleon praised the Samaritan woman 'because she showed the kind of faith that was inseparable from her nature and corresponded to it, in that she did not hesitate over what he told her' (*fragment* 17, p. 169) and 'because she behaved in a way suited to her nature, for she neither denied nor explicitly acknowledged her shame... wanting to learn in what way, and pleasing whom and worshipping God, she might be released from her immorality, she said "Our fathers worshipped on this mountain"' (*fragment* 19, p. 170). The woman must cast out the passions of her false relationships (her immersion in the material, the worldly) and come to the Saviour to receive gnosis and her heavenly bridegroom.

Is faith, then, automatic on the part of the pneumatic? Is the response already predetermined? We need at this point to consider the fragments which deal with the sowing (another picture alongside that of inbreathing).

Heracleon's interpretation of John 4.35-38 is helpful to us for this purpose. He referred the harvest of these verses to 'the souls of believers, saying 'They are ripe, ready for harvest, and suitable for being gathered into the barn, that is through faith into rest, all those who are ready. For they are not all (ready). Some (souls) were already ready, he says, some were on the point of being ready, some are near to being ready, and some are still being sown' (*fragment* 32, p. 174). This extract shows that there are stages of readiness among pneumatics and that some seeds are still being sown. Although Barbara Aland[137] stresses the latter point, the former seems the more significant point, namely that even among pneumatics there are varying degrees of readiness of response. As to the latter point, this argument could still be combined with the automatic response, since the myth of Sophia and the pneumatic seeds is true of every generation.

Probably, overall, we have a phenomenon not dissimilar to the Johannine combination of predestinarian passages alongside the tremendous stress on faith. Thus, Heracleon expresses the grace character of salvation in ontological terms: the pneumatic is such because the seed is sown in him or her from above. But faith is necessary to turn away from one's entanglement in the material and in the state of ignorance of the divine. The experience of the turning away from the material to the divine is due to the power and energy of the Spirit.

---

[137] B. Aland, 'Erwahlungstheologie und Menschenklassenlehre (Die Theologie des Herakleon als Schlüssel zum Verstandnis des christlichen Gnosis ?)', in M. Krause (ed.), *Gnosis and Gnosticism* (NHS III; Leiden: Brill, 1977), p. 164.

Heracleon taught that the pneumatic has an evangelistic responsibility. The experience of 'conversion' leads to speaking to the psychics. The Samaritan woman is a symbol of this. She 'returned to the world to announce the good tidings of Christ's coming to the calling [= psychics]' (*fragment* 27, p. 173). Heracleon picks up the idea of the Samaritans believing because of the woman's report (Jn. 4.39) and equates her report with the witness of 'the unspiritual church' (*fragment* 37, p. 176). The pneumatics, then, can help the psychics to come to saving belief.

This same idea emerges briefly in Heracleon's exposition of the living water passage in John 4.12-15. Origen said 'Not improbably he interprets the "springing up"' (v. 14) as referring to those 'who receive what is richly supplied from above and who themselves pour forth for the eternal life of others that which has been supplied to them' (*fragment* 27, p. 173). In other words, the pneumatic becomes the vehicle by which the Holy Spirit may work in the life of non-pneumatics, the psychics.

Foerster saw a contradiction between Heracleon's interpretation of Jn. 2.13-16 and 4.39,[138] but his view probably underestimates the different theme of the two stories. The cleansing of the temple is primarily concerned with the pneumatics, and Heracleon emphasizes that it is they who elicit the help of the Lord: by the cross and the Spirit he will separate them and constitute them as the true church and house of the Father; whereas the Samaritan woman's evangelism is directed to winning the psychics to a saving knowledge and experience of the Lord.

That psychics may experience salvation is confirmed by Heracleon's treatment of the nobleman's son. Healing takes place through forgiveness: the Saviour raised him to life through forgiveness. The servants (= angels) tell the father (= Demiurge) of the cure: '"Thy son lives" means that he is behaving fittingly and rightly, and no longer doing what is unseemly'.[139]

Commenting on John 8.44, Heracleon said that some psychics 'become sons of the devil by intent', whereas others 'may also be called sons of God by intent'. He adds 'Because they have loved the desires of the devil and performed them, they become children of the devil, though they were not such by nature' (*fragment* 46, pp. 180-81).

Heracleon considered that 'children' must be understood in three ways:

(i) by nature (φύσει): a child is begotten;

(ii) by inclination (γνώμῃ): 'When one who does the will of another person by his own inclination is called the child of him whose will he does';

(iii) by merit (ἀξίᾳ): e.g., by doing the works of the devil they become like him.

Clearly, if one can become a 'child' by inclination, choice and will are involved. Some have by their choice become children of the devil; others, children of God.

We have, then, three types of persons: the pneumatic who responds in true faith to the Saviour; the psychic who responds but not fully to the word and who is

---

[138] Foerster, *GNOSIS*, p. 173.

[139] The father asks the Saviour to help his son, i.e. the nature thus constituted. A few sentences earlier Heracleon had said that John 4.48 was fittingly said to the kind of person whose nature is determined through works and who is convinced by means of sense perception and does not believe the word. See *fragment* 40, pp. 177-79.

convinced by means of sense perception; and the choics who do the works of the devil, and do not respond to the Saviour at all. Religious experience is here involved. The first group are the most 'spiritual'; the last are not spiritual at all; while the middle group are not as spiritual as they might be but cannot be 'written off' totally.[140]

Is then ontology a means of explaining the facts of religious experience? The truly spiritual are predestined to respond, which means that all is of the grace of God. They have a responsibility to others to help them to become true believers. The psychics are explained because of the nature of their response. They can respond and become children of God, or the opposite. It depends on their inclination. Those who make no response are predestined not to do so, because their nature is that of the devil; they are of the same substance as he.[141]

SUMMARY

The fragments of Heracleon are not substantial and we could wish for more before making firm pronouncements. He seems to have emphasized a conversion experience in which there was imparted a sense of release or separation from involvement in the material world, and the Holy Spirit is the agent of this. Faith is a necessary part of this religious experience, and the realization of one's salvation should lead to personal evangelism to convince the psychics of the possibility of their gaining salvation.

5.3. *Ptolemaeus*

In the extracts of Ptolemaeus preserved by Irenaeus and Clement of Alexandria,[142] the interpreter has to seek to press through the mythology to the religious experience of

---

[140] Cf. Elaine Pagels, *The Johannine Gospel in Gnostic Exegesis: Heracleon's Commentary on John* (Nashville, TN: Abingdon, 1973), pp. 112, 120.

[141] In recent years Luise Schotroff, '"Animae Naturaliter Salvandae", zum Problem der himmlischen Herkunft des Gnostikers', in W. Eltester (ed.), *Christentum und Gnosis* (BZNW 37; Berlin: Topelmann, 1969), pp. 65-97, has swung away from the view that the Valentinians assumed an automatic response on the part of the pneumatic. She asserted that the three classes of people illustrate three decisions defining human experience. Aland *Erwahlungstheologie*, p. 154, also argues that the sowing of the pneumatic seed is not limited to a definite group of people, and maintained (p. 171) that all depends on the encounter with the Saviour, which is the moment when sonship is constituted (p. 181). Pagels, *Johannine Gospel*, pp. 114-22, stressed the experiential focus of Valentinian theology and maintained (p. 100) that it was the theology of divine election which led to the description of 'natures'. She believes that hylics and pneumatics have no choice (p. 104); the psychics, however, may choose to be sons of God or the devil. Cf. Hauschild, *Gottes Geist,* p. 165, who said that Heracleon ontologised the thought of election with the help of the pneuma concept.

[142] Irenaeus, *AH* 1.1.1–1.8.6 (called Account A) (= Epiphanius, *Panarion* 31.9.1–31.27.16) runs parallel with Clement of Alexandria, *Excerpta ex Theodoto* 43.2–65.2 (though there are some differences). This can be ascribed to Ptolemaeus. To

which the mythology is the expression. Ptolemaeus makes much of the idea of an angelic counterpart in the Pleroma to the offspring of the Sophia outside the Pleroma.[143] The offspring need to be reunited with the angels in order to enter the Pleroma. Genesis 1.27 is so interpreted that male = angelic, while female = the superior seed (cf. also Adam and Eve who derives from Adam). The union of angel and offspring of Sophia is the ultimate goal of the training of the latter (see below).

What religious experience lies behind the conviction that one has a heavenly bridegroom, that one is part of an entity, the superior half of which is an angel? We have to conjecture here, but it is not stretching the imagination too much to envisage some sort of ecstatic or rapturous experience of the Spirit. Indeed, Hauschild considers that the 'Syzyzy' thought represents a reinterpretation of the concept that Christ or the Spirit is in the Christian.[144] But we perhaps need to go further than this general statement and conjecture a specific religious experience of some intensity which suggested to the recipient the 'invasion' of the earthly by the heavenly. In other words, Valentinian gnostics like Ptolemaeus were intellectual charismatics.

Ptolemaeus likened the seed sown in the pneumatic to gold in the mud. As the gold retains its nature and beauty because the mud cannot harm it, so pneumatics cannot lose or suffer injury to their spiritual substance, whatever material actions they may engage in. How, we may ask, do pneumatics realize that they have the seed within them? As gold is discovered buried in the mud, so we may envisage a special spiritual experience when penumatics 'discover' the seed within them.

According to Ptolemaeus, a period of training was necessary.[145] The seeds were sent forth immature, to be trained and brought up here,[146] and later, when they are accounted worthy of perfection, they will divest themselves of their souls[147] and become intelligent spirits and, without being hindered or seen, will enter into the Pleroma and will be bestowed as brides on the angels around the Saviour who himself will form a pair with Sophia who enters the Pleroma also.[148] Exactly what this training consists of is not spelt out in detail: it could in part refer to ongoing experience of the Spirit which the pneumatic now enjoys after the period of unawareness (like the gold in the mud), though it is linked with the acquiring of knowledge,[149] but had nothing to do with moral discipline according to Irenaeus.[150]

---

this we may add Ptolemaeus' *Letter to Flora* (preserved in Epiphanius *Panarion* 33.3.1–33.7.10). Hippolytus, *Refutatio* 6.29.22–36.4 exhibits certain differences over against Ptolemaeus' views as recorded by Irenaeus, and this is called Account B.

[143] This is the terminology used in Irenaeus, *AH* 1.5.6 and 1.4.5.
[144] Hauschild, *Gottes Geist*, p. 177, note 100.
[145] See *AH* 1.6.1 and *Exc. Ex Theod.* 59.1.
[146] *AH* 1.6.4 ('the seed sent forth thence in a feeble, immature state'); 1.7.5 ('weak').
[147] Cf. *Exc. Ex Theod.* 61.3: divesting of the passions.
[148] *AH* 1.7.1.
[149] See *Exc. Ex Theod.* 59.1.
[150] *AH* 1.6.3-4.

SUMMARY

Behind the recognition that one is an offspring of Sophia, there probably lies an experience which was interpreted as due to the divine Spirit.[151] The pneumatics' experience is expressed in terms of the rediscovery of themselves, of a sense of belonging to the heavenly world and of training to be prepared for the reunion with that heavenly world. This is expressed ontologically in the idea of the pneumatic seed within and mythologically in the idea of the ultimate marriage with an angel. In the mythology, the pneumatics' experience has been projected into the heavenly world. The dangers of this approach are evident in the way that Irenaeus describes gnostic reaction to the vast majority of church members: they were deemed spiritually inferior and would enjoy an inferior salvation.[152]

We have been left to surmise and conjecture from the intellectual framework or theological *raison d'être* back to the religious experience, and we cannot always be sure that our inferences are correct. The gnostic myths explained experience. Pneumatic experiences may have been part of this.

EXCURSUS

There are three further pieces of evidence which might also be considered in this section on Rome.

In the first place, accepting the conclusions of J.N.D. Kelly that the Old Roman Creed developed out of the three article formula at baptismal services and that it may have received its final redaction more than a decade before the end of the second century,[153] we would have a witness to the Spirit in the third section. 'I believe...in the Holy Spirit, the holy church, the forgiveness of sins, the resurrection of the flesh and eternal life'. The final four phrases may be properly described as the 'fruits of the Spirit in action'.[154] They serve to expound something of what is meant by affirming belief in the Holy Spirit. The Spirit created the church, which is 'holy', because indwelt by the Spirit and because it is set apart for God, and, therefore, on the way to moral holiness. The forgiveness of sins is associated with the complex of conversion-baptism-entry into the people of God, in which the Spirit is at work and is given to believers. The Spirit will bring about the great eschatological transformation, 'flesh' being chosen as being especially suitable to counter those who denied the resurrection of the body, especially gnostics (not to mention affirming the resurrection in the face of those who ridiculed it on philosophical grounds).

The Old Roman Creed, thus, becomes a witness to the Roman church's belief in the benefits given to it by God through the Spirit.

---

[151] Cf. H.A. Green, *The Economic and Social Origins of Gnosticism* (Atlanta, GA: Scholars, 1985), p. 239: 'Gnostic sects can be identified as religious groupings characterised by the belief that the Spirit is immediately present'.

[152] *AH* 1.6.2; *Exc. Ex Theod.* 51.2.

[153] J.N.D. Kelly, *Early Christian Creeds* (London: Longmans, Green, 1950), pp. 126-30.

[154] Kelly, *Creeds*, p. 155.

Secondly, another piece of evidence worth mentioning is the emergence of Montanism at Rome.[155] We do not know how strong numerically it became, but three writers refer to it.

When Eusebius commences to tell the story of Montanism, he begins (in *HE* 5.14) with a derogatory remark about the leaders who 'like poisonous reptiles crawled over Asia and Phrygia', mentions the three original leaders by name and then (5.15) continues 'Others flourished in Rome, of which Florinus[156] was the leader.and with him was Blastus'.[157] Both had 'fallen away' (had been excommunicated?) from the presbytery (5.15). Were these two men expelled from office because of their Montanist beliefs, or were they expelled from office and then gravitated towards Montanism?

Eusebius tells us twice that a certain Gaius published at Rome in Zephyrinus' time a work 'as an answer to Proclus, the champion of the Phrygian heresy' (6.20.3; 2.25.6). Possibly Gaius criticised Montanism for composing 'new scriptures' (6.20.3). Gaius himself went so far in his opposition to Montanism as to reject the book of Revelation and John's Gospel (so Hippolytus, *Refutatio omnium haeresium* 6.1.38), presumably in an attempt to deprive Montanism of any scriptural support, and he may have been one of the Alogi.[158]

Heine believed that there was hostility at Rome towards the idea of any new revelation in the period around the end of the second century, and in this atmosphere the Montanists appealed to the Paraclete sayings (especially Jn. 16.12-13).[159]

Tertullian has a fascinating paragraph in *adversus Praxean* 1:

For at that time the bishop of Rome was on the point of recognizing the prophecies of Montanus, Priscilla and Maximilla, and as a result of that recognition was offering peace to the churches of Asia and Phrygia;[160] but this man [Praxeas], by false assertions concerning the prophets themselves and their churches, and by insistence on the decisions of the bishop's predecessors, forced him to recall the letters of peace already issued and to desist from his project of receiving the spiritual gifts. Thus, Praxeas at Rome managed two pieces of the devil's business:

---

[155] For discussions see de Labriolle, *Crise*, pp. 245-90; Trevett, *Montanism*, pp. 55-66; R.E. Heine, 'The Gospel of John and the Montanist Debate at Rome', *Studia Patristica XXI* (Leuven: Peeters, 1989), pp. 95-100.

[156] If Florinus is the same as the Florinus of *HE* 5.20, then he was a native of Asia Minor and known to Irenaeus. He was attracted to or became an adherent of Valentinism. Irenaeus wrote a letter to both him and Blastus (see *HE* 5.20).

[157] Pace Labriolle, *Crise*, p. 276, who denied that Blastus was a Montanist.

[158] The name given by Epiphanius to heretics who opposed Montanism and who rejected John's Gospel and Revelation. Apart from the basic meaning of 'irrational', the term may have been intended to suggest opposition to the Logos of the Fourth Gospel.

[159] So Heine, *Montanist Debate*, pp. 99-100.

[160] Tertullian's remark that recognition by the bishop of Rome would give 'peace to the churches of Asia and Phrygia' seems either disingenuously inaccurate or naively optimistic.

he drove out prophecy [Montanism] and introduced heresy [monarchianism]: he put to flight the Paraclete and crucified the Father.

The remarks of Tertullian indicate the following sequence of events. At least two bishops gave an unfavourable response to Montanism (the inference from the plural 'predecessors'); then a new bishop was inclined to give a different assessment and 'recognize' the new prophecy; but Praxeas (representing the Asia Minor churches?) mounted a strong campaign to get the new bishop to change his mind and was successful, with the result that the new bishop withdrew his recognition.

If Tertullian wrote *adversus Praxean* around AD 210-11 or 213 and he was describing comparatively recent events, this would favour Zephyrinus as the new bishop with Eleutherus (174-89) and Victor (189-99) as his predecessors who were not minded to recognize Montanism, as Labriolle argued,[161] though Trevett prefers Eleutherus as the new bishop with Anicetus (155-66) and Soter (166-74) as those previously hostile,[162] while Lampe goes for Victor (189-99) as the bishop attacked with Soter and Eleutherus as his predecessors.[163] Certainty is not attainable, and for our purposes does not matter greatly. On any of these views, Montanism clearly had its adherents in Rome before 200. Some in Rome were favourably disposed towards it. Perhaps they formed a house congregation within the overall Roman church.

The final writer to mention Montanism at Rome was Hippolytus. In his work, *Refutatio omnium haeresium*, generally reckoned to have been written around the end of the second decade of the third century or later, Hippolytus attacked Montanism and revealed that one section of Montanists had veered over to Monarchianism (10.26).

Thirdly, if the 'traditional' view of the *Apostolic Tradition* as the work of Hippolytus in the early third century and reflecting Roman church practice going back into the second century were correct, there would be a case for including it within our survey. However, Hippolytus' authorship has come under attack, and the editors of the most recent edition (in the Hermeneia series)[164] are clearly sceptical. Furthermore, they argue for 'an aggregation of material'[165] over a period leading to what can now be reconstructed from the variety of witnesses to the *Apostolic Tradition*. Their assessment is that, while there is older material contained within it, perhaps originating as early as the mid-second century, other material may be as late

---

[161] Labriolle, *Crise*, pp. 257-275, esp. 273 (he dates Praxeas' activity to around 198-200, p. 275). Heine, *Montanist Debate*, p. 97, also opts for Zephrinus, whose initial favourable attitude, he believes, was an anomaly in Roman attitudes towards prophecy at the end of the seond century.

[162] Trevett, *Montanism*, p. 58.

[163] Lampe, *Christen*, p. 332 (*Christians at Rome*, p. 394-95).

[164] P.F. Bradshaw, M.E. Johnson and L.E. Phillips, *The Apostolic Tradition* (Hermeneia; Minneapolis, MN: Fortress, 2002).

[165] Bradshaw, Johnson and Phillips, *Apostolic Tradition*, p. 14. For a history of interpretation, including the recent doubts about Hippolytus' authorship, see pp. 1-6, 11-14. J.A. Cessato, *Hippolytus between East and West* (Oxford: Oxford University Press, 2002), pp. 99-100 accepts the doubts about the Roman provenance and Hippolytean authorship of the Apostolic Tradition.

as the mid-fourth century, and that 'it is unlikely that it represents the practice of any single Christian community'. They suggest a core document to which the rest has been added at various intervals.[166]

We may briefly mention that within this suggested core document there appear to be two references to the Spirit. In the section on bishops, the one chosen by all the people to be the bishop is to be ordained in the presence of the faithful who in silence are to pray for the descent of the Spirit on the one being ordained as bishop (2.4). Later on, when advice is being given on times when it is appropriate to pray, the faithful are advised to pray after awaking from sleep, but that if there is a service of 'instruction', they should give this preference and hasten to church in order to hear the Word of God, for the church is 'where the Spirit flourishes' (35.2). The importance of attending to the 'word' and the precedence accorded to public over private prayer emerge clearly. Both these references underline the importance of the believing community as a 'locus' of the Spirit and in its prayer for those elected to office within it.

The editors rightly point out that material added at a later date may not necessarily be a later composition but could be material which is as old as the core itself.[167] Thus, chapter 16 on the whole belongs to the core document, but v. 17 may be a later addition, and yet in its theological outlook it could be said to cohere with the two references to the Spirit just quoted, for the author writes 'If we have left out any other thing, the things themselves will inform you, for we all have the Spirit of God'. Likewise, the Prologue ends with the comment that 'the Holy Spirit bestows perfect grace on those who rightly believe, that they may know how those who preside over the church ought to hand on and preserve all things' (1.5).[168] Both 16.17 and 1.5 reveal a conviction that the Spirit will guide the faithful to discern what is right both in terms of doctrine and in coming to right decisions.

We do not intend to pursue the inquiry into material in the *Apostolic Tradition* any further. The few references to which we have drawn attention could well indicate that towards the end of the second century there was still a deeply held conviction that the Spirit of God was present with the believing congregation, wherever these particular traditions may have originated.

6. Conclusion

We have surveyed the literature emanating from within the Roman church, both 'orthodox' and 'heretical'. It gives us some reflection of what was being taught in all its diversity among Christians and interested inquirers in the period under review.

---

[166] Bradshaw, Johnson and Phillips, *Apostolic Tradition*, pp. 14-15.

[167] Bradshaw, Johnson and Phillips, *Apostolic Tradition*, p. 14.

[168] Bradshaw, Johnson and Phillips, *The Apostolic Tradition*, pp. 13-15, 22-23, do not indicate whether the present chapter might be the introduction to what they call the 'core document' or a later introduction. Even the core document would need some sort of introduction. Arguably, the theology of 1.5 fits an earlier rather than a later period.

At the beginning of our period, we have two writings composed within perhaps a decade of each other and revealing substantial differences. 1Peter seems to base the Christian life in the activity of the Spirit, from its start to its end. The Spirit is active in conversion; is at work within the life of the congregation making it the dwelling place or home of the God who is King, equipping members with various gifts and enabling the church to offer spiritual sacrifices; and sustains Christians amidst persecution. By contrast, Clement seems to subordinate Spirit to order within the church. Though he believes that a common experience of the Spirit binds Christians together, it cannot be said that this appears as a controlling or dominant theme in his lengthy letter. Clement mentions the Spirit occasionally but never discourses on the Spirit.

Both writers agree in seeing the apostolic mission as undergirded by the Spirit's activity (1 Pet. 1.11; 1 Clem. 43.2, cf. 42.4).

At the beginning of our epoch we are confronted with a diversity at Rome: the Spirit is experienced as a vital part of the Christian life in the one case, while the Spirit is a traditional concept but not a vitally significant part of the experience in the other.

The *Shepherd of Hermas* shows us that prophecy was believed to be the mouthpiece of the Spirit, though how far prophecy was a living and widespread phenomenon is difficult to gauge from *The Shepherd* itself in view of the conflicting nature of the evidence. What is surprising is Hermas' teaching on the delicacy of the Spirit as if the Spirit is inherently weak and ultra sensitive and not able to fight against evil. This aspect appears alongside that of the Spirit as power (personified in the twelve virgins around the Tower). If we were right earlier in suggesting that this idea of the delicacy of the Spirit is part of the moral urgency of the preaching of Hermas, it still remains a strange development, for it is shifting the emphasis from God to humans; from God's power available in the Spirit which helps, to the need of men and women so to act as to preserve the Spirit within them.

Justin began teaching in Rome a few years after Hermas published his work. Justin believed that all Christians had been baptized or circumcised with the Holy Spirit. They have been born anew through faith and the Spirit. He also reveals that activities like prophecy, miracle-working and exorcisms were still flourishing and these were seen as the gifts of the Spirit in fulfilment of Psalm 68 and Joel 2. The evidence, though culled indirectly from his writings, is far more positive than Hermas, on the role of the Spirit in Christian experience.

Although we know very little about Montanism at Rome, it did get a footing within the Christian community there and, according to Tertullian, came close to receiving official recognition, but in the end no less than three bishops returned an adverse verdict on it.

Interestingly, if experientially the Spirit does not appear to have been dominant in the writings emanating from Rome, taken as a whole, the blessings associated with the Spirit received acknowledgment in the Old Roman Creed.[169]

Our final block of writings was the 'Italian' school of Valentinus. In Ptolemaeus we observed how the experience of the Spirit had been 'ontologised', so that now the Spirit is a substance or part of a person. If we probe behind the mythology which Valentinian gnosticism developed, we may assume spiritual experiences which were explained in terms of a pneumatic seed implanted in the true Christians and which they rediscovered in conversion. The sense of kinship with the divine in some spiritual experience(s) was elucidated in terms of the heavenly seed sown within the pneumatics and destined to be reunited with an angelic partner. The division of human beings into pneumatics, psychics and choics, with the first being the spiritual elite, ran the risk of spiritual pride and a possible moral laxity.

With Valentinian gnosticism, we meet a speculative branch of Christianity which proved unacceptable to what came to be the mainstream Christian movement. It flowered within the church, only to be ejected from it, because its tenets were deemed incompatible with what was considered the apostolic faith. Whatever the leading Valentinian gnostics may have thought and said, their development went beyond the parameters of apostolic witness about the Spirit. It contravened it at one decisive point—that the gift of the Spirit was open to all who believe, and it developed an explanation of gnostic experience which perverted the basis of apostolic preaching as now deposited in the NT.

With Rome we have come to what we may call 'western Christianity', compared certainly with Syrian Christianity, with Asia Minor standing half way between them, both geographically and theologically. If Clement and Hermas are representative, then it cannot be claimed that it was natural to describe religious experience in terms of the Spirit. In the case of Clement, order seems to have so controlled his thinking that Spirit is subordinate to order. Hermas' view of the delicacy of the Spirit is bound to inhibit a sense of the Spirit as power, blowing like the wind and sweeping a person on in God's ways. We miss the sense of the Spirit which emerges in the Johannine writings and the *Odes of Solomon*, even Tatian, both as teacher and guide and as the mainspring of personal experience.

We sense the nearness, in terms of experience, of Clement, the author of The Pastoral Epistles and Polycarp. Office and order are uppermost; Spirit is controlled by these, rather than vice versa. Though he has visions, Hermas' sense of being the agent of the Spirit is not so pronounced as John of Patmos or Montanus, Priscilla and Maximilla. The sense of authority which pervades what John of Patmos says and which also comes across from Montanist oracles does not somehow emerge as strongly in Hermas. Where John of Patmos and Montanus would see themselves as authorized to speak directly to the churches, Hermas does not feel on the same level as the elders, even though he has a sense of divine call.

---

[169] See, e.g., Kelly, *Creeds*, pp. 155-57; H.J. Jaschke, *Der heilige Geist im Bekenntnis der Kirche* (Munster: Aschendorff, 1976), pp. 21-35.

Our conclusion has to be that overall we seem to have a diminishing stress on the centrality of the Spirit in religious experience as we move westwards.

CHAPTER 6

Southern Gaul

The first piece of extant evidence for Christianity in southern Gaul is the letter of the churches at Lyons and Vienne, which was addressed to their fellow Christians in Asia and Phrygia and gave an account of the horrendous persecution suffered in 177 under Marcus Aurelius and Lucius Verus.[1] This fact and a number of small details—of the martyrs killed in 177 Attalos and Alexander came from Pergamon and Phrygia respectively (*HE* 5.1.17, 49, 53); a slave's name was Pontikos, suggesting that his native area was Pontus in Asia Minor; Irenaeus was born in Smyrna according to his own testimony (*AH* 3.3.4; cf. Eusebius *HE* 5.20.5-6)—have suggested that close ties existed between the two areas, and offer, therefore, a possible clue pointing to the fact that the church in southern Gaul was founded through Christian people moving from Asia Minor. More than this we cannot say.

In the summer of 177, a horrendous and brutally savage persecution of Christians erupted in Lyons. It was probably instigated by the leading citizens and secured the eventual agreement of the emperor Marcus Aurelius. While Irenaeus was out of the city, taking a letter from the church to bishop Eleutherus in Rome requesting toleration for Asia Minor Montanists (Eusebius *HE* 5.4.1-2, 4), bishop Pothinus was martyred. Irenaeus was chosen on his return to succeed him. He later (ca.182-88) wrote a five volume work entitled *Adversus haereses* (*Against Heresies*), which is primarily an attack on Gnosticism, especially the teaching of Valentinus' pupils, and a defence of the Church's tradition (it is extant fully only in Latin translation; only parts of the original Greek have survived). A more popular work from him is entitled *Demonstration of the Apostolic Preaching*, which expounds the main themes of Christian belief according to the church's rule of faith (this has survived only in an Armenian translation). In two extant letters to bishop Victor of Rome, he urged respect for the Quatrodeciman position on Easter (*HE* 5.23.3,4) and action against one Florinus, a presbyter who held Valentinian views (*HE* 5.15.1; 5.20.4-8).

---

[1] Our sole authority for this is Eusebius *HE* 5.1-3. The text and translation is published in H. Musurillo, *The Acts of the Christian Martyrs* (Oxford: Clarendon, 1972), pp. xx-xxii, 62-85.

1. The Letter of the Church at Lyons and Vienne

This letter was probably written soon after the persecution of the summer of 177[2] and soon after Eleutherus had become bishop of Rome in succession to Soter. The bulk of the letter deals with a narrative of the suffering and death of the martyrs, seen as a glorious victory won by Christ through his suffering servants (*HE* 5.1.1-63),[3] to which Eusebius added two sections (5.2-3) with a view to the situation in Asia and Phrygia where there was 'dissension' due to the rise of Montanism.

HE 5.2 stresses the martyrs' charity, tolerance and compassion to those who, under judicial pressure or mob harassment, had denied Christ. They made every effort to persuade them to revoke their recantation and to stand firm in their witness to Christ. They showed love like a mother to them and prayed earnestly to God for them. Indeed, they managed successfully to persuade the lapsed to confess Christ anew (5.2.6: this picks up and repeats what the letter had earlier said as recorded at 5.1.45-46, where those who had initially denied Christ but were brought to re-confess him are likened to 'the dead' who are brought to life again or to miscarriages who are reconceived and given back alive to their mother, the Church). Such behaviour contrasted with 'the inhuman and merciless disposition towards the members of Christ' displayed by others (5.2.8), which may be an allusion to the rigorist attitude of Montanists towards the lapsed, though this has been denied.

Eusebius narrates how a certain Attalus corrected the harsh asceticism of a fellow Christian, Alcibiades, who, when imprisoned, tried to maintain his previous lifestyle. Attalus received a revelation that Alcibiades was not doing the right thing in not making use of God's gifts and was causing offence to others. Accordingly, he persuaded Alcibiades to eat all kinds of food and to thank God for them. The apologetic note is clear: it is not the Spirit's will that the asceticism advocated by Montanism should be imposed on all (5.3.1-3).

Thus, on two issues, the Gallic churches differed from the Montanist approach. This does not necessarily mean, however, that they were unsympathetic to an emphasis on the Spirit.

We turn now to investigate what the letter may reveal about the experience of the Spirit amongst members of these congregations.

A. Divine Presence

The letter recounts something about the activity of two members of the church, Alexander (a Phrygian by origin, who had spent many years in Gaul) and Vettius Epagathus. Alexander, a doctor, 'was known practically to everyone because of his love of God and his outspokenness in speech, for he did in fact possess a share in the

---

[2] W.H.C. Frend, *Martyrdom and Persecution in the Early Church* (Oxford: Blackwell, 1965), pp. 1-30, discusses the historical circumstances of the persecution.

[3] At 5.1.6, the letter quotes Romans 8.18, leading Weinrich, *Spirit and Martyrdom*, p. 189, to make the comment that 'the entire letter is, so to speak, a commentary on Rom.8.18'.

apostolic gift (ἀποστολικόν χάρισμα, 5.1.49). In this thumbnail sketch, we have a fascinating glimpse of how Christianity must have spread in these early years. Here was someone who earned his living through medicine, but whose love for God led him into witnessing to others. He stood in this respect in the apostolic succession and shared the same gift as the apostles. That here the call and empowering of the Spirit are in mind can hardly be doubted. The adjective 'apostolic' may have been applied because either experiences credited to the influence of the Spirit were rare and had come to be confined to the past apostolic era (in which case Alexander would be exceptional) or the apostolic era ('the founding era') was a time when the Spirit had been first poured out on the followers of Jesus and so it was natural to regard subsequent experience of the Spirit as similar to the apostolic charisma. The latter explanation commends itself on the grounds both of the evidence of the letter itself and of Irenaeus (see below, section 2).

Vettius Epagathus had drawn attention to himself, because, indignant at the biased judgments passed by the authorities against his fellow Christians, he asked to be allowed to speak in defence of them. This only led to his eventual martyrdom.

As a result of this and of his martyrdom, he earned himself the title 'the advocate of Christians; he had within himself the Advocate, the Spirit who inspired Zachariah' (παράκλητος Χριστιανῶν χρηματίσας, ἔχων δὲ τὸν παράκλητον ἐν ἑαυτῷ, τὸ πνεῦμα [πλέον] τοῦ Ζαχαρίου[4]). The language of the letter is conditioned by the judicial setting—hence the play on παράκλητος.[5] Clearly, for the writer, Vettius Epagathus was a Christian in whom the Holy Spirit dwelt. 'He was and is a true disciple of Christ, following the Lamb wherever He goes' (*HE* 5.1.10). The source of παράκλητος is clearly the fourth gospel (Jn. 15.26; 16.8-11), but we may ask whether the logion about the Spirit's aid in times of judicial interrogation (Mk. 13.11 par, Lk. 12.11-12) may have exerted some influence also. The difference that Vettius speaks on behalf of others is not an insurmountable one: the Spirit could be seen as using him to defend other believers. We could say that Mark 13.11 envisages a specific situation, whereas the Paraclete Sayings of the

---

[4] *HE* 5.1.9-10. The manuscript tradition varies on whether πλέον should be read or not. The reading without it is probably the 'harder' reading and is preferred by H.J. Lawlor and J.E. Oulton, *Eusebius Ecclesiastical History*, Vol. I (New York/Toronto: Macmillan/London: SPCK, 1927), p. 141, and G.W.H. Lampe 'Martyrdom and Inspiration', in W. Horbury and B. McNeil (eds.), *Suffering and Martyrdom in the New Testament* (Cambridge: Cambridge University Press, 1981), p. 126. Surprisingly, Musurillo, *Acts*, pp. 64-65, does not even mention the manuscript variation and includes πλέον in his printed text, though does not translate it. K. Lake, *Eusebius: The Ecclesiastical History*, Vol. I (Loeb Classical Library; Cambridge, MA: Harvard University Press/London: Heinemann, 1926), p. 411, takes the references to Zachariah in 5.1.9-10 to the father of John the Baptist because of the echoes of Luke 1 in the description of Vettius Epagathus, while for a tradition that Zachariah was martyred, see H. von Campenhausen 'Das Martyrium des Zacharias', *Aus der Frühzeit des Christentums* (Tubingen: Mohr, 1963).

[5] Frend, *Martyrdom and Persecution*, p. 17, sees here a pro-Montanist stance.

fourth gospel do not particularize but use lawsuit imagery. It could be that the description of Vettius Epagathus would turn the minds of Christians to both the Johannine Paraclete Sayings and the more limited, but very pertinent and relevant Synoptic promise of the Spirit's help before tribunals.

In the cases, then, of Alexander and Vettius Epagathus we have individuals who abounded with enthusiasm for the faith, who were motivated by a desire to spread that faith and by love of their fellow Christians and who counted their lives cheap for the gospel's sake. Such were deemed to be inspired by the Holy Spirit, whether it is stated indirectly as in the case of Alexander ('apostolic gift') or directly as in the case of Vettius Epagathus ('having within himself the Advocate').

B. Divine Illumination

When he refers to the incident in which Attalus persuaded Alcibiades, Eusebius concludes by saying of Attalus and the other martyrs: 'They were not inattentive[6] to God's grace, but the Holy Spirit was their counsellor' (5.3.3). This statement agrees with the statement that Attalus received a revelation (5.3.2).[7]

The letter only refers to this particular revelation. It would, strictly speaking, be impossible to judge how far we could generalize from the case of Attalus to others, and assume that others (non-martyrs) were recipients of the Spirit's guidance and revelation of God's will. Certainly, the Spirit is depicted as imparting knowledge of what is right in God's sight through a particular Christian. The Spirit imparted knowledge of God's will to one believer through another. The Letter does not, however, enlighten us as to the mode of this revelation.

C. Divine Power

We meet the idea of the Holy Spirit as power and strength particularly in martyrdom. The letter described Vettius Epagathus as showing the Spirit that indwelt him through the fullness of his love, in that he consented to lay down his life in defence of his fellow Christians (5.1.10). The Spirit led him to such a love for those in Christ that he embraced martyrdom for them.

The letter asserts that 'the joy of their martyrdom, their hope in the promises, their love for Christ and the Spirit of the Father' relieved the burden of the confessors (5.1.34). The first three items are the human attitude (the joy they experienced as they contemplated martyrdom, their hope based on and engendered by

---

[6] The Post-Nicene Fathers Library translation offers 'deprived of', but this sense of ἀνεπίσκεπτος is not attested in either H.G. Liddell, R. Scott, H.S. Jones and R. McKenzie, *A Greek-English Lexicon* (Oxford: Clarendon Press, 1968), p. 134, or G.W.H. Lampe, *A Patristic Greek Lexicon* (Oxford: Clarendon, 1961-68), p. 136.

[7] Lampe, 'Martyrdom and Inspiration', p. 119, commented on the 'pneumatology of martyrdom': 'The martyr's testimony was believed to be inspired by the Holy Spirit and the Christian who confessed his faith in circumstances of persecution was regarded as closely akin to the prophet as a recipient of revelation and a proclaimer of God's word'.

the promises, their love towards Christ), but the last is God's comfort and strength ('the Spirit of the Father').

At the same time, of course, joy, hope and love are among the fruit of the Spirit according to Paul, as is humility, a quality of the martyrs which the letter emphasizes. They begged that they should not be called martyrs before they had actually suffered death and asked for prayers that they might be faithful to the end and become perfected. They were also mindful of Jesus' exclusive right to the title martyr (5.2.2-4).

The idea of the martyrs' being strengthened or empowered frequently occurs. Blandina was filled with such power that her torturers were exhausted (5.1.18). Her confession 'I am a Christian' renewed her strength (5.1.19). Through her Christ 'showed that what human beings reckon as mean and unlovely and despicable are counted by God worthy of great glory, because of the love for Him which she powerfully demonstrated without boasting of it in any form' (5.1.17). Sanctus withstood all the indignities heaped upon him, with superhuman strength (5.1.20), and he remained firm, 'strengthened by the heavenly fountain of the water of life that flows from the side of Christ' (5.1.22): the Johannine echoes here (Jn. 4.10-14; 7.38; 19.34) permit our thinking that the strengthening agent, the crucified Christ's gift, is the Spirit. When tortured a second time, this proved by Christ's grace to be not a torture but a cure (5.1.24).

Those in prison were horribly tortured, but were 'strengthened by the Lord and given power in body and soul, stimulating and encouraging the others' (5.1.28). Even the ninety-year old Pothinus, weak and infirm though he was, did not weaken amidst the interrogation, the howls of the mob and the physical maltreatment accorded to him without any respect for his age. It is said of him that he was 'strengthened ὑπὸ προθυμίας πνεύματος on account of the pressing desire for martyrdom' (5.1.29). Is this a reference to the 'spirit' of Pothinus which was eager or ready or willing,[8] or a reference to God's Spirit who supplies or arouses the eagerness or readiness or willingness[9] (taking πνεύματος as a genitive indicating the author or origin of the quality mentioned in the preceding noun)? Weinrich's case for arguing for a reference to God's Spirit is twofold: the conviction that the narrative is modelled on Mark 14.38, where he takes πνεῦμα as God's Spirit, and the fact that Irenaeus takes the Marcan verse in exactly this way (*AH* 5.9.2). Of these, the latter is more significant as it shows how Mark 14.38 was being interpreted by someone in the leadership of the Lyons and Vienne congregation. We have just noted that in the immediately preceding paragraph (5.1.28) the letter has operated with a body-soul (σῶμα-ψυχή) pair, and a little later in paragraph 29 once again there is a body-soul contrast in respect of Pothinus, so might we not have expected a similar use here instead of σῶμα-πνεῦμα if the writer had the human spirit in mind? But since at

---

[8] Lake, *Eusebius*, p. 421, has 'zeal of spirit'. Musurillo, *Acts*, p. 71, offers 'eagerness of spirit', while the Penguin Classics translation by G. Williamson, *Eusebius: The History of the Church* (rev. and ed. by A. Louth; Harmondsworth: Penguin, 1989), p. 143, renders by 'spiritual enthusiasm'.

[9] Weinrich, *Spirit and Martyrdom*, pp. 193-94, and 211 (note 23).

5.1.9 the letter describes Vettius Epagathus as 'fervent in spirit' (ζέων τῷ πνεύματι) that point is not decisive. Could it be said that the writer wished to convey both a reference to God's help and to Pothinus' own wish in the phrase and deliberately left it ambiguous? That possibility cannot be completely ruled out, but one would expect one sense to be uppermost. The lack of any accompanying phrase with πνεῦμα, such as 'of God' or 'Fatherly' is a further factor making an absolutely firm decision difficult. While it is very tempting to follow Weinrich, we do not feel that his case is absolutely assured.

The letter draws a vivid contrast between those who faithfully confessed Christ and were imprisoned and those who denied him but were also imprisoned. The former went forth to their martyrdom 'gladly; great glory and grace were mingled on their faces, so that they even wore their chains like a beautiful ornament, like a bride adorned with golden tassels embroidered in many colours, and they were perfumed with the sweet savour of Christ, so that some thought that they had been anointed with worldly perfume' (5.1.35). By contrast, the latter were depressed, downcast, wretched and covered with every disgrace, and they still had to bear the insults of the pagan mob. Because of their defection, they had lost the all-honourable, glorious, life-giving Name (5.1.35).

The letter reports of the doctor Alexander, previously mentioned, that amidst the horrible persecution he did not utter any cry of pain but 'held converse with God in his heart' (5.1.51). It also speaks of those, who had been tortured so severely that it seemed impossible for them to survive, actually living on: 'Although deprived of human attention, they were strengthened and given power by the Lord in soul and body', and they continued to encourage their comrades in prison (5.1.28).

We notice also how the concept of Christ in the martyrs or Christ's achieving things through the martyrs pervades the account.[10] Christ, suffering in Sanctus, achieved great glory and overwhelmed the adversary and thus gave an example to those who remained that nothing was to be feared where love of the Father existed and that nothing was painful where Christ's glory was present (5.1.23). Fellow Christians gazed on Blandina who seemed to hang on the post in the arena in the form of a cross, and 'saw in the person of their sister him who was crucified for them' (5.1.41). The letter says of her that 'she had put on Christ, that mighty and invisible Athlete, and had overcome the adversary in many contests and through her conflict had won the crown of immortality' (5.1.42).[11] During her dying moments she did not perceive what was happening 'because of the hope and possession of what she believed in and because of her communion with Christ' (5.1.56).

---

[10] Lampe, 'Martyrdom and Inspiration', pp. 119-20, called this the Christocentric aspect of martyrdom. Von Campenhausen, *Idee des Martyriums*, pp. 89-91, commented on the shift, as time went on, from the Spirit's help in witnessing, to Christ's presence strengthening the martyr.

[11] Lampe, 'Martyrdom and Inspiration', p. 122, wrote, 'The faithful confessor is inspired by the Holy Spirit and dies as an imitator of Christ and a participant in his victory over the demonic powers'.

Frend discussed whether Montanism influenced the Christians of Lyons.[12] While noting many similarities of language and ideas between them and the Phrygian Montanists, he thinks 'The problem would, however, appear to be more one of parallel religious developments rather than allegiances'.[13] This seems an apposite comment, since, while the Lyons Christians display evident experience of the Spirit/risen Christ, their letter breathes a different atmosphere from Montanist rigorism and asceticism (which the redactor exploited).

Summary

If parallel religious development is a correct assessment and the experience reflected in the martyrs of Lyons and Vienne does not owe its inspiration to Montanism, then we have evidence of the independent vitality of Christian experience in the 170s in southern Gaul, coming from the period after the dreadful persecution of 177. Faith before the persecution must have been vibrant for these Lyons and Vienne Christians to stand firm for Christ, when persecution erupted, conscious that the Spirit of God was guiding and empowering them.

The conviction that the martyrs were inspired and upheld by the Holy Spirit or by Christ breathes through the letter. And it is married to a gentle, loving and compassionate outlook. Their spiritual experience did not lead to fanaticism and pride, but humility and courage of the highest order.

The Spirit is also seen as one who guides some believers into what is God's will and corrects mistaken emphases in the lives of others.

2. Irenaeus

Because Irenaeus said that when a boy he heard Polycarp (*AH* 3.3.4), he was presumably a native of Smyrna or a neighbouring town. If he studied at Rome (a conjecture based on *AH* 3.3.3 where he speaks appreciatively of Justin's teaching), then he remained unknown to the leaders of the church.[14] Later, he became a presbyter and then bishop of the church at Lyons and Vienne. While bishop, he wrote *Adversus Haereses*[15] and also *Demonstration of Apostolic Preaching*, which enable us to reconstruct Irenaeus' system of belief. Here we need not go into the

---

[12] Frend, *Martyrdom and Persecution*, pp. 16-17. If Montanism started ca.172/3, the question arises whether it could have directly influenced the southern Gallic churches by 177?

[13] Frend, *Martyrdom and Persecution*, p. 16.

[14] The letter which Irenaeus took from the Lyons-Vienne congregation commended him to the Roman church leaders, as A. von Harnack, *Geschichte der altchristlichen Literatur II: Chronologie I* (Leipzig: Hinrichs, 1897), pp. 324, 332, convincingly argued.

[15] See A. Benoit, *Saint Irénée, introduction à l'étude de sa théologie* (Paris: Presses universites de France, 1960), for an analysis of the structure of *AH*. All quotations are from *AH*, unless specified to be from the *Demonstration*.

issue of Irenaeus' sources.[16] Of recent scholars, G. Wingren and H-J. Jaschke (to mention but two) have argued that Irenaeus has welded his material into a coherent whole.[17] Even Hauschild, who is more favourably disposed to the kind of theory of multiple sources proposed by Loofs,[18] admits that Irenaeus 'lived from many traditions but he has bound them together into a certain unity'.[19]

We need to bear in mind the polemical nature of *AH* and the fact that Irenaeus concentrated mainly on the doctrine of God and the person of Christ,[20] plus the question of the authority on which belief in God is based: revelation, scripture, and true gnosis.[21] Irenaeus had especially to refute the gnostic view that God was remote from the world, because matter is inferior and the divine cannot have contact with it. There were fundamental differences over the Spirit too (the spiritual seed idea and the corollary of this in terms of redemption and ethics), but it was the other topics that engaged Irenaeus' attention particularly. Despite this, Irenaeus' work abounds in references to the Spirit, and we can gain a well-rounded picture from what he says. For example, he wrote: 'For where the church is, there is the Spirit of God; and where the Spirit of God is, there is the church and every kind of grace' (3.24.1). 'Where the Spirit of the Father is, there is a living person' (5.9.3). These two quotations of themselves can serve as an illustration of the central significance, in religious experience, which the Spirit had for Irenaeus:[22] without the Holy Spirit there is neither church nor individual Christian. Without the Spirit there is no life. The first of these quotations warns us always to bear in mind the ecclesiological setting for the experience of the Spirit in Irenaeus' thinking.[23] In pursuing our interest in how far religious experience was 'stamped' by the Holy Spirit for

---

[16] See especially A. Loofs, *Theophilus von Antiochien adversus Marcionem und die anderen theologischen Quellen bei Irenäus* (TU 46; Leipzig: J.C. Hinrichs, 1930), and the important critiques by F.R. Montgomery-Hitchcock, 'Loofs' Theory of Theophilus of Antioch as a source of Irenaeus', *JTS* 38 (1937), pp. 130-139, 255-66; 'Loofs' Asiatic Source IQA and the Ps. Justin, *de resurrectione*', *ZNW* 36 (1937), pp. 35-60.

[17] G. Wingren, *Man and the Incarnation* (Edinburgh: Oliver & Boyd, 1959); H-J. Jaschke, *Der heilige Geist im Bekenntnis der Kirche* (Münster: Aschendorff, 1976).

[18] Hauschild, *Gottes Geist*, pp. 207-208.

[19] Hauschild, *Gottes Geist*, p. 220. The footnote to this sentence runs, 'One can thus speak with a certain degree of correctness of a "unified teaching on the Spirit by Irenaeus" [so Brox, *Offenbarung*, p. 163, n. 147] so long as one does not thereby overlook that it has been built up out of different complexes.' For Hauschild, Irenaeus has blended two basic viewpoints: the prophetic Spirit who empowers to special deeds (e.g. 3.9.3) and the life-giving Spirit who forms the essence of a person (e.g. 5.6-13).

[20] Cf. Jaschke, *Der heilige Geist*, pp. 176-77, 185.

[21] Cf. N. Brox, *Offenbarung, Gnosis and gnostischen Mythos bei Irenäus von Lyons* (Salzburg-München: A. Pustet, 1966).

[22] A. d'Ales, 'La Doctrine de l'Esprit en saint Irénée', *RSR* 14 (1924), pp. 537-38, said of 3.24.1 that it was the most eloquent and complete expression of Irenaeus' doctrine of the Spirit.

[23] Cf. Jaschke, *Der heilige Geist*, pp. 159, 265-77, 341, 347, 349-51.

Irenaeus, it would be wholly wrong for us to envisage the individual in isolation. For Irenaeus the church is in a sense primary and the individual derivative.

Irenaeus' conviction that the OT prophets had received God's Spirit deserves comment. The reason within God's purpose for this is significant: 4.14.2 states that God raised up prophets 'accustoming man upon earth to bear His Spirit (within him) and to hold communion with God'. The prophetic experience is part of God's educative process: He was seeking to counteract the effects of the Fall and to restore human beings to their pristine state and the possibility of developing that state into maturity.[24] The incarnation continued that educative process: the Word/Son 'became the Son of Man that he might accustom man to receive God and God to dwell in man, according to the Father's good pleasure' (3.20.2);[25] the Spirit truly prepared man in the Son of God and the Son led him to the Father (4.20.5); the Spirit became accustomed through the incarnation to dwell in human nature (3.17.1). By his incarnation the Son unites the human and the divine and so prepares the way for the outpouring of the Spirit, thus opening the possibility of the ultimate gift of the vision of the Father and the incorruption of humans.

In another passage (4.20.6), Irenaeus spoke of the prophetic experiences of God (their vision of the advent of the Lord, their audition of the divine voice, their sight of the prophetic Spirit and his influence): such were prefigurements[26] of that ultimate beatific vision of God for 'those who bear His Spirit (in them) and always wait patiently for His coming'. Although Irenaeus is talking about the OT prophets, he describes them and what they foresaw in terms of what he believes a Christian is, namely someone who bears God's Spirit within them and who is looking forward to the consummation of salvation and the vision of God. The present and future aspects of salvation are linked together and seen to be continuous: present experience of the Spirit in fact preparing us for the future glorious experience of God. Irenaeus uses a triadic structure in his summarizing description of the prophetic experience: 'God the Father is shown forth in all these (operations), the Spirit indeed working and the Son ministering, while the Father was approving and man was being prepared for salvation'.

---

[24] Cf. 4.38.3 for the general idea of the development of humans.

[25] Jaschke, *Der heilige Geist*, p. 218, says, 'The Spirit who overshadowed Mary shaped the human nature of the Son in the incarnation and so can also possess the creature in his totality'. Pentecost is thus the result of the process of the divine 'growing accustomed' to dwell in man.

[26] See R. Tremblay, *La Manifestation et la vision de Dieu selon saint Irénée de Lyon* (Münster: Aschendorff, 1978), pp. 71, 91-102 (esp. 94-95, 101), 145, 147, 165-171, for a careful examination of relevant passages to show that, while concrete realities, the prophetic experiences were signs or types, imperfect economies, which only sketch those by which the Word-Son will show himself in the incarnation. They still leave the Word-Son invisible; it is the incarnation that makes him visible. Cf. the same point made earlier but more briefly by A. Houssiau, *La Christologie de saint Irénée* (Louvain-Gembloux: Publications Universitaires, 1955), pp. 87-90, 130.

A little further on (4.20.8), Irenaeus again reverts to the idea of our being prepared in the OT era. He says that 'the Spirit of God pointed out by the prophets things to come, forming and adapting us beforehand that we might be made subject to God'. In one sense the prophetic experience is analogous to Christian experience. Their experience is that necessary discipline and training in order that humans might be received into the future glory of God.[27]

These passages are instructive for our theme: they concern the OT prophets,[28] yet they reveal how Irenaeus was thinking about Christians and how central the experience of the Spirit was in his understanding of the Christian faith. In his description of what the prophets experienced in an anticipatory manner, he helps us see that for him Christians are those who bear the Spirit within them.

The same Spirit who rested on the prophets of old now rests on the church and its members (4.33.9, 15). Pentecost is the fulfilment of God's promises and means the universal outpouring of the Spirit (3.12.1.). The same Spirit who came on the OT prophets had come upon Christians, 'although he has been poured out upon us after a new fashion in these last times' (4.33.15): active from creation onwards, he is received by those who believe God and follow His Word.

The 'vineyard' of Matthew 21.43 has been taken away from the Jews and given to the church, and this 'illustrious church is everywhere, for those who receive the Spirit are everywhere' (4.36.22; cf. *Dem.* 6). While Irenaeus is concerned in context to trace the various stages of the history of salvation back to the one God, we note that 'church' and 'those who receive the Spirit' are set in parallel. The implication is that the heart of Christianity is the experience of the Spirit. The hallmark of the church and its members is the possession of the Spirit.

Thus, even those who are barbarians as regards language have salvation 'written in their hearts by the Spirit, without paper or ink' (3.4.2), alluding to 2 Corinthians 3.1-6. Men and women, despised on cultural grounds as barbarians, have experienced God's Spirit in their hearts, and consequently they preserve the church's ancient tradition which goes back to the apostles. The subjective and objective sides of Christian experience are held together in an exemplary manner. Salvation is a matter of the 'heart'—the Spirit has been at work in the inner experience. Yet the objective side is the faithful adherence to apostolic tradition. The experience of the Spirit does not produce subjectivism on the rampage, but is in harmony with the tradition.

Once again, this paragraph reveals where Irenaeus puts the centre of Christianity: salvation through the mediating work of the Spirit, and, since that salvation has been wrought by the Creator through His Son, Jesus Christ, there is a triadic confession of the Father, Son and Spirit.

---

[27] J. Behr, *Asceticism and Anthropology in Irenaeus and Clement* (Oxford: Oxford University Press, 2000), p. 56, says that for Irenaeus God was seen prophetically in the Spirit in the OT, adoptively in the Son, and paternally in the future Kingdom for those prepared by the Spirit for the Son who leads us to the Father.

[28] Cf. *Demonstration* 56: The righteous of the OT era, 'such as feared God and died in righteousness and had in them the Spirit of God, as the patriarchs and prophets and righteous persons', may obtain salvation at the Last Judgment.

A. Divine Presence

We shall begin our survey by considering when and how for Irenaeus believers receive the Holy Spirit. He states clearly in *Demonstration* 42 that Jesus Christ gave the Holy Spirit in baptism to believers and that the Holy Spirit abides in them continually, provided that they walk in truth and holiness. Christ cleansed 'their [Gentiles'] souls and bodies by the baptism of water and of the Holy Spirit' (*Dem.* 41). According to *Demonstration* 3, three blessings are linked to baptism in the triune name: remission of sins; seal for eternal life; and new birth for God, i.e. adoption. Though here the Holy Spirit is not expressly named as the author of these blessings, nonetheless we may safely assume that he is in mind, both because of the specific mention of him in the Trinitarian formula which precedes the reference to the blessings and in the light of what Irenaeus says in 41-42. The reference to baptism following a confession of the Father, Son and Holy Spirit suggests a kind of elaboration of that confession, especially the work of the Holy Spirit.[29]

After *Demonstration* 6 outlines a Trinitarian basis for our faith, Irenaeus continues in 7: 'And for this reason the baptism of our regeneration proceeds through these three points: God the Father bestowing on us regeneration through His Son by the Holy Spirit.' The Son and Spirit are God's agents to effect regeneration on believers in baptism.

At *AH* 3.17.1, Irenaeus begins by denying that Christ or Saviour descended on Jesus. The apostolic testimony asserted that it was the Spirit of God who descended on him in his baptism, and Irenaeus cites Isaiah 11.2 and 61.1 in support; then declares that it is the same Spirit who, the Lord promised, would help the disciples (Mt. 10.20); and follows this up by saying, 'And again, when giving to the disciples the power of regeneration unto God, he said to them "Go and teach all nations, baptizing them in the name of the Father and of the Son and of the Holy Spirit". For God promised through the prophets that in the last times He would pour out him [the Spirit] upon (His) servants and handmaids'. The cluster of ideas—regeneration, baptism, Holy Spirit—is hardly accidental. The power of regeneration is linked with the execution of the Lord's command to baptize, and the connecting link (*hunc enim promisit...effundere se in novissimis temporibus* [For he promised that he himself would pour him (the Spirit) out in the last times]) binds the Spirit's outpouring with this baptism, and it is clearly the Spirit who effects the regeneration. There is an implicit parallelism between Jesus' baptism and ours in this sequence of thought, the common denominator being the bestowal of the Holy Spirit.

In the next paragraph we read: 'For our bodies have received through the bath that unity which leads to incorruption; but our souls, by means of the Spirit. Therefore, both are necessary, since both contribute towards the life of God' (3.17.2).

---

[29] Cf. Jaschke, *Der heilige Geist*, pp. 131-39. There is widespread evidence of a baptismal confession in which the Third Article confessed belief in the Spirit and the blessings associated with his activity: see *Epistula Apostolorum* 5; Justin *Apol. 1*.61; Irenaeus *AH* 4.33.7; and *Demonstration* 3,6.

Baptism marks the entry of believers into the church—the many become one in Christ. So it is a means of physical unity within God's people. The Spirit is imparted to the soul and this also is a bond of union. Since the Spirit is given in baptism, the two coincide. Both are necessary. This is a clear statement that baptism without the gift of the Spirit is incomplete. The outward rite of baptism has value, but the Spirit is also necessary. Both contribute towards the bestowal of God's life to the believer.

The healing of the man born blind through washing in the pool of Siloam has for Irenaeus a twofold meaning: the man was restored to his original formation (creation) and he was reborn ('that regeneration which takes place by means of the bath', 'inasmuch as man, with respect to that formation which was after Adam, having fallen into transgression, needed the bath of regeneration', 5.15.3). There was a physical restoration, but also a spiritual regeneration. The washing in the pool of Siloam is a symbol of baptism. The thought of the Spirit is below the surface of what Irenaeus writes.

Clearly the one who has responded to the church's proclamation of the gospel with believing faith in Christ receives the Spirit in baptism as far as Irenaeus is concerned. The human response of faith is matched from God's side with the renewing of a person's being through the Holy Spirit.

Certain expressions and concepts which Irenaeus uses lead us to believe that in his thinking the reception of the Spirit was a conscious experience. These may be mentioned as follows:

(i) The Abba prayer, mentioned twice by Paul as being prompted by the Spirit (Gal. 4.4-6; Rom. 8.14-15), is seized upon by Irenaeus. He exploits it in contexts where he mentions adoption (see below). Thus, at 4.9.2 he refers to the Holy Spirit, who is with us and who cries Abba Father, while 5.8.1 quotes Romans 8.15 and mentions the Spirit again as the author of the Abba cry. We may also refer to 3.6.1, though here the Spirit is not specifically mentioned. Irenaeus refers the phrase 'You are gods and all sons of the Most High' from Psalm 82.1 to those 'who have received the grace of adoption, by which we cry Abba Father'.[30]

By itself this point would not, of course, be decisive, but it will be part of a chain of evidence. For the moment, we content ourselves with saying that Irenaeus appears to have found the prayer of Christians addressing God as Abba through the movement of the Spirit within them to be a significant feature of their Christian life.

---

[30] Irenaeus refers the phrase 'God stood in the congregation of the gods, He judges among the gods' to 'the Father and the Son and those who have received the adoption; but these are the church' (3.6.1). The later verses of Psalm 82 (vv. 6-7) are referred to those who have not received the gift of adoption, but who 'despise the incarnation of the pure generation of the Word of God, defraud human nature of promotion to God, and prove themselves ungrateful to the Word of God who became flesh for them' (3.19.1). See A. Rousseau and L. Doutreleau (eds.), *Contre Les Hérésies III/I* (Paris: Les Éditions du Cerf, 1974), p. 254; and Behr, *Asceticism*, pp. 69-70, for a discussion of this passage.

(ii) The Abba cry leads naturally on to the theme of adoption. Irenaeus can often use 'adoption' as an umbrella term for salvation without any elaboration.[31] On other occasions he does elaborate, and it is these passages which are of interest to us.

Baptism is the point of adoption:[32] thus *Demonstration* 3 says that 'this baptism is the seal of eternal life and is the new birth unto God, that we should no longer be the sons of mortals but of the eternal and perpetual God'. The images of new birth and becoming God's children are here fused together. In 4.31.2 Irenaeus points out that it is only God Himself who can bestow the power of giving birth to children on the elder and younger church (Jewish and Gentile respectively). God has made His Word the father of the human race, and the Word poured out the life-giving seed, i.e. the Spirit, through his incarnation. From his incarnation the two synagogues (churches) produced 'living sons to the living God'. The Jewish and Gentile churches' power to produce 'living sons' is due to the Word and the Spirit, i.e., the incarnation when flesh and Spirit were united, while stage two is assumed, namely that after his exaltation this union was extended and universalized by the gift of the Spirit to believers. The fact that there are now 'living sons' is due to the gift of the Spirit. A living son is, like the Word incarnate, a commingling of flesh and Spirit. It is, above all, the gift of the Spirit which makes us children who are alive.

That the experience of the Spirit lies at the heart of what Irenaeus understands by adoption emerges from other passages. At 5.12.2 Irenaeus is distinguishing between the breath of life which all people have and the vivifying Spirit. When the sinner turns from evil to what is good, he receives the quickening Spirit and will find life. To this end he quotes the LXX version of Isaiah 57.16 in a way which has destroyed the parallelismus membrorum of the Hebrew:

'For the Spirit shall go forth from me
And I have made every breath.'

The latter is what everyone shares in; the Spirit, however, is poured forth by God 'upon the human race by adoption of sons'. Adoption and Spirit go together, and this status and experience are open to everyone, though not all respond to God's saving activity.

Adoption means to know and love God the Father and to obey His word (4.16.5). God has widened the scope of 'those laws which are natural and noble and common to all' from their application to the Jews: God 'has generously given human beings (the privilege of) knowing God as Father by adoption and to love Him with the whole heart and to follow His word unswervingly... He has also increased their reverence, for sons should have more respect than slaves and have greater love for their father'. Here we breathe the essence of the filial relationship: it has its side of respect and awe (*timor*), but also of love and affection (*diligere eum ex toto corde*).

---

[31] See 3.6.1-3 (twice); 3.19.1; 3.20.2; 3.21.4; 4.33.4; 5.32.2
[32] Cf. Jaschke, *Der heilige Geist*, p. 167; Behr, *Asceticism*, p. 69.

The 'knowing' is clearly that of personal relations, not something abstract or theoretical.

This is confirmed by 3.18.7. Irenaeus here says that the Mediator between God and humans had 'to bring to friendship and concord, so that at one and the same time God received man and man presented himself to God. For, in what way could we be partakers of the adoption of sons, unless we had received from Him through the Son fellowship with God Himself?' While the Spirit is not expressly mentioned here, the other passages permit us to assume that the Word sets up the possibility of this friendship and the Spirit is the means of realizing it. The Spirit confers what Christ has made possible.

Examination of the relevant passages reveals that adoption is a very meaningful concept and experience for Irenaeus: Christians have been brought into a loving relationship with their heavenly Father and at the heart of this relationship, making it possible, is the Spirit's activity.

(iii) Akin to adoption, but belonging to a different range of ideas, is that of new life, which has already been touched upon in several of the quotations previously utilized. Irenaeus is fond of emphasizing the vivifying effect of the Spirit. Because humanity has been overcome by the devil and is in bondage to sin and death, human beings need to be set free and quickened to life, and this is what the Spirit does. Irenaeus pictures the Spirit continually renewing the youth of the church: the Spirit 'as if it were some precious deposit in an excellent vessel, is rejuvenated and makes the vessel which contains it to be rejuvenated also. For this gift of God has been entrusted to the church, as breath was to the first created person, for this purpose that all its members might receive it and be vivified' (3.24.1).

Here Irenaeus draws a parallel between the creation of Adam in Genesis 2 and the creation of the church: as God breathed into man and he became a living being, so He bestowed His Spirit on the church and gave its members life (cf. the same parallel in 5.12.2: 'The breath of life which made man an animated being is one thing and the vivifying Spirit, who also caused him to become spiritual, is another'). Then Irenaeus uses Isaiah 42.5, in exactly the same way as he used Isaiah 57.16 (see above), namely by separating breath and Spirit: that God gave breath to people on earth and the Spirit to those who walk upon it.

The breath of life is given to all living creatures and is temporal. The Spirit, by contrast, is eternal and 'is theirs alone who tread down earthly desires' (which is a description of believers); and is poured out by God on the human race by adoption of sons (again, a way of referring to believers. The gift is offered to all, but only those who respond receive the Spirit and in that act are thereby adopted as sons).

Irenaeus explains Jacob's wives and concubines allegorically in 4.21.3. That Jacob had sons from his wives and concubines becomes a symbol that 'Christ should present sons to God, both from freemen and from slaves after the flesh, bestowing on all, in the same manner, the gift of the Spirit, who vivifies us'. In this allegory, Jew and Gentile are treated alike—both receive 'the vivifying Spirit', though they come from the free (the Jewish race) and the slave (the Gentiles). The important thing for our purpose is the link between the Spirit and receiving life.

So, then, the Father bestows 'regeneration' on us through His Son by the Holy Spirit (*Dem.* 7); alternatively, Irenaeus can say that it is the Spirit who 'renews' humans to God (*Dem.* 6).

If Irenaeus can use the language of the vivifying Spirit, this strongly suggests that for him the passage from the old life to the new life in Christ is a vivid and memorable one. Again, we would suggest that behind the use of a certain type of language there was a certain type of experience. To those most conscious of a dramatic experience of the Spirit, the language of new life, of being regenerated, of being revivified, springs naturally to the lips.

(iv) Germane to our theme is also Irenaeus' use of the image of water,[33] which is a picture with rich associations in the Bible and which had been used for the Spirit, particularly by the Fourth Gospel (Jn. 4.14; 7.37-39). In 4.14.2 the Spirit is described as 'like many waters', because God is rich and the Word can liberally confer benefits upon his subjects. The 'many waters' thus represent an inexhaustible supply of blessing proceeding from God to humans, in the capacity to supply spiritual renewal and growth.

For Irenaeus, the Son of God, who is always one and the same, gives to believers a well of water springing up to eternal life, a clear allusion to John 4.14, and, therefore, by implication, to the gift of the Spirit (4.36.4). In 4.33.14 Irenaeus recalls God's promise of a new covenant (Jer. 31.31-34) and of a new heart and spirit (Ezek. 36.26) and he quotes Isaiah 43.19-21 which mentions the new Exodus, in the course of which God will cause rivers to arise to give drink to His people. He takes the words of Second Isaiah as a prediction of the liberty of the new covenant: 'the faith in Christ, the way of righteousness sprung up in the desert, and the streams of the Holy Spirit in a dry land, to give water to the elect people of God whom He has acquired that they might show forth His mighty works'. The desert or dry land becomes a symbol of humans apart from God before the incarnation. Christ and Spirit together transform the situation: the former is 'the way of righteousness', while the latter is 'the streams' which give 'water to the elect people of God'.[34] The Holy Spirit's work is to vivify God's chosen people.

In another passage (3.17.2), Irenaeus works extensively with the dryness/water imagery as a picture for the work of the Spirit. He first describes believers as like a lump of dough which must be united by means of liquid; that is, believers needed to be made one in Christ by means of 'the water from heaven'; 'through the bath [of baptism] we have received a union which leads to incorruption'. There is in all probability a dual reference here: Irenaeus has in mind the Holy Spirit ('the water from heaven'), but the phraseology 'water' leads his thought on to the idea of baptism, since that is where the believer first encounters the Spirit and receives him (as expounded above), and so he can speak of 'the bath' as the sacrament of the church's unity, which leads to incorruption.

---

[33] Behr, *Asceticism*, p. 67, has also noticed that Irenaeus was fond of using the image of water for the Spirit.

[34] Rousseau and Doutreleau (eds.), *Contre Les Hérésies, III/I*, (SC), p. 274, see here an echo of Romans 3.22 and John 7.37-39.

Then, secondly, Irenaeus likens people to a dry tree unable to bring forth fruit without rain from above, but believers' souls have been moistened by the Spirit.

Both the union of believers through the one baptism and the gift of the Spirit contribute to the life of God imparted to us. The Lord Jesus received the water which springs up to eternal life and conferred it upon 'those who are partakers of himself, by sending the Holy Spirit upon all the earth'. Union with Christ means receiving the Spirit. John 4 and the Samaritan woman are once more in Irenaeus' mind: the Lord promised her living water 'so that she should thirst no more..., having in herself water springing up to eternal life'.

Irenaeus continues to work with the dryness/water imagery in 3.17.3-4. Gideon's prophecy (Irenaeus uses 'prophesied', whereas, strictly speaking, Gideon's words were a petition) of a dry fleece (Jg. 6.39) is allegorized as a sign that the Israelites would no longer have God's Holy Spirit (and to support this Irenaeus quotes Isaiah 5.6, 'I will also command the clouds that they rain no rain upon it'), 'but that the dew, which is the Spirit of God, ...should be diffused throughout all the earth'. We need the dew of God, Irenaeus continues, for three reasons. Firstly, in order that we should not be consumed by fire: that is, by the devil who has been cast down from heaven like lightning (cf. Lk. 10.18). The Holy Spirit is thus our defence against the attacks of the devil. Secondly, so that we should not be rendered unfruitful: the Holy Spirit revivifies us so that we bear fruit to God. Finally, in order that we might have an Advocate to withstand the accuser: it looks as if here Irenaeus is widening the activity of the Johannine Paraclete-Spirit to include our defence in the heavenly court (in 1 Jn. 2.1-2 the ascended Christ performs such a role), or he may have had in mind Romans 8.26 with its reference to the Spirit's interceding for us.

Finally, we may mention two further references to the Holy Spirit in terms of water. Irenaeus says in *Demonstration* 57 that Immanuel 'makes glad those who drink of him, that is to say, who receive His Spirit, (even) everlasting gladness'. The picture of drinking from Christ means receiving the Spirit, which entails joy and gladness. Union with Christ can be described equally in terms of receiving the Spirit.

In 5.18.2 the Spirit is described as 'in us all and He is the living water which the Lord grants to those who rightly believe in him and love him and who know that "there is one Father who is above all and through all and in all".' The language of indwelling is utilized, and the 'living water' evokes John 7.37-39. To be in a relationship of faith in and love for Christ means to have the Spirit. Once more, it is clear that union with Christ entails the experience of the Spirit.

The use of the water imagery for the Holy Spirit by Irenaeus reinforces the impression conveyed by the 'vivifying' description of the Spirit's work: people cannot of themselves obtain that life which they forfeited in the Fall. They need help from God through the Son and the Spirit ('God's hands'). Thus, the Spirit is described in terms of 'the life-giving seed, that is, the Spirit of the forgiveness of sins, through means of which we are quickened' (4.31.2). Forgiveness of sins and new life belong inseparably together, like two sides of a coin, and both are mediated to the believer by God's Spirit. When the Spirit encounters the believer in baptism, we receive forgiveness and new life (cf. *Dem.* 3).

The idea of being quickened into life by the Spirit suggests an experience which can be looked back upon, recalled and dwelt upon: in other words, a specific experience in which a person is conscious of being taken out of themselves by God and set on a new mode of existence. All this comes filtering through in the imagery used by Irenaeus.

(v) Irenaeus also uses the idea of believers' carrying the Spirit within them. He states this in *Demonstration* 7: 'As many as carry (in them) the Spirit of God are led to the Word, i.e. to the Son; and the Son brings them to the Father... Without the Spirit it is not possible to behold the Word of God, nor without the Son can any draw near to the Father: for the knowledge of the Father is the Son, and the knowledge of the Son of God is through the Holy Spirit; and, according to the good pleasure of the Father, the Son ministers and dispenses the Spirit to whomsoever the Father wills and as He wills'. There is a movement out from the Father through the Son and through the Spirit, and a movement back through the Spirit via the Son to the Father. There is no access to the Son now without the Spirit; and no access to the Father without the Son.

At 5.8.1 Irenaeus says that 'we receive a certain portion of (God's) Spirit' which prepares us 'for incorruption, because we are little by little accustomed to receive and bear God'. To have the Spirit is to receive and bear God in an educative and preparatory way so that ultimately we are prepared 'for incorruption'.

The idea of bearing the Spirit may indicate one of two ideas: the flesh is a receptacle for the Spirit who is now a constituent part of the believer, or a conscious awareness of the activity of the Spirit within one's life. The two are not, of course, necessarily mutually incompatible. In the light of the evidence so far surveyed, we could not exclude the second line of interpretation.

(vi) With some hesitation we mention the language of pouring out the Spirit. The Lord Jesus has not only redeemed us through his own blood 'but has also poured out the Spirit of the Father (*efffundente Spiritum Patris*) for the union and communion of God and man...'(5.1.1).[35] Here Irenaeus might be echoing the language of Acts 2/Joel 2, since he probably has Pentecost in mind (cf. 3.11.9). On the other hand, he is talking about what is true for believers in general. Since that is the case, we have to ask whether 'poured out' signifies a vivid experience in which Irenaeus at any rate had been conscious of being 'drenched' by the divine presence, which he described as the Spirit. It certainly cannot be ruled out, though we cannot be absolutely certain.

(vii) This last passage from 5.1.1 leads us on to the next point: the Spirit is the means of communion with Christ and imparts God to humans. The passage continues: 'leading indeed God down to men by means of the Spirit, and, on the other hand, leading man up to God by his own incarnation'. There is a two-stage process here. By his incarnation Jesus united humanity and God together, because he

---

[35] Cf. 5.12.1, where A. Rousseau and L. Doutreleau (eds.), *Contre les Hérésies V* (SC V/I; Paris: Les Éditions du Cerf, 1969), p. 256, doubt that Acts 2.17 is in mind in view of the fact that the language, Latin *in novissimis temporibus*, Greek ἐπ' ἐσχάτων τῶν καιρῶν, does not correspond to Acts 2.17.

is the Word and the Spirit indwells him[36] (i.e., 'the hands of God' are involved, as in the act of creation). This sets the pattern for believers. Their humanity is now joined by the Spirit. The Lord 'has poured out the Spirit of the Father' on believers and this creates the union of God and humanity in them. Irenaeus uses two phrases—'for union and communion of God and men' and 'imparting God to men by means of the Spirit', and these mean the same thing. Clearly to have the Spirit is to have God.

If Jesus' incarnation establishes a pattern in general, his baptism in particular is also a pattern for us, because the Spirit descended on him in the Jordan and is now given to believers (3.17.1; cf. 3.18.3).

The Spirit is, then, the vital means of our experience of God. Knowing God is a matter of being indwelt by the Spirit. To receive the Spirit is to have fellowship with God. Another way of putting this is that the Spirit is the means of our fellowship with Christ and He is our means of access to the Father. Irenaeus can say that 'the means of communion with Christ has been distributed throughout it [the church], that is the Holy Spirit, the guarantee of incorruption, the means of confirming our faith, and the ladder of ascent to God' (3.24.1). It is tempting to assume that 'the ladder of ascent to God' refers to experience of God now, but probably it refers to the conviction that the Spirit raises our bodies to participate in the life of eternity with God, since the preceding phrase 'the guarantee of incorruption' points in that direction and elsewhere Irenaeus speaks of ascending through the Spirit and through the Son to the Father, on the journey to that part of the Father's house which is appropriate according to our worthiness (5.36.2).

Even so, the Spirit is still described as 'the means of communion with Christ', i.e., the Spirit is the agent of actualizing the risen Lord's presence in the believer. Without the Spirit there is no fellowship with the Son, while to have the Son is to have the Father.

We have to ask ourselves whether this kind of emphasis could be propounded by someone who was not consciously aware of the Spirit's presence. The close link between Spirit and fellowship with God, the stress on knowing God in an obviously experiential manner, seem to demand an affirmative answer to this question. Both because of scriptural promises and because of his own experience, Irenaeus knows that Christians are in fellowship with God because the Spirit is a 'tangible' factor in their lives.

(viii) We might also mention here the way that Irenaeus handles 1 Corinthians 3.16 in 5.6.2. In context, Irenaeus is maintaining that our flesh will be saved. He argues that here and now the Spirit indwells believers and this fact is a guarantee that our bodies will participate in the ultimate salvation (Irenaeus' teaching about recapitulation is the ultimate basis for this).[37] 'How then is it not the utmost blasphemy to allege that the temple of God, in which the Spirit of the Father dwells, and the members of Christ, do not partake of salvation but go to perdition?'

---

[36] Cf. Wingren, *Man*, p. 105: 'By His incarnation our Lord brought God down to men through the Spirit, and man to God by His assumption of human flesh'.

[37] Cf. A. Grillmeier, *Christ in Christian Tradition* (London: Mowbray, rev. ed., 1975), pp. 103-104.

Proof that Christians are God's temple, indwelt by God's Spirit, is afforded by 1 Corinthians 3.16, which Irenaeus applies to the individual believer (not to the church, as Paul does): 'Here he [Paul] manifestly declares the body to be the temple in which the Spirit dwells...not only does he acknowledge our bodies to be a temple but even the members of Christ', and Irenaeus then goes on to quote 1 Corinthians 6.14 also. Yet again, Irenaeus reveals his conviction that Christians possess God's Spirit and this constitutes the decisive characteristic of their life in Christ.

Once again, this argument seems to demand the underlying explanation that for Irenaeus experience of the Spirit is something real, not theoretical.

So far, then, we have considered how the Spirit is given in baptism to those who believe and how Irenaeus uses various concepts which cumulatively suggest a deeply felt awareness of the Spirit's presence in the believer's life. We now turn to consider the concept of the perfect man/person in Irenaeus.

The truly spiritual person is one who has received God's Spirit (4.33.1), not one in whom the pneumatic seed has been sown (as in Valentinian gnosis). Irenaeus can also speak of the 'perfect' as those who have the Spirit remaining in them, i.e. 'perfect' does not stand for some spiritual elite, but for all Christians who have received the Spirit through faith and baptism.[38] Irenaeus writes: 'The perfect man consists in the commingling and the union of the soul which has received the Spirit of the Father, and been mixed with that flesh which was moulded after the image of God' (5.6.1). Spiritual, Irenaeus insists, does not mean to be stripped of one's flesh. That would mean a person was reduced to his spirit. 'But when this Spirit, blended with the soul, is united to (God's) handiwork, man is rendered spiritual and perfect because of the outpouring of the Spirit, and this is he who was made in the image and likeness of God' (5.6.1). Although the ANL translation prints 'spirit' with a small letter[39] and Harvey '*spiritus*',[40] the context points to God's Spirit.[41] It is body (plasma) plus soul (*anima*) plus Holy Spirit (*Spiritus*) that makes people 'spiritual', because the Spirit has been poured out upon them. A few lines earlier too, Irenaeus said that Paul spoke of the 'spiritual': 'they being spiritual because they partake of the Spirit', while a few lines later he said 'But if the Spirit be wanting to the soul, such a person is indeed of an animal nature (*animalis*) and is left carnal, shall be an imperfect being, possessing indeed the image (of God) in their formation (*in plasmate*), but not having received the similitude through the Spirit'.[42] Normally

---

[38] Cf., e.g., d'Arles, *Doctrine*, p. 502; Jaschke, *Der heilige Geist*, pp. 240-41, 262.

[39] A. Roberts and W.H. Rambaut (eds), *The Writings of Irenaeus*, Vol. 2 (Edinburgh: T. & T. Clark, 1869), p. 68.

[40] W.W. Harvey (ed.), *S. Irenaei...Libros quique adversus haereses*, Vol. 2 (Cambridge: Cambridge University Press, 1857), p. 334.

[41] Rousseau and Doutreleau (eds.), *Contre les Hérésies V/2*, p. 77, rightly begin the Greek, Latin and French word with a capital letter.

[42] Cf. *4 Praef.*, where a person is a mixed organisation of soul and flesh, who was formed after the likeness of God and moulded by His hands; 3.22.1 'Everyone will allow that we are (composed of) a body taken from the earth and a soul receiving the Spirit from God'; see also 2.33.5; 5.6.1; 5.9.1. See D.E. Jenkins, 'The Make-Up of Man according to

imago and *similitudo* (the Greek equivalents would be εἰκών and ὁμοίωμα) are synonymous in Irenaeus,[43] but here is one occasion where he distinguishes them, because he wanted to emphasize the difference which receiving the Spirit makes to a person.

Irenaeus interprets 1 Corinthians 15.45-46 not so much Christologically but rather of believers. Just as Adam who had been made a living soul (*anima*) forfeited life when he turned from God, so 'the same individual when he reverts to what is good and receives the quickening Spirit shall find life' (5.12.2). First comes what is animal (i.e. flesh plus soul); then the spiritual: 'Afterwards...it should receive the communion of the Spirit'.

The same distinction between creation and adoption occurs in 5.18.2: 'To some He [the Word] gives after the manner of creation the (spirit) of creation, (the spirit) which is made; but to others (He gives) after the manner of adoption, (the Spirit) which is from the Father, namely His generation' (= the Word grants the Spirit to all as the Father wills). 'The Spirit (is) in us all [i.e. Christians] and He is the living water, which the Lord grants to those who rightly believe in him and love him'.

Clearly, then, for Irenaeus the distinctive feature of the Christian is possession of the Spirit, bestowed by God through His Son. This means a Christian can be called 'spiritual' or 'perfect',[44] in distinction to non-believers (and not, as in Valentinian gnosis, in distinction to the hylics and psychics).

Irenaeus', in F.L. Cross (ed.), *Studia Patristica* 6.4 (Berlin: Akademie-Verlag, 1962), p. 94: 'The Spirit is no part of man's first make-up'; similarly J. Lawson, *The Biblical Theology of St. Irenaeus* (London: Epworth, 1948), p. 206; Jaschke, *Der heilige Geist*, pp. 294-95. Recently, Behr, *Asceticism*, pp. 98-109, has challenged this explanation, and has argued that humans from the beginning have the Spirit of God; however, this seems to mean that humans can see the Creator through creation, while Behr admits that the Spirit is bestowed *in a special manner* on those who have been adopted as sons of God (my italics): they are 'vivified in a stronger fashion'. Behr maintains that for Irenaeus the breath of life created by the presence of the life-giving Spirit in creation, is a type of the vivification to come. This does not seem (if I have understood Behr aright) to be a huge difference over against the view expressed above, since all would agree that God's Hands have always been seeking to draw humans to the Father. E.F. Osborn, *Irenaeus of Lyons* (Cambridge: Cambridge University Press, 2001), pp. 220-25, sees the Spirit of God as the third part of the believer in Irenaeus, but says that the breath of life produces animation, while the Holy Spirit produces vivification: one source of life is received in two ways. When man loses the Spirit of God, he is still a human being shaped by the Hands of God in God's image, but the likeness is not there any longer.

[43] So, e.g., Wingren, *Man*, p. 158; Jaschke, *Der heilige Geist*, p. 314. Osborn, *Irenaeus*, p. 212, however, interprets Irenaeus differently: the 'image' is the body, including physical and intellectual qualities, while the 'likeness' comes through the Spirit and can be lost.

[44] Jaschke, *Der heilige Geist*, p. 177, rightly emphasises that, over against the gnostics, there is in Irenaeus no natural bond between us and the divine *Urgrund* of our being.

Finally, we turn to consider how possession of the Spirit leads out into action and speaking. Specifically, we shall consider what Irenaeus has to say about spiritual gifts.

In *Demonstration* 99–100, Irenaeus refers to heretics who 'do not receive the gifts of the Holy Spirit and cast away from themselves the prophetic grace, watered whereby people bear fruit of life to God... And such are in no wise serviceable to God, seeing that they cannot bear any fruit' (99). 'They do not receive the Spirit, that is, they reject prophecy' (100). It looks as if here Irenaeus has in mind the Alogoi[45] (cf. 3.11.9, where he says that 'others [namely the Alogoi] set aside the gift of prophecy from the church'). The clear implication is that prophecy is for Irenaeus a gift of the Spirit to the church and still current in his day.[46]

In *AH* 2 Irenaeus gives us some information about the presence of spiritual gifts amongst Christians. In 2.28.7 he says that while the Spirit searches all things, even the deep things of God, yet to us 'there are diversities of gifts, diversities of administrations and diversities of operations' and 'at the moment we know in part and prophesy in part' (1 Cor. 12.4-6; 13.9 are being echoed). This is used in context to point out that there are some questions so difficult that all we can do is to leave them in God's hands. Nonetheless, it is interesting that Irenaeus uses the reference to prophecy when a reference to partial knowledge alone would have made his point.

In 2.31.2 he says that Valentinians cannot give sight to the blind or hearing to the deaf nor can they exorcise demons or cure the weak, lame, paralysed etc., nor can they 'raise the dead, as the Lord raised them, and the apostles did by means of prayer and as has been frequently done in the brotherhood on account of some necessity—the entire church in that particular locality entreating (the miracle) with much fasting and prayer, the spirit of the dead man has returned, and (the life of) the man has been granted in answer to the prayers of the saints'. Irenaeus follows this up by saying that the church performs such miracles without payment and gives financial help to those cured since they frequently do not possess the things which they require (2.31.3).

Irenaeus claims in 2.32.4 that while the Lord performed the miracles predicted of him by the prophets, 'those who are truly his disciples, having received grace from him, do in his name perform (miracles) so as to promote the welfare of other people, according to the gift which each one has received from him'. Some exorcise devils. Frequently those thus cured believe and join the church. 'Others have foreknowledge of things to come: they see visions and utter prophetic expressions. Others still heal the sick by laying their hands upon them and they are made whole. Yes, moreover, as I have said, the dead even have been raised up and remained among us for many years. And what more shall I say? It is not possible to name the number of gifts

---

[45] The name given by Epiphanius to those whose opposition led them to reject both the Fourth Gospel with its teaching on the Paraclete, and also the book of Revelation. They were active apparently in Asia Minor towards the end of the second century.

[46] A. Mehat, 'Saint Irénée et les Charismes', in E.A. Livingstone (ed.), *Studia Patristica* 17.2 (Oxford: Pergamon, 1982), p. 720, says that Irenaeus was more upset by the suspicions of antimontanists than by the rebellion of Montanist prophets.

which the church throughout the whole world has received from God in the name of Jesus Christ who was crucified under Pontius Pilate and which she exerts day by day for the benefit of the Gentiles, neither practising deception upon any nor taking any reward from them. For as she has received freely from God, freely also does she minister (to others)' (2.32.4). Though the Spirit is not expressly named in this passage, the references to grace and gift(s) make it indisputable that Irenaeus had the Spirit's gifts in mind.

Irenaeus believed that the OT prophets themselves had predicted these gifts. After quoting Deuteronomy 5.24 ('We shall see in that day that God will talk to man and he shall live'), he said: 'For certain of these men used to see the prophetic Spirit and his active influences poured forth for all kinds of gifts'. Then he quoted Hosea 12.10, that God said 'I have multiplied visions and have used similitudes by the hands of the prophets', and said that Paul was expounding this passage in the church when he wrote 1 Corinthians 12.4-7 (4.20.6). Prophecy in the church in particular was predicted by the OT prophets. 'For (the Word) promised by the prophets that in the last times he would pour him [the Spirit] upon (his) servants and handmaids that they might prophesy' (3.17.1). Joel's language is clearly being employed, though not expressly cited.

As to gifts of the Spirit, Irenaeus said 'We also hear many brothers in the church who possess prophetic gifts and who through the Spirit speak all kinds of languages and bring to light for the general benefit the hidden things of men and declare the mysteries of God' (5.6.1).[47]

The possession of gifts should not, however, be the occasion of pride in us; rather, they should lead to humility (5.22.2).

SUMMARY

Four main areas have occupied us in this first section: believer's baptism as the point of reception of the Holy Spirit; expressions suggestive of a conscious experience of the Spirit (the Abba cry; adoption; new life; the water image; carrying the Spirit within one; the Spirit poured out; the Spirit as the means of our communion with God and our knowing God); the concept of the spiritual or perfect person; and the evidence of spiritual gifts (miracles and prophecy especially) being exercised in current church life. All these substantiate the case that for Irenaeus the Spirit was not a matter of theory but a central factor in Christian experience.

---

[47] Lawson, *Biblical Theology*, pp. 97-98, doubted whether passages like 2.32.4; 3.11.9; and 5.6.1 pointed to a Spirit-given charismatic ministry in Irenaeus' own day. Rather, he felt that these passages vindicated the church's claim that it was she, not the heretics, who possessed the Spirit of God. These two viewpoints are not mutually exclusive. Lawson's view, however, seems refuted by Irenaeus' assertions that raisings from the dead had been frequent; the church helped financially those cured; the healed or exorcised often joined the church; and he himself had heard prophecy and glossolalia in the church. These references point to the presence of the charismatic gifts in the church of Irenaeus' day (so F.R. Mongomery-Hitchcock, *Irenaeus of Lugdunum* [Cambridge: Cambridge University Press, 1914], pp. 259-60).

B. Divine Illumination

We turn now to consider the relation of the Spirit and truth in the believer's experience. For Irenaeus the Spirit 'furnishes us with a knowledge of the truth'; he 'has set forth the "economies" of the Father and Son, in virtue of which he dwells with every generation of people, according to the Father's will' (4.33.7). This knowledge of the truth is, of course, 'the doctrine of the apostles and the ancient constitution of the church throughout all the world and the distinctive character of the body of Christ according to the successions of the bishops' (4.33.8).

Here we see the strong link which Irenaeus forges between the Spirit and the church. The Spirit does not stimulate unrestrained speculation (like Valentinianism), but leads believers to a firm conviction about the teaching which rests on apostolic witness and tradition, which is enshrined in the scriptures, and which is given by the bishops and presbyters in the various congregations of the one church throughout all the world.

Irenaeus' remarks about the spiritual disciple (i.e. one who has received God's Spirit) in 4.33.1-15 confirm this. He says that the spiritual disciple judges everyone but is judged by no one (echoing 1 Cor. 2.15): because of the Spirit who indwells them, Christians can assess and evaluate others, but these cannot reach a considered judgment on Christians because they do not possess the Spirit. Specifically, the spiritual disciple is able to evaluate the idolatrous nature of Gentile religion, the enslavement of the Jews to the law, and the heretical views of Marcion, Valentinus, the Ebionites, the Docetists, false prophets and schismatics (4.33.1-7). Such a person has a firm faith in the one God Almighty, in His Son Jesus Christ and his incarnation and 'in the Spirit of God who furnishes us with a knowledge of the truth' (4.33.7). The spiritual disciple will also understand the prophecies of the OT against those who divide the God of the OT from the God of Jesus (4.33.15).

It is not surprising that Irenaeus, in seeking to rebut gnosticism, should strongly link the Spirit and the tradition inherited from the earliest generation and enshrined in the NT and the Rule of Faith. There is clearly a polemical thrust behind this. There is a twofold line of approach: the Spirit has produced the faith held by the church throughout the world, while those who adhere to such a faith clearly are led by the Spirit.

Irenaeus does not discuss the relationship between this strong adherence to what he believes is apostolic faith and his belief in prophecy as a gift of the Spirit still current in the churches. Perhaps he did not feel that it was a problem since the apostle Paul had placed certain limits on the exercise of prophecy—that it should operate within the conviction that Jesus was Lord (1 Cor. 12.1-3) and should be exercised in accordance with faith (whatever exactly Paul had in mind in Romans 12.8, a later writer could take this as in accordance with the faith).

SUMMARY

Irenaeus saw one aspect of the Spirit's work as leading into the truth, and he equated this truth with the traditional teaching of the church. The amount of material in section B is, however, fairly small. Is there a reason for this? It may be that for

Irenaeus the truth had already been given to the church through the apostles and that the bone of contention with the Valentinians lay elsewhere than in the belief that possession of the Spirit and Truth went hand in hand.

The 'blinding flash' of inspiration is not an aspect on which he dwells, for the truth had been settled.

C. Divine Power

At 3.17.2, one reason Irenaeus gave why Christians need the dew (= the Spirit) of God, was to bear fruit for life. The language has Pauline overtones (Rom.7.4), though it is commonplace enough. We should probably take the bearing of fruit idea in an ethical sense: the Spirit's renewing activity is to lead to an ethically pleasing life in God's sight.

On several occasions, Irenaeus links the newness of the Christian life and the ongoing activity of the Spirit. He maintains that God would not send the redeemed back to Mosaic legislation; on the contrary, He desires them 'to live in newness by the Word, through faith in the Son of God and love' (*Dem.* 89). In *Demonstration* 89–90 Irenaeus interprets the wilderness of Isaiah 43.18-21 (where God will cause streams to flow), as standing for the Gentiles. The Word of God, by disseminating the Holy Spirit over the earth, has 'refashioned the new way of godliness and righteousness and made copious streams to spring forth', as promised. Clearly, the Holy Spirit is the inspiration, power and mainspring of the Gentiles' new lifestyle. He has enabled them to break with their idolatrous, immoral past, and to step forth on a new lifestyle in harmony with God's will and characterized by righteousness. 'Therefore, our calling is by the newness of the Spirit and not in the oldness of the letter', and he adds an extensive quotation from Jeremiah 31.31-34. Clearly, the writing of God's law in the inner being is equated with the gift of the Holy Spirit. The new way of life, the way of 'godliness and righteousness', which fulfils God's laws, is made possible by the Spirit who is the main impetus behind a new ethical direction.

Isaiah 43.19-21 is used on another occasion by Irenaeus, namely 4.33.14, in the context of mentioning the promise of a new covenant (Jer. 31.31-34) and a new heart and spirit (Ezek. 36.26). All these passages 'plainly announced that liberty which distinguishes the new covenant and the new wine which is put into new skins, that is, the faith which is in Christ, the way of righteousness sprung up in the desert and the streams of the Holy Spirit in a dry land'. Again, we note the link between ethics and the Spirit in the way in which there exists a certain parallel between faith, the way of righteousness and the streams/water of the Holy Spirit, whom Christians receive. There is a way of righteousness to be followed (Christ's), but it is the Spirit who helps the Christian to walk that way. God's aim in acquiring such a people is 'that they might show forth His mighty acts, but not that they might blaspheme Him who made these things, that is, God'. While Irenaeus' last phrase is directed against the gnostic division between a supreme Deity and a Demiurge/creator, we may surmise that godly and righteous conduct in the Spirit's power would be one of the ways in which Christians show forth God's mighty acts.

Irenaeus believed that the apostles at the Jerusalem Council 'gave the new covenant of liberty to those who had in a new way believed in God through the Holy Spirit' (3.12.14). He clearly has in mind James' ruling, accepted by the Council, that the Mosaic Law was not to be imposed on the Gentile converts. This was the 'liberty' which had been accorded to Gentile believers. He goes on to say that 'the apostles who were with James allowed the Gentiles to act freely, entrusting us to the Spirit of God' (3.12.15).

Irenaeus links the disciples' power of regeneration with baptism in 3.17.1 because God has fulfilled His promise to pour out His Spirit on His servants and handmaids. 'Therefore, the Spirit descended on the Son of God made Son of Man to become accustomed through him to dwell in the human race, to rest with human beings and to dwell in God's workmanship, *voluntatem Patris operans* (in them) *et renovans eos a vestuste in novitatem Christi*' (working the Father's will in them and renewing them from the old way of life to Christ's new way of life). The indwelling Spirit helps Christians to do God's will. This whole process is a renewal: it brings people from their old habits into Christ's new life. The Spirit is the agent of a new ethical life.

This newness is at the same time a restoration. We receive by the Spirit the image and superscription of the Father and the Son (3.17.3). Human beings were originally made in the image and likeness of God. They lost this by the Fall, but now, through Christ's work as man and the gift of the Spirit, they recover this position, and the possibility of growth is opened up to them. Irenaeus allegorizes the parable of the Good Samaritan. The Lord entrusts to the Holy Spirit the man who fell into robbers' hands. The two denarii given to the innkeeper are the image and superscription of the Father and the Son. After we have received these by the Spirit, 'we should make this denarius entrusted to us multiply and remit it to the Lord thus increased'. So, God will not lose His 'original outlay' but will gain interest on it, as redeemed humans progress to that goal appointed for them. In this process of restoring the image and likeness and enabling people to grow, the Spirit has a key role.

It is fascinating and relevant for our theme to observe how Irenaeus handles the flesh/Spirit theme compared with Paul. For Paul the flesh is weak (Rom. 8.3), and there is a warfare between flesh and Spirit, which may neutralize the believer's attempt to do good (Gal. 5.17).

Irenaeus accepts that the flesh is weak and quotes Jesus' words (Mk. 14.38) to this effect (5.9.2). Indeed, the flesh, 'when destitute of the Spirit of God, is dead, not having life, and cannot possess the kingdom of God' (5.9.3). However, Irenaeus claims that the Spirit of God is 'a stimulus to the weakness of the flesh'; what is strong prevails over what is weak 'so that the weakness of the flesh will be absorbed by the strength of the Spirit'; 'when the infirmity of the flesh is absorbed, it exhibits the Spirit as powerful; and again, when the Spirit absorbs the weakness (of the flesh), it possesses the flesh as an inheritance for itself, and from both of these a living man is formed—living because he partakes of the Spirit, but man, because of the substance of the flesh' (5.9.2).

The power of the Spirit is impressively set forth here. There is no suggestion of a struggle in which the Spirit may be hindered or checked. Here Irenaeus concentrates on the all-powerful, conquering might of the Holy Spirit. As a further illustration of this, the Spirit gives the martyrs strength to despise death and bear their witness.

The second claim of Irenaeus is that the Holy Spirit inherits the flesh, which is dead, and translates it into the Kingdom of Heaven (5.9.4); the Spirit purifies people and raises them up to the life of God (5.9.2). It is clear that this translation into the Kingdom of Heaven and this being raised to the life of God are not purely future ideas but present realities, as can be seen by Irenaeus' words: 'In order that we may not lose life by losing that Spirit who possesses us, the apostle exhorting us to fellowship with the Spirit has said.... "That flesh and blood cannot inherit the Kingdom of God" ' (5.9.4). The Spirit possesses the believer now; and, therefore, he lives now—he is 'a living man' (5.9.2, 32). When Jesus said 'Let the dead bury their dead', he was referring to 'people of this stamp', flesh and soul without God's Spirit, 'because they do not have the Spirit who quickens people' (5.9.1).

The Spirit as life-giver, vivifying what is lifeless, is uppermost here. Life invades death and transforms the situation.

Irenaeus makes a third claim. The Spirit of God 'lays hold of' the flesh. To justify this, Irenaeus quotes 2 Corinthians 3.3 and continues 'If, therefore, in the present time fleshly hearts are made partakers of the Spirit, what is there astonishing if, in the resurrection, they receive that life which is granted by the Spirit?' (5.13.4; cf. the use of 2 Cor. 3.1-6 in 3.4.2).

Here, then, in three images, which cannot be too rigorously separated, Irenaeus sets forth his belief in the aid given to the believer by the Spirit. Hence he can say that although the flesh is weak, it forgets what is its own inherent quality and 'adopts the quality of the Spirit, and is conformed to the Word of God' (5.9.3). In former days when we were without the Spirit, we did not obey God ('we walked...in the oldness of the flesh'); now, however, 'having received the Spirit, let us walk in newness of life, obeying God' (5.9.3).

Thus, once more, we meet the ethical implication of fellowship with the Spirit: the change of lifestyle. The same is true of the assertion 'When a person is grafted in by faith and receives the Spirit of God, they do not lose the substance of their flesh but change the quality of the fruit of their works...and receive another name which shows that they have been changed for the better, being no longer flesh and blood, but a spiritual person and is called such' (5.10.2). Here Irenaeus is taking the Pauline image of the wild olive tree in Romans 11 in an individual sense. If people progress by faith towards better things and receive God's Spirit and bring forth the fruit of the Spirit, they 'shall be spiritual, as being planted in the paradise of God'. If the opposite happens, if they reject the Spirit and desire to be of the flesh rather than of the Spirit, then they will not inherit the Kingdom of God (5.10.1; cf. 5.11.1). It is important that as the good olive tree should not be neglected or else it will itself run wild, so also people should not become unfruitful in righteousness (5.10.1). It is vital that we should 'not neglect the engrafting of the Spirit while pampering the flesh' (5.10.1). Later, Irenaeus says that we must lay aside the lusts of the flesh and receive the Holy Spirit, and then he quotes Colossians 3.5, 9 'Put to death, therefore, your members which are on the earth... Cast off the old person with its deeds' (5.12.3).

God causes us 'to serve Him in holiness and righteousness all our days, in order that a person, who has embraced the Spirit of God, might pass into the glory of the Father' (4.20.4).[48] There are three stages involved: firstly, the conversion experience, here described from the human angle as a person embracing the Spirit of God; then, that same Spirit frees us from wickedness and leads us along the path of holiness; thus the Spirit prepares us for the final stage, which is to pass into the glorious presence of God.[49] In this way, the Spirit is the ethical power for the believer. It is clear that a person's 'embracing' the Spirit is not just a future hope but holds good of the present, producing the desired ethical qualities, and all this prepares the human race for the future communion with the Father in glory.[50]

It is this ethical implication that explains a strand in Irenaeus' thought, which suggests that by doing righteous deeds we preserve the Spirit within us. God's Son made it clear 'that we ought, after our calling, to be also adorned with works of righteousness, so that the Spirit of God may rest upon us' (4.36.6). In a similar way, Irenaeus invokes Paul: 'Because, therefore, we cannot be saved without the Spirit of God, the apostle exhorts us through faith and pure lifestyle to preserve the Spirit of God, lest, having become non-participants of the Divine Spirit we lose the Kingdom of Heaven...' (5.9.3). As Jaschke rightly stresses,[51] we do not in Irenaeus' view dispose of the Spirit; Christians can only preserve the Spirit by a believing life. In demanding the preservation of the Spirit, Irenaeus shows that our possession of the Spirit is not automatic or self-evident.

---

[48] A somewhat similar pattern is presupposed in 5.11.2. To do the works of the flesh brings death. Believers, however, are not in that plight: whereas they have borne the image of the earthly man in their pre-conversion stage, they now bear the image of the One from heaven. This came about when they were washed and received the Spirit. Where Paul himself in 1 Cor. 15.46 is eschatologically orientated, Irenaeus is thinking of the present. The image of the Heavenly Man is *already* being borne by the Christian and 1 Cor. 6.11 is utilised to expound this. Christians have washed away their former vain manner of life, and now, in those very bodies which were doomed to death, 'we are made alive by working the works of the Spirit'.

[49] Behr, *Asceticism*, pp. 38-39, speaks of the *continuity* of the nourishing activity of the Spirit in Irenaeus (my italics).

[50] H-J. Jaschke, 'Pneuma und Moral. Der Grund christliche Sittlichkeit aus der Sicht des Irenaus von Lyon', *Studia Moralia* 14 (1976), p. 281, summarising what is the 'Christian proprium' in moral conduct for Irenaeus, says that people let themselves be grasped by the one God who embraces creation and redemption, so that, possessed by the Holy Spirit and in fellowship with believers, they mature into children of God to find their goal at the end in the vision of the Father.

[51] Jaschke, *Der heilige Geist*, pp. 177-78; 'Pneuma und Moral', pp. 257, 262.

Normally, Irenaeus stresses the initiative and power of the Spirit as in the illustration about the Lord wanting his temple, that is, our flesh, 'to be clean that the Spirit of God may take delight in it, as a bridegroom with a bride' (5.9.4). Just as a bride is wedded, not weds, so the flesh is inherited by the Spirit. The initiative and influence lie with the groom and the Spirit; the bride and the flesh are passive recipients. The flesh is not the dominant partner, but it is 'taken over' by the Spirit, not vice versa.

In 4.38.1 Irenaeus answers the question why God did not make humans perfect from the beginning. He maintains that man was an infant and needed to develop. Hence, our Lord, 'who was the perfect Bread of the Father, offered himself as milk to us, as to infants'. This was to enable us via the nourishment of milk 'to become accustomed to eat and drink the Word of God', that we might 'be able to contain in ourselves the Bread of immortality, which is the Spirit of God' (4.38.1).[52] The incarnation was a stage in the process by which we might be able to 'bear' the indwelling Holy Spirit: it was a preparation, the ultimate aim of which was to assist us to accommodate the Spirit who is the guarantee of immortality ('the Bread of Immortality').

Irenaeus then picks up Paul's rebuke to the Corinthians that he had fed them with milk, not with meat, because they were not able to bear it. He explains this: 'You have been taught the advent of our Lord as a man; but, because of your weakness, the Spirit of the Father does not yet rest upon you... That is, that the Spirit of the Father was not yet with them, because of their imperfection and the shortcomings of their lifestyle'.[53] Irenaeus says that the Corinthians 'could not receive the Holy Spirit because the faculties which can be trained for God were still feeble and undisciplined' (4.38.2).[54]

At first sight this seems to go against Irenaeus' clear emphasis that the distinctive mark of Christians is that they are indwelt by the Spirit of God. Yet we must bear in mind the context and Irenaeus' defence of his idea of man as an infant who needs to grow.[55] Rather, *Demonstration* 42 would be more typical: Irenaeus says about

---

[52] There is no need to read an eucharistic interpretation into this sentence as Jaschke, *Der heilige Geist*, p. 271, does. Wingren, *Man*, p. 161, refers the food and drink to the incarnate Christ or the Spirit. W. Bousset, *Kyrios Christos* (Nashville, TN: Abingdon, 1970), p. 430, while acknowledging that the language is drawn from the eucharist, believes that Irenaeus is thinking of the union of deity and humanity held out to the believer.

[53] Lampe, *Seal*, pp. 118-19, thinks that Irenaeus has in mind Acts 8. He believes that Irenaeus is implying that Paul had not laid hands on the Corinthians, but maintains that Irenaeus does not relate this to the baptismal rite of his own day. Benoit, *Bapteme*, pp. 205-207, also thinks that Irenaeus is interpreting 1 Corinthians in the light of the customs related in Acts, and points out that Irenaeus here ignores 1 Cor. 3.16.

[54] Jaschke, *Der heilige Geist*, pp. 318-19, says that here Irenaeus 'shows yet again the need for a quality response from the human side, without which no union with the Holy Spirit is possible' ('Quality response' is an attempt to render the German *Qualifikation*).

[55] Benoit, *Baptême*, pp. 205-206, stresses that Irenaeus' concern is with the idea of human development, not baptism, but goes no further into this. Irenaeus, in the next

believers: 'In them continually abides the Holy Spirit, who was given by Him [God] in baptism and is retained by the receiver, if they walk in truth and holiness and righteousness and patient endurance'. The conditional clause is again a reminder that believers do not dispose of the Spirit, but may preserve the gift by their conduct.

We may draw this section to a close by quoting Irenaeus' words in 5.20.2. He says that the Lord recapitulated in himself the human condition and situation: 'By uniting man to the Spirit [a reference to the incarnation] and causing the Spirit to dwell in man [a reference to the risen Lord's pouring out of the Spirit] he is himself made the head of the Spirit and gives the Spirit to be the head of man: for through him [the Spirit] we see and hear and speak'. There is a hierarchy here, as it were: Christ-Spirit-the Christian (cf. the hierarchy of God-Christ-the Christian in 1 Cor. 3.23). Through his incarnation and exaltation (cf. Acts 2.33), our Lord is the executive power over the Spirit (cf. 3.11.8). The immediate head over the believer is the Spirit, for the Spirit is the means by whom the Christian spiritually sees and hears and speaks. The believer's spiritual discernment and speech is prompted by the Spirit. Because the Spirit is the source of all that the Christian has and is, he may rightly be termed the 'head' of man. Such is eloquent testimony to the central significance of the Spirit in the life of the believer for Irenaeus.

SUMMARY

Irenaeus believed that the Christian is enabled to live a new life through the indwelling power of the Spirit.[56] Irenaeus' view of the ethical life is firmly anchored in his conviction about the strength imparted by the Spirit. The Spirit is both motivation and power for Christian living so different in quality from paganism. Irenaeus affords an interesting contrast to Hermas in this ethical section. Where Hermas has much on the delicacy and sensitivity of the Spirit, Irenaeus has no such idea, but speaks strongly of the Spirit's power to swallow up the weakness of the flesh. He unambiguously focuses attention on the Spirit as aid to ethical progress. The few statements which indicate that believers preserve the gift in effect teach that our possession of the Spirit is not automatic and so emphasize the importance of our conduct. But we are left in no doubt that the Spirit aids our weakness by his power.

---

paragraph (4.38.3), wrote 'man making progress day by day and ascending towards the perfect, that is, approaching to the uncreated One... Now it was necessary that man should in the first instance be created; and having been created, should grow; and having grown, should become adult; and having become adult, should be increased; and having increased, should grow strong; and having grown strong, should be glorified; and having been glorified, should see his Lord'. Behr, *Asceticism*, p. 124, commenting on this passage, speaks of 'a rhythm and pattern which God has arranged for the growth of man to his full perfection'.

[56] It is significant how on a number of occasions, Tremblay, *Manifestation*, pp. 138-39, 143, 162, 171, stresses that what Irenaeus is talking about is an interior experience or an activity of an interior order by which a person appropriates the very being of God Himself or by which an individual enters personally into communion with God.

Summary

On extant evidence, Irenaeus is the first since Paul to ground the Christian way, in all its aspects, so thoroughly in the work of God's Spirit. While Irenaeus used sources and allowed those sources to speak for themselves, he had thought through the Christian faith theologically. The way in which overall his conception hangs together enables us to see the prominent role which the Holy Spirit plays in Irenaeus' thought both in the experience of Christians and also from Creation to the End.

3. The Valentinian Marcus

Although Hippolytus places Marcus in the 'Oriental School', Irenaeus expressly locates the activities of his followers 'in our own district of the Rhone' (*AH* 1.13.7). Leaving aside Marcus' numerological speculations (1.14-16), we may make some conjectures from what Irenaeus says about Marcus' attitude to the Spirit.

Irenaeus acknowledges that Marcus is inspired, but maintains that he is possessed by 'a demon as his familiar spirit, by means of which he seems able to prophesy' and assist others to prophesy (1.13.3). He reports Marcus as claiming to possess the greatest knowledge, to have received the highest power from above (1.13.1) and to be inspired by Charis whose mediator he was (1.14.1).

Irenaeus accepts too that Marcus is able to command his followers to prophesy, but argues that 'such spirits as are commanded by these men and speak when they desire it, are earthly and weak and audacious and impudent, sent forth by Satan for the seduction and perdition of those who do not hold fast that well-compacted faith which they received at first through the church' (1.13.4).

A further charge made by Irenaeus is that Marcus used manipulative arts in order to deceive and lead astray 'a great number of men and not a few women' (1.13.1). Marcus 'is a perfect adept in magical impostures' (1.13.1). Irenaeus reports how he persuades women by some trick with cups (perhaps at the Marcosian eucharist). Of interest is what Marcus is reported to say to the women: 'May that Charis who is before all things and who transcends all knowledge and speech, fill your inner being and multiply in you her own knowledge, by sowing the grain of mustard seed in you as in good soil' (1.13.2). Clearly, this is a prayer for being filled inwardly with heavenly power and knowledge: that is, a specific experience of the 'invasion' of the human personality by the divine.[57]

Similarly in the case of prophesying, Marcus is alleged to devote himself to wealthy women. He says to them: '"I am eager to make you a partaker of my Charis... Receive first from me and by me (the gift of) Charis. Adorn yourself as a bride who is expecting her bridegroom that you may be what I am, and I what you

---

[57] J. Reiling, 'Marcus Gnosticus and the New Testament: Eucharist and Prophecy', in T. Baarda, A.F.J. Klijn and W.C. van Unnik (eds.), *Miscellanea Neotestamentica* (Leiden: Brill, 1978), p. 169, wrote, 'The purpose of this gnostic eucharist is fulfilment with the Spirit which means at the same time fulfilment with the true gnosis'.

are. Establish the germ of light in your nuptial chamber. Receive from me a spouse, and become receptive of him, while you are received by him. Behold Charis has descended on you; open your mouth and prophesy". When she demurs, he insists and then she utters some nonsense as it happens to occur to her such as might be expected from one heated by an empty spirit... Henceforth she reckons herself a prophetess and expressed her thanks to Marcus for having imparted to her of his own Charis' (1.13.3). This gratitude (Irenaeus alleges) expresses itself in monetary gifts and sexual favours.[58]

Even when allowances have been made for 'smear tactics', it still looks as if Marcus sought to induce a state of inspiration in the women followers: he convinced them that he could pass on divine inspiration to them.[59]

By contrast, Irenaeus' definition of prophecy is worth quoting: 'Only those to whom God sends His grace from above possess the divinely-bestowed power of prophesying; and then they speak where and when God pleases, and not when Marcus orders them to do so'.[60]

Summary

Brief, biased and tendentious as are Irenaeus' remarks, they do at least show clearly the emphasis within Marcus' group on experience of divine power, however questionably induced.

4. Conclusion

Our survey from the southern Gallic churches has covered two sources from the 'orthodox' side and one source concerning heretical Christians. All three reveal an emphasis on the experiential side of the Christian faith. One might say that Irenaeus provides a theological explanation for the kind of religious experience revealed in the *Letter* of the Lyons and Vienne congregations. In the *Letter*, we meet a fervent kind of Christianity which seeks to spread the faith and win others for Christ and which embraces martyrdom for Christ, often enduring atrocious torments with heroic courage born of the conviction that the Spirit/risen Christ was with them to strengthen and support them.

Irenaeus gives us a theological assessment of the work of the Spirit. Faith leading to baptism is the moment when Christians receive the Spirit. Now, in our Syrian section, we met documents which reflected intense religious experience which did not necessarily link that experience with baptism (e.g., *The Odes of Solomon*) or which did not magnify the role of baptism (e.g. the fourth gospel). In Irenaeus, however, there is a very definite link with baptism, as we saw. Our knowledge of the conditions under which people became Christians and joined the church in southern

---

[58] 1.13.5 says that Marcus used love potions to retain his hold on these women.

[59] Reiling, *Marcus Gnosticus*, p. 176, said that Marcus played the role of *Geistmittler* (mediator of the Spirit).

[60] Cf. Hermas, Mandate 11, discussed in 5.3, above.

Gaul is sketchy. Were they baptized immediately and then instructed, or were they instructed as catechumens first and then baptized? In either case, baptism by immersion would provide a dramatic moment, at which a sense of the Spirit's presence would be entirely natural. It crystalized the passage from paganism to Christianity, from darkness to light. Irenaeus' view is comparable to a tradition like Titus 3.4-7, but we do not meet anything like Ignatius' cosmic speculation approach, in which the baptismal water has been purified by Jesus' own baptism.

The implication of a whole series of phrases which Irenaeus uses is that the experience of the Spirit was a conscious one: Christians were aware of the Spirit in their lives, prompting prayer to God as Abba and imparting a new quality of life. They had a sense of the Spirit as a permanent indwelling force who enables communion with Christ and the Father to take place. The perfect person is not someone already morally perfect, but rather a Christian who has received the Holy Spirit. The receiving of the Spirit does indeed involve a changed life style and Irenaeus stressed the new ethical conduct which flows through the inner strength imparted by the Spirit.

Gifts and graces of the Spirit continued to be experienced within the congregations known to Irenaeus, including prophecy, healing and exorcisms.

The Spirit leads into the truth, i.e., the truth known within the universal church, embodied in the church's tradition and Rule of Faith. Irenaeus' position is akin to John's stress on the Paraclete's ministry of leading into the truth. But, once the Johannine reinterpretation of Jesus' ministry was encapsulated in the fourth gospel, it became tradition, part of the basis on which the church's belief was erected. From a standpoint later on, Irenaeus' link between the Spirit and truth was due to the need to preserve apostolic witness. Irenaeus' position is also similar to the Pastorals' emphasis on the 'deposit' to be preserved, and also to Tertullian's stress that the Paraclete does not alter doctrine, the rule of faith (see chapter 7).

The Spirit, one of 'God's Hands', was active in the first creation, is active in regeneration and in the educative process which prepares people for the ultimate vision of God. From start to finish the Spirit, along with the Word-Son of God, is one of God's executive agents in carrying out His work of restoring human beings.

Finally, the Valentinian Marcosians known to Irenaeus seem to stress a religious experience in which some at any rate of their number were seized (as they believed) by a power from above, which enabled them to be the mouthpiece of what they conceived to be the divine pneumatic Pleroma.

The evidence, then, from southern Gaul, orthodox and heretical alike, bears ample testimony to the vitality of religious experience within all shades of Christian opinion. If we compare this with the result of our investigation in other areas, then we could say that these churches were not dissimilar to many of the Syrian churches in their deep sense of the power of the Spirit at work in their midst. Probably in touch with Asia Minor congregations, they also shared the Montanist stress on the Spirit without having certain features which they deemed a fault in Montanism. Irenaeus as a church leader has points in common with the seer John and the author of the Pastorals of earlier generations, and yet differs from them both. He shares in general with the former a sense of the Spirit's present activity, while he himself is at home in the structures of the developed threefold ministry. With the latter he accepts the institutional side of the church, but manages to have a theology of the Spirit's ongoing activity which seems to go far beyond anything hinted at in the Pastorals. Eighty years on, he seems to have a balance between Spirit and institution which the Pastor did not altogether succeed in maintaining.

The southern Gallic churches seemed to have stressed the Spirit more than the church at Rome did, as reflected in extant literature, though we must remember that the Old Roman Creed embodied the conviction that blessings did accompany the gift of the Spirit. Earlier we pointed out that Irenaeus reflected use of such a Trinitarian baptismal confession of faith, and he too expatiated on the blessings of the Spirit. The Spirit is not just an item in a credal statement, but part of the very fabric of the Christian life and experience for Irenaeus.

CHAPTER 7

Northern Africa

The origins of the church at Carthage and the provinces of Roman Africa and Numidia are shrouded in mystery. In AD180 twelve Christians from Scilli (the exact location of which is unknown) were executed in Carthage by the proconsul, Saturninus. The *Acts of the Scillitan Martyrs* quote from a Latin translation of the Bible, which suggests that the church's origins in this part of North Africa must be sought earlier in the second century. Whether the church at Carthage was founded from Rome[1] can be neither proved nor disproved. Certainly, connections between Rome and Carthage were close. Tertullian does not give precise information, though he did claim that Christians were very numerous in Carthage and the provinces (e.g. *Apol.* 37.4; *Scap.* 5.2). W.H.C. Frend has suggested that the origins of the *seniores laici* may go back to a Jewish or Judaeo-Christian environment out of which the North African church developed in the second century AD.[2]

It is mainly from towards the end of the second and the beginning of the third centuries that we get first hand documentation of North African Christianity. In this section, we shall concentrate on two sources of evidence: *The Passion of Perpetua and Felicitas*[3] and the writings of Tertullian (without looking at Tertullian, we would not, in fact, have within our survey any first-hand evidence of Montanism, as we mentioned in our previous remarks on Asia Minor Montanism in 3.8).

---

[1] So, e.g., H. Lietzmann, *The Founding of the Church Universal* (London: Lutterworth, 2nd ed., 1950), p. 217.

[2] W.H.C. Frend, 'The Seniores Laici and the Origins of the Church in North Africa', *JTS* 12 (1961), pp. 280-84.

[3] Many scholars believe that Tertullian was the final redactor of the Passion (e.g. de Labriolle, *Crise*, pp. 338-533, especially 345-51, for tables of the language used by the redactor in the prologue and conclusion of the Passion and by Tertullian; cf. too V. Morel, 'Disciplina, le mot et l'idée représentée par lui dans les oeuvres de Tertullien', *RHE* 40 (1944-45), p. 44; Musurillo, *Acts*, p. xxvii. However, R. Braun, 'Nouvelles observations linguistiques sur le redacteur de la "Passio Perpetuae"', *VC* 33 (1979), pp. 105-17, has cast serious doubts on this hypothesis, and T.D. Barnes, *Tertullian* (Oxford: Clarendon, 1971, reissued with postscript 1985), p. 329; Weinrich, *Spirit and Martyrdom*, pp. 223-25, and D. Rankin, *Tertullian and the Church* (Cambridge: Cambridge University Press, 1995), p. 13, also deny Tertullian's redactorship.

1. The Passion of Perpetua and Felicitas

The Passion of Perpetua and Felicitas is 'a vivid witness to the youth and vigour of the growing African church of the late second century'.[4] It tells the story of the persecutions and martyrdoms suffered by the churches in North Africa in AD 202.

The redactor of the *Passion* either belonged to the Montanist persuasion or shared some of their convictions.[5] In the introduction (ch. 1), he criticized those who would restrict the power of the one Spirit to times and seasons (1.3). Recent events are greater than past events because of being 'a consequence of the extraordinary graces promised for the last stage of time'. Then there follows a quotation from Joel 2.28 (1.4). 'So too we hold in honour and acknowledge not only new prophecies but new visions as well, according to the promise. And we consider all the other functions of the Holy Spirit as intended for the good of the church; for the same Spirit has been sent to distribute all his gifts to all, as the Lord apportions to everyone' (1.5).

He intended to record some of these recent events so that 'no one of weak and despairing faith may think that supernatural grace was present only among those of ancient times, either in the grace of martyrdom or of visions, for God always achieves what He promises, as a witness to the non-believer and a blessing to the faithful' (1.5).

The group of eventual martyrs was still within the church in North Africa,[6] as is shown by the account of Saturnus' vision in which bishop Optatus and the elder and teacher, Aspasius, ask Perpetua and Saturnus to effect a reconciliation between them.[7] The defensive tone of the author in his opening paragraphs, when he asserted that the working of the Spirit was not to be confined to past ages but was present in his own day, is clear and probably suggests that Montanists or enthusiastic Christians, though inside the church, were a minority.

The writer was clearly seeking to refute a view which invested the past with now spiritually unattainable heights. He wanted to undermine the tendency to look back at the past as a golden age and to lament that things were not the same. On the contrary, he believed that the Spirit was at work, inspired the present martyrs and imparted visions and dreams. Was there, then, a deep divide within the congregations known to the author? How strong numerically were those Christians who felt aware of the Spirit's help and power? Were they chafing against the alleged lack of spirituality of the majority? We can only pose such questions; we cannot supply the answers.

---

[4] Musurillo, *Acts*, p. xxv. All quotations are taken from Musurillo's translation.

[5] J.F. Matthews, in a review of Barnes' *Tertullian*, has maintained that while no one will question the Montanist tone of the preface of the *Passio*, the grounds for believing it actually to be Montanist (eagerness for martyrdom and the spiritual ascendancy of confessors over the established clergy) are inadequate (*JTS* 25 [1973], pp. 248-49). Weinrich, *Spirit and Martyrdom*, pp. 228-36, goes further and denies that the redactor was in any way Montanist.

[6] Barnes, *Tertullian*, pp. 164-86.

[7] So, too, Barnes, *Tertullian*, p. 79.

A. Divine Presence

After her baptism, Perpetua says that she was 'inspired by the Spirit not to ask for any other favours after the water [her baptism] but simply the perseverance of the flesh' (3.5). The Spirit guided her petitionary prayers so that her requests focussed only on the prayer to persevere faithful to Christ amidst the physical sufferings ahead.

An instance of charismatic prayer is when Perpetua involuntarily prayed for Dinocrates, her dead brother, and continued to do so because she felt that he was in torment. Later, she has a vision which assured her that he was released from his suffering (7.1-8.4). The Spirit-filled, prospective martyr's prayer avails powerfully for the object of her intercession. In this instance, it reaches beyond this life to the life beyond death.

We might also mention here the prayer for Felicitas, who was eight months pregnant, made by her comrades who were afraid of the postponement of her martyrdom. As a result of the prayer, her labour commenced, and she gave birth to a son. In this way, she was able to go forward with them all to martyrdom (15.1-7).

Along with prayer, there are visions granted to Perpetua. She had two visions which revealed her impending martyrdom to her: the bronze ladder reaching to heaven, symbolizing martyrdom, in 4.3-10, and the fight with a vicious-looking Egyptian, symbolizing the devil, in 10.1-15.

These visions are a mode of revelation. Messages are conveyed to Perpetua from God. Given the writer's introduction, it is clear that, as far he is concerned, such revelatory visions are the inspiration of the Holy Spirit. We notice certain features of these prayers and visions. They were not concerned with the spread of the gospel or some aspect of God's plan; they tend to glorify the Christian rather than Christ; prayer concerned either the martyr's own fate or a relative of the martyr. In these features, there are both similarities to and differences from the visions in the Acts of the Apostles, for example.

C. Divine Power

In a martyrological document, we naturally do not expect to find ethical discussions, but rather we look for whether there is any idea of the martyr's receiving strength to cope with his or her impending ordeal.

When the author narrated the ordeal of Perpetua's martyrdom—she was attacked by a heifer—he said 'She awoke from a kind of sleep (so absorbed had she been in ecstasy in the Spirit) and she began to look around her. Then, to the amazement of all, she said "When are we going to be thrown to that heifer or whatever it is?"'(20.8). The Spirit had answered her prayer (3.5) and lifted her above the consciousness of the pain arising from the wild beast's attacks.

We have mentioned the pregnancy of Felicitas. During what was a difficult labour, a guard reminded her of the even greater pains which she would have to endure when she got in the arena. To this she replied 'What I am now suffering I suffer by myself. But then another will be inside me (*alius erit in me*) who will suffer for me, just as I am suffering for him' (15.6). The martyr is conscious of a reciprocity of suffering due to the mutual indwelling of servant and Master in the Spirit.

Side by side with this, there are passages where the emphasis is on the martyr's steadfastness and endurance. Just before Perpetua's struggle with the Egyptian, the One of marvellous stature (God or Christ?) says of Perpetua, 'If this Egyptian defeats her, he will slay her with the sword. But if she defeats him, she will receive this branch' and then he withdrew (10.9, 13). Weinrich comments that the martyr is essentially on their own before the adversary.[8] While this comment is understandable, it may not be altogether fair. The redactor had already emphasized that no one of weak or despairing faith should think that supernatural grace was only given to those of the past, for God always achieves what He promises (1.6). So, we should certainly assume that he believed that supernatural strength was given to the martyrs.

The author concluded his work: 'These new manifestations of virtue will bear witness to the one and the same Spirit who still operates and to God the Father almighty, to His Son Jesus Christ our Lord, to whom is splendour and immeasurable power for all the ages' (21.11).[9]

All this is hardly a literary motif. Rather, it is a case of men and women possessing a sense of the Spirit within them and as a result developing a kind of theology which eagerly embraces martyrdom, as following in the steps of Christ and being conformed to his sufferings and so bearing witness to him. However, the tendentious nature of the final redaction suggests that the editor saw the martyrdoms as proof of the validity of the position which he had so clearly set out in his prologue and to which he returned in his epilogue.[10] They are seen as proof of the Spirit's present work in the churches: he was not absent as if confined only to previous generations.

Summary

The picture which emerges reveals at least one type of Christianity in North Africa:[11] enthusiastic, Spirit-directed, world-renouncing,[12] eager to embrace

---

[8] Weinrich, *Spirit and Martyrdom*, p. 242; also p. 240.

[9] Cf. 16.11 'Therefore, since the Holy Spirit has permitted the story of this contest to be written down and by so permitting has willed it...'.

[10] Whether or not the Passion was by Tertullian, he certainly believed that martyrdom was a duty and that the Paraclete did urge Christians to martyrdom (cf. Barnes, *Tertullian*, pp. 164-86; Weinrich, *Spirit and Martyrdom*, pp. 254-55, 263).

[11] Frend, *Martyrdom and Persecution*, p. 365, and *The Donatist Church* (Oxford: Clarendon, 1952), pp. 112-18, contrasts this type of Christianity in North Africa with the religion of Clement of Alexandria (see chapter 8 below).

[12] Barnes, *Tertullian*, p. 79, says that the dominant motif of African Christianity was 'an uncompromising rejection of an alien world'.

martyrdom.[13] It may not have been that of the majority, but at least within one church it represented a particular facet of church life and in its stress on the Spirit is reminiscent of the kind of portrait that Luke gives us of the early church. Naturally, martyrdom is to the fore, and, in the sense of being one with Christ in suffering, the outlook is close to Paul.

2. Tertullian

There are difficulties in gaining a true understanding of the Spirit's role in Tertullian's religious experience:

(i) Tertullian was primarily a controversialist, whether attacking heretical views or defending practices which he considered essential to the Christian lifestyle. The controversial nature and style of his writings might not offer much information on our theme. Yet on some subjects treated[14] we might expect references to the Spirit.

(ii) Tertullian's skill in the use of rhetoric[15] also has to be taken into consideration. As an illustration, we may refer to how F. Forrester Church has shown the way in which Tertullian can describe women following in the steps of Eve as 'the gateway for the devil' (*diaboli ianua*), when he wants to appeal for modesty of dress, while elsewhere he blames Adam for the Fall and shows a far more positive view of women and their spiritual potential and capability (e.g. for martyrdom).[16] We might have to take this rhetorical skill into consideration when evaluating some of Tertullian's statements which might seem paradoxical.

(iii) How far did Tertullian change his views due to his adherence to Montanism, or did this strengthen existing ones?[17] Did Tertullian initially hold that all Christians

---

[13] Cf. what *The Acts of the Scillitan Martyrs* (to be dated ca.180, the time of the martyrdoms, see Quasten, *Patrology II*, p. 181) reveals of another North African congregation. This document also exhibits a strong world-renouncing approach (e.g., one Speratus said, 'I do not recognise the empire of this world. Rather, I serve that God whom no one has seen nor can see, with these eyes... I acknowledge my Lord who is the emperor of kings and of all nations', para. 6); a biblically-based Christianity (if one may use the term—When asked what was in their case, Speratus said 'Books and letters of a just man named Paul', para. 12); and an eagerness for martyrdom (Nartzalus said 'Today we are martyrs in heaven. Thanks be to God', para. 15, and all thanked God as they were led out to the execution, para. 17). It is probably only the extreme brevity of the account why no reference to the Spirit occurs. If we were to go by feeling, we sense their vibrant personal experience of the Spirit.

[14] Cf. H. von Campenhausen, *The Latin Fathers* (London: A. & C. Black, 1964), p. 9: 'scarcely a problem in the church of that time about which Tertullian did not express his view, or in some way offer his opinion'.

[15] See R.D. Sider, *Ancient Rhetoric and the Art of Tertullian* (Oxford: Clarendon, 1971).

[16] F.F. Church, 'Sex and Salvation in Tertullian', *HTR* 68 (1975), pp. 83-101.

[17] According to von Campenhausen, *Latin Fathers*, p. 31, 'As a Montanist Tertullian did not become other than he had always been'; so too, Rankin, *Church*, pp. 42, 50; and

received the Spirit, but later believed that only those who accepted the New Prophecy possessed the Spirit? Or are there signs in the earlier writings of a division between spiritual and unspiritual Christians which his move to Montanism only strengthened?[18]

(iv) A fourth issue is that of inner consistency. If a writer like Tertullian alluded to the Spirit's power in a few places, is this a reflex of tradition, an almost unconscious lip service to a NT emphasis, or should it be assumed in the other passages where no explicit reference is made?

(v) A further point needs to be made, namely that Tertullian, under Stoic influence,[19] envisaged spirit as a material substance, extremely fine and rarefied but material nonetheless. For him, *spiritus* is the substance (*substantia*) of divinity,[20] as in *Prax.* 7.8: 'For who will deny that God is a body (*corpus*) although God is Spirit (*spiritus*)? For Spirit has a body of its own kind (*generis*), in its own form (*effigie*)'. *Spiritus* is the substance which passes from the Father to the Son and from the Father through the Son to the Holy Spirit without any division (*Prax.* 3.5; 4.1). Therefore, *spiritus* is the substance (*substantia*) of the Word, while *sermo*, *ratio* and *virtus* are the modes of manifestation (the '*accidens*') (*Apol.* 21.11 continues, 'We have been taught that he [the Word] ... is called Son of God and God because of the unity of the substance. For God too is Spirit [*spiritus*]'. So, 21.12, '[he is] Spirit of Spirit and God of God' [*de spiritu spiritus et de deo deus*]. In *Prax.* 8.4 we read 'But the Word is formed by Spirit and...the body of the Word is Spirit' [*sermo autem spiritu structus est et...sermonis corpus est spiritus*]).

But also Tertullian will use *spiritus* for the Holy Spirit, the third person (*persona*) of the Trinity.

E.F. Osborn, *Tertullian, First Theologian of the West* (Cambridge: Cambridge University Press, 1997), pp. 210-13.

[18] Barnes, *Tertullian,* pp. 43-44, listed certain words or phrases in Tertullian's works which are distinctive of Montanist beliefs, two of which may be mentioned here: the abuse of catholics as '*psychici*' and the employment of '*nos/vos*' or '*noster/vester*', used either explicitly or by implication, to contrast Montanists with catholics. See Rankin, *Church*, pp. 41-51, for a discussion of Tertullian's relationship to the New Prophecy. Among the generally accepted 'Montanist' works of Tertullian are *adv. Val.*, *de anima*, *de resurr.mort.*, *adv. Marc.*, *de corona*, *de virg.vel.*, *de exhort.cast.*, *de fuga in persecutione*, *adv.Prax.*, *de monogamia*, *de ieiunio*, *de pudicitia*.

[19] E.g., S. Otto, '*Natura*' *und* '*Dispositio*'. *Untersuchung zum Naturbegriff und zur Denkform Tertullians* (München: Max Hueber Verlag, 1960), pp. 3, 17, 38, 46, 88; R. Braun, *Deus Christianorum:Recherches sur le vocabulaire doctrinal de Tertullien* (Paris: Publications de la Faculte des Lettres et Sciences Humaines d'Alger XLI, 1962), pp. 149, 201, 206, 285, 554; J. Danielou, *The Origins of Latin Christianity* (London: Dartman, Longman and Todd, 1979), pp. 209-23; A. Grillmeir, *Christ in Christian Tradition*, (London: Mowbrays, 2nd ed., 1982), p. 118.

[20] See Braun, *Deus Christianorum*, pp. 149, 182, for a thorough discussion; also C. Stead, 'Divine Substance in Tertullian', *JTS* 14 (1963), pp. 46-66.

In other words, *spiritus* has a double meaning: the substance of divinity (which the Word and the Spirit share with the Father) and the Holy Spirit. The context must be examined carefully for the sense.[21]

For Tertullian, what has corporeal reality can resist, act or operate on or move something else. 'In God existential density is at its strongest'.[22] 'How could it be that He, without whom nothing was made, is nothing? How could He who is empty have made things which are solid, and He who is empty have made things which are full, and He who is incorporeal have made things which have corporeality?' (*Prax.* 7.7).

There is an interplay of biblical and Stoic thought. John 4.24 was influential as well as Stoicism; and while Spirit in the Bible is a way of expressing God's activity, in Stoicism the activity springs from corporeality.[23]

By way of introduction we shall consider two passages in which Tertullian gives a formal definition of the Paraclete's work:

(a) In *de virginibus velandis*,[24] Tertullian described the Holy Spirit as the vicar of the Lord. Since human mediocrity could not comprehend everything at once (Jn. 16.12), the Lord sent the Paraclete to bring discipline to perfection: 'The Paraclete's administrative office (is) the direction of discipline, the revelation of the scriptures, the re-formation of the intellect, the advancement towards the better things' (11.4-5).

Tertullian then developed his idea of growth and seasons both in nature and the spiritual realm. As regards the latter, he instanced four seasons:

(i) the rudimentary: characterized by the natural fear of God;

(ii) infancy: the era of the law and the prophets;

(iii) the fervour of youth: the gospel era;

(iv) maturity: the time of the Paraclete, who, after Christ, is the only one to be called and revered as Master (1.6-7).

The first work of the Spirit is, then, the establishment of discipline. Arguably, all four items really refer to discipline, since 'the better things' are synonymous with it, while the correct interpretation of scripture and the reshaping of Christian minds appertain to it also.

(b) In *Monogamia*,[25] Tertullian described the work of the Paraclete as twofold. Firstly, he initially bears witness to Christ; then, secondly, he reveals the 'many

---

[21] Cf. H. Bender, *Die Lehr über den heilige Geist bei Tertullian* (München: Max Hueber Verlag, 1961), p. 99.

[22] Danielou, *Latin Christianity*, p. 217.

[23] Otto, *Natura*, p. 4, points to the link between *natura* and activity, between the *substratum* and its result.

[24] Dated before 207 by Quasten, *Patrology II*, p. 307; to 208/9 and after by Barnes, *Tertullian*, pp. 55, 328, the treatise deals with the veiling of virgins lest they should entice men to lust after them and endanger also their own purity.

[25] Barnes, *Tertullian*, p. 55, dates to 210/11; Quasten, *Patrology II*, p. 305, to 217; W.P. le Saint, *Tertullian's Treatises on Marriage and Remarriage* (New York: Newman, 1951), p. 86, also to 217. That is, all three scholars date it within the Montanist period of Tertullian. This work is the last of three treatises dealing with marriage and remarriage.

things' concerning discipline which the disciples could not bear (Jn. 16.12) and which are no less burdensome to Tertullian's day than to the original disciples (2.4).

In these two writings from within the Montanist period, we discern an emphasis on discipline. The Paraclete witnesses to Christ, and then imposes a discipline which goes beyond what Jesus taught, because we are now in the era of maturity. We notice a silence in these passages on whether the Spirit empowers Christians to shoulder this discipline. Does he impose a heavy yoke and expect people to carry it unaided?

The resistance to this discipline, which Tertullian noticed among those whom he branded as the sensualists who do not receive the Spirit (e.g. *de Monogamia* 1), served only to mark off the unspiritual from the truly spiritual.

We now turn to our three areas of concern.

A. Divine Presence

Did Tertullian think of a specific experience of receiving the Spirit? Did he expect Christians to be conscious of having the Spirit?

In *de cultu Feminarum* II.1.1,[26] all Christians are God's temple because they have appropriated the Holy Spirit. The 'appropriation' seems to suggest the conscious acceptance by believers of the gift offered to them.

The family image is used in *Apologeticum*.[27] Christians are brothers—even pagans say 'Look how they love one another'—who possess knowledge of their common Father, have drunk of the one Holy Spirit and have been born into the same light of truth (39.9). The reference to drinking the one Spirit may echo 1 Corinthians 12.13, but the use of such a vivid phrase, when less dramatic ones were available, suggests an experience of which Christians were conscious. One of the common bonds of the Christian family, then, is their mutual possession of the Holy Spirit.

Tertullian's treatise *de baptismo*[28] seems to envisage both an infusion of the water by the Spirit or Angel[29] (to produce cleansing)[30] and, following laying-on of

---

It strongly upheld one marriage as God's will and judged second marriages as unlawful and akin to adultery.

[26] Barnes, *Tertullian* p. 55, dates to 196 or early 197; Quasten, *Patrology II* p. 295: 'before his Montanist period'. Tertullian basically appeals for modesty in female dress to distinguish Christian from pagan women, and condemns cosmetics, jewellery, etc.

[27] Quasten, *Patrology II*, p. 265, dates to 197; T.R. Glover, *Tertullian Apology* (London: William Heinemann, 1966), p. xix, to 197-98; C. Becker, *Tertullians' Apologeticum. Werdung und Leistung* (München:Kösel-Verlag, 1961), p. 44, to 197; Barnes, *Tertullian*, p. 328, to autumn 196 or later. Tertullian defends Christianity against various criticisms made by pagan critics (incest, infanticide, atheism, disloyalty to the state) and protests against the treatment of Christians in the law courts.

[28] Quasten, *Patrology II*, p. 280, dates to 198-200; E. Evans, *Tertullian's Homily on Baptism* (London: SPCK, 1964), p. xi, places it 'about the turn of the century'; Barnes, *Tertullian*, p. 55, dates to 198.

hands and prayer, a personal experience of the Spirit who descends on Christians as he did on Jesus in his baptism and who brings God's peace like the dove after the flood (6.1; 8.3-4).[31] The analogy with Jesus' baptism and the Flood fits in with a personal awareness of the Spirit's activity.

The idea of the Spirit's visitation of the heart to take up his abode there (after repentance has prepared a clean heart) occurs in *de Paenitentia* (2.6),[32] and this language is commensurate with a felt awareness of the Spirit's coming upon the Christian. The common experience of the Spirit is again a mark of Christians (10.4, 6).

Tertullian employs the nuptial image (*de Anima*).[33] The soul is wedded to the Spirit, and the flesh 'follows' as part of the bridal portion, no longer the servant of the soul but of the Spirit (41.4).[34] Since intimacy is the essence of the nuptial metaphor, its usage argues for a conscious experience of possessing the Spirit.

It is true that for Tertullian our present experience of the Spirit is the guarantee of our future experience[35] and when the fullness of the Spirit has been received, then the flesh will become a Spirit-informed body. But this does not lessen the fact that it is assumed that Christians have already received the Spirit.

---

[29] Tertullian equates the Holy Spirit (ch. 4) and the Angel (ch. 5), using John 5.1-9 as a typology of Christian baptism: see J. Danielou, *The Bible and the Liturgy* (London: Darton, Longmann & Todd, 1960), pp. 210-13.

[30] Tertullian says that baptism prepares for the reception of the Spirit (ch. 6). For the tension between what Tertullian says here and elsewhere about the relation of the Spirit and baptism, see Lampe, *Seal*, pp. 157-62, who describes Tertullian's statements on this subject as confusing and inconsistent.

[31] E.C. Ratcliff, *Liturgical Studies* (ed. A.H. Couratin and D.H. Tripp; London: SPCK, 1976), p.129, distinguished between recovering the Spirit of God and receiving the Holy Spirit, but this is hardly convincing (that sort of view was firmly rejected by Lampe, *Seal*, pp. 161-62).

[32] Quasten, *Patrology II*, p. 299, dates to 203; W.P. Le Saint, *Tertullian—Treatises on Penance and on Purity* (London: Longmans, Green, 1959), suggests either between 200 and 206 or between 193 and 202/3, certainly before 207; Barnes, *Tertullian*, p. 55, placed it between 198 and 203.

[33] J.H. Waszink, *De Anima* (Amsterdam: J.M. Meulenhoff, 1947), p. 6, dates to 210-13; similarly Quasten, *Patrology II*, p. 289; while Barnes, *Tertullian*, p. 328 (in the postscript) contents himself with after 208. The treatise refutes false doctrines about the soul and discusses certain questions about the soul.

[34] Cf. *de resurrectione mortuorum* 63.1, 3, also for this image of bride and groom applied to the flesh and the Holy Spirit. Waszink, *Anima*, p. 457, says that the picture of the soul wedded to the Spirit does not seem to occur before Tertullian.

[35] He takes pignus Spiritus of 2 Cor. 1.22; 5.5 (cf. Eph. 1.13 pignus hereditatis nostrae) as a partitive genitive, not an epexegetic one, as *de resurrectione mortuorum* 51.2; 53.18-19 make abundantly clear.

In *de resurrectione mortuorum*,[36] Tertullian interprets God's gifts mentioned in the OT not as material bounties, as the Jews took them, but spiritually. Thus, water stands for the Spirit and wine represents the soul which receives strength from the vine which is Christ: 'even as they reckon the holy land itself to be strictly Jewish territory, though it ought rather to be interpreted as the Lord's flesh, so that flesh thenceforth in all who have put on Christ is a holy land, truly holy through the indwelling of the Holy Spirit, truly flowing with milk and honey through the sweetness of his own hope, truly Judean through the familiar converse of God' (26.10-11).

To put on Christ and to be indwelt by the Spirit are thus two sides of the one coin. The flesh of those 'who have put on Christ is a holy land, truly holy through the indwelling of the Holy Spirit'. This state produces 'familiar converse with God'. If Tertullian can use the idea of *familiaritas* with God, it is clear that conscious awareness of God's presence is in mind.

The implication of what Tertullian says in *Scorpiace*[37] — that one aspect of our continuity with the apostles is the Spirit — is that all Christians have the Holy Spirit, and this is explicitly asserted by him in *de fuga in persecutione*,[38] where Tertullian uses Joel 2.28 to countermand Matthew 10.23: 'No command that shows Judea to be specially the sphere for preaching applies to us, now that the Holy Spirit has been poured out upon all flesh' (6.4). But no hint is given in either passage as to the exact manner of experiencing the Spirit.

Tertullian spoke of the Christian's being clothed with the Holy Spirit, when he allegorized the Parable of the Prodigal Son, and took the prodigal not as a backsliding Christian but as an unbeliever. He denies that an apostate can 'recover his former garment, the robe of the Holy Spirit, and a renewal of the ring, the sign of baptism' (*de puditicia*[39] 9.11). 'The ring which is *signaculum lavacri*' may be paraphrased as 'the ring which stands for that sign which consists of baptism'. Tertullian's order of Holy Spirit and baptism is probably due to the order of robe and ring in the original parable, as earlier he allegorized the prodigal's 'substance' as baptism, the Holy Spirit and eternal hope. The idea of 'being clothed' has a NT ring

---

[36] Quasten, *Patrology II*, p. 283 dates it to 'perhaps 210-12'; Barnes, *Tertullian*, p. 326, to 208-11.

[37] Barnes, *Tertullian*, p. 55, and 'Tertullian's Scorpiace', *JTS* 20 (1969), pp. 105-132, dates to late 203/early 204, convincingly against the later date of 213 during Scapula's persecution, advocated amongst others by Quasten, *Patrology II*, p. 282. Tertullian defended martyrdom against the gnostics (who are the scorpions, because they denied the need or value of martyrdom and hence their teaching is poisonous).

[38] Quasten, *Patrology II*, p. 310, dates to 212; Barnes, *Tertullian*, p. 328, places it after 208 without specifying more closely. In this work, Tertullian withdrew his earlier permission of flight during persecution (*ad Uxorem* 1.3; *de Paenitentia* 13) and discussed Mt. 10.23 at length.

[39] Quasten, *Patrology II*, p. 312, contents himself with saying that this work is violently Montanist. Le Saint, *Penance and Purity*, p. 52, says that it was 'composed some time after 212/3'. Barnes, *Tertullian*, p. 55, dates to 210/211.

about it, as we see in Luke 24.49 of the Spirit; Romans 13.14; Galatians 3.27; Ephesians 4.24; Colossians 3.10 of Christ the new man.

Yet it is also in this treatise that Tertullian enunciated the sharp division between spiritual and psychic people. 'The very church itself is properly and principally the Spirit himself' (21.16). The church consists of those who possess the Spirit. To this church (and not to the psychics) is given the power of forgiving sins, 'the church of the Spirit by means of a spiritual man, not the church which consists of a number of bishops' (21.17).[40]

Thus, it would appear that only in the latest of his writings do we meet a distinction between spiritual and psychic, the true church and an outward hierarchical church. Tertullian certainly began with the assumption that all Christians receive the Spirit.

We turn now to consider the link between the receiving of the Spirit and activity of word and deed resulting from that experience. We shall particularly consider Tertullian's view of prophecy and visions as inspired by the Spirit.

He believed that the former gifts of grace to Israel had been withdrawn and that the Holy Spirit no longer lingered in Jewish synagogues (*adv. Iudaeos*[41] 13.15; cf. *adv. Marc.* 3.23.2; 5.8.4). The law and the prophets were until John the Baptist. Vision and prophecy were 'sealed' by Christ. After him there were no visions, prophecy or miracles in Judaism. All the previous spiritual gifts ceased in Christ (8.14). The disciples of Christ, however, obtained the promised power of the Holy Spirit for the gift of miracles and utterance, and then proceeded into the world and preached the gospel (*de praescriptione haereticorum* 20.4).[42] The initial fulfillment of the promise was at Pentecost and between then and Tertullian's own day spiritual gifts and endowments had existed in the church as is revealed by his ironical comment that truth had to wait for certain Marcionites and Valentinians to set it free. Tertullian used the expression 'new prophecy' and saw Montanus, Priscilla and Maximilla as a fulfilment of the Johannine promise of the Paraclete. He spoke of 'us...whom the recognition of spiritual gifts entitles to be deservedly called spiritual' (*de monogamia* 1.2).

One of Tertullian's criticisms levelled at a certain Praxeas was that at Rome he had done a twofold service for the devil: 'He drove away prophecy and brought in

---

[40] Frend, *Martyrdom and Persection*, p. 378, wrote, 'In this work, the theology of the gathered community was given classic expression... It is a permanent protest against institutional religion in favour of a religion of the Spirit.'

[41] Quasten, *Patrology II*, pp. 268-69, offers no date. H. Trankle, *Tertullian Adversus Iudaeos* (Wiesbaden: Steiner, 1964), p. lxvii, contents himself with saying that it is one of Tertullian's earliest works. Barnes, *Tertullian*, p. 55, assigns it to the summer of 197. The work was sparked off by a dispute between a Christian and a Jewish proselyte and deals with how Christians should interpret the OT.

[42] *Praes. Haer.* denied the right of heretics to use the Bible and maintained that catholic doctrine originated in apostolic tradition, the truth of which is prior to the lateness of falsehood/heresy. Quasten, *Patrology II*, p. 272, dates to ca. 200; Barnes, *Tertullian*, p. 55, to 203.

heresy; he put to flight the Paraclete and he crucified the Father' (*ad Praxean* 1.5).[43] According to Tertullian, Praxeas persuaded a bishop of Rome, who was about to recognise Montanism, to withdraw that recognition[44]—hence Tertullian's sarcastic remark that Praxeas put the Paraclete to flight. In Tertullian's sentence, prophecy and Paraclete stand in parallelism, for the Spirit produces prophecy.

Prophecy was an endowment of God's grace (*de anima* 22.1). For Tertullian it was associated with ecstasy. He also links sleep and ecstasy, and illustrates this by Adam, who during sleep experienced the influence of the Spirit, 'for ecstasy, the Holy Spirit's creative power of prophecy, fell upon him'. As a result he exclaimed 'This is now bone of my bones and flesh of my flesh; therefore, shall a man leave his father and mother and shall cleave to his wife and they two shall become one flesh',[45] the true interpretation of which is the great mystery of Christ and the church (Eph. 5.31-32).

We dream and the memory of those dreams is the gift of the ecstatic condition during which mental function is withdrawn, though not totally extinguished, for the soul is never inactive. It is absent (*amentia*) when ecstasy is at work in us to bring before us images of a sound mind and wisdom.

Tertullian also associates Daniel with ecstasy (*de anima* 48.3-4). This ecstasy, however, was not due to his fasting, for this aimed to please God and not induce a state of the soul amenable to dreams and visions. God alone can give ecstasy. Fasting may, however, 'recommend' the ecstasy to God so that 'it happens in God' (*ita non ad ecstasin summovendam sobrietias proficiet, sed ad ipsam ecstasin commendandam ut in deo fiat*, 48.4). What does Tertullian mean by *ut in deo fiat*? Presumably God acts by sending the ecstatic state within the dream. He is the author of this state of grace.

Ecstasy was the state in which Peter at the Transfiguration made the suggestion about erecting three tabernacles. It was not a mistake on his part, but uttered in a state of ecstasy which is the concomitant of grace. 'For when a man is in the Spirit, especially when he has sight of the glory of God or when God is speaking by him,

---

[43] Quasten, *Patrology II*, p. 284, dates *ad Praxean* to 213; Barnes, *Tertullian*, p. 55, to 210/11. The reference to heresy/crucifying the Father is to the 'modalism', according to which the Father, Son and Spirit are modes of the same being, successive roles adopted to further the divine purpose of salvation, but not indicative of different persons within the Godhead. Hence, Tertullian's polemical remark that Praxeas crucified the Father.

[44] Which bishop it was is a matter of dispute. We need not discuss this issue here. For differing views, see Labriolle, *Crise Montaniste*, pp. 273-75, who favours Zephyrinus (198-217) and thinks that Praxeas' intrigues took place ca.198-200; P. Lampe, *Christen*, p. 332 (*Christians*, pp. 394-95), who believes that the bishop in question was Victor (189-99); and Trevett, *Montanism*, p. 58, who maintains that it was Eleutherus (174-89), ca.178-79. (Note: scholars differ as to whether Zephyrinus suceeded Victor in 198 or 199.)

[45] *de anima* 11.44; 21.1-2; 45.3; cf. *de ieiuniis* 3.21; *adv. Marc.* 4.22.4.

he must of necessity fall out of his senses, because in fact he is overshadowed by the power of God—on which there is disagreement between us and the natural men'.[46]

Dream and an ecstatic state within it are essential features of the experience of receiving prophetic revelation from God. In this way, the Spirit of God bestows the gift of prophecy on chosen vessels such as Montanus, Priscilla and Maximilla. Tertullian wrote about Priscilla: 'Through the holy prophetess Prisca the gospel is thus preached: "The holy minister knows how to minister sanctity". "For purity", she says, "is harmonious and they see visions; and turning their faces downward, they even hear manifest voices as salutary as they are secret"' (*de exhortatione castitatis*[47] 10.5).[48] In *de anima* 9, a famous passage gives an account of a Christian sister's visions. It needs to be quoted in full:

> For because we acknowledge spiritual gifts, we too have merited the attainment of the prophetic gift, although coming after John [the Baptist]. We have today amongst us a sister whose lot it has been to be favoured with spiritual gifts of revelation, which she experiences in the Spirit by ecstatic vision amidst the sacred rites of the Lord's Day in the church: she converses with angels, and sometimes even with the Lord; she both sees and hears mysterious communications; she understands some men's hearts, and to them who are in need she distributes remedies. Whether it be in the reading of the scriptures, or in the chanting of the psalms, or in the preaching of sermons, or in the offering of prayers, in all these religious services matter and opportunity are afforded to her of seeing visions. It may possibly have happened to us, whilst this sister of ours was rapt in the Spirit, that we had discoursed in some ineffable way about the soul. After the people are dismissed at the conclusion of the sacred services, she is in the regular habit of reporting to us whatever things she may have seen in vision (for all her communications are examined with the most scrupulous care, in order that their truth may be probed). 'Amongst other things', she says, 'there has been shown to me a soul in bodily shape, and a spirit has been in the habit of appearing to me; not, however, a void and empty illusion, but such as would offer itself to be even grasped by the hand, soft and transparent and of an ethereal colour, and in form resembling that of a human being in every respect'. This was her vision, and for her

---

[46] *adv. Marc.* 4.22.4-5. As its title suggests, this work, in five books, was written to combat the views of Marcion and his followers. Quasten, *Patrology II*, p. 275, dates to 212; E. Evans, *Adversus Marcionem* (Oxford: Clarendon, 1972), p. xviii, puts it in 207-8, while Barnes, *Tertullian*, p. 327, espouses the view of several editions, the last being post 207-8.

[47] This work was written to a friend, after the death of his wife, to dissuade him from contemplating a second marriage. Quasten, *Patrology II*, p. 305, dates to between 204 and 212; Barnes, *Tertullian*, p. 328, to after 208.

[48] Rankin, *Church*, p. 123, interpreted the phrase 'holy minister' to be 'in fact the Holy Spirit, or, more correctly, the spirit of the pray-er'. This seems to be a case of giving with one hand and taking away with the other! I assume that the primary reference is to a human 'minister', but one indwelt and inspired by the Holy Spirit.

witness there was God; and the apostle most assuredly foretold that there were to be 'spiritual gifts in the church (9.3-4).[49]

Is this a catholic or Montanist service?

(a) Tertullian has preached. Even if he was a layman, he might have been involved in some ministry of the word,[50] given his theological abilities.

(b) 'People' (*plebs*) may mean the congregation as opposed to the leaders, who could be referred-to in the phrase 'reporting to us' (*nobis enunciate*), yet '*nobis*' could refer to a group of Montanist Christians.

(c) The visions were tested by some after the service so that their veracity might be established.[51] Waszinck's comment that 'it is dubious whether such an examination would have taken place after a catholic service; and if so, if Tertullian would have been present', assumes that the examination would have been conducted by catholic ministers. But if the Montanists were still part of the catholic congregation (forming an *ecclesiola in ecclesia*),[52] then 'to us' (*nobis*) could refer to almost a kind of 'after meeting' which Montanists would frequent.

(d) The late date for the composition of *de anima*, upheld by Waszinck and Quasten, would favour a purely Montanist service, with *nobis* referring to their leaders, while the earlier date preferred by Barnes is congruous with a catholic service (see footnote 33).

(e) The elements of the service might point to a catholic service (assuming that scripture reading, chanting of psalms, preaching and prayers suggest a fairly structured Word-Response type of service).[53] Would not Montanist services be more free and less structured?

On the whole, the evidence seems slightly in favour of a catholic service.[54]

---

[49] Cf. the challenge to Marcion to produce evidence of spiritual gifts and graces in his churches, in *adv.Marc.* 5.8.12 and 5.15.5.

[50] So von Campenhausen, *Latin Fathers*, p. 7, though Labriolle, *Crise Montaniste*, p. 461, and Waszink, *de Anima*, p. 169, assumed a Montanist assembly with a sermon by Tertullian.

[51] It is possible that oracles, tested and approved, may have been gathered into a book or books; cf. Epiphanius, *Panarion*, 49.2; Theodoretus, *Haereticarum Fabularum Compendium*, 3.1.

[52] So D. Powell, 'Tertullianists and Cataphrygians', *VC* 29 (1975), pp. 33-54; G.L. Bray, *Holiness and the Will of God* (London: Marshall, Morgan and Scott, 1979), pp. 56-60; C.M. Robeck, *Prophecy in Carthage* (Cleveland, OH: Pilgrim Press, 1992), pp. 130-31, 272-73; Rankin, *Church*, p. 41; Trevett, *Montanism*, pp. 73-76.

[53] From an earlier period, Justin (*Apology* 1.67) intimates that a service consisted of readings from the memoirs of the apostles or writings of the prophets, a discourse, prayers and then communion. Tertullian himself in *Apologeticum* 39 mentions prayer, reading of scripture, exhortation, rebukes and sacred censures, as integral parts of Christian worship, and also says that the Agape began and ended with prayer and included the singing of hymns to God, all of which suggests a certain order in worship.

[54] Rankin, *Church*, p. 35.

We note that apart from visions this prophetess was gifted with the understanding of what was going on in people's hearts and the capacity to offer help to those who were willing to acknowledge their need (et medicinas desiderantibus sumit).

There are several references to exorcisms in Tertullian's writings,[55] though in none of these is the Holy Spirit specifically mentioned. Doubtless they were seen as a sign of his presence and power.

SUMMARY

We have explored the references in Tertullian to Christians' receiving or possessing the Spirit in an endeavour to ascertain whether they lend support to the idea of a conscious awareness of the Spirit's invasion of or presence in the believer's life. We suggested that many of the images (appropriation, drinking, visitation, marriage, indwelling) could indeed be so taken. Confirmation has resulted from Tertullian's views on spiritual gifts, and the illuminating description of the Christian sister who received visions from the Spirit and how these were tested afterwards. Of significance also is Tertullian's analysis of the ecstatic state in which prophecies were received.[56]

B. Divine Illumination

We saw in our introductory section that Tertullian had described the Paraclete as the one who was to reveal those things which Jesus could not impart during his earthly ministry. We, therefore, expect to encounter the idea of the Spirit as one who guides into deeper perception of God's truth. The description of the Spirit as the Spirit of Truth occurs frequently.[57] It is interesting to observe how Tertullian handles John 16.12-13 in *de praescriptione haereticorum* 22. He says that Jesus 'promised the future attainment of all truth by the help of the Spirit of Truth' (22.9) and he fulfilled this promise by sending the Holy Spirit as the Acts of the Apostles shows (22.9-10). Indeed, W. Bender maintained that Tertullian has said little on the way in which the Holy Spirit helps guard the truth. 'The real activity of the Spirit lies for him first and foremost in the past, namely when he taught through the apostles.

---

[55] *Apologeticum* 23.4, 15-16; 27.5, 7; 32.3; 43.2; 46.5, 10-12; *de Spectaculis* 29.3; *de Anima* 57.5; *ad Scapulam* 2.9; 4.5 (Quasten, *Patrology II*, p. 267, dates *ad Scapulam* to 212; Barnes, *Tertullian*, p. 55, agrees. Tertullian addressed this to the proconsul of Africa, pleading for freedom of worship and referring to a recent eclipse of the sun as a sign of God's anger at the persecution carried out by the proconsul).

[56] Interestingly, Danielou, *Latin Christianity*, p. 341, listed among those characteristics of Tertullian which were also to be found throughout Latin Christianity 'a subjectivity, which gives special prominence to inner experience'.

[57] See, e.g., *de praescriptione haereticorum* 8.14; *de corona* 4.6 (the writing of this work was occasioned by the refusal of a Christian Roman soldier to wear a laurel wreath at a military ceremony. Tertullian felt that serving in the Roman army was unacceptable because of its idolatrous nature and practices. Quasten, *Patrology II*, p. 309, assigns it to 211, while Barnes, *Tertullian*, p. 328, places it after 208); *de fuga in persecutione* 14.3; *adv. Praxean* 30.5.

What they preached is handed down to us in the Holy Scriptures. Through the words of Scripture the Holy Spirit also practises today his office as guardian of the faith'.[58] This is probably correct in what it affirms rather than in what it appears to deny, as we shall see below.

We cannot discern the truth without the help of God, Christ, the Spirit and faith (*de anima* 1.4). The Spirit, received through baptism and the laying on of hands, illumines the soul (*de resurrectione mortuarum* 8.3); indeed, *de paenitentia* speaks of God's grace illuminating the world through His Spirit (*gratiam...quam in extremitatibus temporum per spiritum suum universo orbi inluminaturus esset*, ['grace...by which he has illumined the whole world by his Spirit in these latest times'] 2.4).[59] At the same time Tertullian is prepared to argue that the Paraclete is not an innovator opposed to catholic tradition (*de monogamia* 2.1).

Specifically, there are seven areas where the Spirit is thought of as guiding into the truth:

(a) He preaches 'one monarchy' and interprets 'the economy (of Father, Son and Spirit) for those who admit the words of his new prophecy' (*adv. Prax.* 30.5).

(b) He teaches the corporeal nature of the soul, through the visions of a Christian sister (*de anima* 9.4, quoted above).

(c) He teaches the punishment of the soul in Hades before resurrection (*de anima* 5.7).

(d) He teaches monogamy, and has now retracted the concession made in 1 Corinthians 7.39 (*de monogamia* 3–4). The new prophecy outlawed a second marriage: if the infirmity of the flesh was allowed to prevail up till then, the Paraclete has now revoked the indulgence which permitted a second marriage. Accordingly, we cannot completely accept Bender's statement quoted above, since here is an example of the Spirit's 'tightening up' on what even Paul allowed.[60]

This is further illustrated by Tertullian's use of the Pauline expression 'the newness of the Spirit and not the oldness of the letter' (Rom. 7.6) in *de monogamia*. In his exposition, he equates the body of Christ of Romans 7.4 with 'the church, which consists in the Spirit of newness' (13.3), in order to contrast the law and the new dispensation under which a second marriage is forbidden. In Paul 'the newness of the Spirit' stands for the new life freed from sin and under the leading of the Spirit, and Paul would no doubt have believed that the Spirit leads in new directions. Tertullian takes 'the newness' in that sense, but specifically a new ethical demand banning a second marriage.

---

[58] Bender, *Lehre über den heiligen Geist*, p. 115; somewhat similarly, H. Karpp, *Schrift und Geist bei Tertullian* (Gütersloh: C. Bertelsmann, 1955), pp. 58-67 (esp. 63-64) and 70. Osborn, *Tertullian*, p. 243, wrote that for Tertullian the Paraclete brings no strange novelties but testifies to Christ; he is a restitutor rather than an institutor.

[59] Tertullian can refer to the illumination of Christians without expressly mentioning the Spirit: e.g., *Pud.* 7.11; *Apol.* 39.5

[60] Karpp, *Schrift und Geist*, p. 63, refers to this as the only time when a word of scripture is deprived of its authority by the Spirit.

(e) He counsels a willingness for martyrdom (*de anima* 55.5; *de fuga in persecutione* 9.4).[61] And so Tertullian brands those Christians who criticized a soldier for refusing to wear a laurel as having rejected the prophecies of the Holy Spirit and as purposing to refuse martyrdom (*de Corona* 1.4).

(f) He refuses a second repentance to heinous sinners (*de pudicitia* 1.2-21). The prophecy of Montanus is reported to the effect that while the church can forgive sins, he would not do so lest others also sin (21.7). Tertullian defends the consistency of the Spirit. Thus, while exegeting Revelation 2.18-22 concerning the repentance offered to 'Jezebel', Tertullian asserts that 'Jezebel' was never a true Christian but a heretic—a Nicolaitan—on a par with the heathen, and so this was why an opportunity of repentance was offered to her (*de pud.* 19).

(g) He teaches the resurrection of the flesh. Tertullian cites Prisca the prophetess as the mouthpiece of the Paraclete to brand those who denied the resurrection of the flesh as erroneous. 'They are carnal and yet they hate the flesh' (*de resurrectione mortuarum* 11.2).

Of our list of seven items, there is an almost equal division between doctrinal beliefs (the economy of the Trinity; the nature of the soul; its pre-resurrection punishment; the resurrection of the flesh) and ethical issues (no second marriage; no second repentance; willingness for martyrdom). This is in harmony with what Tertullian said in *de virg.vel.* 1.2: the Paraclete brought no alteration to the Rule of Faith (he confirms and clarifies already known truths), but he might alter aspects of customs, conduct and lifestyle.[62]

Tertullian speaks of the New Prophecy pouring in from the Paraclete and dispelling former ambiguities in the scriptures. God, by pouring the Spirit forth, 'has cleared from all obscurity and equivocation the ancient scriptures by the clear light of their words and meanings' (*de resurr.mort.* 63.9). This means that he has removed any support that heresies might have obtained from the ambiguities of scripture: 'It was fit and proper, therefore, that the Holy Spirit should no longer withhold the effusions of his gracious light upon these inspired writings... He has accordingly now dispersed all the perplexities of the past, and their [the heretics'] self-chosen allegories and parables, by the open and perspicuous explanation of the entire mystery through the New Prophecy which descends in copious streams from the Paraclete' (*de resurr.mort.* 63.9).[63]

Tertullian claimed that he was a disciple of the Paraclete, not men (*ad Prax.* 13.5; cf.1.7; 2.1). Having received the Paraclete, he declared that he himself was a better man (*de Pud.* 1.11). In the end, the test was whether people recognized the truth of

---

[61] See Weinrich, *Spirit and Martyrdom*, pp. 253-55, 263, for a helpful survey of how important martyrdom was to Tertullian.

[62] The importance of this passage is stressed by V. Morel, 'Le Développement de la "Disciplina" sous l'action du saint-Esprit chez Tertullien', *RHE* 35 (1939), pp. 243-65; cf., too, Karpp, *Schrift und Geist*, pp. 52-57.

[63] Karpp, *Schrift und Geist*, p. 46, commented that the New Prophecy did not devalue scripture but perfected its use.

the New Prophecy. If they did, then they were led by the Spirit; if not, then such people were unspiritual.

SUMMARY

The teaching ministry of the Spirit, his ongoing ministry of leading to all the truth, his continuous unfolding of the will of God as he takes the things of Christ and applies them to the church, that is to say, above all, his exposition through the scriptures—all this was taken with utmost seriousness and conviction by Tertullian. Thus, there is for Tertullian a close link between the scriptures and the Spirit.[64] The Spirit inspired them in the past, as when Tertullian asserts that Paul's remarks in 1 Corinthians 7.40 are a statement of the Holy Spirit (*ad Uxorem II* 2.4): this admonition to continence and only one marriage has 'divinity for its patron' (*de exhort.cast.* 4.5). And the Spirit has a present role in explaining them: of his own exposition of 1 Corinthians 7.12-14 Tertullian says that he will seek to explain the passage if the Spirit gives ability to him (*ad Uxorem II* 2.8).[65] Indeed, sometimes the Spirit may revoke what he had earlier allowed (e.g. the permission to remarry in 1 Cor. 7), while the command to flee (Mt. 10.23) caused Tertullian considerable problems when in his later writings he forbade all flight in the face of persecution or its threat. The Spirit exercises his office as guardian of the faith through the scriptures and through them he has taken measures against heretics.[66] There is a combination of a past and present role regarding the scriptures, but his inspiration of the scriptures in the past must not obscure his present task of illuminating them.

C. Divine Power

We turn now to consider the vital field of Christian ethics and the Spirit and how Tertullian envisaged the relationship between them. His stern moral demands are well known. Did he dwell on the empowering of the Spirit?

In a fairly early work, *de idolatria*,[67] Tertullian said that as slaves of Christ freed from captivity to the world, Christians have an obligation to act according to Christ's pattern (18.5). Is 'obligation' the note which Tertullian strikes or does he mention the Spirit's help?

---

[64] Cf. *Apologeticum* 20.4: 'The same Spirit inspires them [the prophets and the books of scripture]'.

[65] Quasten, *Patrology II*, p. 302, dates Tertullian's two treatises to his wife to between 200 and 206, whereas Barnes, *Tertullian*, p. 55, conjectures that they were written between 198 and 203, and certainly before 206.

[66] See *de idol.* 15.6; *de praes.haer.* 6.6; *de carne Christi* 23.6; *de resurr.mort.* 24.8; *adv. Marc.* 5.7.1.

[67] It sought to dissuade Christians from anything connected with idolatry including festivities, state office, military service, etc. Quasten, *Patrology II*, p. 310, dates it to the same time as *de corona*, i.e., 211, whereas Barnes, *Tertullian*, pp. 55, 328, dates it to after the *Apologeticum*, i.e., after 196.

(a) In another of Tertullian's early works, *de spectaculis*,[68] we meet an idea not dissimilar to that enunciated by Hermas, namely that the Spirit is tender and sensitive.[69] 'God has enjoined us to deal calmly, gently, quietly and peacefully with the Holy Spirit, because these things alone are in keeping with the goodness of his nature, with his tenderness and sensitiveness, not to vex him with rage or ill-nature or anger or grief' (15.2). So, Tertullian can ask, 'What concord can the Holy Spirit have with the Shows and all their bloodthirstiness?' (15.3). He knows of instances where Christians have attended the Shows and Games and fallen away from Christ (26.1-4).

He had previously said in *de cultu feminarum II* that modesty was necessary lest God should be offended and forsake the polluted abode. We are a temple of the Holy Spirit, and modesty is the sacristan and priestess of that temple (1.1). Accordingly, 'we ought to wish our sphere of pleasing to lie in the graces (*bonis*) of the Spirit, not in the flesh' (3.2).[70] The Christian should seek to please God by behaviour laid down, not by the flesh and its desires, but by the Spirit, for this will be in accordance with God's will. Later, he says that God has put certain things in the world 'in order that there should now be the means of putting to the proof the discipline of His servants' and so we should act usefully and cautiously (10.5). The emphasis is on us, not on God, on how we behave rather than on a divine-human cooperative act.

We meet the idea of shocking the Spirit in *de patientia*.[71] When Christians give precedence to things earthly over things heavenly, when they are impatient over and grieve because of the loss of something, they greatly shock the Spirit for the sake of a worldly matter (7.7). On the other hand, Tertullian believes that patience is a cardinal virtue of the Christian life. Love is trained by it (12.8). Faith makes patience its pre-eminent co-helper for amplifying and fulfilling the law (6.3). When the Spirit descends, patience accompanies him. If we do not admit patience with the Spirit, then the Spirit will not always stay with us (15.7). Here again is the idea of a sensitive Spirit who will desert the uncongenial abode.

---

[68] This work is a bitter condemnation of the public Shows and Games. It is dated by Quasten, *Patrology II*, p. 293, to 197; Barnes, *Tertullian*, pp. 55, 328, to 196.

[69] Not touched upon by A. Adam, 'Die Lehre vom dem hl. Geiste bei Hermas und Tertullian', *ThQ* 58 (1906), pp. 36-61, who is mainly concerned with the relation of Christ and the Spirit. See Appendix 4, a revised version of my contribution 'The "Delicacy" of the Spirit in the Shepherd of Hermas and in Tertullian', in E.A. Livingstone (ed.), *Studia Patristica* 21 (Leuven: Peeters, 1993), pp. 154-57.

[70] Following the reading *in spiritus bonis* advocated by N. Rigaltius, *QSF Tertulliani Opera* (Paris, 1634), followed by Koehler (1854), the *Ante-Nicene Christian Library* translation (1882), Marra (1930), and W. Kok (1934), against A. Kroymann, *de cultu feminarum, Tertulliani Opera I* (Corpus Christianorum Latina Series; Brepols: Turnholt, 1954), who prefers *in spiritu nobis*.

[71] One of the works which is very difficult to date. Barnes, *Tertullian*, p. 55, conjectures between 198 and 203, but acknowledges that because additionally it reveals no Montanist leanings, it should appear under the simple rubric 'before 206'.

The same idea occurs in the *de exhortatis castatis*. Here Tertullian speaks of the spiritual benefit of sexual abstinence even in a first marriage ('By parsimony of the flesh, you will gain the Spirit' 10.1) and implies the dulling effect of involvement in sexuality. 'If this dulling [i.e. of the spiritual faculties], even when the carnal nature is allowed room for exercise in a first marriage, averts the Holy Spirit, how much more when it is brought into play in a second marriage?' (11.1).

Here then in these remarks we encounter the idea that the Spirit's influence is lessened and thwarted by people's behaviour. The Spirit seems to be weaker than the opposing powers.[72]

(b) Alongside of this strand is Tertullian's conviction that the Spirit is an aid and help to the Christian. The conclusion to *de idolatria* begins thus: 'Amid these reefs and inlets, amid these shallows and straits of idolatry, faith navigates, her sails filled by the Spirit of God; safe if cautious, secure if intently watchful' (24.1). A little later he says that the reason why at the apostolic council the Holy Spirit relaxed the bond and yoke of legal observances for us was that 'we might be free to devote ourselves to the shunning of idolatry. This shall be our law...This law must be set before such as approach to the Faith...' (24.3). The law of shunning idolatry is an irreducible minimum. To assist us there is the Holy Spirit like the wind blowing the sails of a boat.

Tertullian says in *de carne Christi*,[73] when exegeting 1 Corinthians 15.47, that we who are in the flesh are being made celestial by the Spirit (8.6). He maintains that this verse is not concerned with any difference of material (*ad materiae differentiam spectat*): rather, it contrasts the earthly substance of Adam's flesh and the heavenly substance of Christ's spirit (*caelestem de spiritu substantiam...Christi*). The passage refers the heavenly man '*ad spiritum*, i.e. that which is the *substantia propria* of the Word and which is the constitutive material of divinity'.[74] Just as Christ was heavenly in an earthly flesh, so also they who are incorporated into him (8.7). His followers are becoming heavenly even in this earthly flesh. The agent of

---

[72] We might compare Tertullian's comments in *de Oratione* where he says that a defiled spirit can receive no recognition from the Holy Spirit. Prayer should be free from anger (he refers to Mt. 5.22-23) and all perturbation of mind, and one's own spirit should be in accord with the Holy Spirit (ch. 10). 'What reason is there in going to prayer with hands indeed washed but the spirit foul?' (13.1). On the other side, Tertullian can say that we offer a sacrifice of prayer in the Spirit (28.3) and that Christian prayer multiplies grace in power (29.1). See also 20.5 for the power of the prayer of the newly baptised (i.e., now possessing the Spirit). Quasten, *Patrology II*, p. 296, dates *de Oratione* to ca. 198-200. E. Evans, *Tertullian's Treatise on the Prayer* (London: SPCK, 1953), places it amongst the earliest of Tertullian's writings. Barnes, *Tertullian*, p. 55, assigns it to between 198 and 203.

[73] Quasten, *Patrology II*, p. 283, dates to 210-12; E. Evans, *Tertullian's Treatise on the Incarnation* (London: SPCK, 1956), p. vii, says, 'The date 206 will not be far out, though it may be somewhat too early'; Barnes, *Tertullian*, p. 326, accepts the view of Braun, *Deus Christianorum*, pp. 267-68, that it was written between 200 and 203, but not published till Tertullian had written *de Resurr.Mort.* some five to eight years later.

[74] Cf. Evans, *Incarnation*, p. 123: 'i.e. Christ's divine substance'.

this is the Spirit, *'spiritu scilicet'*. What sense does *'spiritu'* have here? It seems possible that here the meaning is hovering between substance and the activity of the Spirit, i.e., a combination of Stoic materialism and biblical realism.[75]

In a statement occurring in the reproduction of the Rule of Faith, Tertullian states that it is the power of the Holy Spirit who leads such as believe (*de praesc. haer.* 13.5). He it is 'who was to sanctify man' in the divine person (*ad Prax.* 12.3). The power of God's grace is more potent than nature (*de anima* 21.6). Exegeting John 6.63 in *de resurr. mort.*, Tertullian asserts that the Spirit establishes salvation and is profitable to the flesh and is the giver of life to what is put to death (37.6). The inner man (cf. Eph. 3.16-17) needs renewing by the supply of the Spirit (40.7). In *de patientia* Tertullian referred to the mind as the ruling principle in a person and asserted that it easily communicates the gifts (*invecta*) of the Spirit to its habitation, the body (13.1).

When discussing Jesus' remark about the hardness of men's hearts as the cause of the Mosaic divorce law, Tertullian asserts that 'Hardness of heart prevailed until the coming of Christ; it should be enough that infirmity of the flesh prevailed until the coming of the Paraclete. The new law abrogated divorce, which was a definite abuse that had to be ended; the New Prophecy outlaws second marriage, which is just as truly the dissolution of a prior marriage' (*de monogamia* 14.4). At first sight, it seems as if Tertullian is talking about the Spirit's overcoming the weakness of the flesh. Yet a careful reading of the passage suggests that Tertullian is in fact thinking of correct teaching. Paul had allowed a second marriage because of the infirmity of the flesh (14.2). Now the Paraclete had revoked this indulgence which Paul permitted (14.3). The time is short, and honour demands that marriage should not be repeated (14.4), though Tertullian concedes that church people still appeal to the Pauline permission, evading the force of his dearest convictions and frustrating his intentions (14.5).

Then Tertullian goes on to maintain that if in the days of Jesus' earthly ministry there were things that his disciples could not bear (Jn. 16.12), however, 'there is no one who cannot bear them now, for he is at hand who gives us the ability to do so' (14.6). Jesus himself said that the spirit was willing, though the flesh was weak.[76] He said this that 'the Spirit might overcome the flesh and that weakness might give way to strength' (14.6). Tertullian applies the Deuteronomic assertion—that good and evil had been placed before the people (30.15)—to his readers. 'In proposing both good and evil to your choice He shows that you are able to choose good if you

---

[75] Evans, *Incarnation*, p. 35, translates 'by spirit of course', while the *ANL* prints 'Spirit', and Bender, *Lehre*, p. 132, alludes to this passage while discussing the new birth mediated by the Spirit and water.

[76] See Weinrich, *Spirit and Martyrdom*, pp. 258-59, for the statistics concerning Tertullian's use of Mk. 14.38/Mt. 26.41. He exegetes the text on five occasions, three in his non-Montanist writings where he understands *spiritus* to mean the human spirit (*ad Mart.* 4.1; *de Pat.* 13.7; *ad Uxorem* 1.4), and two in writings from his Montanist period, in both of which he takes *spiritus* to be the divine Spirit (in addition to *de Monogamia* 14.6, the other occurrence is *de Fuga* 8.1-2).

wish' (14.7). Tertullian implies that if they are unable to choose the good, it is because they do not wish to do this, and then they must depart from Christ whose will they do not obey. Teaching is uppermost, not help to do it. The issue is whether people can bear the extra teaching, not whether the Spirit assists them to perform it.

De Pudicitia, one of Tertullian's most violent Montanist treatises, acknowledges that Tertullian is renouncing a previously held opinion (referring to the position that the sin of adultery might be forgiven by the church 1.10). He says that he is not ashamed that he has abandoned an error. 'Rather I rejoice that I am quit of it, since I recognize that I am now a better man and one of greater purity. Nobody blushes when he makes progress' (1.11-12). What he goes on to say shows that he is thinking of the knowledge of the truth. 'In Christ also knowledge has its ages and through these even the apostle [Paul] passed' (1.12—a reference to 1 Cor. 13.11). Tertullian wished that certain in the catholic church would change their views instead of promising 'pardon to adulterers and fornicators in opposition to fundamental Christian discipline' (1.14).

Tertullian exclaims 'What excellent remedies the Holy Spirit has provided to prevent the recurrence of something which he is unwilling to allow for a second time' (16.18). These remedies turn out to be perseverance in widowhood and reconciliation of partners (16.17).

The apostolic decree is quoted in ch. 12 (and interpreted in an ethical sense) with the addition 'with the assistance of the Holy Spirit' (12.4), a phrase which occurs neither in the Greek nor Latin MS tradition of Acts. Does Tertullian mean assistance in the sense of power to abstain from the offences prohibited, or in the sense that the Holy Spirit shows us clearly what are now God's demands? I suspect the latter, since Tertullian goes on to say 'How do the apostles wish to regard those crimes which they single out from the Old Law for special attention and which are the only ones they insist must necessarily be avoided?... They have loosed us from a multitude of obligations so that we may be forced to discharge those whose neglect is more dangerous' (12.6, 8), and then he refers to an engagement which the Holy Spirit has contracted with us. 'The Holy Spirit will not accept what he has remitted [the ceremonial observances of the old Law] nor will he remit what he has retained [the obligation to avoid the three capital sins]' (12.9). We are at the level of revelation of what mode of behaviour is required of Christians.

In ch. 17, Tertullian quotes Romans 8.2, 3-5, but follows this up by saying 'It is to us that he is directing the integrity and plenitude of the rules of discipline' (*sed in nos dirigit integritatem et plenitudinem disciplinarum* 17.11). The law of the Spirit replaces the old Law.

When in ch. 21 he speaks of the Spirit's power as a thing apart,[77] Tertullian is thinking of the authority to forgive sins especially, something which is (he accepts)

---

[77] Assuming the reading '*seorsum, quod potestas (spiritus)*'. The edition of *de pudicitia* in *Tertulliani Opera*, Corpus Christianorum Latina Series vol. 2, p. 1326, reads '*Sed rursum quid potestas?*' = 'But again what power? (The Spirit)'. The sense would not be radically different if the latter reading were accepted.

inherent in the church; but the Paraclete has spoken through one of the new prophets: 'The church can forgive sin, but I will not do it lest others also sin' (21.7).[78]

Our summary of the theme of this sub-section must be that Tertullian does speak of the power of the Spirit, yet it does not occupy a prominent place in what he has written. The picture of the sails of a boat filled by the wind is a graphic and arresting one. It cannot be said, however, that in his writings as we have them Tertullian has much exploited that aspect of the Spirit. There is little of comfort or encouragement or pastoral help in what he says. There is plenty of demand; little of grace or assistance.

Thus, we could say that in (a) above Tertullian is more akin to Hermas than Paul, since both speak of the delicacy or sensitivity of the Spirit, whereas in (b) there is some, though not a great deal of, kinship with Paul, insofar as both speak of the help of the Spirit, but the apostle Paul emphasises this far more than does Tertullian.

(c) We need also to consider a view which Tertullian expressed in *ad Uxorem I*. He said to his wife that some things are bestowed by the Lord through his bounty, while we have others by our own efforts. Those which the Lord has bestowed are governed by his generosity; those which are achieved by us are won at the cost of personal endeavour (8.3). In context, the persistence in widowhood and the avoidance of a second marriage are due to our own efforts. So, he exhorted his wife to cultivate the virtue of self-restraint, industry and temperance (8.3). He maintained that the spirit (which is from heaven) is stronger than the flesh and we have no excuse when we yield to the weaker force. Servants of God ought to scorn the desire of the flesh and the world, since we renounce both lust and ambition (4.1-2), and he appealed to his wife to train herself to imitate the example of continence furnished by Christian widows of the past (4.3-5). To root out desire has its compensation in the blessings of heaven which last forever (4.5).

In Book II he would describe continence as something heroic (1.2), whereas it is the weakness of faith which leads to passion for worldly pleasure, especially among the wealthy (8.2-3)

In *de resurr. mort.*, Tertullian describes himself, who once committed adulteries, as striving towards continence now, for it is this flesh of ours which will receive either God's judgment of fire or His salvation (59.3). As Christ made an alliance of flesh and Spirit in his incarnate life (63.1), so in believers the flesh (the bride) is wedded to the Spirit (the groom) through Christ's redemptive act (63.3), and that union will be brought to pass at the resurrection.

Certainly in these passages, Tertullian gives the impression of Christianity as self effort. This emphasis, brought out in the previous paragraphs, leads us on to

---

[78] The 'I' of the *faciam* may refer to the new prophet who uttered the words, but ultimately the reference is back to the Paraclete. See von Campenhausen, *Ecclesiastical Authority*, pp. 213-37, and also Robeck, *Prophecy*, pp. 117-19, for fuller discussions.

consider how Tertullian regards Christianity as *disciplina*.[79] When, for example, he argues for a physical resurrection, he maintains that salvation is promised to the flesh by Paul, 'for it would on no account have been fitting to demand of it any discipline of its own in holiness and righteousness unless the prize of discipline had pertained to it also' (*de resurrect. mort.* 47.9). Tertullian applies the earthly and heavenly of 1 Corinthians 15.48 to 'such at first in discipline and afterwards in the dignity which has been the aim of discipline' (49.4). Christians must seek to wear the image of Christ here and now 'in this flesh and in this time of discipline' (49.6). The apostle Paul's words 'Let us wear...' point in the direction of discipline (49.8).

Men and women have free choice. God places some actions to our credit and recompenses with an eternal reward. The choice we make shows how we are disposed towards God. So, Tertullian says, if we practise continence, we will amass a great store of sanctity. 'Deny the flesh and you will possess the Spirit.' 'Let us renounce the things of the flesh so that we may in due season bring forth the fruits of the Spirit' (*de exhort. cast.* 10.1). After mentioning pagan examples of chastity he says 'A Christian, then, is all the more guilty if he refuses to embrace a chastity which effects salvation' (13.2).

To visit the Shows and Games is incompatible with *disciplina*,[80] because of the rivalry, madness, bile, anger, pain, etc (*de spect.* 15.3-4). So, it is important not only to abstain from doing certain things but also to keep clear from those who do them (15.8). Tertullian extends the application of Psalm 1.1 to Christian abstinence from the Shows and Games and says that 'divine scripture may always be broadly applied, wherever, agreeably with the sense of the actual matter in hand, discipline is fortified' (3.4).[81]

In those works most strongly influenced by his Montanist views, the question of discipline figures quite prominently. In *de velandis virginibus* Tertullian enunciated the role of the Paraclete as the director of discipline. Whereas the Rule of Faith remains unchanging, points of discipline may be changed (1.4). Appeal is made to John 16.12-13 (1.5). Discipline has advanced from a rudimentary stage until now, under the Paraclete, it is settling into maturity (1.7). In ch. 10 Tertullian draws a distinction between maintaining virginity and the continence practised by widows. 'Constancy of virginity is maintained by grace; of continence, by virtue. For great is the struggle to overcome concupiscence when you have become accustomed to such

---

[79] Cf. P. Labriolle, *History and Literature of Christianity from Tertullian to Boethius* (London: Kegan Paul, Trench, Trubner, 1924), pp. 78-79, who said that to Tertullian Christianity was 'above all else, a discipline, that is a rule of life, and a check upon the will...a closely circumscribed network of regulations...He likes to give rules for everything... Rigidly defined explanations must therefore adapt the injunctions of the law to everyday realities.' See also V. Morel, 'Disciplina: le mot et l'idée représentée par lui dans les oeuvres de Tertullien', *RHE* 40 (1944-45), pp. 5-45, for a detailed analysis of Tertullian's usage.

[80] Morel, *Disciplina*, p. 33, interprets *disciplina* here as the moral laws.

[81] Morel, *Discioplina*, p. 30, interprets *disciplina* here as divine laws.

concupiscence, whereas you will easily subdue a concupiscence the enjoyment of which you have never known' (10.3-4).

The idea of the introduction of a severer discipline by the Paraclete comes out also in *de monogamia*. When Paul claimed to have the Spirit of God in 1 Corinthians 7.40, it was 'his intention to retract, on the authority of the Holy Spirit, any concession which may have been forced from him by necessity' (3.6). Paul was really abrogating the permission given to marry. Therefore, it is not impossible that after apostolic times the same Holy Spirit should come again in order to introduce a discipline according to all truth (3.8). What the Paraclete reveals is no novelty (3.9). What he deferred, he now exacts (3.9). The Paraclete could have forbidden marriage altogether, but has only in fact insisted on monogamy (3.10).

Likewise in *de ieiuniis*,[82] Tertullian says that the Holy Spirit has issued commands for fasting so that Christians might be disciplined (13.5). He contrasts the truly spiritual Christians with the psychics: 'To you your belly is god, and your lungs a temple, and your paunch a sacrificial altar, and your cook the priest, and your fragrant smell the Holy Spirit, and your condiments spiritual gifts, and your belching prophecy' (16.8).

In his stress on fasting, Tertullian maintains that it is 'the instrument of the iniquitous spirit's egress as of the Holy Spirit's ingress' (8.3), and he interprets the pre-baptismal gift of the Spirit to Cornelius in Acts 10 as a sign that his fasting had been heard (8.4).

Strictures on 'psychic' Christians are found in *de pudicitia*: they bring disgrace on the Paraclete by their irregular discipline (1.20). In ch. 11.3 Tertullian asserts that Christian discipline begins after redemption (the passion of the Lord): 'No one was perfect before the economy of faith was revealed; no one was a Christian before Christ was taken up into heaven; no one was holy before the Holy Spirit came from heaven to establish this discipline'. The scriptures—apostolic authorship is assumed— 'are the chief determinants of that discipline which like a priest guards the perfect sanctity of the temple of God and roots out from the church, everywhere, every sacrilegious act committed against chastity—with never a word about its restoration' (Heb. 6.4-8 is cited shortly afterwards) (20.1).[83]

While Morel has convincingly shown that *disciplina* in Tertullian is wider than moral or disciplinary matters, nevertheless, the majority of instances do fall under his category of 'rules and laws and their observance' (in fact, about one third).[84]

Finally, in this section, we turn to consider what Tertullian had to say on the theme of martyrdom and the Spirit. In *ad martyres*,[85] which was addressed to

---

[82] This work attacked alleged laxity in fasting by catholics and upheld Montanist practices. Quasten, *Patrology II*, p. 312, offers no date apart from its being within Tertullian's Montanist period, while Barnes, *Tertullian*, p. 55, puts it at 210-11.

[83] Here *disciplina* shades over into the specific point about non-forgiveness for flagrant sinners and the observance of this, as also at *de pud.* 6; cf. Morel, *Disciplina*, pp. 25, 39.

[84] Morel, *Disciplina*, pp. 27-45.

imprisoned Christians awaiting trial and facing the prospect of martyrdom, Tertullian tells them that the Holy Spirit has entered prison with them. Indeed, they would not be there if he had not been with them (1.3). Presumably he means that it is the Holy Spirit who made them Christians and has led them to confess Christ openly (cf. Mk. 13.10; Lk. 21.14-15), with the result that they are now in prison, awaiting execution. For Tertullian, martyrdom is very much willed by God.[86]

Tertullian asks the martyrs, therefore, not to grieve the Spirit and to do all they can to retain him so that he may lead them from prison to their Lord, in martyrdom (1.3). While 'retain' points to the efforts of believers, the expression 'lead' must carry overtones of help and support in order to endure the ordeal of martyrdom.

They are about to pass through a noble struggle. The living God is their superintendent, and the Holy Spirit (with whom Christ has anointed them) is their trainer. Christ has led them to prison and intends the period of imprisonment as part of their training. The prize is an eternal crown, heavenly citizenship and everlasting glory (3.3-4). They must remember, therefore, that the flesh is weak and make sure that the flesh obeys the Spirit and gains strength from the Spirit (4.1).

Of OT prophets who were persecuted, Tertullian says, 'They who were accustomed to be led by the Spirit of God used to be guided by himself to martyrdoms' (*Scorpiace* 6.4), and the same is true of Christians: 'neither can we suffer on behalf of God except there be in us the Spirit of God, who also speaks concerning us the things which belong to our confessorship' (*ad Prax.* 29.7). Two ideas seem to be intermingled here: firstly, the idea of the Spirit's indwelling Christians—he imparts strength and patience to endure amidst suffering; and, secondly, the idea of the Spirit's inspiring the witness of Christians who are on trial (confessorship).[87]

Tertullian argues that the persecution saying of Matthew 5.10-12 was meant for all Christians and not just the apostles (*Scorpiace* 9.2). Even if initially applicable to the latter, this rule has come down to us as disciples by inheritance and as bushes from the apostolic seed. We are an offshoot of the name (of Christ) and have the Holy Spirit as part of the vine branches (*tradux*)[88] (3.2). The implication of this passage is that the Holy Spirit enables the disciple to endure martyrdom.

---

[85] Quasten, *Patrology II*, p. 292, dates to 202, while Barnes, *Tertullian*, pp. 55, 328, dates to after 196.

[86] Weinrich, *Spirit and Martyrdom*, pp. 253-54, stresses that for Tertullian martyrdom was 'the very form and figure of the Christian life', being a duty and a necessity, for God wills persecution by which He sifts His people.

[87] This double strand must be borne in mind when evaluating the assertion of von Campenhausen, *Idee des Martyriologie,* pp. 90-92, that there was a shift away from the earlier stress on the Spirit as inspiring witness to and confession of Christ before a hostile world, to that of Christ within the martyr prompting martyrdom.

[88] '*Tradux*' is a branch of the vine, a vine-layer, which has been trained for propagation: see C.T. Lewis and C. Short, *A Latin Dictionary* (Oxford: Clarendon, 1894), p. 1885.

This idea becomes explicit in *de fuga in persecutione*. Here Tertullian maintains that the Spirit incites us to martyrdom, not to flight (9.4). If we were to ask advice of the Spirit, he would approve of what he has already uttered (9.4): that perfect love casts out fear and we ought to lay down our lives for the brothers (9.3, quoting 1 Jn. 3.16; 4.18). Indeed, the Spirit brands the runaways (11.2)—in context Tertullian is thinking very much of church leaders: 'When persons in authority themselves—I mean the very deacons and presbyters and bishops—take to flight, how will the layman be able to see with what view it was said, Flee from city to city? Thus too, with the leaders turning their backs, who of the common rank will hope to persuade men to stand firm in the battle?' (11.1).

Tertullian then quotes John 10.12 and alludes to the prophetic threats against the false shepherds who abandon their flock as prey to the beasts (11.2). For Tertullian, it is not 'the duty of those who have been set over the church to flee in the time of persecution' (11.3).

Later, Tertullian refers to the help of the Paraclete in bearing persecution: he 'guides into all truth and animates to all endurance. And they who have received him will neither stoop to flee from persecution nor to buy it off, for they have the Lord himself, One who will stand by us to aid us in suffering as well as to be our mouth when we are put to the question' (14.3). The Paraclete and the risen Lord are an aid to endurance, to bear suffering and an inspiration to speak a word of Christian testimony when under cross-examination. In moving to speak of the risen Lord Tertullian seems to have in mind Luke 21.14-15, which is probably a Lucan reshaping of Mark 13.10/Luke 12.11-12, possibly also a passage like 2 Timothy 4.18.

Tertullian points out to any Christians who may be fearful lest they should under persecution deny their faith, that God has the power to shield us in danger. While countering the idea that he who flees lives to fight another day, Tertullian points out that Christ is in us; we have been clothed with Christ since baptism, and we should rely on the Lord in whose hand we are (10.2-3). Here, then, believers are assured of Christ's presence within them, and that is sufficient guarantee of their being able to stand firm in the faith, against persecution. Christ language and not Spirit language is used, but the overall sense is the same, that of divine empowering to stiffen our resolve and our endurance.

It must be admitted that Tertullian is on the whole more interested in the 'ought', the moral rightness, of enduring persecution. If he can prove that we ought to do it, that is sufficient.[89] Is it indicative that only in the last sentences of *de fuga in*

---

[89] Weinrich, *Spirit and Martyrdom*, describes the principal thrust of Tertullian's approach to martyrdom as 'ethical' (pp. 260-61); it is an exhibition of the martyr's strength and virtue of mind and spirit (p. 262), 'an heroic deed, similar to that of pagan heroes, springing out of the inner recesses of human courage, human virtue and human loyalty to a valued cause' (p. 265). 'The martyr is by and large alone in his martyrdom, required to exercise his virtue and courage lest he prove himself unworthy and become subject to God's condemnation' (p. 266).

persecutione does the stern moralist mention the help that is given to Christians in meeting the rigorous demands imposed on them?

Summary

Arguably, Tertullian was a stern, puritanical rigorist throughout his life. In *de spectaculis*, his opposition to worldly Shows like gladiatorial contests, athletic games and the theatre is plain and trenchant. They are not in harmony with the religion of Christ (15), and Christians expose themselves to the attacks of evil spirits by frequenting them (26): 'How monstrous it is to go from God's church to the devil's...to raise your hands to God and then to weary them in applause of an actor' (25). A few months later, in *apologeticum*, he admitted that 'it is our desire to suffer. We conquer in dying; we go forth victorious at the very time we are subdued... But we go zealously on, good presidents; you will stand higher with the people if you sacrifice the Christians at their wish. Kill us, torture us, condemn us, grind us to dust; our injustice is the proof that we are innocent... The oftener we are mown down by you, the more in number we grow; the blood of Christians is seed' (50.1, 3, 12-13).

To this extent, Montanism only reinforced his existing Puritanism. Tertullian represents a certain religious type. One is inclined to say that psychological factors enter in here rather than theological ones. Tertullian bolstered his position with theological and other arguments. But temperamentally he was a rigorist from the start.[90]

3. Conclusion

The evidence available from North Africa from around the end of the second century and the beginning of the third certainly attests the liveliness of experience of many within the churches there. The *Passion of Perpetua and Felicitas* shows the conviction that the Spirit is still active in the churches of Christ, especially as the inspirer of prayer, prophecy and revelation, vision and dream, and as the imparter of strength in martyrdom. This is also confirmed by Tertullian's description of the visions of a Christian lady, recorded in *de Anima*. The tone of spiritual exaltation discernible in *The Passion* remind us of the spiritual exuberance of the *Odes of Solomon* and the accounts of the martyrdoms narrated in the letter from the Lyons and Vienne congregation.

The comments of the final editor of the *Passion* show, however, that within the congregations known to him there were many who did not look for an activity of the Spirit in the present, and seem to have confined that activity to the past.

---

[90] R.P.C. Hanson, 'Notes on Tertullian's Interpretation of Scripture', *JTS* 12 (1961), p. 279, asserted, 'Having virtually removed the burden of a legalistic Old Testament religion, he introduced a legalistic New Testament one'; Frend, *Martyrdom and Persecution*, pp. 373-74, said that Tertullian developed 'a sort of New Testament *halaka*...a baptized Judaism'.

Tertullian originally believed that all Christians received the Spirit through faith and baptism, but in the end denied the Spirit to catholic Christians, and he could be extremely biting in his sarcasm about their spiritual degeneracy and their sensuality as he deemed it. In his 'them/us' approach, he is rather like the author of 1 John (2.19) in Syria, Jude (19-20) in Asia Minor, also both the Montanists and catholics in Asia Minor in their mutual hostility and the Valentinian gnostics (who set themselves in a category above church Christians). There is an element of judgmentalism and spiritual elitism here. 'Orthodox' and 'heretic' alike may thus display it. The need to carry on a polemic against heretics on the one hand or to bolster one's claims against an 'establishment' regarded as less illuminated and perceptive on the other hand, may well inevitably produce these hardened attitudes.

Tertullian's main emphasis is on the work of the Spirit in 'legislating' for moral discipline within the church. The Spirit's work of helping to interpret the scripture seems in the end to be geared virtually exclusively in Tertullian's works to matters of discipline. Although references to the help of the Spirit in ethical conduct and martyrdom are not lacking in Tertullian, the predominant emphasis is on the Spirit's tightening up on discipline and ethical directives. Tertullian seems almost a charismatic legalist. Duty stands out, rather than a grateful response to God in the power of the Spirit. He lacks the balanced wholeness of Irenaeus' approach and the reiterated stress found in Irenaeus on the Spirit's strength to empower the new lifestyle.

This particular emphasis in respect of the Spirit in Tertullian seems strange in view of his passionate conviction that the Montanist leaders were a fulfilment of the Johannine Paraclete sayings, although the combination of a stress on the Spirit and legalism would not be peculiar to him in the history of the Christian church. Thus, Tertullian confirms the impression we gained from our study of the Asia Minor Montanists.

By his stress on the Paraclete and his claim that the Johannine promise had been fulfilled, Tertullian invites comparison with the fourth evangelist. It is precisely at the point of John's emphasis on the power of the indwelling Christ (chs 15 and 17) that we have found Tertullian lacking. On the other hand, in one sense Tertullian is an heir of John in the way he increasingly draws the lines of demarcation tighter and tighter and excludes those deemed to be spiritually 'unfruitful branches', so that one has the feeling that Tertullian and the author of 1John are not far apart in many respects (as hinted at above).

Tertullian came to be very critical of Hermas, because the latter had preached the possibility of a second repentance for those already Christians, though, as we have previously seen, he actually seems to have shared with Hermas the idea of the Spirit's delicacy, a motif which, we suggested, was far from NT convictions about the Spirit. Tertullian was also bitterly disappointed with a bishop of Rome for not having endorsed Montanism, and he saw this as a sign of the spiritual decline and degeneracy of that church whose praise he had sung in previous works. The isolation of his last years reveals the ultimate outcome of that spiritual pride and elitism noted above.[91]

---

[91] On the issue of whether Tertullian actually seceded from the catholic church, see the article, already referred to in footnote 52, of D. Powell who argued that Tertullian and his followers formed a group within the church (an *ecclesiola in ecclesia*). Osborn, *Tertullian*, pp. 23, 177, 212, 251, also believes that, though Tertullian was dissatisfied with the church universal, he stayed within the community of the church at Carthage.

CHAPTER 8

Egypt

The early history of Christianity in Egypt still remains shrouded in mystery. Since Walter Bauer, it has been considered to have been of a nature later frowned on by the 'orthodox' catholic church. Bauer[1] believed, firstly, that at the beginning of the second century there were two Christian groups in Egypt, each centred on a distinctive gospel and both resting on syncretistic gnostic foundations: Jewish Christians of Alexandria using the Gospel of the Hebrews, native Christians using the Gospel of the Egyptians (the fragments of these which have survived, offer us no help for our theme). Secondly, he drew attention to the fact that well-known personalities originating from Egypt in the second century were gnostics: Basilides, Carpocrates, and Valentinus. Furthermore, at the end of the century, bishop Demetrius of Alexandria was apparently the only Egyptian bishop, a fact which suggested a limited church organisation.

More recently, this view has been challenged by C.H. Roberts:[2]

(i) An examination of the *nomina sacra* (sacred names) in biblical MSS suggests that Christianity developed its own system and was not dependant on Judaism. It is more likely that this system was taken with Christianity to Alexandria by Jewish Christians, whose theology of the Name has been stressed by several scholars, than that it originated in Alexandria.

(ii) Probably the Synoptic Gospels were in circulation, since the *Gospel of the Egyptians* appears to depend on them.

(iii) It would be odd if gnosticism flourished alone, provoked by and provoking no contrary movement.

(iv) The fragment of Irenaeus' *AH* found at Oxyrhynchus, and probably dating from the last part of the second century, shows the orthodox reaction against gnosticism and the close relationship between Alexandria and the church of the west.

(v) Probably, because in Alexandria Christianity was initially closely associated with Jews who were hated and resented, Christians found it a difficult task to

---

[1] W. Bauer, *Orthodoxy and Heresy in Earliest Christianity* (London: SCM, 1973), pp. 44-60.

[2] C.H. Roberts, *Manuscript, Society and Belief in Early Christian Egypt* (Oxford: Clarendon, 1979). This was favourably reviewed by T.C. Skeat in *JTS* 31 (1980), pp. 183-86); see also his earlier article 'The Christian Book and the Greek Papyri', *JTS* 1 (1949), pp. 115-68; also M. Hornshuh, *Studien zur Epistola Apostolorum* (Patrische Texte und Studien 5; Berlin: Akademie-Verlag, 1965), pp. 99-115.

promote mission and gain converts. Only after the Jewish revolt in AD 117 was the movement able to dissociate itself from Jews.

(vi) It was not so clear that Basilides and Valentinus were unorthodox in the early stages of their career, and in any case undue weight should not be attached to two teachers. The rest of Egyptian Christianity may not have shared their views.

(vii) Pantaenus may have been appointed to cleanse the catechetical school of gnostic influence.

(viii) Only one gnostic papyrus dating before the fourth century has been discovered.

There can be no doubt that Roberts has offered a credible alternative to the Bauer hypothesis. He does not deny that gnosticism found a fertile soil in Egypt, but he has shown that a Jewish Christian presence is likely in Alexandria and the provinces (given the close links between the two) from the first century, even if at first it may have been numerically small.[3]

Since the *Epistula Apostolorum* does not offer us material germane to our theme, we turn to a brief examination of Clement of Alexandria, although it is not easy to determine just how typical of Egyptian Christianity Clement was. He certainly presents a contrast to Tertullian in Carthage. Then, we shall look at the teaching of one of Valentinus' followers, Theodotus, extracts from whose writing have been preserved in a work by Clement seeking to rebut Theodotus.

1. Clement of Alexandria

We know very little about Clement. He came to Christian convictions after a long search. He greatly admired Pantaenus, who was head of the catechetical school at Alexandria, and studied under him. Clement eventually succeeded him ca. 190 and taught at Alexandria until he left during the persecution under Severus ca. 202. It is thought that he settled at Antioch and died ca. 214.

Clement[4] does not deal thematically with the Holy Spirit,[5] although references to the Spirit are scattered through his writings. He divides what all people possess into

---

[3] A broadly similar approach to Roberts is taken by C.W. Griggs, *Early Egyptian Christianity* (Coptic Studies 2; Leiden: Brill, 1990). Griggs thinks that Egyptian Christianity was founded on a more broadly based literary tradition and a less defined ecclesiastical tradition than was Christianity in the region from Syria to Rome (p. 34). To explain the silence about details of the establishment of Christianity in Egypt, he makes the suggestion that Demetrius may have been regarded as the 'second founder' of the church at Alexandria and that his predecessors were not considered Christian enough (p. 28).

[4] Clement's major works are *Protrepticus*, which sought to convert outsiders to the Christian revelation; *Paedagogus*, which aimed to provide catechumens and young Christians with instruction in Christian morality and etiquette as they moved in cultured society; and *Stromateis* (which means 'patchwork'), which contains a miscellany of themes about wisdom, philosophy, God, marriage, martyrdom, etc. He also wrote a short treatise on the right attitude to wealth in the form of an exposition of the gospel story of

two spirits,[6] as in *Stromateis* 6.134.1 where the 'flesh' and 'Spirit' of Galatians 5.17 are applied to the two spirits (τοῖς δισσοῖς πνεύμασιν).

There is the subordinate or subject spirit (τὸ ὑποκείμενον πνεῦμα), for which Clement also uses several phrases: the bodily spirit; the fleshly spirit; and the created spirit.[7] 'Through the bodily spirit, then, a man perceives, desires, rejoices, is angry, is nourished, grows' (*Strom.* 6.136.1). Clement says that the command 'You shall not lust' means 'You shall not serve the fleshly spirit but subdue it' (*Strom.* 6.136.2).

There is also τὸ ἡγεμονικόν πνεῦμα (ruling or governing spirit): it rules when it holds sway over desires (*Strom.* 6.136.1). A person faces the danger that the ruling spirit will be dominated by excessive passions, which are contrary to reason. The power of choice belongs to the ruling spirit, and through it a person lives (*Strom.* 6.135.4).[8] This is the reason why human beings are in the image of God (*Strom.* 5.94.5), or rather the image of the Image (= Word) of God.

On these two spirits, shared by everyone, we may quote *Strom.* 4.165.1: 'Always, therefore, the good actions, as better, are attributed to [or, if προσάπτονται is middle, have to do with] the better, the spiritual, whereas voluptuous and sinful (actions) are attributed to the worse, the sinful'.

The distinctive mark of Christian believers, however, is the Holy Spirit whom they have received in baptism.[9] Christians are those with whom the regal gold has been mixed,[10] namely the Holy Spirit (*Strom.* 5.98.4). God has begotten us as His adopted children by the Spirit (*Paed.* 1.21.2). The Holy Spirit has flowed down to us

---

the rich man and Jesus, with the title *Quis Dives Salvetur?* (*The Rich Man's Salvation*). We also have a treatise rebutting the ideas of the Valentinian theologian, Theodotus, and the Eastern branch of Valentinianism, usually referred to under a Latin title, *Excerpta ex Theodoto*.

[5] Cf. P. Galtier, *Le Saint Esprit en nous d'après les Pères grecs* (Rome: Apud Aedes Universitatis Gregorianae, 1946), p. 70; Hauschild, *Gottes Geist*, pp. 16-17.

[6] See C. Bigg, *The Christian Platonists of Alexandria* (Oxford: Clarendon, 1913), pp. 107-108, and Hauschild, *Gottes Geist*, pp. 16-28. For precursors in the idea of the partition of the soul, see S.R.C. Lilla, *Clement of Alexandria: A Study in Christian Platonism and Gnosticism* (Oxford: Oxford University Press, 1971), pp. 80-92, and also S. Sandmel, *Philo of Alexandria: an Introduction* (Oxford/New York: Oxford University Press, 1979), pp. 25, 62, 99-100, 153, for Philo's concept of lower and higher mind, the latter of which can rule man's passions and enable him to live by the law of nature.

[7] τὸ σωματικόν πνεῦμα; τὸ σαρκικόν πνεῦμα; and τὸ πλασθέν (or κατὰ τὴν πλάσιν) πνεῦμα respectively.

[8] As with reference to the first spirit, so also with regard to the ruling spirit Clement uses a variety of terms: νοῦς (mind); ἀπόρροια θεϊκή (divine emanation); ἐμφύσημα (inbreathing); θεία ἔννοια (divine mind); ψυχή λογική (rational soul).

[9] E.g. *Paed.* 1.26.1 draws a parallel between the experience of Jesus at his baptism and that of Christians.

[10] Cf. *Paed.* 2.20.1: a person is mixture (κρᾶμα) with the Spirit, though see *Excerpta ex Theodoto* 17.3-4 (which are Clement's reflections) for a denial that there is a mixture (κρᾶσις), rather a juxtaposition (παράθεσις).

from above (*Paed.* 1.28.1), and our sins have been washed away and we have been spiritually illuminated and awakened from spiritual sleep (*Paed.* 1.26.1-2). Instruction leads to faith, which, with baptism, is trained by the Holy Spirit (*Paed.* 1.30.2).

A. Divine Presence

Clement can use the language of friendship with the Lord (*Strom.* 2.104.2) or being near God in His presence (*Strom.*4.148.2) or entertaining God as a guest in souls free from stain (*Protr.* 9.84.5).

His ideal, which is constantly reiterated, is that Christians should be liberated from all passion, disciplined in pursuit of the good, moderate in such habits as eating and drinking, calmly and rationally contemplating the divine, motivated by love of God, perpetually ascending along the path of moral virtue until at last, through death, they attain the beatific vision of God. Clement's ideal is moderation: a simple diet, simplicity in dress and so on. While God's good gifts are to be accepted with thanksgiving, anything leading to excessive pleasure should be curbed. He even defines marriage as established for the procreation of children, with sexual intercourse being undertaken for that purpose only, and that after child bearing a husband and wife should be like brother and sister (*Strom.* 6.12.30).[11]

Firstly, reason is for Clement the ordering power. Faith is the necessary first step to salvation (*Strom.* 2.31.1), but then knowledge should be the governing principle building on faith. While passions disturb the soul (*Strom.* 2.59.6), reason is unmoved and acts as a sure pilot of the soul. To know the truth imparts stability which avoids passions and adheres to the good and imitates God (*Strom.* 2.51.6). So, faith and knowledge together make the Christian soul uniform and equable (*Strom.* 2.52.3). For Clement, once Christians are armed with reason, it is a case of 'Will and you shall be able': for the true gnostic (by whom Clement does not mean the 'heretical' type of gnostic, against whom he wrote, but one who was part of the Christian community and approached life in the manner described), will, judgment and exertion are identical (*Strom.* 2.77.5-6). Reason, then, is the stabilizing power which the gnostic receives from the Word.

Secondly, Clement saw our friendship with the Word through the Spirit actualized in prayer, study of the scriptures, contemplation and the eucharist:[12] 'By these things, (the gnostic) unites himself with the heavenly choir, being enlisted in it for ever-mindful contemplation, in consequence of his interrupted thoughts (of heaven while on earth)' (*Strom.* 7.49.1; cf. 80.2). Indeed, prayer should be a constant activity of the gnostic, not just at set times (*Strom.* 7.73.1).

---

[11] Behr, *Asceticism*, p. 133, notes in Clement a constant oscillation between an attitude of openness towards the world and a rigorous demand for detachment from it.

[12] E.g., *Strom.* 7.40.3; 44.5-8; 45.1; 49.1-8 (prayer); *Strom.* 3.42.4-5 (scriptures); *Strom.* 4.152.3 (contemplation); *Paed.* 2.19.4–2.20.1 (eucharist, though J.N.D. Kelly, *Early Christian Doctrines* [London: A. & C. Black, 1958], p. 213, sees this as an unusual passage in Clement); cf. Bigg, *Christian Platonists*, p. 130.

Clearly, Clement envisages this communion with the Word/God as having the potential for assimilation to God. The mind will be kept steadfast in its relation to divine matters (*Strom.* 4.139.4). 'I must be in what is Yours, O Omnipotent One, and if I am there, I am near You' (*Strom.* 4.148.2). As those at sea are held by the anchor and brought back to it, so the gnostics in drawing God towards them imperceptibly bring themselves to God (*Strom.* 4.152.2-3; cf. 7.82.2 where Clement speaks of carrying God and being carried by God). In the contemplative life, gnostics in the act of worshipping God attend to themselves and through their own spotless purification behold the holy God in a holy manner (*Strom.*4.152.3). For to know oneself is to know God (*Strom.* 3.1.1; 7.3.1).[13]

By these two means, then, the stabilizing power of reason and communion with God, the true gnostic has reached the state of passionlessness, waiting to put on the divine image (*Strom.* 4.138.1).

With this passionlessness, nonetheless, Clement can also speak of the gnostic's experience of joy throughout the day as such a person utters and does the precepts of the Lord (*Strom.* 7.80.3). There is one noteworthy passage, where Clement appeals to his readers to abandon pagan mysteries and join the worship of the Word: 'O truly sacred mysteries, O pure light, in the blaze of torches I have seen a vision of heaven and of God' (*Protr.* 12.120.1-12.121.3). Clement is describing something of an ecstatic experience which he enjoyed amidst the assembled Christian congregation. It must be admitted, however, that this passage is unusual.

Given Clement's ideal as outlined above, it would be surprising to encounter the note of that rapturous experience, where Christians feel overwhelmed by a power outside of themselves, as the norm.[14] In Clement's writings, we are in a rather different world than that of earlier generations who had certain experiences which 'swept them off their feet' and which they attributed to the Spirit. Heightened emotional feelings, which were for them a sign of the Spirit, are on the whole alien to Clement's understanding of Christianity. The new person created by God's Holy Spirit is for Clement ἀπαθῶν (without passion).

B. *Divine Illumination*

Clement links the Holy Spirit, baptism and illumination. 'While being baptized, we are illuminated' (*Paed.* 1.26.1; cf. 1.25.1). This is explained as follows: 'our sins had obscured the light of the divine Spirit, but now they have been wiped away and the eye of our own spirit is unimpeded and we can contemplate the Divine, because the Holy Spirit flows down from heaven upon us' (*Paed.* 1.28.1). The Spirit is the

---

[13] Cf. E.F. Osborn, *The Philosophy of Clement of Alexandria* (Cambridge: Cambirdge University Press, 1957), p. 93: 'the emphasis is on the gnostic's personal holiness and spiritual fellowship with God. He is joined to God as a spiritual being'.

[14] See the prayer at the end of *Paed.* 3.101.1-2: 'Cause all of us who live in Your peace..., having sailed tranquilly over the billows of sin, to be wafted in calm by Your Holy Spirit...by night and day to the perfect day'.

agent of illumination (alternatively, this is the Saviour's activity, e.g., *Strom.* 1.178.1).

The illuminatory role of the Spirit figures in *Stromateis* 6.137.4 onwards. The seventh day is one of rest (which humans need because of life's troubles), preparing for Christ our primal day, our rest, whom Clement also equates with the first creation of light. He then describes the Holy Spirit in terms of light: 'For the Holy Spirit, who is indivisibly divided to those who are sanctified through faith, is the light of truth, the true light who casts no shadow. He has the task of being a lamp to give knowledge of the things that exist' (*Strom.* 6.138.2).

The Holy Spirit belongs to the whole range of activities called wisdom (understanding, knowledge, science, faith, right opinion, art, experiment). Indeed, the Spirit is a dominant ruling principle. Those who possess the Spirit can search the deep things of God (an echo of 1 Cor. 2.10), particularly of OT prophecies (*Strom.* 2.7.3; cf. 5.25.5, where Clement, citing 1 Cor. 2.9-10, says that Paul recognizes the spiritual and gnostic person as the disciple of the Holy Spirit, whom God dispenses, and who, therefore, possesses the mind of Christ).

Commenting on Romans 8.15, Clement says that we have received the Spirit that we may know the true and only Father (*Strom.* 3.78.5). Whereas for Paul the Spirit prompts the exuberant cry 'Father', Clement envisages the knowledge of God purifying the ruling spirit of the soul, so that nothing stands in the way of its contemplating the Divine and of entering more nearly into impassibility (*Strom.* 4.39.2), i.e., Clement sounds a more intellectual note.

However, Clement finds it more natural to speak of the Word as our Instructor, Teacher and Guide. As the Image of God and genuine Son of Mind (= God, *Protr.* 10.98.4), he sprinkles all with the dew of truth (*Protr.* 11.114.3). So, Clement appeals to all to receive the Word as Teacher: to receive Christ is to receive sight and light and so to know God (*Protr.* 11.113.2-3). He exhorts his pagan audience to abandon customs and sail past this 'wicked island': 'Exert your will only and you have overcome ruin, bound to the wood of the cross you shall be freed from all destruction, the Word of God will be your pilot and the Holy Spirit will bring you to anchor in the haven of heaven' (*Protr.* 12.118.4).

Clement emphasizes study, meditation, contemplation, the pursuit of reason, in order to reach a passionless state. We have moved from a standpoint where a sudden insight or clarification is attributed to the Spirit as in primitive Christianity. Clement sees careful study and contemplation of spiritual things as the guidance of the Spirit, or, more frequently, of the Word.

Clement does assume a differentiation within the ranks of members of the church between the 'ordinary' Christian and the truly gnostic Christian. Simple believers are likely to remain at the level of immaturity, whereas the gnostic Christian presses on towards true maturity and perfection in the Christian life. Clement draws a distinction between the salvation which the simple believer enjoys and the more perfect salvation which is brought about by the true gnostic's asceticism (*Strom.* 6.14.2-3). This 'double standard', as it were, seems to be inbuilt into Clement's approach to the Christian life.

C. Divine Power

Clement had spoken of the Word as the only one who ever tamed the most intractable of all wild beasts, humans (*Protr.* 1.4.1). By the power of the Holy Spirit, the Word of God arranged in harmonious order both this great world and the little world of the human person too, body and soul (*Protr.* 1.5.3). Or Clement can assert that God our teacher alone has the power to conform humans worthily to His own likeness (*Protr.* 9.86.2); but, in fact, it is teaching, rather than the power of the Spirit directly, which effects this conforming. He can also speak of the new man created by God's Holy Spirit (*Protr.* 11.112.3).

When Clement speaks of the indwelling help of the Word[15] or the Spirit, is ethical empowerment in mind?

(i) 'By his own Spirit, he [the Word] will nourish those who hunger for the word' (*Paed.* 1.47.3). Spiritual communion is uppermost in mind rather than ethical transformation.

(ii) When talking of instruction in the truth (leading to contemplating God) and the pattern of holy deeds, Clement says that our Instructor keeps hold of the child (= the individual Christian)'s helm and wafts us on by the favourable breeze of the Spirit of Truth until he brings us safe to anchor in the haven of heaven (*Paed.* 1.54.3). Basically, the idea is that truth keeps us on a safe course in life.

(iii) The Holy Spirit is the true ointment with which Christian women should be anointed (*Paed.* 2.65.2). Alternatively, Clement can say that those women who are adorned with the Word adopt simplicity of lifestyle (*Paed.* 2.126.1; 2.128.1). Here conduct and behaviour are in mind.

(iv) Clement maintains that the person who strives after passionless-ness will prevail by the addition of the power which comes from God. For God breathes power into willing souls, but if they turn away from their eagerness, even the Spirit given by God is withdrawn (*Quis Dives Salvetur?* 21.1-2). When Clement refers to God's breathing power into willing souls, he is presumably thinking of baptism. Here, then, human willingness and divine power cooperate together[16] to achieve that freedom from the wrong passions or that 'enemy within' (*QDS* 25.5). Later, the rich are reminded that they are fortified by the power of God the Father, the blood of the Servant of God and the dew of the Holy Spirit (34.1).

How in practice did all this work out in Clement's view?

(a) Clement has a striking confidence in the power of knowledge/truth itself. Truth is immoveable and so 'the righteous shall not be shaken forever' (*Strom.* 6.81.1, 3, citing Psa. 112.6). This confidence rests on the belief that human beings

---

[15] Osborn, *Philosophy*, p. 107, wrote 'the indwelling Christ...is the source of all that is good'.

[16] Hauschild, *Gottes Geist,* p. 66, calls this 'synergism of man and the Spirit'; cf., too, W.E.G. Floyd, *Clement of Alexandria's Treatment of the Problem of Evil* (Oxford: Oxford University Press, 1971), pp. 88-90. Behr, *Asceticism*, pp. 168-71, also speaks in terms of synergism, and maintains that rather than a new world penetrating the Christian's existence, the Christian stretches upwards, touching the world 'on tiptoe only'. He speaks of 'an external collaboration between two actors'.

were made for close fellowship with God and for contemplation of heaven, a heavenly plant destined to come to the knowledge of God (*Protr.* 10.100.2-3). For Clement, it is intended that we should be saved by ourselves (*Strom.* 6.96.2), for we are all naturally constituted to acquire virtue (*Strom.* 9.96.3).

Once we have responded, then the divine power of goodness clings to the soul which is engaged in contemplation and prophecy and impresses on that soul something of its intellectual radiance, as in Moses' experience (*Strom.* 6.104.1-2). The gnostic is illuminated and becomes kingly (*Strom.* 6.152.2; cf. 6.149.5), can fulfil the divine command to be lord over the wild beasts within us (*Strom.* 6.115.2) and is studying to be θεός (*Strom.* 6.113.3; cf. *Protr.* 1.8.4).

There is a graphic illustration which Clement uses of the Word as a charioteer who leads and drives to salvation the human horse (= the irrational part of the soul) bent on pleasures (*Paed.* 3.53.2).

(b) Clement also assumes a link between knowledge and action (*Strom.* 6.68.3-69.3): knowledge is 'the beginning and author of all rational action'. Knowledge and action go together; the two cannot be separated. The Word may either inspire people with fear of the consequences of an action and so ward them away from it (*Paed.* 1.68.1; *Strom.* 2.37.2; cf. *Protr.* 9.95.1), or rebuke them and so shame them from sin (*Paed.* 1.74.2). Either way, the Word seeks to induce a change of behaviour.

Clement maintains that the character of the life which Jesus enjoins is not very formidable. He commands and so fashions his commands that we can accomplish them (*Paed.* 1.98.1)

In this link between knowledge and action, Clement moves in a different world to Paul's 'divided person' of Romans 7.

(c) Discipline and practice lead to habit (*Strom.* 6.78.4). 'The gnostic associates through love with the Beloved One to whom he is allied by free choice, and by the habit which results from training approaches closer to him' (*Strom.* 6.72.1). The acquiring of knowledge demands application, training and progress. 'In the one, then, who has rendered their virtue indefectible by discipline based on knowledge, habit is changed into nature' (*Strom.* 7.46.9). The disciplined training becomes ingrained habit. In this disposition, there will be no conflict between will, judgment and the corresponding activity.[17]

An essential part of our training is copying Christ. During his incarnate life, the Word was free from passion, envy, ignorance etc (*Strom.* 7.72): he trained the flesh, by nature subject to passion, to a habit of impassibility (*Strom.* 7.7.6). So also the true Christian should emulate his Teacher and Instructor, and strive for a passionless state through undisturbed intercourse and communion with the Lord (*Strom.* 7.13.3), and so he will be like a wrestler victorious over all his opponents (*Strom.* 7.20.3-

---

[17] Behr, *Asceticism*, pp. 200-201, points out how Clement stresses that the true gnostic's disposition becomes unshakeable and infallible (*Strom.* 6.9.4).

5).[18] Not surprisingly, the Word is often pictured as a trainer of the Christian athlete (e.g. *Paed.* 1.57.3).

(d) If knowledge perfects faith, love perfects knowledge. Knowledge terminates in love (*Strom.* 7.57.4). Love is 'celestial food, the banquet of reason' (*Paed.* 2.53). It is 'not desire, but is a relation of affection, restoring the gnostic to the unity of faith' (*Strom.* 6.73.3). Love means affinity to the impassible God and also the friends of God (*Strom.* 6.73.6).

Perhaps surprisingly, Clement never links love and the Spirit as Paul did (Gal. 5.22). We do not meet the antithesis 'Knowledge puffs up, love builds up' of Paul's rebuke to the Corinthians. Where for Paul faith works itself out in love, in Clement there is an ascending order of faith, knowledge and love.

If love brings affinity to God, being in His presence influences our actions, words and temper.[19] We will feel God's inspiration in everything (*Strom.* 7.35.4-7). Indeed, our holiness is Providence's return to itself, a responsive feeling of loyalty from the one who is a friend of God (*Strom.* 7.42.2). God assists the gnostics, honouring such with closer oversight and breathes into them the strength they need for the completion of their salvation (*Strom.* 7.48.1-2).

Somewhat similar are the statements about the Holy Spirit's influence on Christians. 'For, in the first place, the best beauty is in the soul, as we have pointed out on many occasions, when the soul is adorned by the Holy Spirit and influenced by the radiant charms which proceed from him—righteousness, wisdom, fortitude, temperance, love of the good and modesty, than which no more blooming colour has ever been seen' (*Paed.* 3.64.1). The Holy Spirit influences Christians to embrace the kind of ethical virtues listed, thereby producing the true beauty.

(e) Christ's help is mentioned in connection with martyrdom which should be undergone for love, not reward. We can only fight against the spiritually wicked powers by trusting in the Almighty God and the Lord Jesus. 'The Lord says "Lo, here I am". See the invincible Helper who shields us' and Clement also quotes 1 Peter 4.12-14 with its reference to the Spirit's resting on the persecuted (*Strom.* 4.47.1-4).

Martyrdom for Clement is the climax of a process of discipline and training by which gnostics have been freed from fear and pain and become like their Teacher in impassibility (*Strom.* 6.71.4–72.2; cf. 4.78.2).

Finally, we turn to a strand in Clement's thought which needs to be mentioned, namely: provided that Christians continually discipline themselves to eradicate all passions, they will earn the Holy Spirit.[20]

---

[18] Cf. Bigg, *Christian Platonists*, p. 126, 'Self-control, holiness, has made reason the absolute master of the brute in the centaur man.'

[19] Cf. Osborn, *Philosophy*, p. 163, paraphrases Clement: 'How can the gnostic help growing better, when he is always in the company of God?'

[20] Cf. Hauschild, *Gottes Geist*, p. 71: 'Moral progress and ascent to knowledge of God make union with the Holy Spirit possible'; and Floyd, *Problem of Evil*, p. 89: 'Man must dispose himself for the reception of grace through the acquisition of particular virtues'.

(i) 'The more of a gnostic a man becomes by doing right, the nearer is the illuminating Spirit to him' (*Strom.* 4.107.6).

(ii) The body 'becomes receptive of the soul which is most precious to God and is deemed worthy of the Holy Spirit through the sanctification of soul and body, perfected by the Saviour's equipping' (*Strom.* 4.163.2).

(iii) The soul thus beautified becomes a temple of the Holy Spirit when it has acquired a disposition of mind in the whole of life, corresponding to the gospel (*Strom.* 7.64.7).

We meet a duality: through faith and baptism we receive the Holy Spirit; by moral ascent we become fit to receive the Holy Spirit. We are already the temples of the Holy Spirit through baptism; we become temples by moral perfection. There is something of the 'Become what you are' of the NT here, though never in Paul do we meet the idea of becoming fit for the Spirit. Hauschild states it thus: 'What can be fixed anthropologically as the new being must be first realized ethically by a new life'.[21] Behr is more critical and believes that Clement's asceticism severely curtails the effective power of the new life granted to believers in baptism, which Clement nevertheless felt so keenly and described so vividly,[22] and he goes so far as to speak of 'a second saving change' (*Strom.* 7.10.4).

Clement is loyal to the tradition of new creation or new birth, which goes back to primitive Christianity, especially Paul, yet he also wishes to emphasize the need for progress and development, morally and spiritually, and ascent towards the heavenly world and union with God. Divinization is for Clement a process. The Christian is on the way to becoming a perfect person.

Summary

While a person consists of two spirits, the 'subject' spirit and the 'ruling' spirit, Christians have received the Holy Spirit following their rebirth and adoption through faith and baptism. The Holy Spirit is an 'addition' to the created natural person. The Holy Spirit reinforces the 'ruling' spirit. In the Christian life, there should be a progression from faith to increasing knowledge of the truth through the continual exercise of reason, and on to love, in a spiritual journey towards passionlessness and assimilation to God or divinization. Increasing stability comes to the true gnostic through reason's grasp of the truth and this enables contemplation of God.

Not surprisingly, illumination is a key idea linked with the Holy Spirit in Clement, though more often with the Word. Study, meditation, prayer, contemplation, are all means by which the process of moving forward along the way of virtue and of drawing nearer to God takes place.

Knowledge and action go together. Disciplining oneself leads to the formation of habit, which in time becomes nature. Occasionally, Clement can speak of the necessity of making moral progress in order to become a temple for the Holy Spirit

---

[21] Hauschild, *Gottes Geist*, p. 76.

[22] Behr, *Asceticism*, p. 183, and he repeats that assessment on pp. 203 and 213.

to dwell in us. On the other hand, from time to time, Clement ties the taming of our passions and the progress in virtue to the Holy Spirit, though again more frequently to the Word who is preeminently our teacher. Divine help and human endeavour are both there in Clement, yet he has unquestionably put tremendous stress on our striving for moral perfection.

2. Theodotus

As stated earlier, Hippolytus mentioned a western and eastern branch of Valentinianism (*Ref.* 6.35.5-7). Among those whom he allocated to the latter was one Theodotus. We owe our knowledge of what Theodotus taught to Clement of Alexandria, who wrote *Excerpts from the works of Theodotus and the so-called eastern school at the time of Valentinus*.[23] Clement intersperses his extracts from Theodotus with comments of his own. He uses 'Theodotus says', 'he says', 'they say' or 'the Valentinians say', and these act as markers for us to discern where Clement is quoting.[24]

The *Excerpts* fall into four main sections, of which the third (43-65) bears a striking resemblance to a section in Irenaeus' *AH*, where Irenaeus is describing the teaching of Ptolemy (the so-called 'Great Notice'). This raises, of course, the question whether in this section Clement has incorporated material from a different source (especially as the linguistic 'markers' just alluded-to never occur in this section). This issue raised, it remains true, however, that there are considerable similarities between sections 1-28, 29-42, and 66-86 on the one hand and 43-65 on the other.[25] Even Sagnard is undecided whether Clement has joined material from the different Valentinian schools together.[26] We will point out whenever material from section 43-65 is being discussed and try not to make any major point which depends only on material from that section.

A. Divine Presence

In a famous passage, oft quoted,[27] Theodotus reveals the kinds of questions which concerned and troubled the gnostic type of person.

> 'Who were we? What have we become? Where were we?
> Where has our lot been cast? Towards where are we hastening?
> From what are we being redeemed? What is birth? What is rebirth?' (78.3).

---

[23] We have consulted F. Sagnard, *Clément d'Alexandrie: Extraits de Théodote* (SC 23; Paris: Les Éditions du Cerf, 1970 = reprint of 1948 edition with some small corrections).
[24] Sagnard, *Extraits*, p. 30.
[25] See Sagnard, *Extraits*, p. 48.
[26] Sagnard, *Extraits*, p. 28.
[27] E.g., Jonas, *Gnostic Religion*, p. 45; Schnackenburg, *John* I, p. 146; H. Conzelmann, *An Outline of New Testament Theology* (London: SCM, 2nd ed., 1969), p. 12; Rudolph, *GNOSIS*, p. 71.

Ignorance is the essence of existence in this world, and so revelation is necessary to convey the knowledge needed and longed-for.[28] The gnostics are convinced that they possess that knowledge as a divine gift and so are assured of salvation.[29]

As with the western Valentinians, so also with Theodotus, judging by the language employed, the conversion experience was probably a dramatic, life-changing one. In conversion, the 'pneumatics' realize who they are. In chapter 2, Theodotus interpreted the sleep of Adam in Genesis 2 symbolically. The male seed[30] was deposited by the Logos in the soul of Adam while he was asleep. This seed is an emanation (ἀπόρροια) of the angelic element. It acts like a yeast, making into one what seems to be divided, namely soul and flesh. Adam's sleep is 'the forgetfulness of the soul'. This is why the Saviour said 'Save yourself and your soul'.[31] Therefore (3.1), the Saviour came and 'awakened the soul and ignited the spark'.

Theodotus quotes 'Let your light shine before others' (Mt. 5.16) and then refers to the insufflation of John 20. 'After the resurrection, he breathed the Spirit into the apostles; he divided and separated the dust like ashes; he ignited the spark and quickened it into life' (3.2). We note the terminology employed in these passages: an awakening from sleep; igniting of a fire (twice); a quickening into life. All of these are striking and memorable images and are indicative of the powerful experience undergone. We also note how Scripture is used: Genesis 2 and John 20 are both so interpreted as to secure a Valentinian sense, and a possible allusion to Jesus' words now recorded in Luke is again given a Valentinian twist.

Later, Theodotus says that the Saviour has appeared and describes with various images what he has done. He has 'filtered' the seeds (41.2).[32] meaning separated them from the inferior elements which were mixed up with them and which were not really compatible with the pneumatic nature of these seeds. He 'formed' (μορφώσαντος) these seeds (at 68 they are described as imperfect, without understanding, foolish, weak and formless,[33] and hence in need of being formed[34] or corrected[35]). Finally, the image of light is utilized: the Saviour-Light has illuminated the seed so that it could know the Man of the superior seed. This is how John 1.9 is taken: the Light enlightens every (inner) man who has come into the world (41.3). The light banishes the darkness which has surrounded the seed.

---

[28] Jonas, *Gnostic Religion*, p. 45.

[29] Sagnard, *Extraits*, p. 203, n. 3.

[30] The terminology used here is unusual: normally Theodotus refers to the female seed or the children of the woman from above (e.g., 21.2-3; 67.3-4; 68.1; 79.1), or more generally, the pneumatic or superior seed.

[31] An allusion to Lk. 17.28-33; 12.20; 9.24-25, in the opinion of Sagnard, *Extraits*, p. 57, note 5.

[32] Here the verb συνδιυλίζω is used, while in 41.4, the verb χωρίζω is used to express a similar idea: 'he separated the passions which darkened and were mixed with it'.

[33] Theodotus even says that they were brought forth like ἐκτρώματα, a deliberate echo of Paul's description of himself at his conversion in 1 Cor. 15.8.

[34] μόρφωσις occurs at 45.1; and also at 57.1; 60.1 in the third section.

[35] διόρθωσις occurs at 30.2; 35.2.

All these modes of expression point to an experience which has transformed the self-understanding of the recipient. The experience has brought light where there was darkness, knowledge where there was ignorance, order where there was confusion.

At 24.1, Clement reports that 'the Valentinians say', which introduces another reflection of theirs on the Spirit. 'The Spirit, whom each of the prophets had for his ministry, has been poured out on all who are of the church. Therefore, the signs of the Spirit—healings and prophecies—are fulfilled through the church'. What is meant here by 'all who are of the church'? The occurrences of the 'church' in the parts of the *Excerpts* which are from Theodotus seem to have in mind the pneumatics, the superior seed, which comprise the body of Jesus.[36] Both Sagnard and Rudolph interpret the phrase at 24.1 in this way.[37] Interestingly, Clement does not challenge the claim of healings and prophecies, but criticizes the Valentinian belief in an Ineffable Father and a Demiurge who was used by Sophia to create the world. He says, 'But they fail to understand that the Paraclete, who works now continuously in the church, is of the same substance and power as the One who operated continuously according to the old covenant' (24.2).

Given that baptism continued in the second century to be baptism of believers, whether directly from paganism or from Christian homes, and given that conversion or commitment to Christ and baptism were held together,[38] it is natural that baptism should be a memorable experience. That would seem to be the case in what Theodotus says about baptism. Broadly speaking, there are two main aspects about baptism which emerge from what Theodotus says.

Firstly, baptism delivers from the evil powers. In baptism we put off the evil powers (77.1). We become superior to all the other powers (76.4). The baptized person becomes servant of God and master of the unclean spirits. Whereas prior to baptism these spirits used to be active against those baptized, now they shudder before them (77.3). The power of Fate controlling destinies through the stars has been ended with baptism (78.1). The one who has been 'sealed' through the name of the Father, Son and Holy Spirit is no longer subject to the attacks of all the powers, and through the three names he has been liberated from the 'triad of corruption'.[39] The baptized has received 'power to walk on scorpions and serpents, the evil powers' (76.2, which picks up Lk. 10.19).

In 81.1-3, Theodotus drew a distinction between material fire and immaterial (or spiritual or rational) fire. The former attacks the body, while the latter attacks immaterial beings like demons, bad angels and even the devil. By analogy, baptism

---

[36] See 22.3; 26.1; 40.1; 41.2; 42.3; and, in the third section, 58.1.

[37] Sagnard, *Extraits*, p. 33 (in his 'Notes', Sagnard takes this comment as 'an invitation made to Christians to recognise in them this "pneuma" and adhere to Valentinian doctrines' (p. 108). Presumably, Sagnard has in mind those psychics who have an inclination to good and who as a result might gain salvation, though an inferior one to the pneumatics, i.e. to have a place in the Ogdoad but outside the Pleroma); Rudolph, *GNOSIS*, p. 207.

[38] Even if a period of instruction preceded the actual baptism itself.

[39] Sagnard, *Extraits*, p. 205, does not feel able to say what this triad consists of.

has a perceptible side, which quenches the perceptible fire, and an intelligible side[40] which is, through the Spirit, a remedy[41] against the intelligible fire (81.2). Clearly, 'fire' is being used as a technical term. Jonas helpfully explains how the Valentinians elaborated the eminent position of fire among the elements of the universe solely for the sake of its spiritual correlation. What to the Stoics was 'rational fire', 'the fiery Mind of the universe', the bearer of cosmic Reason, is for the Valentinians the embodiment of ignorance.[42]

Because the Spirit is from above and is immaterial, he not only controls the elements but also the evil powers and rulers (81.3).

The example of the Lord's life—he was baptized, was in the wilderness with the wild beasts and was supported by the angels—is stressed. We must clothe ourselves with the weapons of the Lord, which are able to quench the arrows of the devil (an allusion also to Eph. 6.16), thus keeping body and soul invulnerable (85.3).

In view of the frequency with which this theme is mentioned and concentrated so much in these chapters (76–85), it must be held to give an insight into the experience associated with baptism in the mind of Theodotus. There must have been an exultant sense of relief at liberation from the evil and hostile powers who would keep the 'pneumatics' in ignorance and deprive them of their heavenly birthright.

The second major theme associated with baptism is that of regeneration through union with Christ and the power of the Spirit, or to express this in a Valentinian way, a 'formation' or 'correction'.[43] Baptism is into God (εἰς Θεὸν, 76.2) and in the name of the Father, Son and Holy Spirit (76.3), into whom we are born again (76.4). Baptism means the death and end of the old life (βίος) and Life (ζωή) according to Christ (77.1), who is the sole Lord of this life. We become servants of God (77.3). When 'formed', the seed becomes changed into a man and becomes 'son of the Bridegroom', no longer weak and subject to cosmic powers but male fruit (79; cf. 68 where the designation 'children of the male and of the bridal chamber' occurs. See also 21.3 where it is said that the 'female seeds' are changed into male, are united to the angels and go into the Pleroma).

The one to whom Christ has given rebirth is transferred into life, into the Ogdoad.[44] They die to the world and live to God. Death and corruption are destroyed by the death and resurrection of Christ and ours (80.1-2).

According to Theodotus, the Spirit purifies (exorcises) the baptismal water, and this means that not only does the water of baptism separate the inferior element but also adds sanctification (82.2). In what sense is 'sanctification' used here? Is it used of moral holiness or a reawakening of the pneumatic seed and union with the realm

---

[40] The Greek is τὸ νοητός.

[41] Or 'protects from' which is how Sagnard, *Extraits*, p. 205 translates ἀλεξητήριον. Both these meanings are possible.

[42] Jonas, *Gnostic Religion*, p. 198.

[43] See footnotes 34 and 35.

[44] I.e., the eighth heaven, where the pneumatics wait until the number of the elect is complete and then they, with their angelic counterparts, will enter into the Pleroma. The psychics who are saved remain forever in the Ogdoad; they never enter the Pleroma.

of Pneuma? Since in 82.1 Theodotus has just said that the bread and oil (while the bread seems likely to be a reference to the Lord's Supper, the oil could refer to an anointing before/during the baptismal ceremony, or possibly anointing for healing as in James 5.14)[45] are consecrated by the power of the Name of God and transformed into spiritual power, the latter seems more likely.[46]

Baptism is also a 'sealing' (σφραγίς) in 83.1. The rest of the paragraph seems to imply that evil spirits can somehow sneak into the act of baptism and secure the seal, which makes them for the future incurable, which is a strange concept![47] — as if God was bound by His own seal. It seems all the more strange in view of the fact that at 80.3 Theodotus says that the one sealed by the (Name of the) Father, Son and Holy Spirit is no longer exposed to the attacks of every other power, and through the threefold Name has been released from the entire triad of corruption.[48] Then, in support, Theodotus quotes in his own way 1 Corinthians 15.49: 'After having borne the image of the earthly, then he carries the image of the heavenly', giving it a present connotation and obliterating Paul's future reference to the End.[49]

In the final section (86), the seal is mentioned again, but as 86 is exactly parallel to a passage in Clement's *Eclogae Propheticae* 24, there is every possibility that 86 is a comment by Clement himself and Sagnard seems inclined to that position.[50] We shall, therefore, not use it in our discussion of Theodotus' views.

---

[45] Sagnard, *Extraits*, p. 207, n. 2, suggests the former, while Lampe, *Seal*, p. 125, hesitantly ('perhaps') opts for the latter.

[46] The adjective ἅγιος occurs at 58.2 in a quotation from Rom. 11.16. Otherwise all other uses of the ἁγι- group of words in the *Excerpts* occur in remarks made by Clement (see indices of Greek words provided by Sagnard, *Extraits*, pp. 255-76). No judgment is thereby being made on the ethical teaching or behaviour of Theodotus; merely, that, in this context, ἁγιασμός is not concerned with moral conduct.

[47] Lampe, *Seal*, p. 127, went so far as to include this in his verdict 'On the whole, however, Gnostic conceptions of the seal are crude in the extreme and represent the beliefs and superstitions of the popular or half-educated mind'. If he were writing today, he might express himself more cautiously, but even so the strangeness of what Theodotus said remains. Perhaps it was a pastoral warning for the pneumatic not to be over confident once he/she had been illuminated and saved.

[48] Even Sagnard, *Extraits*, p. 205, admits to being unable to define what this triad of corruption is.

[49] Theodotus also drops the καθώς and makes the first verb into a participle (φορέσας), and changes the main verb into the present indicative active in the third person singular where Paul has the future indicative active in the first person plural.

[50] *Extraits*, p. 211, where he heads his French translation with 'Clement?' and in note 1 quotes the whole of the relevant section from the *Eclogae Propheticae*. Clement draws the passage about the tribute money (Mt. 22.15-20) into his exposition, and the ἐπιγραφή is interpreted as the Name of God and the εἰκών as the Spirit of God. As animals are branded and carry a mark as an indication of their owner, so the believing soul has received the 'seal' of truth and carries about (as Paul had said in Gal. 6.17) 'the marks of Christ'. The true believer knows the truth and this is God's mark of ownership.

C. Divine Power

What was Theodotus' teaching on the way in which Christians should behave and did he envisage the Holy Spirit as a help to ethical conduct pleasing to God?

In 48.2, he refers to the creation of evil spirits. 'For us there is a battle against them. This is why Paul said "Do not grieve the Holy Spirit of God" [Eph. 4.30]'. Sagnard sees here a play on words: 'Do not put on the Spirit the sadness of evil' [= the hylic].[51] There is presumably some allusion to Sophia's passions because she could not know the unknowable Father and was expelled from the Pleroma.

Whereas Ephesians 4.30 is set within ethical injunctions before and after (on the one hand, commands like to have done with lying and speak the truth v. 25, not to nurse anger v. 26, not to steal v. 27, etc., and, on the other hand, the command to put away bitterness, anger, wrangling, slander, and to be kind and forgiving, vv. 31-32), what Theodotus seems to be concerned with is that the pneumatic should lose his or her status by letting the pneumatic spark be submerged by hylic elements. Ethical considerations do not seem to be uppermost.

Theodotus maintains at 67.1 that Paul's statement in Romans 7.5, 'When we were in the flesh', refers to 'that weakness, the emission from the Woman Above'. In other words, Paul is being used in an un-Pauline way. For the apostle, 'flesh' is human nature under the power of sin, and this has serious ethical consequences leading to death, whereas Theodotus is referring to the pneumatic seed trapped in the fleshly element, in a state of ontological weakness, ignorant of its origin, needing its male (angelic) counterpart.[52] A similar argument is found in 68 and 79—indeed 67–68 and 79 form a distinct group within the last section (66–86).[53]

Section 69–73 deals with astrology: how the evil Powers control the course of the stars and govern through them and so dominate human beings as if they were their children (69.1-2). A human being is a feeble animal (73.3), and inclined to choose the worse and to assist those who hate him/her (namely, the evil powers). Even the good powers are not able to save and guard us. It needed the Lord to rescue us and bring us peace (72–73, 74–75). The Good Shepherd has descended and given his life for his sheep (73.2, alluding to Jn. 10.11-14). The Saviour's birth and the events of his life have broken the stranglehold of Destiny (Εἱμαρμένη) and brought us peace (74). The star at the birth is mentioned in 74-75 as having destroyed the ancient astral order and inaugurated the new way of salvation.

We are not specifically told in any of these passages what entanglement in the hylic actually involves in terms of concrete behaviour. All attention is focussed on deliverance from involvement in the fleshly-material. 'Because of the opponents [= evil Powers], who, through the body and things external, encroach upon the soul

---

[51] Sagnard, *Extraits*, p. 161, n. 4.

[52] Sagnard, *Extraits*, p. 191, n. 2, says that flesh is taken 'in a figurative sense': 'it is the element issued from the passion of Wisdom'. 'The pneumatic element, being mixed with this world, is in a state of weakness...'.

[53] Sagnard, *Extraits*, p. 191, n. 2.

(ἐπιβατεύουσι τῆς ψυχῆς) and seize hold of it to enslave it', even the good angels cannot save and guard us (73.1).

Theodotus argues at 52.2 (which is part of the third section) that we 'should not nourish or strengthen the fleshly element'—which the Saviour called 'the Adversary' [alluding to Mt. 5.25] and Paul 'the law at war with the law of my mind' [Rom. 7.23]—'by the power of our sins but should put it to death and show its fallen character by abstaining from evil so that (this fleshly element) might be secretly scattered and blown away...and might not have the strength to remain alive in the journey through the fire' (into the Pleroma). On the surface this might seem to be thoroughly Pauline, even though using slightly different phrases, but still equating 'flesh' and evil. However, 'the fleshly element' seems actually to be the material, the physical, and all associated with it.

Desjardins believes that this section 52 is addressed to the psychics who are in mind in the section 50.1 to 53.1 (pneumatics come in view at 53.4 and through to 54).[54] Assuming that this is a correct interpretation, it fits in with the idea that of the three types of humanity, the psychic can choose good or evil, and this view seems to be implied also at 34.2, where the redeemed psychics occupy the place previously occupied by Sophia outside the Pleroma.

In conclusion, we have to say that the *Extracts* give us little or no information about the ethical teaching of Theodotus. His own life may have been a morally good one, and he may have expected the pneumatics to live good lives, but that is not his concern within the *Extracts* given by Clement. It may be significant, though it is an argument from silence, that Clement does not attack Theodotus personally or the Valentinians in general on grounds of immoral behaviour. We might have expected that, if there were grounds for doing so.

In the *Extracts*, Theodotus' concern is to try and ensure that the pneumatics, once awakened, do not succumb again to involvement in the material world. Perhaps the reference to 'fastings, supplications, prayers' at the time of baptism (84) point in the direction of moral seriousness, but on the evidence available we cannot go farther.

Conclusion

What we learn from the *Extracts* suggests that Theodotus had undergone an experience which radically changed his life and outlook. The accompanying ritual act, namely baptism, obviously was also highly significant and memorable for him. A sense of enlightenment and liberation must have flooded into his life, giving direction and purpose to him.

That said, the theological frame of reference used to interpret that experience differs considerably from what we have seen elsewhere in Christian circles in the second century outside of the Valentinians. The Spirit in Theodotus' writing hardly agrees with that which we might call 'orthodox' Christian belief.

---

[54] Desjardins, *Sin*, pp. 31-40, discusses Excerpt 52; see p. 38 for his argument that it is the psychic who is addressed. Cf. Sagnard, *Extraits*, p. 164.

3. Conclusion

Why does someone like Clement present baptism and the reception of the Holy Spirit as illumination? What does that tell us about his religious experience and its main features, particularly as in Clement's case this fits in with the stress on faith proceeding to knowledge and on reason and truth as guides in the Christian life? Clement represents an intellectual rather than an ecstatic approach to Christianity. At a time when Montanism was making its impact in Asia Minor and in North Africa, Clement represents an opposite pole.[55] This does not mean that there is nothing of what we might call 'passion' in his religion. One thinks of some of his lyrical outbursts in praise to Christ (*Strom.* 2.21.1-5) and prayer (*Paed.* 3.101.1-3) or the evangelical appeals to receive God's grace (*Protr.* 9–10). Clement's ideal of passionlessness means, of course, getting rid of the impure passions of anger, jealousy, lust, etc. Clement is no 'desiccated calculating machine', even if he is an 'intellectual' and sought to counter heresy without surrendering the intellectual approach.[56]

Of all writers surveyed in our period, Clement seems to exemplify best the Christian intellectual (or, as he might have said, the true Christian gnostic). In *Strom.* 1.11.2 he describes how he listened to various teachers in Greece, Syria, the east and finally in Egypt, where he heard a teacher (probably the reference is to one Pantaeus, head of the catechetical school at Alexandria, whom Clement eventually succeeded), whom he likens to a bee gathering the spoil of the flowers of the prophetic and apostolic meadow. When he tracked him down, he found rest. The Alexandrine tradition of redemptive knowledge coming through the Spirit's gift of illumination clearly fitted Clement's experience.

Within the Christian church of the second century, Clement stands as an example of the scholar who consciously brought his scholarship into the service of the church as the gift of the Spirit.

In the spectrum of Egyptian Christianity we have also come across Theodotus, of the Valentinian persuasion. Theodotus represents the type of person troubled by many questions to do with what it means to be human in this world. He was attracted to a theological solution of these questions which was to take him and those like him on an intellectual journey which would lead them outside the 'mainstream' of the Christian movement. His own religious experience was probably a memorable and dramatic one, bringing with it a sense of enlightenment as to his true purpose and destiny in the world of reality and a sense of liberation from those forces which would drag him down or away from that purpose and destiny. But the interpretation espoused by him put those who had had his type of experience into a special category—the pneumatics—over against others within and outside the Christian communities, and this was a radical departure from the

---

[55] Hauschild, *Gottes Geist*, p. 60, sees the reaction of the church against Montanism exemplified in Clement.

[56] H. Chadwick, *Early Christian Thought and the Classical Tradition* (Oxford: Clarendon, 1966), p. 33.

conviction of Christians in the NT era that all who confessed Jesus as Saviour and Lord were part of the people of God and led by the Spirit of God.

CHAPTER 9

Conclusion

I.

As we seek to draw together the results of our study, we can see that the claim to have the Spirit of God on the part of Christians may be understood as part of their 'self-understanding'. The sense of having received the Spirit may be seen as marking Christians off from others outside the movement, or as characterizing some, but not all, within the movement, with certain consequences being drawn from this.

Early Christianity was a 'sect' in the sense that it was very much a minority movement, on the 'outside' of society, often suspect and likely to be the victim of social abuse and popular violence. Arguably that did not alter in our period, although Christianity had grown considerably and spread widely by the end of the second century. Whereas Paul had cast longing eyes towards Spain in the late fifties, just over a century later, in 177, Christianity was strong enough in southern Gaul to withstand and survive some horrendous persecution. Of course, Paul himself had an ecumenical and universal outlook in the sense that he both sought to keep the Jewish and Gentile wings of the church together and had a global sense of mission; while in the second generation the author of Ephesians had a deep sense of the universal Lord exercising his sovereignty through his body, the church, and Luke held strong convictions about the church's mission beginning from Jerusalem and going out to the ends of the earth. Nonetheless, Christianity was still a comparatively small movement around AD 90.

At the beginning of the period which our study embraces, 1 Peter combines a sense of a persecuted and abused minority with the awareness that the 'brotherhood' is spread through the world. At the end of the era, Irenaeus can speak of the universal church, of a succession of bishops going back to the apostles and of a rule of faith adhered-to by all the churches. This stress is, of course, in opposition to gnosticism; it is part of the apologetic/polemic to stress the all-embracing, universalist aspect of the 'orthodox' church over against the elitist, exclusive claims of the heretics; but it is, nonetheless, real for all that. We might wonder, however, how would Irenaeus have spoken, had he been setting the church over against the world/the Roman Empire? The *Letter* of the southern Gaul congregations to those in Asia Minor concerning the martyrs of 177 reveals all too clearly how the might of the state as well as mob violence could be turned against Christians, how cruel torments as well as false accusations could be unleased against them.

In the light of all this, we can ask whether the sense of the Spirit's presence acted as a Christian distinctive, the 'theological' conviction dovetailing into the sociological factor: a minority movement bolstered its morale by claiming to have the Spirit of God, whereas the world did not possess the Spirit? Certainly traces of this can be found in Syrian Christianity. We meet this position in the Fourth Gospel: 'I will give you another Paraclete that he may be with you forever, the Spirit of Truth, whom the world cannot receive, because it does not see him nor knows him. You know him because he remains beside you and will be in you' (Jn. 14.16-17). The piety of the *Odes of Solomon* is akin to that of Johannine Christianity. The author is aware of a sharp division between believers and the world. There is nothing quite as explicit as John 14.16-17, but we read of the experience of the Spirit as leading away from vanity and folly to the present entry into Paradise (cf. the imagery like release from captivity, the passage from darkness to light or from death to life). Possibly Tatian should be mentioned here in view of his sharp criticisms of the Greeks and his conviction that receiving the Spirit means a return to what a person ought to be, i.e., body-soul-Spirit. Only those who have the Spirit are completed human beings.

In Asia Minor, the nearest expression of this appears in the Book of Revelation: John of Patmos feels himself inspired by the Spirit to speak a word to the churches in the crisis when the power of the beast will stir the earth's inhabitants against the followers of the Lamb. If there is a holy 'Trinity' (God, the Lamb, the Spirit) plus the woman of ch. 12, there is a satanic trinity (Satan/the dragon, the beast, the three unclean spirits of 16.13) plus the great whore of ch. 17. As the seven Spirits of God are sent forth into all the world, so the three unclean spirits go forth to the kings of the whole world to make them fight at Armaggedon.

1 Peter reveals how the minority group of Christians at Rome compensated for lack of status in the world's eyes by their conviction that they were elected by the Father, redeemed by the blood of Jesus Christ and sanctified by the Spirit (1.2). Even when faced by the world's persecution, they were assured that God's Spirit would rest upon them (4.14). They were God's family indwelt by the Spirit (2.5), whereas unbelievers were rejected (2.8).

In a similar fashion, Tatian and Clement of Alexander see the Holy Spirit as the distinctive mark of the Christian over against the rest of humanity. For the latter, it is the 'tenth' quality which completes a person.

(b) We may say that this church/world antithesis is similar to that when the church claims to have the Spirit and denies it to Judaism. The Spirit becomes a sign of being the true people of God. Thus, the implication of *Barnabas* 6.11-16 and 16.6-10 is that Christians filled by the Spirit are the fulfillment of the promise of a land flowing with milk and honey and of a new heart/spirit to replace the heart of stone. A strong anti-Jewish note runs through Barnabas, and he sees the OT as a Christian book which the Jews have misunderstood and which has come true in the Christian era and is now fully understood. Justin Martyr in his *Dialogue with Trypho* argues that the Spirit ceased to operate amongst the Jews and has baptized Christians. The OT prophecies about God's gifts to men and women have been fulfilled in the outpouring of the Spirit upon Jesus' followers. Tertullian also advances the idea that the Spirit ceased to work in the Jewish people, but has been poured out on Christians (*adv. Iud.* 13.15; 8.14).

(c) We can go a step further and say that it is an extension of the use of the contrast just discussed when we meet an 'internal' application. This may take one of two forms: what we may call a struggle for power and what we may call a doctrinal dispute. We shall differentiate these two for the sake of clarity, though in practice they may not necessarily be so clearly separated and may overlap: the latter may be overt and the former latent or vice versa.

In a struggle for power within a church, one group may claim exclusive possession of the Spirit and deny it to the rival group. There may be no doctrinal differences of any significance. Thus, Clement of Rome, who exhorts the Corinthian congregation to restore unity and harmony and reinstate the ejected elders, claims to have written under the guidance of the Spirit, and, therefore, urges that his advice be followed, while he brands the ringleaders of the troubles as arrogant, proud, boastful upstarts, qualities clearly alien to the Spirit of God. One is inclined to see this as a tactical move in view of the general tenor of Clement's theology with its stress on order and the absence of stress on the Spirit elsewhere. (There may have been latent different theologies of the church or of the way in which the Spirit inspires people.)

A little later in Rome, Hermas denied that certain who claimed to be prophets by foretelling the future were in fact true prophets: they are inspired by the devil and possess an earthly, vain spirit empty of any real power (*Mand.* 11).

In Asia Minor, the outbreak of Montanism produced fierce division. Catholic bishops did not deny that Montanus, Priscilla and Maximilla were inspired, but attributed their inspiration to the power of evil. In North Africa, Tertullian was to return the compliment and brand catholics as sensualists and denied them the possession of the Spirit. The example of Ignatius points in two directions. He claimed to be inspired by the Spirit when he involuntarily cried out 'Pay attention to the bishop and elders and deacons' (*Phld.* 7.1). Here the Spirit 'supports' the emergent institutional structure. But it is true that those who were in opposition to the bishop appear to be more judaistically inclined than Ignatius felt appropriate (5.2-6.2).

In a doctrinal dispute, one group may claim to have God's Spirit and, therefore, the truth, and deny God's Spirit to their opponents (Those who believed that they were inspired by the Spirit would naturally assume that they ought to have the leadership of a church). There are a number of examples of this in the literature which we have surveyed.

Within Syria, the Elder of the Johannine epistles encouraged his flock by assuring them that they and not the heretics possessed the Spirit and proffered tests by which to expose false inspiration and confirm true inspiration. The members of his congregation did not need a teacher: their anointing from God meant that they all had knowledge, whereas the opponents were anti-christs. In Asia Minor, the author of the Pastorals wanted reliable men to be appointed to ministerial office in order to ensure the preservation of the true tradition, and the indwelling Holy Spirit assists in this task of guarding the deposit (2 Tim. 1.14; 2.2), over against heretical perversions and falsifications. The heretics may have a form of religion, but lack its power. Jude denied the heretics the Spirit and branded them as unspiritual, while 2 Peter believed that as the Spirit moved the prophets to speak, so he guided the church's official teachers to interpret the OT scriptures in the contemporary scene. The author denied 'private' interpretation of the scriptures. He seems to link Spirit and Office.

Irenaeus in southern Gaul denied gnostic views about a threefold division of the human race into the hylics, who would never be saved, the psychikoi, who might be saved if they responded, and the elect, in whom dwelt the pneumatic seed, linking them 'by nature' to the divine pleroma above. For Irenaeus, the Spirit, who is active in creation and redemption, has been poured out on all believers, having first become accustomed to dwell in humanity through the incarnation.

Thus, at many points along the spectrum, the Spirit becomes the touchstone of whether a person is 'in' or 'out', whether a person belongs or is excluded, whether a person's views are acceptable or to be rejected. Possession of the Spirit and orthodoxy go hand in hand. Or, alternatively, possession of the Spirit and being cooperative with church leaders are synonymous. The Spirit becomes a 'bone of contention' in an inner-church struggle. From having been a hallmark of the church over against the world, the Spirit becomes the hallmark of the true church over against the false.

II.

Within the overall idea of the Spirit as a hallmark of the church over against the world, as something which should characterise believers, one of our major interests has been whether possession of the Spirit was something consciously felt, a sense of being encountered by the divine power from outside of oneself and enhancing one's existence, an experience which is not appropriately attributed to latent human powers but comes from God (= our section A, *Divine Presence*). We probed behind language and concepts used to the religious experience underlying them. We have assumed that the use of a certain type of language is wedded to a certain type of religious experience. Someone who has undergone a certain type of religious experience finds it natural to use certain phrases. Thus, the dramatic conversion may be described as 'seeing the light', 'born again', 'my chains fell off', 'the dungeon flamed with light' (a glance at the hymn book of any Christian denomination reveals the type of language we have in mind). Of course, language can become traditional and repeated as a matter of habit and inheritance, which the group expects to hear it. Yet careful reading of a text will usually or often disclose whether the language has become ossified or whether genuine experience suffuses it.

The evidence for a continuing experience of the Spirit is 'patchy'. Thus, the Johannine communities of Syria at the beginning of our period seem to have had a strong awareness of the Spirit who is present as 'the Friend from Court', teaching and guiding them, while the roughly contemporary Pastoral Epistles from Asia

Minor reflect a growing institutionalism and credalisation of the faith, with less stress on the Spirit's help.

Around the middle of the century, we have the spiritual exuberance of the *Odes of Solomon* (Syria) and the prosaic moralism of *2 Clement* (Corinth?). Later, both Justin and Irenaeus attest the continuing existence of miraculous healings and exorcisms, and prophecy and speaking with tongues. Justin was a widely travelled man, while Irenaeus had been brought up in Asia Minor, knew something of Rome and ministered in southern Gaul. While Montanism may have had special features (e.g., a stress on ecstasy), it would be erroneous to see it as an isolated phenomenon as if there were no manifestations of prophecy or inspired speaking either during the decades before its emergence or contemporaneous with it.

At the end of our period, the North African congregations clearly contained within them men and women who experienced dreams, visions and revelations, which they felt came to them from the Spirit. However, the editor of the *Passion of Perpetua and Felicitas* was clearly attempting to combat a viewpoint which saw the Spirit as present in power in the past rather than in the present. Thus, there was a difference of opinion and experience in the churches of that area.

Unfortunately we do not possess much evidence from Egypt. Clement of Alexandria's type of Christianity was probably not typical, and we do not possess documents which let us glimpse the experience of more 'popular' Christianity. The excerpts from the writings of the Valentinian theologian, Theodotus, which we possess, suggest that people like him had had a life-changing experience, but the 'grid' by which they interpreted it led them away from what was deemed acceptable to the developing 'great church'. Thus, there is variety and diversity over our period.

Within any given geographical area, there is not a picture of a uniform experience (as later an Antiochene and an Alexandrine emphasis in theological thinking emerged; or an east/west division).

In Syria, the evidence points to a continuing experience of the Spirit over our period, in the Johannine communities, Ignatius, the Odes of Solomon and Tatian. Yet, even here, the *Didache*, with its evidence that 'the first fine careless rapture' was not being maintained and that respect for itinerant prophets claiming the Spirit's inspiration was tempered by the recognition of the need to test their claim (so that this third generation writing did what Paul had had to do at Corinth in the first), rubs shoulders with the *Odes of Solomon*, while Matthew seems to have had an even deeper suspicion of the charismatic miracle worker-prophet than the *Didache*. If Ignatius was himself a charismatic bishop, his overall emphasis is on the institutional side as a way of preserving unity and doctrinal purity: he believes that all Christians have the Spirit, but they must submit to and obey the bishop. If Matthew's Gospel and Ignatius represent Antioch, the Johannine congregations and those within which the *Odes of Solomon* originated may come from eastern Syria. The *Didache* may represent the situation among rural congregations, which depended on itinerant prophets, though were now beginning to move to an established ministry of their own.

Again, a uniform picture does not emerge from Asia Minor. The Spirit-inspired seer, John of Patmos, seems an unusual figure amidst the growing trend towards institutionalism as exemplified by the Pastorals, Jude and 2 Peter. Yet *Barnabas* seems to reflect a spirituality in which the Spirit is experienced as recreating, cleansing power and Christians are seen as a temple of God whose Spirit indwells them. Montanism thus came on the scene in an area where the threefold ministry had established itself. Although in public disputations the catholic bishops were not preeminently successful, they produced a stream of literature: Apolinarius of Hierapolis, Miltiades (*HE* 5.17.1), Apollonius (*HE* 5.18.1) and the anonymous anti-Montanist (*HE* 5.16.2). Labriolle felt that the church in Asia Minor was not so mediocre as the Montanists made out, and that it exhibited a certain moral rigorism rather than worldliness.[1]

It is interesting that when Miltiades traced a prophetic succession from NT times, those whom he mentions outside the NT era are associated with Asia Minor: the daughters of Philip (at least they moved there, according to Eusebius in *HE* 3.31.3-4; 3.39.9; 5.24.1-2), Quadratus and Amnia in Philadelphia (*HE* 5.17.1-2); while Polycrates, bishop of Ephesus, in his letter to Victor of Rome, mentioned Melito as one who lived entirely 'in the Holy Spirit'. Certainly, if Polycarp is in any way typical, the Asia Minor churches were well served. Although absolute certainty is impossible because of the fragmentary nature of our sources, Montanist attacks on the catholic bishops of Asia Minor probably were not completely fair (just as the reverse was true). Westwards at Rome, Clement and Hermas represent very different types of spirituality, the one rational, sober, orderly, and the other more enthusiastic and charismatic. With hindsight we may say that Clement was to be the more typical of the future, though the *Shepherd of Hermas* remained very popular for some considerable time after its composition. Justin taught at Rome for perhaps fifteen years, and it seems from his writings that the Spirit was not a negligible factor in the life of Christians. If the *Gospel of Truth* represents teaching which was heard at Rome, whether Valentinus is the author or not, then certainly the experience of God plays an important role in the writer's life, though this is not prominently defined in terms of the Spirit.

Irenaeus, leader of the churches in southern Gaul, gives the impression of a Christianity in which the Spirit undergirds all aspects. The Spirit was not an intellectual abstraction, but experienced as a living, envigorating power. There is no Christian or Church without the Spirit. The idea of Christians bearing the Spirit within them means for Irenaeus that believers are conscious of the Spirit's presence and help. To receive the Spirit is to know God and experience His adoption and the privilege of addressing Him as Abba-Father. The *Letter* from the congregations of Lyons and Vienne confirms that vitality and strength of the experiential side of the life of Christians as seen theologically in Irenaeus. Here, then, we meet congregations whose sense of the Spirit's nearness, leading and power enabled them

---

[1] De Labriolle, *Crise*, pp. 136-38.

to face persecution and yet also avoid the extremes of a severe and unatttractive fanaticism.

Most of our North African evidence comes from a pro-Montanist source, Tertullian, and so it is not surprising that there should be a stress on the Spirit. We have seen how Tertullian began by asssuming that all Christians received the Spirit, though he later restricted this experience to those who accepted the New Prophecy and its ethical directives. He gives a vivid picture of the experiences of a Christian sister in ecstasy during which she received revelations from the Spirit, and he also reports the prophetic utterances of Priscilla and Maximilla.

The editor of the *Passion of Perpetua and Felicitas*, whether a Montanist or not, was troubled by the fact that some Christians believed that the Spirit was only active in past periods, which suggests that they were not conscious of the presence and power of the Spirit in their lives.

When we turn to Egypt, we only have Clement of Alexandria who represents a highly intellectual, rational type of faith, which, nonetheless, affirms very strongly that Christians do possess the Spirit. His ideal is freedom from passions of an evil sort into a calm, immovable state based on contemplation of the Divine and nearness to God.

There is, then, variety and diversity within a given area. Mere geographical proximity does not ensure similarity of religious experience. Perhaps this is what we might have expected a priori.

III.

We turn to pose the question whether within our sources we can observe different types of experience, though claimed as stemming from the same Spirit, or similar types of experience, but which are interpreted by their recipients in a manner doctrinally unacceptable to others. We shall look at three possible examples drawn from the *Shepherd of Hermas*, Valentinian Gnosticism and Montanism.

Was Hermas describing different types of experience when he examined the true and false prophets? Or did the two types of prophets have similar types of experience, but, in the case of the false prophets, they debased them by the use to which they put them (namely, by fortune telling to the personal profit of the prophet concerned)? In actual fact, Hermas does not expatiate on the actual experience[2] except to say that the false prophet is struck dumb when he enters the gathering of righteous people, whereas the true prophet 'finds voice' in such company. We may speculate how such people ever gained a reputation in the first place: it is clear that pagan practices have infiltrated the church, perhaps on the 'fringes' of the church, where church members of not very strong faith and some pagan enquirers whose understanding of the Christian faith was not very profound, 'rubbed shoulders'.[3]

---

[2] Reiling, *Hermas*, p. 93.

[3] Reiling, *Hermas*, p. 91, located this activity on the borderline between the church and the pagan world, and believed that Mandate 11 showed how easily prophecy could change into divination and assume pagan forms.

Within such types, a person might build up a coterie of followers and win a reputation for fortune telling, while at the same time being paid for 'services rendered'.

Thus, milieu seems all-important: within their own 'group' and within the company of righteous people. We are not told, however, what the false prophet did when enquiries were made: did he induce some trance-like state or did he possess some mechanical means to aid fortune-telling?

Since the true prophet speaks involuntarily, i.e., when the Lord wills, and not when humans wish, we may assume that there was some sense of inner compulsion in his case. The true prophet spoke because he could not do anything else.

Thus, we may conclude that, if Hermas was being fair to the two types of prophets, we are dealing with basically different experiences in *Mandate* 11. At least, on his view, they were different.

Next, we turn to Valentinian Gnosticism. Here we use the *Gospel of Truth* as an indicator of the type of personal experience involved. We are on more solid ground than in the discussion on *Mandate* 11, since this work represents the author's own views and not someone else's about him (whether the author was Valentinus or a pupil of his is, therefore, at this point unimportant). We notice that the questions are more man-centred: Who am I? Where have I come from? etc., and not Where is God? How do I find Him? How can I be right with Him? Though these questions are anthropologically centred, we cannot rule out such questions as illegitimate simply because the canonical scriptures are predominantly theocentric.[4] But what people like Irenaeus objected-to was the interpretative framework imposed on the experience. No doubt as a church leader Irenaeus would have agreed that there were spiritually keen members of the church; some church members who were not deeply committed; and some men and women who seemed impervious to any spiritual matters. When, however, the Valentinians talked about a pleroma of thirty aeons, the passion of Sophia and the pneumatic seed and so on, Irenaeus resisted with all his vigour.

Though we cannot say with certainty, the spiritual experiences of some Valentinians may have been akin to 'orthodox' church members—a sense of peace, of being born again, of being enlightened and so on, but how these were explained was unacceptable to Irenaeus. Of course, there were bad Valentinians and (even allowing for exaggeration) some were no doubt morally lax or manipulated the feelings of others (see Irenaeus' description of Marcus). But there were also orthodox members who were guilty of moral laxity and financial dishonesty (for the latter, see the reference to an elder called Valens mentioned by Polycarp in his *Letter to the Philippians* 11.1-4).

Why did Irenaeus accept one conceptual framework or one 'grid' of tradition, while the Valentinians accepted another? We may, in the end, have to admit that we have not the evidence to answer this fully, but we can offer some suggestions. In the

---

[4] E.g. E. Schweizer, 'Two Early Creeds Compared', in W. Klassen and G.N. Snyder (eds.), *New Testament Issues Today* (London: SCM, 1962), pp. 166-77, convincingly showed that the questions behind 1 Cor. 15.3-5 and 1 Tim. 3.16 were very different and reflected the different cultural milieux in which these two creeds originated.

first place, what Irenaeus charged Marcus with was deluding wealthy women, who enriched him with monetary gifts (*AH* 1.13). While one must be careful about using standard anti-heretical smear tactics, this may afford us a hint: were there sociological factors for some conversions to Valentinian Gnosticism? Social position and wealth were bolstered by the thought of being among the spiritually elite.[5] Certainly, the abstruseness of Valentinian speculation would need a fair degree of education and intelligence to master.

Secondly, it is clear that many Valentinians continued to be within the catholic church and wanted to remain there. Did Valentinus' failure to become bishop at Rome (so Tertullian) have any effect on his thinking? Were the second generation pushed into more extreme speculation because of factors like that or other factors?

Thirdly, the syncretistic nature of Gnosticism, in which 'unchristian' elements are mingled with 'Christian' ones, forces us to ask whether there were certain types of people to whom syncretism would be almost 'natural'?

Finally, we might mention that the difficulties which some people experienced with the OT might be a factor in inducing them to turn to a form of Gnosticism.

Some or all of these considerations may have played some part in disposing one thinker to go along one plane of thought, and another along a totally different plane; for one to remain loyally within the parameters of an inherited tradition and for another to venture off into a different terrain of thought.

Finally, we turn to Montanism. In our discussion, we saw that, while there was some sort of ecstatic condition involved, the actual oracles were uttered in rational, intelligible language. No point of doctrine was involved, and the early Montanists were doctrinally orthodox. Why, then, were they branded by the catholics as inspired by evil spirits? The experience per se does not seem to have been unusual, since prophecy and glossolalia had occurred in NT times; Justin argued that prophetic gifts still remained in the church of his day (*Dial.* 82) and he also stressed the passivity of the prophet when inspired; Irenaeus knew of prophecy and inspired speech in the churches (*AH* 5.6.1). But the mode of the experience did become an issue at the heart of the controversy. The catholics turned the stress on ecstasy against the Montanists and denied that ecstasy was an inseparable accompaniment of true prophecy (e.g. Miltiades wrote a treatise with the thesis that a prophet need not speak 'in ecstasy', *HE* 5.17).

---

[5] Green, *Origins*, pp. 173, 190, 210, 262, sees disenfranchised intellectual Alexandrian Jews as the catalyst for the *origins* of Gnosticism. What was the appeal of Gnosticism, once launched, in *other* areas of the Mediterranean world? P. Lampe, *Christen*, pp. 251-68 (*Christians at Rome*, pp. 292-318), while rejecting the Weber-Kippenberg theory that gnostics were intellectuals and members of the socially privileged strata, recognised that in Rome some intellectual gnostics became world-denying because as Christians they could no longer be politically active, but that the Valentinian doctrine would help to restore the self-worth of the Christian intellectual and wealthy and help maintain the sense of being an elite.

The rift came[6] about for a number of reasons. The Asia Minor bishops resented the personal attacks on their supposed lack of spirituality (cf. *HE* 5.16.9), and they considered the claims of Montanus, Priscilla and Maximilla to be the mouthpiece of the Paraclete as objectionable (*HE* 5.14). They believed that it was blasphemous of the Montanists to want to add to the precepts of Jesus (*HE* 5.18.5) and found offensive Themiso's composition of 'a general letter' (5.18.5). Later, in the third century, Origen argued in his commentary on 1 Corinthians that women had no right to teach in public, but that does not seem to be present in what the second century catholic opponents brought up against the movement (at least as reported by Eusebius in *HE* 5.14-19).

There was a struggle for the nature of the church, and the bishops in the end succeeded in driving the Montanists out of the church.

If we confined ourselves to the first four arguments mentioned above, none of these is strictly speaking theologically grounded. The first is personal as is the second, since, from the earliest days of the church, men and women had been regarded as the mouthpiece of the Spirit. Similarly, the third seems to be of the same nature, once one accepts that the Gospel tradition had been augmented and adapted and shaped to meet the ongoing needs of the churches, and once one takes into consideration that a writing like *The Shepherd* enjoyed wide popularity. The fourth again invites the same comment: writings like *The Shepherd* or *Epistula Apostolorum* were intended for wide circulation.

We are driven to acknowledge that there were personality factors in the case of Montanism. This would be comparable to Paul's dispute with the Judaisers, where we could surmise that not only did cultural factors become involved with points of theology (adherence to the Law, circumcision, etc., with belief in Jesus as messiah), but that these may have been exacerbated by personal ones (e.g. Paul's temperament). Paul claimed that there existed theological unanimity between himself and Jerusalem (1 Cor. 15.11), yet he knew that he was mistrusted by the congregation there (Rom. 15.30-31). When Luke told how the church had settled the issue of the admission of Gentiles to the church, he stressed that Peter had been deeply impressed that the Gentiles had received the same Spirit as Jewish believers (Acts 10–11; 15). Yet even Luke had to acknowledge that, though the Spirit had been given to Gentile believers, some Jewish Christian refused to accept that this was enough (Acts 15.1), and that Paul, though a chosen vessel of the Lord and vouched for by devout men like Ananias and Barnabas (Acts 9.15-18, 27), was suspect in the eyes of many Jerusalem Christians (Acts 21.20-22).

To return to our survey, we have looked at three groups of people who claimed to have the Spirit of God (or to be inspired or possessed of oracular powers): those whom Hermas calls false prophets, the Valentinian Gnostics and the Montanists. The historian may legitimately conclude on the basis of what Hermas said that the false prophets of *Mandate* 11 did not have an experience of God's Spirit comparable with the true prophet; whereas it is conceivable that the best representatives of

---

[6] Labriolle, *Crise*, pp. 131-43.

Valentinian Gnosticism had spiritual experiences not necessarily dissimilar to many who held orthodox views, but that their interpretation of these experiences proved unacceptable. The Montanists' stress on ecstasy cannot be said to be unheard-of or unique, but other factors led to their being condemned by the catholic bishops.

Thus, in two out of the three samples, it does not seem that the type of experience per se was the root cause of division: rather, it was the interpretation placed on it that aroused opposition. In the case of Montanism, the opposition then seized on the mode of experience as a handle with which to undermine the influence of the new prophets.

This conclusion can fit in with general observations, for it is clear that people are both shaped by their experiences and in turn shape their experiences. On the one hand, our experiences may often have a profound affect on us and shape our approach to life. Thus, conversion to Christianity, the sense of receiving a new awareness of the presence and power of what is described as the Spirit of God, may produce a different lifestyle or a changed personality (e.g., more loving and gentle, less selfish than before) or a change of career, resulting from a new sense of vocation. All that would not be denied. But, on the other hand, the kind of person we are or have become may exert a determining influence on the type of experience to which we are open. Some types of people are more susceptible to certain types of experience. Furthermore, the person who has experienced a dramatic conversion often may not be able to understand the person who has not undergone such an experience and dismiss them as unspiritual. Training in what is often termed academic theology may produce a rift between what the person has become and his or her previous background. That is, their ongoing experience has produced a changed outlook or modified their approach to life, and they may have moved away from the circle of previously accepted assumptions. To hold office in the church for a lengthy period also may exert its influence in this way and act as a conditioning for the way we expect to experience God through the Spirit.

These general considerations agree with the particular examples which we have surveyed. They serve to back up the difference between 'experience' and the 'interpretation of experience' which, we have suggested, emerges from our study.

IV.

In all three cases, the implications of the alleged experience passed from the sphere of the individual into the corporate life of the church: the false prophets of *Mandate* 11 were influencing some church members; Valentinus or his followers were teaching a version of Christianity and making followers; Montanism attempted to lead the church in a certain direction. The church was forced to test and evaluate.

The validity of a claim to be inspired was a notoriously difficult one to evaluate and had had a long history. It vexed Israel in connection with prophecy, as, for example, Deuteronomy 13.1-11; 1 Kings 13.22; Isaiah 28.7-8; Micah 3.5-12; Jeremiah 27–28 amply show; and it was a problem in earliest Christianity. Paul enunciated tests to measure the claim: a confessional one (Jesus is Lord), a behavioural one (love and a Christ-like pattern of dying to self and rising to new life) and an ecclesiological one (building up the church), none of which centred on the experience itself but on its discernible effects, both in the life of the individual and the congregation (see 1 Cor. 12.3, 10; 14.12, 29; 1 Thess. 5.19-22; 2 Thess. 2.1-2), while the Synoptic tradition contains warnings against false prophets (Mk. 13.5-6, 21-23) who may be unmasked by the type of message which they proclaim (self-claims as part of the proclamation of the approaching End).

In our period, the problem surfaces again and again, and it is interesting to observe the type of tests which various writers draw up:

Matthew 7.13-23: behaviour ('fruits'), doing God's will.

Didache 11–12: disseminating false teaching; not stopping long in one place; asking for money, behaviour, etc.

Revelation 2.20: association with idolatry and immorality.

1 John 4.1-21: doctrinal test (incarnation) and behaviour (love).

Ignatius: doctrine, behaviour (too Jewish or lack of care for the needy), obedience to the bishop and elders.

Hermas: the people among whom the prophet functions; whether he responds to human requests or inner-divine-compulsion; character and conduct.

Montanism: some criticism (fair or unfair) of the character and conduct of Montanist leaders; plus the argument that prophets did not have to be in ecstasy in order to prophesy.

With the partial exception of the very last of these, none of the other tests proposed really centre on the actual experience itself. Thus, no one says that someone must feel certain emotional stirrings within. The tests proposed are external ones: subscription to doctrine; character; conduct; relation to church authorities and the congregation; practical tests like attitude to money, hospitality. Tertullian seems unique in arguing for ecstasy as a component part of prophecy. In this general approach, then, second century Christianity followed the pattern set by Paul.

V.

We have already seen how the idea of possession of the Spirit was intertwined on occasions with disputes over different interpretations of the Christian faith. We suggested that this was an extension of the original belief that Christians as the messiah's people and the new people of God had received the Spirit of God. A blend of Joel 2.28-32 and Jeremiah 31.31-34 would, of course, produce the conviction that the Spirit mediated the presence of God and inscribed the knowledge of His will on the human heart.

The link between the Spirit and a sense of illumination, being guided into possession of the truth, an awareness of God's will, a feeling of a deepening of one's knowledge of spiritual things (= B: *Divine Illumination*, throughout our study), can be found in our period. This may take various forms, and once more we have to be prepared to ask whether writers were so convinced that their interpretation was the correct one that they argued that, *therefore*, it was given by the Spirit. Perhaps it is

Clement of Alexandria who in our period claims illumination most insistently, though there is little direct link up with the Spirit in his writings, and he emphasizes study and contemplation, rather than sudden illumination attributed to the Spirit.

Arguably, there are five facets of the Spirit's ministry in this respect. Firstly, Scripture can be understood now through the Spirit. Barnabas expounds the OT scriptures in a pneumatic way. He claims that the Lord has circumcised his hearing and heart that he might understand the truth concealed in the scriptures (10.12). This circumcision of hearing and heart is probably an allusion to the work of the Spirit. Barnabas contrasts his exegesis of the OT with the erroneous way of interpreting it by the Jews. They took literally what God meant figuratively all along. There is a polemical thrust even if Barnabas is not in his writing expressly combating Jewish teachers.

Much the same can be said of Justin, whose *Dialogue with Trypho* claims that the OT is only properly understood if referred to Jesus and the church. Among the gifts of the Spirit are those of understanding, counsel, foreknowledge and teaching, and within this array it is legitimate to see the capacity to understand the OT. Clearly, Justin believed that his interpretation is 'correct', while Trypho is in error.

2 Peter believed that as the Spirit originally inspired prophecy, so he inspired the official teachers to interpret it (and not private individuals).

Clement of Alexandria was also convinced that the gift of the Spirit enabled Christians to understand the sense of the OT scriptures.

Secondly, the truth has been given in Jesus Christ, but there is need to understand it better and more fully by the help of the Spirit. This is particularly the approach of the Fourth Gospel (Jn. 14.26; 16.12-15): the Spirit takes the things of Christ and proclaims them to the disciples. He teaches by reminding disciples of what Jesus said and helping them to understand it. The Paraclete sayings may well be the evangelist's defence of what he has done in his Gospel: an interpretation that draws out of the tradition what was implicit in it. Thus, there is both freedom (reinterpretation of the tradition) and control (a basic fidelity to the tradition). This emphasis has not been totally ignored by the Elder of 1 and 2 John, for, while he says that his readers have received an anointing (= the Spirit), who teaches them about everything so that they do not need anyone to teach them (1 Jn. 2.27), this assertion has certainly been strongly balanced by the command to adhere to what they had been originally taught.

For Irenaeus the Spirit of God 'furnishes us with a knowledge of the truth' and it is he who 'has set forth the dispensations of the Father and the Son' (*AH* 4.33.7). He too knows the blend of freedom and control, the latter being the church's Rule of Faith, the apostolic faith, which is adhered-to by the churches everywhere.

Tertullian believed that one of the Paraclete's task was 'the revelation of the scriptures', i.e. the NT, and that meant for him particularly ethical matters, for he was in the fourth age, the era of the Paraclete, the time of maturity. Accordingly, Tertullian grappled with the interpretation of dominical and Pauline statements, and sought to interpret them in terms of a more rigorist demand, for this was what the Paraclete was now saying to the church.

In the third place, the truth has been given and there cannot be any additions. We must preserve what we have been given. This is a feature of the post-apostolic era, for that epoch faced the problem of preserving the true apostolic proclamation amidst the welter of rival interpretations.

This strand appears in the Johannine Epistles: the Spirit is the teacher of Christians, but he has already given them the truth in what they heard from the beginning and they must abide or continue in it. In the Pastorals, Jude and 2 Peter, there is a similar emphasis on the tradition, the faith once for all delivered to the saints. The idea of reinterpretation seems foreign. The stress is holding on to the truth in which they are already established. The Spirit's task in the Pastorals is to aid ministers to preserve the Pauline tradition, and, by implication, in 2 Peter, to refute those who twist not only the OT but also Paul's letters.

Irenaeus often wrote in a similar vein, because of the need to combat gnostic reinterpretations of the gospel and apostolic preaching. The Spirit leads believers/the church to certainty about the teaching which is enshrined in the scriptures and which has been handed down from the apostles in the various congregations of the one church throughout the whole world. Tertullian spoke of the new prophecy, but did not believe that the Paraclete brought new doctrinal revelations, while for Clement of Alexandria adherence to the apostolic faith was essential and the Spirit's illuminating activity did not infringe that.

Fourthly, the understanding of God's will for a specific situation. Here John of Patmos claimed to be God's messenger to the churches in what he believed would be the hour of trial about to burst over the whole world. Hermas believed that the true prophet spoke as God willed, within the believing congregation and that he personally had been given a message from God about a second repentance before the approaching End. Justin attests that prophetical gifts were still present in the church (*Dial.* 82.1). Montanus and the prophetesses, Priscilla and Maximilla, believed that they were the mouthpiece of God and the Paraclete, burdened with a message for the church of their day. Tertullian agreed with this, and his later writings stridently affirm that the New Prophecy ought to be heeded and Christians should follow the Paraclete's directives and eschew second marriages, embrace the opportunity of repentance, discipline the body and refuse a second repentance to flagrant sinners. The Paraclete was now imposing sterner measures.

Irenaeus is also a witness to the presence of prophecy in southern Gaul (e.g. *AH* 5.6.1; 3.17.1). Prophets bring to light the hidden things of people and declare the mysteries of God.

Both the *Letter of the churches at Lyons and Vienne* and the *Passion of Perpetua and Felicitas* reveal a conviction that the Spirit may impart a revelation of God's will. In the former, Attalus received a revelation to persuade Alcibiades to give up a too rigorist lifestyle; in the latter, Perpetua is led through two visions to a realization that martyrdom awaits her, while through other visions she sees her dead brother and is led to pray for him.

Finally, in the gnostic experience of conversion, believers are led from a sense of alienation and purposelessness to a knowledge of their true self: who they are, where they are from, and what their true destiny is. The *Gospel of Truth* portrays this as like an awakening from sleep, the coming-to after the stupor of drunkenness, the emergence from the terrors of a nightmare and the realization of how all the terrors and fears were groundless. Just occasionally, the *Gospel of Truth* links this experience of conversion with the work of the Spirit, though it does not appear that the Spirit plays a prominent role in this document. This type of experience was linked, as we have seen, with a theology which was unacceptable to catholic thought and belief.

By contrast, Clement of Alexandria, who also expressed the idea that to know oneself was to know God, might be described as an orthodox Christian gnostic who sought to remain loyal to what was held to be the apostolic faith within the mainstream catholic tradition.

VI.

The evidence that Christians in the period under review were aware of the help and power of the Spirit, enabling them to live better and more Christ-like lives varies, but on the whole there seems less holding together of the ethical demand and the Spirit's help than is characteristic of Paul in the first generation (= C: *Divine Power*, throughout our study).

In Syria, the Johannine Epistles linked possession of the seed of God (= Spirit) and a sinless lifestyle and believed that God's indwelling power in the believer was greater than the power of evil in the world. Ignatius described the Holy Spirit as the rope which winches Christians into place as stones in God's temple, while another image describes Christians as carrying God and Christ around, rather as pagans carry their idols. Obedience to Christ's commands is the garment that adorns Christians, who are πνευματικοὶ who cannot do the things of the flesh. Helped by the Spirit, they live for God within the fleshly realm.

Concurrently with this, we have the approach of the *Didache* and Matthew. Ethical lapses by charismatic persons have led to either a cautious or hostile view towards prophecy. If the *Didache* takes over and shapes a Jewish Two Ways ethical teaching, it does not interpolate references to the Spirit's help. Matthew nearly sets obedience to God's commands over against charismatic activity in 7.15-23. He does, however, set ethical teaching forth as a consequence of the proclamation of the Kingdom of God by Jesus.

Within the *Odes of Solomon*, there are a few ethical references, some mentioning the Spirit, others not doing so. The genre of the work, however, does not lend itself so readily to ethical discussion. Clearly, however, the Odist envisages a holy lifestyle resulting from commitment to Christ and the experience of the Spirit. If Tatian uses the picture of the soul, bereft of the Spirit, going astray into idolatry and of conversion as recovering hidden treasure which needs to be cleaned up because of its long involvement in the material, the implication is that the Christian lifestyle resulting from receiving the Spirit will be a morally pure and holy one.

In Asia Minor, we noted the tendency not to hold together the ethical imperative and the divine help to fulfil the demands laid upon Christians (2 Peter, Barnabas, Polycarp), though the two elements are there. Similarly, in Montanism there appears to be an ethical strictness and a sterner approach to discipline, but no mention in extant sources of the Spirit's gracious assistance and power to help the weak progress along the Christlike way.

Rome represents a mixture. 1 Peter speaks about Christians offering 'sacrifices' produced by the Spirit, while Clement stresses Christian morality but does not mention the Spirit as the powerhouse of Christian living. Hermas, who is concerned with the question of post-baptismal repentance and forgiveness, knows of the strength supplied by the Spirit, but equally seems to have introduced the idea of the 'delicacy' of the Spirit who retreats from a person when confronted by evil, and thus abandons that person. Here the emphasis seems to be the preservation of the *Spirit's* purity rather than people's purity.

Ethics are not the dominant concern where Justin speaks about the Spirit. The *Gospel of Truth* is concerned mainly with the experience of the call or conversion, though Valentinus (according to Clement of Alexandria (*Strom.* 2.20) referred to the ethical transformation of the gnostic: evil spirits are banished, the Father visits and sanctifies the heart, and hence the gnostic will see God. But this idea is not touched upon by the *Gospel of Truth.*

It is Irenaeus in southern Gaul, who of all the writers in the second century seems to be closest to the Pauline view of the Spirit as undergirding the Christian's ethical life. For him, the experience of the Spirit leads to a newness of life. The Spirit is power and lifts our weakness up and forward along Christ's way, enabling us to grow spiritually and bear ethical fruit for God. The Spirit works the Father's will in us and restores God's image and likeness in us. The Spirit is active from creation through redemption to consummation as one of 'God's hands', the Word being the other hand.

Tertullian in North Africa confirmed the impression, gained from a study of Asia Minor Montanism, of charismatic legalism. He does speak of the Spirit's aid and strength occasionally, but the dominant impression is of the duty of fulfilling the high ethical demands imposed by the Paraclete. Tertullian (like Ephesians) has the idea of grieving the Spirit and (like Hermas) the concept of the delicacy of the Spirit, who will desert an uncongenial abode. Christianity is often described in terms of self-help, and the note of pastoral help and encouragement seems lacking. There is, then, in Tertullian plenty of demand, but little of grace or assistance.

Occasionally, Clement of Alexandria mentions the help of the Spirit, but he does not develop this with any consistency. His emphasis on reason as a force for stability, to overcome the ruinous effects of passion, was no doubt a factor inhibiting such a development.

We are forced to ask whether this widespread failure to hold together grace and demand, power and command, Spirit and ethics, is linked to the varied picture obtained from our survey of religious experience per se. The link between the two would not be surprising. Where a deep sense of the presence and power of the Spirit has been experienced, it would be natural to translate that into daily living and moral victory. Where there is no sense of the Spirit's indwelling, there would always be the possibility of seeing Christianity in moralistic terms without the divine help to live out such an ideal. But clearly this cannot be pressed too far, as Montanism and Tertullian reveal.

VII.

Finally, we touch on a question which seems to push itself to the fore more sharply from material towards the end of the second century. Was there in the period under review any shift in understanding the nature of the Spirit as God's power *ab extra*, towards the Spirit's becoming (as it were) an integral part of a human being's makeup? Is there a shift away from the Spirit's residing in a person (yet always remaining God's Spirit and never a person's to control) to an ontological view of a human being as body-soul-spirit/Spirit (in which it might be difficult to distinguish human spirit and divine Spirit)? Is there an anthropologization of the Spirit?

Yet, on the other hand, we must be careful not to exaggerate the differences between these two perspectives. A glance at the literature from Syria warns us to be cautious. John's Gospel speaks of the Spirit's residing in the believer and yet the strongly personal traits of the Paraclete-Spirit are well-known and need not be rehearsed here. We have also seen that the experiential awareness of the Spirit is assumed in John. Without the Spirit, the disciples would be like helpless orphans without protection in a hostile world; without him, they would be incomplete and his coming leads the work of salvation to its culmination.[7]

Ignatius frequently uses flesh and spirit in connection with believers[8] and also (though to a lesser extent) Jesus.[9] When at Smyrnaeans 12.2 he describes Jesus' resurrection as both fleshly and spiritual, he cannot be referring to the Holy Spirit, as such an idea would be inconceivable. In other words, 'flesh and spirit' is a description of the whole person.[10] In the case of Jesus, the phrase underlines his true and full humanity, while for believers it denotes what one might call the outer and inner aspects of a person. For Ignatius this inner side of the Christian has been brought to a new dimension, because the Christian is born of and belongs to the Spirit, and the Spirit is 'the rope' which hoists Christians into place in the building which is God's temple. Thus, it would probably be wise to allow for some

---

[7] Cf. the overall thesis of W.H. Cadman, *The Open Heaven* (ed. G.B. Caird; Oxford: Blackwell, 1966).

[8] *Eph.* 10.3; *Mag*.1.2; 13.1-2; *Trall. insc.* 12.1; *Rom. insc.*; *Smyrn.* 13.2; *Pol.* 1.2.

[9] *Eph.* 7.2; *Mag.* 1.2.

[10] Schoedel, *Ignatius*, pp. 23-24, discusses Ignatius' use of flesh and spirit. He comments: 'It is characteristic of Ignatius to speak of unity in terms of polarities...that together serve to express totality... One of the most important of these polarities is that of "flesh" and "spirit"...' (p. 23).

oscillation in the phrase 'flesh and spirit', i.e., the inner side of the Christian is what it is because the Christian is indwelt by the Spirit. Clearly, however, those who are born of the Spirit have to live in the flesh and should act in a spiritual manner. But we have seen also how the Spirit came upon Ignatius and inspired him to speak in a particular way which exceeded the bounds of his own knowledge. Thus, ideas of inspiration and indwelling coexist in what he writes.

Likewise, in the *Odes of Solomon*, we have language which, while speaking of the Spirit's residing within believers (e.g. *Ode* 28), also speaks of the Spirit as acting upon them, lifting them to heaven (36.1-2), imparting the 'milk' of spiritual nourishment (19.5), and inspiring the composition of Odes (6.1-2; 14.7-8; 16.5-7), etc.

Tatian clearly has a tripartite view of the redeemed person: such a person is body-soul-Spirit. However, it must be noticed that he speaks of the Spirit as being originally the soul's companion (13.2), but as leaving the soul when the latter refused to follow the Spirit. When reunited with the Spirit, the soul 'mounts to realms above where the Spirit leads it' (13.2) or the believer is the temple indwelt by the Spirit of God (15.2). Reunited with the Spirit, a person becomes what they once were ('his ancient kinship' 20.3).

It seems difficult to say that Tatian has completely ontologized the Spirit, when he can use the idea of the Spirit's being a companion of the soul and leaving the soul. A person is not perfect without the Spirit, but the Spirit controls that person, not vice versa.

There is certainly no evidence for any shift in extant literature from Asia Minor. At the end of our period, the Montanist prophets were passive recipients of ecstatic experiences: the Spirit came upon them and they claimed that they did not control the Spirit. As Maximilla remarked, she was *compelled* to speak, whether she wished to or not.

The evidence from Rome is more instructive. On the one hand, there is Hermas. He sees a person's flesh as a vessel for the Spirit to dwell in. So a person is flesh-Holy Spirit.

We have seen the strands in Hermas which envisage the Spirit in different ways. The Spirit is like a deposit to be returned to God (*Mand.* 3.2), which may be diminished, spoilt or contaminated by Christians (*Sim.* 9.32); or as delicate and either forced to flee before evil as something which is uncongenial and restrictive, or crushed by human sorrow, angry temper or double-mindedness (*Mand.* 5, 10). The first envisages the Spirit as something static, almost a thing; whereas the second sees the Spirit at least as personal, for he can be upset, worn out or crushed or feel restricted.

Perhaps it is significant that in the first strand Hermas is using illustrations, a deposit or a garment. In pursuing the moral implications of our receiving God's Spirit, Hermas has in all probability pushed too far his illustration and ended up by implying that God's Spirit could be changed into a lying spirit. We believe that this can explain the statements which meet us especially in *Mandates* 3 and 10:[11] thus, in *Mandate* 3.1, Hermas speaks about the Spirit whom God made to dwell in our flesh (parallel to saying that the Lord dwells in us); in 3.2 he speaks about our receiving 'the Spirit who is free from falsehood' (πνεῦμα ἄψευστον) from God and how some Christians have returned 'the Spirit marred by falsehood' (πνεῦμα ψευδὲς); in 3.4 the servant of God is warned that the Spirit of truth has no complicity with evil. Also, *Mandate* 10.3.2 speaks of the sad person's grieving the Holy Spirit given to them because the Spirit is cheerful. The Spirit wants to produce cheerfulness, but the sad person has thwarted his efforts. *Similitude* 9, as we saw, can speak of various holy spirits and can personify the virtues produced by the one Holy Spirit as virgins (9.13.2; 9.15.1-2).

We have earlier had occasion to comment on the fact that Hermas is not a systematic theologian, and that is apparent in this area of ethical teaching. Hermas can move from speaking of God's Spirit to the human spirit or speak of holy spirits. Yet equally *Mandate* 11 on true and false prophecy emphasizes the power of God which lies outside of human manipulation or control and which works in sovereign freedom.

On the other hand, we have Valentinus and his followers. It is when we come to them that we encounter the idea of the divine pneumatic seed within the elect, which constitutes that person's essence. Although training is necessary, the elect will be saved and ultimately the pneumatic seed will be united with its angelic partner. We believe that Hauschild is right when he said that the concept of election has been ontologised, though we would want to argue for some experience, some sense of the divine presence, which has to be taken to be an assurance of election. The Pneuma is a substance or part of a person. Even here there is need of a call to reveal to the gnostics that they do in fact possess the pneumatic seed and that their real self comes from on high. They are among the elect and of the same substance with the Divine, but their true self comes *ab extra* and their present state is that of strangers in a foreign land and their destiny is to be reunited with the divine world above.

Turning to southern Gaul, we find that for Irenaeus the true, perfect person is body-soul-Holy Spirit. The Holy Spirit became accustomed to dwell in humanity through the incarnation, and then the Spirit was poured out on all believers, and thus they are in turn prepared for the ultimate vision of God and incorruption. Irenaeus uses 1 Corinthians 3.16 in an individual sense: the individual believer is a temple of God in which the Spirit of God dwells. The believer does not dispose of the Spirit; hence the idea of our *preserving* the Spirit by faith and pure conduct, which we do encounter occasionally in Irenaeus. We have seen, however, that there is ample evidence for assuming that experience of the Spirit as the life-giving power of God was something real and vivid for Irenaeus. Once again, we have to say that ideas of

---

[11] Lawson, *Introduction*, p. 239, went so far as to say on *Mandate* 5: 'It is characteristic of Hermas that he is vague in his conception of the Holy Spirit. The Spirit is here written of almost as though He were merely the higher side of man's natural faculties, rather than an empowering and indwelling divine Presence.' Cf. the comment made by Carolyn Osiek, which we quoted on p. 163.

inspiration/empowering and of indwelling are present in a Christian thinker and leader.

In North Africa, for Tertullian Christians are a temple of the Holy Spirit. The Spirit takes up his abode in us. He is wedded to the soul, and the flesh is part of the soul's bridal portion, while the soul communicates the gift of the Spirit to its habitation, the body. We meet (as in Hermas) the idea that the Spirit is tender and sensitive; hence we ought to live holy lives such as please the Spirit. Martyrs should not grieve the Spirit, but retain him so that he can lead them from prison through martyrdom to their Lord. Believers can shock the Spirit if they become impatient over the loss of something and give precedence to earthly above heavenly things, and he will leave them. So Tertullian's advice is to deny the flesh and the Christian will possess the Spirit. Fasting is a means of 'the Holy Spirit's ingress'.

Thus, like Tatian and Irenaeus, Tertullian sees the true person as body/flesh-soul-Holy Spirit, and there is no doubt that for him the Spirit is fully personal. But, as we saw earlier, there is a tendency in Tertullian to emphasize the moral duties of Christians without much corresponding stress on the power of the Spirit to help. In fact, we glean more of the experiential side of the Spirit from the small document *The Passion of Perpetua and Felicitas* than from Tertullian's writings.

Finally, we mention Clement of Alexandria, who sees the Christian as comprised of body/flesh plus soul (itself divided into the subject and the ruling spirit) plus the Holy Spirit. There is virtually no sense in Clement of ecstatic experience or invasion by the Spirit. With his stress on rationality, there is no room in Clement for the Spirit to blow like the wind where he wills. At the same time, he uses the language of friendship with the Lord through the Spirit and of entertaining God as a guest in spotless souls. This friendship is actualized at certain special moments (prayer, study, contemplation), but equally is something which ought to go on all the time, as the Christian gnostic progresses in detachment from passion and becomes more and more assimilated to God.

All in all, our brief survey leads us to bring a negative answer to the query of this last section. Clearly, in the second half of the second century, we are meeting writers whose basic presuppositions concerning human nature are different from those who come from a predominantly Hebraic-Jewish milieu. There is a greater assumption that a person is a body and soul. But, notwithstanding this, the inheritance from the earliest Christian tradition of a combination of the Spirit as power from on high and indwelling companion is not lost.

VIII.

We have come to the end of our survey which set out to examine how far the generations of the sub-apostolic era were consciously aware of the Holy Spirit and how far they describe their religious experience in terms of the Holy Spirit. Our conclusion must be that the truth lies somewhere between the impression created by the letters of Paul that true Christianity is the experience of the Spirit of Christ and the assumption made by many scholars that experiences of the Spirit were much rarer even by the end of the first century, never mind the second century. We may not live in the atmosphere of the Pauline letters, but, equally, we do not descend to the impoverished level painted by some. The literature surveyed leaves us with a variegated picture, and in that, at least, it probably reflects faithfully second century Christianity.

APPENDIX 1

Who were the Spiritual? A Second-Century Debate[1]

Because of the limits of time, I shall confine myself to three topics to illustrate my contention that quite a lively discussion went on in the second century on the issue 'Who were the spiritual?'

1. Justin Martyr

I choose Justin Martyr as an example of a Christian response to Judaism, the parent body, around the middle of the second century.[2] Over against Judaism, Justin claims that Christians are 'the true spiritual Israel' and descendants of the patriarchs, 'who have been led to God through this crucified Christ' (*Dial.* 11.5). We 'have received not fleshly but spiritual circumcision, which we received through baptism by God's mercy' (*Dial.* 43.2). Justin argues also that the sacrifices, of which, for example, Malachi 1.10-12 spoke, are not animal ones but 'true and spiritual praises and giving of thanks', such as Christians do offer (*Dial.* 118.2). Thus, Christians, 'through the calling of the new and eternal covenant, that is of Christ', are 'more intelligent and God-fearing than yourselves, who are considered to be lovers of God and men of understanding but are not', he says to Trypho (*Dial.* 118.2).

All this is fairly standard stuff and can be found more or less in Paul. Justin appears, however, to be *the first to argue that spiritual gifts have ceased in Judaism with the descent of the Spirit on Jesus at his baptism in the river Jordan.*

The relevant passage is *Dial.* 87. Trypho raised a question concerning Justin's application of Isaiah 11.1-10 to Jesus: if Jesus was filled with the Spirit's powers at a particular moment, how can Justin claim that Jesus had been pre-existent and then become incarnate, born of a virgin? Justin acknowledges that there is something of a difficulty here, but goes on to maintain that the Spirit's powers did not come on Jesus because he needed them, but because they would stop or cease in him.

While prior to the incarnation, Justin argues, the Spirit gave partial gifts to some of the Jewish people, e.g. to Solomon (wisdom), Daniel (understanding and counsel), Moses (might and godliness), Elijah (fear), Isaiah (knowledge), since the

---

[1] A paper delivered to the Bristol Theological Society in 1988.
[2] See now Judith Lieu, *Image and Reality: The Jews in the World of the Christians in the Second Century* (London: T. & T. Clark, 1996), pp. 103-53, for a lengthy discussion of Justin's approach as revealed in the *Dialogue with Trypho*. She has not, however, discussed the theme in which we are interested.

incarnation the Spirit rested (ἀνεπαύσατο) [Isaiah 11.1] that is, ceased (τουτέστιν ἐπαύσατο)—to dispense his gifts and powers among the Jews.

Justin has interpreted the middle voice of ἀναπαύω of Isaiah 11.1, meaning 'to rest', as equivalent to the middle voice of παύω meaning 'to stop or cease'. In fact, Justin argues that there had been no Jewish prophet since Jesus. The Spirit had ceased to inspire the Jews, whereas, however, he gives gifts to those who believe in Christ 'according as he deems each person worthy of them'. Justin follows this up by quoting Psalm 68.18 and Joel 2.28-29 in defence of his case. He then asserts 'Now it is possible to see amongst us women and men who possess gifts of the Spirit of God' (*Dial.* 88.1).

Justin in effect says to the old mother community: 'You do not possess the Spirit; but we do, and, therefore, we are the true people of God, the spiritual Israel'.[3]

2. Irenaeus and the Valentinian Gnostics

Irenaeus provides evidence of a fierce dispute over who were the spiritual. He had to face Valentinian Gnosticism in the area of the Rhone valley at Lyons and Vienne, where he was the spiritual leader, the local bishop.

Again, because of the limits of time, let me just mention that in the Valentinian system, one of the thirty aeons which constituted the Pleroma or the Spiritual (τὸ πνευματικόν), Sophia, chaffing under the lack of knowledge of the Highest Deity and working herself up into a passion, is cast out of the Pleroma, and, outside, is separated from her passions by an aeon sent for this purpose, Horos. Eventually, these spiritual seeds are sown in some of the humans created by the Demiurge: they are sent from the world above to the world below to receive 'formation'.

The Valentinians' system postulated three types of humans: the choics (or hylics), destined for complete destruction; the psychics who might be saved if they responded to spiritual truth aright and if they produced good works. 'Such, namely, as are established by their works and by a mere faith, while they have not perfect knowledge. We of the church, they say, are these persons' (*AH* 1.6.2). Finally, 'the spiritual' possess perfect knowledge and are capable of judging all things, whereas the psychics do not receive the things of the Spirit (*AH* 1.8.3, echoing 1 Cor. 2.14-15). They are 'the firstfruits' of Romans 11.16, whereas, Irenaeus reports, 'we the church of the psychic' are the lump. The spiritual are not saved by works, but, because they possess the spiritual seed, a portion of the Pleroma deposited within them, they will be saved by nature (φύσει) (*AH* 1.6.2). According to Irenaeus, the majority of them allege that they are already perfect and claim the title spiritual. 'They call themselves spiritual' *AH*.3.15.2; cf. 2.17.3; 2.29.1). They believed that they could not lose their spiritual substance (no more than gold, submerged in mud, can lose its qualities). Indeed, they can act as they wish, Irenaeus alleges (*AH* 1.6.2-3). He accuses them of committing many abominations and impieties. 'They run us

---

[3] This would be part of what Lieu calls 'the language of competition and take-over', *Image and Reality*, pp. 136-40.

down...as utterly contemptible and ignorant persons, while they highly exalt themselves, and claim to be perfect, and the elect seed. For they declare that we simply receive grace for use; therefore also it will again be taken away from us; but that they themselves have grace as their own special possession, which has descended from above by means of an inexpressible and indescribable conjunction' (*AH* 1.6.4).

Bizarre as their overall system may strike us today as being, I want us to ask why did such men and women as the Valentinian gnostics think like this? To what, for example, does their concept of a divine seed deposited in them correspond? What were they expressing? Of what were they giving a mythological explanation? I would conjecture that they had some sort of religious or spiritual or mystical experience in which they felt inwardly invaded by what they considered the heavenly world. These spiritual experiences are ontologized as the divine seed planted within them. The experience is interpreted by a 'conceptual grid', which involves giving metaphysical expression to the sense of being empowered from on high.

We are not, however, left to mere speculation, and I should like to draw your attention to the *Gospel of Truth* and to remnants of the work of Heracleon preserved for us within Origen's commentary on John's Gospel. The experience of conversion, or 'the call', is described by the author of the *Gospel of Truth* in a series of quite vivid images expressing a reversal of what the author felt before. He woke up as from a sleep disturbed by a frightening nightmare (28.28–30.12, 13-19); he sobers up after drunkenness and becomes his true self (22.13-15, 16-20); the state of forgetting is abolished (18.5-12, 16-18, etc); light replaces darkness (24.32–25.3; 35.27-29); he receives rest (42.21.22; 35.23, 25-27) instead of torment (31.21-22, 26-27); he has a sense of completeness (19.3-7; 25.35–26.15; 34.28-32); warmth replaces coldness (34.28-29, 32). The Son 'gave them thought and wisdom and mercy and salvation and the Spirit of power from the infinitude of the Father and from kindness. He caused the torments and scourgings to cease...and with power he abolished them and defeated them by gnosis' (31.15-22, 26-27).

Heracleon, a member of the so-called 'western school' of the Valentinians, interpreted the Johannine incident of the cleansing of the temple in this way: the cord and wood of the whip symbolise the Spirit and the cross respectively. By these means the Saviour purifies and cleanses 'the spiritual', separating them from the rest who are evil and so the church consists no longer of a den of robbers and merchants but is a house of Christ's Father.

The Samaritan woman is another type of 'the spiritual', whom the Saviour assisted to cast out the passions of her false relationships (her immersion in the material) and so she came to the Saviour to receive gnosis and her heavenly bridegroom. She then spoke of Christ to the psychics. The 'spiritual' have an evangelistic responsibility and they must announce to the psychics the good tidings of Christ's coming and try and help them to saving faith. The springing up of the water in John 4.14 referred to the 'spiritual' pouring out for others what had been supplied to them. Heracleon said 'For through the Spirit and by the Spirit the soul is drawn to the Saviour'.

Irenaeus describes for us what we might call a—degenerate—form of the Lord's Supper held by Marcus and his followers (*AH* 1.13.2-7). Irenaeus was dependent on the evidence of women who had been attracted away from his church into Marcus' group, but had found their way back again.

Marcus, another disciple of Valentinus, claimed to be the mediator of Charis, and he urged and induced women to receive Charis in their inner being and prophesy. 'I am eager to make you a partaker of my Charis, since the Father of all continually beholds your angel [literally, your mightiness] before His face. Now the place of your angel is among us: we ought to become one. Receive first from me and by me (the gift of) Charis. Adorn yourself as a bride who is expecting her bridegroom, that you may be what I am and I what you are. Establish the germ of light in your nuptial chamber. Receive from me a spouse and become receptive of him, while you are received by him. Behold Charis has descended upon you; open your mouth and prophesy'.

Irenaeus portrays these women as basically silly people, easily aroused emotionally, who are deceived by a plausible rogue, who not only gains financially by his tricks but also receives sexual favours (the Church Fathers were adept at smear tactics, but the imagery attributed to Marcus is certainly erotic). What is clear, however, is that Marcus led his followers to expect some sort of experience, in which they were possessed by a power, as they believed, from the world above and united with the divine Charis, whose mediator he himself is.

It would be dangerous to generalise from one example, but it is a firm example. Thus, where we do possess a description of worship, there is clear evidence of some experience interpreted as the receiving of the divine seed.

In summary, I would want to suggest that within Valentinian gnostic circles 'the spiritual' are those who have received certain experiences, and who interpret these experiences as an awakening or call, the receiving of a divine seed, which renders the recipient aware of their destiny to be saved.

How did Irenaeus react to the teaching of the Valentinian gnostics? Due to the limits of time, I will pass over his criticisms of a theological nature directed against the Valentinian Pleroma, Sophia, etc, and concentrate on *his view of what a spiritual person really is*. His view comes out most forcefully when in fact he is discussing the resurrection of believers, in *AH* Book 4.

Irenaeus sharply attacks the Valentinian notion that the spiritual will divest themselves of their fleshly bodies and their souls, and be united with an angelic partner. For him, the truly spiritual or perfect person consists of body, soul and Holy Spirit. The spiritual are those who partake of the Spirit, not because their flesh has been stripped off and taken away (*AH* 5.6.1). Flesh and soul constitute a psychical and fleshly condition (ψυχικός καὶ σαρκικός): such a person has indeed the image of God, but only if such a person receives the Spirit of God can they be said to possess the likeness or similitude (usually Irenaeus equates image and similitude; here in the interests of polemics he has separated them). It is, then, the union of flesh, soul and Holy Spirit which constitutes the perfect person. Irenaeus calls on Paul's prayer in 1 Thessalonians 5.23 for support. It is clear that Irenaeus takes the phrase τὸ πνεῦμα in 1 Thessalonians 5.23 to refer to the Holy Spirit: 'Those are the perfect who present to the Lord the three without offence. Those, then, are the perfect who have had the Spirit of God remaining in them and have preserved their souls and bodies blameless...' (*AH* 5.6.1).[4]

Later, he says that the portion of the Holy Spirit that we receive prepares us for incorruption and accustoms us gradually to receive and bear God and 'renders us spiritual even now' (*AH* 5.8.1). People who possess the first instalment of the Spirit and are subject to the Spirit are properly called 'spiritual' by the apostle Paul (referring to Rom. 8.9, 15), because the Spirit of God dwells in them. It is the union of flesh and soul receiving the Spirit of God which makes up the spiritual person, whereas those who are the slaves of fleshly lusts and who reject the advice of the Spirit are those whom the apostle Paul rightly calls fleshly (*AH* 5.8.2-3).

The soul is the middle ground between flesh and God's Spirit. Sometimes it follows the flesh and falls into fleshly lusts; sometimes it follows the Spirit who saves us and forms us for eternal life. Those who fear God, trust in His Son's advent and have God's Spirit established in their hearts, can be called 'pure', 'spiritual' and 'those who live to God', 'because they possess the Spirit of the Father' (*AH* 5.9.2).

Let me give you some examples of how this fundamental conviction of Irenaeus shapes and influences his exegesis of the Bible. Firstly, he separates the Hebrew parallelism of breath and spirit in both Isaiah 42.5 and 57.16, and interprets breath as that which God gives to all people, but 'spirit' he takes as the Holy Spirit whom God gives to believers whom He adopts as His sons (*AH* 5.12.2). A second instance is the words of Jesus in Gethsemane: 'The flesh is weak; τὸ πνεῦμα is willing' is taken to refer to the Holy Spirit. He believes that the Spirit can be a stimulus to the weakness of the flesh for what is strong will prevail over what is weak, 'so that the weakness of the flesh will be absorbed by the strength of the Spirit' (*AH* 5.9.2). The flesh adopts, as it were, the quality of the Spirit and is made conformable to the Word of God. Thirdly, the apostle Paul's eschatological discussions in 1Corinthians 15.49 and especially verse 50 are treated by Irenaeus, because they were quoted 'by all the heretics in support of their folly' (*AH* 5.9.1). Irenaeus takes 15.49 to be referring to our pre- and post-conversion experience. He asks when did we bear the image of him who is of the earth, and answers when we did the works of the flesh. To the further question when do we bear the image of the heavenly, the answer is when we were washed in the name of the Lord and received his Spirit (*AH* 5.11.2), i.e. all we who have been baptized and received the Holy Spirit bear the image of the heavenly man. Irenaeus then takes 'flesh and blood' of 1 Corinthians 15.50 to mean people who do not have the Spirit: as such, they cannot inherit the Kingdom of God (*AH* 5.9.1). Finally, I mention that Irenaeus applies the Pauline imagery of the wild olive branch grafted into the cultivated olive tree, to all believers. Just as a branch does not lose the substance of its wood but changes the quality of its fruit and receives another name, so those who believe and receive God's Spirit do not lose the

---

[4] Cf. H-J. Jaschke, *Der heilige Geist im Bekenntnis der Kirche* (MBT 40; Münster: Aschendorff, 1976), pp. 296-97.

substance of the flesh but change the quality of their works and receive another name. They show that they have changed for the better; they are not now just flesh and blood, but a spiritual person and are called such (*AH* 5.10.2).

To sum up, we may say that for Irenaeus, to be spiritual means to have God's Spirit, and God's Spirit is given to believers on believing in Christ and being baptized and as they continue in faith, love and obedience. The Spirit is given to all believers and not just a select few.

3. Tertullian and the Catholics

As is well know, Tertullian became a supporter of 'the new prophecy', which we call Montanism. Whether he actually formally seceded from the catholic church at Carthage and formed a separately organised group is disputed, but need not detain us here.[5] What is clear is that Tertullian felt himself increasingly alienated from the majority of the catholic church, whom he felt to be unspiritual and whom he branded as *psychici*.[6]

Early Montanism was doctrinally orthodox, as is generally accepted by modern scholarship, and certainly Tertullian would not have accepted anything that was not. I shall select three subjects on which Tertullian wrote, to illustrate the debate about who were the spiritual. On each of these, Tertullian took what we might call a 'hard line' approach, in opposition to what he thought was a too soft or gentle, too lax and too unspiritual and undisciplined approach.

The first topic we shall look at was the question of a second marriage (after the death of the first partner). In *de exhortatione castitatis*, Tertullian maintained that a man, separated from his wife, feels better and thinks of spiritual things. He argued that if the use of sex in a first, permissible marriage repels the Holy Spirit and produces spiritual insensibility, how much more would this be the case if the practice continues in a second marriage (chs 10-11).

De Monogamia followed a few years later and launched into a savage attack on those in the church who did not share his views that one should not marry a second time after the death of the first partner. In the opening chapter he alleged that the *psychici* encourage more than one marriage: 'We who are deservedly called the spiritual...consider that self restraint is as worthy of veneration as freedom to marry is worthy of respect'. Then comes the charge that the *psychici* do not receive the Holy Spirit and take no pleasure in such things as are of the Spirit, but they take pleasure in the things of the flesh.

---

[5] D. Powell 'Tertullianists and Cataphrygians', *VC* 29 (1975), pp. 33-54, argues that Tertullian did not secede, and that the supporters of the new prophecy remained inside the church as an *ecclesiola in ecclesia*. Many scholars have subsequently agreed with his assessment.

[6] The use of psychici is often held to be a lexical indication of the writings from Tertullian's Montanist period: e.g. Barnes, *Tertullian*, p. 44, though this has been challenged by Bray, *Holiness*, pp. 57-58.

The prophetess Anna of Luke 2 was for Tertullian an illustration of the type of person who should be adherents of the spiritual temple, the church, i.e. married only once (ch. 8), while Christ the second Adam is himself a model of monogamy because he has only one spouse, the church. The spiritual monogamy of Christ and his church ought to lead to monogamy in the flesh (while virginity is the highest ideal, monogamy is the next highest, chapter 8).

Tertullian believed that while Paul had by way of concession allowed a second marriage in 1 Corinthians 7, now the Paraclete through the new prophecy was tightening up on discipline and was revoking the Pauline concession (Incidentally, this appears to be the one place where Tertullian accepted that the Paraclete had actually set aside a NT passage.[7] Otherwise, the role of the Paraclete was to expound Scripture and clarify any obscurities and reveal God's will more clearly and openly than had sometimes been the case).

The second area which I want to examine is fasting. Montanists had tightened up spiritual discipline in the area of fasting and had gone so far as to forbid the use of liquids during fasts.

Tertullian launched into a ferocious attack on members of the catholic church in his treatise *de ieiunio*. He maintained that they did not like spiritual discipline (1.2), and they oppose the new prophecies and their spiritual declarations (1.2), branding them as devil-inspired (11.2-4). Tertullian says that they are like Adam who yielded to his belly rather than God, and they like feasts, not fasts (3.2). Tertullian also likened them to Esau who sold his birthright for a mess of pottage (17.1-3). 'Their love shows its fervour in saucepans; their faith, its warmth in kitchens; their hope, its anchorage in waiters; their love—your young men sleep with their sisters [fellow members of the church]' (17.2-3). 'You', he says, 'as men of only mind and flesh (*homines solius animae et carnis*) you refuse spiritual things' (17.5). He ends up with the assertion that an overfed Christian will be more bloody (*sanginatior*) for bears and lions than for God, except that he ought to fight against wild beasts (17.9). I take this terse statement to mean that such a Christian will provide a juicy meal for the animals in the arena, but will not be of the stuff that martyrs are made of, though they ought to be fighting the beasts, not offering them an easy meal.

Tertullian's language is violent and extreme. Anyone not agreeing with his viewpoint is stridently written off as unspiritual.

The final issue which I want to look at is that of readmitting erring church members back into fellowship. Again, we need not discuss whether it was the local bishop at Carthage or the bishop at Rome whose decision to readmit repentant adulterers into the fellowship of the church provoked Tertullian's wrath in *de Pudicitia*.[8]

---

[7] Cf. Karpp, *Schrift und Geist*, p. 63.
[8] See the discussions in de Labriolle, *Crise*, pp. 415-55, esp. pp. 416-17, 433 and 453-55; K. Beyschlag, 'Kallist und Hippolyt', *TZ* 20 (1964), pp. 103-24; and most recently, Trevett, *Montanism*, pp. 114-19.

Tertullian's position on this issue was threefold: (a) the unspiritual catholic church under its bishops had no right whatsoever to forgive sins; (b) Spirit-filled men have such a right; but,

(c) the Paraclete does not wish them to use this power lest it should encourage other sinners to indulge in sinful behaviour in the knowledge that they could obtain readmission to the church: 'The right to forgive sins is given to the church, but it is the church of the Spirit through spiritual men; it is not the church which consists of a number of bishops' (21.17).

For Tertullian, a church which is unspiritual cannot *ipso facto* forgive sins; it has forfeited any right or authority. In any case, the church must be kept unspotted and clean from any defilement by sinful behaviour. Thus, adulterers and others guilty of serious sins have forfeited any right to come back into the church. There is no grace for those who have committed such heinous sins. Spiritual law blocks the way back and keeps the doors of the church firmly shut here on earth.

Tertullian at this point graphically illustrates that perennial tension with which the church has to live, namely whether it is a society of saints or a home and school for forgiven sinners. W.H.C. Frend described *de Pudicitia* thus: 'In this work, the theology of the gathered community was given classic expression.... It is a permanent protest against institutional religion in favour of a religion of the Spirit.'[9]

Although occasionally Tertullian could speak of the empowering help of the Spirit, it *is* only occasionally, and the more prominent note in his writings is that of spiritual law, not grace. The era of the new prophecy had ushered in for him the time of 'maturity' in spiritual matters, after the seasons of the rudimentary, infancy and youth (*de virginibus velandis* 1.6-7). 'The Paraclete's administrative office is the direction of discipline, the revelation of the Scripture, the re-formation of the intellect, the advancement towards better things' (1.4-5). Probably the 'better things' relate to spiritual discipline, while the correct interpretation of Scripture and the reshaping of Christian minds appertains to it also.

In *de Monogamia* Tertullian said that the work of the Paraclete, after bearing witness to Christ, consisted of revealing the 'many things' concerning discipline which the disciples could not bear (Jn. 16.12) and which (Tertullian acknowledged) are no less burdensome to Tertullian's own day than to the original disciples (2.4). The resistance to discipline served only to mark off the unspiritual from the truly spiritual.

As a postscript, I want to refer briefly to the *Martyrdom of Perpetua and Felicitas*, whose editor supplied it with an introduction (chs 1–2) and a conclusion (chapters 14-21). For a long time it has been customary to regard Tertullian himself as the editor, but recently R. Braun has subjected the redactional chapters to minute scrutiny and has come to the conclusion that Tertullian was not the author.[10] For our

---

[9] Frend, *Martyrdom and Persecution*, p. 378.

[10] See R. Braun's two studies: 'Tertullien est-il le redacteur de la Passio Perpetuae?', *Revue des etudes Latines* 33 (1955), pp. 79-81, and 'Nouvelles observations linguistiques sur le redacteur de la "Passio Perpetuae"', *VC* 33 (1979), pp. 105-17. More recently,

purposes, whether Tertullian was or was not the editor does not greatly matter. The *Martyrdom* is a witness to enthusiastic (if not necessarily Montanist[11]) Christianity in Carthage and North Africa, and to some of the tensions and differing viewpoints concerning the contemporary activity of the Spirit, present in the church at Carthage.

The editor points out that just as deeds in ancient times were recorded to promote God's glory and offer spiritual strengthening to believers, so more recent examples should be committed to writing for the same purposes: 'Let those then who would restrict the power of the one Spirit to times and seasons look to this: the more recent events should be considered the greater, being later than those of old, and this is a consequence of the extraordinary graces promised for the last stage of time'. (Then Acts 2.17-18 is quoted.) 'So we too hold in honour and acknowledge not only new prophecies but new visions as well, according to the promise.... Thus no one of weak or despairing faith may think that supernatural grace was present only among those of ancient times, either in the grace of martyrdom or of visions, for God always achieves what He promises, as a witness to the non-believer and a blessing to the faithful' (1.3, 5).

In his conclusion, referring to the martyrdoms which he has recounted, the editor says 'For these new manifestations of virtue will bear witness to one and the same Spirit who still operates (*usque adhuc operari*) and to God the Father Almighty, to His Son, Jesus Christ our Lord, to whom is splendour and immeasurable power for all the ages. Amen.' (21.11).

4. Conclusion

In this appendix, I have looked at three areas which may be described as Christianity versus Judaism; Orthodoxy over against heterodoxy; Dispute within orthodoxy Christianity itself. These three areas indicate that there was a lively debate in the second century over who might truly be described as 'the spiritual'. We saw in Justin that the Christian church claimed to have the Spirit of God over against its rival, the Synagogue (in what might be described as rivalry between siblings over their heritage). The catholic church responded to those within its ranks who strayed into error and espoused a different doctrinal system and framework by which to describe experience: in the person of Irenaeus it sought to wrest the claim to be the spiritual from those whom it deemed heretical. Finally, we saw, through Tertullian's writings, how within orthodox Christianity itself there could be quite sharp differences of opinion over who was responding to the contemporary guidance and

---

Weinrich, *Spirit and Martyrdom* (Washington DC: University of America Press, 1981), pp. 224-29; Barnes, *Tertullian*, p. 329; and Trevett, *Montanism*, p. 270, have also rejected the view that Tertullian was the redactor of *The Martyrdom*. Robeck, *Prophecy*, p. 17, regards the view as not yet proven.

[11] J.F. Matthews, reviewing Barnes' *Tertullian*, accepted the Montanist tone of the Preface to the *Martyrdom*, but did not think that there were adequate grounds for labelling it Montanist (*JTS* 25 (1973), pp. 248-49). Similarly, Weinrich, *Spirit and Martyrdom*, pp. 227-28.

leading of the Spirit, indeed, over whether the Spirit was in fact at work in the contemporary church. One comes from the second century back into our own day with a sense of *déjà vu*. The debate of the second century is not dissimilar to what has happened in the last thirty to forty years right across the church spectrum. The same polarisation may be observed then as now.

APPENDIX 2

The Meaning ἀκοίμητον πνεῦμα in Ignatius' Letter to Polycarp 1.3

Most translators of the Apostolic Fathers have assumed that Ignatius is referring to Polycarp's own spirit when he urged him:

γρηγόρει ἀκοίμητον πνεῦμα κεκτημένος.[1]

Thus, for example, Lightfoot translated 'Be watchful and keep thy spirit from slumbering', and C.C. Richardson rendered, 'Be ever on the watch by keeping your spirit alert'.[2]

I have come across only two scholars who have taken the phrase to refer to the Holy Spirit and both do so without any justification or argument. O. Perler translated our phrase 'Be vigilant for you have received a Spirit who does not slumber' and maintained that the Spirit is the principle of an extremely active apostolate. A. Benoit said of Ignatius' views: 'The hierarchy is united to the Spirit, it is strengthened by the Spirit, it has received the gift of the Spirit (*Pol.* 1.3)', but he did not elucidate the reference further.[3]

Now it must be admitted straightaway that the surrounding exhortations directed to Polycarp might well be felt to favour a reference to Polycarp's own spirit, especially as Ignatius encourages him to justify his office, be concerned for unity in the church, to put up with and bear with everyone, to pray unceasingly, to ask God for greater wisdom, to be watchful, and to speak to everyone in a manner befitting godly unity. That said, Ignatius in the same paragraph also refers to the grace with which Polycarp is clothed, and to a 'fleshly and spiritual diligence'; he mentions the example of the Lord and of God's character; and encourages Polycarp to ask God for wisdom. Thus, if the gaze of Ignatius is firmly directed to Polycarp, there are enough reminders of the divine dimension of how a church officer should carry out his duties for us to say, at the very least, that the issue of the meaning of ἀκοίμητον πνεῦμα is not completely foreclosed.

---

[1] J.B. Lightfoot, *The Apostolic Fathers* (London: Macmillan, Part 2, Vol. 3, 1889), p. 228, lists no variants for this phrase.

[2] Lightfoot, *Apostolic Fathers*, p. 160; C.C. Richardson, *Early Christian Fathers* (London: SCM, 1953), p. 118.

[3] O. Perler, 'L'evêque représentant du Christ selon des documents des premiers siècles', in Y. Congar and B-D. Dupuy (eds.), *L'Episcopat et l'Église Universelle* (Paris: Presses Universitaires de France, 1962), p. 38; Benoit, B*aptême,* p. 76.

In this short note, I wish to offer tentatively reasons why we should consider that Ignatius had in mind *God's* Spirit. The adjective ἀκοίμητος/ον is not a word used frequently. According to Liddell-Scott-Jones, it is used in classical Greek of the sea by Aeschyllus (sixth–fifth century BC); of nymphs by Theocritus (third century BC); of fire by Plutarch (first–second century AD); and of tears (found on the inscription P.Oxy. 1468.7). W. Bauer pointed to the *Apocalypse of Peter* 27;[4] *Sibylline Oracle* 2.181;[5] *Wisdom of Solomon* 7.10; and Philo (without specifying references). No one, so far as I know,[6] has followed up the reference to *Wisdom* 7.10, although this passage, which concerns Wisdom, is the sole occurrence of ἀκοίμητος in the Greek OT. The passage in *Wisdom* 7.10 runs as follows:

ὑπὲρ ὑγείαν καὶ εὐμορφίαν ἠγάπησα αὐτήν
καὶ προειλόμην αὐτὴν ἀντὶ φωτὸς ἔχειν
ὅτι ἀκοίμητον τὸ ἐκ ταύτης φέγγος.
('I loved her above health and beauty
And I chose to have her rather than light
Because her radiance *never goes out*').

Could it be that Ignatius had this passage in mind and transferred the idea from the figure of Wisdom to the Spirit of God? As Wisdom's radiant light never ceases and is never extinguished, so God's Spirit is ceaselessly at work, and thereby assists the Christian minister. The Spirit is unsleeping, and he will help bishop Polycarp maintain an unceasing watchfulness. Such a transfer from Wisdom to Spirit would not be a difficult or impossible step.[7] If this is correct, we could then translate 'Watch, because you have received (or you possess) the Spirit who never sleeps'.

Certain objections suggest themselves. In the first place, the writings of the OT and the Apocrypha do not seem to exert much influence on Ignatius, who, E.F. von

---

[4] Those who persecute or betray the righteous were cast into a place of darkness where they were scourged by evil spirits and worms *that never sleep* consumed their entrails (27). In W. Schneemelcher (ed.) *New Testament Apocrypha*, Vol. 2 (trans. and ed. by R. McL. Wilson), C. Maurer dates the *Apocalypse of Peter* to the first half of the second century (p. 675).

[5] 'O blessed servants, as many as the master, when he comes, finds awake; for they have all stayed awake all the time looking expectantly with *sleepless* eyes.' This is clearly a Christian interpolation based on Mt. 24.45-51/Lk. 12.42-46.

[6] Not even W.R. Schoedel in his magnificent commentary, *Ignatius*.

[7] J.A. Davis *Wisdom and Spirit* (Lanham, MD: University Press of America, 1984), pp. 47-62, after maintaining that there is a large measure of common outlook between the author of *Wisdom of Solomon* and Philo (cf. too D. Winston, *The Wisdom of Solomon* [AB 43; New York: Doubleday, 1979], pp. 3, 59-63), goes on to argue for a close link between Spirit and Wisdom in Philo's thought. The Spirit bestows illumination on the mind, which seeks within the Law for a deeper meaning than the literal sense. This higher wisdom is a step on the way to being drawn into mystical communion with God. Wisdom is obtained through the assistance of God's Spirit.

Goltz alleged,[8] came to Christ without it. More recently, Schoedel has written: 'It is generally recognised that Ignatius reflects scant interest in the Hebrew Scriptures'.[9] However, is there any evidence for the fact that Ignatius might have been acquainted with the *Wisdom of Solomon*, either directly or indirectly through Christian teaching? Certainly, M. Rackl thought that in *Magnesians* 8.2, where Jesus Christ is described as God's Son, who is His Word who proceeded from silence, Ignatius might have had in mind *Wisdom* 18.14-15 'All things were lying in peace and silence....when Your almighty Word leapt from Your royal throne in heaven'. Though subsequently gnostic thought was held to be behind Ignatius' thought,[10] recently M. Elze also felt that *Wisdom* 18.14-15 offers the best parallel to *Magnesians* 8.2,[11] while Schoedel also quotes *Wisdom* 18.14-15 as a parallel to Ignatius *Ephesians* 19.1 ('three mysteries of a cry which were done in the stillness of God').[12]

If Rackl, Elze and Schoedel are right, then Ignatius knew the *Wisdom of Solomon*. This is an important point for our enquiry.

A second objection is that such an accompanying adjective for the Holy Spirit might be thought strange and unusual. In response, we might begin by considering the introduction to the *Letter to the Smyrnaeans*. Ignatius describes the church as 'filled with faith and love, lacking in no gift, most godly and bearing holy things' and then greets it ἐν ἀμώμῳ πνεύματι καὶ λόγῳ Θεοῦ. There are two possibilities of taking this passage. One is to refer the blameless spirit to the human spirit and the word of God to the Christian message or gospel. But the other is to take the referents as the Holy Spirit and Christ (the Word of God).[13] In his Lexicon, Bauer clearly took the phrase with πνεῦμα to the Holy Spirit (though he did not comment on the phrase in his commentary). If Bauer is right, then Ignatius would be saying that all the gifts and qualities which the Smyrnaeans possess come from the activity of the Spirit and Word in their lives. The purity of the Spirit guarantees the

---

[8] E.F von Goltz, *Ignatius von Antiochen als Christ und Theologe* (TU XII; Berlin: Akademie-Verlag, 1895), p. 85. M. Rackl, *Die Christologie des heiligen Ignatius von Antiochien* (Freiburg: Herder, 1914), p. 296, noted many echoes but few quotations from the OT.

[9] Schoedel, *Ignatius*, p. 9.

[10] Schlier, *Religionsgeschlichtliche Untersuchungen*, pp. 38-39; Bartsch, *Gnostisches Gut*, pp. 53-71.

[11] M. Elze, *Uberlieferungsgeschichtliche Untersuchungen zur Christologie der Ignatiusbriefe* (Tübingen unpublished thesis: Universität Bibliothek, 1963), pp. 56-59; quoted with approval by Schoedel, *Ignatius*, p. 121(15).

[12] Schoedel, Ignatius, p. 91 (23), and quotes in support H. Lietzmann, *The Beginnings of the Christian Church* (New York: Scribner, 1937), pp. 323-24, and A Cabaniss, 'Wisdom 18.14f: An Early Christmas Text', *VC* 10 (1956), pp. 97-102.

[13] A small pointer to accepting a reference to the Word of God is that where Ignatius attaches a phrase to his greetings in the introduction or inscription of the letters, there is always a reference to God the Father or Jesus Christ. The *Letter to the Smyrnaeans* would be unique, therefore, if, having an attached phrase, it did not include a reference to Jesus Christ.

godliness of the church. So, to describe the Spirit as blameless offers some sort of parallel to describing the Spirit as ever-vigilant and never sleeping.

We ought to draw *Magnesians* 15.1 into the discussion also. Ignatius bids the Magnesians farewell, adding: κεκτημένοι ἀδιάκριτον πνεῦμα ὅς ἐστιν Ἰησοῦς Χριστός. Either the participle has an imperatival force and Ignatius has issued a final command, 'Possess a steadfast spirit, which is Jesus Christ', or the participle indicates a state into which the Magnesians have already entered and still enjoy. If we take it as an imperative, it would be hard to avoid the conclusion that the human spirit is in mind, but the addition of 'which is Jesus Christ' indicates that Ignatius believes that the Magnesian believers are somehow enveloped by Christ and strengthened by him—Christ is the source of that unwavering spirit so desirous if the church is to live in that unity and harmony of God, which Ignatius so persistently advocated. If we opt for the alternative, and the perfect participle might point to something which the Magnesians have entered into and continue to enjoy, then we could not rule out entirely the possibility that πνεῦμα is God's Spirit, whose steadfast character will enable the Magnesians to remain steadfast in unity and harmony. Ignatius's comment 'which is Jesus Christ' would then indicate that the experience of the Spirit is the experience of Christ himself (compare how for Paul, in terms of experience, Christ is life-giving Spirit and how he said that the Lord is Spirit).

It is time to turn to Philo, to whom Bauer referred as using ἀκοίμητος though without actually specifying any instances. The concordances of J. Leisegang and of G. Mayer[14] indicate that Philo uses ἀκοίμητος ten times. Of these ten occurrences, two refer to God, one to Justice personified as God's assessor and one to the heavenly world; the remaining six instances refer to the human mind and the faculty of understanding. God beholds and watches everything with an eye (or eyes) that never sleep (*de mutatione nominum* 40; *de specialibus legibus* I.330). This should be an inducement to people to abstain from evil behaviour, and especially from maltreating unfortunate people like the deaf or blind (*de specialibus legibus* IV.201). While the earth is sunk in sleep, the heavenly world is kept in unsleeping wakefulness (*de Iosepho* 147).

Philo attributes the quality of unsleepingness to the eye(s) of the human mind or soul (νοῦς, διάνοια, ψυχή are used). The human mind or soul is what is most akin to its Creator, and, therefore, the quality which is appropriate to God is also appropriate to it.

Given a common Alexandrine background to both Philo and the author of the *Wisdom of Solomon*, it should occasion no surprise that the latter should have used ἀκοίμητος of the Divine Wisdom. Schoedel believes that Hellenistic Judaism may have mediated philosophical elements in Ignatius' doctrine of God.[15]

---

[14] J. Leisegang, *Philonis Alexandrini Opera quae supersunt*, Vol. 7.1 (Berlin: Georgius Reimerus, 1926); G. Mayer, *Index Philoneus* (Berlin-New York: Topelmann, 1975).

[15] Schoedel, *Ignatius*, p. 17.

Summary

We have seen that it is probable that Ignatius was acquainted with the Wisdom of Solomon, a work which describes Wisdom as ἀκοίμητος, the sole occurrence of this word in the Greek OT.

Philo described God's eyes as 'unsleeping' and he can also describe the eye(s) of the mind or soul in a similar way, since for him the mind or soul is most akin to the Creator.

It could be claimed that *Wisdom of Solomon* 7.10 and Philo provide an intelligible background against which a Christian writer at the beginning of the second century AD could describe the Holy Spirit as 'unsleeping', set in the context of encouraging a Christian minister to be watchful in the execution of the duties of his office

I do not claim that I have proved that ἀκοίμητον πνεῦμα in *Pol.* 1.3 must refer to the Holy Spirit, but at least this ought to be reckoned as a real possibility more seriously in the future.

APPENDIX 3

The Experience of the Spirit in the Odes of Solomon[1]

To read and reread the *Odes of Solomon* is to be brought in touch with probably the most vibrant, passionate and exuberant Christian experience in the period roughly AD 100-170. While 'truth' is important for the Odist, it is the intensity of his experience which strikes us most of all. No writer, not even Ignatius, has quite bared their soul to us in the way that the Odist has. He pours out to us his feelings in an uninhibited manner. One might call the Odes (using contemporary jargon) 'a charismatic song book' from the second century. As such, it affords a fascinating glimpse into one section of early Christianity, probably somewhere in Syria.

I.

I take Ode 25 to be about conversion.[2]

> I was rescued from my chains,[3]
> And I fled unto Thee, O my God,
> Because Thou art the right hand of salvation
> And my helper.

The imagery used expresses the sense of deliverance and liberation from a previous enslavement. At the same time the conversion has produced scorn and emnity in those who cannot understand the new life and its motivation:

> But I was despised and rejected in the eyes of many,
> And I was in their eyes like lead. (verse 5, compare verse 11a)[4]

---

[1] A slightly altered version of a Short Communication delivered at the 1983 Oxford Patristic Conference and printed in *Studia Patristica* 18.3 (Leuven: Peeters, 1989), pp. 173-81. All quotations are from the translation made by J.H. Charlesworth, *The Odes of Solomon* (Oxford: Oxford University Press, 1973).

[2] Not specifically about baptism as Bernard, *Odes,* assumes, in accordance with his general approach to the Odes. Harris, *Odes,* p. 126, wrote: 'The writer...has been brought out of spiritual bondage into liberty.'

[3] Cf. the lines of the verse in Charles Wesley's great hymn ('And can it be'):
'My chains fell off, my heart was free,
I rose, went forth, and followed Thee.'

But God proved a source of strength in such testing times (v. 6). The Odist uses two pictures. God gave him a lamp both on his right and his left. The conversion experience is here seen in terms of illumination. The implication is that God's light has replaced the former darkness in his life.

The other picture is that God gave him a new set of clothes:

> And I was covered with the covering of Thy Spirit,
> And I removed from me my garments of skin. (verse 8)

We have here an allegorical, spiritualised exposition of Genesis 3.[5] The garments of skin stand for the 'old man', the sinful person. This has been replaced by a new garment which consists of the Holy Spirit. *The experience of being filled with the Spirit is thus a central part of the conversion experience.*

Probably the removal of sickness in verse 9 is intended symbolically and not literally.[6] The Ode concludes:

> And I became mighty in Thy truth
> And holy in Thy righteousness....
> And I became the Lord's by the name of the Lord
> And I was justified by His kindness,
> And His rest is forever and ever. (verses 10, 11b, 12)

II.

Living the Christian life is also under the direction and help of the Holy Spirit. Ode 28 opens with the picture of the dove spreading its wings over its young and sees this as analogous to the Spirit's protection and care:

> As the wings of doves over their nestlings,
> And the mouths of their nestlings towards their mouths,
> So also are the wings of the Spirit over my heart.

The close association of the Spirit and dove in Jesus' baptism has probably led to the use of the wings of doves/ wings of the Spirit parallel. This imagery, conducive to suggest the Holy Spirit as the spiritual Mother of believers, has probably also led the thought of the Odist on in the next verse:

> My heart continually refreshes itself and leaps for joy,

---

[4] Cf. Bernard, *Odes*, p. 107: 'The new Christian is despised by those who do not know the gospel'. See 23.20 for another reference to 'enemies' (at 22.3; 42.5, it is the enemies of Christ himself).

[5] Harris, *Odes*, pp. 67-70, esp. 69. Cf. *Odes* 11 and 21.

[6] *Pace* Bernard, *Odes*, p. 108.

Like the babe who leaps for joy in his mother's womb'. (verse 2)[7]

In trusting in the Lord the Odist experiences rest, because the one in whom he trusts is trustworthy (verse 3), and has greatly blessed him (verse 4a). So close is the relationship that it can be described as a lover on his/her beloved's lap—so I take the brief verse 4b 'And my head is with Him.' Compare verse 7:

> And immortal life embraced[8] me
> And kissed me.

The Odist has no fear that any circumstance (dagger or sword or destruction) can divide him from the Lord (verses 5-6). Verse 8 is significant for our inquiry:[9]

> And from that (life) is the Spirit within me,
> And it cannot die because it is life.

We see here the conviction that the Spirit dwells within the believer; the Spirit comes from the Lord who is Immortal Life, and shares in immortality.

The Odist can contemplate the threatening experiences of life[10] in confidence that the immortal Spirit sustains his life and will continue to do so.

III.

A further area of the Spirit's influence is that of the composition of odes and songs.

> I rested on the Spirit of the Lord,
> And she lifted me up to heaven;
> And caused me to stand on my feet in the Lord's high place,
> Before His perfection and His glory,
> Where I continued glorifying (Him) by the composition of His odes.

So run the opening two verses of Ode 36.[11] Here we have a realised eschatology reminiscent of Ephesians 2.6, except here the reference is personal and individual, whereas in Ephesians 2.6 the plural 'we' is used.

---

[7] Possibly Luke 1.41 has influenced the phraseology too.

[8] Following the reading of N: see Charlesworth, *Odes*, p. 110, note 4.

[9] The versification is different in Harris and Mingana, *Odes*, p. 358, and Bernard, *Odes*, p. 111. Charlesworth's v. 8 = their v. 7.

[10] Harris, *Odes*, p. 129, rightly says that this Ode recalls the 'Who shall separate us?' of Romans 8

[11] The classification of Bernard, *Odes*, p. 121: 'A song of the baptised Christian'—is inappropriate and springs from the straitjacket he has imposed on the Odes. Furthermore, vv. 3-8 are *ex ore Christi*, so rightly Harris and Mingana, *Odes*, p. 384, and Charlesworth, *Odes*, p. 127. The Odist could be applying to the believer the kind of

The Holy Spirit enables the Odist, while on earth, to experience heaven, the glorious presence of the Lord, and so inspired by this is he that he continues to compose.

Elsewhere the Odist likens himself to a harp whose strings the Spirit plucks to make melody about the Lord's love (6.1-2), while he prays to the Lord in Ode 14.7-8:

> Teach me the odes of Thy truth
> That I may produce fruits in Thee
> And open to me the harp of Thy Holy Spirit, O Lord.

Alongside of songs and hymn writers as inspired by the Holy Spirit, we ought probably to set also the preachers of the Word. Within the Odes there is very little indication of any ecclesiastical hierarchy or set ministry, but in two places preachers seem to be mentioned: Odes 6 and 12. In the former, the Odist imagines a stream (= Christian message[12]) flowing over the world.

> Blessed, therefore, are the ministers of that drink,
> And lived by the living water of eternity. (v. 18)

Although the Holy Spirit is not mentioned specifically, it seems likely from the Odist's description of them 'as the Lord's' and as living 'by the living water of eternity' (verse 18) that he believed that they too were inspired by the Holy Spirit.

Ode 12 lists those to whom the Most High has given His Word:

> the interpreters of His beauty
> and the narrators of His glory,
> and the confessors of His purpose,
> and the preachers of His mind,
> and the teachers of His works.

The source of their inspiration is the Lord who has imparted His truth to them, stimulated them by the Word and spoken to them (see verses 10-13).

Poets and preachers proclaim the truth, grace and love of the Lord, and they are inspired to do so.

IV.

In several Odes *the Odist glides over to speak as Christ*. In his first edition Harris had some difficulty in deciding whether the Odist was speaking in his own name or

---

assertion made in the Fourth Gospel about Jesus (e.g. Jn. 3.13; 8.23; 13.1) and the promise that believers should be where he is (Jn. 12.26; 13.36; 14.3; 17.24).

[12] Harris and Mingana, *Odes,* p. 239; Charlesworth, *Odes,* p. 32, notes 15-16.

that of the Messiah.[13] In the second edition he and Mingana wrote[14] on Ode 8: 'This is the first of the Odes that is clearly marked by a dual personality, the Odist becoming at a certain point in the song the Lord Himself.'

Now how do we account for this phenomenon which characterises several of the Odes? Must not *one* of the contributory factors be the Odist's sense of being filled and inspired by the Holy Spirit? The experience of the Holy Spirit is the experience of fellowship with the Lord, a relationship which the Odist describes in terms of lovers:

> I love the Beloved and I myself love Him....
>   I have been united [to Him], because the lover has found the Beloved. (3.5, 7)

And this relationship and its blessings are further delineated in these words at verse 10: 'This is the Spirit of the Lord'.

There are other factors no doubt (e.g. the prophets' sense of being the mouthpiece of Yahweh and speaking as if they were Yahweh). But the Spirit's presence mediating the Lord must be counted as a vital facet of this unusual phenomenon.

V.

I close by briefly raising the question why should these compositions and this author stand almost unique in the period 100-170?

If we look just before his time, we might list as examples of those who felt inspired by the Spirit.

The author of the Qumran *Hymns of Thanksgiving*[15] (e.g. *1QH* 7.6-7; 9.32; 12.11-12; 14.12-13; 16.1, 6-7, 11-12).

The author of the Fourth Gospel (e.g. the Paraclete sayings).

The author of the book of Revelation (e.g. 1.10).

The author of the Johannine Letters (e.g. 1 John 3.24; 4.13).

Ignatius (e.g., *Romans* 7.1-3; *Philadelphia* 7.1-2).

---

[13] E.g. *Odes*, p. 134, about Ode 36, whereas in 1920 he and Mingana divided Ode 36 as follows: vv. 1-2 Odist, vv. 3-8 Christ, and also attributed Ode 22 to Christ.

[14] Harris and Mingana, *Odes*, pp. 256-57.

[15] This is not the place to discuss the links of thought between Qumran and the Odes which have been pointed out, especially by J. Carmignac, 'Un qumranien converti au Christianisme: l'auteur des Odes de Salomon', in H. Bardtke (ed.), *Qumran-Probleme* (SSAW 42; Berlin: Deutsche Akademie der Wissenschaften zu Berlin, 1963), pp. 75-108, and J.H. Charlesworth, 'Qumran, John and the Odes of Solomon', in J.H. Charlesworth (ed.), *John and Qumran* (London: Geoffrey Chapman, 1972), pp. 107-36, both of whom favour the hypothesis that the Odist was a converted member of Qumran. It is sufficient for our purposes here that the author of the *Hodayot* believed that God's Spirit inspired and directed him.

If we assume with many scholars that the author of the Apocalypse was probably a Jewish Christian, a migrant from Palestine,[16] and that the Fourth Gospel originates from Syria,[17] then we would have an interesting concentration in the Palestinian-Syrian milieu. Again to use a modern term, we could say a trajectory[18] in which the experience of the Spirit is the hallmark of true religion.

---

[16] E.g. G. Kretschmar, 'Ein Beitrag zur Frage nach dem Ursprung frühchristlicher Askese', *ZThK* 61 (1964), p. 44; Müller, *Zur frühchristlichen Theologiegeschichte*, pp. 46-50.

[17] E.g. D.M. Smith, 'Johannine Christianity: Some Reflections on its Character and Delineation', *NTS* 21 (1975), esp. pp. 237-38 (reprinted in *Johannine Christianity: Essays on its Setting, Sources, and Theology* [Edinburgh: T. & T. Clark, 1987], p. 22).

[18] I assume here a date for the Odes sometime in the second century (and not in the late third century as advocated by H.J.W. Drijvers in many publications during 1978–82).

APPENDIX 4

The 'Delicacy' of the Spirit in the Shepherd of Hermas and in Tertullian[1]

1. The Shepherd of Hermas

The idea occurs in two of the *Mandates*, though τρυφερός is only used in one of them (*Mandate* 5).

(a) In *Mandate* 5, the Shepherd says that if Hermas is patient, the Holy Spirit will not be darkened by another, that is, evil spirit. The Holy Spirit will be content with the vessel where he dwells (that is, a person's flesh): it will be like living in a spacious room. If, however, the reverse happens and bad temper enters, this will adversely affect the Holy Spirit who is delicate. He feels confined, choked by the evil spirit, and polluted by it. The Spirit does not have enough room to serve the Lord (5.1)

Chapter 2 goes on to discuss this 'overcrowding'. The vessel cannot contain the two spirits. 'The delicate spirit, because it is not accustomed to dwell with an evil spirit or harshness, departs from that kind of person and seeks to dwell with gentleness and tranquillity.' The Shepherd, therefore, exhorts Hermas to refrain from bad temper, the most evil of spirits, and to cultivate patience.

In *Mandate* 10, the warning this time is directed against sadness, the sister of doublemindedness and bad temper. Grief wears out (ἐκτρίβει)[2] the Holy Spirit (10.1.1-2) and grieves him (10.2.2). The Shepherd also says: 'Sadness wears out the Holy Spirit and yet again saves.' This combination, which is strange to Hermas, is partially elucidated in ch. 2: when the doubleminded person fails to achieve their aims, sadness enters them and grieves and wears out the Holy Spirit. Then, when bad temper takes control of a person, they are sad at what they did and *repent*. (Presumably, the sadness that enters the doubleminded person brings about the same result, although this is not expressly stated). This sadness, therefore, seems to bring salvation, *because* the person repented at having done wrong.

---

[1] A slightly altered version of a short communication delivered at the 1987 Oxford Patristic Conference and printed in *Studia Patristica* XXI (Leuven: Peeters, 1993), pp. 154-57.

[2] In his 'Der Hirt des Hermas', *Die Apostolischen Väter* (HzNT Ergänzungsband; Tübingen: Mohr, 1923), pp. 514, 517-19, 534, Dibelius described the overcrowding idea of *Mandate* 5 and the wearing out of the Spirit in *Mandate* 10 as non-Christian ideas taken over by the author.

So, the Shepherd exhorts Hermas to put away sadness and not to afflict the Holy Spirit lest he intercedes with God. For God's Spirit given to this flesh does not endure either sadness or distress.

From where did Hermas get this idea of the delicacy of the Spirit? In view of the brevity of time, I can only make assertions baldly. Firstly, Liddell-Scott-Jones *Dictionary of Classical Greek* offers no examples of the use of τρυφερός for gods or spirits. Secondly, the LXX offers no real starting point for the idea. Thirdly, G. Mayor's *Index Philoneus* does not list τρυφερός, nor does the *Concordance to Josephus* (Vol. IV) edited by K.H. Rengstorff.[3] The NT offers no real parallel, although Ephesians 4.31 speaks of grieving the Spirit. However, we need to remember the OT concept of sin affecting the holiness of the Temple and causing the Divine to retreat from it: God will only remain while His dwelling place is pure;[4] together with the fact that twice the *Damascus Document* speaks of men sullying the Holy Spirit (7.12; 8.20),[5] and the *Manual of Discipline*, as is well known, speaks of the two spirits of good and evil in conflict in a person.

We may draw the following conclusions:

Hermas seems to be unique in the use of τρυφερός of the Holy Spirit.

The *general idea* of the delicacy of the Spirit fits best on to a Jewish, especially late Jewish, background.

The *context* of the idea is a pastoral aim to raise the standard of Christian ethics.

The idea involves a *weakening* of the NT emphasis on the Spirit as power.

2. Tertullian

Despite Tertullian's violent attacked on *The Shepherd of Hermas* in *de Pudicitia*, he actually shared with Hermas the idea of the delicacy of the Spirit. Two passages may be cited which use *delicatus* and/or *tener* of the Spirit.

We begin with *de Spectaculis*, usually dated to ca. AD 197. At the beginning of ch. 15, Tertullian asserted that it is not places *per se* which pollute us but what is done in them, and he goes on to say: 'God has instructed us to deal with the Holy Spirit—who by His natural goodness is tender and delicate[6]—in tranquillity and gentleness, in quietness and peace, and not to upset him with madness, bitterness of feeling, anger and grief. How can the Holy Spirit have anything to do with the

---

[3] G. Mayor, *Index Philoneus* (Berlin/New York: Topelmann, 1975); K. Rengstorff, *Concordance to Josephus* (Leiden: Brill, 1983).

[4] For a full discussion, see K. Newton, *The Concept of Purity at Qumran and in the Letters of Paul* (Cambridge: Cambridge University Press, 1985), pp. 1-51.

[5] Cf. J-P. Audet, 'Affinites litteraires et doctrinales du "Manuel de Discipline"', *RB* 60 (1953), pp. 64-65.

[6] The text runs *'utpote pro naturae suae bono tenerum et delicatum'*: M. Turcan, *Les Spectacles* (SC 332; Paris: Les Éditions du Cerf, 1986), p. 227.

Shows? There are no public games without violent agitation to the (human)[7] spirit...' (15.2, 3a, 4). The whole thrust of the passage is that the Shows and Games arouse feelings and emotions incompatible with the presence of the Holy Spirit. The violence of passions excited is inimical to the tenderness and delicacy of the Spirit. The frenzy stimulated is hostile to the continuing presence of God's Spirit who is holy and peaceable. Later, Tertullian remarks that it is impossible to think of God in a situation where there is nothing of God: 'What sort of conduct is it to go from the assembly of God to the assembly of the devil? From sky to stye, as the proverb has it?'(25).[8] He quotes 'What has light to do with darkness and what have life and death in common?' (26).

In *de Patientia* Tertullian uses a striking image: 'Patience is seated on the throne of His very gentle and kind Spirit, who is not enveloped by the whirlwind nor made dark by the cloud which Elijah saw for the third time, but who is of a serenity full of delicacy, open and simple... For where God is, there also is His disciple [alumna], as is also patience' (15.6).[9] Here there is a juxtaposition of Spirit, patience, calmness, delicacy and discipleship.

According to G. Claesson's *Index Tertullianus*,[10] there is no other instance of Tertullian's use of *delicatus* or *tener* which applies to the Spirit. We may, however, briefly allude to passages where a similar idea occurs.

According to *de Cultu Feminarum II*, all Christians are a temple of the Holy Spirit. But unclean or profane behaviour will offend God and He will leave the polluted abode.

De Oratione 12.1 says that an impure spirit cannot be acknowledged by the Holy Spirit nor a sad spirit by the Spirit of joy.

In *de Patientia* 7.7, Tertullian says that an impatient spirit greatly shocks [*concutit*[11]] the Spirit. 'If we will not admit patience with the Spirit, will He always stay with us? No, on the contrary, he will not remain long' (15.7).

During *de Exhortatione Castatis*, Tertullian argued that sexuality dulls spiritual sensitivity. 'If it turns away [*avertit*] the Holy Spirit in a first marriage, how much more when indulged-in in a second marriage?' (11.1).

We note the dominance of ethical concern. Tertullian endeavoured to jolt his readers into an awareness of the moral dangers of the Shows and Games. His picture of the delicacy of the Spirit fits into his assertion of the incompatibility of the ethos of the Shows and Games and the theatre with a Christian life style. Likewise, he is concerned both for the spiritual wellbeing of women themselves and that they do not

---

[7] The context demands that the human spirit is in mind. See also T.R. Glover, *de Spectaculis* (Loeb Classical Library; London: Heinemann, 1931), p. 271, and Turcan, *Spectacles*, p. 227.

[8] '*de caelo....in caenum*' was rendered 'from sky to stye' by Glover, *de Spectulis*, p. 227.

[9] See J.C. Fredouille, *De La Patience* (SC 310; Paris: Les Éditions du Cerf, 1984), pp. 110-111. The relevant part of the text runs '*sed est tenerae serenotatis...*'.

[10] Paris: Études Augustinnienes, 1974.

[11] Fredouille, *Patience*, p. 85, translates by 'maltraite'.

cause others to go astray. The same moral concern is discernible in what Tertullian says on prayer, the lack of patience, and the expression of our sexuality (whatever other factors also contributed to his views).

The theme of the delicacy of the Spirit and the allied theme of shocking him and causing his departure both serve the moral earnestness of Tertullian.

3. Concluding Remarks

The concept of the delicacy of the Spirit, while alien to the NT, seems so striking that we have to ask whether Tertullian derived it from Hermas, or, did both derive it from a source prior to both of them?

As no evidence exists to support the latter, and as Tertullian certainly knew *The Shepherd of Hermas*, it seems likely that Tertullian was indebted to Hermas for the basic idea,[12] and this is strengthened by the consideration that like Hermas Tertullian sees anger, impatience and grief/sadness as qualities that cause the Holy Spirit to depart from believers.

---

[12] Cf. Danielou, *Latin Christianity*, p. 154; Turcan, *Spectacles*, p. 226.

APPENDIX 5

The Cessation of the Holy Spirit from Judaism in Justin Martyr, Irenaeus and Tertullian

The earliest Christians were soon involved in discussion and debate with fellow Jews and their leaders. That did not cease to occur after the separation of Christian congregations from the synagogue. Whereas there was a tendency among scholars to fix this separation around the 90s and link it with the so-called *Birkath-ha-Minim* and to see AD 135 as almost a cut-off point for any dialogue betweeen the two movements, more recent studies have shown that the separation was a much longer affair and that contacts continued well beyond the end of the second Jewish Revolt.[1]

The purpose of this appendix is to draw attention to one argument put forward (it would seem) in the second century, which does not appear to have attracted much, if any, attention among scholars, namely the cessation of the Holy Spirit from Judaism. This argument appears first in Justin, also in Irenaeus and then in Tertullian. Thus, this paper has a very limited purpose and seeks only to expose a small facet of the discussions which took place between Jewish and Christian scholar-writers.

1. Justin Martyr

In his Dialogue with Trypho, Justin maintains that prophetic gifts, previously present among the Jews, remain with Christians, even to the present time, for 'they have been transferred to us'. The parallel is taken as far as false prophets: as the Jews knew the phenomenon of false prophets in the past, so now Christians also know it (82.1-2).

What is hinted-at here is taken up at greater length in chs 87–88. At 87.2, Trypho is reported as having raised a question concerning Justin's application of Isaiah 11.1-2 to Jesus: if Jesus was filled with the Spirit's powers at a particular moment, how can it be that he was pre-existent and then became incarnate, born of a virgin?

---

[1] See now Judith Lieu, *Image and Reality: the Jews in the World of the Christians in the Second Century* (London: T. & T. Clark, 1996), for a discussion of Jewish–Christian relationships in general in Asia Minor during the second century. Our theme does not figure in her treatment, although she does discuss Justin's approach both in the *Dialogue with Trypho* and the *Apologies*.

Acknowledging that there is something of a difficulty,[1] Justin goes on to maintain that Scripture did not say that the Spirit's powers came on Jesus because he needed them, but because they would stop or cease in him: ἐπ᾽ ἐκείνου ἀνάπαυσιν μελλόντων ποίεισθαι. He goes on to explain his meaning: spiritual powers find their accomplishment (πέρας ποίεισθαι) in Christ, so that after him, there would be no more prophets in the Jewish nation as previously. Justin alleges that in fact there has been no prophet after Jesus among the Jews.

Then Justin maintains that the Jewish prophets had each received one or two powers from God (e.g., Solomon received wisdom; Daniel, understanding and counsel; Moses, might and godliness; Elijah, fear; Isaiah, knowledge). Now, however, since the incarnation, the Spirit has rested, that is ceased (ἀνεπαύσατο οὖν τουτέστιν ἐπαύσατο) to dispense his gifts and powers *among the* Jews,[2] but he does give (δίδωσιν) them to those who believe in Christ, 'according as he deems each person worthy of them', and Justin proceeds to quote Psalm 68.18 and Joel 2.28-29 in defence of this argument.[3]

At the beginning of ch. 88, Justin asserts that it is possible to see amongst Christians both women and men who possess gifts from God's Spirit (as the Joel 2 quotation predicted).

Thus, Justin has a theory which divides the history of inspiration by the Spirit into three phases: firstly, the OT era, with the partial bestowal of the powers of the Spirit upon the Jews; secondly, the era of Jesus, with the full bestowal of the Spirit on him and the ceasing by the Spirit to inspire any Jews thereafter; finally, the era of the Church: the resumption of the bestowal of the Spirit and his gifts on Christian believers. Diagrammatically, this could be represented as follows:

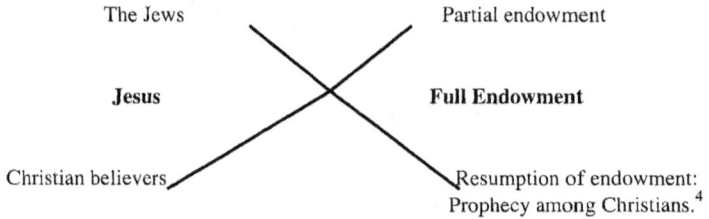

[1] O. Skarsaume, *The Proof from Prophecy* (Leiden: Brill, 1987), p. 197, thinks that here Justin diverged from his source which in all probability did understand the baptism of Jesus as a messianic anointing with the Spirit on the basis of Isaiah 11.2-3 (with John the Baptist as the new Elijah anointing Jesus, p. 277).

[2] Just as in *Dial.* 49–51, 52, Jesus made John cease to prophesy and baptize. Justin is interpreting the compound ἀναπαύεσθαι as equivalent to παύεσθαι.

[3] In the NT, Joel 2.28-29 is quoted in Acts 2.18-21, while Eph. 4.8 uses Ps. 68.18 as OT proof of Jesus' ascension and the bestowal of gifts (through the Spirit) to believers, who comprise the Body of Christ.

[4] Cf. Osborn, *Justin Maryr,* p. 92, also recognises three stages which he characterises as 'dispersion, concentration and dispersion' and speaks of the visual image of an hourglass. I would dissent from this equation of the first and third periods ('dispersion'),

By comparison, the inspiration of Christian believers is fuller and greater than their Old Testament counterparts. Now that any inspiration in Judaism has ceased, only the Church can claim to be 'the true spiritual Israel' and descendants of the patriarchs, 'who have been led to God through the crucified Christ' (11.5).

2. Irenaeus

Irenaeus' main aim was to combat the influence of the teaching of gnostics, especially Valentinian gnostics. He was not engaged in any particular dialogue with Jewish scholars. Significantly, therefore, at *AH* 3.17.3-4, we meet the idea that God no longer sends the Spirit to the Israelites. Irenaeus refers to the story of Gideon and the fleece in Judges 6. He allegorised the dry fleece in the story as a sign that the Israelites would no longer have God's Holy Spirit. To support this, he also quotes Isaiah 5.6: 'I will also command the clouds that they rain no rain upon it', 'but that the dew, which is the Spirit of God...should be diffused throughout all the earth' (see below for Tertullian's use of this verse). The primary concern of Irenaeus is the universal gift of God's Spirit from Pentecost onwards, so the fact that he actually mentions the cessation of the Spirit to Israel could be a pointer to the fact that here he is picking up a tradition known to him.

3. Tertullian

In *adversus* Iudaeos,[5] Tertullian says that after Christ had come and after his passion, there was no need any longer for 'vision or prophet' to announce his coming (the Jews cannot point to any prophetic works or visible miracles subsequent to Christ's advent (8.13), an assertion supported by 'The law and the prophets were until John the Baptist' from Luke 16.16. 'For when he was baptised (the occasion when he sanctified the waters by his baptism), all the fullness of past spiritual gifts ceased in Christ who sealed all visions and prophecies which he fulfilled by his coming.'[6]

Here Tertullian shares with Justin the thought that spiritual gifts ceased in Judaism with the coming of Christ and that this cessation was linked with his baptism.

A similar idea that spiritual gifts ceased in Judaism with Christ's coming is repeated in 13.13.[7] In commenting on the fact that the Jews have not received Christ,

---

as it seems that Justin stresses that in the OT era there was only partial endowment of prophetic figures, whereas he stresses that Christian prophets are more fully endowed.

[5] See Trankle, *Adversus Iudaeos,* esp. pp. xi-lxxxviii, for a convincing defence of Tertullian's authorship, along the lines of an uncompleted work, probably published without Tertullian's consent, perhaps even posthumously.

[6] Tertullian's gaze here is wholly directed on the Jews. Clearly he believed that the Spirit had been given to Christians.

[7] Trankle, *Adversus Iudaeos,* pp. li-lii, suggests that 13.1-23 represented the earliest supplement to *Adversus Iudaeos* 1-8; this was then followed by chs 9–12, with

Tertullian refers to the synagogues 'in which the Holy Spirit no longer lingers, as in time past he was accustomed to tarry in the temple before the advent of Christ who is the true temple of God.'

The prophet Isaiah had said that the Jews should suffer this thirst of the divine Spirit and Tertullian quotes Isaiah 65.13, 16 in the following form: 'Behold, they who serve Me shall eat, but you shall be hungry; they who serve Me shall drink but you shall thirst; and you shall howl from tribulation of spirit: for you shall transmit your name to My elect. But the Lord will destroy you; but a new name shall be given to those who serve Me, who shall be blessed in the lands.'

A little later (13.24), Tertullian maintains that though the Jews still contend that the messiah has not yet come, they ought to recognise their fate. This was constantly foretold as destined to occur after the advent of the messiah, because of their godlessness and their murder of the messiah.

God has taken away the wise architect who builds the church, God's temple and the holy city and the house of the Lord. Here language from Isaiah 3.1-3 is used, and there can be little doubt that the wise architect is the Holy Spirit,[8] 'for thenceforth God's grace desisted (from working) among them'. Tertullian then quotes Isaiah 5.6 'The clouds were commanded not to rain a shower upon the vineyard of Sorek'[9] and proceeds to interpret the clouds as celestial benefits which God commanded should no longer be forthcoming to Israel. 'And thus, the former gifts of grace were withdrawn; the law and the prophets were until John'.

Even the pool of Bethsaida ceased to heal Israelites after Christ's advent (Tertullian then pursues the physical devastation of the land, applying Is. 1.7-8, 20 and Ps. 59.11 to what happened to the Jews, i.e., in AD 70 and 135).

Tertullian was later to use material from *adversus Iudaeos* in *adversus Marcionem*.[10] In Book III.23.2-3, Tertullian quotes Isaiah 3.1-3 in abridged form (he only refers to prophet and the wise architect) and applies it to God's taking away the Holy Spirit from Jewry: God's grace has ceased among the Jews from the time of Christ. 'And so because the dews of spiritual graces were withdrawn from them, the law and prophets were until John'.

Then, in Book V.8.4-5, Tertullian quotes Isaiah 11.1-3 and argues that this predicted that Christ would spring from the virgin of the Davidic line. On Christ the whole *substantia Spiritus* would have to rest. This did not mean that there would be no subsequent acquisition accruing to him, who even before his incarnation was the Spirit of God (in other words, the Isaiah text does not support an 'adoptionist' interpretation—compare Justin's concern to avoid this).

Isaiah predicted that the entire operation of the Spirit of grace would have to rest on him, but would cease and come to an end as far as the Jews were concerned. And, indeed, after that time of Christ's appearance, 'the Spirit of the Creator never

---

13.24–14.13 intended to replace 10.17–12.2. This analysis is of no consequence for our theme, as 13.13, 24 add nothing new to 8.13-14.

[8] So also Bender, *Lehre über den heilige Geist,* p. 107.

[9] The phrase 'of Sorek' may come from Isaiah 5.2 (LXX).

[10] See Trankle, *Adversus Iudaeos*, pp. liii-lxvii.

Appendix 5

breathed upon them.' Again Tertullian uses the language of Isaiah 3.1-3 and Luke 16.16, and then goes on to quote both Psalm 68.19 and Joel 2.28-29 (cf. Justin *Dial.* 87[11]). Christ has in these last days appeared as the dispenser of spiritual gifts: the gift of the Spirit belongs to Christ. Tertullian then quotes 1 Corinthians 12.8-11 mingled with Isaiah 11.1-3.

4. Other Evidence

In the *Didascalia Apostolorum*,[12] generally dated to the first half of the third century, but incorporating material which could obviously be considerably older in origin, we read: 'When He [God] abandoned the people, He left their temple desolate; He rent the veil, He withdrew His Holy Spirit and shed him upon them that believed from among the Gentiles, as He said by Joel: "I will pour out My Spirit upon all flesh". For He took away from that people His Holy Spirit and the power of His word, and all the ministry and established it in His church' (23.5.7 = *Apostolic Constitutions* 6.5).

Here we encounter our theme with its positive counterpart, the bestowal of the Spirit on Gentile believers in accordance with Joel 2 and the establishment of the ministry in the church. What is a new theme, over against Justin, Irenaeus and Tertullian, is the link with the abandonment of the temple, actualised in the rending of the veil (see Mk. 15.38).

Two of these themes—the rending of the veil and the giving of the Spirit to the Gentiles—appear in the *Testament of Benjamin*: 'The veil of the temple shall be rent, and the Holy Spirit shall descend on the Gentiles like a spreading fire' (9.4). Our theme of the cessation of the Spirit in Judaism is not specified, though it is implied in the rending of the veil, which symbolises the abandonment of the temple.

The *Testaments of the Twelve Patriarchs* have been the subject of much discussion. There seems to be a general consensus of scholarly opinion that they received their present form sometime in the second half of the second century in Christian circles[13], and that *Benjamin* 9.4 would be among the *Christian* interpolations or enlargements to a basically Jewish work.

Assuming this as a reasonable working hypothesis, we may tentatively suggest that among some Christians there was a *topos* of God's abandonment of the temple at the death of Jesus (symbolised in the rending of the veil), the withdrawal of the

---

[11] P. Prigent, *Justin et l'Ancien Testament* (Paris: Gabalda, 1964), p. 116, thinks that Tertullian used Justin's now lost *Syntagma* which announced the spiritual gifts which the glorious, raised Lord bestowed on Christians, a belief resting on Isa. 11, Ps. 68 and Joel 2.

[12] See *Didascalia Apostolorum*, ed. R.H. Connolly, revised by H. Chadwick (Oxford: Clarendon, 1968).

[13] H.W. Hollander and M. de Jonge, *The Testaments of the Twelve Patriarchs* (Leiden: Brill, 1985), p. 85 (see pp. 434-47 for a discussion of *Test.Benj.* 9.4); J. Becker, *Untersuchungen zur Entstehungsgeschichte der Testamente de zwölf Patriarchen* (Leiden: Brill, 1970), pp. 375-76.

Holy Spirit from the Jews and the giving of the Spirit to Gentiles. This *topos* finds a place in the *Didascalia*.

5. Older Roots

There is in the NT no express statement to the effect that God had withdrawn the Spirit from the Jewish people, although it could be deduced from what is said. Thus, Paul says that the blessing promised to Abraham is that in Christ the Gentiles might receive the Spirit by faith (Gal. 3.14), while he also asserts that Christians are 'the circumcision who worship God in the Spirit' (Phil. 3.3).

In someone with a more negative approach to Israel, this could lead to the idea that God had ceased to allow the Spirit to inspire the Jews. In the fourth gospel, for example, the Jews are, broadly speaking representatives of the unbelieving world, and the world cannot receive the Paraclete-Spirit sent after Jesus' glorification (14.17).

If we turn to the Apostolic Fathers, the *Epistle of Barnabas* is a writing characterised by a wholly negative approach to Judaism. No express statement to the effect that God had withdrawn the Spirit occurs, but it is a theologoumenon with which the author would no doubt have agreed. Indeed, the author might have queried whether the Jews ever possessed the Spirit (if they never received the covenant, the corollary would seem to be that God's Spirit was never given to them).

6. Conclusions

Justin Martyr appears to be the first writer to develop the idea that God withdrew the Spirit from Israel and to do so on the basis of an exegesis of Isaiah 11.1-3, in which the verb ἀναπαύομαι (to rest) is taken as an equivalent of παύομαι (to stop, bring to an end or cease). It is quite possible that Irenaeus and fairly certainly Tertullian have taken over this idea from Justin.[14]

The theme was part of Justin's polemic against Judaism and apologetic on behalf of Christianity. It was a part of the contention that Christians are the true people of God: they possess the Spirit of God in their midst, inspiring believers to speak God's words or distributing various gifts for other forms of service.

---

[14] So Trankle, *Adversus Iudaeos*, pp. lxi, lxxix-lxxxviii (Trankle merely alludes to the similarity between *Dial.* 87.3-5 and *Adv. Iud.* 8.13; 13.25-26 and *adv. Marc.* 5.8.4-5 on p. lxi and later argues from other examples for Tertullian's use of Justin, pp. lxxix-lxxxviii). Prigent, *Justin et l'Ancient Testament*, p. 115, refers to Justin as Tertullian's favourite author and thinks that Tertullian was in *adv. Marc.* 5.8.4-5 indebted to Justin's now lost *Syntagma* rather than *Dial.* 87. See also the comment by C. Aziza, *Tertullien et le Judaisme* (Paris: Belles Lettres, 1977), p. 70, 'Justin from whom Tertullian often borrowed...'. Skarsaune, *Proof*, pp. 435-53, while expressing his conviction that the problem of whether Irenaeus and Tertullian used Justin's sources or Justin's own writings is very complex, does in the end assert that Irenaeus' and Tertullian's 'use of the Apology and the Dialogue is manifest' (p. 445).

Appendix 5

We also get a glimpse of another stream of Christian tradition in which a similar idea is discernible, this time linked with the death of Jesus and the rending of the Temple veil and the consequent bestowal of the Spirit on Gentiles and the Church (*Test. Benj.* 9.4; *Didascalia* 23.5.7).

This theme should be incorporated into future discussions of Jewish–Christian dialogue, as a small feature of 'the parting of the ways'.

Select Bibliography

Abbott, E.A, *Light on the Gospel from an Ancient Poet* (Cambridge: Cambridge University Press, 1912).
Abramowski, R., 'Der Christus der Salomoden', *ZNW* 35 (1936), pp. 44-69.
Adam, A., 'Die Lehre von dem hl. Geiste bei Hermas und Tertullian', *ThQ* 58 (1906), pp. 36-61.
Adam, A., 'Erwägungen zur Herkunft der Didache', *ZKg* 68 (1957), pp. 1-47.
Aland, Barbara, 'Erwählungstheologie und Menschenlehre (Die Theologie des Herakleon als Schlüssel zum Verstandnis der christlichen Gnosis)', in M. Krause (ed.), *Gnosis and Gnosticism* (NHS III; Leiden: Brill, 1977), pp. 148-81.
— , 'Gnosis und Christentum', in B. Layton (ed.) *The Rediscovery of Gnosticism I: The School of Valentinus* (Leiden: Brill, 1980), pp. 319-42.
Aland, K., 'Der Montanismus und die kleinasiatische Theologie', *ZNW* 46 (1955), pp. 109-16.
—, 'Bermerkungen zum Montanismus und zur frühchristlichen Eschatologie', *Kirchengeschichtliche Entwurfe* (Gütersloh: Gerd Mohn, 1960), pp. 105-48.
d'Arles, A., 'La Doctrine de l'Esprit en saint Irénée', *RSR* 14 (1924), pp. 497-538.
Ashton, J., *Understanding the Fourth Gospel* (Oxford: Clarendon, 1991).
Audet, J-P., 'Affinités littéraires et Doctrinales du "Manuel de Discipline"', *RB* 59 (1952), pp. 219-38; *RB* 60 (1953), pp. 41-82.
— , *La Didachè* (Paris: Gabalda, 1958).
Aune, D.E., *The Cultic Setting of Realised Eschatology in Early Christianity* (Leiden: Brill, 1972).
— , 'The Odes of Solomon and Early Christian Prophecy', *NTS* 28 (1982), pp. 435-60.
— , *Prophecy in Early Christianity and the Ancient Mediterranean World* (Grand Rapids, MI: Eerdmans, 1983).
— , *Revelation 1–5* (WBC 52A; Waco, TX: Word, 1997); *Revelation 6–16* (WBC 52B); and *Revelation 17–22* (WBC 52C; Nashville, TN: Thomas Nelson, 1998).
Balch, D.L., *Let Wives be Submissive* (Missoula, MT: Scholars, 1981).
Bammel, E., 'Jesus und Paraklet in Johannes 16', in B. Lindars and S.S. Smalley (eds.), *Christ and Spirit in the New Testament* (Cambridge: Cambridge University Press, 1973), pp. 199-217.
Bardy, G., *La Théologie de l'Église de saint Clement de Rome à saint Irenée* (Paris: Les Éditions du Cerf, 1945).
Barker, Margaret, *On Earth as it is in Heaven: Temple Symbolism in the New Testament* (Edinburgh: T. & T. Clark, 1995).
Barnard, L.W., 'A Note on Barnabas 6.8-17', in F.L. Cross and E.A. Livingstone (eds.), *Studia Patristica* 4 (TU 79; Berlin: Akademie-Verlag, 1961), pp. 263-67.
— , *Studies in the Apostolic Fathers* (Oxford: Blackwell, 1966).
— , 'The Shepherd of Hermas in Recent Study', *HJ* 9 (1968), pp. 29-36.

—, *Studies in Church History and Patristics* (Thessalonica: Patriarchikon Hudryma Paterikon Mileton, 1978).
Barnes, T.D., 'Tertullian's Scorpiace', *JTS* 20 (1969), pp. 105-32.
—, 'The Chronology of Montanism', *JTS* 21 (1970), pp. 403-408.
—, *Tertullian* (Oxford: Clarendon, 1971, reprinted with appendix, 1985).
Barrett, C.K., 'The Holy Spirit in the Fourth Gospel', *JTS* 1 (1950), pp. 1-15.
—, *The Pastoral Epistles* (Oxford: Clarendon, 1963).
—, *The Signs of an Apostle* (London: Epworth, 1970).
—, 'Jews and Judaisers in the Epistles of Ignatius', *Essays on John* (London: SPCK, 1982), pp. 133-58.
—, *The Gospel according to St. John* (London: SPCK, 2nd ed., 1978).
Bartsch, H-W., *Gnostisches Gut und Gemeindetradition bei Ignatius von Antiochien* (Gütersloh: Bertelsmann, 1940).
Bauckham, R.J., 'The Great Tribulation in the Shepherd of Hermas', *JTS* 25 (1974), pp. 27-40.
—, *Jude 2Peter* (WBC 50; Waco, TX: Word, 1983).
—, 'The Role of the Spirit in the Apocalypse', *EQ* 52 (1980), pp. 66-83 (= *The Climax of Prophecy: Studies on the Book of Revelation* [Edinburgh: T. & T. Clark, 1993], pp. 150-73).
—, *The Theology of the Book of Revelation* (Cambridge: Cambridge University Press, 1993).
Bauer, W., 'Die Briefe des Ignatius von Antiochia' and 'Der Brief des Polykarp von Smyrna an die Philipper', in *Die apostolischen Väter* (HzNT; Ergänzungsband. Tübingen: Mohr, 1923).
Bauer, W., *Orthodoxy and Heresy in Earliest Christianity* (London: SCM, 1972).
Beare, F.W., *The First Epistle of Peter* (Oxford: Blackwell, 2nd ed., 1948).
Beasley-Murray, G.R., *Baptism in the New Testament* (London: Macmillan, 1962).
—, *The Book of Revelation* (NCB; London: Oliphants, 1974).
—, *John* (WBC 36; Waco, TX: Word, 1987).
Becker, C., *Tertullian: Apologeticum. Werden und Leistung* (München: Kösel Verlag, 1961).
Becker, J., 'Das Geist und Gemeindeverstandnis des vierten Evangelisten', *ZNW* 89 (1998), pp. 217-34.
Beker, J.C., *Heirs of Paul: Paul's Legacy in the New Testament and in the Church Today* (Edinburgh: T. & T. Clark, 1992).
Beckwith, I.T., *The Apocalypse of John* (New York: Macmillan, 1920).
Behr, J., *Asceticism and Anthropology in Irenaeus and Clement* (Oxford: Oxford University Press, 2000).
Bender, W., *Die Lehre über den heiligen Geist bei Tertullian* (München: Max Hueber Verlag, 1961).
Bengsch, A., *Heilsgeschichte und Heilswissen. Eine Untersuchung zur Struktur und Entfaltung des theologischen Denkens im Werk "Adversus Haereses" des hl. Irenäus von Lyon* (Leipzig: St. Benno-Verlag, 1957).
Benko, S., *Pagan Rome and the Early Christians* (London: Batsford, 1984).

Bennema, C., *The Power of Saving Wisdom: An Investigation of Spirit and Wisdom in Relation to the Soteriology of the Fourth Gospel* (WUNT 148; Tübingen: Mohr Siebeck, 2002).
Benoit, A., *Le Baptême Chretien au 2 siècle* (Paris: Presses Universitaires de France, 1953).
— , *Saint Irénée, introduction a l'étude de sa Théologie* (Paris: Presses Universitaires, 1960).
Bernard, J.H., *The Odes of Solomon* (Texts and Studies VIII; Cambridge: Cambridge University Press, 1912).
Berthouzoz, R., *Liberté et Grâce suivant la théologie d'Irénée de Lyon* (Paris: Editions du Cerf/Fribourg: Editions Universitaires Fribourg Suisse, 1980).
Best, E., '1 Peter 2.4-10: A Reconsideration', *NT* 11 (1969), pp. 270-93.
— , *1 Peter* (NCB; London: Oliphants, 1971).
Betz, H.D., *Lukian von Samosata und das NT* (TU 76; Berlin: Akademie-Verlag, 1961).
Betz, O., *Der Paraklet: Fürsprecher im häretischen Spätjudentum, im Johannes-Evangelium und in neu gefundenen gnostischen Schriften* (AGSU 2; Leiden: Brill, 1963).
Beyschlag, K., 'Herkunft und Eigenart der Papiasfragmente', in F.L. Cross (ed.), *Studia Patristica* 4.2 (TU 79; Berlin: Akademie-Verlag, 1961), pp. 268-80.
— , *Clemens Romanus und der Frühkatholizismus* (Tübingen: Mohr, 1966).
— , '1 Clemens 40-44 und das Kirchenrecht', in F.W. Kantzenbach (ed.), *Reformatio und Confessio* (Festschrift für D.W. Maurer) (Berlin-Hamburg: Lutherisches Verlaghaus, 1965), pp. 9-22.
— , 'Kallist und Hippolyt', *TZ* 20 (1964), pp. 103-24.
Bianchi, U., 'Religio-Historical Observations on Valentinianism', in B. Layton (ed.), *The Rediscovery of Gnosticism I: The School of Valentinianism* (Leiden: Brill, 1979), pp. 103-14.
Bigg, C., *The Christian Platonists of Alexandria* (Oxford: Clarendon, 1913).
Blackman, E.C., *Marcion and his Influence* (London: SPCK, 1964).
Blum, G.G., *Tradition und Sukzession. Studien zur Normbegriff des Apostolischen von Paulus bis Irenäus* (Berlin-Hamburg: Lutheranisches Verlagshaus, 1963).
Bogart, J., *Orthodox and Heretical Perfectionism in the Johannine Community as evident in the first Epistle of John* (SBLDS 33; Missoula, Montana: Scholars, 1977).
Bonwetsch, N., *Die Geschichte des Montanismus* (Erlangen: Andreas Deichert, 1881).
Boring, M.E., *The Continuing Voice of Jesus: Christian Prophecy and the Gospel Tradition* (Louisville, KY: Westminster/John Knox, 1991).
W. Bousset, *Kyrios Christos* (Nashville/New York: Abingdon, 1970).
Bowe, Barbara E., *A Church in Crisis: Ecclesiology and Paraenesis in Clement of Rome* (HSR 23; Minneapolis, MN: Fortress, 1988).
Bower, R.A., 'The Meaning of ΕΠΙΤΥΓΧΑΝΩ in the Epistles of St. Ignatius of Antioch', *VC* 28 (1974), pp. 1-14.

Bradshaw, P.F., M.E. Johnson and L.E. Phillips, *The Apostolic Tradition* (Hermeneia; Minneapolis, MN: Fortress, 2002).
Bray, G.L., *Holiness and the Will of God: Perspectives on the Theology of Tertullian* (London: Marshall, Morgan & Scott, 1979).
Braun, F.M., *Jean le Théologien et son Évangile dans l'Église ancienne* (Paris: Gabalda, 1959).
Braun, R., *'Deus Christianorum'. Recherches sur le Vocabulaire doctrinal de Tertullien* (Paris: Publications de la Faculte des Lettres et Sciences Humaines d'Alger XLI, 1962).
—, 'Nouvelles Observations Linguistiques sur le redacteur de la "Passio Perpetuae"', *VC* 33 (1979), pp. 105-17.
Brooke, A.E., *The Johannine Epistles* (ICC; Edinburgh: T. & T. Clark, 1912).
Brown, R.E., *The Gospel according to John* (AB 29 and 29A; New York: Doubleday, 1966 and 1970).
—, *The Epistles of John* (AB 30; New York: Doubleday, 1982).
—, *The Churches the Apostles Left Behind* (New York: Paulist, 1984).
Brown, R.E. and J.P. Meier, *Antioch and Rome* (New York: Paulist, 1983).
Brox, N., *Offenbarung, Gnosis und gnostischen Mythos bei Irenäus von Lyon* (Saltzburg-München: A. Pustet, 1966).
—, *Die Pastoralbriefe* (Regensburg: Friedrich Pustet, 1969).
—, 'Zur pseudepigraphiscen Rahmnung des ersten Petrusbriefes', *BZ* 19 (1975), pp. 78-96.
—, *Der Hirt des Hermas* (KAV 7; Göttingen: Vandenhoeck & Ruprecht, 1991).
Bruce, F.F., 'The Spirit in the Apocalypse', in B. Lindars and S.S. Smalley (eds.), *Christ and Spirit in the New Testament* (Cambridge: Cambridge University Press, 1973), pp. 333-44.
Brunner, G., *Die theologische Mitte des Klemensbriefes* (Frankfurt: Josef Knecht, 1972).
Bultmann, R., 'Ignatius and Paul', *Existence and Faith: The Shorter Writings of Rudolf Bultmann*, ed. by S.M. Ogden (London: Hodder & Stoughton, 1961).
—, *The Gospel of John* (Oxford: Blackwell, 1971).
Burge, G.M., *The Anointed Community: The Holy Spirit in the Johannine Tradition* (Grand Rapids, MI: Eerdmans, 1987).
Burgess, S.M., *The Spirit and the Church: Antiquity* (Peabody, MA: Hendrickson, 1984).
W.H. Cadman, *The Open Heaven: The Revelation of God in the Johannine Sayings of Jesus*, ed. G.B. Caird (Oxford: Blackwell, 1969).
Caird, G.B., *The Revelation of St. John the Divine* (London: A. & C. Black, 1966).
Campbell, R.A., *The Elders: Seniority within Earliest Christianity* (Edinburgh: T. & T. Clark, 1994).
Campenhausen, H. von, *Die Idee des Martyriums in den alten Kirche* (Göttingen: Vandenhoeck & Ruprecht, 1936).

—, 'Polykarp von Smyrna und die Pastoralbriefe', *SHAW* (1951), pp. 5-51 (= *Aus der Fruhzeit des Christentums* [Tübingen: Mohr, 1963], pp. 197-252).
—, *The Latin Fathers* (London: A. & C. Black, 1964).
—, *Tradition and Life in the Church* (London: Collins, 1968).
—, *Ecclesiastical Authority and Spiritual Power in the Church of the First Three Centuries* (London: A. & C. Black, 1969).
—, *The Formation of the Christian Bible* (London: A. & C. Black, 1972).
Carleton-Paget, J.N.B., 'The Outlook and Background of the Epistle of Barnabas' (PhD thesis, Cambridge University 1991).
Carmignac, J., 'Un Qumranien converti au Christianisme: l'auteur des Odes de Salomon', in H. Bardtke (ed.), *Qumran-Probleme* (Berlin: Deutsche Akademie der Wissenschaften zu Berlin, 1963), pp. 75-108.
Carpenter, H.J., 'Popular Christianity and the Theologians in the Early Centuries', *JTS* 14 (1963), pp. 294-310.
Casurella, A., *The Johannine Paraclete in the Church Fathers* (Tübingen: Mohr, 1983).
Cessato, J.A., *Hippolytus between East and West* (Oxford: Oxford University Press, 2002).
Chadwick, H., 'The Silence of Bishops in Ignatius', *HTR* 43 (1950), pp. 169-72.
—, 'Justification by Faith and Hospitality', in F.L. Cross (ed.), *Studia Patristica*, 4.2 (Berlin: Akademie-Verlag, 1961), pp. 281-85
—, 'Justin Martyr's Defence of Christianity', *BJRL* 47 (1964-65), pp. 275-97.
—, *Early Christian Thought and the Classical Tradition* (Oxford: Clarendon, 1966).
—, *The Early Church* (Harmondsworth: Penguin, 1967).
—, 'Some Reflections on the Character and Theology of the Odes of Solomon', in P. Granfield and J.A. Jungmann, *Kyriakon* I (Münster: Aschendorff, 1970), pp. 266-70.
Charlesworth, J.H., 'The Odes of Solomon—not Gnostic', *CBQ* 31 (1969), pp. 357-69.
—, 'Les Odes de Salomon et les manuscripts de la mer morte', *RB* 76 (1970), pp. 524-49.
—, 'Qumran, John and the Odes of Solomon', in J.H. Charlesworth (ed.), *John and Qumran*, (London: Geoffrey Chapman, 1972), pp. 107-36.
—, *The Odes of Solomon* (Chico, CA: Scholars, 1977).
Charlesworth, J.H., and R.A. Culpepper, 'The Odes of Solomon and the Gospel of John', *CBQ* 35 (1973), pp. 298-322.
Chevalier, M-A., *Souffle de Dieu* (Paris: Editions Beauchesne, 1978).
Clark, K.W., 'Worship in the Jerusalem Temple after AD70', *NTS* 6 (1959-60), pp. 269-80.
Cothenet, E., 'Les prophètes chrétiens dans l'évangile selon Matthieu', in M. Didier, *L'Évangile selon Matthieu* (Glembloux: J. Duculot), pp. 281-308.
—, 'Les prophètes chrétiens comme exégètes charismatiques de l'écriture', in J. Panagopoulus, *Prophetic Vocation in the New Testament and Today* (Leiden: Brill, 1977), pp. 77-107.

Conzelmann, H., 'Was von Anfang war', in W. Eltester, *Neutestamentliche Studien für Rudolph Bultmann* (Berlin: Topelmann, 1954), pp. 194-201.
— , *Heiden-Juden-Christen* (Tübingen: Mohr, 1981).
Corwin, Victoria, St. *Ignatius and Christianity at Antioch* (New Haven, CT: Yale, 1960).
Cullmann, O., *Early Christian Worship* (SBT 10; London: SCM, 1953).
— , *The Johannine Circle* (London: SCM, 1976).
Dahl, N.A., 'La terre où coulent le lait et le miel selon Barnabé 6.18-19', in *Aux Sources de la Tradition Chrétienne. Mélanges offerts à M. Goguel* (Neuchâtel-Paris: Delachaux & Niestlé, 1950), pp. 62-70.
Danielou, J., *The Bible and Liturgy* (London: Darton, Longman & Todd, 1960).
— , *A History of Early Christian Doctrine: Vol. I. The Theology of Jewish Christianity* (London: Darton, Longman & Todd, 1964).
— , *A History of Early Christian Doctrine: Vol. 2 Gospel Message and Hellenistic Culture* (London: Darton, Longman & Todd, 1973).
— , *A History of Early Christian Doctrine: Vol. 3 The Origins of Latin Christianity* (London: Darton, Longman & Todd, 1977).
Daube, D., 'τρία μυστήρια κραυγῆς: Ignatius Ephesians 19.1', *JTS* 16 (1965), pp. 128-29.
Davies, J.G., 'Tertullian, *de Resurrectione Carnis* LXIII: A Note on the Origins of Montanism', *JTS* 6 (1955), pp. 90-94.
Davies, S.L., 'The Predicament of Ignatius of Antioch', *VC* 30 (1976), pp. 175-80.
Desjardins, M.R., *Sin in Valentinianism* (SBLDS 108; Atlanta, GA: Scholars, 1990).
Dibelius, M., 'Der Hirt des Hermas', in *Die apostolischen Väter* (HzNT Ergänzungsband; Tübingen: Mohr, 1923).
— , 'Die Mahl-Gebete der Didache', *ZNW* 37 (1938), pp. 32-41 (= *Botschaft und Geschichte*, Zweiter Band [Tübingen: Mohr, 1953], pp. 117-27).
— , 'Rom und die Christen im ersten Jahrhundert', *SHAW* 1942, pp. 18-29 (= *Botschaft und Geschichte*, Zweiter Band [Tübingen: Mohr, 1953], pp. 177-228).
Dibelius, M., and H. Conzelmann, *The Pastoral Epistles* (Hermeneia; Philadelphia, PA: Fortress, 1972).
Dietzfelbinger, C., 'Paraklet und theologischer Anspruch im Johannesevangelium', *ZThK* 82 (1985), pp. 389-408.
Dodd, C.H., *The Johannine Epistles* (London: Hodder & Stoughton, 1946).
— , *The Interpretation of the Fourth Gospel* (Cambridge: Cambridge University Press, 1953).
Dodds, E.R., *The Greeks and the Irrational* (Berkeley: University of California Press, 1951).
Donahue, P.J., 'Jewish Christianity in the Letters of Ignatius of Antioch', *VC* 32 (1978), pp. 81-93.
Donelson, L.R., *Pseudepigraphy and Ethical Argument in the Pastoral Epistles* (HUT 22; Tübingen: Mohr, 1986).
Donfried, K.P., 'The Theology of Second Clement', *HTR* 66 (1973), pp. 487-501.

—, *The Setting of Second Clement in Early Christianity* (SNT 38; Leiden: Brill, 1974).
—, (ed.), *The Romans Debate* (Minneapolis, MN: Fortress, 1977).
Drijvers, H.J.W., 'Die Oden Salomos und die Polemik mit den Markioniten im Syrischen Christentum', *Orientalia Christiana Analecta* 205 (Rome: Symposium Syriacum 1976, 1976), pp. 39-55.
—, 'Kerygma und Logos in den Oden Salomos dargestellt am Beispiel der 23 Ode', in A.M. Ritter (ed.), *Beiträge zu den geistesgeschichtlichen Beziehungen zwischen Antike und Christentum* (Göttingen: Vandenhoeck & Ruprecht, 1979).
—, 'The 19th Ode of Solomon: Its Interpretation and Place in Syrian Christianity', *JTS* 31 (1980), pp. 337-55.
—, 'Odes of Solomon and Psalms of Mari—Christians and Manichaeans in Third Century Syria', in R. van den Broek and M.J. Vermaseren (eds.), *Studies in Gnosticism and Hellenistic Religions* (Leiden: Brill, 1981), pp. 117-30.
—, 'Facts and Problems in early Syriac-speaking Christianity', *The Second Century* 2 (1982), pp. 157-75.
Dunn, J.D.G., *Baptism in the Holy Spirit* (London: SCM, 1970).
—, *Jesus and the Spirit* (London: SCM, 1975).
—, *Unity and Diversity in the New Testament* (London: SCM, 1977).
—, 'Baptism in the Spirit: A Response to Pentecostal Scholarship on Luke-Acts', *JPT* 3 (1993), pp. 3-27.
—, *The Theology of Paul the Apostle* (Edinburgh: T. & T. Clark, 1998).
Ehrhardt, A., *The Apostolic Succession in the First Two Centuries of the Church* (London: SPCK, 1953).
Elliott, J.H., *The Elect and the Holy* (SNT 12; Leiden: Brill, 1966).
—, 'A Catholic Gospel: Reflections on "Early Catholicism" in the New Testament', *CBQ* 31 (1969), pp. 213-33.
—, 'Ministry and Church Order in the New Testament: A Traditio-Historical Analysis of 1 Pet. 5.1-5 and Parallels', *CBQ* 32 (1970), pp. 367-91.
—, *A Home for the Homeless* (Philadelphia, PA: Fortress, 1981).
—, *1 Peter* (AB 37B; New York: Doubleday, 2000).
Ellis, E.E., 'Prophecy in the New Testament Church—and Today', in J. Panagopoulos (ed.), *Prophetic Vocation in the New Testament and Today* (Leiden: Brill, 1977), pp. 46-57.
—, *Prophecy and Hermeneutic in Earliest Christianity* (Tübingen: Mohr, 1978).
Elze, M., *Tatian und seine Theologie* (Göttingen: Vandenhoeck & Ruprecht, 1960).
Evans, E., *Tertullian's Treatise against Praxeas* (London: SPCK, 1948).
—, *Tertullian's Treatise on Prayer* (London: SPCK, 1953).
—, *Tertullian's Treatise on the Incarnation* (London: SPCK, 1956).
—, *Tertullian's Homily on Baptism* (London: SPCK, 1964).
—, *Adversus Marcionem* (Oxford: Clarendon, 1972).
Filson, F.V., 'The Significance of the Early House Churches', *JBL* 58 (1939), pp. 105-112.

Floyd, W.E.G., *Clement of Alexandria's Treatment of the Problem of Evil* (Oxford: Oxford University Press, 1971).
Foerster, W., 'Die Grundzüge der ptolemäeischen Gnosis', *NTS* 6 (1959-60), pp. 16-31.
—, *Gnosis I: Patristic Evidence* (Oxford: Oxford University Press, 1971).
Forbes, C., *Prophecy and Inspired Speech in Early Christianity and its Hellenistic Environment* (Peabody, MA: Hendrickson, 1997).
Fornberg, T., *An Early Church in a Pluralistic Society: A Study of 2Peter* (CB NT Series 9; Lund: CWK Gleerup, 1977).
Forrester-Church, F., 'Sex and Salvation in Tertullian', *HTR* 68 (1975), pp. 83-101.
Fox, R., *Pagans and Christians in the Mediterranean World from the Second Century AD to the Conversion of Constantine* (Harmondsworth: Viking, 1986).
Franck, E., *Revelation Taught: The Paraclete in the Gospel of John* (CB NT Series 14; Lund: CWK Gleerup, 1985).
Freeman-Grenville, G.S.P. 'The Date of the Outbreak of Montanism', *JEH* 5 (1954), pp. 7-15.
Frend, W.H.C., 'The Seniores Laici and the Origins of the Church in N. Africa', *JTS* 12 (1961), pp. 280-84.
—, *Martyrdom and Persecution in the Early Church* (Oxford: Blackwell, 1965).
Galtier, P., *Le Saint Esprit en nous d'après les Pères grecs* (AG 35; Rome: Aedes Universitatis Gregorianae, 1946).
Gerke, F., *Die Stellung des ersten Clemensbriefes innerhalb der Entwicklung der altchristlichen Gemeindeverfassung und des Kirkenrechts* (TU 47; Leipzig: J.C. Hinrichs, 1931).
Gibbard, S.M., 'The Eucharist in the Ignatian Epistles', in F.L. Cross (ed.) *Studia Patristica* 8.2 (Berlin: Akademie-Verlag, 1966), pp. 214-18.
Glover, T.R., *Tertullian: Apology and de Spectaculis* (Loeb Classical Library; London: Heinemann, 1931).
Goguel, M., *L'Eucharistie des Origines à Justin Martyr* (Paris: Fischbacker, 1910).
Goldstein, H., *Paulinische Gemeinde im ersten Petrusbriefe* (SBS 80; Stuttgart: KBW, 1975).
Goppelt, L., *Christentum und Judentum im ersten und zweiten Jahrhundert* (Gütersloh: Bertelsmann, 1954).
—, 'Kirchenleitung in der palästinischen Urkirche und bei Paulus', in F.W. Lantzenbach (ed.), *Reformatio und Confessio* (*Festschrift für D.W. Maurer*) (Berlin-Hamburg: Lutherisches Verlaghaus, 1965), pp. 1-8.
—, 'Kirchenleitung und Bischofsamt in den ersten drei Jahrhundert', in I. Asheim and V.R. Gold (eds.), *Kirchenprasident oder Bischof?* (Göttingen: Vandenhoeck & Ruprecht, 1968), pp. 9-35.
—, *Der erste Petrusbrief* (Göttingen: Vandenhoeck & Ruprecht, 1978).
Goltz, E.F. von, *Ignatius von Antiochen als Christ und Theologe* (TU 12; Berlin: Akademie-Verlag, 1895).
Grant, R.M., 'The Odes of Solomon and the Church at Antioch', *JBL* 63 (1944), pp. 363-77.

—, *Augustus to Constantine* (London: Collins, 1971).
—, *Early Christianity and Society* (London: Collins, 1978).
—, *Gods and the One God* (London: SPCK, 1986).
Grant, R.M., and D.N. Freedman, *The Secret Sayings of Jesus* (London: Collins, 1960).
Green, H.L., 'Suggested Sociological Themes in the Study of Gnosticism', *VC* 31 (1977), pp. 169-80.
—, *The Economic and Social Origins of Gnosticism* (Atlanta, GA: Scholars, 1985).
Greenslade, S.L., 'Scripture and other Doctrinal Norms in Early Theories of the Ministry', *JTS* 44 (1943), pp. 162-76.
Greeven, H., 'Propheten, Lehrer, Vorsteher bei Paulus', *ZNW* 44 (1952-53), pp. 1-43.
Gregor-Smith, R., 'Tertullian and Montanism', *Theology* 46 (1943), pp. 127-36.
Griggs, C.W., *Early Egyptian Christianity* (Coptic Studies 2; Leiden: Brill, 1990).
Grillmeier, A., *Christ in Christian Tradition* (London-Oxford: Mowbrays, 2nd ed., 1975).
Grobel, K., 'Shepherd of Hermas, Parable II', *Vanderbilt Studies in the Humanities* 1 (1951), pp. 50-55.
—, *The Gospel of Truth* (London: A. & C. Black, 1960).
Grundmann, W., 'Die Apostel zwischen Jerusalem und Antiocha', *ZNW* 39 (1940), pp. 110-37.
—, 'χρίω-χρῖσμα', in G. Friedrich (ed.), *TDNT* (Grand Rapids, MI: Eerdmans, 1974), Vol. IX, p. 572.
Guthrie, D., *New Testament Introduction* (Leicester: Apollos and Downers Grove, Illinois: Intervarsity Press, 4th rev. ed., 1990).
Haacker, K., *Die Siftung des Heils: Untersuchungen des Struktur des johanneischen Theologie* (Stuttgart: Calwer Verlag, 1972).
Hagner, D.A., *The Use of the Old and New Testaments in Clement of Rome* (SNT 34; Leiden: Brill, 1973).
Hainz, J., *EKKLESIA, Strukturen paulinischer Gemeinde-Theologie and Gemeinde-Ordnung* (Regensburg: Friedrich Pustet, 1972).
—, 'Die Anfänge des Bischofs- und Diakonenamtes', in J. Hainz (ed.) *Kirche im Werde* (München-Paderborn-Wein: Schoningh, 1976), pp. 91-107.
Hall, S.G., 'Repentance in 1 Clement', in F.L. Cross (ed.), *Studia Patristica* 8.2 (Berlin: Akademie-Verlag, 1966), pp. 30-43.
Hamman, A., 'La Signification de σφραγίς dans le Pasteur d'Hermas', *Studia Patristica* 4.2 (Berlin: Akademie-Verlag, 1961), pp. 286-90.
Hanson, A.T., *The Pastoral Epistles* (NCB; London: Marshall, Morgan & Scott, 1982).
Hanson, R.P.C., 'Notes on Tertullian's Interpretation of Scripture', *JTS* 12 (1961), pp. 273-79.
—, *Tradition in the Early Church* (London: SCM, 1962).
Harnack, A. von, *Die Lehr der Zwölf Apostel* (TU 2; Leipzig: Hinrichs, 1886).

—, 'Das Zeugnis des Ignatius über das Ansehen der romischen Gemeinde', *SBPAW* 1 (1896), pp. 111-31.
—, *Die Chronologie der altchristlichen Litteratur bis Eusebius* (Leipzig: J.C. Hinrichs, 1897).
—, *The Expansion of Christianity in the First Three Centuries* (London: Williams & Norgate, Vols. 1-2, 1904-5).
—, *Marcion: Das Evangelium vom fremden Gott* (Leipzig: J.C. Hinrichs, 2nd ed., 1924). (English Translation without the Appendices of the original: *Marcion: The Gospel of the Alien God* [Durham, NC: Labyrinth Press, 1990].)
—, *Einführung in die alte Kirchengeschichte: Das Schreiben der romischen Kirche an die korinthische aus der Zeit Domitians (1 Clemensbriefe)* (Leipzig: J.C. Hinrichs, 1929).
Harris, J.R., *The Teaching of the Apostles (Διδαχή τῶν ἀποστόλων)* (London: Clay and Baltimore: John Hopkins University Press, 1887).
—, *The Odes and Psalms of Solomon* (Cambridge: Cambridge University Press, 1909).
Harris, J.R., and A Mingana, *The Odes and Psalms of Solomon* (Manchester: Manchester University Press, Vols. 1–2, 1916, 1920).
Harrison, P.N., *The Problem of the Pastoral Epistles* (Oxford: Oxford University Press, 1921).
—, *Polycarp's Two Epistles* (Cambridge: Cambridge University Press, 1936).
—, *Paulines and Pastorals* (London: Villiers, 1964).
Harvey, A.E., 'Elders', *JTS* 25 (1974), pp. 318-32.
Hauck, F., *Die Kirchenbriefe* (NDT 10; Göttingen: Vandenhoeck & Ruprecht, 1957).
Hauschild, W-D., *Gottes Geist und der Mensch: Studien zur frühchristlichen Pneumatologie* (München: Chr.Kaiser Verlag, 1972).
Haykin, M.A.G., 'The Fading Vision? The Spirit and Freedom in the Pastoral Epistles', *EQ* 57 (1985), pp. 291-305.
Headlam, A.C., 'The Odes of Solomon', *CQR* 71 (1911), pp. 272-97.
Hedrick, C.W., and R. Hodgson (eds.), *Nag Hammadi, Gnosticism and Early Christianity* (Peabody, MA: Hendrickson, 1986).
Heine, R.E., 'The Gospel of John and the Montanist Debate at Rome', in E.A. Livingstone (ed.), *Studia Patristica* 21 (Leuven: Peeters, 1989), pp. 95-100.
Hengel, M., *Property and Riches in the Early Church* (London: SCM, 1974).
Hill, D., *Greek Words and Hebrew Meanings: Studies in the Semantics of Soteriological Terms* (SNTSMS 5; Cambridge: Cambirdge University Press, 1967).
—, 'Prophecy and Prophets in the Revelation of St. John', *NTS* 18 (1971-72), pp. 401-18.
—, 'On the Evidence for the Creative Role of Christian Prophets', *NTS* 20 (1974), pp. 262-74.
—, 'False Prophets and Charismatics: Structure and Interpretation in Matthew 7.15-23', *Biblica* 57 (1976), pp. 327-48.

—, 'Christian Prophets as Teachers or Instructors in the Church', in J. Panagoulos (ed.), *Prophetic Vocation in the New Testament and Today* (Leiden: Brill, 1977), pp. 108-30.

—, *New Testament Prophecy* (London: Marshall, Morgan & Scott, 1979).

Holladay, C.H., *THEIOS ANER in Hellenistic Judaism: A Critique of the Use of this Category in New Testament Theology* (Missoula, MT: Scholars, 1977).

Holwerda, D.E., *The Holy Spirit and Eschatology in the Gospel of John* (Kampen; Kok, 1959).

Horbury, W.H., 'Jewish-Christian Relations in Barnabas and Justin', in J.D.G. Dunn (ed.), *Jews and Christians: The Parting of the Ways AD 70 to 135* (Grand Rapids, MI: Eerdmans, 1999), pp. 315-45.

Horrell, D.G., *The Social Ethos of the Corinthian Correspondence: Interests and Ideology from 1 Corinthians to 1 Clement* (SNTW; Edinburgh: T. &. T. Clark, 1996).

Hoskyns, E.C., *The Fourth Gospel* (ed. F.N. Davey) (London: Faber & Faber, 2nd ed., 1947).

Houssiau, A., *La christologie de saint Irénée* (Louvain-Glembloux: Publications Universitaires, 1955).

Hvalvik, R., *The Struggle for Scripture and Covenant: The Purpose of the Epistle of Barnabas and Jewish-Christian Competition in the Second Century* (WUNT 82; Tübingen: Mohr, 1996).

Isaacs, Marie E., *The Concept of Spirit: A Study of Pneuma in Hellenistic Judaism and its Bearing on the New Testament* (Heythrop Monographs 1; London: Heythrop College, 1976).

Jaschke, H-J., *Der heilige Geist im Bekenntnis der Kirche* (MBT 40; Münster: Aschendorff, 1976).

—, 'Pneuma und Moral. Der Grund christliche Sittlichkeit aus der Sicht des Irenäus von Lyon', *Studia Moralia* 14 (1976), pp. 239-81.

Jaubert, Annie, 'Les Sources de la conception militaire de l'Église en 1 Clement 37', *VC* 18 (1964), pp. 74-84.

—, 'Thèmes lévitiques dans la Prima Clementis', *VC* 18 (1964), pp. 193-203.

—, *Clément de Rome—Épître aux Corinthiens* (SC 167; Paris: Les Éditions du Cerf, 1971).

Jeffers, J.S., *Conflict at Rome: Social Order and Hierarchy in Early Christianity* (Minneapolis, MN: Fortress, 1991).

Jenkins, D., 'The Make-up of Man according to Irenaeus', in F.L. Cross (ed.), *Studia Patristica* 6.4 (Berlin: Akademie-Verlag, 1962), pp. 91-95.

Jeremias, J., *Die Briefe an Timotheus und Titus* (NTD 9; Vandenhoeck & Ruprecht: Göttingen, 1963).

Jeske, R.L., 'Spirit and Community in the Johannine Apocalypse', *NTS* 31 (1985), pp. 452-66.

Johnson, S.E., 'Unsolved Questions about Early Christianity in Anatolia', in D.E. Aune (ed.), *Studies in the New Testament and Early Christianity* (Leiden: Brill, 1972), pp. 181-93.

Johnston, G., *The Spirit-Paraclete in the Gospel of John* (SNTSMS 12; Cambridge: CUP, 1970).
Joly, R., 'Hermas et le Pasteur', *VC* 21 (1967), pp. 201-18.
—, *Hermas le Pasteur* (SC 53; Paris: Les Editions de Cerf, 2nd ed., 1968).
Jonas, H., *The Gnostic Religion* (Boston: Beacon, 2nd ed., 1963).
Karpp, H., *Schrift und Geist bei Tertullian* (Gütersloh: C. Bertelsmann, 1955).
Karavites, P., *Evil, Freedom and the Road to Perfection in Clement of Alexandria* (Leiden: Brill, 1999).
Käsemann, E., *New Testament Questions for Today* (London: SCM, 1963).
—, *Essays on New Testament Themes* (London: SCM, 1964).
Keener, C.S., *The Spirit in the Gospels and Acts: Divine Purity and Power* (Peabody, MA: Hendrickson, 1997).
Kelly, J.N.D., *Early Christian Creeds* (London: Longmans, Green, 1950).
—, *Early Christian Doctrines* (London: A. & C. Black, 1958).
—, *The Pastoral Epistles* (London: A. & C. Black, 1963).
—, *The Epistles of Peter and Jude* (London: A. & C. Black, 1969).
Kertelge, K., 'Das Apostelamt des Paulous, sein Ursprung und seine Bedeutung', *BZ* 14 (1970), pp. 161-81.
Kettler, F-H., 'Enderwartung und himmlischer Stufenbau im Kirchenbegriff des nachapostolischen Zeitalters', *TLZ* 79 (1954), pp. 385-92.
Kingsbury, J.A., 'The Verb AKOLOUTHEIN ("to Follow") as an Index of Matthew's View of his Community', *JBL* 97 (1978), pp. 56-73.
Klevinghaus, J., *Die theologische Stellung der apostolischen Väter zur altestamentliche Offenbarung* (Gütersloh: Gerd Mohn, 1948).
Knight, J., *2 Peter and Jude* (New Testament Guides; Sheffield: Sheffield Academic Press, 1995).
Knoch, O., *Eigenart und Bedeutung der Eschatologie im theologischen Aufriss des ersten Clemensbrief* (Bonn: Peter Hanstein, 1964).
—, *Die "Testamente" des Petrus und Paulus: die Sicherung der apostolischen Überlieferung in der spätneutestamentlichen Zeit* (SBS 62; Stuttgart: KBW, 1973).
Knopf, R., *Das nachapostolische Zeitalter* (Tübingen: Mohr, 1905).
—, Die Lehre der zwölf Apöstel and Die zwei Clemensbriefe, in *Die apostolischen Väter* (HzNT Ergänzungsband; Tübingen: Mohr, 1923).
Koester, H., *Synoptischen Überlieferung bei den apostolischen Vätern* (TU 65; Berlin: Akademie-Verlag, 1957).
—, 'Gnomai Diaphorai: The Origin and Nature of Diversification in the History of Early Christianity', *HTR* 58 (1965), pp. 279-318 (= in J.M. Robinson and H. Koester, *Trajectories through Early Christianity* [Philadelphia, PA: Fortress, 1971], pp. 114-57).
Korschorke, K., 'Die Polemik der Gnostiker gegen das kirchliche Christentum', in M. Krause (ed.), *Gnosis and Gnosticism* (NHS 3; Leiden: Brill, 1971), pp. 43-49.
Kortner, U.H.J., *Papias von Hierapolis* (Göttingen: Vandenhoeck & Ruprecht, 1983).

Kraft, H., 'Die altkirchliche Prophetie und die Entstehung des Montanismus', *TZ* 11 (1955), pp. 249-71.
—, 'Vom Ende der urchristlichen Prophetie', in J. Panagopoulos (ed.), *Prophetic Vocation in the New Testament and Today* (Leiden: Brill, 1977), pp. 162-85.
Kraft, R.A., 'Barnabas' Isaiah Text and the "Testimony Book" Hypothesis', *JBL* 79 (1960), pp. 336-50.
—, 'In Search of Jewish Christianity and its Theology', *RSR* 60 (1972), pp. 81-91.
Kretschmar, G., 'Ein Beitrag zur Frage nach Ursprung frühchristlichen Askese', *ZTK* 61 (1964), pp. 27-67.
Kuhnert, W., 'Die antimontantistische Anonymus bei Eusebius', *TZ* 5 (1949), pp. 436-46.
Kümmel, W.G., *Introduction to the New Testament* (London: SCM, 1966).
Kydd, R.A.N., *Charismatic Gifts in the Early Church* (Peabody, MA: Hendrickson, 1984).
Kyrtatas, D.J. *The Social Structure of the Early Christian Communities* (London/New York: Verso, 1987).
Labriolle, P. de, *Les Sources de l'histoire des Montanisme* (Fribourg: Librairie de l'Université and Paris: Ernest Leroux, 1913).
—, *La crise Montaniste* (Paris: Ernest Leroux, 1913).
—, *History and Literature of Christianity from Tertullian to Boethius* (London: Kegan,Paul, Trench, Tribner, 1924).
—, 'La polémique antimontaniste contre le prophétie extatique', *RHPR* 11 (1925), pp. 97-145.
Lampe, G.W.H., *The Seal of the Spirit* (London: Longmans, Green, 1951).
—, '"Grievous Wolves" (Acts 20.29)', in B. Lindars and S.S. Smalley (eds.), *Christ and Spirit in the New Testament* (Cambridge: Cambridge University Press, 1973), pp. 253-68.
—, 'Martyrdom and Inspiration', in W. Horbury and B. McNeil (eds.), *Suffering and Martyrdom in the New Testament* (Cambridge: Cambridge University Press, 1981), pp. 118-35.
—, 'The Testimony of Jesus is the Spirit of Prophecy', in W.C. Weinrich (ed.), *The New Testament Age* (Macon, GA: Mercer University Press, 1984), pp. 245-58.
Lampe, P., *Die stadtrömische Christen in den ersten beiden Jahrhunderten* (Tübingen: Mohr, 1987) (English Translation with revisions and partial updating: *From Paul to Valentinus: Christians at Rome in the First Two Centuries* [Minneapolis, MN: Fortress, 2003]).
Lattke, M., *Die Oden Salomos in ihrer Bedeutung für Neues Testament und Gnosis* (OBO 25.1; Göttingen: Vandenhoeck & Ruprecht, 1979).
Law, R., *The Tests of Life: A Study of the First Epistle of John* (Edinburgh: T. & T. Clark, 1909).
Lawson, J., *The Biblical Theology of St. Irenaeus* (London: Epworth, 1948).
—, *A Theological and Historical Introduction to the Apostolic Fathers* (New York: Macmillan, 1961).

Layton, B. *The Gnostic Scriptures* (London: SCM, 1987).
Liebart, J., *Les Enseignements moraux des Pères apostoliques* (Gembloux: Duculot, 1970).
Lietzmann, H., *The Founding of the Church Universal* (London: Lutterworth, 2nd ed., 1950).
Lieu, Judith, *The Second and Third Epistles of John* (SNTW; Edinburgh: T. & T. Clark, 1986).
— , *The Theology of the Johannine Epistles* (Cambridge: Cambridge University Press, 1991).
Lightfoot, J.B., *The Apostolic Fathers*: Vol.1.1-2. *St. Clement of Rome* (London: Macmillan, 2nd ed., 1890); Vol. 2.1-3. *St. Ignatius. St. Polycarp*, (London: Macmillan, 2nd ed., 1889).
— , *The Apostolic Fathers* (London: Macmillan, 1898).
Lilla, S.R.C., *Clement of Alexandria: A Study in Christian Platonism and Gnosticism* (Oxford: Oxford University Press, 1971).
Lindars, B., *The Gospel of John* (NCB; London: Oliphants, 1972).
Lindblom, J., *Gesichte und Offenbarungen: Vorstellungen von gottlichen Weisungen und übernatürlichen Erscheinungen im ältesten Christentum* (Lund: C.W.K. Gleerup, 1968).
Lips, H. von, *Glaube-Gemeinde-Amt: zum Verstandnis der Ordination in den Pastoralbriefen* (Göttingen: Vandenhoeck & Ruprecht, 1979).
Lohse, B., *Das Passafest der Quartadecimaner* (Gütersloh: Gerd Mohn, 1953).
Lohse, E., 'Ursprung und Prägung des christlichen Apostolats', *TZ* 9 (1953), pp. 259-75.
— , 'Die Entstehung des Bischofsamtes in der frühen Christenheit', *ZNW* 71 (1980), pp. 58-73.
Loofs, F., *Theophilus von Antiochien adversus Marcionem und die anderen theologischen Quellen bei Irenäus* (TU 46; Leipzig: J.C. Hinrichs, 1930).
Lowther-Clarke, W.K., *The First Epistle of Clement to the Corinthians* (London: SPCK, 1937).
Lowy, S., 'The Confrontation of Judaism in the Epistle of Barnabas', *JJS* 11 (1960), pp. 1-33.
Lüdemann, G., 'Zur Geschichte des ältesten Christentums in Rom', *ZNW* 70 (1979), pp. 86-114.
— , *Heretics: The Other Side of Early Christianity* (London: SCM, 1996).
Lusk, D.C., 'What is the Historic Episcopate?', *SJT* 3 (1950), pp. 255-77.
MacDonald, Margaret Y., *Early Christian Women and Pagan Opinion: The Power of the Hysterical Woman* (Cambridge: Cambridge University Press, 1996).
MacMullen, R., *Christianizing the Roman Empire AD100–400* (New Haven and London: Yale, 1984).
McDonald, L.M., and S.E. Porter, *Early Christianity and its Sacred Literature* (Peabody, MA: Hendrickson, 2000).

Maier, H.O., *The Social Setting of the Ministry as Reflected in the Writings of Hermas, Clement and Ignatius* (Waterloo, ON: Wilfred Laurier University Press, 1991).
Malatesta, E., *Interiority and Covenant* (AB 69; Rome: Pontifical Biblical Institute, 1978).
Markschies, C., *Valentinus Gnosticus? Untersuchungen zur valentinianischen Gnosis mit einem Kommentat zu den Fragmenten Valentins* (WUNT 65; Tübingen: Mohr, 1992).
Markus, R.A., 'Pleroma and Fulfilment', *VC* 8 (1954), pp. 193-224.
Marshall, I.H., *The Epistles of John* (Grand Rapids, MI: Eerdmans, 1978).
— (with P.H. Towner), *The Pastoral Epistles* (ICC; Edinburgh: T. & T. Clark, 1999).
Marxsen, W., *Der Frühkatholizismus im NT* (Neukirchen-Vluyn: Neukirchener Verlag, 1958).
— , 'Die Nachfolge der Apostel', *Der Exeget als Theologe* (Gütersloh: Gerd Mohn, 1968), pp. 75-90.
Massyngberde-Ford, Josephine, *Revelation* (AB 38; New York: Doubleday, 1965).
— , 'Was Montanism a Jewish-Christian heresy?', *JEH* 17 (1966), pp. 145-58.
Maurer, C., *Ignatius von Antiochien und das Johannesevangelium* (Zurich: Zwingli-Verlag, 1949).
McGuire, Anne, 'Conversion and Gnosis in the Gospel of Truth', *NT* 28 (1986), pp. 338-55.
Meeks, W.A., and R.L. Wilken, *Jews and Christians in Antioch in the First Four Centuries of the Common Era* (Missoula, MT: Scholars, 1978).
Mehat, A., 'Saint Irénée et les Charismes', in E.A. Livingstone (ed.), *Studia Patristica* 17.2 (Oxford: Pergamon, 1982), pp. 719-24.
Meinhold, P., 'Geschehen und Deutung im ersten Clemensbrief', *ZKG* 58 (1939), pp. 82-129.
— , 'Geschichte und Exegese im Barnabasbrief', *ZKG* 59 (1940), pp. 255-303.
— , *Studien zu Ignatius von Antiochien* (Wiesbaden: Franz Steiner Verlag, 1979).
Menard, J.E., 'Die Erkenntnis im Evangelium der Wahrheit', in W. Eltester, *Christentum und Gnosis* (Berlin: Topelmann, 1969), pp. 59-64.
Molland, E., 'The Heretics Combatted by Ignatius of Antioch', *JEH* 5 (1954), pp. 1-6.
— , 'La Thèse "La prophétie n'est jamais venue de la volonté de l'homme" (2 Pierre 1.21) et les Pseudo-Clementines', *ST* 9 (1955), pp. 67-85.
— , 'La circoncision, le baptême et l'autorité de décret apostolique (Actes 15.28f) dans le milieux judeo-chretiens des Pseudo-Clementines', *ST* 9 (1956), pp. 1-39.
Montgomery-Hitchcock, F.R., *Irenaeus of Lugdunum* (Cambridge: Cambridge University Press, 1914).
— , 'Loofs' Theory of Theophilus of Antioch as a Source of Irenaeus', *JTS* 38 (1937), pp. 130-39, 255-66.
— , 'Loofs' Asiatic Source IQA and the Ps. Justin *de* resurrectione', *ZNW* 36 (1937), pp. 35-60.

Morel, V., 'Le Développement de la "Disciplina" sous l'action du saint-Esprit chez Tertullien', *RHE* 35 (1939), pp. 243-65.
Morgan-Wynne, J.E., 'A Note on John 14.17b', *BZ* 24 (1979), pp. 93-96.
— , 'The Holy Spirit and Christian Experience in Justin Martyr', *VC* 38 (1984), pp. 172-77.
— , 'The Experience of the Spirit in the Odes of Solomon', in E.A. Livingstone (ed.), *Studia Patristica* 18.3 (Leuven: Peeters and Kalamazoo: Cistercian, 1989), pp. 173-81.
— , 'The Delicacy of the Spirit in the Shepherd of Hermas and Tertullian', in E.A. Livingstone (ed.), *Studia Patristica* 21 (Leuven: Peeters, 1993), pp. 154-57.
— , 'References to Baptism in the Fourth Gospel', in S.E. Porter and A.R. Cross (eds.), *Baptism, the New Testament and the Church: Historical and Contemporary Studies in honour of R.E.O. White* (SNTSSS 171; Sheffield: Sheffield Academic Press, 1999), pp. 116-35.
Mosbech, H., 'Apostolos in NT', *ST* 2 (1948), pp. 166-200.
Moule, C.F.D., 'Sanctuary and Sacrifice in the Church of the New Testament', *JTS* 1 (1950), pp. 29-41.
— , 'A Note on Didache IX.4', *JTS* 6 (1955), pp. 240-43.
Moxnes, H., 'God and His Angel in the Shepherd of Hermas', *ST* 29 (1974), pp. 49-56.
Müller, U.B., 'Die Parakletenvorstellung im Johannesevangelium', *ZTK* 71 (1974), pp. 31-78.
— , *Prophetie und Predigt in Neuen Testament* (Gütersloh: Gerd Mohn, 1975).
— , *Zur frühchristlichen Theologiegeschichte. Judenchristentum und Paulinismus in Kleinasien an der Wende vom ersten zum zweiten Jahrhundert nach Christus* (Gütersloh: Gerd Mohn, 1976).
Munck, J., 'Presbyters and Disciples of the Lord in Papias', *HTR* 52 (1959), pp. 223-43.
— , 'Jewish Christianity in Post-Apostolic Times', *NTS* 6 (1959-60), pp. 103-16.
— , 'Primitive Jewish Christianity and later Jewish Christianity: Continuation or Rupture?', in *Aspects du Judeo-Christianisme* (Colloque de Strassburg 1964) (Paris: Presses Universitaires de France, 1965), pp. 77-91.
Murray, R.J., 'Jews, Hebrews and Christians: Some Needed Distinctions', *NT* 24 (1982), pp. 194-208.
Mussner, F., 'Die johanneische Parakletsprüche und die apostolische Tradition', *BZ* 5 (1961), pp. 56-70.
— , *The Historical Jesus in the Gospel of John* (London: Burns & Oates, 1967).
Musurillo, H., (ed.), *The Acts of the Christian Martyrs* (Oxford: Clarendon, 1972).
Nauck, W., 'Probleme des frühchristlichen Amtsverstandnisses', *ZNW* 48 (1957), pp. 200-20.
— , *Die Tradition und der Charakter des ersten Johannesbriefes* (Tübingen: Mohr, 1957).
Nautin, P., 'Notes critiques sur la Didachè', *VC* 13 (1959), pp. 118-20.

—, *Lettres et Écrivains Chrétiens des II et III siècles* (Paris: Les Éditions du Cerf, 1961).
Neufeld, V.H., *The Earliest Christian Confessions* (NTTS 5; Leiden: Brill, 1963).
Niederwimmer, K., *The Didache* (Hermeneia; Minneapolis, MN: Fortress, 1998).
Nielson, J.T., *Adam and Christ in the Theology of Irenaeus of Lyons* (Assen: van Gorcum, 1968).
Niewalda, P., *Sakramentssymbolik im Johannesevangelium?* (Limburg: Lahn-Verlag, 1958).
Nock, A.D., *Conversion, the Old and the New in Religion from Alexander the Great to Augustine of Hippo* (Oxford: Oxford University Press, 1933).
Norris, R.A., *God and the World in Early Christian Theology* (New York: Seabury Press, 1966).
Norris, F.W., 'Ignatius, Polycarp and 1 Clement: Walter Bauer reconsidered', *VC* 30 (1976), pp. 23-28.
Oberlinner, L., *Die Pastoralbriefe: Erste Folge: Erster* Timotheusbrief; Zweite *Folge: Zweiter* Timotheusbrief; Dritte *Folge: Titusbrief* (HTKNT XI.2.1, 2 and 3; Freiburg-Basel-Vienna: Herder, 1994, 1995 and 1996).
Oesterreicher, J., 'Um Kirche und Synagoge im Barnabasbrief', *ZKT* 74 (1952), pp. 62-70.
O'Hagan, A.P., 'The Great Tribulation to come in the Pastor of Hermas', in F.L. Cross (ed.), *Studia Patristica* 4.2 (Berlin: Akademie-Verlag, 1961), pp. 305-10.
Opitz, H., *Ursprünge frühkatholischer Pneumatologie* (Berlin: Evangelische Verlagsanstalt, 1960).
Osborn, E.F., *The Philosophy of Clement of Alexandria* (Cambridge: Cambridge University Press, 1957).
—, *Justin Martyr* (Tübingen: Mohr, 1973).
—, *Tertullian, First Theologian of the West* (Cambridge: Cambridge University Press, 1997).
—, *Irenaeus of Lyons* (Cambridge: Cambridge University Press, 2002).
Osiek, Carolyn, 'Wealth and Poverty in the Shepherd of Hermas', in E.A. Livingstone (ed.), *Studia Patristica* 17.2 (Oxford: Pergamon, 1982), pp. 725-30.
—, *Rich and Poor in the Shepherd of Hermas: An Exegetical Social Investigation* (CBQMS 15; Washington DC: Catholic Biblical Association, 1983).
—, *The Shepherd of Hermas: A Commentary* (Hermeneia; Minneapolis, MN: Fortress, 1999).
Otto, S., *"Natura" und "Dispositio": Untersuchung zum Naturbegriff und zur Denkform Tertullians* (MTS 2.19; München: Max Hueber, 1960).
Pagels, Elaine H., *The Johannine Gospel in Gnostic Exegesis, Heracleon's Commentary on John* (SBLMS 17; Nashville and New York: Abingdon, 1973).
—, *The Gnostic Paul* (Philadelphia, PA: Fortress, 1975).
—, *The Gnostic Gospels* (Harmondsworth: Penguin, 1982).
Painter, J., 'The Farewell Discourses and the History of Johannine Christianity', *NTS* 27 (1981), pp. 525-443.
—, 'The "Opponents" in 1 John', *NTS* 32 (1986), pp. 48-71.

—, *The Quest for the Messiah: The History, Literature and Theology of the Johannine Community* (Edinburgh: T.& T. Clark, 1991).
Panagopoulos, J., 'Die urchristliche Prophetie: ihr Charakter und ihre Funktion', in J. Panagopoulos (ed.), *Prophetic Vocation in the New Testament and Today* (Leiden: Brill, 1977), pp. 1-32.
Patsch, H., 'Die Prophetie des Agabus', *TZ* 28 (1972), pp. 228-32.
Paulsen, H., *Studien zur Theologie des Ignatius von Antiochien* (Göttingen: Vandenhoeck & Ruprecht, 1978).
Paulsen, H., 'Die Bedeutung des Montanismus fur die Herausbildung des Kanons', *VC* 32 (1978), pp. 19-52.
Pearson, B.A., *Gnosticism, Judaism and Egyptian Christianity* (SAC; Minneapolis, MN: Fortress, 1990).
Pearson, B.A., and J.E. Goehring (eds.), *The Roots of Egyptian Christianity* (SAC; Minneapolis, MN: Fortress, 1986).
Peel, M., *The Epistle to Rheginos* (London: SCM, 1969).
Perler, O., 'L'évêque, represéntant du Christ selon des documents des premiers siècles', in Y. Congar and B-D. Dupuy (eds.), *L'Épiscopat et l'Église Universelle* (Paris: Les Éditions du Cerf, 1962), pp. 31-66.
Pernveden, L., *The Concept of the Church in the Shepherd of Hermas* (STL 27; Lund: Gleerup, 1966).
Peterson, E., 'Beiträge zur Interpretation der Visionen im Pastor Hermae'; 'Kritische Analyse der fünften Vision des Hermas'; and 'Die Begegnung mit dem Ungeheuer', in E.Peterson, *Frühkirche Judentum und Gnosis* (Rome-Freiburg-Wien: Herder, 1959), pp. 254-309.
Petze, G., *Die Traditionen über Apolonius von Tyana und NT* (Leiden: Brill, 1970).
Piana, G. la, 'Foreign Groups in Rome during the first century of the Empire', *HTR* 20 (1927), pp. 183-403.
—, 'The Roman Church at the End of the Second Century', *HTR* 18 (1925), pp. 201-277.
Porsch, F., *Pneuma und Wort. Ein exegetischer Beitrag zur Pneumatologie des Johannesevangeliums* (Frankfurt: Knecht, 1974).
Potterie, I. de la, 'L'impeccabilité du Chrétien d'après 1 Jean 3.6-9', in *L'Évangile de Jean* (Recherches Bibliques 3; Bruges: Desclée de Brouwer, 1958), pp. 161-77.
Potterie, I. de la, and S. Lyonnet, *La vie selon l'Esprit. Condition du Chrétien* (Paris: Les Édition du Cerf, 1965) (English Translation: *The Christian Lives by the Spirit* [Staten Island, NY: Alba House, 1971]).
Powell, D., 'Tertullianists and Cataphrygians', *VC* 29 (1975), pp. 35-54.
Prast, F., *Presbyter und Evangelium in nachapostolischer Zeit* (Stuttgart: KBW, 1979).
Prigent, P., *Les Testimonia dans le Christianisme primitif. L'Épître de Barnabé I-XVI et ses sources* (Paris: Gabalda, 1961).
—, *Justin et l'AT. Les Testimonia dans le Christianisme primitif* (Paris: Gabalda, 1964).

—, 'L'Hérésie Asiate et l'Église confessante de l'Apocalypse à Ignace', *VC* 31 (1977), pp. 1-22.
Prigent, P., and R.A. Kraft, *L'Épître de Barnabé* (SC 172; Paris: Les Éditions du Cerf, 1971).
Quasten, J., *Patrology* (Westminster, MD: Newman Press, Vols. I–III, 1950, 1953 and 1960).
Quispel, G., *Lettre à Flora–Ptolémée* (SC 24; Paris: Les Éditions du Cerf, 2nd ed., 1966)
—, 'The Discussion of Judaic Christianity', *VC* 22 (1968), pp. 81-93.
—, 'Genius and Spirit', in M. Krause (ed.), *Essays on Nag Hammadi Texts* (NHS VI; Leiden: Brill, 1975), pp. 155-169.
—, 'Valentinian Gnosticism and the Apocryphon of John', in B. Layton (ed.), *The Rediscovery of Gnosticism I: The School of Valentinus* (Leiden: Brill, 1980), pp. 118-27.
Rackl, M., *Die Christologie des heiligen Ignatius von Antiochien* (FTS 14; Freiburg: Herder, 1914).
Rahner, J., 'Vergegenwärtigende Erinnerung: die Abschiedsreden, der Geist-Paraklet und die Retrospektive des Johannesevangelium', *ZNW* 91 (2000), pp. 72-90.
Rasthke, H., *Ignatius von Antiochien und die Paulusbriefe* (TU 99; Berlin: Akademie-Verlag, 1967).
Ratcliff, E.C., *Litugical Studies*, ed. A.H. Couratin and D.H. Tripp (London: SPCK, 1976).
Reiling, J., *Hermas and Christian Prophecy: a Study of the Eleventh Mandate* (SNT 37; Leiden: Brill, 1973).
—, 'Prophecy, the Spirit and the Church', in J.Panagopoulos (ed.), *Prophetic Vocation in the New Testament and Today* (Leiden: Brill, 1977), pp. 58-76.
—, 'Marcus Gnosticus and the New Testament: Eucharist and Prophecy', in T. Baarda, A.F.J. Klijn and W.C. van Unnik, *Miscellanea Neotestamentica* (Leiden: Brill, 1978), pp. 161-79.
Rhode, J., 'Häresie und Schisma im ersten Clemensbrief und in den Ignatiusbriefen', *NT* 10 (1968), pp. 217-33.
Richardson, C.C., *The Christianity of Ignatius of Antioch* (New York: Columbia University, 1935).
Richter, G., *Studien zum Johannesevangelium* (ed. J. Hainz) (BU 13; Regensburg: Pustet, 1977).
Riesenfeld, H., 'Reflections on the Style and Theology of St.Ignatius', in F.L. Cross (ed.), *Studia Patristica* 4 (TU 79; Berlin: Akademie-Verlag, 1961), pp. 312-22.
Robeck, C.M., *Prophecy in Carthage: Perpetua, Tertullian and Cyprian* (Cleveland, OH: Pilgrim Press, 1992).
Roberts, C.H., *Manuscript, Society and Belief in Early Christian Egypt* (London: The British Academy, 1979).
Robinson, J.A., 'The Immediate Sources of the Didache', *JTS* 35 (1934), pp. 113-46.

Robinson, J.A.T., *Redating the New Testament* (London: SCM, 1976).
— , *The Priority of John* (London: SCM, 1984).
Rogge, J., 'ἕνωσις und verwandte Begriffe in den Ignatiusbriefen', in *Und fragten nach Jesus, Beiträge aus Theologie, Kirche und Geschichte, Festschrift für E. Barnikol* (Berlin: Evangelische Verlaganstalt, 1964), pp. 45-51.
Roloff, J., *Apostolat-Verkündigung-Kirche: Ursprung, Inhalt und Funktion des kirchlichen Apostelamtes nach Paulus, Lukas und den Pastoralbriefen* (Gütersloh: Gerd Mohn, 1965).
Rudolph, K., *GNOSIS: The Nature and History of an Ancient Religion* (Edinburgh: T. & T. Clark, 1983).
Rusch, T., *Die Entstehung der Lehre vom heiligen Geist bei Ignatius von Antiochia, Theophilus von Antiochia und Irenäus von Lyon* (Zurich: Zwingli, 1951).
Sagnard, F.M.M., *La Gnose Valentinienne et le Témoignage de saint Irenée* (EPM 36; Paris: Librairie Philosophique J. Vrin, 1947).
— , *Extraits de Théodote: Clément d'Alexandrie* (SC 23; Paris: Les Éditions du Cerf, 1970).
Saint, W.P. le, *Tertullian's Treatises on Marriage and Remarriage* (ACW XIII; London: Longmans, Green, 1951).
— , *Tertullian: Treatises on Penance* (ACW XXVIII; London: Longmans, Green, 1959).
Sand, A., 'Anfänge einer Koordinierung verschiedener Gemeindeordungen nach den Pastoralbriefen', in J. Hainz (ed.), *Kirche im Werden* (München-Paderborn-Wien: Schöningh, 1976), pp. 214-37.
Satake, A., *Die Gemeindeordnung in der Johannesapokalypse* (WMANT 21; Neukirchen-Vluyn: Neukirchener Verlag, 1966).
Sauser, E., 'Tritt der Bischof an die Stelle Christi? Zur Frage nach der Stellung des Bischofs in der Theologie des hl. Ignatius von Antiocheia', in V. Flieder (ed.), *Festschrift für Franz Loidl* (Vienne: Hollinek, 1970), pp. 325-39.
Schafer, P., *Die Vorstellung vom heiligen Geist in der rabbinischen Literatur* (SANT 28; München: Kösel-Verlag, 1972).
Schelkle, K.H., *Die Petrusbriefe. Der Judasbriefe* (HTKNT 13.2; Freiburg-Basel-Vienna: Herder, 1961).
— , 'Spätapostolische Briefe als frühkatholisches Zeugnis', in J. Blinzer, O. Kuss and F. Mussner (eds.), *Neutestamentliche Aufsätze, Festschrift für J. Schmid* (Regensburg: Friedrich Pustet, 1963), pp. 225-232.
Schepelern, W., *Der Montanusmus und die Phrygischen Kulte* (Tübingen: Mohr, 1929).
Schille, G., 'Zur urchristliche Tauflehre: stilische Beobachtungen am Barnasbrief', *ZNW* 49 (1958), 31-52.
— , *Die urchristliche Kollegialmission* (ATANT 48; Zurich: Zwingli, 1967).
Schlier, H., *Religionsgeschlichtlicher Untersuchungen zu den Ignatiusbriefen* (Giessen: Topelmann, 1929).
— , 'Die Ordnung der Kirche nach den Pastoralbriefen', in *Glaube und Geschichte, Festschrift für F. Gogarten* (Giessen: Topelmann, 1948), pp. 38-60 (= H. Schlier,

Die Zeit der Kirche [Freiburg: Herder, 2nd ed., 1972], pp. 129-47; = in K. Kertelge, *Das kirchliche Amt in NT* [Darmstadt: Wissenschaftliche Buchgesellschaft, 1977], pp. 475-500).
Schnackenburg, R., *The Gospel according to John* (London: Burns & Oates, Vol. I, 1968; Vol. II, 1980; Vol. III, 1982).
— , *The Johannine Epistles* (Tunbridge Wells: Burns & Oates, 1984).
Schneider, J., *Die Kirchenbriefe* (NTD 10; Göttingen: Vandenhoeck & Ruprecht, 1961).
Schnelle, U., 'Johannes als Geisttheologe', *NT* 40 (1988), pp. 17-31.
— , 'Die Abschiedsreden im Johannesevangelium', *ZNW* 80 (1989), pp. 64-79.
Schoedel, W.R., 'A Blameless Mind "Not on loan" but "By nature" (Ignatius Trall. 1.1)', *JTS* 15, 1964, pp. 308-16.
— , 'A Neglected Motive for Trinitarianism', *JTS* 31 (1980), pp. 356-67.
— , *Ignatius of Antioch* (Hermeneia; Philadelphia, PA: Fortress, 1985).
Schoeps, H.J., *Urgemeinde Judenchristentum Gnosis* (Tübingen: Mohr, 1956).
Schottroff, Luise, 'Animae Naturaliter Salvandae, zur Problem der himmlischen Herkunft des Gnostikers', in W. Eltester (ed.), *Christentum und Gnosis* (Berlin: Topelmann, 1969), pp. 65-97.
Schröger, F., 'Die Verfassung der Gemeinde des ersten Petrusbriefes', in J. Hainz (ed.), *Kirche im Werden* (München: Schöningh, 1976), pp. 239-52.
Schulz, S., 'σπέρμα', in G. Friedrich (ed.), *TDNT* (Grand Rapids, MI: Eerdmanns, 1971), Vol. VII, p. 545.
Schüssler Fiorenza, Elisabeth, *Priester für Gott: Studien zum Herrschafts- und Priestermotiv in der Apokalypse* (NTAbh.7; Münster: Aschendorff, 1972).
— , *The Book of Revelation: Justice and Judgment* (Philadelphia, PA: Fortress, 1985).
Schwarz, R., *Bürgerliches Christentum im NT? Eine Studie zu Ethik, Amt und Recht in den Pastoralbriefen* (OKB 4; Klosterneuburg: Verlag OKB, 1983).
Schweizer, E., *Church Order in the New Testament* (London: SCM, 1961).
— , 'πνεῦμα', in G. Friedrich (ed.), *TDNT* (Grand Rapids, MI: Eerdmans, 1968), Vol.VI, pp. 389-451.
— , 'Observance of the Law and Charismatic Activity in Matthew's Gospel', *NTS* 16 (1969-70), pp. 213-30.
— , *Matthäus und seine Gemeinde* (SBS 71; Stuttgart: KBW, 1974).
Segelberg, E., 'Evangelium Veritatis. A Confirmation Homily and its Relation to the Odes of Solomon', *Orientalia Suecana* 8 (1959), pp. 3-42.
Segovia, F.F., 'The Theology and Provenance of John 15.1-17', *JBL* 101 (1982), pp. 115-28.
Selwyn, E.G., *The First Epistle of St. Peter* (London: Macmillan, 1946).
Sider, R.D., *Ancient Rhetoric and the Art of Tertullian* (Oxford: Oxford University Press, 1971).
— , 'On Symmetrical Composition in Tertullian', *JTS* 24 (1973), pp. 405-23.
— , 'On the Shows: An Analysis', *JTS* 29 (1978), pp. 339-56.

—, 'Approaches to Tertullian: A Survey of Recent Scholarship', *SC* 2 (1982), pp. 228-60.
Simon, M., 'La Migration à Pella: Legende ou réalité?', in *Aspects du Judeo-Christianisme*, Colloque de Strassburg 1964 (Paris: Presses Universitaires de France, 1965), pp. 37-54.
Skarsaume, O., *Proof from Prophecy: A Study in Justin Martyr's Proof-Text Tradition: Text-Type, Provenance, Theological Profile* (SNT 66; Leiden: Brill, 1987).
Smalley, S.S., *1, 2, 3 John* (WBC 51; Dallas TX: Word, 1984).
Smith, D.M., 'Johannine Christianity', *NTS* 21 (1975), pp. 222-48.
Smith, J.P., *St. Irenaeus: Proof of the Apostolic Preaching* (ACW 16; New York/Ramsey, NJ: Newman, 1952).
Spicq, C., *Les Épitres Pastorales* (EB; Paris: Gabalda, 1947).
—, *Les Épitres de Saint Pierre* (SB 4; Paris: Gabalda, 1966).
Standaert, B., 'L'Évangile de Vérité: Critique et Lecture', *NTS* 22 (1975-76), pp. 243-75.
Stead, G.C., 'Divine Substance in Tertullian', *JTS* 14 (1963), pp. 46-66.
—, 'The Valentinian Myth of Sophia', *JTS* 20 (1969), pp. 75-104.
—, 'In Search of Valentinus', in B. Layton (ed.), *The Rediscovery of Gnosticism I: The School of Valentinus* (Leiden: Brill, 1980), pp. 75-102.
Steichele, H., 'Geist und Amt als kirchenbildende Elemente in der Apg.', in J. Hainz (ed.), *Kirche im Werden* (München: Schöningh, 1976), pp. 185-203.
Story, C.I.K., *The Nature of Truth in the "Gospel of Truth" and in the Writings of Justin Martyr* (SNT 25; Leiden: Brill, 1970).
Strecker, G., *Der Weg der Gerechtigkeit: Untersuchung zur Theologie des Matthaus* (FRLANT 82; Göttingen: Vanhoeck & Ruprecht, 2nd ed., 1966).
—, *Das Judenchristentum in den Pseudo-Klementinen* (TU 70; Berlin: Akademie-Verlag, 2nd ed., 1981).
Streeter, B.H., *The Primitive Church* (London: Macmillan, 1929).
Sweet, J.P.M., *Revelation* (Phildelphia, PA: Westminster, 1979).
Swete, H.B., *The Holy Spirit in the Ancient Church* (London: Macmillan, 1912).
Talbert, C.H., '2 Peter and the Delay of the Parousia', *VC* 20 (1966), pp. 137-45.
Tarvainen, O., *Glaube und Liebe bei Ignatius von Antiochien* (Joensun: Pohjois-Karjalan Kirjapaino Oy, 1967).
Telfer, W., 'The Origins of Christianity in Africa', in F.L. Cross (ed.), *Studia Patristica* 4.2 (TU 79; Berlin: Akademie-Verlag, 1961), pp. 512-17.
Telfer, W., *The Office of a Bishop* (London: Darton, Longman & Todd, 1962).
Thierry, J.J., 'Note sur τὰ ἐλάχιστα τῶν ζώων au chapitre XX de la 1 Clementis', *VC* 14 (1960), pp. 235-44.
Thüsing, W., *Die Erhöhung und Verherrlichung Jesu im Johannesevangelium* (NA 21.1-2; Münster: Aschendorff, 1960).
Tiede, D.L., *The Charismatic Figure as Miracle Worker* (Missoula, MT: Scholars, 1972).

Tinsley, E.J., 'The imitatio Christi in the Mysticism of St. Ignatius of Antioch, in K. Aland and F.L. Cross (eds.), *Studia Patristica* 2.2, (TU 64; Berlin: Akademie-Verlag, 1957), pp. 553-60.
Tollinton, R.B., *Clement of Alexandria* (London: Williams & Norgate, 1914).
Torrance, T.F., *The Doctrine of Grace in the Apostolic Fathers* (Edinburgh-London: Oliver & Boyd, 1948).
Towner, P.H., *The Goal of our Instruction: The Structure of Theology and Ethics in the Pastoral Epistles* (JSNTSS 34; Sheffield: Sheffield Academic Press, 1989).
Trankle, H., *Adversus Iudaeos* (Wiesbaden: Steiner, 1964).
Tremblay, R., *La Manifestation et la Vision de Dieu selon St. Irénée de Lyon* (MBT 41; Munchen: Aschendorff, 1978).
Trevett, Christine, *A Study of Ignatius of Antioch in Syria and Asia* (SBEC 29; Lewiston: Edwin Mellen, 1992).
— , *Montanism: Gender, Authority and the New Prophecy* (Cambridge: Cambridge University Press, 1996).
Trites, A.A., *The New Testament Concept of Witness* (SNTSMS 31; Cambridge: Cambridge University Press, 1977).
Turner, H.E.W., *The Pattern of Christian Truth* (London: Mowbray, 1954).
Unnik, W.C. van, 'Is 1 Clement 20 purely Stoic?', *VC* 4 (1950), pp. 181-89.
— , '1 Clement 34 and the "Sanctus"', *VC* 5 (1951), pp. 204-48.
— , 'The Teaching on Good Works in 1 Peter', *NTS* 1 (1954-55), pp. 92-110.
— , 'The Gospel of Truth and the New Testament', in F.L. Cross (ed.), *The Jung Codex* (London: Mowbray, 1955), pp. 79-129.
— , 'Christianity according to 1 Peter', *ET* 68 (1956-57), pp. 79-83.
Verner, D.C., *The Household of God: The Social World of the Pastoral Epistles* (SBLDS 71; Chico, CA: Scholars, 1983).
Vögtle, A., 'Die Schriftwerdung der apostolischen Paradosis nach 2 Petr. 1.12-15', in H. Baltensweiler and B. Reicke (eds.), *Neues Testament und Geschichte: Historisches Geschehen und Deutung im Neues Testament* (Zurich: Theologischer Verlag/Tübingen: Mohr, 1972), 297-306.
Vokes, F.E., *The Riddle of the Didache: Fact or Fiction, Heresy or Catholicism?* (London: SPCK/New York: Macmillan, 1938).
Vööbus, A., *Liturgical Traditions in the Didache* (Stockholm: ETSE, 1968).
Waszink, J.H., *De Anima* (Amsterdam: J.M. Meulenhoff, 1947).
Weinel, H., *Die Wirkungen des Geistes und der Geister im nachapostolischen Zeitalter bis auf Irenäus* (Freiburg: Druck von H. Lampp, 1899).
Weinrich, W.C., *Spirit and Martyrdom: A Study of the Work of the Holy Spirit in Contexts of Persecution and Martyrdom in the New Testament and Early Christian Literature* (Washington DC: University Press of America, 1981).
Weiss, H-F., 'Paulus und der Heretiker, zum Paulusverstandnis in den Gnosis', in W. Eltester (ed.), *Christentum und Gnosis* (Berlin: Topelmann, 1969), pp. 116-28.
Wengst, K., *Tradition und Theologie des Barnabasbriefes* (AKG 42; Berlin-New York: Walter de Gruyter, 1971).

—, *Häresie und Orthodoxie im Spiegel des ersten Johannesbriefes* (Gütersloh: Gerd Mohn, 1976).

—, *Bedrängte Gemeinde und verherrlichter Christus: Der historische Ort des Johannesevangeliums als Schlüssel zu seiner Interpretation* (BTS 5; Neukirchen-Vluyn: Neukirchener, 1983).

Wenk, M., *Community-Forming Power. The Socio-Ethical Role of the Spirit in Luke-Acts* (Sheffield: Sheffield Academic Press, 2000).

Whittaker, Molly (ed.), *Oratio ad Graecos* (Oxford: Clarendon, 1982).

Widmann, M., 'Irenäus und seine theologische Väter', *ZTK* 54 (1957), pp. 156-73.

Wilckens, U., 'Der Paraklet und die Kirche', in D. Lührmann and G. Strecker (eds.), *Kirche* (Tübingen: Mohr, 1980), pp. 185-203.

Wilken, R.L., 'Collegia, Philosophical Schools and Theology', in S. Benko and J.J. O'Rourke (eds.), *Early Church History: The Roman Empire as the Setting of Primitive Christianity* (London: Oliphants, 1972), pp. 268-91 (= revised version of 'Towards a Social Interpretation of Early Christian Apologetics', *CH* 39 [1970], pp. 437-58).

—, *The Myth of Christian Beginnings* (London: SCM, 1979).

—, *The Christians as the Romans saw Them* (New Haven, CT: Yale, 1984).

Williams, Jacqueline A., *Biblical Interpretation in the Gnostic Gospel of Truth from Nag Hammadi* (SBLDS 79; Atlanta, GA: Scholars, 1988).

Wilson, R.McL., 'Jewish Christianity and Gnosticism', in *Aspects du Judeo-Christianisme*, Colloque de Strassburg 1964 (Paris: Presses Universitaires de France 1965), pp. 261-272.

—, 'The Spirit in Gnosticism', in B. Lindars and S.S. Smalley (eds.), *Christ and Spirit in the New Testament* (Cambridge: Cambridge University Press), pp. 345-55.

—, 'Valentinus and the Gospel of Truth', in B. Layton (ed.), *The Rediscovery of Gnosticism I: The School of Valentinus* (Leiden: Brill, 1980), pp. 133-41.

Wilson, W.J., 'The Career of the Prophet Hermas', *HTR* 20 (1927), pp. 21-62.

Wilson, W.C., *Five Problems in the Interpretation of the Shepherd of Hermas: Authorship, Genre, Canonicity, Apocalyptic, and the Absence of the Name 'Jesus Christ'* (MBPS 34; Lewiston-Queenston-Lampeter: Mellen, 1995).

—, *Toward a Reassessment of the Shepherd of Hermas: Its Date and Pneumatology* (Lewiston: Edwin Mellen, 1993).

Windisch, H., 'Der Barnabasbrief', in *Die Apostolischen Väter* (HzNT Ergänzungsband; Tübingen: Mohr, 1923).

—, *The Spirit-Paraclete in the Fourth Gospel* (Facet Books Biblical Series 20; Philadelphia, PA: Fortress, 1968) (= English Translation of 'Die fünf johanneischen Parakletsprüche', in H. von Soden and R. Bultmann [eds.], *Festgabe für A. Julicher* [Tübingen: Mohr, 1927], and 'Jesus und der Geist im Johannesevangelium', in H.G. Wood [ed.], *Amicitiae Corolla: Essays Presented to J.R. Harris* [London: University of London Press, 1933]).

Wingren, G., *Man and the Incarnation. A Study in the Biblical Theology of Irenaeus* (Edinburgh: Oliver & Boyd, 1959).

Winslow, D.F., 'The Idea of Redemption in the Epistles of St. Ignatius of Antioch', *GOR* 11 (1965), pp. 119-131.

Woll, D.B., 'The Departure of "The Way": The First Farewell Discourse in the Gospel of John', *JBL* 99 (1980), pp. 225-39.

Wong, D.W.F., 'Natural and Divine Order in 1 Clement', *VC* 31 (1977), pp. 81-87.

Wray, Judith H., *Rest as a Theological Metaphor in the Epistle to the Hebrews and the Gospel of Truth: Early Christian Homiletics of Rest* (SBLDS 166; Atlanta, GA: Scholars, 1998).

Wrede, W., *Untersuchungen zum ersten Clemensbriefe* (Göttingen: Vandenhoeck & Ruprecht, 1891).

Young, Francis M., *The Theology of the Pastoral Epistles* (Cambridge: Cambridge University Press, 1994).

Ziegler, A.W., *Neue Studien zum ersten Clemensbrief* (München: Manz, 1958).

Zimmerman, A.F., *Die urchristlichen Lehrer* (Tübingen: Mohr, 1984).

Zwaan, J. de, 'The Essene Origin of the Odes of Solomon', in R.P. Casey, Silva Lake and A.K. Lake (eds.), *Quantulacunque: Studies Presented to Kirsopp Lake* (London: Christophers, 1937), pp. 285-302.

— , 'Some Remarks on the "Church Idea" in the Second Century', *Aux Sources de la Tradition chrétienne. Mélanges offerts à M. Goguel* (Neuchâtel-Paris: Delachaux & Niestlé, 1950), pp. 270-78.

Author Index

Abbott, A.E., 67
Abramowski, R., 61
Adam, A., 44, 240
Aland, Barbara, 178, 180
Aland, K, 7, 123-24, 129
d'Arles, A., 196, 207
Andreson, C., 79
Ashton, J., 23
Audet, J-P., 44-47, 160-61, 314
Aune, D.E., 44-45, 50-51, 54-55, 58, 60-62, 64, 68-70, 79, 89-90, 93-95
Aziza, C., 322

Baarda, T., 218
Balch, D.L., 144
Baltensweiler, H. 4
Bammel, E., 5, 31
Barclay, J.G.M., 16
Bardtke, H., 70, 311
Barker, Margaret, 42, 89
Barnard, L.W., 119, 125, 150-51, 164-65
Barnes, T.D., 8, 125, 222-23, 225, 227-34, 236, 239-40, 246-47, 297, 300
Barrett, C.K., 6, 9, 26, 29-31, 34, 48, 96-97, 128
Barth, G., 50
Barth, M., 14
Bartsch, H-W., 58
Batiffol, P., 79
Bauckham, R.J., 90-95, 104-6, 108
Bauer, W., 58, 79, 142, 252
Beasley-Murray, G.R., 3, 22, 24-25, 34, 89, 91, 93-94, 97-98
Beare, F.W., 48-50, 139, 145
Becker, C., 229
Becker, J., 5, 25, 27, 29, 321
Beckwith, I.T., 91
Behr, J., 198, 200-1, 203, 208, 215, 217, 255, 258-59, 261
Bender, W., 8, 228, 237, 242, 320

Bennema, C., 5
Benoit, A., 58, 114, 167, 195, 216, 302
Bernard, J.H., 62-63, 66-67, 79, 307-9
Berger, K., 51
Berthouzoz, R., 171
Best, E., 139, 141
Betz, H.D., 10-11
Betz, O., 5
Beyschlag, K., 148-150
Bigg, C., 254-55, 260
Black, M., 94
Blass, F. (and Debrunner, A.) 144-45
Blinzer, J. 141
Bogart, J., 42
Bonnard, P., 50
Bonwetsch, N., 7
Boring, M.E., 31-32, 39, 41, 44, 46, 50-51, 90-91, 94
Bornkamm, G., 5, 46, 50, 52, 95, 129
Bousset, W., 116, 216
Bowe, Barbara E., 129, 148-49
Bradshaw, P.F., 184-85
Braun, F-M., 70, 79, 110
Braun, R., 222, 227, 241, 299
Bray, G.L., 8, 235, 297
Brock, S., 79
van Broek, R., 79
Brooke, A.E., 35, 42
Brown, R., 5, 22, 26-30, 32-34, 36-39, 42, 73, 85, 135
Brox, N., 96-97, 151-52, 157-59, 196
Bruce, F.F., 10, 13, 91
Brunner, G., 149
Büchsel, F., 42
Bultmann, R., 5, 28, 30, 38, 41-42, 45, 58
Burge, G.M., 5, 25-26, 28-31, 33, 35
Burgess, S.M., 5

Canabiss, A., 304
Cadman, W.H., 287
Caird, G.B., 89, 91, 93-94, 287
Carlton-Paget, J.N.B., 110, 112, 114
Carmignac, J., 70, 311
Carson, D.A., 22
Case, S.J., 5
Casey, R.P., 79
Cessato, J.A., 184
Chadwick, H., 59, 70, 76, 125, 169, 269, 321
Charlesworth, J.H., 22, 59-60, 63, 67, 70-73, 75-76, 79, 307, 309, 311
Chester, A., 118
Chevalier, M-A. 3, 6
Church, F.F., 226
Claesson, G., 315
Congar, Y., 302
Connelly, R.H., 321
Conzelmann, H., 96-97, 102, 262
Cothenet, E., 50
Couratin, A.H. 230
Court, J., 89
Cranfield, C.E.B., 104-105, 139
Cross, A.R., 25
Cullmann, O., 22, 24

Dahl, N.A., 112
Danielou, J., 44, 79, 227-28, 230, 236, 316
Daube, D., 142
Davey, N.F., 28, 32
Davies, J.G., 123
Davies, W.D., 50, 161
Davis, J.A., 4, 303
de Jonge, M., 321
de Labriolle, P., 7, 122-23, 125, 183-84, 222, 233, 245, 276, 280
de la Potterie, I., 32, 40, 42
Desjardins, M.R., 172, 176, 268
de Zwaan, J. 79
Dibelius, M., 45, 96, 102, 152, 155, 157-60, 162, 313
Didier, M., 50
Dietzfelbinger, C., 5, 29, 33
Dodd, C.H., 36, 39, 42, 111
Donelson, L.R., 102

Donfried, K.P., 128, 131, 135
Doutreleau, L., 200, 203, 205, 207
Drijvers, H.J.W., 61, 65-66, 79, 312
Dunn, J.D.G, 3, 4, 6, 9-13, 24-26, 30-33, 40-43, 95-100, 107, 118, 140-42, 146, 150.
Dupuy, B-D., 302

Elliott, J.H., 139-42, 144, 149-50
Ellis, E.E., 96, 104, 128
Eltester, W., 52, 180
Elze, M., 82-83, 304
Evans, E.E., 229, 234, 241-42

Farrer, A., 91
Fee, G.D., 4, 96-97
Feuillet, A., 89
Fiorenza, Elizabeth S., 23, 94
Fleming, J., 78
Floyd, W.E.G., 258, 260
Foerster, W., 173, 177-78
Forbes, C., 12
Ford, Josephine M., 89-90, 92, 125
Fornberg, T., 105-106
Fox, R.L., 125
France, R.T., 50
Franck, E., 5, 30
Fredouille, J.C., 315
Freeman-Grenville, G.S.P., 125
Frend, W.H.C., 125, 190, 191, 195, 222, 225, 232, 249, 299
Friedrich, G., 101, 107

Galtier, P., 254
Gerke, F., 129
Glover, T.R., 229, 315
Gnilka, J., 13, 14, 48
Goguel, M., 44, 112
Goodspeed, E.J., 49
Goppelt, L., 16, 44, 139
Granfield, P., 59
Grant, R.M., 125, 171
Green, H.A., 182, 279
Green, M., 105-106
Gregg, J.A.F., 63
Griggs, C.W., 253
Grillmeir, A., 206, 227
Grobel, K., 171-76

Grundmann, W., 39
Gundry, R.H., 49
Gunkel, H., 8
Guthrie, D., 13, 36, 50, 96, 98, 104-105, 139

Haacker, K., 5
Haenchen, E., 12
Hafeman, S.J., 4
Hagner, D.A., 149
Hamilton, N.Q., 4
Hanson, A.T., 96, 99
Hanson, R.P.C., 249
Hare, D.R.A., 49
Harris, J.R., 45, 47, 61-63, 65, 67, 69, 76, 79-80, 307-11
Harrison, P.N., 96, 118
Harvey, W.W., 207
Hauck, F., 39, 41-42
Hauschild, W-D., 6, 80-81, 83, 180-81, 196, 254, 258, 260-61, 269
Haya-Prats, G., 3
Headlam, A.C., 63, 78
Heine, R.E., 7, 183-84
Held, H-J., 50
Hermann, I., 4
Hill, D., 49-50, 70, 91, 95, 101
Hollander, H.W., 321
Holwerda, D.E., 5, 28
Horbury, W., 110, 191
Horn, F.W., 4
Hornshuh, M., 252
Horrell, D.G., 148
Hoskyns, E.C., 28, 32
Houlden, J.L., 41
Houssiau, A., 197
Howard, W.F., 35
Hull, J.H.E., 3
Hümmel, R., 50
Hvaalvik, R., 110-12, 116

Isaacs, M.E., 161

Jaschke, H-J., 7, 187, 196-97, 199, 201, 207-8, 215-16, 296
Jaubert, A., 147
Jenkins, D.E., 207
Jeremias, J., 45, 96

Jeske, R.L., 90
Johnson, A.R., 77
Johnson, M.E., 184-85
Johnston, G., 5, 31
Joly, R., 150, 161
Jonas, H., 171-73, 262-63, 265
Jungmann, J.A., 59

Karpp, H., 237-38, 298
Käsemann, E., 51, 97, 107, 149
Kearsley, R., 8
Keener, C.S., 5, 6, 26
Kelly, J.N.D., 1, 96-97, 104-8, 139, 145-46, 182, 187, 255
Kiddle, M., 94
Kilpatrick, G.D., 49-50, 52
Kingsbury, J.A., 50-52
Klassen, W., 278
Klijn, A.F.J., 218
Knight, J., 104, 106
Knoch, O., 149-50
Knopf, R., 1, 3, 46-47, 106, 113, 129, 147
Koester, H., 16
Körtner, U.H.J., 24, 117
Kraft, H., 7, 124-25
Kraft, R.A., 109, 111-15
Kremer, J., 3
Kretschmar, G., 312
Kroymann, A., 240
Kümmel, W.G., 22, 36, 49, 96, 104-105
Kydd, R.A.N., 8

Labourt, J., 79
Lake, A.K., 79
Lake, K., 191, 193
Lake, S., 79
Lampe, G.W.H., 1, 3, 14, 63, 79, 91, 97, 117, 130-31, 191-92, 194, 216, 230, 266
Lampe, P., 135-38, 151, 170, 184, 233, 279
la Piana, G., 135
Lattke, M., 65, 69, 76, 80
Law, R., 35
Lawlor, H.J., 123, 191

Lawson, J., 45, 58, 130-31, 208, 210, 289
Layton, B., 79, 171, 173, 176
Leaney, A.R.C., 161
Leisegang, J., 305
Leroy, H., 38
le Saint, W.P., 228, 230-31
Lewis, C.T. (and Short, C.), 247
Liddell, H.G. (Scott, R., Jones, H.S. and McKenzie, R.) 192
Lietzmann, H., 222, 304
Lieu, Judith, 37, 39-40, 42-43, 292-93, 317
Lightfoot, J.B., 128, 159, 302
Lightfoot, R.H., 23, 31
Lilla, S.C.R., 254
Lincoln, A.T., 13
Lindars, B., 5, 23, 27, 29, 31, 78, 91, 111, 169
Livingston, Elizabeth A., 209.
Lohmeyer, E., 91
Lohse, E., 89
Loofs, A., 196
Louth, A., 193
Lüdemann, G., 135
Lührmann, D., 33
Lull, D.J., 4
Luz, U., 3, 15

Maier, H.O., 151
Manson, T.W., 23
Markschies, C., 170, 172, 176
Marshall, I.H., 36-38, 40-42, 96-99, 102
Martin, R.P., 14, 22, 105, 139
Marxsen, W., 149
Matthews, J.F., 223, 300
Maurer, C., 54, 303
Mayer, G., 305, 314
McDonald, L.M., 14, 89, 96, 104-5, 139
McGuire, A., 172-73
McNeill, B., 79, 191
Meade, D.G., 13, 77
Mehat, A., 209
Meier, J.P., 15, 49, 135
Meinhold, P., 57-58, 129, 147-48
Menzies, R.P., 4

Michaels, J.R., 139
Michel, O., 52
Miller, J.D., 96
Minear, P.S., 136
Mingana, A., 63, 76, 79, 309-11
Mitton, C.L., 10, 13-14
Molland, E., 107-108
Moloney, F.J., 22
Montgomery-Hitchcock, F.R., 196, 210
Morel, V., 222, 238, 245-46
Morgan-Wynne, J.E., 6, 25, 27, 41, 240
Morris, L., 22, 50
Moule, C.F.D., 4, 6, 141-42
Muddiman, J., 14
Müller, U.B., 5, 23, 27, 31, 33, 312
Murray, R.J., 73, 79
Musurillo, H., 189, 191, 193, 222-23
Mussner, F., 5

Neufeld, V.N., 37
Newton, K., 160, 314
Neyrey, J.H., 104-106
Niederwimmer, K., 44-47
Nineham, D.E., 3
Nock, A.D., 172

Oberlinner, L., 96-99, 101
Opitz, H., 6, 129, 160
Osborn, E.F., 164, 208, 227, 237, 251, 256, 258, 260, 318
Osiek Carolyn, 137, 151-52, 156, 158-59, 162-63, 289
Otto, S., 227-28
Oulton, J.E., 23, 191
Overman, J.A., 49-50

Pagels, Elaine, 180
Painter, J., 27
Patsch, H., 12
Paulsen, H., 7, 58, 125
Percy, E., 13
Perler, O., 302
Pfister, W., 4
Phillips, L.E., 184-85

Porsch, F., 5, 24-25, 28, 30, 32-33, 40, 42
Porter, S.E., 14, 25, 89, 96, 104-105, 139
Powell, D., 123, 235, 251, 297
Prigent, P., 109, 111-15, 169

Quasten J., 59, 109, 119, 128, 226, 228-34, 236, 239-41, 246-47

Rackl, M., 304
Rahner, J., 5, 30, 33
Rambaut, W.H., 207
Rankin, D. 222, 226, 234-35
Ratcliff, E.C., 230
Reicke, B., 4
Reiling, J., 6, 151, 164, 218-19, 277
Rengstorff, K., 314
Richardson, C.C., 57, 302
Ritter, A.M., 79
Roberts, A., 207
Roberts, C.H., 252
Robinson, J.A.T., 13-14, 16, 22, 36, 44, 49, 104-5, 139
Robinson, J.M., 52
Robeck, C., 235, 244, 300
Rousseau, A., 200, 203, 205, 207
Rudolph, K., 171-72, 262, 264
Rüsch, T., 6
Russell, D.S., 77

Sagnard, F.M.M., 171, 173-74, 262-68
Salmon, G., 125
Sand, A., 101
Sandmel, S., 254
Satake, A., 89, 95
Schäfer, P., 107
Schneemelcher, W., 303
Schelke, K., 107-108
Schepelern, W. 7, 123
Schlatter, D.A., 50
Schlier, H., 13-14, 56, 58, 304
Schnackenburg, R., 13-14, 22-27, 29-30, 32-34, 36-39, 41-42, 98, 262
Schneider, J., 36, 39, 41-42, 104-5, 139

Schnelle, U., 5, 25-27, 29-30, 33, 35
Schoedel, W.R., 54-58, 287, 303-5
Schotroff, Luise, 180
Schulz, S., 42
Schweizer, E., 1, 43, 50-52, 91, 95-96, 100, 278
Selwyn, E.G., 139, 144
Shelton, J.B., 4
Shepherd, W.H., 4
Sider, R.D., 226
Sidebottom, E.M., 104
Skarsaume, O., 109, 169
Skeat, T.C., 252
Smalley, S.S., 5, 22, 31, 37, 91
Smith, D.M., 22, 312
Snyder, G.N., 278
Southwell, P., 72
Spicq, C. 96, 139, 145
Stalder, K., 4
Standaert, B., 171
Stanton, G.N., 49-50
Stauffer, E., 89
Stead, C., 227
Stendahl, K., 52
Stonehouse, N.B., 49
Story, C.I.K., 164, 170, 174, 176
Strathmann, H., 91
Strecker, G., 33, 36, 49-51, 107
Streeter, B.H., 50
Stronstadt, R., 3, 4
Sweet, J., 91, 93-94
Swete, H.B., 8

Taylor, J.V., 6
Thüsing, W., 32
Torrance, T.F., 130, 163
Towner, P.H., 96-98, 102
Trankle, H., 232, 319-20, 322
Tremblay, R., 197, 217
Trevett, Christine, 7, 54-56, 58, 121-25, 183-84, 233, 235, 298, 300
Tripp, D.H., 230
Trites, A.A., 91
Turcan, M., 314-16
Turner, M., 4

van Roon, A. 13
van Unik, W.C., 144, 171, 218

Vermaseren, M.J., 79
Vielhauer, P., 141
Vögtle, A., 104-106
Vokes, F.E., 44, 47
von Campenhausen, H., 1, 46, 96, 99, 119-20, 226, 235, 244, 247
von Goltz, E.F., 304
von Harnack, A., 44, 78, 129, 135, 146, 150, 195
von Lips, H., 99, 101
Vööbus, A., 45

Wainwright, A.W., 6
Walls, A.F., 7, 125
Waszink, J.H., 230, 235
Weinel, H., 2, 8, 25
Weinrich, W.C., 57-58, 91, 119, 144, 190, 193, 222-23, 225, 238, 242, 247-48, 300
Wengst, K., 22, 109-14, 116

Wenk, M., 4
Westcott, B.F., 35, 41
Whittaker, M., 80
Wilckens, U., 33
Wilcox, M., 128
Williams, Jacqueline A., 171
Williamson, G., 193
Wilson, J.C., 151, 153-54, 156, 162
Wilson, R. McL., 303
Wilson, W.G., 35
Windisch, H., 5, 27, 110-12
Wingren, G., 196, 206, 208, 216
Winston, D., 303
Witherington, B., 48
Wray, Judith H., 171, 175
Wrede, W., 129, 146, 148-50

Young, F., 102

Ziegler, A.W., 147, 149

Scripture Index

Old Testament

Genesis
1.1-2 165
1.26-27 81
1.27 133
2 202, 263
2.7 81
3 308
3.21 62
49.11 166

Exodus
33.1-3 112

Numbers
11.25-26 145
11.29 17

Deuteronomy
5.24 210
13.1-11 281
19.15 93
30.6 116
30.15 242
31.6 119
31.8 119
31.23 119

Joshua
1.9 119

Judges
6.39 204

1 Samuel
16.14 160

1 Kings
13.22 281
18 168.

2 Kings
9.30 75

1 Chronicles
28.20 119

2 Chronicles
32.7 119

Psalms
1 245
1.3-6 113
8.6 157
19 169
24 169
47 169
59.11 320
68.18 167-69, 293, 318
72 169
82 200
99 169
110 169
112.6 258

Isaiah
1.7-8 320
1.20 320
3.1-3 320-21
5.6 204, 319-20
11.1-10 17, 167-68, 292
11.1-3 320-22
11.1-2 317
11.1 293
11.2-3 169, 318
11.2 145, 199
11.4 93
22.15-25 77
22.17-18 77
22.19-23 77
28.7-8 281
40.6-8 141
42.1-4 166
42.5 202, 296
43.18-21 212
43.19-21 203, 212
44.1-3 63
53 149
57.16 201-2, 296

59.1-2 160
59.15-19 160
61.1 199
65.13 320
65.16 320
66 169

Jeremiah
4.30 75
5.14 93
27-28 281
31.31-34 203, 212, 282

Ezekiel
8.3 153
10.18 160
11.1 153
11.19 112
11.22-23 160
11.24 153
23.40 75
36.26 112-113, 203, 212
40.2 153
47 67
47.1-12 117
47.1 113
47.7 113
47.12 113

Daniel
7 169
10.19 119

Hosea
12.10 210

Joel
2 12, 168-69, 205, 321
2.28-32 111, 282
2.28-29 167, 293, 318, 321
2.28 98, 110, 231.

Micah
3.5-12 281

Zechariah
4 92-93
4.1-14 92

4.6 92

Malachi
1.10-12 292

Non-Biblical Jewish Writings

Damascus Document (Zadokite Fragment)
7.12 (5.11) 161, 314
8.20 (7.4) 161, 314

4 Ezra
3.22 160

Manual of Discipline
3.13 – 4.26 160

Philo
de Iosepho
147 305

de mutatione nominum
40 305

de specialibus legibus
1.330 305
4.201 305

Sibyline Oracles
2.181 303

Wisdom of Solomon
7.10 303, 306
18.14-15 304

New Testament

Matthew (49-53)
1.23 52
4.23-25 53
5-7 53
5.8 176
5.10-12 247
5.16 263
5.17-20 21
5.21-26 51
5.22-23 241

Scripture Index

5.32 51
5.37 51
7.11 13, 126
7.13-23 282
7.13 126
7.15-23 52, 285
7.16-20 50
7.17-18 53
7.21-23 50
7.21 50
7.23 84
8.17 52
10 51
10.5-6 51
10.19-20 53
10.20 199
10.23 51, 231, 239
10.28 131
10.40-41 51
12.18-21 52
12.33 53
13.35 52
13.40-43 124
15.24 51
17.17-20 51
18.20 52, 84
19.9 51
19.21 48
21.43 198
22.15-20 266
23.2-3 51
23.8-12 51
23.34 51
24.45-51 303
26.41 242
28.18-20 21
28.20 53, 84-85

Mark
3.28-29 46
13.5-6 282
13.9 92
13.10 247-48
13.11 92-93, 120, 145, 191
13.21-23 282
14.38 193, 213, 242
15.38 321
16.17-18 52

Luke
1.41 309
4.18 39
6.43 53
9.24-25 263
10.18 204
10.19 264
11.13 13, 26
11.49 51
12.4-5 131
12.11-12 120, 145, 191, 248
12.20 263
12.42-46 303
16.16 319, 321
17.28-33 263
21.14-15 247-48
24.49 13, 232

John (22-35)
1.1-3 42
1.9 263
1.10 42
1.13 24, 38
1.14 41
1.18 30
1.32-33 27
2.22 30-31, 42
3.1-15 44
3.1-10 38
3.3-13 24
3.3-8 25, 34
3.4 24
3.5-8 25
3.5 24
3.6 24, 56
3.8 24, 54
3.14-16 25
3.14-15 26
3.34 27
3.35 32
4.10-14 193
4.14 26, 58, 203, 294
4.24 228
5.1-9 230
6 27
6.27 52
6.42 52
6.63 242

7.37-39 26, 35, 58, 203-204
7.37-38 26-27
7.38 193
7.39 26-27, 35
7.41-42 52
7.52 52
8.14 54
9.22 43
10.11-14 267
10.12 248
10.16 36
11.51-52 36
12.16 30-31, 42
13-17 27
13.7 30
13.33 27
13.36 27
14.1 27
14.2 27
14.16-17 28, 35, 272
14.16 27
14.17 27-28, 30, 322
14.18-19 28, 35
14.18 28
14.22 29
14.23 29, 35
14.26 29-30, 32, 35, 42, 85, 283
14.27-28 27
15 256
15.1-17 35
15.26-27 34
15.26 34, 191
15.27 34
16.4 27
16.7-11 34
16.8-11 191
16.12-15 31-32, 42, 85, 174, 283
16.12-13 32, 236, 245
16.12 32, 228-29, 242, 299
16.13-15 28, 32
16.13 31
16.14-15 32
16.25 33
17 250
17.20-23 36
17.26 33
18.14 31
19.34 193

20 263
20.21-22 52
20.22 174
21.14-15 22

Acts of the Apostles
1.8 13, 15, 52
2 13
2.1 13
2.4 12
2.5 13
2.8 12
2.12 98, 111
2.17-18 300
2.18-21 318
2.33 169, 217
4.8 12, 153
5.1-11 12, 164
6.10 153
7.55 153
8 216
8.4-24 15
8.14-24 13
8.18-24 164
9.1-2 20
9.15-18 280
9.17-19 20
9.19-22 20
9.27 280
10-11 280
10 13
10.38 39
10.45 111
10.46 12
11 21
11.16 13
11.19-26 20
11.28 12
13-14 20, 87
13.1 12, 20
13.2 12
13.9 12, 153
15 21, 280
15.1-29 20
15.1 280
15.28 12
15.32 12
16.6 15

16.7 12
16.8 15
16.10 15
17.16-34 128
18.2 135
19 87
19.6 12
19.11-20 15
20.22 18
20.28 13, 15
21.4 12, 18
21.9 12
21.10-11 12
21.20-22 280
28.14 136
28.15 136
28.30-31 136
28.31 13

Romans
1.8 135
2.29 116
5.5 98
7-8 160
7 160, 259
7.4 237
7.5 267
7.6 237
8.2 243
8.3-5 243
8.3 213
8.4 10
8.5 56
8.9 10, 296
8.12 154
8.14-15 200
8.14 10, 200, 257
8.15 10, 296
8.23 12
8.26 204
8.35-39 65
9-11 135
11 214
11.16 266, 293
11.25 11
12.1-3 11
12.1-2 144
12.1 146

12.6-8 10
13.14 232
14-15 136
14.27 56
15.18-19 12
15.19 9, 12, 52
15.29 135
15.30-31 280
16.5 87, 135
16.9 136
16.10 136
16.14 135, 151
16.15 135

1 Corinthians
2.4 9
2.9-10 257
2.10 257
2.12 10
2.14-15 293
2.15 211
3.16-17 82
3.16 115, 141, 206-7, 216, 289
3.23 217
5.3-5 12
6.11 215
6.14 207
6.17 156
6.19-20 82, 115
6.19 10, 156
7 239
7.12-14 239
7.39 237
7.40 9, 239, 246
10.14-22 94
10.15 11
11.13 11
12-14 4, 100, 149
12 10
12.1-3 43, 211
12.3 10, 282
12.4-7 210
12.4-6 15, 209
12.7 43
12.8-11 10, 321
12.8-10 12
12.8-9 55
12.10 282

12.13 10, 229
12.28-30 10
12.31-14.1 43
13 11
13.9 209
13.11 243
14.1 11
14.12 43, 282
14.14 11
14.18 9
14.19 11
14.20 11, 48
14.24-33 12
14.24-25 11-12, 54
14.26-28 11
14.29 55, 282
14.34-35 168
14.37-38 61
14.37 55
15.3-5 278
15.11 280
15.12 131
15.45-46 208
15.46 215
15.47 241
15.48 245
15.49 266, 296
15.50 296
15.51 11
16.8 87

2 Corinthians
1.21 39
1.22 12, 230
2.12-13 87
3.1-6 198, 214
3.3 214
3.17-18 10
3.17 4
3.18 4, 11
5.5 12
5.13 9
6.16 10, 141
8-9 11
8.2 11
8.5 11
8.21 11
11.14 10

12.1-9 60
12.1-4 9
12.9 11
12.12 9, 52

Galatians
1.20 21
1.21 87
2.1-10 21
2.2 11
2.6 –8 20
2.6 48
2.9-10 20
2.11-14 21
3.1 48
3.2-5 10
3.2 10
3.14 10, 322
3.27 232
4.1 48
4.3 48
4.4-6 200
4.6 10
5.16-26 56
5.16 10
5.17-18 10
5.17 10, 118, 213
5.18 10
5.21 260
5.22 48
5.25 10
6.1 48
6.17 266

Ephesians (13-15)
1.13 14, 230
1.17 14
2.6 309
2.18 14
2.19-22 82
2.21-22 141
2.22 14
3.16-17 242
3.16 14
4 169
4.3-4 14
4.4 156
4.8 318

4.11 15
4.24 232
4.25 267
4.26 267
4.27 267
4.29 14
4.30 14, 164, 267
4.31-32 267
4.31 14, 314
5.5 230
5.18 14
5.19 14
5.31-32 233
6.10-20 14

Philippians
3.3 322
3.15 48
4.8 11
4.18 146

Colossians
1.7 87
3.5 215
3.9 215
3.10 232
4.13 87

1 Thessalonians
1.6 146
4.8 10
5.12 48
5.14 48
5.19-22 282
5.19-21 37
5.19-20 55
5.19 11, 164
5.23 295-96

2 Thessalonians
2.1-2 282

The Pastoral Epistles (96-103)
1 Timothy
1.3-4 100
1.10 100
1.18 100
2.2 97

2.9-15 168
2.9-10 102
3.1-13 102
3.7 97
3.15 97, 100.
3.16 278
4.7 100
4.9 102
4.11-13 101
4.14 99, 100
5.8 100
5.17-20 102
5.22 101
6.1 97
6.3 100
6.9-10 97
6.17-19 97, 102
6.20 99

2 Timothy
1.6-7 99, 103
1.6 99
1.12 99
1.13 100
1.14 98-99, 103, 274
2.2 274
2.3 97
2.14 100
2.18 131
2.20-21 102
2.23 100
3.1-5 98
3.5 98-99, 103, 155
3.6 118
3.12 97
3.14 100

Titus
1.5-9 102
1.9 100
1.13 100
2.1-12 102
2.1 100
2.5 97
2.9-10 97
2.12 97
2.13 97
2.14 97

3.3-7 97
3.3 98
3.4-8 97-98
3.4-7 98-99, 220
3.5-7 102-03, 126
3.5 111
3.9 100

Hebrews
2.4 12, 52
3.2-6 141
5.11-6.12 48
6.4-8 246
10.14 48
10.21 141
13.16 144

James
5.14 266

1 Peter (139-46)
1.1-2 140
1.2 140-41, 146, 272
1.3-12 140
1.3 143
1.6-7 140
1.11 140
1.12 140-41
1.13-2.3 142
1.13-25 143
1.14 140
1.18 140
1.21 140
1.23 140-41
2.2 140
2.4-7 144
2.4-5 140-41
2.5 82, 144, 146, 272
2.6-8 141
2.8 272
2.9-10 140-41, 143
2.9 141, 144, 146
2.12 140, 144
2.20 144
2.21-25 143
3.1 144
3.13-17 140
3.13 144

3.15 144
3.16 144
3.17 144
3.18-20 143
4.1-6 146
4.2-4 140
4.4 140
4.10-11 142-43
4.12 140
4.12-14 260
4.12-17 139
4.14 144-46, 272
5.1-5 143
5.12 139

2 Peter (105-9)
1.3-11 109
1.3-4 109
1.5-7 109
1.5 109
1.9 109
1.10 109
1.11 109
1.12-15 109
1.16-18 109
1.19-20 106
1.21 106-8
2.1 109
3.1-2 109
3.11-13 109
3.14 109
3.15-16 108
3.16 106
3.17 109

The Johannine Epistles (35-43)
1 John
1.1-4 40
1.1-3 174
1.6 43
1.10 43
2.1-2 44, 204
2.1 42
2.7 40
2.10 43
2.14 39
2.18-27 39
2.19 36, 84, 250

2.20 40, 85
2.22-23 40
2.22 37
2.24 40
2.27 40, 85, 283
2.29 38
3.2 44
3.3 44
3.6 42-43, 86
3.9 38, 42-43, 86
3.10-11 43
3.11 40
3.14 43
3.16 248
3.23 43
3.24 36-38, 311
4.1-21 282
4.1 36-37, 55, 163
4.2-3 37, 164
4.5 36-37
4.6 37-38
4.7-12 38, 43
4.7 38, 43
4.9 38
4.10 38
4.11 38
4.12 38
4.13 36-38, 311
4.18 248
4.20-21 43
5.1-2 43
5.1 37-38
5.4 38, 41
5.5 41
5.6-8 41, 85
5.6 41
5.7-8 41
5.8 41
5.16-17 42
5.16 42
5.18 38, 42-43, 86

2 John
2 39
5-6 40
7 36

3 John 36, 49, 117

Jude (104-05)
4 105
8 105
11-12 105
19-21 105
19-20 250
24-25 105

Revelation (89-96)
1.2 91
1.4 92
1.6 93
1.9 91
1.10 90, 311
1.11 90
1.12-20 90
1.16 93
1.20 93
2-3 61
2.12 93
2.14-16 94
2.16 93
2.18-22 238
2.20-23 94
2.20 282
3.12 93
3.21 93
4.1 90
4.2 90
4.5 92
5 92
5.6 92
5.10 93
11 93
11.5-6 93
11.8 94
11.11 94
11.12 94
11.13 94
12 272
12.17 91
14.4 94
14.13 91
16.6 95
16.13 272
17 272
17.3-18 90
17.3 153

18.20 95
18.24 95
19.10 91
19.15 93
20.6 93
21 124
21.10 90, 153
22.16-17 91

Early Christian Writings

Apocalypse of Peter
27 303

Apostolic Tradition (184-85)
1.5 185
2.4 185
16.17 185
35.2 185

Barnabas (109-18)
1.2-3 112
1.2 111
 1.3 111-112, 116
1.4-5 116
1.3 111
1.4 111
1.5 111, 117
1.8 116
2-16 117
2.2 112
2.10 116
4.1 112, 116
4.6 116
4.9-10 112
4.9 116
4.11-12 112, 116
4.11 112
5.3 116
6.8-18 113
6.8 112
6.9 112
6.10 116
6.11-16 112; 272
6.13 116
6.14 112, 116
6.15 112, 116-17
6.16 112, 116

6.17 112, 116
6.18-19 112, 116
9.9 116
10.10 116, 282
11.1 113
11.6 113
11.8 113
11.9-11 113, 116
11.9 113
11.10 113-14, 117
11.11 112-14, 117
11.13 112
11.14 113
11.16 113
12 113
16.3-4 110
16.6-10 114, 272
16.6 114
16.8-9 114, 117
16.7 114
16.8-10 114
16.8 114
16.9 115
16.10 115
16.14-15 114
17.1 116
19.7 116
19.9-10 45
21.5 116
21.6 117

1 Clement (146-50)
1-3 148
1-2 147
1.1-2.1 147
2 148
2.1 147
2.2 147-48
4-6 148
5 136
6.1 136
8.1 147
13.1 147
14.1 129
16 149
16.2 147
20 150
21.5 129

21.7 129
30.1 129
30.3 129
35.5 129
37-38 150
38.2 129, 137
42-44 150
42.3 147
42.4 147, 186
43.2 186
45.2 147
46.5 147-48
46.6 147-48
47.3 147
48.5 129
54.2 147
55.2 137
57.2 129
59.1 148
63.2 128
65.1 137

2 Clement (130-34)
1.1-2 130
1.3 120
1.5 120
1.6-7 130
1.7 130
2.4-5 120
2.6-7 130
2.7 130
3.1 130
3.4 132
4.3 130, 132
5.1-7 132
5.1 130, 132
5.5-6 130
6.1-7 132
6.7-9 130
6.9 130, 133
7.1-5 130
7.6 130, 133
8.1-6 132
8.1-3 132
8.4 130, 132-33
8.6 130, 133
9.1 131-32
9.2 130-31

9.4 131-32
9.5 130, 132
9.8 132
9.11 132
10.1 132
10.2 132
10.4 132
10.5 132
11.1 132
11.6-7 130-31
11.7 131
13.1 132
13.3-4 132
14 130
14.1-2 133
14.2 133
14.3 130, 133
14.4 133
14.5 131
15.3 132
15.5 130, 132
16.1 132
16.4 132
17.1 132
17.3 130, 132
17.4 132
17.5-7 132
17.7 132
18.1 132
19.1 130, 132
19.3-4 132
19.3 132
20.1-4 132

Clement of Alexandria (253-62)
Eclogae Propheticae
24 266

Excerpta de Theodoto (262-68)
1-28 262
2 263
3.1 263
3.2 263
17.3-4 254
21.2-3 263
21.3 265
22.3 264
24.1 264

24.2 264
26.1 264
29-42 262
30.2 263
34.2 268
35.2 263
40.1 264
41.2 263-264
41.3 263
41.4 263
42.3 264
43-65 262
45.1 263
48.2 267
50.1-53.1 268
51.2 182
52 268
53.4 268
57.1 263
58.1 264
58.2 266
59.1 181
60.1 263
61.3 181
66-86 262, 267
67-68 267
67.1 267
67.3-4 263
68 263, 265, 267
68.1 263
69-73 267
69.1-2 267
72-73 267
73.1 268
73.2 267
73.3 267-68
74-75 267
74 267
76-85 267
76.2 264-65
76.4 265
77.1 264-65
77.3 264-65
78.1 264
78.3 262
79 265, 269
79.1 263
80.1-2 265

80.3 266
81.1-3 264
81.2 265
81.3 265
82.1 266
82.2 265
83.1 266
85.3 265
86 266

Paedagogus
1.21.2 254
1.25.1 256
1.26.1-2 255
1.26.1 254, 256
1.28.1 255-56
1.30.2 255
1.47.3 258
1.54.3 258
1.57.3 260
1.68.1 259
1.74.2 259
1.98.1 259
2.19.4-20.1 255
2.20.1 254
2.53 260
2.65.2 258
2.126.1 258
2.128.1 258
3.53.2 259
3.64.1 260
3.101.1-3 269
3.101.1-2 256

Protrepticus
1.4.1 258
1.5.3 258
1.8.4 259
9.84.5 255
9.86.2 258
9.95.1 259
10.98.4 257
10.100.2-3 259
11.112.3 258
11.113.2-3 257
11.114.3 257
12.118.4 257
12.120.1-121.3 256

Quis Dives Salvetur?
21.1-2 258
25.5 258
34.1 258

Stromateis
1.11.2 269
1.178.1 257
2.7.3 257
2.21.1-5 269
2.31.1 255
2.37.2 259
2.51.6 255
2.52.3 255
2.59.6 255
2.77.5-6 255
2.104.2 255
2.114.3-6 176
3.1.1 256
3.42.4-5 255
3.78.5 257
4.38.1 256
4.39.2 257
4.47.1-4 260
4.78.2 260
4.107.6 261
4.139.4 256
4.148.2 255-56
4.152.2-3 256
4.152.3 255-56
4.163.2 261
4.165.1 254
5.25.5 257
5.94.5 254
5.98.4 254
6.12.30 255
6.14.2-3 257
6.68.3-69.3 259
6.71.4-72.2 260
6.72.1 259
6.73.3 260
6.73.6 260
6.78.4 259
6.81.1 258
6.81.3 258
6.96.2 259
6.96.3 259
6.104.1-2 259

6.113.3 259
6.115.2 259
6.134.1 254
6.135.4 254
6.136.1 254
6.137.4 257
6.138.2 257
6.149.5 259
6.152.2 259
7.3.1 256
7.7.6 259
7.10.4 261
7.13.3 259
7.20.3-5 259-60
7.40.3 255
7.42.2 260
7.44.5-8 255
7.45.1 255
7.46.9 259
7.48.1-2 260
7.49.1-8 255
7.49.1 255
7.57.4 260
7.64.7 261
7.72 259
7.73.1 255
7.80.2 255
7.80.3 256
7.82.2 256

Didache (44-49)
1-6 47
4.10 47, 116
5.1-2 46
6.2 47
9-15 45
9.1-10.6 47
9.1-10.5 45
9.3 47
10.2 45
10.3 45, 47
10.6 45
10.7 46
11-15 45
11-12 117, 282
11.7-8 55
11.7 46
11.8-9 46

11.8 46
11.9 47
11.10 46
11.11 46
11.12 47
12.1 55
14 45

Didascalia Apostolorum
23.5 321, 323
23.7 321, 323

Didymus of Alexandria
De Trinitate
3.41.1   121

Epiphanius
Panarion
48.1-2 120
48.4 121
48.10 123
48.12 121
48.13 121
49.2 235

Eusebius
Chronicle
287-88 120

Historia Ecclesiastica
Book 1
13 279

Book 3
31.3-4 276
31.3 23
39.9 23, 276

Book 4
4.10 170
4.27 120
23.10 138

Book 5
Preface 120
1.1-63 190
1.9-10 191
1.9 194

1.10 191
1.17 193
1.18 193
1.19 193
1.20 193
1.22 193
1.23 194
1.24 193
1.28 193-94
1.29 193
1.34 192
1.35 194
1.41 194
1.42 194
1.45-46 190
1.49 191
1.51 194
1.56 194
2-3 190
2 190
2.2-4 193
2.6 190
2.8 190
3.1-3 190
3.2 192
3.4 120, 122
4.1-2 189
4.4 189
5.1-3 189
5.1 189
5.17 189
5.20 183
5.49 189
5.53 189
6.1 279
14-19 280
14 280
14.1 121
15.1 189
16-17 121-22
16.2 276
16.4 89
16.7 122
16.8 122
16.9 280
16.16-17 89
16.17 121
16.18-19 124

16.19 123
16.20 122
16.22 122
17 279
17.1 276
17.1-2 122, 276
17.2-3 122
17.4 125
18.1 276
18.2 124
18.3 122, 124
18.5 122, 280
18.6 123
18.12-13 122
19.3 122
20.4-8 189
20.5-6 189
24.1-2 276
24.2 23, 89
24.3 89
24.4-5 89
24.6 89

Hippolytus
Refutatio
6.29.22-36.4 181
6.30 171
6.35.5-7 262
10.26 184

Ignatius (53-58)
Ephesians
2.2 55
4.1 55
4.3 55
6.1 55
7.1 55
7.2 56-57, 287
8.1 56-57
8.2 55-56
9.1 55, 57
10.3 287
17.1-2 39
19.1 304
20.2 55

Magnesians
1.2 287

8.2 304
13.1-2 287
13.1 57
15.1 305

Trallians
Inscr. 287
15.2 55

Romans
Inscr. 137, 287
7 57
7.1-3 311
7.2-3 58

Philadelphians
5.2-6.2 273
7.1-2 311
7.1 54, 273
7.2 54
8.2 110

Smyrneans
Inscr. 304
12.2 287
13.2 287

Polycarp
1.2 287
1.3 302-6

Irenaeus (195-218)
Adversus Haereses
Book 1
4.5 181
5.6 181
6.1 181
6.2-3 293
6.2 182, 293
6.3-4 181
6.4 181, 294
7.1 181
7.5 181
8.3 293
13.1 218
13.2-7 295
13.2 218
13.3 218-19

13.4 218
13.5 219
13.7 218
14-16 218
14.1 218

Book 2
17.3 293
28.7 209
29.1 293
31.2 209
31.3 209
32.4 209-10
33.5 207

Book 3
3.3 195
3.4 195
4.2 198, 214
6.1-3 201
6.1 200
11.8 217
11.9 205, 209-10
12.1 198
12.14 213
15.2 293
17.1 197, 199, 206, 210, 213, 284
17.2 199, 203, 212
17.3-4 204, 319
17.3 213
18.3 206
18.7 202
19.1 200-01
20.2 197, 201
21.4 201
22.1 207
24.1 196, 202, 206

Book 4
Praef. 207
9.2 200
14.2 197, 203
16.5 201
20.4 215
20.5 197
20.6 197, 210
20.8 198
21.3 202

31.2 201, 204
33.1-7 211
33.1 207
33.4 201
33.7 199, 211, 283
33.8 211
33.9 198
33.14 203, 212
33.15 198, 211
36.4 203
36.6 215
36.22 198
38.1 216
38.2 216
38.3 197, 217

Book 5
1.1 205
6-13 196
6.1 207, 210, 284, 295-96
6.2 206
8.1 200, 205, 296
8.2-3 296
9.1 207, 214, 296
9.2 213-14, 296
9.3 196, 213-15
9.4 214, 216
9.32 214
10.1 214-15
10.2 214, 297
11.1 204
11.2 215, 296
12.1 205
12.2 201-02, 208, 296
12.3 215
13.4 214
15.3 200
18.2 204, 208
20.2 217
22.2 210
32.2 201
36.2 206

Demonstration of Apostolic Preaching
3 199, 201, 204
6 198-99, 203
7 199, 203, 205

Scripture Index 373

41-42 199
42 216
57 204
89 212
99-100 209

Justin (164-70)
1 Apology
13.1 138
14.2 138
61 165, 199
64.2 165
65-66 165
67 235
67.6 138

2 Apology
6 168
6.6 168
12 164

Dialogue with Trypho
1 164
8.1 165
10.4 168
11.5 292, 319
29.1 165, 170
30.3 168
39.2 167-69
43.2-3 166
43.2 292
49-52 318
54.1 166
76.6 168
82 279
82.1-2 317
82.1 167-68, 284
85.3 168
87-88 317
87 168-69, 292, 321
87.2 167, 317
87.3-88.1 167
87.3-5 322
87.3-4 168
87.5-6 168
87.5 167-68
87.6-88.1 170
87.6 167

88.1 167-68, 293
88.2 169
114.4 166
118.2 292
135.3 166
135.4-5 166
135.9-10 166

Martyrdom of Polycarp (119-120)
Inscr. 88
2.2-3 119
3.1 119
5.2 120
7.2 119
8.2 88
9.1 120
10.2 88
12.2 88
13.1 88
13.3 119
14.2 119
15.2-3 119
16.2 118, 120
17.1 120
17.2 88
18.1-2 120
18.1 88, 119
20 88
20.2 120

Minucius Felix:
Octavius 138

Odes of Solomon (59-80)
1.1 71
1.2 71
1.4 72
3.3 61
3.5 61
3.7-9 61
3.7 61
3.8-11 71
3.10 61, 74, 85
4.3 63
4.6-7 62-63
4.9 63
4.10 63
4.15 71

6.1-2 66-67, 288
6.1 67
6.3 66
6.7 66
6.11 67
6.12 67
6.14-18 67
6.15 71
6.16-24 71
6.17 71
6.18 310
7.4 71
7.6 71
7.7-12 71
7.10 71
7.12-24 71
7.17-29 70
7.20-21 71
7.26 72
8 76, 311
8.1-2 75
8.1 68
8.3 311
8.5 311
8.6 75
8.7 311
8.10 311
8.13 64
9.4 71
9.5 71
9.7 71
9.10-12 71
10.1-3 70
10.1 71
10.2 68
10.3 71
11.1 59
11.2-3 59
11.2 72
11.3 74
11.4-5 74
11.5 59, 72
11.6 60
11.11 71
11.12 60
11.14-21 71
11.14 71
11.16-17 60

11.18-19 60
11.18 75, 86
11.20 75, 86
11.23 75
12 70
12.1-4 70
12.1-2 74
12.1 72
12.2 68
12.3 71
12.10-13 310
12.10-12 70
12.13 72
13.3 75
14.2 71
14.7-8 67-68, 72, 74, 288, 310
14.7 68
15.2 71
15.4-6 72
15.8-10 71
16.1-3 68
16.2 68
16.5-7 68, 288
16.8-16 71
16.9-20 68
16.18 71
17.2-3 71
17.4-5 72
17.4 71
17.5 74, 85
17.6 71
17.7 71
17.8-16 71
17.12 71
17.16 71
18.4 72
18.6-7 74
18.7 71
19.1 65
19.2 65
19.4 65
19.5 65
19.6-7 65
20.1 76
20.3 62
20.4-5 76
20.6 71, 76
20.7 60, 71

21.1 71
21.3 71
22.7 71
22.8-10 71
22.8 70
24.5 71
25.1 62, 71, 307
25.2 74
25.4 62
25.5 307
25.6 74, 308
25.7 62, 71, 74
25.8 62, 74-75, 308
25.9-10 62
25.10-11 74
25.10 74-75, 86, 308
25.11 307-08
25.12 71, 308
26 68
26.1-3 69
26.5-7 69
26.8 69
26.10 69
28 64, 288, 308
28.1-2 64, 308
28.2 309
28.4 64, 309
28.5-6 309
28.5 65
28.7 64, 309
28.8 309
28.9-18 71
28.17 71
28.19 71
29.5 71
31.1-11 71
31.1-2 71, 74
31.2 71
31.7-11 74
31.7 71
31.8-10 71
32.1 65, 71
33 72
33.8 74
33.12 71
35.7 71
36.1-2 65, 288, 309, 311
36.2 69

36.3-8 309, 311
38 74
38.1 72
38.4 72
38.5 71
38.17 71
38.18-21 65
38.20 65
41.4 71
41.8 71
41.12 71
41.14 71
42 69
42.2 71
42.4 69-70, 77
42.6 69-71, 77
42.8-9 71
42.10 71

Passion of Perpetua and Felicitas
(223-26)
1-2 299
1 223
1.3 223, 300
1.4 223
1.5 223, 300
1.6 225
3.5 224
4.3-10 224
7.1-8.4 224
10.1-15 224
10.9 225
10.13 225
14-21 299
15.6 225
16.11 225
20.8 224
21.11 225, 300

Polycarp (118-19)
Philippians
1.3 118
2.2 118
3.2-3 118
4.1 118
5.2 118
5.3 118
7.2 118

8.2 118
11.1-4 278
11.2 118
12.2 118
13.1 118
13.2 118

Shepherd of Hermas (150-64)
Vision 1 (150)
1.3 151-52

Vision 2
1.1 152
2.6 151
4.2-3 151, 153
4.3 137

Vision 3 (151-52, 154-55)
1.8-9 151
8.2 155
8.8 155
8.11 153
9.7-10 152

Vision 4 (152)
4.5-6 153

Vision 5 (150, 152)
4.3 151
5.7 153

Mandate 3 (289)
1 154, 157, 289
2 157, 288-89
4 157, 289

Mandate 5 (158, 288, 313)
1.3 158
1.4 158
2 154, 313
2.4-7 160
2.5-6 158
2.7 158
5 158
6.5 163
7 154

Mandate 9
1.1-12 158

Mandate 10 (158, 288-89, 313)
1.1-3 158
1.1-2 313
1.1 158
1.2 158
2.2-6 158
2.2 158, 313
2.3-4 158
2.4-6 158
2.4 158
2.5 158
3.2-3 158
3.2 289
5-6 154

Mandate 11 (6, 151, 153-54, 156-57, 162, 219, 273, 278, 280-81, 289)
2 153
7 153
8 153
9-10 153
9 153
11 55
12 153, 157
14 153
16 55
17 153-54
18-20 154
21 154

Mandate 12 (157)
1.1 157
2 157
3.4 157
4.3 157

Similitude 5
5.2 155
6.5 154
6.6 154
6.7 154
7.1-2 154
7.1 154

Similitude 8
7.4 152
8.1 156

Similitude 9 (25, 117, 154-55, 157)
1.1 155, 163
2-4 155
13 156
13.2-3 155
13.2 155, 289
13.5 155-56
13.7 155-56
13.9 156
15 156
15.1-2 289
20.1-2 156
24.2 155
24.4 155
26.2 152
27.1-3 152
32 288
32.3 158

Tatian
Oration (80-83)
7.3 81
11.2 81
12.1 81
13.1 82
13.2-3 82
13.2 80-81, 288
13.3 82-83
15.1 81
15.2 80-81, 83, 288
15.3 82-83
16.3 83
20.1 81
20.3 82-83, 288
21.1 83
22.1 83
30.1 82
33.2 83

Tertullian (226-51)
de anima
1.4 237
5.7 237
9.3-4 234

9.4 237
11.44 233
21.1-2 233
21.6 241
22.12 33
41.4 230
45.3 233
48.3-4 233
48.4 233
55.5 238
57.5 236

Apologeticum
20.4 239
21.11-12 227
23.4 236
23.15-16 236
27.5 236
32.3 236
39 235
39.5 237
39.9 229
43.2 236
46.5 236
46.10-12 236

de baptismo
4 230
5 230
6.1 230
8.3-4 230

de carne Christi
8.6 241
8.7 241
23.6 239

de corona militi
1.4 238
4.6 236

de cultu feminarum II
1.1 229, 240
3.2 240
10.5 240

de exhortatione castitatis
4.5 239

10-11 297
10.1 241, 245
10.5 234
11.1 241, 315
13.2 245

de fuga in persecutione
6.4 231
8.1-2 242
9.3 248
9.4 238, 248
10.2-3 248
11.1 248
11.2 248
14.3 236, 248

de idolatria
15.6 239
18.5 239
24.1 241
24.3 241

de ieiuniis
1.2 298
3.2 298
3.21 233
8.3 246
8.4 246
11.2-4 298
13.5 246
16.8 246
17.1-3 298
17.2-3 298
17.5 298
17.9 298

adversus Iudaeos
1-8 319
8.13 319
8.14 232, 273
9-12 319, 322
10.17-12.2 320
13.1-23 319
13.13 319
13.15 232, 273
13.24-14.13 320
13.24 320
13.25-26 322

adversus Marcionem
Book 3
23.2-3 320
23.2 232

Book 4
22.4-5 234
22.4 233

Book 5
7.1 239
8.4-5 320, 322
8.4 232
8.12 235
15.5 235

ad martyras
1.3 247
3.3-4 247
4.1 242, 247

de monogamia
1 297
1.2 232
2.1 237
2.4 229
3-4 237
3.6 246
3.8 246
3.9 246
3.10 246
8 298
13.3 237
14.2 242
14.3 242
14.4 242
14.6 242
14.7 243

de oratione
10 241
12.1 315
13.1 241
20.5 241
29.1 241

de paenitentia
2.4 237

2.6 230
10.4 230
10.6 230

de patientia
6.3 240
7.7 240, 315
12.8 240
13.1 242
13.7 242
15.6 315
15.7 240, 315

de praescriptione haereticorum
6.6 239
8.14 236
13.5 242
20.4 232
22.9-10 236
22.9 236
30 170

ad Praxean
1 183-84
1.5 233
1.7 238
2.1 238
3.5 227
4.1 227
7.7 228
7.8 227
8.4 227
12.3 241
13.5 238
29.7 247
30.5 236-37

de puditicia
1.2-21 238
1.11-12 243
1.11 238
1.12 243
1.14 243
1.20 246
6 246
7.11 237
9.11 231
11.3 246

12 243
12.4 243
12.6 243
12.8 243
12.9 243
15.2 315
15.3 315
15.4 315
16.17 243
16.18 243
17.11 243
19 238
20.1 246
21.7 244
21.16 232
21.17 232, 238, 299
25 315

de resurrectione mortuorum
8.3 237
11.2 238
24.8 239
26.10-11 231
37.6 242
40.7 242
47.9 244
49.4 244
49.6 244
49.8 244
51.2 230
53.18-19 230
59.3 244
63.1 230, 244
63.3 230, 244
63.9 238

ad Scapulam
2.9 236
4.5 236
6.63 241

de scorpiace
3.2 247
6.4 247
9.2 247

de spectaculis
3.4 245

15 249
15.2 240
15.3-4 245
15.3 240
15.8 245
25 249
26 249
26.1-4 240
29.3 236
50.1 249
50.3 249
50.12-13 249

ad uxorem I
1 244
1.3 231
1.4 242
8.3 244

ad uxorem II
1.2 244
2.4 239
2.8 239
4.1-2 244
4.3-5 244
4.5 244
8.2-3 244

de virginibus velandis
1.2 238
1.4-5 228, 299
1.4 245
1.5 245
1.6-7 228, 299
1.7 245
2.4 299
10.3-4 246

Gnostic Writings

The Gospel of Truth (171-77)
17.8 173
17.10-11 172
17.22 173
18.5-12 173, 294
18.16-18 173, 294
18.32 173
19.3-7 173, 294

20.2 173
22.13-15 173, 294
22.16-20 173, 294
22.16-19 172
24.10-11 176
24.32-25.3 173, 294
25.12-18 173
25.35-26.15 173, 294
26.18-27 175
26.32-27.8 173
26.34-27.1 176
27.11-14 173
28.19-28 175
28.28-30.12 172, 294
30.12-16 174
30.13-19 294
30.16-31 174
30.16 175
30.32-35 174
30.34 173
31.4-7 175
31.9-15 175
31.15-22 175, 294
31.21-22 173, 294
31.26-27 173, 175, 294
31.32-33 175
32.32-34 173
32.23 173
32.37 172
33.32 175
33.39-34.1 175
34.9-12 174
34.9-14 174
34.15-16 175
34.28-32 173, 294
34.28-29, 32 294
35.23 175
35.23, 25-27 173, 294
35.24-28 175
35.25-26 172
35.27-29 173, 294
36.1-13 173
36.17-37.3 175
36.17-20 175
37.37-39 173
42.18 176
42.21-22 173, 175, 294
42.26-30 175-76

42.31-33 173, 176
43.19-23 173, 176

Heracleon (177-80)

Ptolemaeus (180-82)

Studies in Christian History and Thought
(All titles uniform with this volume)
Dates in bold are of projected publication

David Bebbington
Holiness in Nineteenth-Century England
David Bebbington stresses the relationship of movements of spirituality to changes in their cultural setting, especially the legacies of the Enlightenment and Romanticism. He shows that these broad shifts in ideological mood had a profound effect on the ways in which piety was conceptualized and practised. Holiness was intimately bound up with the spirit of the age.
2000 / 0-85364-981-2 / viii + 98pp

J. William Black
Reformation Pastors
Richard Baxter and the Ideal of the Reformed Pastor
This work examines Richard Baxter's *Gildas Salvianus, The Reformed Pastor* (1656) and explores each aspect of his pastoral strategy in light of his own concern for 'reformation' and in the broader context of Edwardian, Elizabethan and early Stuart pastoral ideals and practice.
2003 / 1-84227-190-3 / xxii + 308pp

James Bruce
Prophecy, Miracles, Angels, *and* Heavenly Light?
The Eschatology, Pneumatology and Missiology of Adomnán's Life of Columba
This book surveys approaches to the marvellous in hagiography, providing the first critique of Plummer's hypothesis of Irish saga origin. It then analyses the uniquely systematized phenomena in the *Life of Columba* from Adomnán's seventh-century theological perspective, identifying the coming of the eschatological Kingdom as the key to understanding.
2004 / 1-84227-227-6 / xviii + 286pp

Colin J. Bulley
The Priesthood of Some Believers
Developments from the General to the Special Priesthood in the Christian Literature of the First Three Centuries
The first in-depth treatment of early Christian texts on the priesthood of all believers shows that the developing priesthood of the ordained related closely to the division between laity and clergy and had deleterious effects on the practice of the general priesthood.
2000 / 1-84227-034-6 / xii + 336pp

Anthony R. Cross (ed.)
Ecumenism and History
Studies in Honour of John H.Y. Briggs
This collection of essays examines the inter-relationships between the two fields in which Professor Briggs has contributed so much: history—particularly Baptist and Nonconformist—and the ecumenical movement. With contributions from colleagues and former research students from Britain, Europe and North America, *Ecumenism and History* provides wide-ranging studies in important aspects of Christian history, theology and ecumenical studies.
2002 / 1-84227-135-0 / xx + 362pp

Maggi Dawn
Confessions of an Inquiring Spirit
Form as Constitutive of Meaning in S.T. Coleridge's Theological Writing
This study of Coleridge's *Confessions* focuses on its confessional, epistolary and fragmentary form, suggesting that attention to these features significantly affects its interpretation. Bringing a close study of these three literary forms, the author suggests ways in which they nuance the text with particular understandings of the Trinity, and of a kenotic christology. Some parallels are drawn between Romantic and postmodern dilemmas concerning the authority of the biblical text.
2006 / 1-84227-255-1 / approx. 224 pp

Ruth Gouldbourne
The Flesh and the Feminine
Gender and Theology in the Writings of Caspar Schwenckfeld
Caspar Schwenckfeld and his movement exemplify one of the radical communities of the sixteenth century. Challenging theological and liturgical norms, they also found themselves challenging social and particularly gender assumptions. In this book, the issues of the relationship between radical theology and the understanding of gender are considered.
2005 / 1-84227-048-6 / approx. 304pp

Crawford Gribben
Puritan Millennialism
Literature and Theology, 1550–1682
Puritan Millennialism surveys the growth, impact and eventual decline of puritan millennialism throughout England, Scotland and Ireland, arguing that it was much more diverse than has frequently been suggested. This Paternoster edition is revised and extended from the original 2000 text.
2007 / 1-84227-372-8 / approx. 320pp

Galen K. Johnson
Prisoner of Conscience
John Bunyan on Self, Community and Christian Faith
This is an interdisciplinary study of John Bunyan's understanding of conscience across his autobiographical, theological and fictional writings, investigating whether conscience always deserves fidelity, and how Bunyan's view of conscience affects his relationship both to modern Western individualism and historic Christianity.
2003 / 1-84227-223-3 / xvi + 236pp

R.T. Kendall
Calvin and English Calvinism to 1649
The author's thesis is that those who formed the Westminster Confession of Faith, which is regarded as Calvinism, in fact departed from John Calvin on two points: (1) the extent of the atonement and (2) the ground of assurance of salvation.
1997 / 0-85364-827-1 / xii + 264pp

Timothy Larsen
Friends of Religious Equality
Nonconformist Politics in Mid-Victorian England
During the middle decades of the nineteenth century the English Nonconformist community developed a coherent political philosophy of its own, of which a central tenet was the principle of religious equality (in contrast to the stereotype of Evangelical Dissenters). The Dissenting community fought for the civil rights of Roman Catholics, non-Christians and even atheists on an issue of principle which had its flowering in the enthusiastic and undivided support which Nonconformity gave to the campaign for Jewish emancipation. This reissued study examines the political efforts and ideas of English Nonconformists during the period, covering the whole range of national issues raised, from state education to the Crimean War. It offers a case study of a theologically conservative group defending religious pluralism in the civic sphere, showing that the concept of religious equality was a grand vision at the centre of the political philosophy of the Dissenters.
2007 / 1-84227-402-3 / x + 300pp

Byung-Ho Moon
Christ the Mediator of the Law
Calvin's Christological Understanding of the Law as the Rule of Living and Life-Giving

This book explores the coherence between Christology and soteriology in Calvin's theology of the law, examining its intellectual origins and his position on the concept and extent of Christ's mediation of the law. A comparative study between Calvin and contemporary Reformers—Luther, Bucer, Melancthon and Bullinger—and his opponent Michael Servetus is made for the purpose of pointing out the unique feature of Calvin's Christological understanding of the law.

2005 / 1-84227-318-3 / approx. 370pp

John Eifion Morgan-Wynne
Holy Spirit and Religious Experience in Christian Writings, c.AD 90–200

This study examines how far Christians in the third to fifth generations (c.AD 90–200) attributed their sense of encounter with the divine presence, their sense of illumination in the truth or guidance in decision-making, and their sense of ethical empowerment to the activity of the Holy Spirit in their lives.

2005 / 1-84227-319-1 / approx. 350pp

James I. Packer
The Redemption and Restoration of Man in the Thought of Richard Baxter

James I. Packer provides a full and sympathetic exposition of Richard Baxter's doctrine of humanity, created and fallen; its redemption by Christ Jesus; and its restoration in the image of God through the obedience of faith by the power of the Holy Spirit.

2002 / 1-84227-147-4 / 432pp

Andrew Partington,
Church and State
The Contribution of the Church of England Bishops to the House of Lords during the Thatcher Years

In *Church and State*, Andrew Partington argues that the contribution of the Church of England bishops to the House of Lords during the Thatcher years was overwhelmingly critical of the government; failed to have a significant influence in the public realm; was inefficient, being undertaken by a minority of those eligible to sit on the Bench of Bishops; and was insufficiently moral and spiritual in its content to be distinctive. On the basis of this, and the likely reduction of the number of places available for Church of England bishops in a fully reformed Second Chamber, the author argues for an evolution in the Church of England's approach to the service of its bishops in the House of Lords. He proposes the Church of England works to overcome the genuine obstacles which hinder busy diocesan bishops from contributing to the debates of the House of Lords and to its life more informally.

2005 / 1-84227-334-5 / approx. 324pp

Michael Pasquarello III
God's Ploughman
Hugh Latimer: A 'Preaching Life' (1490–1555)

This construction of a 'preaching life' situates Hugh Latimer within the larger religious, political and intellectual world of late medieval England. Neither biography, intellectual history, nor analysis of discrete sermon texts, this book is a work of homiletic history which draws from the details of Latimer's milieu to construct an interpretive framework for the preaching performances that formed the core of his identity as a religious reformer. Its goal is to illumine the practical wisdom embodied in the content, form and style of Latimer's preaching, and to recapture a sense of its overarching purpose, movement, and transforming force during the reform of sixteenth-century England.

2006 / 1-84227-336-1 / approx. 250pp

Alan P.F. Sell
Enlightenment, Ecumenism, Evangel
Theological Themes and Thinkers 1550–2000

This book consists of papers in which such interlocking topics as the Enlightenment, the problem of authority, the development of doctrine, spirituality, ecumenism, theological method and the heart of the gospel are discussed. Issues of significance to the church at large are explored with special reference to writers from the Reformed and Dissenting traditions.

2005 / 1-84227-330-2 / xviii + 422pp

Alan P.F. Sell
Hinterland Theology
Some Reformed and Dissenting Adjustments
Many books have been written on theology's 'giants' and significant trends, but what of those lesser-known writers who adjusted to them? In this book some hinterland theologians of the British Reformed and Dissenting traditions, who followed in the wake of toleration, the Evangelical Revival, the rise of modern biblical criticism and Karl Barth, are allowed to have their say. They include Thomas Ridgley, Ralph Wardlaw, T.V. Tymms and N.H.G. Robinson.
2006 / 1-84227-331-0 / approx. 350pp

Alan P.F. Sell and Anthony R. Cross (eds)
Protestant Nonconformity in the Twentieth Century
In this collection of essays scholars representative of a number of Nonconformist traditions reflect thematically on Nonconformists' life and witness during the twentieth century. Among the subjects reviewed are biblical studies, theology, worship, evangelism and spirituality, and ecumenism. Over and above its immediate interest, this collection provides a marker to future scholars and others wishing to know how some of their forebears assessed Nonconformity's contribution to a variety of fields during the century leading up to Christianity's third millennium.
2003 / 1-84227-221-7 / x + 398pp

Mark Smith
Religion in Industrial Society
Oldham and Saddleworth 1740–1865
This book analyses the way British churches sought to meet the challenge of industrialization and urbanization during the period 1740–1865. Working from a case-study of Oldham and Saddleworth, Mark Smith challenges the received view that the Anglican Church in the eighteenth century was characterized by complacency and inertia, and reveals Anglicanism's vigorous and creative response to the new conditions. He reassesses the significance of the centrally directed church reforms of the mid-nineteenth century, and emphasizes the importance of local energy and enthusiasm. Charting the growth of denominational pluralism in Oldham and Saddleworth, Dr Smith compares the strengths and weaknesses of the various Anglican and Nonconformist approaches to promoting church growth. He also demonstrates the extent to which all the churches participated in a common culture shaped by the influence of evangelicalism, and shows that active co-operation between the churches rather than denominational conflict dominated. This revised and updated edition of Dr Smith's challenging and original study makes an important contribution both to the social history of religion and to urban studies.
2006 / 1-84227-335-3 / approx. 300pp

Martin Sutherland
Peace, Toleration and Decay
The Ecclesiology of Later Stuart Dissent

This fresh analysis brings to light the complexity and fragility of the later Stuart Nonconformist consensus. Recent findings on wider seventeenth-century thought are incorporated into a new picture of the dynamics of Dissent and the roots of evangelicalism.

2003 / 1-84227-152-0 / xxii + 216pp

G. Michael Thomas
The Extent of the Atonement
A Dilemma for Reformed Theology from Calvin to the Consensus

A study of the way Reformed theology addressed the question, 'Did Christ die for all, or for the elect only?', commencing with John Calvin, and including debates with Lutheranism, the Synod of Dort and the teaching of Moïse Amyraut.

1997 / 0-85364-828-X / x + 278pp

David M. Thompson
Baptism, Church and Society in Britain from the Evangelical Revival to *Baptism, Eucharist and Ministry*

The theology and practice of baptism have not received the attention they deserve. How important is faith? What does baptismal regeneration mean? Is baptism a bond of unity between Christians? This book discusses the theology of baptism and popular belief and practice in England and Wales from the Evangelical Revival to the publication of the World Council of Churches' consensus statement on *Baptism, Eucharist and Ministry* (1982).

2005 / 1-84227-393-0 / approx. 224pp

Mark D. Thompson
A Sure Ground on Which to Stand
The Relation of Authority and Interpretive Method of Luther's Approach to Scripture

The best interpreter of Luther is Luther himself. Unfortunately many modern studies have superimposed contemporary agendas upon this sixteenth-century Reformer's writings. This fresh study examines Luther's own words to find an explanation for his robust confidence in the Scriptures, a confidence that generated the famous 'stand' at Worms in 1521.

2004 / 1-84227-145-8 / xvi + 322pp

Carl R. Trueman and R.S. Clark (eds)
Protestant Scholasticism
Essays in Reassessment

Traditionally Protestant theology, between Luther's early reforming career and the dawn of the Enlightenment, has been seen in terms of decline and fall into the wastelands of rationalism and scholastic speculation. In this volume a number of scholars question such an interpretation. The editors argue that the development of post-Reformation Protestantism can only be understood when a proper historical model of doctrinal change is adopted. This historical concern underlies the subsequent studies of theologians such as Calvin, Beza, Olevian, Baxter, and the two Turrentini. The result is a significantly different reading of the development of Protestant Orthodoxy, one which both challenges the older scholarly interpretations and clichés about the relationship of Protestantism to, among other things, scholasticism and rationalism, and which demonstrates the fruitfulness of the new, historical approach.

1999 / 0-85364-853-0 / xx + 344pp

Shawn D. Wright
Our Sovereign Refuge
The Pastoral Theology of Theodore Beza

Our Sovereign Refuge is a study of the pastoral theology of the Protestant reformer who inherited the mantle of leadership in the Reformed church from John Calvin. Countering a common view of Beza as supremely a 'scholastic' theologian who deviated from Calvin's biblical focus, Wright uncovers a new portrait. He was not a cold and rigid academic theologian obsessed with probing the eternal decrees of God. Rather, by placing him in his pastoral context and by noting his concerns in his pastoral and biblical treatises, Wright shows that Beza was fundamentally a committed Christian who was troubled by the vicissitudes of life in the second half of the sixteenth century. He believed that the biblical truth of the supreme sovereignty of God alone could support Christians on their earthly pilgrimage to heaven. This pastoral and personal portrait forms the heart of Wright's argument.

2004 / 1-84227-252-7 / xviii + 308pp

Paternoster
9 Holdom Avenue,
Bletchley,
Milton Keynes MK1 1QR,
United Kingdom
Web: www.authenticmedia.co.uk/paternoster

www.ingramcontent.com/pod-product-compliance
Lightning Source LLC
Chambersburg PA
CBHW071141300426
44113CB00009B/1045